# THE EUROPEANS

**TEXTS IN REGIONAL GEOGRAPHY**
**A Guilford Series**
Edited by James L. Newman, Syracuse University

The Europeans: A Geography of People, Culture, and Environment
*Robert C. Ostergren and John G. Rice*

Africa South of the Sahara: A Geographical Interpretation
SECOND EDITION
*Robert Stock*

# THE EUROPEANS

## A Geography of People, Culture, and Environment

ROBERT C. OSTERGREN
JOHN G. RICE

**THE GUILFORD PRESS**
New York   London

© 2004 The Guilford Press
A Division of Guilford Publications, Inc.
72 Spring Street, New York, NY 10012
www.guilford.com

This book is printed on acid-free paper.

Last digit is print number: 9   8   7   6   5   4   3   2

**Library of Congress Cataloging-in-Publication Data**
Ostergren, Robert Clifford.
    The Europeans: a geography of people, culture, and environment / Robert C. Ostergren,
John G. Rice.
        p. cm. — (Texts in regional geography)
    Includes bibliographical references and index.
    ISBN 1-59385-006-9 (alk. paper) — ISBN 0-89862-272-7 (pbk.: alk. paper)
    1. Europe—Economic conditions.   2. Europe—Social conditions.   3. Geography—
Europe.   I. Rice, John G.   II. Title.   III. Series.
    HC240.O35 2004
    940—dc22

                                                                                    2003027822

# Contents

# List of Figures and Tables

**FIGURES**

## TABLES

# Acknowledgments

This book is both a product and a reflection of the many rewarding years we have devoted to teaching courses on the geography of Europe to undergraduate students at the University of Wisconsin–Madison and the University of Minnesota, Twin Cities. Above all we wish to extend our gratitude to the great many students who have passed through these courses and inspired us with their curiosity about Europe and their enthusiasm for learning. It is to students and learning that we dedicate this book.

There are also many people who contributed in more specific ways to the writing and production of this book. We wish to extend our thanks to Jim Newman and the editors at The Guilford Press for their encouragement along the way, and the production staff at Guilford for the skill with which they brought the final product to fruition. We owe a debt of gratitude to the individuals who read and commented on all or portions of the manuscript, including Joshua Hagen, Jerry Kramer, Jason Ostergren, Helga Leitner, and two anonymous reviewers. We also want to thank Mike Daniels, Joshua Hagen, Anne Knowles, Jerry Kramer, and Jason Ostergren for the photos they contributed to the text. And last but not least, a special thanks goes to Marieka Brouwer of the University of Wisconsin Cartographic Laboratory for her careful and professional attention to the design and production of the many maps that appear in this volume.

# CHAPTER 1

# Introduction

## EUROPE AS A CULTURE REALM

It's a typical summer morning in Strasbourg, France, the Alsatian city of nearly 400,000 situated on the upper Rhine border with Germany. On the Place Gutenberg, which fronts Strasbourg's imposing red-hued 12th-century cathedral, crowds of tourists are beginning to queue to ascend the 328 steps to the viewing platform atop the ornately fili-greed Gothic spire. From this vantage point, visitors can look down upon the steep-pitched roofs of the well-preserved half-timbered me-dieval houses that cluster below in the city's historic center. Or, casting their gaze a bit farther afield, they can take in the sprawling surrounding urban landscape of modern high-rises and residential suburbs. Farther out across the Alsatian Plain to the east lies the bluish-gray ridgeline of the Vosges, ending at its southern extremity in the Belfort Gap lead-ing to the south of France and the Mediterra-nean. Far to the east in Germany lie the dark heights of the Black Forest, and stretched out before them the broad upper valley of the Rhine, which flows north to the Rhineland and the North Sea. As the historic meeting place of water and land routeways from all corners of Europe, the city has long been re-

**FIGURE 1.1. The Cathedral Quarter of Strasbourg.** Tourists gather before the towering Gothic west front of Strasbourg's 12th-century Cathédrale Notre-Dame. The single tower, which rises to a height of 142 meters, was the tallest in Europe at the time of its com-pletion. It is visible from much of the Alsace Plain.

1

puted, as its name implies, to be one of the major crossroads of Europe. The expansive view in all directions from high atop the cathedral tower is dramatic confirmation of that fact.

Strasbourg is, in many ways, the perfect place to begin this book, for it epitomizes much of what we may think of as important to an appreciation of today's Europe. While historically known as one of Europe's great crossroads, the city today likes to think of itself as the "capital of Europe," an icon of European unity and cooperative integration. In the aftermath of World War II the city became the headquarters of the Council of Europe, the continent's oldest intergovernmental organization, which was headquartered here on the border between France and Germany as a symbol of the postwar rapprochement between these two warring rivals. It is also the permanent home of the European Parliament, which makes Strasbourg, along with Brussels and Luxembourg, one of the main centers of the European Union (EU), the federalized organization of 25 states dedicated to the democratic integration of decisions at the European level governing matters of mutual interest to the member states. Strasbourg is also home to a host of other international organizations, including the International Human Rights Institute, the European Science Foundation, the European Center of Regional Development, and the Assembly of European Regions. The city likens itself to Geneva and New York as a world city and home to major international organizations, without being a national capital.

But the city may be thought of as representative of Europe in many other ways as well. It is a provincial capital (and certainly looked upon as no more than that from Paris) and a regional center. Like many other such places in today's Europe, the city takes special pride in its historic heritage, its cultural leadership of its regional hinterland, and its modern economic prosperity and development. Strasbourg was founded more than 2,000 years ago as a Celtic settlement, and later as a Roman camp. It rose to commercial prominence in the Middle Ages, when it became a free

**FIGURE 1.2. The European Parliament in Strasbourg.** In sharp contrast to the highly decorated Gothic west front of Strasbourg's medieval cathedral is the modern glass-fronted headquarters of the European Parliament, opened in 1999.

city within the Holy Roman Empire, and remained so for a time even after its incorporation into France through the Treaty of Westphalia in 1648. As the capital of Alsace, tucked between Germany and France, sovereignty over the city and its region has bounced back and forth between these two rivals. After two centuries of French rule, it was annexed by Germany between 1871 and 1918, and again from 1940 to 1944, before being finally returned to France. The culture features a local living language, Alsatian (*Elsässisch*), which is a High German dialect; a cuisine that is distinctively German but influenced by French practices and tastes; a rich folklore; and a unique vernacular style of architecture. The city and its region have both a strong Catholic and Protestant tradition and a prominent Jewish minority. Indeed, the Protestant work ethic is often cited as an influence that helped to make the city and its region one of the wealthiest in Europe, built on a healthy mix of industries in the food, transportation, and luxury sectors.

Thus, as in so many European places, the citizens of Strasbourg belong to many Europes. Their city plays an active role in the new supranationally integrated Europe epitomized by today's newly enlarged European Union, and to which we will return so often in the pages to follow. At the same time, and certainly just as importantly, it is an integral part of an established national state. Europe, after all, is the birthplace of the modern nation-state, and every European and European place is an active participant therefore in a national economy and culture. Yet, at another level, the city is unique in the context of its own regional and cultural environment. Strasbourgians interact with one another in a way that is reflective of their distinctive past, they work and recreate together, and look to the future with much the same perspective. Like most Europeans, they live very modern lives and are affected daily by the homogenizing effects of today's economy and society. Nonetheless, they do what they can in the face of such trends to preserve some sense of their own local history, culture, and identity.

This book is about the geography of a people—the Europeans—their culture, and the environments in which they live. It is a regional geography, that is, an exploration of a particular part of our world, the region (or cultural realm) that we call *Europe*. Our treatment of these people and their region is topically organized and both contemporary and historical in its approach. And, as our brief opening comments about the city of Strasbourg and its inhabitants suggest, we focus on the multiplicity of influences and conditions that underlie the way in which Europeans live their daily lives and see their place in Europe and the world.

We begin in this chapter by defining and delimiting Europe as a cultural space and examining the cultural variation within that space. In subsequent chapters we explore the environmental contours of the region and the ways in which Europeans have come to inhabit and interact with their environmental surroundings, both in the past and in the present. From there we turn to discussions of language, religion, and polity, three topics that help us to delve more deeply into the cultural traits and historical traditions that we believe lend Europe its distinctive regional personality and help to define the important subregional differences that exist among its people and places. Later in the book we examine the evolution and contemporary fea-

tures of the urban environments within which the vast majority of Europeans live their daily lives. We follow that by treating two of the most salient aspects of daily life: the ways in which people make and prepare to make a living, and the ways in which they use the fruits of their labor to consume and recreate. Finally, in an epilogue, we try to look ahead a bit to see what the future may hold in store.

## THE CONCEPT OF REGION

A region may be defined as a bounded segment of earth space; yet, the term is used by different people to mean different things. Because the notion is so important in geography and so central to how we wish to introduce Europe as a geographical place, it is worth beginning with an examination of its meanings. We will discuss three kinds of regions here: *instituted*, *naively perceived*, and *denoted*. It is important to recognize that all regions are products of the human mind. Regions do not exist without the agency of humankind. They do, however, differ in who creates them, why they are created, and how they function.

### Instituted Regions

Instituted regions are perhaps the most familiar to the lay public. Open any atlas and the pages are cluttered with them. They are created by authorities within some organization—for example, national, state, or local governments, religious organizations such as the Roman Catholic Church, private businesses, and so on. The regions are created so that the organization can more easily administer whatever activity it is engaged in, whether carrying out planning for the future, collecting revenues, assembling data, or the like. Once instituted, these regions are recognized as existing entities and have boundaries that are clearly demarcated, on paper if not always on the ground; these are usually, but not always, agreed on by everyone.

Systems of instituted regions are often *hierarchical*; that is, they nest within one another.

The secular instituted region at the highest level of the hierarchy is the independent state. In the United States the second level is represented by the constituent state (e.g., Minnesota); below that is the county, then the city or rural township. The regions at different levels have different functions, but it is not easy to generalize about their importance. In the United States, for example, local authorities control education, while in European countries decisions about education are typically made at much higher levels. In Switzerland the greatest power over most matters is held by the communes and the cantons into which they are grouped rather than by the federal government.

## Naively Perceived Regions

In contrast to instituted regions, which are the formal creations of authorities, naively perceived regions are created informally. They come into existence through popular recognition and without official sanction. Recognition may come from people living either within the region or outside of it. In the first case the regions are *internally perceived*. They are closely associated with the notion of *community* in that they are the result of a closely knit group of people identifying in their own minds a territory that "belongs to *us* rather than to *them*."

Before the development of modern transportation technology, when movement over space was costly and time-consuming, small spatial communities, each with its own cultural traits and dialect, were common, especially in long-settled areas. The boundaries between these communities were seldom formally drawn, but they were well known to the community members. Often a grove of trees, a pile of rocks or perhaps a stream was recognized as the limit of "our land." Beyond it one entered "foreign" territory. Regions of this kind have been far more numerous in Europe, with its long history of settlement, than in North America. Yet, urbanization and modern developments in transportation and communication have begun to erode their significance for people. As we move more widely

and easily across earth space, our identification is with ever larger regions.

Similar to the naively perceived region or community, and central to much current writing on the identification and demarcation of informal places and regions, is the "imagined community." The emphasis here is on the idea that regional designations are socially constructed and therefore subject to continuous debate and reinterpretation. The imagined community may often reflect the views of an elite that wishes to foster the idea of a bond between a group and a place to realize certain political, cultural, or economic goals. The role of language, rhetoric, and naming can therefore be critical in forming these spatial frameworks and communicating them to others. We see this often in the struggles for political recognition waged by ethnic minorities in European states. It also has played an important role in the development of a sense of nationhood.

## Denoted Regions

Maps of denoted regions are commonly found in geographic and other academic writings. They are created by scholars, perhaps most frequently by geographers, in order to reduce the complexity of the real world so that it can better be understood. For this reason they might also usefully be designated as *pedagogical* regions. The process of creating denoted regions (regionalization) is exactly analogous to the process of *classification*. When any area (piece of space) is being divided into regions, what is actually happening is that the *places* that make up that space are being grouped together because they have something in common. It is important to note that such regions are entirely the product of the mind of the person who has created them and have no independent existence.

Denoted, or pedagogical, regions are of two kinds. *Uniform regions*, sometimes called formal, are homogeneous (or uniform) with respect to certain selected phenomena. Such a region may be defined, for example, by the dominance of Lutherans within its boundaries or by the fact that most of its agricultural land produces wheat, or by a combination of such factors. *Nodal regions*, sometimes called functional, are also denoted but differ from uniform regions in that the places included in them are defined as similar not because they are homogeneous with respect to certain selected criteria but rather because they are all tied to the same central place by the movement of people, ideas, and things. In other words, they all experience more spatial interaction with the same central place or node than they do with any other.

## EUROPE AS A CULTURE REALM

With the meanings of the term *region* defined we can now turn to the question of how Europe meets the definition of the term. Our prime purpose here is to define Europe as a uniform denoted region, to identify those traits that distinguish it from the eight or nine other major culture realms of the world. Before doing this, however, it may be useful to review the history of Europe as a naively perceived region and to comment on its conception as an instituted region.

### Naively Perceived Europe

In general parlance Europe is often called a continent. This word is derived from the Latin and is cognate with the words *continuous* and *contain*. It means literally "a *continuous* body of land *contained* within water." A cursory glance at the map tells us at once that Europe does not qualify for the appellation *continent*. It is, rather, only a small western peninsula of the great landmass we call Eurasia. The reason people have come to think of Europe as one of the seven continents of the world is because it is perceived, both internally and externally, as a distinctive culture region.

It was the Greeks who invented Europe. The Greeks were given to dichotomous thinking—that is, the penchant for dividing things into two mutually exclusive groups. Their primary division of the world was into the *ecumene*, the known, inhabited world, and the

*anecumene*, the unknown, presumably uninhabited, world. The ecumene occupied the temperate zone of the northern hemisphere, where the Greeks themselves lived, while the anecumene occupied the rest. The ecumene was also divided into two parts, *occidens*, the land to the west (associated with pleasure and happiness), and *oriens*, the land to the east (associated with uncivilized peoples). Occidens developed into Europe and oriens into Asia, although the derivations of the terms are not clear. Greece, then, occupied the center of the ecumene, a not unusual cosmological view for human societies. Europe probably originally referred to northwestern Greece, but the concept was expanded as the Greeks colonized the western Mediterranean and learned more about the lands north of the Alps.

With the rise of the Roman Empire, the Greek distinction between east and west, Europe and Asia, became blurred. The Empire occupied the lands all around the Mediterranean Sea, even in North Africa, on the fringe of the fiery Sahara Desert. For the Romans, Europe, Asia, and this third realm, Africa, were drawn together by "our sea," *mare nostrum*. Although the Greek dichotomy had no meaning for the Romans, they too divided the world into two parts. Their distinction was between Civilization, the Empire or *Romania*, and all the land that lay beyond the Empire, *Barbaria*. Civilization was associated with urban life (both the words *city* and *civilization* come from the Latin *civis*, citizen). *Barbaria* was rural and non-Roman (the Latin word derives from the Greek *barbaros*, foreign). For the Romans, then, Europe was not a useful concept, and it was simply discarded.

When the Empire fell apart, however, the Roman dichotomy, too, lost its relevance. Although the Empire in the East continued to exist for many centuries, at least in fragmentary form, in the West a variety of new "empires," creations of the barbarian invaders from the north, came and went. One institution, however, did preserve the legacy of the Roman Empire, the Christian Church. Civilization now came to be identified with Christianity. The new, medieval, dichotomous dis-

a

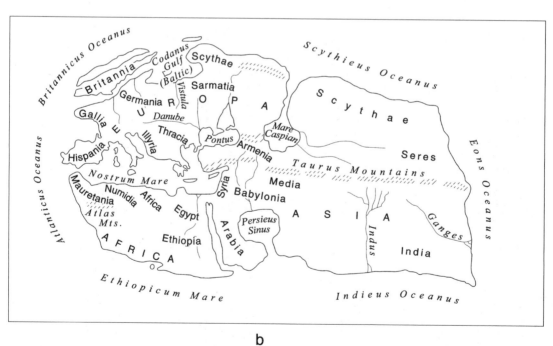

b

**FIGURE 1.3 (a and b). The Greek and Roman worlds.** These two maps represent Greek and Roman perceptions of the known world. The first is from Hecataeus, a geographer and travel writer from Miletus, a Greek city in Asia Minor. The second is from the Roman Pomponius Mela, who created a geography of the world in the first century A.D.

tinction was between *Christendom*, the world of the universal Christian Church, and the *pagan* world (the word *pagan* carries the same rural connotation as *barbarian*, coming from the Latin *paganus*, country dweller).

One cannot stress too much the role of the Church in the lives of "Europeans" during the Middle Ages. Its territorial administrative system was far more stable than that of the secular kingdoms, principalities, and other states, and people identified more strongly with the parish in which they lived than with the territory of their secular lord. An individual enjoyed full civil rights only if he was a member of the Christian community. Excommunication was synonymous with outlawry.

Initially Christianity had global aspirations; it is a universalizing religion. However, with the spread of Islam, beginning in the seventh century, Christianity became spatially confined, largely to the area the Greeks had called Europe. Contacts with the Indian and Chinese civilizations to the east were few and those with the sub-Saharan African civilizations to the south virtually nonexistent. The great ocean to the west prevented communication with the American civilizations of the Mexican highlands and the Andes.

At the end of the Middle Ages, however, three important things happened to change the medieval view and to restore the idea of Europe. First, the east–west split that had developed between the Orthodox and Roman Catholic worlds took on the appearance of irrevocability. Second, the unity of Western Christendom was shattered by the Protestant Reformation. At the same time secular states rose to attain equal or greater importance than the Church as foci for the loyalty of their subjects. Religion became for most people just a part of life rather than the focus of life itself. Third, with the Great Discoveries that took Europeans and their religion to distant shores as explorers, conquerors, and colonists, Christianity broke out of Europe and achieved its goal of worldwide distribution.

Even as the Christian populations of Europe spread their religion, their social and cultural values, and their technology beyond the confines of medieval Christendom, they became aware that their part of the world was still quite different, a very special part of the new and wider Christendom. It has been said that "in discovering the world Europe discovered herself." And so the ancient Greek designation of "Europe" returned. In the modern world, then, as in the world of the Greeks, Europe is a naively perceived region. As such it stands as one of the seven continents of the world. Its boundaries may be a topic of some dispute, but its existence is not questioned.

## Instituted Europe

Now, in our times, Europe bids, for the first time in history, to become an *instituted region*. World War II put an end to European hegemony around the world. From the late 1940s to the middle 1960s the great European colonial powers lost almost all of their overseas empires. It is interesting that this is exactly the period during which the states of Europe began to explore the possibility of creating a larger economic and political community. Ironically, just as the peoples of Asia and Africa celebrated a newly won national independence, the peoples of Europe started to look for ways in which they might profitably limit, or give up entirely, their own national independence.

The quest for a more broadly instituted Europe has been one of the major strands of European political development over the post-World War II period. Originating in the West—first as a simple customs union, then as a larger economic block known as the European Community—today's European Union (EU) represents a seemingly inexorable force destined to bring most of Europe together under some kind of federalized political structure. This is particularly true since the demise of European communism in the 1990s. Indeed, for some, "Europe" has become synonymous with the European Union, which with the latest enlargement of 2004 has expanded to include many, but not all, of the former Soviet bloc countries. The EU is now an institution that pervades the lives of Europeans, a fact that will be amply and repeatedly demon-

FIGURE 1.4. Europe and the European Union.

strated in the discussions in subsequent chapters.

Nonetheless, the realization of a completely unified Europe still lies in the future. The region continues to be a composite of smaller instituted regions—the nation-states—that in many cases cling tenuously to their individual identities, powers, and prerogatives. For our purposes, then, we prefer to define Europe for now as a uniform denoted region, a realm whose people share a cultural tradition that sets them apart from peoples elsewhere in the world and gives them their own personality. It is to this Europe that we now turn.

## Europe as a Denoted Region

We pointed out earlier that a uniform denoted region is a delimited piece of earth space created by grouping together places that share common characteristics. At the world scale culture realms are usually formed through the amalgamation of whole countries, which then are taken to be discrete places. The region we will define as Europe consists of 44 independent states. This is more than one-third again as many as existed just a little over a decade ago (32) before the collapse of Soviet power in eastern Europe. These states occupy the western peninsula of the Eurasian landmass, bounded on the north by the Arctic Sea, the west by the Atlantic, and the south by the Mediterranean. In the east we include Belarus, Ukraine, and that part of Russia lying to the west of the Urals. The latter has historically been known as European Russia and has been sharply distinguished from Asiatic Russia, or Siberia, to the east. In our view Siberia is neo-Russian in the same sense that Canada, the United States, Australia, and New Zealand are neo-British and Latin America is neo-Iberian.

In addition to the European space defined above, from time to time in our discussion we will consider a number of peripheral countries. These include, in the southeast, the secular Islamic state of Turkey, which currently awaits a decision to begin formal negotiations for entry into the EU. Also on the periphery, and figuring into our discussion on occasion, are the Arab Islamic states of the Maghreb in North Africa—Morocco, Algeria, and Tunisia—with their strong historic ties to France. In the following section we discuss the cultural traits and historical traditions that we believe give the European core a personality distinct from that of any other major world region.

## THE PERSONALITY OF EUROPE

### The Middle Eastern Heritage

At the outset it is important to note that the basic fabric of European civilization has been borrowed from the Middle East. Anatolia, Mesopotamia, the Levant, and Egypt comprise the homeland of the complex of intellectual and technological innovations that occurred during the so-called Environmental Transformation and which subsequently gave rise to European or, more broadly, Western civilization. In every realm of human activity—economy, government, religion and morality, science, the arts, and the humanities—the cultures of the Middle East had achieved high levels of development at a time when most Europeans were eking out a living as hunters and gatherers, or primitive farmers.

These innovations began with the domestication of plants and animals that led initially to the development of a shifting form of cultivation. The hill lands surrounding the Mesopotamian basin provided very favorable conditions for experimenting with plant and animal breeding. This "Fertile Crescent" offered a variety of biotic niches, each with its own complex of plant and animal communities. Archeologists have uncovered farming villages as much as 10,000 years old and discovered remains of barley, wheat, peas, lentils, and bones of domesticated goats, sheep, and possibly cattle and pigs.

Before 5000 B.C. cultivators began to move down the mountain slopes into the valley of the Tigris and Euphrates Rivers. Here they had to adjust to a new environment. The flood plain soil was very fertile, but the climate was dry and the heat in summer fierce. The agriculturalists learned to manage water and to irrigate their fields. The greater yields obtained in this new environment enabled them to settle down and abandon the shifting cultivation that they had practiced in the hills. Here the plow was developed, and domesticated oxen were used to pull it. Thus, a system of field agriculture was established that was based on the growing of grain and the use of the plow and the draft animal.

Plant and animal domestication was the core of the Environmental Transformation, but a number of other major innovations followed. Metallurgy started with the use of native copper, followed by silver and gold. More important was the discovery, around 3500 B.C., that a mixture of copper and tin produced a hard alloy, bronze, from which superior weapons and tools could be made. These were expensive, however, and most people continued to use stone, wood, or bone. Between 3500 and 3000 two revolutionary developments in transportation occurred: the invention of the wheel for use on land and of the sail for use on water. Another major development in transportation was the domestication of the horse, perhaps in the steppe lands to the north of the Black and Caspian Seas. It probably was introduced into the Middle East during the early part of the second millennium B.C.

As agriculture became more efficient, fewer workers were needed in it. Occupations became more specialized and division of labor increased. Surplus populations began to concentrate in towns, even large cities. By 4000 B.C. the trend toward urban living was well under way in Lower Mesopotamia, the region south of modern Baghdad. The urban places became centers of states, of trade, of philosophical religions, and of scientific inquiry. The art of government, designed to organize and protect society, was raised to a high level. In the realm of commerce, business contracts and credit systems were established, and gold and silver adopted as standards of value. Philosophy, the inquiry into the first causes of things and their final significance, led to the elaboration of complex religious systems and to the establishment of religious institutions and priestly castes. Systems of writing were developed; mathematics, astronomy, and the calendar were invented. The invention of writing led to the creation of poetry, drama, and history and to the development of schools.

One of the crowning achievements of the Environmental Transition was the development of a successful way of extracting large amounts of iron ore from the earth and a means of converting it into a useful material. This metal was used to produce a multitude of things, from pots to swords and plowshares. It is thought that iron-working techniques were first developed in eastern Anatolia or Armenia about 1500 B.C. Another achievement of great magnitude was the invention of the alphabet, again in the second millennium B.C. It was devised by Semitic peoples living in the Sinai Peninsula and was much superior to the older Sumerian cuneiform or Egyptian hieroglyphic systems. Its principal advantage was that it could be easily learned and was applicable to any language. The alphabet would eventually displace all the other writing systems developed in the Old World except the Chinese. It is truly remarkable what the peoples of the Middle East achieved in the years from 8000 B.C. to 1500 B.C. All of these innovations were transmitted to the peoples of Europe, principally through the agency of the Greeks and the Romans.

## Greek and Roman Thought

More than any other people the Greeks were responsible for adapting Middle Eastern culture to the European scene. The Greeks advanced science and philosophy in almost every way, developing both theoretical and empirical work. But perhaps the greatest contribution of the Greeks to European culture was their invention of the *individual*. The states of the east were monumental, bureaucratic, and autocratic. The weight of the state lay heavily upon its subjects. The Greek *polis*, by contrast, was small, a community in which all members (at least free men) could participate. The Greeks conceived of the freeman as a citizen rather than as a subject. They endowed citizens with political liberty, civil rights, and a great deal of mental and moral freedom. Essentially the Greeks created democracy and established reason as the guiding principle in government and all other aspects of life. Of course, they did not know democracy as we know it today, but they laid the groundwork for later developments in this area, which would be among the major ingredients distinguishing European culture from other cultures of the world. Greek thought found its way into later European culture via

**FIGURE 1.5. The Athenian agora.** The agora was the heart of ancient Athens—the place where citizens participated in the cultural, political, commercial, and administrative life of the *polis*. The agora was also a religious center. The building at the top-center of the photo is the Temple of Hephaestus, dedicated to the two gods Hephaestus and Athena during the fifth century B.C. (Photo: J. L. Kramer)

three channels: Roman thought, Christianity, and the Renaissance.

The role of Rome was to take the culture of the Greeks, both what they had inherited from the East and what they, themselves, had invented, spread it throughout the Mediterranean world, and then transmit it through the Latin language and literature to the peoples of northern Europe. The Romans made some contributions of their own, among them a new, more independent status for women, never known in the Greek world, and new principles of political organization and social security expressed in a law code, which is still the foundation of many European legal systems. They also developed a hierarchy of cities and bequeathed much of that hierarchy, albeit in a weakened condition, to medieval Christendom.

## Christianity

It was a Greek, the apostle Paul, who interpreted Christ's teachings to his people (the Gentiles, as the Jews called them) and laid the foundation for Christian dogma. Greek thought, and Neoplatonic philosophy, in particular, imparted a structure to Christian doc-

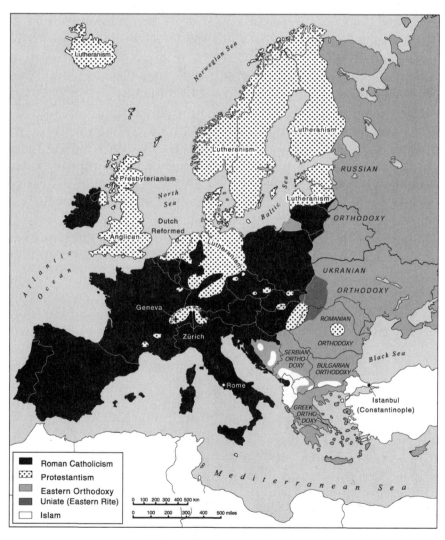

FIGURE 1.6. Religions in Europe, ca. 2000.

trine that had no biblical foundation. Nonetheless Christianity has contributed much to European culture that is not Greek in origin. Most important, perhaps, is the Judeo-Christian code of ethics, which elaborates what is acceptable and what is unacceptable behavior in European societies. This ethical system is founded on the notion that there is a moral code of law handed down by God. Out of this law came the seven virtues and the seven deadly sins. Jewish tradition emphasized the necessity to follow this code to the letter; Christ emphasized rather the spirit of the law, especially love of God and one's neighbor. This ethic is radically different from that of the Greeks and Romans, who had no conception of a divinely dictated moral code. For them, everything that one did was a matter of practical reasoning. One could do well or poorly. In the Judeo-Christian view doing badly in school or at sports is entirely different from failing to help someone in need. The former is a fault, but the latter is a transgression against the virtue of charity. This distinction between a divine and a human moral code affects the very way questions are framed in European and neo-European cultures.

Christian ethics also emphasizes the equal moral status of all human beings. This is because all are potentially immortal and equally precious in the sight of God. This led to sanctions in European culture against infanticide, abortion, and suicide. It also led to the abolition of slavery in Europe by the High Middle Ages, although the practice was to return later, applied not to Europeans but to black Africans. Early Christians accepted slaves into their congregations. This was not difficult to do because for Christians the highest virtues were meekness, obedience, patience, and resignation. The Greeks and Romans, on the other hand, respected independence, self-reliance, magnanimity, and worldly success. As they conceived virtue, a "virtuous slave" was a contradiction in terms. For Christians, however, there was nothing in the state of slavery that was incompatible with the highest moral character.

Like most philosophical religions, Christianity has been susceptible to theological disagreements that have led to schisms. These rifts in the Christian Church have meant that many subsequent cultural developments were specific to particular regions. The most prominent cultural boundary in Europe is that between Western and Eastern Christianity. Western Christendom took its heritage from Greece through the medium of Rome. Eastern Christendom also took its heritage

FIGURE 1.7. **St. Peter's Basilica.** St. Peter's is the hub and principal shrine of the Catholic Church, which has attracted the largest number of Christians in Europe. The present structure, which is the largest in all Christendom and is said to stand on the final resting place of St. Peter, was built during the 16th and 17th centuries. The obelisk that marks the center of the piazza in front of the Basilica was brought here from the Roman circus where Peter was martyred.

from Greece but via Byzantium, a Greek civilization that had been only very slightly Romanized. In the East, Christianity remained Orthodox, that is, early Christian doctrine was little changed. In the West, however, points of theology were constantly questioned, and the tenets of the faith underwent steady change. In time the Eastern Church came to view many of the beliefs of the Roman Church as heretical. Partly for this reason many of the Western philosophical movements that we have described as fundamental to European culture were rejected in the East. Thus, the cultures of Western Christendom often appear more European than those of the Orthodox realm.

One must also remember that the Orthodox realm stands on the eastern boundary of Christendom, where it has been more open to Asian influences than most of the rest of Europe. The Russians held the gates against the Mongols, and, although they were forced into submission for two centuries, they ultimately triumphed and themselves subdued all of northern Asia. For several centuries the Byzantines held the Ottoman Turks at bay before finally succumbing. Greco-Christian culture survived both the Mongols and the Ottomans. There can be no question that the Orthodox world is a part of Europe.

The second major schism occurred within the Western Church in the 16th century and led to the establishment of a variety of "national" Protestant Churches. A defining element of the Protestant world is often said to be an ethic in which hard work and the accumulation of capital holds a central position. This has been explained by some as a result of the Calvinist belief in predestination, the idea that the salvation of any individual has already been decided before that person's birth. Success in this world was seen as a sign of a future in heaven among the "elect." Proponents of this idea see this work ethic as closely linked to the development of the capitalist commercial–industrial society in northwestern Europe.

Some cultural differences have resulted not from theological disagreements but rather from the different attitudes of the Churches as social institutions. Much evidence suggests that, in the early Middle Ages, the Western Church strove very hard to sever the lateral ties in the extended family (to siblings and their families) and to establish the stem family (grandparents, parents, and children), as opposed to the extended family, as the primary economic unit. Some scholars believe that this was done to decrease the lateral flow of resources and increase the probability that wealth would be left to the Church during life and at death. Under the stem family system a young man had to wait until he had personal access to land before he could start a family. The result, they argue, was to produce, by the 17th century, the European marriage pattern, in which both men and women married late and many did not marry at all. This had an enormous effect on birthrates, which were much lower than in the rest of the world. That this is a uniquely western European phenomenon may well be due to the fact that no other world religion had so strong or centralized an institutional organization as the Roman Catholic Church.

## The Indo-European Legacy

The overwhelming majority of Europeans speak languages of the Indo-European family. Most of these languages belong to the Germanic or Balto-Slavic subfamilies, or are descended from Latin, a member of the Italic subfamily. Fewer than 3% of the European population speak the five languages (Hungarian, Finnish, Estonian, Saami, and Basque) that do not belong to this group. Language would then also appear to be a factor unifying the culture realm, though it must be pointed out that many more Indo-European speakers live outside of Europe. Nearly 45% of the world's population speak languages belonging to this family, and just over a quarter of these are Europeans. Roughly the same number of Indo-European speakers live in the state of India alone.

It is difficult to pinpoint the ways in which a common language family lends unity to a group of cultures. However, it can be argued that, more than any other cultural trait, lan-

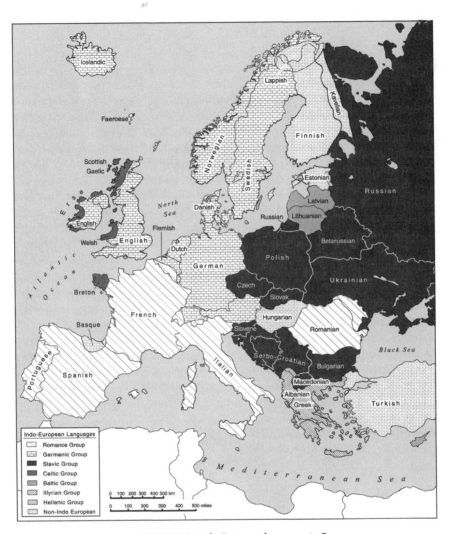

FIGURE 1.8. Indo-European languages in Europe.

guage reflects culture because it is the bearer of culture. Thus, the way in which any people express themselves is shaped by the view that their culture has of the world. This is reflected both in the way that the language is structured and in the vocabulary. There are commonalities among the grammars and lexicons of Indo-European languages that are not shared by other language families. It is easier for an English speaker to learn Russian than Chinese not only because the former languages share some similarities in vocabulary and structure but also because English and Russian speakers are closer to each other in

the way they think about the world than either is to speakers of Chinese.

A common linguistic heritage also implies similar mythologies and customs. Christianity has absorbed not only many elements of Greek and Roman culture but also a great many features of other pre-Christian Indo-European cultures. Our celebration of Halloween goes back to the pagan Celtic observance of New Year. The New Year for the Celts began on November 1. The festival of Sambain was observed on October 31, the last day of summer. It was a time when the herds returned from summer pasture and laws and land tenures were renewed. The souls of the dead were also said to revisit their homes on this date. It was a night when ghosts, witches, hobgoblins, fairies, and black cats were thought to be roaming about. To frighten these evil spirits away, the Celts hollowed out turnips, carved faces in them, and placed them in their windows with lighted candles inside. Rather than proscribe this deeply ingrained celebration, the Christian Church incorporated it into its festival of All Hallows Eve, celebrated on the same date. Gradually Halloween became a secular observance and was introduced into the United States by Irish immigrants in the 19th century.

Lucia, martyred in Sicily in the early fourth century and later canonized, is, because of her name, associated with light (Latin *lux*). In Sweden her feast day, December 13, came to replace the pre-Christian celebration of the winter *blot*, a festival marking the winter solstice, when the days become longer once again. Today the tradition specifies that the youngest daughter in the family dress in a white robe and wear a crown of lighted candles (both symbols of light). European cultures are replete with examples of this kind of survival of pre-Christian Indo-European myths and practices.

## The Renaissance and Humanism

Although Greek thought had a great impact on European culture directly through both Roman society and Christianity, much of it was incorporated during the rebirth of interest in classical learning that occurred toward the end of the Middle Ages, a development conventionally referred to as the Renaissance. Its earliest expression was in the intellectual movement known as humanism, led by secular thinkers in reaction to what they saw as the failed Scholastic philosophy of the Catholic Church. Its first successes were in Italy, and it received an enormous boost from the many eastern scholars who fled to Italy as the Ottoman Turks advanced against the Byzantine Empire. These refugees brought with them important books and manuscripts and, of course, a knowledge of the Greek language,

which had become rare in Western Christendom.

As its name suggests, humanism emphasized the potential good in human beings rather than their sinful nature, which was the preoccupation of the Scholastics. Whereas medieval thought began with the idea that man was flawed and needed to do constant penance in order to gain his reward in heaven, humanist thinking started with the inherent worth of human beings and viewed life as a precious time of inquiry and discovery. Humanism marks the beginning of the transition from the Age of Faith to the Age of Reason. The Renaissance, then, was a return to the true Hellenic sources of Western culture that had been corrupted by the Scholastics and their distorted Latin translations.

The Renaissance scholar, following the ancient Greek model, espoused the objective analysis of perceived experience and exhibited a concern for detail and a highly critical attitude toward all knowledge. This kind of empiricism led ultimately to the development of modern science and, above all, promoted the study of mathematics, which was viewed as the key to human understanding of the universe. Underpinning all of this new intellectual exploration was the Greek notion of the worth of the individual and the dignity of mankind. There was, however, one important

**FIGURE 1.9. Cambridge University.** One of the great seats of learning and a hotbed of Protestant thought at the time of the Reformation, Cambridge University was founded in the midst of a great wave of university establishments that spread across Europe from Italy between the 12th and 16th centuries. King's College and its famous Gothic chapel are viewed here across the "Backs," the name given to the lush meadows that line the River Cam.

Christian addition, and that was the stress on social responsibility as the goal of learning.

This empirical and critical movement, which freed the individual from conformity to the group, set the stage for the many discoveries that launched the Scientific Transformation. The Scientific Transformation began with the Great Discoveries and continued with the revolutions in transportation, agriculture, and industry that gave Europe two or three centuries of hegemony over the rest of the world.

Not until the very end of the 15th century did Christian civilization, pent up for a thousand years in this small western peninsula of the Eurasian continent, finally break out. Through long ocean voyages Europeans discovered the rest of the world and, either politically or economically, conquered most of it. Only two peoples are known to have made persistent voyages far into the open ocean before this time. One was the Vikings, the Scandinavians of pre-Christian times, who sailed to the Shetlands, Orkneys, Iceland, Greenland, and North America. The other was the Polynesians who settled the Pacific islands, but this feat is thought to have been more the result of drift voyages than of intentional navigation. Neither had an appreciable impact on the history of the world.

One French historian, Denis de Rougemont, sees in these voyages of discovery something he feels is crucial in defining European culture, and that is the willingness to take risks. This is arguably a result of the emphasis on the individual over the group. When group security is given high priority, the individual is discouraged from taking risks and the tone of the society is highly conservative. De Rougemont argues that, of all the peoples of the earth, the Europeans are the only ones who have consistently gone beyond the limits set by nature, beyond the traditions fixed by their ancestors. A strict interpretation of this claim would deny technological innovation in other societies, which would be absurd. But it might be justified to say that no other people took such giant strides across the boundaries set by nature.

## The Philosophy of the Enlightenment

The European enthronement of the individual continued during the 17th and 18th centuries in the intellectual movement known as the Enlightenment. Central to the Enlightenment was the celebration of reason as the principal power by which human beings can understand the universe and improve their condition. The goals of rational mankind were considered to be knowledge and understanding, freedom and happiness. It was thought that correct reason could discover useful knowledge. The 18th century is the acme of the Age of Reason. Together with humanism, the Renaissance, and the Reformation, which shattered the monolithic authority of the Roman Catholic Church, this movement fueled the Scientific Transformation in Europe.

Unlike humanism, however, the Enlightenment separated science from theology. The Reformation and the Thirty Years' War had destroyed the hope that the Christian faith and scientific learning could be reconciled. The Enlightenment totally divorced the realms of scientific and theological thought and prepared the way for the secularization of European culture. The privatization of religion, its removal from the public sphere to the sanctity of the home, was to have an enormous impact on European culture, including fertility behavior in the 19th century. Another major element of the Enlightenment was the development of a set of ideas about the fundamental freedom of the individual, formulated largely in England in the 17th century, which led to new definitions of political democracy and parliamentary government. Finally, the Enlightenment fostered the idea of education for the masses, laying the ground for the establishment of truly democratic political institutions.

From the Renaissance through the Enlightenment what we have seen, then, is (1) the rediscovery of Greek notions about both the dignity and freedom of the individual and rational thinking in humanism, which tries to reconcile these two ideas with Christian thought; (2) the disillusionment with Christian teaching brought about by the Protestant Reformation and the subsequent century of wars; (3) the separation of reasoned thinking about nature from theological teachings; and (4) the application of the idea of individual freedom in the political arena, paving the way for the development of the democratic state.

## Nationalism and Romanticism

The new theories of political democracy insisted that states and their governments belonged to the people, not to ruling families. This led ultimately to the uniquely European idea of nationalism, the notion that if political states coincide exactly with homogeneous peoples, or nations, the tensions between the people seeking freedom of action and the governments seeking public order will be minimized. Briefly put, people who feel themselves to be related will want the same things. This represents an extension of the idea of freedom of the individual to freedom of the related group.

Although it had its origins in the spirit of the Enlightenment, nationalism became deeply involved with the Romantic Movement of the late 18th and 19th centuries. Romanticism was a reaction against the rational thinking of the Enlightenment, a rejection of the precepts of order, calm, harmony, balance, and reason that typified that movement. Romanticism stressed the subjective, the irrational, the imaginative, the personal, the spontaneous, the emotional. It also emphasized the common people, rejecting high, cosmopolitan culture, which was Pan-European, in favor of the simple popular cultures of nations, attached to their native soil. Its association with Romanticism greatly changed the shape of nationalism, as we shall see in Chapter 7.

## The Commercial–Industrial Society

There is one further element of European culture that needs to be mentioned. Europe, and Europe alone, developed an economic system that freed the great bulk of its people from the task of producing the basic necessi-

ties of life and produced a division of labor that allowed enormous specialization. Initially this took a capitalist form. Subsequently it was translated into a Marxist form. Both are European.

This economic system was, of course, made possible by the Scientific Transformation, whose roots we have explored, and by the rise of the middle class to great importance, a feature of the Enlightenment. Born in the northwestern part of Europe, it ultimately spread in some form to all other areas of the region and, eventually, on the wings of European imperialism to most of the rest of the world. Its impact on the Third World has often been called "Westernization" or even "Americanization" and today may lie at the core of what we call "globalization," but it often is unaccompanied by other aspects of European culture. However, the fact that European culture, alone among all the cultures of the world, is available as a model to be accepted in part or rejected in toto is also something that makes this region distinctive.

## CULTURAL VARIATION WITHIN THE REALM: DIVERSITY IN UNITY

These, then, are the main elements of the culture that we now call European. Clearly, not all Europeans share to an equal degree in every one of them. Europe has been called a "family of cultures," its historical traditions and cultural heritages overlapping, each figuring in a number of examples but not in all. Before leaving our discussion of Europe as a culture realm, it will be useful to look briefly at how culture varies across the realm.

Just as it is useful to distinguish Europe as one among a number of culture realms in the world, so it is also useful to identify relatively homogeneous culture regions within Europe. Again, the point is to reduce the complexity of reality, making it easier to comprehend the diversity within European culture. The regional scheme presented here has been constructed with a mind to cultural similarities among people, especially with regard to language

FIGURE 1.10. A regionalization of European culture.

and religion, common historical experience, and the role that major cities have played in providing foci for human activity. Our intent has been to create regions that reflect enduring associations rather than modern political or economic alliances, which are important and cannot be completely ignored but also may be quite fleeting. The "places" grouped together to form the regions are whole countries. This is at variance with some of the current thinking, which we will discuss in a later chapter, about the decline of the nation-state and the transfer of political and economic power to the supranational and local levels.

However, our scheme reflects the fact that, for the foreseeable future, the lives of Europeans are still most affected by the institutions, laws, and cultures of the states within which they live.

The regional system adopted here recognizes eight regions within Europe proper and four peripheral regions, which are transitional to other culture realms. In addition, we identify a European "heartland," a region whose people demonstrate the traits of the European culture realm, as they were defined above, more completely than any other Europeans. This "heartland" region includes the London and Paris Basins, much of the Low Countries, the Rhineland, the Bavarian and Swiss plateaus, and the western part of the Po Basin in Italy. It is somewhat reminiscent of "Lotharingian" Europe, the middle portion of Charlemagne's empire as it was divided among his three grandsons. It also somewhat approximates the area known as the "Blue Banana," identified by a group of French geographers in the 1980s as the modern economic and industrial spine of western Europe. While occupying only a relatively small portion of the total area of Europe, it contains almost a fifth of its population.

The heartland, which defies the conventions of national boundaries, lies mainly in what we will identify in our regional scheme as the British Isles, western and west-central Europe, suggesting a twofold division of Europe proper. The inner zone contains the three aforementioned regions, while the outer zone is composed of the other five. This scheme is not meant to suggest that the peoples of the inner zone have been more important than others in European history but rather that they have been more exposed to those ideas and movements that we regard as central to European culture.

## EUROPE PROPER: THE INNER ZONE

### Western Europe

In a sense, since the end of the Middle Ages western Europe can be considered the "headquarters" or "cornerstone" of Europe. From a historical perspective, this is largely because of France, which was one of the most important players on the European scene from the late 16th to the early 20th century. For much of European history Paris was the largest or the second-largest city in Europe. In the Middle Ages the University of Paris was the greatest center of learning in the world, and by the 17th century French culture had become the model for *haute culture* everywhere. French became the language of choice at many European courts and by the 18th century was the international language of diplomacy. The French Revolution was an important early

step in the establishment of the rights of the individual and the evolution of the idea of nationalism, two keystones of European culture. Secularized postrevolutionary France was the first country, as we shall see in Chapter 3, to institute family-size limitations and led the transition from high to low fertility, which totally transformed European life.

Paris remained the cultural focus of Europe and the world well into the 19th century, and with just under 10 million inhabitants Paris today is officially Europe's largest city. It has grown mainly as the capital of a highly centralized French state. As new territories were added to the state, their cultures were suppressed by the central authorities, and their economies were tied very closely to the capital city. The road and railroad systems were focused on Paris, and it is hard to travel any considerable distance in France without passing through the city. In recent years there has been some decentralization, but Paris remains the hub of the French state. To a great extent Paris has also been the center to which the French-speaking Belgian Walloons have looked for cultural guidance.

While Paris has been denied any of the administrative functions of the European Union, all of these are nonetheless located within

FIGURE 1.11. The Champs-Elysées. Open to strollers on a Sunday afternoon in May, the Champs-Elysées carries on in its legendary role as the French capital's most elegant promenade and triumphal way. Crowning the avenue is the Arc de Triomphe, completed in 1836 to celebrate the victories of the Napoleonic Empire.

what we have defined as western Europe. Brussels has housed the headquarters of NATO since 1967. The Berlaymont in the Belgian capital is the seat of the European Commission, the most powerful body of the EU. Every year one meeting of the European Council is held in Brussels, and the city hosts regular meetings of European parliamentary and political groups. Luxembourg is the seat of the European Investment Bank, the Court of Justice, and the Secretariat of the European Parliament. And, as we have seen, the meetings of the European Parliament are held in Strasbourg, which is also the seat of the Council of Europe, a non-EU institution.

The other urban focus of western Europe is the cluster of cities north of the Rhine delta in the Netherlands known as Randstad (Ring City). The Randstad conurbation is anchored by Rotterdam with its Europoort, the continent's largest port in volume of goods handled; Den Haag, the seat of the national government; and Amsterdam, the nominal capital and cultural center of the Netherlands. The latter is the creation of merchants who built the Dutch Empire between the 16th and 18th centuries, fostering an independent spirit that won, first Holland, and then the other northern counties their independence. Just as Paris has been the cultural capital of western Europe, Randstad has been its mercantile capital.

Culturally western Europe sits astride the boundary between what we will later identify as the Germanic and Romanic linguistic subrealms. French is spoken over most of the region, but Dutch prevails in the north, and forms of German may be heard in eastern Belgium, Luxembourg, and Alsace. The populace is predominantly Roman Catholic, though both the French and the Dutch Catholic Churches have been among the most liberal in Europe for many decades. However, islands of Protestantism may be found, especially in the Netherlands. Here both the Dutch Reformed and Christian Reformed Churches are strong in the northern counties, and there is a large Humanist community. A second cultural boundary might be that which separates metropolitan France and the Low Countries from the western and southern peripheries of France. Western France looks toward the Atlantic and has traditionally lagged behind in terms of economic development. It has certain affinities with other Atlantic facing lands in Britain, Scandinavia, and Iberia. The Mediterranean south of France also maintains its cultural distinctiveness from the center, and lately has increasingly allied itself economically, as we shall later see, with its neighbors along the northern rim of the western Mediterranean.

## Britain and Ireland

Britain and Ireland have traditionally been seen as separate from western Europe because they are islands. The British, especially, have regarded the Channel as something that keeps them apart from the rest of Europe, which they refer to as "the continent." Some years back a headline in the *Times* of London read "Fog in Channel, Continent Isolated," a telling commentary not only on Britain's sense of standing apart from Europe but also on its assessment of the relative importance of the two. This is to a large extent based on the aloofness that the British have historically strived to maintain from the turmoil in the lands across the Channel. While armies have swarmed back and forth across the continent, Britain has not been invaded since the Normans did it back in the eleventh century A.D. That same aloofness may be said to characterize British dealings with today's EU. The government in London often seeks special consideration or exemptions for Britain with regard to decisions that may be generally amenable to the rest of her continental neighbors.

Nonetheless, the British broke out of their island fortress in the 16th century and created the greatest overseas empire the world has ever known. Between 1500 and 1600 London tripled in population. Over the next 300 years it became not only the most powerful political capital in the world but the world's premier commercial and financial capital as

**FIGURE 1.12. The London Royal Exchange.** This building with its neoclassical façade was erected in 1842. It is the third building to occupy the site since Sir Thomas Gresham founded the Exchange in 1566 with the intent of supplanting the Bourse of Amsterdam as Europe's foremost marketplace. The Exchange is a symbol of London's long supremacy in the world of finance.

well. The 20th-century collapse of colonialism and the decline of British industrial might have taken their toll on the economy; yet, today London, along with New York and Tokyo, is still one of the three leading financial centers of the world. This has nothing to do with the British stock and bond markets or the strength of the pound sterling, but is related to the international connections forged by London bankers during Britain's period of world hegemony.

Like western Europe, this region shares more fully than most other regions in the characteristics we have identified as defining European culture. English philosophers of the Enlightenment laid the groundwork for modern democracy, and the English are arguably the first modern nation to emerge. Britain is the home of both the Agricultural and the Industrial Revolutions, which brought about the commercial–industrial society as we know it today. Its leading role in shaping what has become our modern global economy is a major reason why English became the language of science and commerce and has surpassed French as the prime medium for international communication.

Just as western Europe is a zone of contact between Romanic and Germanic cultures, this region is a meeting place between Germanic and Celtic cultures. Before the Roman occupation of Britain, the population of the two islands was entirely Celtic. Romanization did not penetrate the society very deeply, and the Latin language did not persist after the Roman troops left. It was the Anglo-Saxon invaders of the fifth century A.D. who brought the ancestral West Germanic dialects of English and drove the Celts into the western parts of the islands and across the Channel into Brittany where Celtic is still spoken today. Later the settlement of Norwegians and Danes brought further (this time North) Germanic influence. Linguistically the region today is English-speaking, though there are still some speakers of Celtic, mostly Welsh, but Gaelic on the western fringes of Scotland and Ireland. While western Europe is mainly Catholic, this region is predominantly Protestant with the exception of a rather conservative Catholic Ireland and Irish Catholic enclaves in the major industrial cities of Britain. For cultural as well as political reasons, a fairly sharp divide still persists between Catholic Ireland and the island of Great Britain.

## West-Central Europe

West-central Europe is German-speaking Europe, largely Catholic in the south and west (except in many urban areas), Protestant in the north and east. Politically it corresponds to the core of the German state as it emerged in the late 19th century plus the core of the Austrian Empire and the Swiss Confederation, which is mainly German-speaking. While thus possessing some cultural unity, the constituent parts of the region have traditionally looked in different directions.

The Rhineland, with its major urban foci at Frankfurt and the Rhine-Ruhr conurbation, has long been oriented toward western Europe. Frankfurt is one of Europe's leading financial centers, while Rhine-Ruhr developed into Germany's greatest center of heavy industry. Hamburg has historically looked to the North Sea and the world at large. Its title of "Free and Hanseatic City" recalls its deep involvement in trade and shipping over the centuries. Even today Hamburg contains more consulates than any other city in the world apart from New York. Berlin's traditional orientation has been eastward. It originated as the capital of Brandenburg, a marchland that guarded the eastern frontiers of the German lands and fostered the further advance of German settlement in the east. Vienna, founded at the strategic point where the Danube flows into the Great Hungarian Plain, played the same role with regard to the German advance to the southeast. In its role as capital of the Austrian Empire, its involvement has been mainly with the Danubian lands. Although smaller cities with historically more local regional associations, both Munich and Zürich, by virtue of their proximity to the Alpine passes, have been more open to influences coming from the south.

Although often lacking cohesion historically, and prone to looking in different directions, west-central Europe constitutes the third regional leg of our inner zone. The German-speaking lands have always been full, if not leading, participants in the advancement of Western culture, science, and political development. As such, it would be difficult to separate them from the West. Politically, this has been especially evident over the decades since World War II, as Germany—by far the

major player in the region—has made partnership with the West the cornerstone of its national policy and identity. This has included rapprochement with its traditional western enemy, France, with which it has attempted to share leadership in the building of a larger European community.

The effect of German reunification since 1989 has been to draw the land and people of former East Germany, however painfully, out of their long isolation under socialist rule and into the western economy and life of the larger German nation. Despite the transfer of the German capital from Bonn, on the west bank of the Rhine, to the former capital of Berlin, a mere 50 kilometers from Germany's eastern frontier, and the lure of new markets and opportunities in east-central Europe, the postwar political and economic alignment of Germany with its western neighbors has not changed. What has changed, however, is perhaps an eastward shift of the center of gravity within what we have delimited as the Inner Zone of Europe proper. Germany's absorption of the formerly socialist *Länder* in the East, along with the absorption now of most of east-central Europe into the EU, has made west-central Europe, and Germany in particular, a more important part of Europe's political and economic core than may have been the case just a decade or so ago.

FIGURE 1.13. The new Reichstag. Originally opened in 1894, this controversial building survived World War II only as a hollowed-out shell of itself. Although restored after the war, the building lost its parliamentary function with the removal of the capital of West Germany to Bonn. Since the reunification of Germany in 1990, Berlin has once again become the capital city, and a newly refurbished Reichstag building, with a striking new glass dome, is the home of the German Parliament, or *Bundestag*.

## EUROPE PROPER: THE OUTER ZONE

### East-Central Europe

East-central Europe is the region within which the Germanic and the Slavic cultures have historically met. Once almost wholly Slavic, much of the region became Germanized during the medieval "Drang nach Osten," when large numbers of German crusaders, merchants, landowners, and peasants settled here. Some of the territory became part of the German and Austrian empires, but even in other parts of the region Germans came to dominate the economy and to define high culture. The deep penetration of Germans and German culture into this region contributed to the idea of *Mitteleuropa*, which came into fashion among German geographers following the unification of Germany in 1871. The term was used to mean "greater Germany," a vast German Folk Area (*Volksgebiet*) centered on Berlin and Vienna and including nearly all of what we define here as west-central and east-central Europe. The notion provided an important rationale for German political expansionism, which brought on the two great world wars. However, with the defeat of Nazi Germany and the forced migration of millions of ethnic Germans out of east-central Europe, the *raison d'être* for *Mitteleuropa* was largely laid to rest.

Language was not all that divided the German invaders from the indigenous population, however. While the Germans, except in the Austrian south, turned to Protestantism during the Reformation, the Slavs remained Catholic or were reconverted during the Counter-Reformation. From the 14th century on, the region also became home to large numbers of Jews who found refuge from the pogroms of western Europe in the lands of more enlightened east European rulers such as Casimir the Great of Poland. Thus, before World War II very large numbers of ethnic Germans and Jews lived in these eastern territories. Almost all of the Jews died in Hitler's extermination camps. After the war some 12–13 million ethnic Germans were forcibly ejected from their homes and resettled in the West, and only a tiny minority live in east-central Europe today (e.g., 500,000 in Poland). These two separate acts of "ethnic cleansing" increased the Catholic and Slavic dominance in the region and thus gave it far more cultural unity than it ever previously possessed.

More than the regions we have discussed so far, east-central Europe lacks clear urban foci. After the partition of Poland in the late 18th century, the great imperial capitals of the East—Berlin, Vienna, and Moscow—all lay beyond its borders. Prague was a great city in the Middle Ages when it served for a time as the seat of the Holy Roman Empire, but its incorporation into the Austrian Empire greatly reduced its status. Budapest rose to prominence in the late 19th century when the Hungarians were given "equal" status with the Austrians in the new Dual Monarchy, but the breakup of the empire following World War I was to leave the city with little territorial influence. The only other candidate for leadership is Warsaw. However, not made capital of the powerful Polish-Lithuanian state until the late 16th century, the city on the Vistula never achieved more than national importance.

Today the states of this region look to the European Union to give them focus. For decades during the long postwar period of socialist rule, there was a sort of nostalgia for a bygone "central Europe," which was kept alive for the most part by exiles from the region living in the West. This nostalgia was of a romanticized central Europe of the Hapsburg era, rather than of the German ideal of a *Mitteleuropa*. After the fall of communism there was some talk of a renewed central European identity and a number of efforts at regional cooperation between some of the states in the region, but this seems to have died away before a wave of enthusiasm for joining the EU and becoming part of the West. Nonetheless, even with the accession now of nearly the entire region to the EU, east-central Europe will likely remain a distinctive European region by virtue of the differences in culture and economy between these countries and the rest of the EU.

**FIGURE 1.14. Budapest.** The capital of Hungary and one of the largest cities of east-central Europe, Budapest straddles the Danube just as it passes through the hills of western Hungary and opens onto the vast Hungarian Plain. It consists of two parts: Buda on one bank is the old medieval center; Pest on the other bank is the newer, more commercial, part of the city. This view looks upstream from the castle hill in Buda with the neo-Gothic-style Parliament building on the right in Pest. The city gained a reputation during the socialist years for its openness to Western influences, which in turn gave it a head start in making the transition to a Western-style market economy.

The one anomaly within the region is Kaliningrad, the isolated piece of Russian territory situated on the Baltic coast between Poland and Lithuania. Kaliningrad oblast consists of the port city of Kaliningrad and its immediate hinterland, and has a population of just under a million. Until the end of World War II, the area, part of the province known as East Prussia, belonged to Germany, and the city was known as Königsberg. After the war East Prussia was partitioned between Poland and the Soviet Union, the German population moved out and in the Soviet part was replaced with Russians. Under Soviet rule, Kaliningrad became an important industrial city and, as the Soviet Union's only ice-free Baltic port, the home of the Russian Baltic Sea Fleet, a function it still retains. Today, Kaliningrad stands out strikingly from the rest of east-central Europe. It has become an enclave of smuggling and other illicit activities, industrial decay, unimaginably difficult pollution problems, and abject economic ruin. Even by Russian standards Kaliningrad is poor, having one of the worst economies in the Russian Federation. It has become surrounded entirely by countries that have been successful in raising their political systems and economies to a level acceptable for mem-

bership in the EU. As a lone and troubled Russian outpost, it is likely to remain outside the mainstream of development and a source of concern for its east-central European neighbors and for Europe as a whole.

## Nordic and Baltic Europe

The core of this far northern region is Scandinavia (Denmark, Norway, and Sweden), whose peoples speak very closely related Germanic languages. In the Viking period the Norwegians extended Scandinavian settlement far out into the Atlantic (the Færoes, Iceland, and Greenland) and in the early Middle Ages the Swedes gained political domination over most of the Finnish population to the east and established Swedish colonies east of the Gulf of Bothnia. Denmark later gained control of Norway and her possessions, while Sweden extended her empire into the lands of the Estonians and Latvians. Thus, the Scandinavians have historically faced in two directions: the Norwegians, and until recently the Danes, have looked to the west while Swedes have been concerned with the east. This "bipolar" Norden, with Copenhagen and Stockholm as its two foci, persisted from the end of the Middle Ages to the early 20th century when, first Norway (1905), then Finland (1917), and later Iceland (1944) gained complete independence.

After centuries of war between Danes and Swedes, the peoples of northern Europe began to foster cooperation among themselves in the 19th century and following World War II. Especially important in this process was the founding in 1952 of the Nordic Council, an international consultative body dedicated to promoting a spirit of cooperation and mutual self-interest within the broad areas of cultural, political, and economic affairs. Also important was the reinforcement of this effort in 1971 through the creation of the Nordic Council of Ministers to serve as an intergovernmental vehicle for cooperation in specific policy areas. The Nordic Council and Council of Ministers have done much to promote the concept of Norden, and its definition as the five Nordic states plus the three autonomous areas of the Færoes, Greenland, and Åland. These efforts have led to the establishment of many common institutions, such as a passport union, common labor market, common diplomatic representation, and a common stance in the United Nations, as well as a rather comfortable sense that Nordic institutions and culture represent a sensible alternative to what goes on elsewhere in Europe.

Now that three of the Nordic countries (Denmark, Sweden, and Finland) belong to the EU and two (Norway and Iceland) do not, the future of the Nordic Council and of Nordic identity and unity has been called into question. Some have even pointed to signs of a crisis of confidence. Growing integration with Europe threatens to reduce the sense of Nordic distinctiveness. It replaces the belief in a "Nordic alternative" with a sense that the region has now become peripheral to an increasingly dominant European core, and as such needs to find new ways to assert itself. The answer seems to lie, in part, with the Baltic, which has emerged since the breakup of the Soviet Union as an attractive new focal point for regional identity and cooperation in northern Europe.

At least two of the Baltic republics (Estonia and Latvia) now appear to be moving toward becoming integral parts of an expanded Nordic/Baltic realm, although their addition also serves to highlight historic East–West differences in orientation between the Nordic states. The interest in generating ties with the Baltic republics, which have now also become new members of the EU, has come mainly from eastward-facing Finland, Sweden, and Denmark. Estonia is the most easily integrated of the Baltic republics. The Estonians are close cultural relatives of the Finns, and Finland has been quite active in promoting economic development in that country since independence. More questionable is the position of Latvia. The Latvian language is related to Lithuanian (both are Baltic), but Latvians, like Estonians, have historically been mainly Lutherans. A further complication is the large number of ethnic Russians still living in Latvia. They are not Russian citizens, but, since independence, have been having difficulty getting Latvian citizenship. The same is true, of course, of ethnic Russians in Estonia. Because of the long involvement of the capital and port city of Riga in Baltic affairs, however, it seems reasonable to include Latvia also in what we have termed Nordic and Baltic Europe. Because of its Catholic religion, long historic ties with Poland, and considerable Polish minority, the third Baltic republic and new EU member, Lithuania, fits fairly comfortably into our east-central Europe region.

**FIGURE 1.15. Neste service station in Narva.** Since the breakup of the Soviet Union, car owners in the Estonian border city of Narva have been able to gas up at this modern Neste service station. Like many other Finnish companies, Neste has invested heavily in Estonia.

## The Western Mediterranean

This region consists of two peninsulas, the Iberian and the Italian. The situation of the Iberian peninsula in Europe bears some striking similarities to that of the Scandinavian peninsula. Both have for most of history lain outside the mainstream of European life. Just as the peoples of Scandinavia have looked both to the west and to the east, so have those of Iberia. At the close of the Middle Ages, when the Reconquista (reconquest of the peninsula from the Moors) had been completed, Barcelona, the capital of Catalonia, became increasingly involved in the trade and politics of Italy, and the southern part of Italy fell under Spanish domination. The Portuguese, on the other hand, pioneered the navigation of the Atlantic and established the colony that would grow into the fifth-largest country in the world (Brazil). Castile joined in the great venture across the western ocean when Isabel agreed to underwrite Christopher Columbus's epic voyage in 1492. The position of Castilian (Spanish) as a world language is a legacy of this.

Both the Italian and the Iberian peninsulas are culturally diverse, but almost everyone except the Basques, who occupy a small region in the north of Spain, speaks a language derived from Latin, and both areas have historically been centers of Roman Catholic orthodoxy. That conservatism has drastically changed in

**FIGURE 1.16. Tower of Belém.** Built in 1515–1521 to protect the entrance to the Tagus River, the Tower of Belém is a symbol of Portugal's historic orientation to the western seas and its seminal role in the great maritime discoveries of the 16th century.

the past few decades, however, and it is revealing that today, because of widespread family planning, Spain and Italy are two of the countries with the lowest fertility rates in the world.

The cultural diversity of the western Mediterranean has manifested itself in the granting of autonomy to a large number of regions. Spain is completely divided into 17 autonomous regions, while in Italy autonomy has been granted to five regions. These are the culturally distinctive islands of Sicily and Sardinia, two regions in the northeast, one with a large German-speaking population and one with a significant Friulian minority, and one, French-speaking, in the northwest. Spanish regional autonomy is the result mainly of pressure from the Catalans and Basques, who have historically felt the greatest oppression from the Castilian center but to some extent also from the Galicians.

There is also great economic diversity within the region. The contrast in wealth between northern Italy and the Mezzogiorno is enormous. There are even some voices in the north calling for secession from Italy because of the perceived burden on the north of supporting an "indigent" south. Even culturally the Po Basin is far closer to the "European heartland" than the Mezzogiorno, as our inclusion of the Milan and Turin regions in that area indicates. The contrast is not quite so great in Spain, but Andalusia is far less well-off than Catalonia and has a much higher rate of unemployment. A recent boom in "Sun Belt" high-tech economic development has been instrumental in drawing parts of the region together. The main beneficiaries are the cities that form an arc following the Mediterranean coast from Catalonia through the south of France and down into western Italy as far as Rome. Known variously as the "Latin Crescent" or "Second Banana," economic cooperation and development along this strip has made it one of the fastest-growing areas in Europe.

## Eastern Europe

Eastern Europe comprises the two republics of Ukraine and Belarus and the European part of Russia. Russia, of course, also embraces territory in Asia—more, in fact, than in Europe. Siberia is, however, treated here not as a part of Europe proper but rather as a peripheral region. These three republics, though independent, are linked to nine other former Soviet republics through membership in the Commonwealth of Independent States (CIS). The CIS was proclaimed by the leaders of the three Slavic republics on December 8, 1991, at the same time the death of the USSR was formally announced.

The region is East Slavic in language and historically Orthodox in religion and thus has more cultural unity than the other regions we have discussed. As we have already pointed out, the most prominent cultural boundary in Europe is that between Western and Eastern Christianity. Orthodoxy has long stood on the eastern boundary of Christendom where it was most open to Asian, principally Muslim, influences. From the middle of the 13th to the end of the 14th century, the Russian principalities endured what came to be known as the "Mongol Captivity," giving rise to myth that, because of this Asian legacy of despotism, Russians could not truly understand democracy and thus lay outside the European realm. During the early 18th century, Peter the Great, keenly aware of this perception of his people, opened Russia to ideas from western Europe in an attempt to "modernize" his country. While much of his work was successful, significant portions of Russian society, including the Orthodox Church, resisted his reforms. Because of the rift with Western Christendom and long interaction with Asian cultures, eastern Europe, together with the Balkans, demonstrates the fewest number of culture traits we have defined as European.

The region's focus is unquestionably Moscow, which became the capital of an expanding Russian empire in the 16th century and remained the political heart of the region until Peter the Great built his new capital, St. Petersburg, in the early 18th century. Moscow's prominence was reestablished after the Bolshevik Revolution with the return of capital functions, and the city continues today to be the major urban focus, not just of Russia but of most of the former USSR. St. Peters-

**FIGURE 1.17. Moscow.** The city of Moscow was founded here along the banks of the Moskva River in the 13th century. The early settlement, sheltered alongside the Kremlin citadel, grew to be the capital of Muscovy, and eventually a Russian Empire that covered large parts of two continents. The Kremlin walls, shown here along the river embankment, encircle the historic administrative and religious center of the city.

burg, Peter's "window on the west," has been historically just that, eastern Europe's point of contact with the rest of the realm. To most Russians it seems far too "western," especially visually, ever to vie with Moscow as the center of the region.

Eastern Europe today continues to grapple with the conversion from a centrally planned to a "free-market" economy. Most obvious to the visitor in Moscow are the tremendous contrasts in level of prosperity. As we shall see, there is also ample evidence of new investment and wealth, much of it however gained by illicit means in Russia's virtually unregulated capitalist economy.

## The Balkans

The Balkans constitutes the poorest region we have yet discussed. Over the past decade or so the region has been highly unstable politically, in large part due to the efforts of the new nationalist Serbian government (then the Republic of Yugoslavia, now known as Serbia and Montenegro) to create an ethnically pure Serbian state at the expense of neighboring Bosnians, Croatians, and Kosovars. Linguistically the region is highly varied, and this, of course, is one reason for the political instability. It is, however, religion that is at the root of the ethnic strife. Although dominantly East-ern Orthodox in religion, the Balkans con-tains substantial Muslim minorities, the result of centuries of dominance by the Ottoman Turks. The Roman Catholic communities, most located just to the north, further compli-cate the picture. Even as the Russians in the 18th century were attempting their rap-prochement with the West, the peoples of the Balkans were still largely cut off from cultural developments in the rest of Europe by their inclusion in the dying Ottoman Empire. Not really until the 20th century did many of the ideas we have earlier defined as "European" penetrate this region.

The Balkans has no clear focus. Under the Turks the political capital was Istanbul (then Constantinople), but this city today is in the Turkish Republic, which we treat below as part of the Southeastern Periphery. Greece, as the richest country in the region and the only one belonging as yet to the EU, would seem to be the natural focus, and Athens is the larg-est city in the region. The Greeks have, in fact, invested fairly heavily in Bulgaria and have taken up the slack left by western Euro-pean companies that have been leery of in-vestment in the region as a whole. Some parts of Greece have long had strong connections with the lands that directly lie to the north. Thessalonica is closer to Sofia than it is to Ath-ens.

Greece has a real problem, however, in playing the role of leader in the region. First, the Greeks do not like to be associated with the term "Balkan," even though they brought the Eastern Orthodox religion to the other Balkan peoples. They regard themselves as the heirs of classical Greek culture and see the peoples of the rest of the Balkans as cul-turally inferior. Second, they are too much at odds with their neighbors to be credible in a leadership role. Confrontation rather than di-plomacy has most often been the route taken by the Greek government in its approach to disputes.

A case in point is that of Macedonia. With the breakup of the state of Yugoslavia, Catho-lic Slovenia and Croatia declared their inde-pendence. Fearful of total Serbian domina-tion, both Bosnia and Macedonia declared theirs. Macedonia, in particular, was in need of international recognition, but the Greeks made every effort to block this because they could not tolerate an independent state bear-ing the name of a region sacred in Greek his-tory as the birthplace of both Socrates and Al-exander the Great. This incident was seen in the rest of the EU as more evidence of Balkan pettiness, and the Greek government was chastised severely for it. Nevertheless, in def-erence to the Greeks, the country is now known officially as "The Former Yugoslav Re-public of Macedonia," and while spokesper-sons for the EU are careful to use this term, it is clear that they regard the Greek position as deplorably small-minded.

Another case is that of Turkey. The enmity toward the Turks goes back, of course, to their long subjugation of the Greeks within the Ot-toman Empire. So bitter was the feeling on both sides that massive population exchanges were arranged between the two countries af-ter the establishment of the Republic of Tur-key in 1923. The situation of Cyprus, where one-fifth of the population is Turkish and the rest Greek, has long kept the sores open. This has been the case since a coup on the south-ern and predominantly Greek side of the is-land during the early 1970s provoked a Turk-ish occupation of the north. This led to a partition of the island into a Greek–Cypriot Republic of Cyprus (internationally recog-nized) and a Turkish Republic of North Cy-prus (recognized only by Turkey). Only now with Cyprus's admission as a new member of the EU does there seem to be a chance for a healing process that reunifies the island after 30 years of discord, and a grudging accep-tance of the fact by the Greek and Turkish governments.

## THE EUROPEAN PERIPHERY

Beyond the boundaries of the European realm, as we have delimited it, lie four regions that may be considered transitional to the non-European world. These regions either contain large numbers of Europeans in their populations or have contributed significant numbers of their own populations to Europe. Although they lie outside the focus of this book, and only occasionally figure into our discussion, it is important to recognize their presence. One is Siberia, an integral part of the Russian state but clearly also a part of the landmass commonly understood as Asia. Two regions, Western Turkestan and the Southeastern Periphery (Turkey and Transcaucasia), include territories that were formerly parts of the Soviet Union, and the last of these regions, the Maghreb, is a former colonial domain of France.

## Siberia

It can be argued that Siberia, Asiatic Russia, constitutes a culture region of its own. Like Anglo-America and Latin America, it may be thought of as a neo-European realm. This vast region was absorbed into the Russian Empire between the middle of the 16th and end of the 17th centuries. It was during this same period that the Spanish, French, and British were building their American empires. The only real difference between Siberia and the Americas is that the colonies in the latter were separated from their mother countries by a large ocean and were eventually able to assert their independence.

Culturally the situation in Siberia is similar to that in Anglo-America. The indigenous population, largely Turkic-speaking, was sparse, and the institutions and language of the region became, and remain, those of the mother country. As in Canada, the population is highly concentrated along the southern border of the region, especially along the routes of the Trans-Siberian and Baykal-Amur rail lines. The indigenous population is scattered in the vast lands of the Arctic north, particularly in the basin of the Lena River.

## Western Turkestan

"Turkestan" is an old regional name applied to the largely Turkic-speaking, Muslim parts of inner Asia (*stan* is an Iranian word meaning "country"). During the Soviet period the western part of this region was known as Kazakhstan and central Asia. The eastern part lies mainly in the Chinese province of Xinjiang, the home of the Turkic Uighur people. Since the breakup of the Soviet Union the five former republics of western Turkestan have declared their independence. The native peoples of four, Kazakstan, Turkmenistan, Uzbekistan, and Kyrgyzistan, are linguistically Turkic, while that of the fifth, Tajikistan, is Iranian.

Under the Soviets the pressures of Russification were strong. Russian was the language of the schools, and the native languages all received Cyrillic scripts. In addition, large numbers of Russians and Ukrainians moved into the region, especially into northern Kazakhstan, where the Soviets established a major iron and steel center on the Karaganda coalfield. Communist ideology, including atheism, was here, as elsewhere in the Soviet Union, a staple of the educational system. Despite the antireligious propaganda of the Soviet period, however, Islam survived and is now enjoying a revival, much as Christianity is in eastern Europe. Thus western Turkestan forms a cultural bridge between Europe and the Islamic world.

## The Southeastern Periphery

This region, containing the four states of Turkey, Armenia, Georgia, and Azerbaijan, provides another such bridge. Turkey and Azerbaijan are secular states with populations that are nearly 100 percent Muslim. Armenia and Georgia are very old Christian states. Georgia is Eastern Orthodox; Armenia has its own separate Apostolic (Monophysite) Church. Armenians are generally ostracized by the other three populations. There has been some rapprochement between Turkey and Azerbaijan, but the Turks belong to the Sunni sect, which dominates the Islamic world, while the Azeris are Shiites, their bitter rivals. Thus, even though the governments of both countries are secular, doctrinal differences pose some problems. Also, the Caucasus region contains literally hundreds of peoples who are ethnically distinct from the four major groups.

The Turks are by far the most numerous people in the region. They are also the best represented within the European core (especially in Germany), where several million reside today as a result of the guest worker migrations initiated during the early 1970s. One can argue that the Turks are neither fully European nor fully Middle Eastern but take an intermediate position between the two cultures. The Turks are an Altaic people, closely related to those of inner Asia, whence they originally came. In the 13th century they invaded the Byzantine Empire and in 1453 dealt it a final deathblow when they seized Constantinople. Rather than accepting the legacy of Greek culture, however, the Turks have vehemently rejected it. After finally subduing the city of Constantinople in 1453, Mehmed the Conqueror declared that he had avenged the Trojans by defeating the Greeks. The long-standing bitter rivalry between Turks and Greeks remains the principal problem in the Aegean region.

Nonetheless, the Turkish intelligentsia today firmly believes that the future of Turkey lies with Europe. On the other hand, as a Muslim, non-Indo-European society, little touched by European philosophy, many (especially the Greeks) would argue that the Turks do not belong in the European family. It is true that they did not share in the great European intellectual movements of the 15th through the 18th centuries, but neither, it should be remembered, did those Balkan subject peoples of the Ottoman Empire whom we unhesitatingly call European today.

If the Turks are not Europeans, then, who are they? They certainly do not fit comfortably with the Islamic peoples of the Middle East. Modern Turkish national identity is a creation of the Ottoman elite of the 19th century and the Kemalist Republicans who seized power from them in the early 1920s. This nationalism is neither strongly Islamic nor ethnically Turkish. The Ottoman rulers, in spite of their political power, were always viewed by the Arabs as inferior newcomers to Islam and, as such, were marginalized in the Muslim world. It is therefore natural that the Republicans who shaped modern Turkey would promote a secular ideology that prioritized the state over religion and rejected a society organized exclusively on religious principles. Religion was made a private matter, personalized, individualized, and secularized, much as Christianity was during the Euro-

**FIGURE 1.18. Monument of the Republic.** Erected in 1928 in the center of Istanbul's sprawling Taksim Square, this monument commemorates the birth of Mustafa Kemal Ataturk's modern Turkish Republic. The soldiers with flags, who stand on either side of the monument, symbolize Ataturk's motto of "Peace at home, peace abroad." One is an unknown soldier who guards the Turkish nation, the other a soldier of peace.

pean Enlightenment. The growth of Turkish Islamist movements since the 1980s has not done much to change this situation. In spite of their anti-Western stance, most Islamists accept the need for coexistence with the institutions and values of the secular establishment and reject the kind of fundamentalism evident in some Arab countries and in Iran.

We would argue here that the Turks are more European than Middle Eastern and that their future lies with Europe. The greatest danger is that the Europeans will reject them. This has happened a number of times, and as we shall see is being repeated again in the recent expansion of the EU to include 10 new countries. Turkey is not being offered any concrete assurances of consideration in the near future despite recent Turkish efforts to institute a host of legal and political reforms that bring them close to meeting the minimal democratic norms required of applicants for EU membership.

## The Maghreb

For the Arab conquerors and bearers of Islam this was the "land of the setting sun" (*maghreb*), the far western reaches of the empire they established during the seventh and eighth centuries across North Africa, the Middle East, and into south Asia. Most of the region was conquered by the Ottomans in the 16th century, but in the 19th and early 20th centuries much of it became a part of the French colonial empire, and it is this association that links the three countries of the Maghreb—Morocco, Algeria, and Tunisia—to Europe today. During the colonial period well over a million French citizens moved into the region, especially Algeria, where they became a vital part of the economy and established the French language as a *lingua franca*.

Although all three states achieved independence after World War II and most of the French returned home, the ties with France have remained strong. Almost 1.5 million Arabic speakers live in France today, the great majority of them from the Maghreb. All three

countries have expressed an interest in joining the European Union, although economic and other problems would seem to indicate that EU membership lies quite a long way down the road. A ray of hope for the Maghreb states did appear in March 1998, however, when Tunisia attained associate status with the EU. The potential for unity in the region is underscored by the Arab Maghreb Union (including also Libya), which was established in the late 1980s but has been largely inactive since. Both Tunisia and Morocco have recently encouraged its revival. Like western Turkestan and the Southeastern Periphery, this region provides a bridge between Europe and the Islamic world.

## FURTHER READING

Ahnström, L. (1993). Europe: Culture area, geoideological construct, or illusion? *Norsk Geografisk Tidsskrift*, 47, 57–67.

Brunt, B. M. (1995). Regions and western Europe. *Journal of Geography*, 94, 306–316.

Chisholm, M. (1995). *Britain on the edge of Europe*. London: Routledge.

Davies, N. (1996). *Europe: A history*. Oxford, UK: Oxford University Press.

Delamaide, D. (1994). *The new superregions of Europe*. New York: Dutton.

Delanty, G. (1995). *Inventing Europe: Idea, identity, reality*. Basingstoke, UK: Macmillan.

de Rougement, D. (1966). *The idea of Europe*. New York: Collier-Macmillan.

Enyedi, G. (1990). East-Central Europe: A European region. *Geoforum*, 21, 141–143.

Fontana, J. (1995). *The distorted past: A reinterpretation of Europe*. Oxford, UK: Blackwell.

Graham, B. (Ed.). (1998). *Modern Europe: Place, culture, and identity*. London: Arnold.

Hagen, J. (2003). Redrawing the imagined map of Europe: the rise and fall of the center. *Political Geography*, 22, 489–517.

Hay, D. (1968). *Europe: The emergence of an idea* (2nd ed.). Edinburgh: Edinburgh University Press.

Kinzer, S. (2001). *Crescent and star: Turkey between two worlds*. New York: Farrar, Straus & Giroux.

Kormoss, I. B. F. (1987). The geographical notion of Europe over the centuries. In H. Brugmans

(Ed.), *Europe: Dream—adventure—reality* (pp. 81–94). New York: Greenwood Press.

Mycklebost, H. (1993). Regionalism in western Europe. *Norsk Geografisk Tidsskrift, 47,* 79–91.

Szücs, J. (1988). Three historical regions of Europe: An outline. In J. Keane (Ed.), *Civil society and the state: New European perspectives* (pp. 291–332). London: Verso.

Wilson, K., & van den Dussen, J. (Eds.). (1993). *The history of the idea of Europe*. London: Routledge.

Wintle, M. (Ed.). (1996). *Culture and identity in Europe: Perceptions of divergence and unity in past and present*. Aldershot, UK: Avebury.

Wolff, L. (1994). *Inventing Eastern Europe: The map of civilization on the mind of the Enlightenment*. Stanford, CA: Stanford University Press.

# PART I

## People and Environment

# CHAPTER 2

# European Environments

While we have taken pains in our introduction to define Europe largely in cultural and political terms, it is also important to see this "continent" that Europeans call home as a unique and highly varied segment of the physical world. More specifically, in this chapter and the two chapters that follow, we hope to highlight the interactions between Europeans and the unique physical settings in which they live, both now and in the past. As geographers we see these linkages between human populations and physical environments as basic to understanding how Europeans live their lives and define the limits of their everyday space.

We will begin our consideration of European environments by emphasizing their great diversity. These differences are easily captured. Any long-distance train or car trip, for example, cannot help but expose the traveler to significant landscape change, for it is actually difficult to travel very far across most parts of Europe without encountering different natural or humanized environments. Or, consider the brief sequence of "bird's-eye" impressions of Europeans and their environments that may be garnered from the window of a trans-Atlantic jetliner as it makes its gradual descent along the final stages of a great circle route to a popular international European terminus like Amsterdam.

On such a flight, our first sighting of Europe usually comes somewhere off the Atlantic coast of Scotland in the form of a scattering of small islands. These islands pass silently beneath us, their barren and rocky surfaces silhouetted against the diamonds of reflected morning sunlight that glint up at us from the wind-blown surface of the North Atlantic. They are the lonely far outposts of northwestern Europe, standing vigil against the open sea. But before too many of them have passed beneath our plane, we begin to see the first signs of human habitation. Barren and remote as they may be, some of these small islands contain settlements, in most cases the remote homes of sheep herders; and here and there on a few of the larger islands we see a clustered settlement—a sort of minimally developed place, with one or two larger buildings, a number of dwellings, and a small harbor. What we are viewing from our high vantage point is but one of Europe's many distinctive environments. As we look down, we are drawn to reflect on what it must be like to live there: perched upon a rocky and barren island, exposed to the harsh North Atlantic weather but at the same time quietly secluded from the rush and bustle of our modern world.

Since it is not uncommon for the offshore islands and mainland coast of western Scotland, as well as the highland interior, to be obscured by early morning fog or low clouds, our next airborne impression of Europe might consist of brief glimpses of Northumberland moors, fields, and villages, caught through breaks in the cloud cover as we pass over the northeast corner of England on our way out over the North Sea. This time the scene seems much more abundantly humanized. There are numerous farmsteads and village settlements, and the upland landscape is lushly green and neatly organized into irregularly shaped fields and pastures. We also note that there are sizable towns. These towns appear to consist of irregularly shaped commercial centers, surrounded by a patchwork of industrial parks and residential areas. We can distinguish from the air that some parts of the townscape are older, some newer. Emanating from the towns are the unmistakable long curves and straight lines of railroad rights-of-way and of highways.

Then we pass out over the North Sea and are suddenly free of land as the gray-brown headlands of the English coast slip behind us. We have been passing rapidly over Europe now for nearly three-quarters of an hour, but are nonetheless still able to look down on an open sea, with no land in sight! But even this vast watery environment shows signs of human activity. The choppy waters below are dotted with craft, large and small. There are heavily loaded freighters and tankers, lying

low in the water. There are ferries, fishing boats, and pleasure craft. As we pass overhead, we can see them all fairly clearly, along with their wakes, which indicate the direction of their travel. We are amazed at the volume of seaborne human activity below and wonder about the origin, destination, and purpose of each craft.

Finally we cross at low level over the coast of Holland; our plane swings inland before lining up for the final approach to Amsterdam's Schiphol Airport. The Dutch coastline is nearly straight and clearly marked by a narrow stretch of beaches and sand dunes. Behind the dunes extend the polder lands—great flat and green expanses of reclaimed land, broken into tiered rows of elongated fields separated from one another by long ribbons of bright reflection given off by the waters of ditches and canals. Human settlement is everywhere dense. In the countryside, closely spaced houses and outbuildings, many of them glass-roofed hothouses, line the canals and roads. Nearby are sprawling areas of urban settlement, consisting of neat rows of semidetached houses with small gardens, or clusters of multistory blocks of flats. Interspersed are large parks of flat-roofed factories and warehouses. We are struck by the constant movement of people and goods below. The canals are full of barges and small craft; and the Dutch road system, perfectly engineered and neatly organized into care-

**FIGURE 2.1. Polder landscape.** Rows of houses, glass-roofed hothouses, water-filled ditches and canals, and elongated flat fields of reclaimed land glide beneath the wing of a trans-Atlantic jetliner cleared for landing at Amsterdam's Schiphol Airport.

fully marked traffic lanes and turnouts, hums busily beneath us as we glide to our touchdown at one of the world's busiest airports.

Our gradual descent has taken us from the outer Atlantic fringes of Europe to one of its great metropolitan centers. We have flown over a mere 1,000 kilometers of European space and seen but a tiny and narrow fragment of the whole, but in such a short distance and restricted area we have noted at least four completely different European environments along with their human habitations and uses. Taken all together, Europe is a vast collection of equally distinctive environments, each of which has been, of course, uniquely humanized to some degree. Our purpose in this chapter is to explore more fully the range and pattern of European environments and at least some of the human uses of them.

## PHYSICAL SETTING

We might begin our exploration by thinking very broadly about a few of the more general physical features of the European continent: its shape, location, and terrain. We have already suggested that Europe is not so much a continent in a physical sense as it is in a cultural sense. We understand that Europe as a physical continent lacks appropriate mass and, at least along its eastern extremities, lacks a clearly defined boundary. From a physical point of view, Europe is more aptly described as a complexly structured peninsular appendage to the great landmass of Eurasia— a subcontinent rather than a true continent. Nonetheless, we will acknowledge the accepted notion of its continentality and proceed to make a few "grand-scale" observations about Europe as a physical setting.

Certainly one physical quality that makes the European continent so distinctive is its outline. It stands out as an area on the globe where land meets sea in a strikingly complex manner. Europe is essentially surrounded on three sides by great bodies of water: the Atlantic Ocean on the west; the Mediterranean and Black Seas to the south; the combined waters of the North Sea, Baltic Sea, and Arctic Sea to the north. Between and among these bodies of water, the continent extends outward from its Eurasian roots as a long and intricate assemblage of major and minor peninsulas, and islands.

Along with Australia, Europe is markedly smaller in area than any of the other continents, but stands alone in its very high proportion of islands and peninsulas to total area—or, seen in another way—in its exceptionally high ratio of shoreline to landmass. This deep interpenetration of land and sea has historically rendered large portions of the continent accessible to seaborne outside influences and, conversely, has made the sea accessible from inland areas in a way not found in many other parts of the world. Most Europeans, although certainly not all, would count the sea as an environmental influence of some importance in their lives, whether it be physical, economic, or simply recreational. Indeed, as we will suggest in a later chapter, the close relationship between Europeans and the sea constitutes one deep and long-standing theme in European people–environment interactions.

Another way in which we might think very broadly about Europe as a physical place is to consider its relative position on the surface of the earth. As a westward extension of the Eurasian landmass, the continent is, and has often acted historically as, a "land bridge" linking Asia with both the western seas and with northern and western Africa. As such, it has historically played a major role in facilitating the movement of people and ideas between east and west. Indeed, geographers have traditionally been fond of pointing out that Europe occupies a rather unique world position that places it near the center of what has been called the "land hemisphere." By this term they mean the half of the planet's surface that contains the greatest possible land area. The implication is that Europe, of all the continents, enjoys the best natural connections with the rest of the inhabited world. While the real meaning of this might be a bit difficult to fully appreciate, it is clear that the continent has benefited, and sometimes suffered,

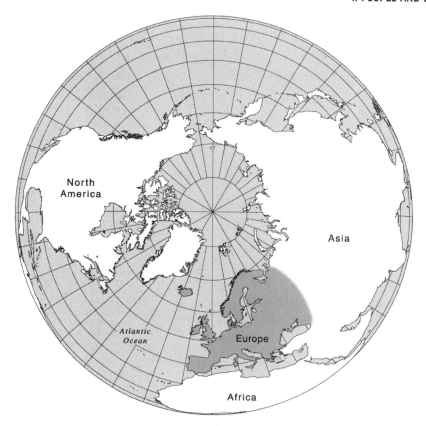

FIGURE 2.2. Europe in the world.

from what might be seen as a naturally central and highly accessible position vis-à-vis much of the rest of the world. In particular, its exposure to the western seas has presented Europeans with special opportunities for overseas trade and colonization that have worked to establish their home as one of the great crossroads of the globe.

Another important aspect of Europe's global position is its high latitude. The continent extends from roughly 35 degrees north latitude on the island of Crete to more than 71 degrees at North Cape, the northernmost point of the Scandinavian peninsula. Americans are, in fact, often surprised to learn that Mediterranean Europe is at a latitude roughly comparable to that of the northeastern "metropolitan" area of the United States, or that the great cities of western and central Europe lie at latitudes comparable to the sparsely settled coast of Labrador or the southern por-

tions of Hudson's Bay. More northerly European cities such as Oslo, Stockholm, or St. Petersburg are actually situated nearly as far north as Anchorage, Alaska. While none of this implies an especially harsh or inhospitable environment, primarily because so much of the continent is affected climatically by its exposure to the moderating influences of the surrounding seas, it does mean that Europeans live in an environment that lies high on the curved surface of our planet.

In fact, position is the key to a basic understanding of the continent's individual climatic regimes. Europe stands in the path of the North Atlantic Drift, the strong oceanic current that brings relatively warm waters to the western and northern margins of the European landmass. Much of Europe also stands in the path of the prevailing westerlies, which, in the absence of any significant north–south-oriented mountain barriers, means that Atlantic-based weather systems are carried eastward almost unhindered for long distances across the continent.

Because of this general eastward movement of air masses over the continent, two Atlantic-based weather-generating systems, the Icelandic Low and the Azores High, play key roles in determining climatic conditions over Europe. Also important, though, is the constant presence of cold Arctic air to the north of the continent, as well as two seasonal sys-

tems, the Siberian High, a cold Asian air mass that extends westward over Russia in winter, and the Asian Low, which generates low-pressure systems over southwest Asia in the summertime. Changes in European weather patterns largely result from the interplay of incoming Atlantic air with these air mass systems over the continent.

The Icelandic Low is an area of persistent low pressure situated over the North Atlantic. It generates a succession of eastward moving

FIGURE 2.3. Climatic zones.

cyclonic fronts that carry mild, moist air in over the western and northwestern portions of the continent. These North Atlantic air masses have a moderating influence on terrestrial temperatures. The general effect is to make summers cooler and winters warmer than one would otherwise expect them to be. These North Atlantic air masses can also sometimes combine, especially in winter, with dry and cold Arctic air penetrating down from the north. When this happens, a long and sinuous polar front is formed that tends to produce churning, stormy, and even chilling weather.

The moderating effect of the intruding North Atlantic air masses extends far to the east, often well into Russia, but as these moist Atlantic air masses pass deeper into the interior of the Eurasian landmass to confront the dry continental air masses of the Eurasian interior, they gradually lose their maritime characteristics. Thus, annual temperature ranges north of Alpine and Mediterranean Europe tend to increase as one moves from the more maritime west to the more continental east, and precipitation totals tend to decrease. In winter, the Siberian High can expand to the west, blocking the eastward movement of the North Atlantic air masses and locking large parts of Europe under bitterly cold conditions. This is the infamous "General Winter" that helped Russia turn back the invasions of Napoleon's Grand Army in 1812 and halt the advance of Hitler's armies during the winter of 1941–1942. Alternatively, in summer the Siberian High is replaced by the Asian Low, which draws the moisture-bearing Atlantic air masses into the interior bringing rainfall, while solar heating of the landmass ensures warmth.

The interplay between the maritime and continental air masses produces three major climatic types north of the Alps. The Marine West Coast climate, which embraces those parts of northern and western Europe most heavily exposed to the intrusion of North Atlantic air masses, is characterized by mild, wet winters and cool, moist summers. The Humid Continental climate, which prevails over all of eastern Europe and the Baltic,

experiences cold, relatively dry winters and warm summers with moderate rainfall. In between the two is a Transitional climate that results from the interaction of maritime and continental influences. It covers an area extending from the east of France into central and southeastern Europe and evidences elements of the two more extreme types.

The fourth and last major European climatic type is the very distinctive, subtropical Mediterranean regime. This results from the annual movement of a second persistent pressure system, the Azores High. This system (also known as the Bermuda High) lies out over the Atlantic well to the west of Europe. In the summer, the Azores High is displaced northward and eastward, bringing it closer to the continent. The effect is to block the southward intrusion of North Atlantic air masses and produce the hot, dry conditions so typical of summer in the Mediterranean Basin. The onset of the Azores High-induced summer weather patterns may be heralded in the spring by a hot and desiccating wind–known as *scirocco*–that rushes northward, carrying with it to Spain, Italy, and sometimes even Greece and Turkey the intense heat of the Sahara. Greece and Turkey are also affected during the summer by a dry northeasterly wind, the *meltemi*, which originates in the steppe lands above the Black Sea and often blows with such force as to cause severe navigational problems in the Aegean Sea.

The typical Mediterranean summer is therefore placid, hot, and droughty. For months on end the skies are blue and the sun shines down upon the land, and, for the most part, the winds are light. With almost no rain the vegetation dries out and browns with the exception of moisture-hoarding species of trees such as the eucalyptus, olive, and holm oak. This is in stark contrast to wintertime, when the Azores High displaces southwestward and North Atlantic air masses bring extended periods of cold and turbulent wet weather—some of the rains can be torrential and last for weeks—to the western Mediterranean. These air masses penetrate also to the eastern Mediterranean, but the Siberian High is often able to send bitterly cold and dry northeasterly winds into this region, reducing winter rainfall there.

But, important as climate is, our most significant grand-scale observation about the European environment is the one with which we began this chapter: the fact that European landforms exhibit an amazingly high degree of variation over relatively small distances. This small continent is quite amazing in that it not only encompasses the whole gamut of basic terrain features, coastal plains, interior plains, uplands, and mountains but also the area that each feature occupies is quite small and the topographic characteristics are so intricately intermingled. Europe appears, at a glance, to be highly compartmentalized. Even the relatively broad interior expanses of the North European Plain, which may appear a uniform green on most relief maps, can be quite differentiated over relatively short distances. In its eastern and northern sections, as we shall soon see, the plain is highly segmented by glacial and drainage features. In the west, on the other hand, the gentle folding and eroding of sedimentary strata have created well-defined basins and successions of alternating scarps and valleys, the best examples of which may be found around the cities of Paris and London. In a large sense, the continent may be viewed as an immense patchwork of distinctive landscapes or natural regions, which are in turn often connected to one another by narrow routeways—the well-known straits, river valleys, coastal plains, mountain passes, and upland gaps that have served throughout European history as conveyors of people, goods, and ideas.

## TERRESTRIAL ENVIRONMENTS

To make some sense of the physical diversity of the continent, it is customary to group terrain features into major landform zones or regions. Here we will identify and briefly describe four such regions, which are arranged roughly as latitudinal belts running across the continent. Ranging from north to south, they are (1) the Northwestern Highlands, (2) the North European Plain, (3) the Central or Hercynian Uplands, and (4) the Alpine and Mediterranean South.

## The Northwestern Highlands

The Northwestern Highlands, as the name implies, are found along the northwestern margins of the continent—and may in some ways be thought of as the "rooftop" of Europe. They include the mountainous backbone (the Kjølen Range) of the Scandinavian peninsula, the North Sea and Atlantic islands that lie immediately to the north and west of Scotland, the Scottish Highlands, the uplands of the Scottish–English borderlands, the northern portions of Wales, and large parts of Ireland. We will refer collectively to the above-mentioned formations as the Caledonian Highlands. We also include within our Northwestern Highlands zone, although physically different in many respects, portions of the Fennoscandian Shield, the vast and ancient geologic formation that underlies much of Sweden, Finland, and Russian Karelia.

Geologically speaking, these Northwestern Highland formations are among the oldest in Europe. The Caledonian Highlands date from, and derive their name from, the Caledonian orogeny, a period of mountain building caused by crustal movements in the Atlantic Basin that took place some 450 million years ago. In essence, a widening of the Atlantic Basin produced crustal movements that uplifted, folded, and transformed ancient layers of sedimentary rocks lying on the ocean floor along the northwestern edge of the continent, creating in the process a vast and formidable mountain chain. The adjacent Fennoscandian Shield, along the western margins of which the Caledonian system was formed, is made of hard Precambrian rock and is one of the world's most ancient and stable geologic formations (more than 540 million years old).

The mountains, high plateaus, and uplands that make up the Caledonian Highland system today are the severely eroded remnants of the once rugged and high formations created so long ago during the Caledonian period of mountain building. They are, in fact, forma-

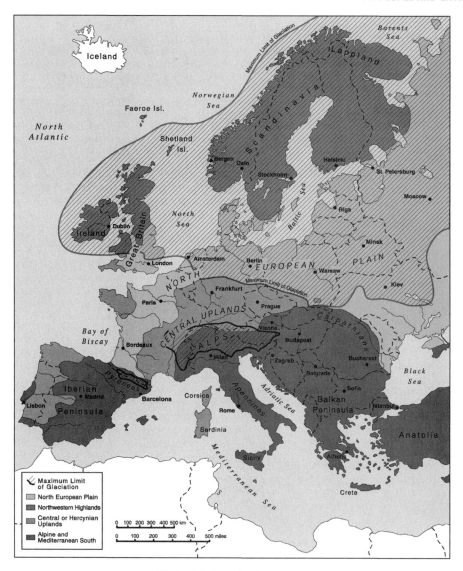

FIGURE 2.4. Major landform zones.

tions that have been uplifted and eroded away several times over the course of geologic history. Glacial erosion, from the Pleistocene era (ca. 10,000–12,000 years ago) in particular, has most recently rounded the surfaces of these old formations and is responsible for cutting the familiar deep fjords and U-shaped valleys of Scotland and western Norway into the faults and depressions of the bedrock. Compared to younger mountains elsewhere in Europe, elevations are relatively low, with peaks rarely exceeding 1,500 meters. The highest peak in Scotland, for example, is Ben Nevis, which reaches just 1,343 meters, while the highest point in the Welsh Highlands is Mount Snowden at 1,085 meters. The Caledonian system is at its highest in parts of the Kjølen Range of western Scandinavia, where some peaks reach heights of more than 2,000 meters.

Their location along the northwestern margins of Europe and their generally southwest to northeast orientation puts the Caledonian formations in a blocking position vis-à-vis the

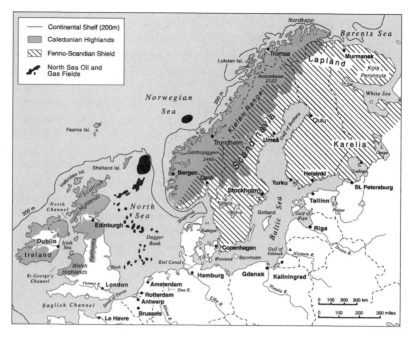

FIGURE 2.5. Northwestern Highlands.

eastward moving frontal systems that sweep in, one after another, off the North Atlantic. These moisture-bearing weather systems produce heavy precipitation as they are forced to rise over the western slopes of the Caledonian highlands. Persistently gray and wet, with stony or boggy soils and a regime of low and stunted vegetation, many highland landscapes project a rather bleak and brooding appearance and are only marginally hospitable to human occupation. With the exception of narrow coastal flats that skirt the margins of islands, bays, and fjords, where marine deposits uplifted out of the sea offer a modicum of agricultural potential, human settlement is generally sparse.

FIGURE 2.6. High fjell. This photo is typical of the ice-scoured and exposed rock of the Kjølen Range, which forms the mountainous backbone of the Scandinavian Peninsula. The landscape is largely barren; the only vegetation comes in the form of small plants that cling to crevices between the rocks.

FIGURE 2.7. Balsfjorden. This fjord is typical of the many "U-shaped" glacially carved valleys found up and down the length of western Norway. Note how settlement clings to the "strandflat," the narrow zone of arable soils along the water's edge. Most of this narrow coastal resource was uplifted from the sea in postglacial times.

The range of natural vegetation and fauna in the Caledonian Highland zone is remarkably narrow compared to other parts of Europe. These areas were among the last to be freed of the great ice sheets that covered much of northern Europe during the last glacial period, and were consequently at the tail end of the process of biotic recolonization that followed the retreat of the glaciers. This is especially true for Ireland, which was quickly cut off from the continent by rising seas. There was perhaps only about a 1,500-year window of opportunity during which migrating species might have reached Ireland. In addition, constant exposure to the stormy North Atlantic placed a high value on the adaptive capabilities of the few biotic species that did manage to establish themselves there. The isolation of Ireland and the difficulties of biotic establishment are reflected in the fact that the island has fewer than half of the floral species native to nearby Britain. Lacking such species as snakes, moles, weasels, fallow deer, and elk, Ireland can also be said to possess a comparatively impoverished range of native fauna.

The Caledonian highland zone is, economically speaking, regarded as a relatively weakly endowed environment. As we have already noted, it offers only limited opportunity for intensive agriculture. And, although histor-

ically somewhat important in the production of metallic minerals—particularly copper, iron, and tin—little of economic value can be competitively produced today (although parts of Norway and Scotland have certainly benefited from their proximity to the North Sea oil fields). Good hydroelectric potential is one compensating factor, but the land is primarily used for extensive agricultural pursuits and increasingly for tourism.

Closely associated with the Caledonian Highlands in our regional scheme is the Fennoscandian (or Baltic) Shield, the great mass of crystalline rock that underlies a large area of northern Europe centered on Scandinavia. The shield tilts slightly downward from north to south. Over much of Sweden, Finland, and Russian Karelia the shield is often at or very near to the surface. Farther south and east, where it extends beneath the Baltic to reach parts of northern Poland, the Baltic States, and Russia, it lies more deeply beneath the surface. The massiveness of the shield has made it a relatively stable part of the earth's outer crust, resistant to the movements of other formations around its periphery. As we have already noted, the great lateral pressures of a widening Atlantic basin that originally built the Caledonian Highlands did much of their mountain-building work along the unyielding northwestern fringes of the shield.

In the north, where the shield is so near the surface, it is often exposed. This is due to the scraping and scouring actions of the last ice sheet, which in many areas simply removed all surface materials and laid bare the hard crystalline rock of the shield. Indeed, the direction of the movement of the ice may be seen in some places by deep grooves and striations left by the glaciers on the exposed rock. Elsewhere the glaciers randomly strewed heavy deposits of erosional material across the surface of the shield— boulders, stones, earth, gravel, and sand—leaving a highly chaotic, and often poorly drained, landscape of hills, ridges, lakes, and marshes.

While very resistant to lateral pressures, the shield did succumb to the immense weight of the ice sheets that covered it during the last ice age. The weight of the ice sheets,

**FIGURE 2.8. Glacial erratic.** The power of glacial processes is evident in many Nordic landscapes. Here large boulders left on the land by the glaciers may be seen strewn among a recently thinned stand of pine trees in western Sweden.

which were up to 4 kilometers thick, caused the shield to subside—settling downward into the more liquid mass of basaltic rock that lies beneath it. With the retreat of the ice sheet, the weight was removed and the shield began slowly to rebound, a process that continues to the present. As a consequence, the slow uplift of the land (nearly 1 meter per century at the upper end of the Gulf of Bothnia) and a corresponding gradual retreat of the sea are physical facts of considerable significance to human settlement in northern Europe. Indeed, some Swedish port towns, founded at river mouths along the Bothnian Gulf during the early part of the 17th century, have been forced by uplift to build modern downstream port facilities because the original town sites are no longer situated on the coast. A compensating submergence of the earth's crust along the southern margins of the shield has meant that human settlement in low-lying lands along the North Sea coastlines of the Low Countries, Germany, and western Den-

mark has faced environmental circumstances that are quite the reverse.

The natural landscape of the shield, then, is one that is profoundly influenced by its geological and glacial history. It is a landscape of exposed rock or heavy glacial deposition, often chaotically arranged and poorly drained, with most settlement clustered along coastal areas, rivers, and lakes where uplift and stream action have provided small areas of arable soils. Uplift also explains why the small settlements of western Norway are strung out along the *strandflat*, a narrow and discontinuous shelf of land whose uplifted marine deposits offer a tenuous foothold for agricultural settlement along the rocky edge of the Caledonian coast. The ancient crystalline rocks of the shield offer important mineral resources, chiefly in the form of metallic ores, such as iron, copper, nickel, zinc, manganese, lead, silver, and gold. Sweden, in particular, has been known historically for its high-grade iron ores. The industrial exploitation of natural resources of all kinds, including extensive forestlands, has been an important part of the region's economic history. The shield also has abundant hydroelectric potential, which has been systematically developed in partial compensation for its lack of fossil fuel deposits.

Given the extremely high latitude of this part of Europe (large areas lie north of the Arctic Circle), there is a marked north–south zonation of vegetational regimes and, much like the Caledonian Highlands to the west, the shield is home to a relatively narrow range of native species. In the extreme north, high latitude and altitude combine to produce a sparse alpine-tundra vegetation of dwarf shrubs and grass heath. Farther south and at lower altitudes, the vegetation cover turns to cold-hardy species of birch, before giving way to a largely coniferous forest of spruce and pine that stretches southward to the Mälaren Basin of south-central Sweden and the southern coastal areas of Finland. There a mixed forest of coniferous and deciduous trees takes over, with oak, birch and aspen figuring prominently among the latter. Sheltered in part from the Atlantic weather systems by the Caledonian Mountains to the west in Norway, the

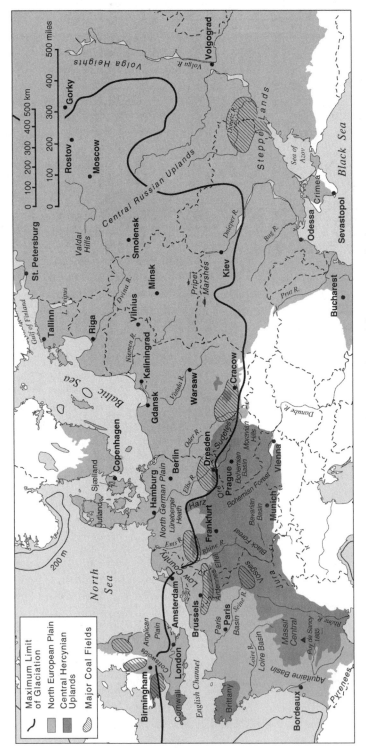

FIGURE 2.9. The North European Plain and the Hercynian Uplands.

landscapes of the shield have a more continental climate, with moderate levels of precipitation and substantial seasonal temperature differences.

## The North European Plain

To the south and east of the Northwestern Highlands lies the North European Plain, our second major landform region. This large yet surprisingly differentiated lowland extends from east to west across the entire continent in a giant but narrowing arc. The broad base of the arc, nearly 2,000 kilometers wide from north to south, is found in the interior plains of European Russia. From there, the plain sweeps westward across Ukraine, Belarus, the Baltic States, and Poland to reach northern Germany, Denmark, and the southernmost extremities of Sweden. It then continues westward through the Low Countries, where it becomes confined to a narrow belt along the North Sea. Farther west, the plain broadens again to include Britain's Anglican plain and much of northern France before swinging southwest through the constricting Gateway of Poitou to reach the Aquitaine Basin of extreme southwestern France, beyond which the plain terminates at the line of the Pyrenees.

Extending as it does across the breadth of Europe, the North European Plain has historically been one of the world's great avenues of human contact. Yet, it is also much broken into distinctive parts, which are separated by great rivers, embayments of the sea, and by local relief; or distinguished from one another by differences in surface materials and vegetation. Large parts of the plain also lie submerged beneath the shallow waters of the Baltic Sea and the English Channel or extend far out beneath the surface of the North Sea.

The geologic formations that underlie the plain are relatively young (65–245 million years old). They consist of strongly cemented layers of sedimentary rock that have accrued over the ages through the laying down of marine deposits during periods when the land was covered by ancient seas, or through the accumulation of material brought down by streams from adjacent upland areas. Elevations are modest, seldom exceeding 200 meters, but can be nonetheless locally significant. Especially in the west, lateral pressures have caused the layers of sediment that underlie the plain to bend and warp to produce a gently undulating surface, on which erosional activity has cut into the tilted softer layers and sometimes left sharp-faced scarps or cuestas. Paris and its basin, for example, are

FIGURE 2.10. Les Andelys. Here at Les Andelys the Seine River cuts away the rich soils of the North European Plain to expose the chalky stone that lies beneath the surface. This photo is taken from the site of an enormous fortress, built in 1196 by Richard the Lionheart, who was both Duke of Normandy and King of England, to command the river and the major land route between Paris and the Channel coast.

**FIGURE 2.11. The Cotswolds.** The English village of Broadway lies at the foot of the sharp western-facing slope of the Cotswold Hills. From the crest of the Cotswold escarpment, a product of the gentle folding of the sedimentary strata that underlie the North European Plain, one can see for miles across the Severn Valley toward Wales.

ringed, especially to the east, by a series of outward-facing cuestas. Escarpments such as the Cotswolds, the Chilterns, and the North and South Downs of lowland Britain similarly provide sharp instances of local relief in the Anglican plain.

In the central and more easterly parts of the North European Plain, surface features are more often associated with the effects of glaciation. The last great ice sheet to advance down out of Scandinavia reached far enough south and west to affect surface features in parts of Belgium and northern France. Farther east and to the south of the Scandinavian centers of glacial advance, the southward-moving ice sheets affected nearly all of the northern lowlands of Germany, Poland, the Baltic States, and Belarus. In Russia and Ukraine, the glaciers penetrated far to the south in the form of two giant lobes of ice that followed the valleys of the Dnieper as far as Kiev and the Volga to a point above Volgograd. Thus, the Valdai Hills, which rise from the Russian plain between St. Petersburg and Moscow and form the main watershed of north-central Russia, derive from the accumulation of erosional material during glacial times. On the other hand, the open plains and steppe landscapes of southern Russia and Ukraine were never glaciated. They are differentiated, instead, by a series of broad east-facing cuestas that rise above the valleys of the Dnieper, Don, and Volga Rivers.

The North European Plain is Europe's greatest agricultural resource. Sizable areas endowed with rich agricultural soils are common. Finely textured and fertile loess soils laid down by strong winds at the end of the last period of glaciation are found, for example, in thick mantle-like layers across large parts of northern France and the Low Countries. They are also found in a series of embayments located along the line in Germany and Poland where the southern margins of the plain meet the Hercynian Uplands (known in German as the *Börde*, or "edge"). Extensive loess deposits are also found in parts of southern Russia. In addition, some of the best agricultural resources in Europe stretch for great distances across the vast plains of southern Russia and Ukraine, where the natural grassland vegetation of the steppes has provided the decayed organic material necessary to produce rich dark chernozem, or "black earth" soils. Alluvium deposits along major rivers, such as the Dordogne in France's Aquitaine Basin, provide additional quality resources. Elsewhere on the plain, exposed marine deposits have provided the basis for productive agriculture in low-lying or reclaimed lands in southern Scandinavia, northern Germany, and the Low Countries. The abundance of such agricultural resources has made the North European Plain one of the most densely populated parts of Europe.

**FIGURE 2.12. Farmland.** The inherent fertility of this rolling agricultural landscape just north of Krakow in eastern Poland comes as a result of the thick layer of glacial deposition laid down long ago over this section of the North European Plain.

At the same time, it is important to recognize that not all parts of the plain are so favorably endowed for the purposes of agriculture. The plain also contains broad expanses of droughty sand and gravel, bands of relatively infertile morainic hills and ridges, or soggy low-lying stretches covered with marshes, peat bogs, and lakes. Such features are usually of glacial origin. The Lüneburger Heath of north-central Germany is one example of a large and sparsely settled sandy outwash plain left by glacial action. The Danish Heath on the western side of the Jutland Peninsula is another. Stages of glacial retreat are marked here and there on the plain by low belts of morainic features, such as the intermittent line of hills and small lakes, known as the Baltic Heights, that runs parallel to the Baltic coast from northeastern Germany to the Baltic States. Elsewhere are wide expanses of thick and somewhat more agriculturally productive glacial till. The old Prussian lands of eastern Germany along with parts of northern Poland are famous for their broad expanses of sandy and relatively infertile soils, while the Baltic States, Belarus, and northern Russia are known for their extensive marshes, peat bogs, and lakes, and their heavily forested and confused morainic landscapes. The Pripet Marshes, a large region encompassing some

270,000 square kilometers of dense forests and low-lying bogs and separating Belarus from Ukraine, have a long reputation as one of the most inhospitable of European environments.

Much of the North European Plain was once extensively forested, although the diversity of species was not as great as those found at similar latitudes elsewhere in the world. This is due again to the effects of the last glaciation, which caused the extinction of a wide range of species that were unable, because of the barrier imposed by Europe's belt of alpine ranges, to migrate southward to safety.

The natural vegetation pattern that developed in the aftermath of glacial retreat differed from west to east. In the west (France, England, the Low Countries, Denmark, western Germany, and southern Sweden) the plain and its adjoining uplands belong to a western European deciduous forest region, which consisted originally of great forests of beech, oak, elm, linden, ash, and other broad-leaved species. What remains today are the last vestiges of these forests, which were systematically cleared over a period stretching from early times to somewhere around the end of the 18th century. With the exception of the grasslands of southern Russia and Ukraine, the remainder of the plain to the east was originally completely covered with a mixed coniferous–deciduous forest. These eastern forestlands have withstood the ravages of human actions to a much greater extent than their counterparts to the west. It is a general rule that the proportion of woodland to agricultural or otherwise improved land rises steadily across Europe's northern plain as one travels from west to east.

One of the most salient features of the North European Plain is its system of navigable rivers. The plain is drained by a series of fairly evenly spaced, high-volume, if somewhat short, watercourses that flow into the Baltic and North Seas, or the Atlantic Ocean. These include, from west to east, the Garronne, Dordogne, Loire, Seine, Thames, Meuse, Rhine, Ems, Weser, Elbe, Oder, Vistula, Nieman, and Divina Rivers. The exception, of course, is in southern Russia and

**FIGURE 2.13. Heath.** Meltwater flowing from beneath the ice pack during the last period of glaciation created a vast outwash plain across the entire west side of the Jutland Peninsula. This extensive area of poor, sandy soils came to support a low, brushy vegetation known as the Danish Heath, which remained neglected and peripheral to agricultural settlement until the late 19th century.

Ukraine, where much longer river systems with a far more pronounced seasonality to their flow, such as the Prut, Dniester, Bug, Dnieper, Don, and Volga, make their way southward across the steppe to the Black and Caspian Seas. Most of the rivers that cross the plain originate in adjacent upland areas and play a major role as arteries of movement and commerce between coastal areas and the interior of the continent. For nearly all of these rivers, the strategic point where estuary meets stream, or where the stream is first fordable or bridgeable when ascending the river, has been fortified and occupied for commercial reasons from very early times.

In the areas that front on the Baltic and North Seas, moraine belts along the coast have acted as a barrier, causing many northward-flowing rivers such as the Vistula, Oder, Elbe, and Weser to make sharp, almost right-angle jogs in order to find an easy exit to the sea. Such adjustments have been facilitated by the existence of broad east–west depressions formed in glacial times by meltwater spillways that ran parallel to the melting edge of the ice sheet. These abandoned spillways, which lie just to the south of the coastal moraine belts, have also made it relatively easy for human populations to construct con-

necting canals between rivers. Northern Germany's highly developed canal system, which consists of the Mitteland Canal and its eastern extensions, the Elbe–Havel and Oder–Havel, was built to take advantage of these features and link together the waters of four major rivers: the Ems, Weser, Elbe, and Oder. Russia too has a highly integrated inland waterway system that connects the Black, Caspian, Baltic, and Arctic Seas by navigable rivers and canals. Inland waterways have been intensively developed across the entire length of the North European Plain and have played an important and early role in fostering movement and communication across the plain in ways that run counter to the grain, and far beyond the limits, of the natural drainage system.

The North European Plain also contains significant fossil fuel resources. A feature of historic importance is the widespread occurrence of major deposits of coal. Most of the continent's great coalfields—those of Lancashire, the English Midlands, South Wales, Sambre-Meuse-Lys, the Saar, the Ruhr, Saxony, Upper Silesia, and the Donets Basin—are found along the margins of the North European Plain or in nearby basins nestled among Hercynian upland formations. During

**FIGURE 2.14. Pitheads and slagheaps.** Coal seams that lay near the surface along the margins of Europe's uplands underwent heavy development and exploitation during the industrial revolution of the 19th century. In this photo, taken in the Rhondda Valley of southern Wales, slagheaps and pithead scar the natural beauty of the landscape.

FIGURE 2.15. Hercynian land-scape. Many of the hills stretching out before these hikers are the remains of ancient and long dormant volcanoes, a common feature of the Hercynian formations near Dolsky in the Czech Republic. A medieval castle, lookout, or ruin often sits atop these heights. (Photo: J. M. Daniels)

the 19th and early 20th centuries, these fields, which were often found in close proximity to the continent's richest and most extensive agricultural areas and well situated with respect to supplies of other industrial raw materials such as iron, copper, lead, and zinc, became the loci of massive concentrations of industry and population. The production of coal from these fields, however, has declined steadily since the middle of the 20th century due to the exhaustion of reserves and significant shifts in energy demands toward other sources, principally oil and natural gas but also nuclear power.

Taken as a whole, Europe's reserves of oil and natural gas are inadequate to meet demand. The reserves that do exist, however, are found for the most part on the North European Plain or its extensions beneath the surface of the seas. The largest are found in the Volga, Caspian Sea, and western Urals region of Russia. Oil and gas produced in Russia are exported via pipeline to many parts of Europe. Also significant are the oil and natural gas reserves discovered beneath the surface of the North Sea since the late 1960s and early 1970s. Indeed, North Sea oil and gas production has helped somewhat to ease the energy import situation of the Netherlands and Denmark. They have also made the UK more or less self-sufficient in fossil fuel en-

ergy, at least temporarily, and have turned Norway into the world's third-largest exporter of oil and the richest of the Scandinavian countries. Elsewhere, though, the plain yields little in the way of petroleum resources, with the exception of a few minor sources in France's Aquitaine and Paris Basins.

## The Central or Hercynian Uplands

Directly to the south of the western and central portions of the North European Plain lies our third major landform region. Like the Caledonian system of the Northwest Highlands, the Central or Hercynian Uplands are the heavily eroded and structurally disturbed remnants of an ancient system of mountains. In this case, however, the parent system is of more recent origin, having first emerged some 200 million or more years ago as a result of seafloor spreading and the collision of continental plates.

The core of the system is a more or less continuous belt of uplands, plateaus, valleys, basins, and corridors sandwiched between the North European Plain and what we have referred to as Alpine and Mediterranean Europe. The Hercynian belt begins in southern Poland in the form of a low-lying plateau to the north of Krakow, and extends westward to the headwaters of the Oder River, where it rises up in a series of massifs, uplands, and basins that encompass the whole of the Czech Republic and the Czech–German borderlands. From there it extends westward in a broad arc across Germany, Belgium, and Luxembourg, as well as across the southern tip of the Netherlands and the northern part of Switzerland, into western France and eventually the south of France. Included are such well-known formations as the Sudeten Mountains, Moravian Hills, Ore Mountains, Bohemian Basin and Bohemian Forest, the Harz Mountains (from which the name Hercynian derives), the Rhenish Slate Mountains (including such formations as the Eifel, Westerwald, Taunus, and Hunsrück), the Bavarian Plateau, Black Forest, Ardennes, Vosges, Jura, and Massif Central. Farther north and west are a number of outlying formations, including the Armorican Massif (Brittany), the Cornwall peninsula, and some portions of southern Wales. Related in age and material, but structurally somewhat different, are the high plateau and low mountain ranges of the Spanish Meseta, which is the dominant feature of central and western Iberia, and the massifs that constitute the western Mediterranean islands of Corsica and Sardinia.

For the most part, the Hercynian formations are made up of older crystalline and metamorphic rock, covered in some areas

with layers of younger sedimentary rock. Movements of the earth's crust have caused much dislocation, uplifting and tilting some blocks to form plateaus and massifs while dropping others to form basins and trenches. In some places, such as the Massif Central in France and in the uplands flanking the upper course of the Rhine River in Germany, volcanic activity has been introduced through deep fissures. The Rhine Graben, a 300-kilometer-long trench or rift valley between Basel and Mainz, through which the Rhine River flows, is an excellent example of a down-faulted block. The Graben is flanked on either side by the uplifted block plateaus of the Vosges and the Black Forest. Along the edges, occasional volcanic features (e.g., the Kaiserstuhl) may be seen that mark the location of recent volcanic extrusions, while nearby hot mineral springs are evidence of continued high geothermal activity.

Most of the Hercynian Uplands are too low in elevation to have been affected by alpine glaciation or are situated too far south to have been touched by the continental ice sheets based in northern Europe. Among the higher points are some of the extinct volcanic peaks of the Auvergne Mountains, which form the core of the Massif Central. The highest of these, the Puy de Sancy, reaches 1,886 meters. The Feldsberg of Germany's Black For-

**FIGURE 2.16. Rhine Gorge.** Between Mainz and Cologne, the Rhine cuts deeply through the Rhenish Slate Mountains, a series of uplifted plateaus and ridges that cover much of west-central Germany. The narrow river gorge is flanked on either side by strings of settlement that cling to the edge of steep slopes covered with woods and vineyards.

**FIGURE 2.17. Massif Central.** This deeply incised valley near Millau in France's Massif Central is the product of stream action and typical of the ruggedness for which this beautiful but forbidding region is known.

est rises above surrounding formations to an impressive 1,493 meters. The crests of the Bohemian Forest rise to 1,457 meters and the Ore Mountains to 1,244 meters, but the Hercynian Uplands are for the most part significantly lower. Much of the erosion in these upland regions has been water-based. Where softer sediments cover the older rocks, rivers or streams have often cut deeply incised V-shaped valleys, along which human settlement follows the valley floors while pasture and woodland cover the slopes.

Taken as a whole, Hercynian landscapes may be seen as a complex jumble of high plateaus, forested ridges, fertile valleys, deep basins, and small plains. They offer up the quintessentially compartmentalized European environment, in which terrain affords a delicate balance between naturally protected refuge and easy connections to the outside world. Some of the most famous linking routeways and gateways in Europe are found within the Hercynian upland zone including the Rhône–Saône Corridor, which links the Mediterranean coast of France with the Paris Basin through the Dijon Gap and with the upper Rhine through the Belfort Gap; the Rhine Valley itself, which links the North European Plain with the alpine passes leading to the Mediterranean south, as well as with Danubian Europe via the Bavarian Gap. Farther to the east lies the Elbe Gap, which opens the otherwise highly enclosed Bohemian Basin to

the North European Plain; and the Moravian Gate, through which north–south movement is facilitated between the Vienna basin and the plains of Poland.

The Hercynian Uplands are not generally known for their abundant energy resources, although coal-bearing rifts are important in such places as the Ore Mountains, the Bohemian Forest, South Wales, and the Massif Central. Europe's most important coalfields are, however, often situated on the margins of the uplands where the deeper fossil-bearing strata of plains and basins are upturned and exposed, and historically have been used in conjunction with the abundant and varied mineral deposits that are found in some Hercynian regions. The Ore Mountains, for example, were famous between the 14th and 19th centuries as a rich source of silver and iron, and are mined today for uranium, lead, zinc, copper, and sulfur. The Harz Mountains are similarly known for their deposits of silver and other minerals, including uranium. Copper, lead, and zinc deposits are found in Hercynian formations located in Spain and Poland, while tin, tungsten, and uranium have been mined in Cornwall and the Massif Central.

The Hercynian region is unevenly settled. The uplands consist of relatively sparsely populated ridges and plateaus, interspersed with more intensely occupied valleys and basins. The region is known for its diverse scenery, both physical and cultural, and exerts a profound attraction as a nearby recreational retreat for the major population centers of the North European Plain. A particularly important recreational lure since early times is the widespread occurrence of hot mineral springs, which are the sites of resorts and health spas. Famous examples include the town of Spa in the Belgian Ardennes (from which the name for this kind of resort derives), the world-renowned spas of Karlovy Vary (Karlsbad) and Mariánske Lázne (Marienbad) in the Ore Mountains, the spa town of Lamalou Les Bains in the Orb Valley of the Massif Central, and the glamorous Black Forest health resort city of Baden-Baden. Once the exclusive domain of the rich

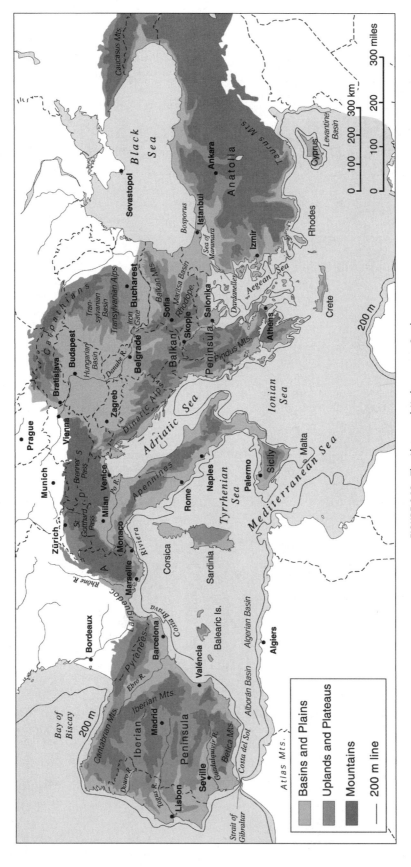

FIGURE 2.18. The Alpine and Mediterranean South.

and famous, many of the region's famous spas have enjoyed a modern renaissance as health retreats for Europe's rapidly aging population.

## The Alpine and Mediterranean South

Our final major landform region is a complex zone of rugged mountains, plateaus, deep basins, coastal plains, and islands that spans the entire southern reaches of the continent. The region contains the youngest and most spectacular mountains in Europe, whose origins lie in the great but relatively recent tectonic pressures created by the northward movement of the African plate, which plunges beneath the European landmass all along the length of its Mediterranean margin. These tectonic pressures emanating from the south have been at work for roughly 20 million years and continue today, as evidenced by the frequent and widespread earthquake and volcanic activity for which southern Europe is all too tragically known. The grain of the southern mountain system runs roughly parallel to the Mediterranean coast and at right angles to the thrusts of the pressures that have created it. Many of these formations were built from material laid down on the floor of an ancient sea, the Tethys, which once covered much of

**FIGURE 2.19. Vulcanism.** Stromboli is one of seven volcanic islands, known collectively as the Aeolian Islands, which lie off the coast of Sicily. With its small white houses, olive groves, and citrus orchards precariously clinging to the flanks of its huge volcanic cone, the island broods majestically but ominously over the quiet waters of the Mediterranean.

the region. Their marine origins are revealed in the widespread occurrence of limestone and sandstone formations and the exposure of marine fossils.

This southern mountain system is actually a series of mountain chains, many of which have distinctive geologic and topographic features. Beginning in the west, they appear in Iberia as several ranges or *cordilleras*, including the steep Atlantic-facing Cantabrian and difficult-to-traverse Pyrenees Mountains in the north, and the less rugged Central Sierra, Iberian, Sierra Morena, and Bética ranges that so neatly compartmentalize the central and western portions of the Iberian Peninsula. These ranges also combine with the major westward-flowing rivers of the Iberian Peninsula, the Porto, the Tagus, and the Guadalquivir, to orient the central plateaus and western valleys of Iberia toward the Atlantic, leaving the remainder of the peninsular land mass to turn its face toward the Mediterranean.

From the Iberian Peninsula the system extends eastward beneath the surface of the western Mediterranean Basin, reemerging briefly as the Balearic island group before establishing itself again on the Riviera coast as the French Maritime Alps. From there, the Alpine system runs north for a distance along the Franco–Italian frontier. These ridge lines reach their highest elevations—Mont Blanc (4,807 meters) and the Matterhorn (4,478 meters)—as they turn eastward and fan out to form a wide band of rugged longitudinal ridges, separated by glacial river valleys, that traverses the length of Switzerland, Austria, and northernmost Italy, before ending in Slovenia as the Julian Alps. A southward trending offshoot, consisting of the Apennine and Sicilian Mountains, forms the backbone of the Italian peninsula and the island of Sicily.

Farther to the east, the system appears again in the form of the Carpathian Mountains, which run in a great arc from the Vienna Basin to the Iron Gate and links the Alps with the many and complexly situated mountain ranges of Balkan Europe (the Transylvanian and Dinaric Alps, and the Pindus, Balkan, and Rhodope Mountains). From the Balkans, the southern system continues eastward, the peaks of countless underwater mountains forming the Greek islands of the Aegean Sea. It reappears on the Anatolian peninsula of Turkey in the form of a pair of coastal mountain chains (the Kuzey Anadoglu along the Black Sea coast and the Taurus along the Mediterranean coast) and a central high plateau. The system reaches its eastern terminus as the rugged Caucasus Mountains, which contain Europe's highest summit in the Elbrus Massif (5,642 meters).

The relative youth of the southern mountain system means that many of its ranges are sufficiently high and rugged to obstruct communication and movement, although few have actually proven to be a serious obstacle for long. Of all of the ranges in the system, the 430-kilometer-long Pyrenees chain, which separates Iberia from the rest of mainland Europe, seems to have been the most effective transportation barrier. The northward-facing steep slope of the Pyrenees and the lack of easily negotiated passes have historically constrained most traffic to the narrow coastal areas at either end of the range.

Other ranges have proved to be less of a barrier, imposing restrictions on movement rather than closing it off altogether. The grain of the Alps in Switzerland, Italy, and Austria,

for example, which consists of a series of east–west running ridges and longitudinal valleys, might be seen as a natural barrier to north–south movement. Yet, they are traversable at a number of points where streams have cut deeply enough into ridgelines to produce low passes. The distances over these passes are relatively short. Famous alpine passes such as Mont Cenis, Great Saint Bernard, Simplon, Saint Gotthard, Splügen, Semmering, and Brenner have played important roles in linking the Mediterranean with northern Europe since early times. The western passes leading from Italy to the Rhône Valley have a particularly long history, while in the east the Brenner Pass, which links the lower Po Plain with Austria and Bavaria, was heavily used as far back as the Stone Age.

The St. Gotthard Pass, which was really not used much before the 13th century, proved in the long run to be especially important because it links northern Italy to the Swiss plateau in a single ascent and decline. Although only a single track, incapable of supporting vehicular traffic until 1830 when an all-weather road was built, the St. Gotthard route was for centuries the most important north–south link across the Swiss Alps. A railroad line was added in 1882 and a motorway tunnel in 1980.

FIGURE 2.20. Mountain barrier. High and rugged, the Pyrenees separate Spain from France. Seen here from the Spanish side, a road leads north toward one of the high passes, as well the micro-state of Andorra, which nestles among some of the highest peaks in the range.

FIGURE 2.21. Alpine longitudinal valley. This photo taken at daybreak, from the window of a passing train, captures the misty quietude of one of the many long valleys that run between the parallel ridges of the Swiss Alps.

Farther to the east, the Carpathians are by contrast relatively low. They are also deeply penetrated by rivers and have many low passes and gaps. They have never really been a major barrier to movement. This is especially true of the Northwestern and Central Carpathians. With the exception of the Tatras massif, which rises to 2,665 meters along the Polish–Slovak border, these two sections often appear more like a series of long hilly plateaus than mountain ranges. In Romania, the Eastern Carpathians are generally a bit higher and more rugged, but the Transylvanian Alps, which form the southern arm of the horseshoe-shaped Carpathian system, are traversed by a number of low-altitude passes that provide relatively easy access between the Wallachian Plain and the Transylvanian Basin.

The mountains of the Balkan Peninsula are far more rugged and complex (the word *Balkan* means mountain). The Dinaric Alps, which parallel the Dalmatian coast of the Adriatic Sea, are a fairly effective barrier to travel. The limestone ranges of these mountains are relatively high, reaching 2,692 meters in northern Albania, and there are no easily negotiated natural passes. On the other hand, the hinterlands of the Dinaric Alps, which extend deep into the interior of the Balkan Peninsula, contain a number of important connectors in the form of interior basins and river corridors. The valleys of the east-

ward-flowing Sava and Morava Rivers, for example, connect the upland regions of eastern Croatia and Bosnia with the Danube and the lowland heart of Serbia. The Morava–Vardar Corridor links the Aegean Sea with the Danube Valley by connecting the northward-flowing Morava River with the southward-flowing Vardar River at their headwaters near the Macedonian–Kosovo border above Skopje, and has served as a major north–south transportation route across the Balkan region since the amber trade of prehistoric times.

FIGURE 2.22. Carpathians. This Carpathian peak in Slovakia, with its gentle and heavily wooded slopes, hardly seems intimidating. Although the Carpathians form an almost continuous horseshoe-shaped arc running through Slovakia, western Ukraine, and Romania, they are relatively easily traversed and have never been a serious barrier to movement.

The Balkan Mountains of Bulgaria, which run east for some 450 kilometers from the Serbian border to Cape Emine on the shore of the Black Sea, seem to cut the country in half, separating the Danube Valley in the north from the Maritsa Basin, sometimes known as the Thracian Plain, in the south. The mountain barrier is actually not particularly high, reaching only 2,376 meters at Botev Peak. More than two dozen passes allow traffic to cross easily from north to south, except in winter when snow hinders passage. Farther to the south the Rhodope Mountains, while not particularly high at 1,000–2,000 meters, have a sufficiently difficult topography to make them one of the more inaccessible parts of the Balkan Peninsula. The Pindus Mountains, which sweep down from Albania and Macedonia to form the backbone of mainland Greece, are rugged enough to constitute a formidable physical barrier, but are broken in key places by passes.

FIGURE 2.23. The Peloponnese. This scene is typical of the rugged, heavily eroded mountain landscapes of Greece. The sparse vegetation on the slopes of this valley in the eastern mountains of the Peloponnese is made up primarily of drought-resistant species.

While rarely an effective barrier to communication, the southern mountain system often does play a significant role as a climatic divide, helping to separate the Marine West Coast, Transitional, and Humid Continental climates of temperate Europe from the Mediterranean climate of southern Europe. In the summertime, for example, the Pyrenees and their westward extension, the Cantabrian Mountains, effectively block the southward movement of moist air masses that come in off the North Atlantic. While their northern slopes enjoy abundant rainfall, the southern slopes and adjacent high plateaus farther to the south have a dry, steppe-like climate induced by the persistent heat of the dry, stable air mass that dominates the Mediterranean summer. Similarly, the various alpine ranges along with the mountains of the Balkan peninsula help to accentuate the differences between the warm and pleasant climatic conditions found in Italy and the coastal areas of the Balkans from the harsher climates of central Europe and the eastern interior of the continent.

The climatic barrier imposed by the southern mountain system is not, however, entirely effective. The southward displacement of the Atlantic air masses affecting Europe in wintertime enables wet and stormy Atlantic weather systems to slide south of the barrier from time to time and enter into the Mediterranean Basin. This produces the intense periods of winter precipitation from which the bulk of the basin's annual supply of atmospheric moisture derives. The movement of winter storms through the basin can also have the effect of drawing cold, damp winds down through the gaps in the mountains or even over the crests of the mountain ranges. The *mistral* is a breathtakingly cold wind that is drawn, in this fashion, down the Rhône–Saône Corridor and into the western Mediterranean basin. In the same way the cold *bora*, a wind that has been known to top 130 kilometers per hour, rushes over the alpine mountain barrier to chill the Adriatic and the eastern coast of Italy. The many basins and corridors strewn about the mountainous Balkans region also provide the passageways that enable cold

FIGURE 2.24. **Montes de Toledo.** In the high interior of the Iberian Peninsula, the open and seemingly endless Meseta landscape stretches out to meet the sky, not unlike the high plains landscapes of the American West.

winter temperatures to creep far southward. Conversely, Mediterranean air sometimes spills northward over the alpine mountain barrier in the form of a warm, desiccating wind known as the *Föhn*. The *aspre* is a similarly warm wind of Mediterranean origin that invades the Garonne Plain in southwestern France.

The landscapes of the Alpine and Mediterranean South are among the most varied in Europe. The highest mountain ranges in the western Alps are permanently snowcapped at around 2,500 meters on the shaded north-facing slopes and at about 3,000 meters on the south-facing, or *Sonnenseite*, slopes. Melted water from glaciers feeds the headwaters of many of the alpine rivers. Heavy glaciation

was prevalent throughout these mountains during the Pleistocene, leaving behind a distinctive alpine landscape of arêtes, cirques, matterhorns, U-shaped and hanging valleys, and long moraine-blocked lakes. Below the snowline is a treeless zone of alpine pastures, and below that the coniferous forests that blanket the foothills and the alpine valleys, at least in places where people have allowed them to remain undisturbed. The Pyrenees were also once glaciated, but no ice sheets remain today. The Carpathians and many of the Balkan mountain chains are very heavily forested in coniferous and deciduous species, and can be snow-covered in winter.

The mountain ridges, slopes, and plateaus most immediately surrounding the Mediter-

FIGURE 2.25. **Lake Lucerne.** The Alpine barrier is often penetrated by long finger lakes, which were dammed behind the terminal moraines produced by the glaciers as they worked their way down out of the mountains. These lakes, as can be seen in this photo of Lake Lucerne near Thun, often serve as points of entry to mountain passes.

ranean were once covered extensively with an open forest of widely spaced and drought-resistant evergreens and wooded shrubs set among rich grasslands, but many centuries of deforestation, soil erosion, and grazing have removed most of this original vegetative cover. Today many mountainous and upland areas in Iberia, the south of France, Italy, the western Balkans, Greece, and Turkey are either barren or covered with a vegetation regime consisting primarily of one of two drought-resistant types. The first is most commonly known by the French word *maquis*, but also as *macchia* in Italian, *mattoral* in Spanish, *longos* or *xerovoúnii* in Greek, and *al arachd* in Arabic. It is a scrubby evergreen vegetation, usually about two meters in height, consisting of such plants as juniper, holm oak, and broom heath. A second kind of plant cover, which is lower, more varied in its species, and covers the ground even more sparsely is known in French as *garrique* (*tommillares* in Spanish, and *phrygana* in Greek). It typically consists of a variety of aromatic plants, such as rosemary and thyme. The absence of deep forest cover, coupled with steep slopes and unstable soils, renders many Mediterranean mountain and upland landscapes susceptible to dramatic erosion during the winter rainy season.

In addition to its mountain and upland landscapes, the Alpine and Mediterranean South contains numerous coastal plains and embayments, as well as a wide variety of interior valleys, basins, and corridors. Intensive Mediterranean agriculture, relying heavily on the cultivation of olives, citrus fruits, and grapes, is focused on the numerous small pockets of coastal plain or embayments (known as *huertas* in Spanish) that dot the coasts of mainland and islands alike. Major coastal lowlands, such as the Andalusian Lowland, the Plain of Languedoc, and the Po River Valley, figure prominently in the region's distinctive landscape mix. So do the highly varied landscapes of the great eastern intermontane basins, such as the vast Hungarian Basin, the Transylvanian Basin, the Wallachian Plain, the Morava–Vardar Corridor, and the Maritsa Basin, which offer every-

thing from the steppe-like environmental conditions found on the Hungarian Plain to the deltaic flood plains of the Danube in eastern Wallachia. A few of the coastal lowlands, such as the Plain of Salonika, the Pontine Marshes, and the Ebro delta, present special problems of drainage and malarial disease that have, until relatively recently, defied human development.

In many parts of this region deposits of industrial minerals of various kinds are important. The Iberian Peninsula has been known historically for the production of copper, tin, silver, and gold, and has also become an important modern source of tungsten, zinc, and uranium. Greece produces bauxite in considerable quantities, as well as nickel and asbestos, and the Greek islands were historically important as sources of copper, silver, and lead. Switzerland, Austria, and Italy, on the other hand, are almost entirely bereft of significant deposits of industrial resources. The Balkan Peninsula is perhaps best endowed, although most of its mineral resources are of limited quantity or quality.

The Alpine and Mediterranean South is relatively poorly endowed with energy resources. The Iberian and Italian peninsulas and the Alpine regions can claim few petroleum or coal reserves of any size or quality. Minor reserves of oil and natural gas are found in some of the interior basins of the Balkan Peninsula and in the Danube corridor, most notably in Romania near Ploesti, and in offshore locations in the northern Aegean Sea. There are also scattered pockets of coal production here and there throughout the Balkan countries. Hydroelectric power is an important source of energy in some areas, particularly in Switzerland and Austria, but also in the Danube Valley after the narrow Iron Gate gorge became the site of a major dam and power station project jointly undertaken and completed by Romania and the former Yugoslavia in the early 1970s.

For the most part, rivers all across this region tend to be short, with highly seasonal flows. In the wet winter season they are often swollen. During the dry summer season they are reduced to only a small flow, and can even dry up entirely. They therefore lack the navigable qualities of their northern and eastern European counterparts. The major exceptions are the Ebro, the Rhône, and the Po; and especially the long Danube, all of which enjoy a more or less constant supply of water from mountain snows. The Danube is the region's longest river. It flows eastward for some 2,850 kilometers from its headwaters in southwestern Germany to the Black Sea. Now linked to the Rhine by the Main-Danube Canal, the Danube has become a major artery for the movement of goods by barge between northwestern and southeastern Europe.

Surface water is an important resource in the drier parts of the Iberian Peninsula, as well as in Italy and Greece. Dams and reservoirs are common landscape features there, especially since the advent of large-scale irrigation projects in the middle and latter parts of the 20th century. In Spain, the government is currently contemplating an ambitious scheme to divert huge amounts of water south from the Ebro via an elaborate system of tunnels and aqueducts to the country's dry Almeira region, where farmers will use it to grow winter fruits and vegetables for the

**FIGURE 2.26. Iron Gate.** As it passes along the Serbian–Montenegrin and Romanian border, the Danube River is suddenly forced to work its way through a gap between the Carpathian and Balkan Mountains. The narrow gorge, known as the Iron Gate, was long a major choke point for movement along the river. Only since 1896 has river traffic been able to bypass the gorge by way of the Sip Canal. Today the Iron Gate is the site of a large hydroelectric power dam, which fills the riverbed behind the dam with backed-up water.

north European market. If the controversial plan is approved, it will be Europe's largest irrigation project.

## The Special Case of Iceland

The physical geography of Iceland is a special case that warrants separate treatment. Geologically speaking, Iceland is the youngest of European environments. The oldest formations on Iceland are only about 16 million years old. The origins of the island are volcanic. It is a remnant of a vast basaltic dome that rose up from the floor of the Atlantic and then collapsed suddenly, leaving a group of small basalt islands that were eventually connected to one another through continued volcanic activity to form a single land mass. Volcanism persists on and around Iceland even today. There are around 200 active volcanoes on the island, and new eruptions occur at the rate of about one every 5 years. The island has many hot water springs and natural steam fields, especially in the younger volcanic areas. Glaciation also remains an active force on Iceland. Glaciers cover extensive parts of the island. Since the soft volcanic rock is easily eroded, the effects of glacial movement on the land are especially marked.

Iceland is very much a natural landscape still in the making—a landscape that gives the impression of immaturity in the ruggedness of its outline and the presence of strong physical forces at work. The island is nearly devoid of forest cover. Compared to many other parts of Europe, the Icelandic landscape seems naked, especially in the interior. A small number of tree species are found on the island, but their distribution is quite limited. This is due in part to natural conditions. But there has also been a profound human effect. Extensive birch woods and woody scrublands did exist in many coastal areas when settlers first arrived a little more than a thousand years ago. These woodlands were largely cleared by settlers and given over to grazing. Only a small part of the original woodland survived the impact of such human activity, although modern reforestation and conservation has increased the vegetative cover somewhat.

FIGURE 2.27. Herðiebreid. The origins of Iceland are volcanic, and volcanic formations, both active and inactive, dominate the landscape. The flat top of Herðiebreid is due to the fact that the volcano's development took place beneath an ice sheet. Note the barren, treeless Icelandic landscape in the foreground.

## MARINE ENVIRONMENTS

In addition to the four major terrain regions described above, it is important not to forget the marine environments that both surround and penetrate the European landmass. The most useful way to organize the marine environments is to think of Europe as being bounded on the west by the Atlantic (and its deep-water northern extensions, the Norwegian and Arctic Seas) and enveloped in the north and south by two symmetrical arcs of continental and interior seas. The northern arc is made up of a complex assemblage, including the English Channel and Irish Sea, the North Sea, the Skaggerak, the Kattegat, the Øresund and Danish Belts, and the Baltic Sea along with its three major extensions, the Bothnian Gulf, the Gulf of Riga and the Gulf of Finland. Although not strictly connected by open water, we might also add to this northern arc the White and Barents Seas, which are linked to the Baltic by canal via the Karelian depression. The corresponding southern arc consists of the Mediterranean and its various component and offshoot seas (the Ligurian, the Tyrrhenian, the Adriatic, the Ionian, and the Aegean Seas), which are connected by the Dardanelles, the Sea of Marmara, and the Bosporus to the Black Sea and its smaller northern annex, the Sea of Azov.

## The Northern Seas

The marine environments of the northern arc have one physical characteristic in common. They all occupy portions of a submerged continental shelf that extends far beyond the shorelines of northern and western Europe. As a consequence, all are relatively shallow, rarely exceeding 200 meters in depth. The average depth of the North Sea is only 90 meters. The sea has many extensive shallows such as the Dogger Bank, a vast underwater moraine feature from the last glacial age, which is covered to depths of only 15 to 30 meters. The only really great depths, reaching nearly 700 meters, are found in a long trench off the western and southern coasts of Norway that links the Skaggerak to the deep waters of the North Atlantic. The average depth of the Kattegat is less than 25 meters; and the Baltic is quite shallow nearly everywhere, with an average depth of just 55 meters.

At the same time, the component parts of the northern arc all have distinctive characteristics of their own. The westernmost seas and straits are much influenced by the Atlantic. They lie directly in the path of the Atlantic Drift, which means that their waters are relatively warm and remain free of ice throughout the winter. The warm and well-mixed waters of these marine environments are also ideally suited to the growth of plankton and a wide variety of fish, including cod, haddock, mackerel, plaice, sole, and whiting. Their abundantly productive fisheries have traditionally been an important resource, although nowadays overfishing has become a serious problem.

Exposure to the ocean also means that these westernmost northern seas can be stormy and treacherous for seafarers. Nonetheless, the North Sea and adjacent waters have long been one of the world's busiest shipping areas. By the late Middle Ages, a lively maritime trade had developed between the towns that surround the sea, and from these great ports intrepid seafarers ventured out in the 16th and 17th centuries to found and profit from the commerce of overseas empire. These waters today are alive with merchant and fishing vessels. The Europoort complex at Rotterdam handles more tonnage than any other port in the world. The large port complexes at La Havre, Antwerp, London, Bremen, and Hamburg also contribute to the ever-present volume of North Sea shipping. More recently, the discovery of major beds of petroleum and natural gas beneath the floor of the North Sea has proven, as we have already pointed out, to be a major boon to the economies of surrounding states. The commerce of the North Sea now includes the piped output of an array of oil platforms that extend southward all the way from the Shetland Islands to the Dogger Bank, as well as the production of a line of natural gas fields that stretches from the east coast of England to the Frisian Islands.

Farther to the east, the Baltic claims distinction as the world's largest brackish-water sea. The salinity of its waters is much reduced by the great quantities of fresh water that flow into it from the many long rivers along its coast, and by the fact that its connections with the western seas are restricted by the narrow Danish straits and the shallow Kattegat. The salt water that enters through these shallow western outlets is cold and heavy, which causes it to sink and not to mix well with surface waters. The waters of the Baltic are generally less than one-third as saline as ordinary

FIGURE 2.28. Wind farms. The northern seas provide a source of energy beyond that of North Sea oil. Wind farms, such as this one, are an increasingly commonplace coastal sight across all of northern Europe.

seawater. Levels of salinity are especially low at the northern end of the Gulf of Bothnia. Nearly landlocked and sheltered from North Sea tides, the Baltic seems more like an inland lake than a sea. It is easily navigated, although parts freeze over in winter due to low salinity, shallowness, and exposure to cold continental air. Icebreakers are needed during most winters to keep ports along the upper shores of the Gulf of Bothnia free of pack ice. Drift ice often forms in the Gulf of Finland, and during severe winters may sometimes close ports for days along the Polish and German coasts. Drift ice has even been known to impede traffic on the Øresund.

Like the North Sea, the Baltic has always played an active commercial role. The 110-kilometer-long Øresund is the most direct natural link between North Sea and Baltic shipping, and one of the world's busiest sea-lanes. Between 1429 and 1657, Denmark controlled both shores of this strategic strait and levied tolls, from its great fortress of Kronoborg at Helsingør, on all shipping that passed through the strait. Even after Sweden took possession of the eastern shore of the Øresund in 1658, the Danes continued to collect the Sound Dues on shipping until forced by the British to suspend the practice in 1857. Commerce to and from the North Sea was also facilitated in 1895 by the construction by Prussia of the Kaiser Wilhelm Canal (Kiel Ca-

**FIGURE 2.29. Øresund.** Visible on the far side of the Øresund from the Swedish city of Helsingborg is the coast of Denmark at Helsingør. The 112-kilometer-long strait has long been one of the most heavily used waterways in the world. Here, at its narrowest point, the Danish coast is just a little over 4 kilometers away.

nal) across the base of the Jutland Peninsula. In Russia, the completion of a White Sea–Baltic Canal system, using penal labor during the 1930s, made it possible for ships of seagoing size to move not only back and forth between the White Sea and the Baltic but also to reach the Black Sea via Russia's internal canal and river system. Thus, taken all together, the assemblage of seas and straits that makes up the northern arc plays an important role as a bridge between all the lands and peoples of northern Europe.

## The Southern Seas

The southern arc begins with the Mediterranean, the world's largest inland sea. The Mediterranean is nearly 4,000 kilometers in length and attains great depths, reaching 4,900 meters in the Ionian Basin off Cape Taíneron on the southern coast of Greece, 4,517 meters off the Isle of Rhodes, and 3,785 meters off the west coast of Italy near Naples. The sea may be divided quite naturally into two large basins, a western and an eastern, separated by an underwater ridge (less than 400 meters depth) that runs between the island of Sicily and the coast of North Africa. These two basins, in turn, may be divided into smaller basins. The western sea breaks down into the Alborán Basin between Spain and Morocco, the Algerian Basin between Algeria and France, and the Tyrrhenian Basin be-

tween Italy and the islands of Corsica, Sardinia, and Sicily. The eastern Mediterranean can be subdivided into the Adriatic Sea between Italy and the Balkan Peninsula, the Ionian Basin between Greece and Libya, the Levantine Basin between Turkey and Egypt, as well as the island-dotted waters of the Aegean Sea between Greece and Turkey.

The Mediterranean is connected to the Atlantic by the narrow (13 kilometers wide) Strait of Gibraltar, through which Atlantic and Mediterranean waters are exchanged—the Atlantic waters flowing in on racing surface currents, while the heavier Mediterranean waters flow beneath the surface in the opposite direction. The waters of the Mediterranean, however, are distinctly different from their Atlantic counterparts in that they are saltier and warmer, the former quality coming from the fact that the evaporation of water from the surface far exceeds the inflow of fresh water from the rivers that drain the surrounding land. Indeed, the sea receives more water from the Atlantic than it does from tributary streams. Mediterranean waters are also quite warm and are governed by a complex system of surface currents. Marine life is abundant, including hundreds of species of fish, sponge, and coral. There is little variation in tides, a feature that facilitates shipping. Winter storms, however, can be a severe threat to navigation. The Ottoman Turks, who were a major naval presence in the eastern

Mediterranean in the 16th and 17th centuries, actually refrained from sending their fleet out during the winter months for fear of losing it.

The Mediterranean is connected to the Black Sea by way of the Sea of Marmara and a pair of very narrow and strategic straits—the Dardanelles and the Bosporus—through which run strong and dangerous currents in the direction of the Mediterranean. The Dardanelles–Sea of Marmara–Bosporus connection between the Mediterranean and the Black Sea is one of the four great Maritime Gateways in Europe, the other three being the Strait of Gibraltar, the English Channel, and the Øresund. Ships passing north to the Black Sea must first negotiate the Dardanelles. Known to the ancients as the Hellespont, the Dardanelles has a fabled history filled with great armies ferrying across its narrow waters (only 1.2 kilometers wide) in search of conquests in Europe or Asia, historic castles and fortresses built to control its traffic, and a bitterly fought World War I campaign on Gallipoli, the long peninsula that encloses the strait on its western side.

On the northern shore of the Sea of Marmara and nestled between the waters of the Golden Horn and the entrance to the Bosporus lies Istanbul, long known as Constantinople, the ancient city of Roman and Byzantine emperors and fabled center for nearly five centuries of the Turkish Ottoman Empire. Above the city of Istanbul, the Bosporus leads north past villages, palaces, and castles and, since the 1970s, past two enormous suspension bridges to the waters of the Black Sea. The narrow Bosporus is one of the world's busiest waterways, carrying three times as much traffic as the Suez Canal and four times as much as the Panama Canal. Ironically, it is also a difficult passage for the fleets of oil tankers and cargo freighters that use it. The waters of the Bosporus "slope" downhill by some 20 degrees from north to south. Southbound ships are carried along by the swift current, which can easily cause a captain to lose control of his vessel. Accidents are fairly frequent and today's sharply increased tanker traffic carrying crude from

Russian oil fields have caused many to worry about new disasters. According to the 1936 Treaty of Monteaux, which governs traffic on the strait, ships have the right to pass through without any "formalities," including the payment of taxes and tolls, or the requirement that they accept local pilots to help them navigate the passage. As a result, only about 40 percent of the large ships take on local pilots. The authorities maintain that the ships in the worst condition to successfully negotiate the strait are, unfortunately, the least likely to seek assistance.

The Black Sea has peculiar water qualities. There is a heavily saline bottom layer that has little movement, contains heavy concentrations of hydrogen sulfide, and has absolutely no marine life. The upper layer, which receives great quantities of fresh water from the long and heavy-flowing rivers that empty into the sea around its northern shores, has low salinity, a marked counterclockwise current, and abundant marine life. These rivers, with their great loads of silt, have also turned the northern and western shore of the Black Sea into an extensive area of deltas, sand bars, and shallow lagoons. The Sea of Azov, which is fed by the Don and Kuban Rivers, has a maximum depth of only 13 meters. Its outlet to the Black Sea, the Strait of Kerch, is a mere seven

**FIGURE 2.30. Bosporus.** This vessel is moving south along the Bosporus past the fortress of Rumeli Hisar, built by Mehmet II (the Conqueror) in 1452 as a strategic move in his plan to capture Constantinople. This is the narrowest point on the waterway and the site of the second of two modern suspension bridges that span the Bosporus to link Europe to Asia.

meters deep. On the other hand, like the Mediterranean, the Black Sea is capable of attaining great depths. Just offshore of the steep and rocky Anatolian coast, the floor of the sea reaches a depth of 2,245 meters.

## The North Atlantic

Facing Europe on the west is the North Atlantic. As a marine environment, the ocean is less intimately European. Unlike the northern and southern seas, the Atlantic is a vast body of water with great depths and distant shores. Those parts that might be regarded as European consist primarily of the coastal zone of the continental shelf, the extent of which varies considerably along the continent's long Atlantic margin but is quite narrow overall.

On the western coasts of Portugal and Spain the continental shelf drops off quickly, seldom extending out for more than 50 kilometers. Deep trenches and dark abysses lie not far beyond. Farther north, the Bay of Biscay forms a wide indentation in the Atlantic face of Europe, bounded on the east and northeast by the French coast from Bordeaux to the tip of Brittany, and on the south by the Cantabrian coast of northern Spain. The floor of the bay drops off steeply, especially in its southeastern corner, in the form of great canyons that reach depths of more than 4,500 meters. Here, the Atlantic can seem forbidding. The waters of the bay have a notorious reputation among sailors for their sudden squalls and ferocious gales.

Farther north, the continental shelf marks the Atlantic approaches to the British Isles by reaching out far to the west. From across this broad shelf the ocean waters penetrate eastward to the English Channel and their junction with the North Sea at the narrow Straits of Dover, as well as to the sheltered waters of the Irish Sea via St. George's Channel. Along the western coasts of Ireland and Scotland, the deep Atlantic presses close once again to the continent's margins. Above the British Isles in the Norwegian Sea, the warm water currents of the Atlantic Drift mix with cold Arctic currents to create rich fishing grounds off the coasts of Iceland, around the Shetland and Faeroe Islands, and along the length of Norway's long coast.

Although physically more forbidding in many ways than the northern and southern seas, the Atlantic has always beckoned Europeans westward. The Atlantic coast is dotted with ports, both large and small, and fishing has long been a principal industry. As we shall point out in a later chapter, the Atlantic has played and continues to play a special role as the great avenue by which western Europeans, at least, have sought external riches both from the sea and through connections with the rest of the world.

## FURTHER READING

Allen, H. D. (2001). *Mediterranean ecogeography.* Harlow, UK: Prentice Hall.

Ashwell, I. Y., & Jackson, E. (1970). The sagas as evidence of early deforestation in Iceland. *Canadian Geographer, 14,* 158–166.

Bryson, B., & Ludwig, G. (1992). Main-Danube Canal: Linking Europe's waterways. *Naional Geographic, 182,* 3–31.

Cumbers, A. (1995). North Sea oil and regional economic development. *Area, 27,* 208–217.

Flohm, H., & Fantechi, R. (Eds.). (1984). *The climate of Europe: Past, present, future: Natural and man-induced climatic changes: A European perspective.* Hingham, MA: Kluwer Academic.

Grove, A. T., & Racham, O. (2001). *The nature of Mediterranean Europe: An ecological history.* New Haven, CT: Yale University Press.

John, D. (1983). *Geology and landscape in Britain and Western Europe.* Oxford, UK: Oxford University Press.

Kirby, D., & Hinkkanen, M.-L. (2000). *The Baltic and the North Seas.* London: Routledge.

Parish, R. (2002). *Mountain environments.* Harlow, UK: Prentice Hall.

Wallén, C. C. (1970). *Climates of northern and western Europe.* Amsterdam: Elsevier.

Wallén, C. C. (1977). *Climates of cental and southern Europe.* Amsterdam: Elsevier.

# CHAPTER 3

# Population

At just over 680 million, Europe's population today is at a historic high. But it is also a population whose growth by natural increase has come to almost a complete standstill. This is due to the fact that fertility nearly everywhere in Europe has fallen to the point where it is at or below replacement level. Fertility rates have, in fact, fallen so low in recent years that many demographers now predict that, barring a sudden baby boom or great surges of immigration, a substantial drop in Europe's population will inevitably take place over the next half-century.

Europe also has the oldest population in the world. People across most of Europe enjoy important advantages in health care, diet, and working environments, and they are living longer lives. The extremely low fertility and greater longevity that characterizes European populations today ensures that an ever larger part of these populations will consist of elderly people in the future. We are witnessing a "graying" of Europe, and there is considerable concern about how a much-reduced work force can in the future care for the growing population of elderly. One by one, European governments are coming to the inescapable and alarming conclusion that the only solutions to this pending problem are some combination of higher taxes, later retirement, and reduced pension benefits—and that set-

ting such policies in motion is going to be quite difficult politically.

In a world where total population is expected to increase from roughly 6 billion today to nearly 9 billion by midcentury, and where populations are characterized more often than not by their relative youthfulness, Europe's presently shrinking and graying population stands in sharp contrast to that of most of the rest of the world. The present demographic situation, however, is but one of many that Europeans have known over the ages. We need to remember that today's situa-

FIGURE 3.1. The "graying" of Europe. An older couple crosses a city street in eastern Germany. As longevity increases and birth rates remain low, Europe's population is becoming progressively older.

tion is just the most recent stage of a long evolutionary process, and that it is often useful to see the present in the context of the past.

Our purpose in this chapter, therefore, is to trace the growth and distribution of Europe's human population, from earliest times to the present, with special attention to the dynamics of population change. We begin by surveying the long, slow course of human progress stretching from the Paleolithic era to the end of the 18th century, and providing some general sense of the way in which historic human populations came to occupy and utilize the earth space we have defined as Europe. Later in the chapter we focus on the dramatic surge in population growth that swept over Europe from the end of the 18th century until well into the 20th century. We examine the underlying mechanism behind this unprecedented growth, the Demographic Transition, how the timing and circumstances of the transition varied over European space, and how in a post-Transition age recent demographic trends have brought Europe's population to its present shrinking and aging state.

## POPULATION AND SETTLEMENT TO THE END OF THE 18TH CENTURY

### The First Europeans

The first distant ancestors of modern humankind were members of a species known as *Homo erectus*. They had originated in Africa. About one million years ago members of this population migrated across the Red Sea land bridge and gradually spread over the Eurasian landmass. They used stone tools, and we call the period of their dominance the Lower Paleolithic. The most recent evidence suggests that they were present in Europe roughly half a million years ago, during the glacial period known as the Middle Pleistocene. Relatively few traces of these earliest inhabitants have survived, however, and much controversy remains over whether these first hominids may have appeared in Europe at a much earlier time. We do know that in time various archaic forms of *Homo sapiens* evolved out of different *Homo erectus* populations, ushering in the

Middle Paleolithic period. In Europe this new species is known as Neanderthal man (*Homo sapiens neanderthalensis*), a more advanced but still very primitive species of hunters and gatherers.

They in turn began to be replaced, perhaps as early as 40,000 years ago, by what may be regarded as anatomically modern humans (*Homo sapiens sapiens*). A debate exists over whether this new subspecies evolved out of different *Homo sapiens* populations already present in Europe or whether they too originated solely in Africa and spread from there about 100,000 years ago to Eurasia. In any case, the appearance of *Homo sapiens sapiens* introduced to Europe human populations whose Upper Paleolithic practices and technological skills, numbers, and degree of local concentration were sufficient to begin to affect natural environments, although the effect was small compared both to the changes wrought by nature and those that human beings would be capable of effecting later.

### The First Farmers

The conclusion of the last period of glaciation, around 10,000 years ago, ushered in a particularly critical time in the human settlement of the continent. At this time the climate was improving. The ice sheets were in full retreat, and sea levels around the world were rising. Forest vegetation and fauna were spreading northward and to higher elevations. Southeast of Europe, in the Fertile Crescent, the arc of uplands rimming the Mesopotamian Plain, human populations were in the process of domesticating plants and animals, a process we referred to in Chapter 1 as the "Environmental Transformation." This momentous event fundamentally altered human history because it marked the beginning of agriculture and sedentary populations. The great increase in the food supply enabled human beings to turn their attention to matters not directly related to sustaining daily life and resulted in the rise of civilization. On the darker side, the greater densities at which people now lived meant that infectious diseases became the prime killers in human populations.

Climatic improvement in Europe was accompanied, however, by the advent of much drier conditions in the Middle East. This induced many of these agricultural populations to leave their homes in search of more hospitable climes. This is the backdrop against which the scattered Paleolithic and Mesolithic hunting, fishing, and gathering economies that had clung precariously to the southern margins of the ice sheet in Europe were gradually replaced over thousands of years by new peoples and material cultures. We call the cultures of these new sedentary farmers and herders Neolithic.

The waves of Neolithic peoples who migrated into Europe from southwestern Asia during this period followed several routeways. Some worked their way across the North European Plain to the valleys of the Oder, the Elbe, the Rhine and beyond, or were deflected northward into Scandinavia. Others entered the Balkans, reaching the Central Danubian Basin via the Maritsa Valley or the Morava–Vardar Corridor, and followed the Danube upstream to settle first in the Hercynian Uplands and later on the plains of central Europe, from which they spread in all directions. Still others moved

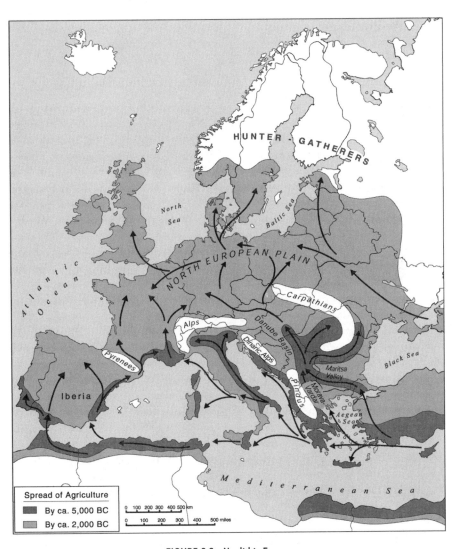

FIGURE 3.2. Neolithic Europe.

westward by sea, making their way along the Mediterranean shores of Greece, Italy, and the Iberian Peninsula, and then by way of the Rhône–Saône Corridor and the Gap of Carcassonne into northern France and Britain.

In this way, the frontiers of Neolithic settlement moved northward and westward to touch nearly all of Europe. The then abundant Mediterranean evergreen forest began to give way in favored places along the coast to the cultivation of grain crops and to open land for grazing. North of the Alps, suitable sites for agricultural settlement were found here and there on the lighter and well-drained soils of river terraces, limestone and chalk formations, and on the great loess deposits that stretch across the foothill margins of the Hercynian Uplands.

## Europeans Learn Metalworking

The Bronze Age, like most of the other innovations thus far, began in the Middle East and spread gradually from there to northwest Europe beginning some 4,000 years ago. Now people began to work deposits of tin and copper, which could be combined to produce bronze, a much more durable and more easily shaped substance than stone. In the process they came to occupy new sites, particularly in the Hercynian Uplands of Germany, Bohemia, Iberia, Brittany, and Cornwall, where deposits of these minerals were found. Silver and gold were mined in Transylvania, Iberia, and the Greek islands, while the Baltic coast became the source of amber, a hard fossilized resin of coniferous trees that has long been prized for its beauty and used to make ornamental jewelry. Here and there the wood fuel requirements of mining and smelting operations began to devour sizable tracts of forest. The introduction during the Bronze Age of a light plow that could be drawn by oxen furthered the expansion of agriculture, as would the new metalworking techniques and greater organizational skills of the Iron Age that followed.

During the Iron Age, which dawned in southeastern Europe about 800 B.C., the pace of civilization quickened. Pig iron was soft

and malleable but tough and slow to rust. It could, however, also be worked into steel to produce the finest of weapons and tools. Combinations of iron, leather, and wood were used to fashion the basic tools with which humans of the time, and long thereafter, worked the land, constructed homes, and fashioned clothing. The iron sources were different than those we know today. Iron ore was found in bogs scattered across the glaciated areas of northern Europe or in some of the mountainous areas of the Mediterranean South, and was worked by small groups of men with hand hammers and small furnaces. Lead, which also abounded in many areas, became important as a bonding layer in masonry and for roofing (lead [Latin *plumbum*] was later used by the Romans for plumbing).

## Europe's Earliest Civilization

Because of their proximity to the Middle East, it was the Greeks who benefited first from the many innovations that had led to the rise of Middle Eastern civilizations. The Minoan civilization of Crete was the first to arise in the territory we have called Europe, about 2500 B.C. This was followed some 600 years later by the Mycenaean civilization of the Peloponnese. Both of these were eclipsed, but after a Dark Age of some 300–400 years the classical Greek civilization began to take shape around 800 B.C. By 400 B.C., when this civilization was at its height, the population of Europe as we have defined it probably numbered no more than 20 million, only 3% of its current size. More than two-thirds of the people lived in the lands adjoining the Mediterranean Sea and were part of a much larger population core that extended to North Africa and the Middle East. This concentration was one of the three great centers of population that had by that time developed on the earth, the others being in South Asia and China. Together, these three realms contained more than three-quarters of the world's total population, considerably more than they do today. North of the Alpine mountain system Europe was only sparsely settled by peoples yet to be brought into the fold of civilization.

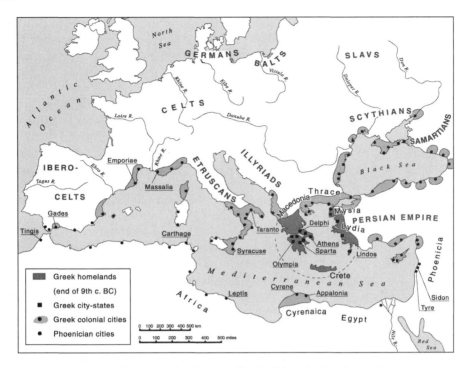

FIGURE 3.3. Classical Greek civilization: The Greek homelands and colonial areas.

Within the European part of the ancient western world Greece was certainly the most densely populated region. With perhaps as many as a quarter of a million people, Athens may have rivaled Babylon in Persia as the largest city on earth. The pressure that the growing Greek population had placed on the limited agricultural land that the peninsula has to offer prompted from the early seventh century onward a massive colonization of the Aegean and the western Mediterranean by peoples from a variety of Greek city-states. On the island of Sicily, Syracuse (originally a colony of Corinth) was among the 10 largest cities in the world. The Greek colonists added to growing indigenous populations in other parts of Mediterranean Europe, notably the Etruscans and the Romans in the Italian peninsula, but also populations near the Rhône delta (Massilia, modern Marseilles) and in Iberia.

Athenian hegemony in the Greek world was brought to an end by the long, exhausting Peloponnesian War in which Sparta and her allies emerged victorious over the Athenian Empire. Sparta, in turn, would suffer defeat in the following century, and power in the Balkans passed to Macedonia in the north. The Balkans, however, would never again be the population focus of Europe. Between 400 B.C. and 200 A.D. the population of Greece fell from 3 to 2 million while that of Italy rose from 4 to 7 million. By 600 A.D. there were fewer than a million people in Greece, and the region would not have 3 million again until the middle of the 19th century.

## The Rise of Rome

The westward shift in the center of gravity of the European population was, of course, the result of the rise of the Roman Republic (founded in 501 B.C.) and its subsequent establishment of a vast empire, which drew together the peoples of the entire Mediterranean basin. For the first time the ancient Western world had something approaching political unity. By 200 A.D Europe's population had reached 36 million. The Roman Empire as a whole had about 46 million people,

28 million of whom lived in Europe. Although the Empire was already beginning to show signs of decline, Rome, with more than half a million people, was still the largest city in the world, and Alexandria in Egypt, the "capital" of the eastern part of the Empire, was a close second or third. On the other side of the Eurasian landmass the Han Chinese had built another empire embracing more than 60 million people. These two great population cores, together with the one in South Asia, still contained about three-fourths of the world's population.

Within the frontiers of the Roman Empire could be found an elaborate network of cities and central places, linked together by carefully engineered all-weather roads and supported to varying degrees by well-ensconced agricultural populations capable of producing surplus foodstuffs. In some places the Romans introduced a considerable degree of engineering, reworking the landscape into ter-

races and providing much-needed moisture through irrigation. By this time, the ancient and venerable triad of wheat, wine, and the olive, in tenuous coexistence with the transhumant husbandry of sheep and goats, had become the mainstay of life in Mediterranean regions. Cereals made up the bulk of the diet, and wheat was the most widely cultivated grain. Grains were grown in a two-field system, in which their cultivation was alternated with a period of fallow and fields were worked with a light plow. Wine was widely produced and consumed. Olive oil, which was the chief cooking oil and shortening used in the preparation of food, was a necessity of life.

The quickening pace and extent of human agricultural, mining, and grazing activities had begun to have a noticeable disturbing effect on the Mediterranean environments of coastal lowland and upland areas. The Romans aggressively stripped the slopes of forest to meet the demand for fuel and build-

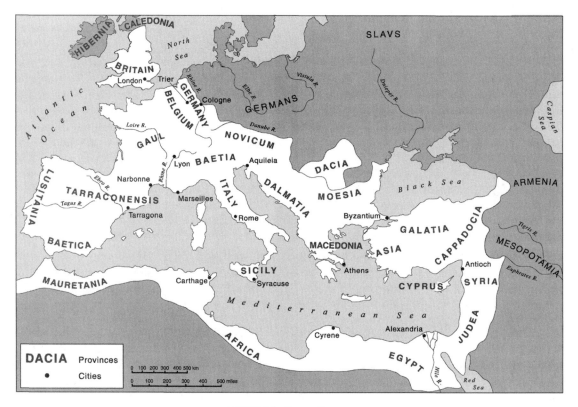

FIGURE 3.4. Roman Europe.

**FIGURE 3.5. The Pontine marshes.** These low-lying lands along the Tiber River were densely populated in early Roman times but were later abandoned when they became infested with malarial mosquitoes. Despite several attempts by Roman emperors and popes to restore the region's productivity and population, the unhealthful marshlands remained uninhabited until modern reclamation projects were initiated under Mussolini during the 1930s.

ing materials and burned away any heavy vegetation to create pasturage for the wandering flocks of goats and sheep. The denudation of the hillsides led to considerable erosion and the accelerated formation along the coasts of silt-laden deltas, which in turn became infested with malarial mosquitoes.

## The Decline of the Mediterranean World

Although by 200 A.D. most Europeans still lived in the Mediterranean Basin, the Romans had conquered considerable territory in western Europe (in Gaul, the Rhineland, and Britain), and the population of these peripheral regions had grown substantially. Containing just over a tenth of Europe's population in 400 B.C., Europe north of the Alps now accounted for nearly an eighth. The years between 200 and 600 saw the decline and fall of the Roman Empire in the west, and the population in all of the Mediterranean lands dropped dramatically. A sharply reduced labor supply meant that much cultivated land could no longer be tended and had to be abandoned. The result was a deterioration of the humanized landscape, as Roman terraces, irrigation systems, and soil conservation practices were neglected.

Sometime around 800 southern Europe lost its population leadership permanently to the lands north of the Alps and the Pyrenees. Both the barbarian invasions of the Empire and a series of deadly epidemics, which ravaged the region from the mid-sixth to the

mid-eighth centuries, took a great toll. Europe's total population had now dropped to 29 million, and it was no longer in any sense the center of the world's western population core. The rapid spread of Islam from its Arabian hearth in the seventh and eighth centuries had produced a brilliant new Islamic civilization stretching from Spain to the gates of India. The seat of the Caliph at Baghdad had nearly three-quarters of a million people and probably was the second-largest city in the world after Changan (Xi'an) in China. By contrast Rome had shrunk to just a tenth of its size at the height of the Empire. In Europe Muslim culture was centered in Spain, where an intensive garden horticulture based on sophisticated irrigation systems and exotic subtropical crops such as sugar cane, rice, and citrus fruits was introduced.

## The Rise of Europe North of the Alps

Between 800 and 1300 demographic recovery was general across Europe, and its portion of the world's population rose from 11% to almost 18%. Between 1100 and 1300 the average annual rate of net increase was nearly 0.3%, a pace never even approached before in the whole of human history. One reason for this burgeoning population was the tremendous amount of arable land added through the assault on the woodlands. The period is known as the "Great Age of Clearing" and, together with the use of the horse, the heavy-wheeled moldboard plow, and the new three-

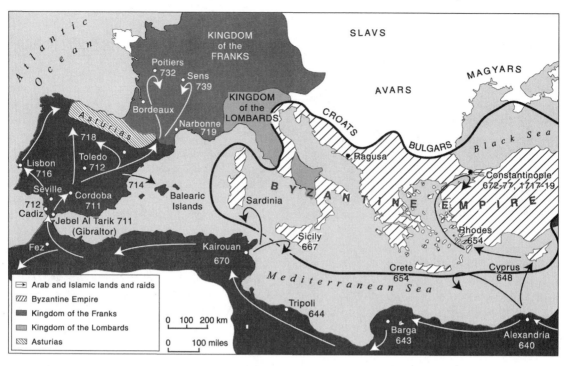

FIGURE 3.6. The spread of Islam in the seventh and eighth centuries.

field system, which allowed two-thirds of the arable land to be planted to crops each year rather than the traditional one-half, food production was enormously increased. Population spread to heavier clayey soils heretofore deemed unworkable and allowed an unprecedented growth of urban life north of the Alps, especially in western Europe. By 1300 Paris had replaced Constantinople as the largest city in Europe.

Farther to the east, and roughly during the same period, German settlers carried forward a second great colonization effort. This movement began in earnest during the 1100s, as Germans extended their political control over areas that were then only sparsely settled by Slavic populations. Earlier efforts at eastern colonization in the 900s had taken German settlement down the Danube valley as far as the Vienna basin, but now the advance of German settlement was directed due east, first across the Elbe-Saale Rivers and then across the Oder. Later it was extended northeastward into the Baltic region. The colonization effort was exceptional for its high level of or-

ganization and planning. The German nobility and clergy, who had acquired rights to vast new lands in the east, moved with great energy to recruit large numbers of land-hungry peasants for the purpose of establishing agricultural villages on their lands. The movement reached its peak in the early 1200s and resulted in the clearing of a broad expanse of territory stretching from the Oder to the Gulf of Finland.

By 1300 there were few lands left to be occupied, and the European population had grown to 80 million, more than twice its size 300 years earlier. Yet, the optimism with which the Europeans of the 12th and 13th centuries must have viewed their world of expanding opportunities came crashing down in the disasters of the 14th century. In the early years a worsening climate brought colder and wetter conditions with attendant widespread crop failures, famine, and disease. But the *sine qua non* of human catastrophes struck in 1347 with a massive onslaught of plague, an event we know today as the Black Death. The initial horror was followed by more outbreaks.

Fields and villages were abandoned in many parts of Europe. Forest and scrub advanced to reconquer parts of what had been once been field, pasture, and fallow. The decline reached its low point somewhere around the middle of the 15th century, and recovery was slow. By 1500 Europe's population stood scarcely higher than it had 200 years earlier. The region had just 16% of the world's population, about the same portion it had had at the pinnacle of Greek civilization.

The gradual population recovery that began at the end of the 15th century continued fitfully for several centuries. By 1780 Europe's population reached 160 million, roughly twice what it had been at the end of the Middle Ages. While this represents a substantial gain overall, much of the increase had, in fact, been confined to two periods: the early 16th century and the middle to later parts of the 18th century. The intervening decades, stretching from the mid-16th to the beginning of the 17th centuries, were a difficult time characterized by substantial fluctuations in population. In some parts of Europe—especially in the western Mediterranean, as well as in France and Germany—serious contractions in the size of the population actually took place.

The generally slow growth and frequent contractions of these centuries underline the very difficult conditions under which the bulk of the European population continued to live. The founding of new worlds and the intellectual and cultural transformations brought to Europe at this time by the Renaissance and Reformation had done little to protect the population form the all too familiar ravages of famine, disease, and warfare. Disastrous crop failures and famines continued to be common throughout Europe to the end of the 18th century and in some areas persisted well into the 19th. There were numerous outbreaks of plague, particularly in cities, during the late 16th and early 17th centuries. The Great Plague of London in 1665 is said to have

TABLE 3.1. The Population of Europe and Its Regions, 400 B.C.–1750 A.D.

| | Population (in millions) | | | | | | |
|---|---|---|---|---|---|---|---|
| | 400 B.C. | 1 A.D. | 600 | 1000 | 1300 | 1500 | 1750 |
| Northern Europe | 0.3 | 0.6 | 0.8 | 1.1 | 2.0 | 2.3 | 3.7 |
| Britain and Ireland | 0.4 | 0.8 | 0.9 | 2.0 | 5.0 | 5.0 | 10.0 |
| Western Europe | 2.8 | 5.5 | 5.0 | 7.2 | 18.0 | 17.1 | 28.2 |
| West-Central Europe | 1.3 | 3.8 | 3.7 | 4.5 | 11.8 | 11.8 | 17.0 |
| East-Central Europe | 1.2 | 2.6 | 1.9 | 3.6 | 8.6 | 9.1 | 15.6 |
| Eastern Europe | 1.4 | 1.9 | 2.8 | 3.7 | 8.4 | 11.2 | 24.3 |
| Balkans | 4.8 | 5.1 | 3.0 | 4.2 | 5.8 | 5.9 | 10.4 |
| Western Mediterranean | 7.5 | 12.0 | 7.5 | 9.5 | 18.8 | 17.8 | 27.0 |
| Europe | 19.7 | 32.2 | 25.6 | 35.8 | 78.3 | 80.1 | 136.2 |

| | % of total population | | | | | | |
|---|---|---|---|---|---|---|---|
| | 400 B.C. | 1 A.D. | 600 | 1000 | 1300 | 1500 | 1750 |
| Northern Europe | 1.7% | 1.7% | 3.1% | 3.1% | 2.5% | 2.9% | 2.7% |
| Britain and Ireland | 2.0% | 2.5% | 3.5% | 5.6% | 6.4% | 6.2% | 7.3% |
| Western Europe | 14.5% | 17.1% | 19.5% | 20.1% | 23.1% | 21.4% | 20.7% |
| West-Central Europe | 6.6% | 11.8% | 14.5% | 12.6% | 15.1% | 14.7% | 12.5% |
| East-Central Europe | 5.9% | 8.1% | 7.4% | 10.1% | 11.0% | 11.4% | 11.5% |
| Eastern Europe | 7.3% | 5.8% | 10.9% | 10.4% | 10.7% | 13.9% | 17.8% |
| Balkans | 24.4% | 15.8% | 11.6% | 11.6% | 7.4% | 7.4% | 7.6% |
| Western Mediterranean | 38.1% | 37.3% | 29.3% | 26.5% | 24.0% | 22.2% | 19.8% |
| Europe | 100.0% | 100.0% | 100.0% | 100.0% | 100.0% | 100.0% | 100.0% |

*Note.* Data from McEvedy and Jones (1978).

killed as many as 100,000 residents in just 18 months. The peak of the epidemic occurred in September when 12,000 died in a single week. Outbreaks of smallpox and typhus also took a dreadful toll. The period is also known for the terrible deprivations caused by warring armies, who laid waste to the land and spread disease wherever they went. Population losses in Germany during the rapacious Thirty Years War (1618–1648) are thought to have reduced the population of many areas by more than half.

## DYNAMICS OF POPULATION GROWTH TO THE END OF THE 18TH CENTURY

### Life Expectancy

Rates of natural increase in Europe during the Middle Ages were very low, rarely exceeding 0.3% per year over any protracted period of time. These rates compare with those currently obtaining in France, Switzerland, and the Low Countries, but occurred in the absence of the family-size limitations employed by these modern populations. What dampened population growth was, of course, the extraordinarily high rates of mortality. From the time human beings developed agriculture, a sedentary lifestyle, and the habit of living together in close quarters, the great majority of people have died of infectious diseases. It was little over a century ago that humankind learned what caused these diseases and only within the past 70 years have we been able to cure some of them.

The bacteria, viruses, or other microorganisms that caused infectious disease in this period could be endemic in a population and kill a few people in any year, but often they became epidemic and wiped out large numbers of people in what are called "crisis years." These epidemics might result from the weakened resistance of the human host, caused by crop failure and malnutrition, or, in the case of viral diseases, they could simply break out when the number of new members of the community who lacked immunity given by the last outbreak reached a critical mass. Epidemics might also occur when diseases not endemic in the population, and to which no one was immune, were introduced from outside. War and invasion was one mechanism producing such outbreaks, but they could also be triggered by peaceful trade. Background mortality, the deaths occurring from infectious and noninfectious (degenerative) diseases every year probably caused fewer deaths overall than the diseases that struck during crisis years.

Before late medieval and early modern times, when church burial registers provide us with some data, our estimates of life expectancy are based on the examination of skeletal remains found in cemeteries, a discipline known as human osteo-archeology. Evidence from ancient Greece suggests that life expectancy at birth was not much more than 20–25 years, indicating a crude death rate of 40–50 per thousand. This figure is heavily influenced by extremely high infant and child mortality, of course, but even for those who survived childhood, males could not expect to live on average beyond 45 and females not much past 36. In classical Rome it has been estimated that half the population reached 20, a third 40 and a sixth 60. Skeletal remains in Sweden and documentary evidence in Britain suggests that the life expectancy at birth of the poor in the Middle Ages was not much more than 20 and that of the aristocracy a scant 7 or 8 years longer. This means that someone reaching the age of 20 could look forward on average to only 25–30 years more.

An interesting finding of virtually all osteo-archeological studies in the world is that women died significantly earlier than men in premodern societies, an observation that is at stark variance with what we know of modern populations, especially those in developed countries, where females normally live longer than males. Crucial to this discrepancy would seem to be the very young age at marriage (13–14) of women in classical and medieval times and the corresponding early onset of childbearing. Their incomplete anatomical and physiological development exposed them to unusual dangers throughout the course of pregnancy, which, if they didn't cause death initially, put them at greater risk during subsequent confinements. It has also been pointed out that women were more exposed than men to infectious disease because they were the nurses. Finally, since pregnancy works to suppress the immune system in an effort to prevent abortions (fetuses differ genetically from their mothers), early and frequent conceptions worked to place young females at even greater risk.

## Mortality and Disease

What, then, were the diseases that afflicted Europeans in classical and medieval times? The pathogens involved in the epidemics of the past are many and often cannot be specified. The Old Testament, as well as many Greek and Roman writings, tell of "plagues" and "pestilences" that ravaged the people of antiquity. These terms are, of course, not used with much precision, and we cannot easily discern the disease or diseases involved. Some have been argued to be true plague, the disease caused by the bacterium *Pasteurella pestis*, which caused the Black Death of the 14th century, but other infections may well have been involved.

The first really well-documented plague is the one that struck Athens in 430 B.C., the second year of the Peloponnesian War, and raged on and off for 3 years. The source of our knowledge of this epidemic is Thucydides' history of this war. He tells us that the sickness arose in Ethiopia, spread down the Nile into Egypt, and entered Athens through its port of Piraeus. He is careful to describe the symptoms of the disease in some detail so that it might be recognized if it ever appeared again. We must infer from this that it was a relatively new sickness among the Greeks. Implicit in Thucydides' description is an understanding of the disease's infectious nature and of the immunity conferred on those victims who were fortunate enough to recover their health. As is the case with most plagues of the distant past, no agreement has been reached as to the specific disease or diseases

involved. Cogent arguments have been made for both measles and typhus, but typhoid fever, smallpox, and plague have also been suggested. Whatever the culprit, the Plague of Thucydides dealt a grievous blow to the Athenian war effort, killing a quarter of the land army and probably contributing substantially to Athens's ultimate defeat.

Two severe plagues struck the Roman Empire in 165–180 A.D. (the Antonine Plague) and again in 251–266. It has been suggested that these might have been epidemics of measles or smallpox and may represent the establishment of these diseases as endemic to the European population for the first time. We know, for example, that measles requires a population of half a million to keep it going. If the great plague of Athens had involved measles, the population would have been too small to accommodate it, and it would have died out when potential hosts were no longer available. On its return during Roman times it would initially have had a devastating effect but would then have become endemic, attacking at intervals those lacking immunity and becoming the childhood disease so familiar to us until quite recently. Smallpox would have made a similar transition. These two epidemics began the sustained decay of population in the Mediterranean Basin, which we noted earlier. It has even been suggested that the onset of these diseases and probably others may have hastened the acceptance in the Empire of Christianity, a religion whose other-worldly orientation was well positioned to provide comfort to people in a demographic crisis.

The greatest blow to befall the late classical world, however, came in the form of the Plague of Justinian, which raged in 542 and 543. This was almost surely true plague, primarily in its bubonic form. By this time *Pasteurella pestis* appears to have been endemic among burrowing rodents in two parts of the world: east-central Africa and the Himalayan foothills of northeast India, Burma, and Yunnan province in China. The disease was known to break out intermittently in the port cities of the Indian Ocean and was almost certainly carried by the black rat (*Rattus rattus*) and its flea (*Xenopsylla cheopsis*). Since the rat traveled by ship, and there was no water connection between the Indian Ocean and the Mediterranean, the peoples of the latter area had apparently never experienced the disease before. When by chance the black rat did reach the Mediterranean, it carried the plague with it and the results were devastating. Over the next 200 years recurring epidemics of plague, together with outbreaks of other diseases, led to major declines in the region's population.

## The Black Death

As noted earlier, while stagnation characterized the demographics of southern Europe, population numbers north of the Alps surged upward. Certainly there were epidemics, but none of truly great magnitude until the 14th century. The plagues of the Mediterranean had not reached northern Europe, probably because the black rat had not yet established itself there. This situation changed in 1347 when *Pasteurella pestis*, spread across the

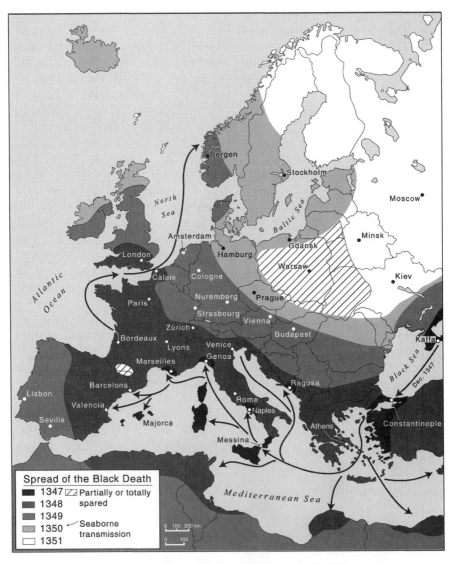

**FIGURE 3.7.** The spread of the Black Death, 1347–1351.

Eurasian steppes from the east by Mongol armies, reached the Black Sea port of Kaffa. From there it was carried to Italy on Genoese ships, unleashing a pandemic that engulfed nearly all of Europe and did not subside until 1351. Rates of mortality are difficult to determine, but probably a third of Europe's population died during the 4 years that plague stalked the land. The havoc it wrought was uneven, however. Italy as a whole was hard-hit, yet the Milanese were spared almost completely. Norway lost half its population, while the people of Bohemia and Poland were hardly touched. As with the Plague of Justinian, epidemics of a more local kind continued to strike for the next few centuries. Plague was probably responsible for the stagnation of the Spanish population in the 17th century and must have contributed to the loss of Spain's great-power status. The last outbreak in western Europe occurred in Marseille in 1720, although the disease remained endemic to eastern Europe and the Middle East.

In spite of the fact that medical practitioners in the Middle Ages lacked any scientific knowledge, some suspected that plague could be transmitted through close contact and recommended isolation of the sick. In the late 14th century, the Republic of Venice, in constant contact with the east, where plague was more common, began to isolate ships and their crews on arrival. At first the isolation lasted 30 days, but when this seemed inadequate it was extended to 40 days, the time both Moses and Christ had spent alone in the desert. In Italian this period was called "the forty," the *quarantina*, a term that has entered the English language to mean the separation of the sick from the healthy.

Plague, at least in its bubonic form, is, as we have seen, an insect-borne disease. Other diseases important in early European history have been transmitted via infected food and water and via droplets in the air expelled through coughing and sneezing. Among the water- and food-borne diseases, dysentery and typhoid fever, both produced by a form of *Salmonella*, have been the most widespread, although cholera, the scourge of the 19th century, has probably received more attention.

The most important airborne diseases, besides measles and smallpox and pneumonic plague, were tuberculosis and influenza. The incidence of tuberculosis appears to have risen sharply after the Black Death, coinciding with an equally abrupt decline in leprosy. This affliction of the skin, extremely widespread in the high Middle Ages, causes the same immune antibodies as one form of pulmonary tuberculosis. It may be that the latter, which is far more virulent than leprosy, simply outcompeted the skin disease and emptied the leper hospitals of Europe. Influenza may also have been present in the European population as early as the 12th century, but the presence of plague makes its certain identification difficult until the 18th century.

## Fertility

From the beginning of the Neolithic to the end of the Middle Ages Europeans experienced high mortality, primarily caused by infectious diseases, and compensated for this by early marriage and high fertility. The result was still only a very slow growth of population. High levels of fertility, however, may have been more a feature of the Middle Ages than it was of Classical times. There is some evidence that the Greeks were interested in limiting family size. The fact that brides were often in their early teens worked against this, but Aristotle, for example, recommended abortion to achieve this goal. A later age at marriage for females would have been a solution, but it would also have threatened male dominance, since men were 10–15 years older than their brides. Exposure of unwanted infants occurred, but it was not the rule. The Greek ideal was to have one son to maintain the family name and one daughter to cement a suitable marriage alliance with another family, and in many instances this ideal was achieved.

In Rome, too, couples seem to have been able to limit the number of children they produced. While they probably had on average at least 15 years of married life, they rarely seem to have had more than two or three children. How did they achieve this? As in Greece abortion was common if the husband concurred. The Romans shared the Greek view that the fetus had no independent existence until birth, so that an unapproved abortion by the wife was considered a crime against the husband, not against the fetus. As in Greece, a small percentage of infants were killed, probably more girls than boys, but a major difference between the two civilizations was that, in Rome from the first century A.D. sex in marriage was touted as a means of procreation alone. Sexual pleasures came to be regarded as dangerous to the health, and the idea of excess became anathema to the Romans.

The early fathers of the Christian Church continued this hostile attitude toward sensuality and at first viewed any sexual intercourse, even within marriage, with some distaste. Gradually, however, the Church came to take the view that marriage was justifiable, but as a vehicle for procreation alone. Thus, any attempts to thwart conception or to abort the fetus were regarded as grave sins. This stance, if accepted by the majority of the population in the Christian Middle Ages, would appear to open the door to increased fertility. Such a development seems even more likely if we believe, as the Greeks and Romans did, that contraception was almost unknown among northern Europeans.

This lack of contraception and resultant high fertility among Europeans during the Middle Ages may have also had its roots in northern European mortality patterns. We have already noted the very low life expectancy in the Middle Ages. Their high mortality simply did not give northern Europeans the luxury of attempting to limit their progeny. It has been calculated that in a population where life expectancy at birth is 20 years each woman must give birth to 6.8 live infants during her lifetime into order to assure that 2.1 reach maturity. That number is required if each mother is to be replaced by another in the next generation and the population is not to decline. In actuality, of course, some women would have to bear more than this number to compensate for those not living through their fecund period. It seems likely that the average medieval European woman married quite early and gave birth to her first

child by age 17. Assuming, then, a birth interval of 29 months, a woman could have achieved eight births by age 34, at which time she would have another 2 years or so to live.

## The Early Modern Demographic System

During the 16th and 17th centuries the medieval demographic system underwent a significant change in Europe. Death rates everywhere dropped from very high to moderately high levels, and in western Europe fertility also declined. These changes define the early modern demographic system. The fall in mortality resulted from the fact that, as populations grew in size, they reached the thresholds needed for many viral diseases (e.g., smallpox and measles) to become endemic, that is, continuously present, in the population. In the case of many viral diseases, victims who recover are normally given lifetime immunity to the disease. Therefore endemic viral diseases become epidemic only when the number of children born since the last outbreak reaches a critical mass. These ailments are thus transformed into regularly recurring childhood diseases to which adults are not susceptible. The conversion of many deadly afflictions into diseases of childhood, of course, had a direct effect on lowering the death rate. But it also had an indirect one in that, because adults were not sick so often, food production and other vital tasks were not so frequently interrupted. The widespread sickness of adults in epidemics disrupts community functions to such an extent that the crisis is greatly exacerbated.

Declining death rates meant that the population could survive even if birth rates declined. This is just what happened in western Europe. The earliest vital statistics we have for national populations are for the countries of northern Europe. During the 1750s the birthrate in Sweden varied between 33 and 39 per thousand and in Norway between 31 and 36. Death rates were not much lower, so that natural increase was slow. East of a line drawn roughly from the Adriatic Sea to the Gulf of Bothnia, however, the situation was very different. In Finland birthrates in the

1750s were in the middle 40s, while in Russia, even as late as the end of the 19th century, they ranged between 46 and 53 per thousand. Thus, while the Russian population tripled between 1500 and 1800, that of most western European countries only doubled.

The lower levels of fertility observed in western Europe in the 18th century are associated with a nuptial behavior that appears to be unique to that region. This "European marriage pattern" involved a relatively high age at first marriage for both women (mid- to late 20s) and men (late 20s to early 30s) and the failure of many people to marry at all. It is important to note that there was at this time no deliberate attempt to limit family size. Rather, people continued to practice natural fertility. The drop in the birthrate was due solely to the fact that the proportion of their reproductive years during which women were at risk to become pregnant was greatly reduced.

This unusual marriage pattern appears to be related to the development of a family structure in western Europe that differed sharply from that in almost all other societies. Virtually alone among the societies of the world, western Europeans placed the burden of agricultural production on the nuclear family. A husband and his wife, together with their children, worked the land for their sustenance. The family might contain retired parents (called a stem family), and the household might include hired help, but fundamentally the married couple was responsible for the tending of animals and the growing of crops. This contrasts sharply with the situation in eastern Europe and much of the rest of the world where a larger unit, comprising a number of related married couples (the joint family), worked the land, decisions usually being made by the eldest male, or patriarch.

The vital difference between these two models where family formation is concerned is that, in the case of the joint family, work was always available for a young man on the family land, and he could begin his nuptial life while quite young. In western Europe, on the other hand, in order to marry and start a family a young man had to have *personal* access to land. Where land was scarce, as it was in western Europe after 1500, this meant that he had to buy land himself (which took more capital than he was likely to have) or he had to wait to inherit land from his father. In areas where impartible inheritance was practiced, sons other than the heir often could never marry but lived out their lives as bachelors, either remaining on their brother's farm or taking employment elsewhere.

The reason why this unusual situation arose nowhere but in western Europe has been the subject of much speculation. One view is that the Catholic Church in the Middle Ages undertook to sever the lateral bonds among siblings. The value of this from the Church's point of view was that wealth would not be spread throughout the extended family but rather would be concentrated within the nuclear family and thus be more easily available to the Church through death bequests. Although the spatial correlation between the occurrence of the nuclear family as the primary economic unit and the realm of Roman Catholicism is not perfect, there is a general correspondence.

By the middle of the 18th century life was still dominated by the specter of infectious disease. Death governed the growth of populations and was a familiar event in everyone's lives. No one could readily anticipate the changes that the 19th century would bring, first in the dramatic lowering of mortality, then in the equally stunning decline in fertility. The people of Europe were about to lead the world into a new demographic era.

## THE DEMOGRAPHIC TRANSITION

In 1780 Europe's population stood at 160 million, just twice what it had been at the beginning of the 14th century. During the next 160 years it more than tripled, to reach 515 million on the eve of World War II. The significant changes that occurred in the demographic behavior of most European populations during a period of less than 150 years is what we know as the Demographic Transition. The drop in mortality is called the

Epidemiologic Transition, while the fall in fertility is referred to as the Fertility Transition. These events spread from Europe to the European populations overseas and then to the other culture realms of the world. It was in western Europe that it was first experienced, however, and it is here that it has been most thoroughly studied.

The Demographic Transition in Europe fell broadly into two phases. In the first phase mortality began to decline, but fertility did not. In this Early Expanding Phase, as the fall in mortality continued, population grew at an ever accelerating rate. The second phase began with the first drop in fertility. Mortality also continued to decline, but not so rapidly as fertility. In this Late Expanding Phase, therefore, population increased at a decelerating rate. Both before and after the transition populations experienced slow growth, but the human condition of these populations was vastly different. Before the transition, when mortality controlled growth, annual change was uneven, substantial losses in a few years being made up by smaller gains in quite a number of others. Life expectancy at birth was low, and most deaths occurred among infants and young children. After the transition, with population growth controlled by fertility, annual increases are relatively even, but changes in fertility may result in baby booms and busts over longer periods of time. Life expectancy at birth is high, and most deaths occur among the elderly.

## The Epidemiologic Transition

The early lowering of the death rate was very clearly the result of a considerable reduction in crisis mortality, that is, in deaths from infectious diseases that occurred during epidemics (hence the term for the transition). The explanation for such a reduction may be sought in three areas: (1) spontaneous declines in the virulence of major diseases, (2) advances in medical knowledge and technology, and (3) improvements in the living environment.

As for the first, while it is thought that plague may have lost some of its pathogenic vigor, perhaps as a result of quarantine, there is no evidence that any of the endemic diseases underwent significant natural alteration. As for medical technology, no advances sufficient enough to substantially reduce death from disease were made until the 1930s when chemotherapy, penicillin, and the sulfa drugs were developed. The one exception to this generalization is the development of smallpox vaccination. The practice quickly became widespread in Europe, and, where it was correctly administered and adequately enforced, it had an immediate effect on death rates from this disease. By itself, however, even this medical advance could not achieve a substantial decline in overall death rates.

It would seem that improvements in the living environment provide the only explanation for the early decline in death rates during the European Epidemiologic Transition. One such improvement was a marked increase in the food supply. Substantial advances in agriculture were achieved during the Agricultural Revolution, which began in England in the 17th century. They included new crops bred from older ones, such as the turnip and clover, which not only helped to improve soils impoverished by growing grains but also provided winter fodder for animals that otherwise would have had to be destroyed. There were also the New World crops, such as maize and the potato, that would produce bumper yields in very marginal conditions, and the tomato, which brought a rich source of vitamins to southern Europeans. All of these innovations meant that agricultural production began to increase more rapidly than population.

The building of canal systems in the 18th century, the improvement of roads, and later the introduction of the railroad provided the means to transport food over significant distances. This served to weaken the effect of local crop failures by allowing authorities to move food from surplus to deficit regions. Given the means to counter natural catastrophes in this way, governments became more interested in organizing such efforts. The end result of all these developments was to greatly reduce malnutrition, which in turn raised resistance to infectious diseases.

Another factor that seems to have been of importance during the early decline in mortality was an improvement in the environment of children. Many people believe that better nutrition produced a more optimistic attitude among parents. This was partly because the parents themselves were healthier, both in mind and body, but also because, as they realized that an increasing number of their children would grow into adulthood, they had more incentive to invest time and energy in caring for them. This is in sharp contrast to pretransition Europe, where children often suffered from benign neglect. In families where food and other resources were scarce, an additional child could be a real burden, especially if it was likely not to grow up to be of help on the farm or provide for its parents in old age. Even if they did not consciously wish for their children's deaths, many parents were at least indifferent to them because they died so frequently. Some scholars suggest that in pretransition Europe children were not regarded as full-fledged people until they reached the age of 6 or 7, when they could begin to help with chores and were less apt to contract fatal diseases.

Once initiated, the drop in death rates continued in phase 2, but for rather different reasons. The effects of the Industrial Revolution began to be felt in several ways. Mass production meant that many goods could be manufactured in large quantities and sold more cheaply than before. Even poor people, for example, could afford to buy soap for everyday use. The British middle class, it is thought, was bathing weekly by the last decades of the 19th century. The introduction of inexpensive cotton, which could be made into washable underclothes, nightclothes, and bed linens helped against body lice, fleas, and ticks, all carriers of disease. One of the great results of the Industrial Revolution was certainly a major improvement in personal hygiene, lowering the incidence of disease and the frequency of death from it.

The Industrial Revolution also had a beneficial impact on agriculture through the development of chemical fertilizers, improved pumping systems, tile drainage, and the like, allowing food production to expand even further and nutritional levels to rise still higher. Another result of industrialization was the installation in the larger cities of public utility

drainage systems, which for the first time assured the separation of human waste materials from drinking water. Cities had always been cesspools of disease, and even as late as the middle of the 19th century drinking water contaminated by human feces and urine was a major medium for the transmission of intestinal diseases such as typhoid fever and dysentery. Perhaps the major impetus behind public health measures in European cities was provided by the appearance of a deadly new disease on the scene, cholera.

Cholera is a water- and food-borne disease that has long been endemic in Bengal. From time to time it would spread to other parts of India, carried by Hindu pilgrims returning from holy places in the lower Ganges valley. In the early 19th century, however, the disease was carried well beyond South Asia, and in the 1830s it invaded Europe for the first time. During an 1854 cholera epidemic in London a doctor, John Snow, mapped the residences of those who died. His map showed a "cholera field" centered on the Broad Street pump. This was the first time a relationship had been shown between contaminated water and the spread of cholera. His discovery had little impact on public policy, however, and it wasn't until several decades later, when Pasteur and Koch discovered that germs cause infectious disease, that most European cities began to undertake improvements in water provision and sewage disposal. After this, cities, once sewers of disease, became the leaders in mortality decline.

Of all the factors involved in effecting the Epidemiologic Transition in Europe, medicine played by far the latest role. It is important to keep in mind that until the late 19th century there was no understanding of germs and their role in causing disease. It was during the last two decades of the 19th century that medical researchers learned how germs were reproduced and transmitted and which ones caused which diseases. Antiseptic surgery, anesthetics, the use of masks and scrubbing did not begin until the 1880s. Before that, major surgery was attempted only as a last resort and most often resulted in death. Even after the relationships between germs and infectious diseases were understood, it was not until the 1930s that any really effective means of killing infectious microorganisms were developed. Indeed, some people argue that until very recent times doctors and hospitals probably did more harm than good. Hospitals were certainly unhealthy, germ-ridden places, and it was not uncommon for a patient to die there of a disease quite different than the one for which he had been admitted.

From the late 18th to the mid-20th century the Epidemiological Transition brought about a startling decline in mortality among Europeans and left them with life expectancies that were among the highest in the world. This was accomplished largely by greatly improving diet, personal and public living environments and, finally, by identifying the causes of diseases and providing effective means of their prevention and cure. At the end of World War II there was great optimism among health authorities not only that vaccines and medicines were available to control the great diseases of human history but also that mankind was in a position to eradicate many of them from the face of the earth. By half a century later, as we shall see, much of this optimism had faded.

## The Fertility Transition

The beginning of fertility decline, which heralds the opening of phase 2 of the Demographic Transition, was made possible by the Epidemiologic Transition. Only when the survival rates among infants and children had greatly improved could people afford to think about limiting family size. The fall in fertility was brought about through a change from natural fertility behavior to family planning. Clearly family planning was not possible under conditions of high mortality since at no time could parents be sure that the number of children they then had would still be alive next year. Family limitation also depended on the acceptance by the community of the small-family norm. While high fertility was necessary to maintain the population, the notion had arisen, supported by social institutions such as the Church, that large families (meaning large numbers of births) were nor-

mal and desirable. Major changes in social values would have to take place if any long-term decline in fertility were to occur. In particular, a degree of secularization was needed before people became comfortable with the idea of family-size limitations. Once this happened, however, more people married and the age at first marriage dropped. The well-established European marriage pattern was abandoned.

We now have conclusive evidence that the Fertility Transition began in France, more specifically in the French-speaking areas of France. Birthrates here were already falling in the 1820s and 1830s and by 1880 had sunk below 25 per thousand for good. Meanwhile, in most of western Europe they were still above 30, in central Europe over 35, and in Russia around 50. While the transition may have begun in the towns, we find it much earlier in French rural areas than we do in the industrialized areas of England or the Ruhr Valley. In Belgium it appears much earlier in Francophone Wallonia than in the Flemish-speaking north. In Switzerland the French-speaking cantons experienced fertility declines before those in the German-speaking parts of the country. This suggests that the acceptance of the small-family norm may be less related to the level of economic development than to cultural factors. That is, once this new idea became established within a particular cultural community, it spread more readily within the community than to people outside. In this light the small-family norm is seen more as a culture trait than as a rational response to changing economic and social conditions. The diffusion of the culture trait was facilitated by similarities in language and value systems. It was accepted quickly where cultural barriers to it were low, but resisted where they were high.

## The Spread of the Demographic Transition

The Demographic Transition in Europe took a very long time to complete. The first long-term declines in mortality began in Norway in the late 18th century; the Fertility Transition in Albania has been concluded only within the past decade. Thus, the Transition spanned two centuries, its time of onset and its duration varying greatly from one country to another. This is one of the fundamental differences between the European experience of the Transition and that of the Third World, where the process has taken far less time. A major reason for this is that Europeans achieved lowered mortality and fertility on their own, while Third World countries have had the advantage of Western technology.

The spread of the Demographic Transition across Europe may be followed in Figures 3.8 and 3.9. When interpreting the maps it is im-

portant to remember several things. First, they treat the populations of modern states as whole and are meant to convey only a general impression of the progress of the Demographic Transition across Europe. Clearly the timing of the Transition varied within countries, so the maps are generalizations of a much more complex picture. Second, the rate at which mortality and fertility fell in any population was quite uneven over time. Thus, while in one decade the fertility in one population might be substantially higher than that in another, 30 or 40 years later it could well have fallen to the same level.

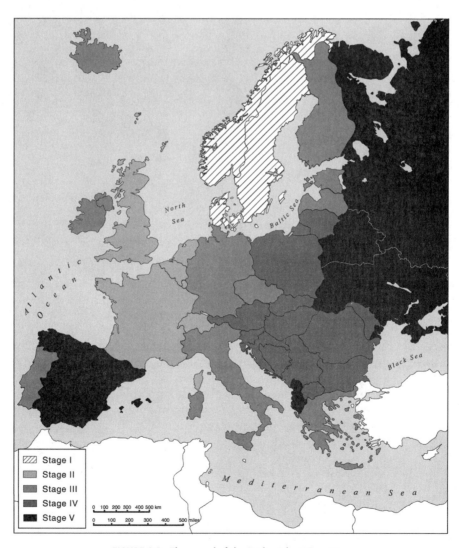

FIGURE 3.8. The spread of the Epidemiologic Transition.

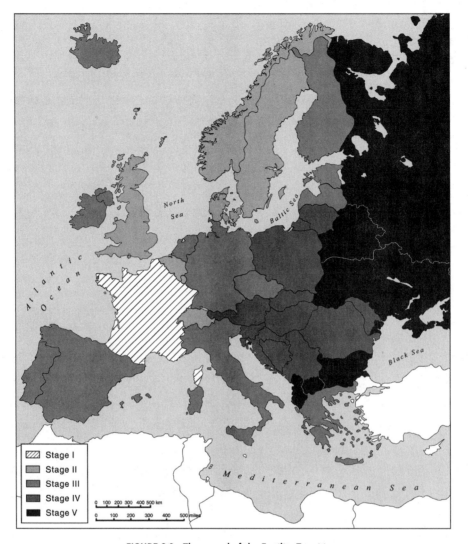

FIGURE 3.9. The spread of the Fertility Transition.

A comparison of the two maps reveals striking similarities. Both the Epidemiologic and the Fertility Transition had their origin in northwestern Europe, but in different countries. Whereas the French led the Fertility Transition, it was in Scandinavia that mortality first began to fall. The early leadership of the French in fertility decline is often explained by the secularization of society brought on by the French Revolution. Secularization can mean either a movement of the people away from religion, or at least from strict religious teachings, or a relaxation by the Church of its position on the matter of

childbearing and family formation. In postrevolutionary France both probably happened. By the 1850s the birthrate in France had dropped below 27 per thousand, while in no other country was it yet below 30. In the same decade Norway's infant mortality rate was just over 100 per thousand, two-thirds of that in Great Britain and well under half the rate in Germany and Russia. From these two cores the Fertility and Epidemiologic Transitions spread in much the same fashion: first to the rest of western Europe, then into central and southern Europe and finally to eastern Europe and the Balkans.

**TABLE 3.2. Birthrates and Death Rates
in Selected European Countries, 1901–1910**

|  | Death rates per thousand | Birthrates per thousand |
|---|---|---|
| Norway | 14.2 | 27.5 |
| England and Wales | 15.4 | 27.2 |
| Ireland | 17.4 | 23.3 |
| France | 19.4 | 20.5 |
| Germany | 18.7 | 33.0 |
| Spain | 25.1 | 34.3 |
| Romania | 25.8 | 39.9 |
| Russia | 30.3 | 46.8 |

*Note.* Data from Rothenbacher (2002).

The major anomaly in all of this would seem to be Ireland. Mortality in Ireland was still relatively high in 1847 when the potato famine struck. The large number of deaths that accompanied this catastrophe weeded out the weaker members of the population and greatly reduced death rates in subsequent years. In a sense the famine prevented the Irish from experiencing the classic Epidemiologic Transition. In the wake of the disastrous potato famine, overall fertility in Ireland remained low—not because the population was practicing family planning but because the Irish were still clinging to the old European marriage pattern involving late marriage and high rates of celibacy. Marital fertility was actually quite high in Ireland, but marriages were of shorter duration and large numbers of both men and women did not marry at all. In the late 1960s the Irish marriage rate finally began to rise. Married couples started to limit their fertility, and the Irish population has now completed the Fertility Transition.

## The Great Atlantic Migrations

Between the end of the Napoleonic wars and the beginning of the Great Depression a massive emigration of Europeans took place. Over 54 million people left for other parts of the world, and, although some returned, the effect of the exodus was to lessen significantly the burden of the population boom that resulted from the Demographic Transition. Indeed, it is remarkable that, despite this massive outpouring of people, Europe's proportion of the world's total population rose from 20% to 24% during the course of the 19th century. It should also be noted that Europeans are unique among the peoples of the world in that they had access to sparsely settled lands as they experienced their rapid population expansion. Those populations that have passed through the Demographic Transition since then have had no such "safety valve."

Most of the emigrants made their way to the Americas, though many from Britain and Ireland found new homes in Australia, New Zealand, and other parts of the British Empire. Within the New World, the United States was the principal destination, taking in nearly 35 million European immigrants during this period. Many others went to Canada, however, and millions of people who left Spain and Portugal, and to some extent Italy, settled in Argentina, Uruguay, Brazil, and Cuba.

In seeking explanations for population migrations it is common to distinguish between push factors and pull factors. The former are things that people perceive to be negative about their present place of residence and cause them to consider alternative locations. The latter are features of other places that are perceived to be positive and act as attractions, reinforcing any push factors that might exist. Besides these, there are facilitating factors, things that make moving easier, physically, economically, or psychologically. All three of these migration stimuli must be considered if one is to gain an understanding of how this massive movement of human beings came about.

During the course of the 19th and early 20th centuries many things happened in Europe to induce people to think about leaving. There were political upheavals such as the failed liberal revolutions of 1830 and 1848, and many who advanced the cause of nationalism became discouraged with the intransigence of conservative political regimes. In western Europe, nonconformist religions were appealing to evergrowing numbers of people, who encountered the staunch opposition of established state churches. Some young men wanted to leave to avoid compulsory military service. However, all these factors notwithstanding, the overwhelming reason people left was economic. In phase 1 of the Demographic Transition employment opportunities could not keep up with the growing numbers of people. The farming population, which was in the clear majority, was especially hard-hit, but during the early stages of the factory system many craftsmen were also put out of work.

The intensity of emigration in different parts of Europe and the timing of emigration across Europe varied significantly. The general pattern was a diffusion of emigrant activity from the western and northern to the southern and eastern parts of the continent. France is the major exception to this rule. The reason is not difficult to understand if one considers the very low rate at which the French population grew during the 19th century, compared to the populations of other northern and northwestern European countries. The pressures that built up in other European countries during the Demographic Transition simply did not exist in France.

Eastern Europe, as a whole, experienced a similarly light emigration, albeit slightly heavier than the French. An important facilitating factor at work here was government policy toward emigration. In the early 19th century virtually all governments were opposed to emigration. In mercantilist economic theory a country's population was one of its chief resources and was to be preserved at all cost. Gradually, as free-trade and laissez-faire policies became more widely accepted, state governments relaxed restrictions on emigration. The Russian Empire was just about the last to do so, and the people who left were not the Russians but rather the minorities— Ukrainians, Poles, Finns, and Jews.

Emigration from east-central Europe was also not especially high relative to the population size. It must be remembered that this region, together with Russia, was quite distant from the major west European ports of embarkation. Literacy was also much lower than

in the West, and, even if the propaganda material published by the American states and the railroad companies had been written in the languages of these regions, most people could not have read them. Many of the factors that facilitated emigration from western Europe simply did not operate in the East.

As far as the timing of the emigration is concerned, a general correlation with the eastward and southward progression of the Demographic Transition is evident. But it is also important to realize that a later decline of emigration in the western and northern parts of Europe is also associated with the industrialization of these countries. By the 1890s the redundant rural populations that had hitherto sought new farming opportunities in the Americas could find work in the cities of their own countries. And even if they preferred to remain farmers, by then little agricultural land was left in the New World, especially in Canada and the United States.

This period marked an enormous shift in the origin of immigrants to the United States. In place of the western Europeans, who were viewed by Americans as easily assimilated into the dominant Anglo-Saxon culture, those who now passed through Ellis Island were "strange-looking" and subscribed to faiths that many in the United States thought would undermine the Protestant ethic. They came from Italy and the eastern parts of Europe and settled in the large cities of the East and Middle West, where they often formed "ghettos" and resisted assimilation. This "New Immigration," as it was called at the time, eventually created a wave of xenophobia and ultimately led to stringent restrictions on immigration during the 1920s.

The large emigration from Spain and Portugal that occurred during the same period, as well as a considerable stream from Italy, was directed toward Latin America. As a colony of Spain until 1898 Cuba was attractive to many Spanish emigrants, while the Portuguese flocked to Brazil with its prosperous coffee plantations in the south and rubber boom in the Amazon Basin. In Argentina, British and other foreign capital built railways that opened up vast areas for agriculture and ranching. Between 1869 and 1914 the Argentine population increased from 2 million to almost 8 million.

Finally, a word needs to be said about Ireland, which fits no more comfortably into the emigration picture than it does into the Demographic Transition. No other European country was so heavily hit by emigration. The 4.6 million people who left represent 87% of the 1875 population. The Irish emigration was also the earliest in Europe; by 1867 half of all those who would leave between 1820 and 1930 were gone. Of course, the unusual pattern is again related to the potato famine that began in 1847. Many died in that tragedy, but, of those who did not, millions elected to leave the meager farming existence that had failed them and to settle in the cities of Britain, the United States, Canada, and Australia. Although they arrived in America while there was still much farmland to be had, they did not want it. They had had enough.

As noted earlier, despite the unprecedented emigration of the 19th and early 20th century, the European population rose dramatically. The distribution of the population also changed during this period. The populations of northern Europe, Britain and Ireland, and west-central Europe grew relative to other regions primarily because of the early fall in mortality. The growth in the Balkans, east-central and eastern Europe was mainly because of the persistence of high fertility. The big losers were western Europe and the western Mediterranean. The former, dominated by France, suffered from a long period of low fertility. The latter lost ground because of persistent high mortality and very heavy emigration.

By 1930, the Demographic Transition was over in western Europe and emigration was being greatly curtailed, both by the American restrictions and the onset of the worldwide economic depression. A new era was opening

TABLE 3.3. The Population of Europe and Its Regions, 1750–1950

| | Population (in millions) | | | | |
|---|---|---|---|---|---|
| | 1750 | 1800 | 1850 | 1900 | 1950 |
| Northern Europe | 3.7 | 6.2 | 9.5 | 15.0 | 21.5 |
| Britain and Ireland | 10.0 | 16.0 | 28.0 | 42.0 | 54.0 |
| Western Europe | 28.2 | 34.2 | 43.5 | 53.2 | 61.0 |
| West-Central Europe | 17.0 | 22.8 | 33.5 | 52.5 | 81.8 |
| East-Central Europe | 15.6 | 22.1 | 29.4 | 47.8 | 53.7 |
| Eastern Europe | 24.3 | 33.5 | 55.8 | 93.0 | 111.7 |
| Balkans | 10.4 | 14.4 | 19.8 | 28.1 | 47.0 |
| Western Mediterranean | 27.0 | 33.0 | 43.0 | 57.0 | 82.0 |
| Europe | 136.2 | 182.1 | 262.5 | 388.6 | 512.5 |

| | % of total population | | | | |
|---|---|---|---|---|---|
| | 1750 | 1800 | 1850 | 1900 | 1950 |
| Northern Europe | 2.7% | 3.4% | 3.6% | 3.9% | 4.2% |
| Britain and Ireland | 7.3% | 8.8% | 10.7% | 10.8% | 10.5% |
| Western Europe | 20.7% | 18.8% | 16.6% | 13.7% | 11.9% |
| West-Central Europe | 12.5% | 12.5% | 12.8% | 13.5% | 16.0% |
| East-Central Europe | 11.6% | 12.1% | 11.2% | 12.3% | 10.5% |
| Eastern Europe | 17.8% | 18.4% | 21.3% | 23.9% | 21.8% |
| Balkans | 7.6% | 7.9% | 7.5% | 7.2% | 9.2% |
| Western Mediterranean | 19.8% | 18.1% | 16.4% | 14.7% | 16.0% |
| Europe | 100.0% | 100.0% | 100.0% | 100.0% | 100.0% |

*Note.* Data from McEvedy and Jones (1978).

in which many European governments began to fear that their populations were growing too slowly. In the next section we will examine the events that have brought Europe's population growth to a standstill and reduced its share of the world's total population from 24% in 1900 to not much over 10% today.

## POPULATION SINCE THE DEMOGRAPHIC TRANSITION

### Pronatalism in Prewar Europe

The very low fertility prevalent across western Europe after World War I was a completely new phenomenon in human experience. Even though mortality had also dropped to all-time lows, populations were growing extremely slowly. The abandonment of mercantilist economic theory notwithstanding, this was a great concern to many governments. The French in particular were worried. Since the beginning of the century, their population had been growing at a rate of little more than 0.1 percent per year, and they had just emerged from a war with Germany in which, although they and their allies had been victorious, they lost a million people. Moreover, their traditional enemy across the Rhine had humiliated them only 50 years earlier in the Franco-Prussian War. The fact that Germany's population since then had increased by 20 million while theirs had grown by a scant 3 million did not escape the French.

In 1920 France, the world leader in family limitation, launched a pronatalist policy. Population policies are measures adopted by governments specifically to alter population dynamics. They are almost always aimed at fertility and migration; except where ethnic cleansing becomes an issue, all governments normally strive to reduce mortality as a matter of course. In the sphere of fertility, policies may be designed to increase reproduction (pronatalism) or to reduce it (antinatalism). To encourage people to have more children the French prohibited abortion, outlawed the sale of all contraceptives, and forbade the spread of any information about birth control. But

added to these negative measures were some positive ones. Women were paid by the state to stay at home and have children, and high monthly allowances were awarded for each child in the family. Some other countries, such as the United Kingdom, provided similar positive incentives without, however, imposing strictures.

In the 1930s Sweden adopted a specific population policy, but it was designed to improve the quality of family life rather than to explicitly encourage or discourage childbearing. Sponsored by Social Democrats Alva and Gunnar Myrdal, the legislation offered a wide range of financial and social benefits to families with children. At the same time, however, people were given access both to the means of birth control and to abortion. The idea was that people should be free to choose to have as many or as few children as they were comfortable with. The genius of the Myrdal plan was partly that the Conservatives bought it as a pronatalist policy but mainly that benefits were extended to the entire population. The issue of providing social welfare for an underprivileged class was not allowed to arise.

True pronatalist policies were carried farthest in Nazi Germany. By 1933 the crude birthrate had dropped to 14.7, and when Hitler took power in the same year he put into place the most stringent policy ever conceived to raise fertility. Not only were birth control and abortion banned, but a special tax was placed on unmarried adults. Besides the usual family allowances, loans were offered to couples to help them get married and establish a family. These loans could be written off by having children; the more children one had, the less money one had to repay. Perhaps the most powerful measure, however, was the launching of an intensive propaganda campaign promoting the building of a master race. People were made to believe that it was the duty of every good German to have many children so that enough glorious Aryans would be available to manage the world under the New Order. Accomplishments in the field of reproduction were duly recognized. History has not shown us many examples of successful pronatalist policies, but

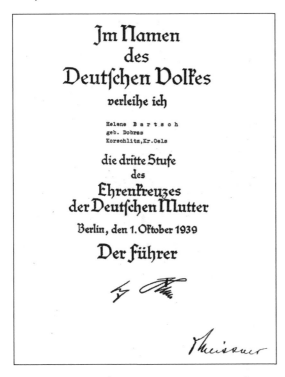

**FIGURE 3.10. Pronatalism in Nazi Germany.** Propaganda was a large part of Nazi Germany's pronatal policy. Mothers received meritorious awards of increasingly higher rank as they had children. This certificate found in an abandoned farmhouse in Silesia by a downed American bomber crew reads: "In the name of the German people I confer on Helene Bartsch, born Dobras, Korschlitz, Kreis Oels, the third degree of the Cross of Honor of the German Mother, Berlin the 1st of October 1939, Der Führer, Adolf Hitler."

Nazi Germany's was one. The crude birthrate rose from 14.7 in 1933 to 20.4 on the eve of World War II.

## Fertility in Postwar Europe

The war, itself, of course, caused large population losses. Millions of Europeans lost their lives: soldiers, sailors, and aviators in military battles, civilians in the brutal bombing and shelling of cities, and the enemies of Nazism in Hitler's concentration camps (estimates place the total death toll in Europe at approximately 40 million). The greatest losses were in east-central and eastern Europe, especially the Soviet Union and Poland, where the Germans pursued a "war of annihilation," but the Germans themselves paid a horrendous price.

Nonetheless, much of the concern in western Europe about the threat of population decline was dissipated after World War II by the baby boom. We have noted that in pretransition populations the death rate varied more than the birthrate. In posttransition populations the opposite has been true. Since infectious diseases have largely been put to rest and fertility has become a matter of conscious choice, the birthrate has varied more than the death rate.

Postwar fertility behavior in Europe falls into three broad patterns. Within the populations that had completed the Demographic Transition before the war, there was a sustained baby boom rather like the one experienced in the United States. The major differences between the European and the American versions are that, in the former, the peak levels of fertility were considerably lower, and the baby boom occurred somewhat later. In the United States the conversion to a peacetime economy was very rapid, and the baby boom began almost immediately. In western Europe it was delayed because many countries had suffered massive destruction of industry, housing, and infrastructure. Only after Marshall Plan aid from the United States secured recovery from the war did the baby boom in western Europe get underway. Among the countries where the transition had not been concluded during the prewar period there was a return to high fertility, but in eastern Europe this was not sustained while in western Europe it was (the Albanian anomaly will be discussed later).

## The Experience of Eastern Europe

Marshall Plan aid was offered to all countries that had been involved in the war, but the Soviet Union rejected it, not only for itself but for its satellites as well. This is a major reason why high fertility was not sustained in the east. The countries of eastern Europe had no one to help them recover but the Soviet Union, where war damage had been more severe than anywhere outside Germany and Poland. Fear of the capitalist West led the Soviet bloc to emphasize the rebuilding of industry and infrastructure at the expense of housing. As industry grew so did cities, and the new housing that was built was needed to accommodate in-migrants from the countryside. People simply could not afford to have large families. By 1965, only Poland and the German Democratic Republic enjoyed fertility rates that approached those of the rest of Europe, and in Hungary, Romania, and Bulgaria fertility had dropped below replacement levels.

Before the development of highly effective contraceptive devices (the pill and the IUD) by the mid-1960s, this very low fertility was only possible because eastern Europe was the forerunner in allowing free access to abortion. The USSR in 1920 was the first country ever to legalize abortion without restrictions during the first 12 weeks of pregnancy. In 1936 it was banned again but reinstated in 1955. All of the Soviet bloc countries except Poland followed this lead and permitted abortions on request for varying periods from the middle 1950s onward. On the other hand, all the countries of eastern Europe have taken some measures, both negative and positive, intended to stimulate fertility. For the most part they have come to naught, however, and, since 1995, even staunchly Catholic Poland's fertility has dropped well below replacement levels. The populations of eastern Europe completed the Fertility Transition not so much because they chose to limit their family size but because their economic circumstances forced them to do so.

## The Rear Guard of the Fertility Transition

While the principal demographic contrast in postwar Europe was between the posttransition populations of the west, with their long baby boom, and the pretransition populations of the east, with their abbreviated one, a word must be said about those countries fitting neither pattern. In none of these populations had the Fertility Transition been completed when the war broke out, but all returned to high fertility and sustained it for several decades after the war's end.

Following the war, Italy, Spain, and Portugal were among the most conservative Catho-

lic countries on earth. A process of liberalization began in the 1970s, however, and in all three the influence of the Church began to wane in certain social spheres. In Spain and Portugal this was associated with the deaths of longtime dictators Franco and Salazar. In Italy it was signaled by the passage in 1978 of a bill allowing free abortion on demand for women over the age of 18 and of a proposal under which Roman Catholicism would cease to be the state religion. In all of these countries fertility levels today are among the very lowest in Europe.

The 1990s have also seen something of a sexual revolution in Ireland. Rulings by the Irish Supreme Court in 1992 and 1995 gave Irish women wide-reaching abortion rights. The 1993 Family Planning Bill provided for the sale of condoms through public vending machines and decriminalized homosexual acts, both in an effort to fight the spread of AIDS. Between 1990 and 1995, fertility dropped by 25 percent to below replacement levels for the first time in Irish history.

High postwar fertility in the Netherlands has been interpreted by many as an attempt by its major religious communities not to lose demographic ground to their rivals. There is a major rift within Dutch society between Protestants and Catholics, but the Protestants themselves are also divided between Dutch Reformed and Christian Reformed communities. A fourth group consists of the Humanists. The major decline in Dutch fertility during the early 1970s may reflect lesser importance attached to religious affiliation as a source of personal identity.

Sexual permissiveness and high fertility in Iceland have a history going back to the Middle Ages. Women have long borne children from a very early age, whether in marriage, after formal engagement, or in the absence of any ritual. There has always been more of a stigma placed on a child because it has no siblings than because it was born out of wedlock. Simply put, the Christian mores of marriage never penetrated Icelandic folk culture, and, even though evangelical Protestantism placed strong sanctions on sexual relations outside marriage, they had little impact on the Icelanders. Though just below replacement levels today, Icelandic fertility, along with Albanian, is the highest in Europe.

In demographic terms Albania was a Third World country in the 1950s. Its fertility was as high as that of any country in the world. This was maintained by a social organization in which a person's greatest allegiance was to the clan. Disputes among clans were resolved by warfare and might result in blood feuds persisting over many generations. Reproduction for the survival of the clan was of paramount importance. The centralized communist regime, established in 1946, did much to undermine the old way of life and reduce the need for large families. By 1995 Albania's fertility was just below replacement level and the Demographic Transition there may now be said to be complete.

## THE EUROPEAN POPULATION TODAY

We noted that changes in attitudes toward family formation were responsible for the changes in fertility that accompanied the Demographic Transition. This is true also of a modern phenomenon that some demographers have come to call the Second Fertility Transition. Those changes during the first transition have been characterized as *altruistic*, while those that have brought about the second transition have been called *individualistic*. That is, the former transition was dominated by a concern for the quality of life of the family as a unit, and especially the children. The latter, on the other hand, emphasizes the right to self-fulfillment of all members of the family, including the parents.

We have already looked at the economic theory of fertility, which suggests that couples placing a higher value on material possessions will limit the number of children they have or choose to have none at all. But beyond this economic calculation, broader changes in social and cultural values are playing a role in this new transition. There is an increasing recognition on the part of society as a whole that all people have a right to equality and to freedom within the sociocultural sphere. As long as one's behavior does not interfere with the freedom of others to act freely, one is free to behave as one sees fit. This new point of view stresses the need for both equality of opportunities (income, education, etc.) and freedom of choice in behavior (dress, sexual behavior, etc.). Equality of opportunity stimulates the growth of the welfare state; freedom of choice fosters changes in fundamental societal values regarding many things, including fertility and family formation.

The effects of these new values on fertility and family formation are many. They include a shift from marriage to cohabitation (stable union without marriage), a shift from children to the adult couple as the focus of family, and a shift from contraception to prevent unwanted births to deliberate "self-fulfilling" choices about whether and when to conceive a child. In addition there has been a decline in the average number of children born to each woman in the population and a shift from families and households with quite similar makeups to ones with very different compositions. While the majority of European households still consist of traditional families, the family norm is being eroded as progressively larger proportions of the adult population are found to be living alone, or living as married or unmarried couples without children.

These changes were made possible by the introduction during the mid-1960s of the pill and the IUD, which revolutionized contraception. This was also about the time that access to abortion became freer in western Europe. Once it was generally accepted that sexual relations in marriage were not solely or even primarily aimed at procreation and contraceptives of high quality had become available, young people began to marry with the intention of delaying childbearing for several years. It then became clear to many that, if children were not to be immediately involved, it shouldn't be necessary to seek public approval of such an arrangement. Gradually the pressure to marry eased so much that couples no longer felt the need to marry before having children. Women, especially older ones, began to choose to bear children without having a stable relationship. By now there also was no stigma on married couples for voluntary childlessness. In short, marital status ceased to be a factor in fertility.

Only three European countries appear to have completed this second transition: Denmark, Norway, and Sweden. In all three, the proportion of births out of wedlock has risen from about 10 percent in the late 1950s to nearly 50 percent or more today. In Iceland, the proportion of children born out of wedlock has reached more than 60 percent, although as we have seen the birth rate there still remains high by European standards. Other countries, particularly in the Mediterranean region and the East are more conservative where the institution of marriage is concerned, but their birthrates are low because of severe family limitations within marriage.

We began this chapter by noting two salient trends in Europe's current demographic situation—that the size of the population is likely to decline over the coming decades and that the population is becoming dramatically older. While not all European countries are

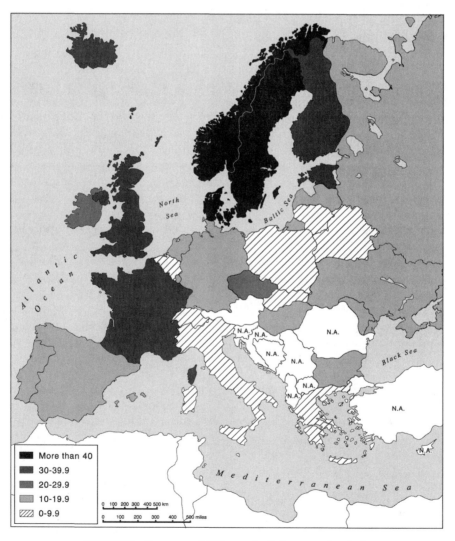

FIGURE 3.11. Percentage of children under 15 born out of wedlock.

facing a population decline, the majority of them will experience little or no growth, and for those with particularly low fertility rates the decline may be substantial. Two prime examples of the latter are Italy and Spain, whose populations are predicted by the year 2050 to fall from a current level of nearly 58 million to just 45 million in the case of the Italians, and from around 40 million to 37 million in the case of the Spanish.

The aging trend is equally striking. For much of Europe, life expectancies have been on the rise throughout the post-World War II decades, the principal exception being Russia, where life expectancies have declined somewhat since the breakup of the Soviet Union. On average, children born today in most European countries can expect to live well into their 70s in the case of boys, and in a majority of countries into their 80s in the case of girls. The long-term trend toward greater longevity coupled with the aging of the outsized "baby boom" generation, which will begin reaching retirement in the decades around 2010, is accelerating what is often referred to as the "graying of Europe."

The share of the elderly across Europe is expected to rise to 37% by 2050, up sharply from roughly 20% today. More than a quarter of the elderly will be over 80 years of age by that time, as opposed to just 15% today. At the same time, given prevailing low levels of fertility, the share of the younger, economically active population will fall to historic lows. In the pay-as-you-go social protection systems common to most European countries, the currently economically active population pays through its taxes for the state pensions and medical benefits of the elderly. Today across the whole of Europe there are roughly 100 working people for every 20 pensioners, but by midcentury the number of pensioners supported by 100 workers is forecasted to rise to 50, precipitating profound consequences for

**TABLE 3.4. The Population of Europe and Its Regions, 1950–2025**

| | Population (in millions) | | | |
| --- | --- | --- | --- | --- |
| | 1950 | 1999 | 2010 | 2025 (est.) |
| Northern Europe | 21.5 | 28.0 | 28.4 | 28.8 |
| Britain and Ireland | 54.0 | 63.1 | 64.5 | 66.4 |
| Western Europe | 61.0 | 85.5 | 89.0 | 92.0 |
| West-Central Europe | 81.8 | 97.2 | 97.3 | 95.5 |
| East-Central Europe | 53.7 | 74.8 | 75.9 | 75.2 |
| Eastern Europe | 111.7 | 162.1 | 157.4 | 149.9 |
| Balkans | 47.0 | 65.4 | 65.3 | 63.6 |
| Western Mediterranean | 82.0 | 107.6 | 107.7 | 103.7 |
| Europe | 512.5 | 683.7 | 685.5 | 675.1 |

| | % of total population | | | |
| --- | --- | --- | --- | --- |
| | 1950 | 1999 | 2010 | 2025 (est.) |
| Northern Europe | 4.20% | 4.10% | 4.14% | 4.27% |
| Britain and Ireland | 10.54% | 9.23% | 9.41% | 9.84% |
| Western Europe | 11.90% | 12.51% | 12.99% | 13.63% |
| West-Central Europe | 15.95% | 14.22% | 14.20% | 14.15% |
| East-Central Europe | 10.48% | 10.94% | 11.07% | 11.14% |
| Eastern Europe | 21.79% | 23.71% | 22.96% | 22.20% |
| Balkans | 9.16% | 9.57% | 9.53% | 9.42% |
| Western Mediterranean | 16.00% | 15.74% | 15.72% | 15.37% |
| Europe | 100.00% | 100.00% | 100.00% | 100.00% |

*Note.* Data from McEvedy and Jones (1978) and Encyclopedia Britannica Staff (2003).

the comprehensive and generous social protection systems that Europeans have come to enjoy.

The countries with the highest proportion of elderly today are Italy, Greece, Germany, Spain, Belgium, and Sweden. Over half of Sweden's social welfare budget already goes to meet the needs of its rapidly growing elderly population, and the burden is expected to increase by midcentury, when the number of pensioners supported by 100 workers in Sweden is expected to reach 54! As time goes on, the highest burdens of an aging population will be borne in the Mediterranean re-

gion and in central and eastern Europe. In Spain and Italy, where the projected ratio of pensioners to workers is expected to be one-to-one by 2050, the scale of the coming crisis is especially daunting. The populations of Greece, Austria, and the Czech Republic will have aged to the point that more than 40% or more of the total are seniors, with most of their central and east European neighbors not far behind. In all of Europe, only Albania, Moldova, Ireland, and Iceland can look forward to an elderly population of less than 30%, but still significantly higher than today's.

Governments have begun to cope, pushing

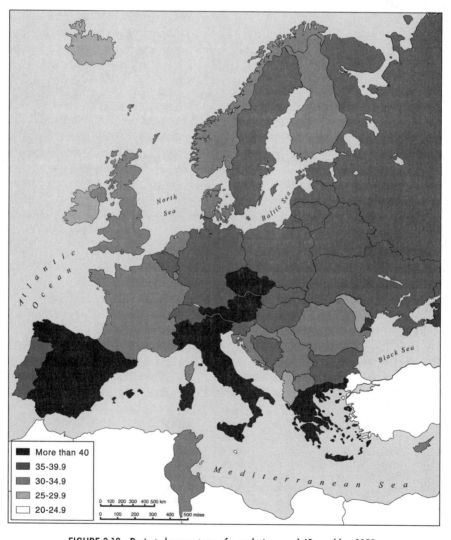

FIGURE 3.12. Projected percentage of population aged 60 or older, 2050.

forward schemes to reduce benefits or delay the statutory onset of retirement (which varies between 60 and 65 in most countries), but such proposals have met with just mixed acceptance so far and in most cases have unleashed storms of protest and labor unrest. The political process of bringing about reforms will likely be a long and difficult one, especially in light of the fact that so many of the voters who must be persuaded to cut back on benefits and eligibility are in those generations that are already retired or soon to retire. Indeed, earlier retirement has become so ingrained in recent years that the proportion of European men aged 55 to 65 who still work has dropped to just under 40%. These people are more likely to demand higher taxes in order to preserve the benefits to which they believe they are entitled than they are likely to vote for fewer benefits and later retirement. In short, the resolution of the problem is one that potentially pits generation against generation.

Some countries will face these stresses to a lesser degree than others. Those who currently enjoy higher levels of fertility and are likely to have more stable populations may feel somewhat less pressured, although they too, given current age structures, will have to support a larger elderly population than they do now. The countries that will experience

FIGURE 3.13. **The younger generation.** Fashionably dressed and prosperous looking, this young couple and many like them may soon have to bear the extraordinary burden of supporting Europe's rapidly growing population of retirees.

the least pressure include Iceland along with some of the least developed countries in the Balkans (Albania, Macedonia, and Moldova). Countries such as Britain and the Netherlands, where private pension plans are more common, may also be spared somewhat.

It is also important to remember that the elderly are seldom evenly distributed geographically even within countries and that the burden of providing the necessary infrastructure—for example, clinics, retirement homes, and recreational facilities (for an increasingly active retired population)—to support the aged may vary from place to place. Major cities, especially the capitals and those with expanding economies, tend on the whole to have much younger populations, while predominantly rural or economically declining urban regions have significantly older populations. Examples of such regions include the high Meseta of northern Spain, the southwestern portions of England and France, much of Italy outside the large cities of the north, and the Baltic coastal regions of northeastern Germany.

Increasingly, as people live longer lives, we are seeing a distinction made between the active and self-supporting elderly, sometimes referred to as "third-age" elderly, and the infirm and dependent, or "fourth-age" elderly. This means that not all of the retired population is necessarily in need of public support and that the onset of such need may be delayed beyond what was previously the norm. Nevertheless, the demands of an ever growing segment of "frail" and impoverished elderly people means continued pressure on financially strapped health and social care services, and the real prospect that this group may suffer from the neglect of society in the years to come.

How, other than raising taxes, reducing benefits, and delaying the age of retirement, can the larger problems of supporting an aging population be solved? Increased immigration is one answer. Indeed, a number of countries in northwestern Europe have admitted large numbers of immigrants over the past three or four decades. This process began during the immediate postwar decades to

FIGURE 3.14. The "third-age elderly." As benefi-ciaries of excellent health care and other benefits, many of Europe's retired population live relatively ac-tive lives. This group of "socially engaged" senior women, standing in front of a travel agency, seems anything but frail and dependent.

fill labor shortages in the rapidly recovering economies of these countries and continued into the 1970s, when economic recession re-duced the need for imported labor and even-tually brought the inflow of foreign "guest workers" to a halt. Unfortunately, these peo-ple, many of whom were later united with their families and settled down permanently in their host countries, have frequently been perceived by the native population as a threat to their national cultural heritage. Their pres-ence, along with more recent waves of asylum seekers and illegal immigrants, is not popular among many Europeans and has recently helped to fuel the fortunes of anti-immigra-tion politicians in many western European countries.

The other rather obvious solution is to in-crease fertility in the native population. Pro-natalist policies are not popular, however, in most of western Europe. For many they have a racist ring about them and invoke unpleas-ant memories of the Nazi era, but there is also a feeling of guilt about advocating increased fertility at a time when the population of the world as a whole is growing so rapidly. Only in France have significant measures, such as state-funded child care, been undertaken to encourage parents to have more children, and

this has paid off to some extent, as the French birthrate has risen. Sweden also achieved a temporary boost in its birthrate in the early 1990s by raising tax benefits for families with children. A number of countries have made efforts to make society more "child-friendly," but this is done more out of a humanitarian concern for the quality of life of the popula-tion than out of an explicit desire to promote

FIGURE 3.15. Anti-immigrant graffiti. As this graffiti on a wall in Venice demonstrates, a high level of resentment exists with regard to the waves of immigrants that Europe has already accepted over the past two or three decades. Although certainly one answer to the prob-lem of finding ways to support an aging population, accepting larger numbers of immigrants is politically difficult. (Photo: J. L. Kramer)

fertility and has not had any appreciable effect. Unless Europeans spontaneously decide they want to have more children or can be accepting of the presence of millions of new immigrants, declining population levels and a further graying of Europe must be anticipated.

## FURTHER READING

Allen, H. D. (2001). *Mediterranean ecogeography*. Harlow, UK: Prentice Hall.

Ashwell, I. Y., & Jackson, E. (1970). The sagas as evidence of early deforestation in Iceland. *Canadian Geographer, 14*, 158–166.

Bryson, B., & Ludwig, G. (1992). Main-Danube Canal: Linking Europe's waterways. *National Geographic, 182*, 3–31.

Cumbers, A. (1995). North Sea oil and regional economic development. *Area, 27*, 208–217.

Encyclopaedia Britannica Staff, Britannica Editors. (2003). *Britannica book of the year 2003*. Chicago: Encyclopaedia Britannica.

Flohm, H., & Fantechi, R. (Eds.). (1984). *The climate of Europe: Past, present, future: Natural and man-induced climatic changes: A European perspective*. Hingham, MA: Kluwer Academic.

Grove, A. T., & Racham, O. (2001). *The nature of Mediterranean Europe: An ecological history*. New Haven, CT: Yale University Press.

John, D. (1983). *Geology and landscape in Britain and Western Europe*. Oxford, UK: Oxford University Press.

Kirby, D., & Hinkkanen, M.-L. (2000). *The Baltic and the North Seas*. London: Routledge.

McEvedy, C., & Jones, R. (1978). *Atlas of world population history*. Hamondsworth, NY: Penguin.

Parish, R. (2002). *Mountain environments*. Harlow, UK: Prentice Hall.

Rothenbacher, F. (2002). *The European population, 1850–1945*. Basingstoke, UK: Palgrave Macmillan.

Wallén, C. C. (1970). *Climates of northern and western Europe*. Amsterdam: Elsevier.

Wallén, C. C. (1977). *Climates of central and southern Europe*. Amsterdam: Elsevier.

# CHAPTER 4

# Human–Environment Interaction

Europeans interact with their physical surroundings in many specific ways, and have done so for centuries. Human interaction with the environment is one of the most basic facts of life. It is also, quite appropriately, one of the oldest and most enduring themes that geographers, among others, feel compelled to write about. This is mainly because what happens on the human–environment interface has so many implications. To a considerable extent, environment influences human action. Environmental conditions may, for example, dictate that certain actions are impossible. At the same time, environment offers a range of opportunities, and humans, depending on their state of cultural and technological development, make critical choices as to how they will interact with their environmental surroundings. Those interactions will ultimately affect both their own well-being and the environment itself, and in turn may be reflected in European cultures and identities.

Foodways are an obvious example of the role of environment in culture. While it is true today that modern processing and importation of low-cost foodstuffs allow most Europeans considerable freedom in what they choose to eat, consumption patterns can still be reflective of long-standing connections between culture and environment. Take, for example, the use of vegetable oils and animal fats as cooking oils. In Mediterranean Europe, the dominant source of cooking oil, both in the past and today, is the olive, while elsewhere in Europe it is butter and lard. The olive, which until the most recent century was the only edible oil-bearing crop that could be grown in Europe, is produced for climatic reasons only in the Mediterranean South. For most of the rest of Europe, environmental conditions conducive to the production of swine and cattle, and the absence of any kind of edible oilseed, led to a traditional reliance on butter and lard, and to a lesser extent on oils derived from fish. Modern food processing has, of course, made it possible to produce cooking oil from a wide variety of imported and domestically produced oilseeds, such as rapeseed, and these products have expanded greatly in popularity, both north and south of the Alps. Nonetheless, due to the imprint that long-established patterns of people–environment interactions have made on traditional culture, a marked regional distinction in the use of traditional cooking oils remains.

Another example is found in the appearance of buildings. Cultural geographers have long expressed fascination with the great differences that may be seen across Europe in the use of traditional building materials. These variations usually have environmental explanations. Stone constructions of various kinds, for example, are found throughout the Mediterranean South, as well as in many parts of France and the British Isles. This zone of stone construction coincides with regions in which extensive deforestation occurred long ago. These are areas where wood has long been in short supply but where building stone of various types has always been relatively abundant. Conversely, traditional wood constructions are widespread throughout the more extensively forested parts of east-central Europe and across most of eastern Europe and Scandinavia. Half-timbered constructions, in which timbers are used to frame structures and plastered wattles of small sticks and branches or rows of bricks are placed between the timbers, seem to occupy an intermediate zone. Half-timbered constructions are found primarily in Germany and adjacent parts of the North European Plain but also in northern France and lowland England. The practice of half-timbering seems to have emerged primarily in areas of moderate deforestation, where supplies of timber could be obtained for the purpose of framing houses but where other materials constituted a more economical solution to filling in the walls.

It would be impossible here to describe fully the immense variety of specific relationships that may exist in Europe between people and environment. We do, however, want to provide some kind of overall sense of the role that environment plays in people's lives and attitudes and how human action has affected European environments. In this chapter, we explore the range and significance of these relationships in three ways. We begin very broadly, by briefly sketching a few general themes that attempt to capture some of the most essential and symbolic connections between Europeans and their environments. Then we turn to the long history of environmental change, highlighting some of the major ways in which the continent's natural environments have been altered over the millennia by human action. Finally, we turn to the issues of contemporary environmental crisis that challenge Europeans today.

## EUROPEANS AND THEIR ENVIRONMENTS

### The Lure of Adventure: Europeans and the Sea

Perhaps no single natural environment has more meaning for Europeans than the sea. We have already pointed out in a previous chapter how intimately Europeans live with the influence of the sea. As inhabitants of a

FIGURE 4.1. Half-timbered construction. The "Little Square" leading to one of the medieval gates in the town of Rothenburg ob der Tauber is one of the most often photographed places in Europe. Rothenburg, which is one of Germany's most romantic tourist attractions, makes a special effort for the sake of image to expose the half-timbered construction of many of the town's houses. Somewhat ironically, this is at variance with historical practice, in which owners have traditionally plastered over half-timbering to give their property a more prosperous, less rustic, appearance.

land of interpenetrating peninsulas and seas, most Europeans are never very far from it. The sea affects their daily weather, their diet, quite possibly their pocketbook, and continually beckons to them as a place to spend their leisure time. Most European nations depend, at least in part, on its resources or its trade to sustain them; even the landlocked ones are connected to it by the continent's great inland waterways and thereby rely on it as a source of resources and trade. In general, Europeans have been regarded historically as a seafaring people. The legacy of that fact is that even today the sea seems to enjoy a certain mystic power over the European imagination. The surrounding seas, however, are not all the same. They have personalities that have attracted Europeans to them in different ways.

The Mediterranean is the peaceful and sundrenched sea of antiquity, the "lungs and breast" of ancient and medieval Europe. The Romans called it "mare nostrum" (our sea), and regarded it as the central medium that held the ancient world together. Indeed, the word *Mediterranean* means "in the midst of land." In medieval and Renaissance times it became a major focus of the merchant's world, conveying at profit the spices and riches, as well as the culture, of the East to satisfy the voracious demands of a Europe emerging from the deep sleep of the Dark Ages.

Since Roman times, however, the Mediterranean has done little to unite those who live around its shores. Competing empires and commercial powers took root around its shores, none of them ever powerful enough to completely subdue the others. Thus, it came to pass that most of the Mediterranean's old coastal and island cultures became bound politically to large mainland states. Moreover, the historic rise of Islam in the Levant during the sixth century, its long and bitterly contested advances into Iberia, and the nearly 500-year hegemony of the Ottoman Empire over the entire eastern Mediterranean basin and the Balkan Peninsula had the effect of turning the Mediterranean into a permanent divide between the Christian lands along its European shores and the Muslim lands along its Balkan, African, and Asian littorals. More recently the Mediterranean has come to stand between a more developed but demographically stagnant Europe and a less developed, youthful, and Arabic north Africa.

Today the Mediterranean is also the holiday mecca for tens of millions from all over Europe: a romantic region of azure waters, rocky coastlines, and sandy beaches set among worn and venerable landscapes. Its coastal regions and islands—especially in Spain and increasingly in the south of France, Italy, and Greece, as well as in Turkey—are literally overrun during holiday seasons by swarms of pleasure-seeking holiday makers from northern Europe who travel briefly to the south in search of Mediterranean sun and warmth. So strong is this desire that tourism easily dominates the local economy of large parts of the Mediterranean region.

The great western ocean, the Atlantic, is the modern sea of profit and power, a "field of dreams" (and confrontations), as one writer has described it. It was the Atlantic that long ago drew adventurous Europeans out of home waters to fish the rich banks off the Newfoundland coast of North America. The Atlantic also drew enterprising Europeans to new worlds that they might conquer, exploit, and settle. It opened the possibility of expanding the spatial bounds of what might be considered European. On its distant shores, Europeans would scramble to proclaim their

**FIGURE 4.2. French Riviera beachfront.** Even on a late autumn afternoon, sun worshippers stake out places in the sun along the seawall of this popular French Riviera beachfront.

New Spains, Frances, Englands, Swedens, Amsterdams, and so on.

The Atlantic soon became the principal medium of wealth and opportunity for the competitive seafaring nations of western Europe, lending to them a certain importance and power in European affairs that they previously lacked. It became the focus of an "Atlantic economy" that ultimately bound the fortunes of western Europe to those of the New World. To the Americas flowed European goods, technologies, and investments, and most significantly the tens of millions of European emigrants who uprooted themselves—first from northern and western Europe and later from southern and eastern Europe—to pursue economic opportunity or political freedom. In return came raw materials, foodstuffs, repatriated earnings, and, in the most recent century, massive military aid and intervention in two world wars.

There is much that happened in the 20th century to underline the importance of the Atlantic as a bridge between Europe and the Americas. Perhaps most importantly, the Atlantic became the focus of a modern alliance (NATO) that bound western Europe and America together as allies for the more than half a century that has elapsed since World War II. But equally important is the fact that the Atlantic is traversed today by a growing network of transnational corporate linkages that are rapidly integrating not only the economies of Europe and America but those of the entire world.

The role of the northern seas is different again. They seem to have a less romantic reputation. They are the seas of hard work, busy with the harvesting of essential marine resources—principally fish, but today also oil and gas—and bustling with the all-important conduct of trade. The northern seas are accessible. They are the ones that penetrate most deeply into the European landmass. They touch in some significant way nearly all of the countries located north of the Alps. They have been, by their very presence and easy accessibility, a continual challenge to the peoples of these countries to profit from them. This is no less the case today than it was in the past.

In some cases, a part of the challenge has been just to hold the seas at bay. The Dutch, for example, have carried on a more or less continuous struggle since the 13th century to claim new lands from the sea and to protect themselves from the devastating storms from the North Sea that have threatened to flood and destroy the fields and settlements of the low-lying Dutch countryside. For centuries the battle swayed back and forth, with substantial gains coming only after the introduction of steam-powered pumping systems in the latter part of the 19th century. Over the past century the process has culminated in two major achievements. The first was the reclamation project that diked off the Zuiderzee, an old arm of the North Sea that deeply penetrated the Dutch coastline. The diking turned the old sea into a fresh water lake, the Ijsselmeer, from which massive polders were systematically drained to produce hundreds of thousands of hectares of reclaimed farmland. The second was the Delta Plan, under which massive dams and barrier sluices were built across the many arms of the Rhine Delta to provide a barrier against massive sea storms, such as the terrible storm of February 1953 in which 1,800 people and many thousands of livestock were lost.

The need to ensure access to the resources

**FIGURE 4.3. La Rochelle.** Once just a sleepy fishing village on the west coast of France, La Rochelle became by the 16th century the principal port for the trans-Atlantic trade with French possessions in North America and the Caribbean. Parts of the town's elegant arcaded streets are paved with granite stones brought back from Canada as ballast in the holds of ships.

**FIGURE 4.4. The Afsluitsdijk.** In 1932 the Dutch completed this 31-kilometer-long dike to isolate the Zuiderzee, a large inland arm of seawater, from the North Sea. Freshwater soon replaced salt water in the old Zee, seen to the right of the dike in this photo. Large areas (polders) were reclaimed for agriculture in a series of projects, and the remainder was preserved as a freshwater lake, now known as the Ijsselmeer.

of the northern seas has been reason for northern Europeans to work together. One recent example of this willingness is the cooperative effort undertaken since the 1970s by countries bordering on the North Sea to partition and exploit the substantial oil reserves that lie beneath its surface. The countries that make up the European Union similarly agree to pursue a common fisheries policy, which seeks to ensure for the future a continued annual harvest of North Sea fisheries for all. There is also growing international cooperation in the battle against pollution in both the Baltic and North Seas.

While the northern seas and their connecting straits may be viewed as a kind of common ground for northern Europeans, they have not been the focus of any kind of lasting political or cultural unity. While various powers have attempted from time to time to impose their will over portions of the region, their hegemony has usually been ineffective or short-lived. In the 14th century, for example, the Baltic was dominated by the sprawling and monopolistic network of north European merchant cities that made up the Hanseatic League. For more than a hundred years, the Hansa succeeded in exerting tremendous economic control over the Baltic

and the resources of the lands that surrounded it, but the organization was never able to achieve any real political unity. Later, in the 17th century, an expansionist Sweden succeeded in transforming the Baltic into a Swedish lake, but this too was not to last. To the present day, a never-ending rivalry between Germans, Danes, Swedes, Poles, and Russians has ensured that no political unity would prevail over the Baltic.

Indeed, many of the modern descendants of the old Hansa cities still compete for their share of the capital and productive power of the Baltic region. One example is the city of Copenhagen, whose port authority styles itself as the "strategic gateway to the Baltic region and 500 million consumers." Strategically located on the Øresund, the heavily traveled strait that connects the Baltic to the North Sea, the port of Copenhagen serves more than 23,000 ships every year. The recently bridged (after years of international debate) Øresund is also the link between burgeoning urban developments along both its Danish and Swedish shores. Despite these advantages, Copenhagen still vies for commercial influence over the Baltic economy with a host of other ports in northern Germany, Poland, Sweden, Finland, and the Baltic States and Russia. In today's Europe, the Baltic seems once again to be at the center of a natural region of growing importance in European affairs. Indeed, as we shall see in Chapter 7, while there has recently been a concerted effort to foster a "Baltic identity" among the peoples who surround the sea, there is as yet no one political or economic focus to the region, and the sea remains as much a separator as a unifier.

The North Sea and its connecting straits also divide and unite. The English Channel, which links the North Sea with the Atlantic and separates Britain from the rest of Europe, has long been hailed by the English as a historic barrier against unwanted influences. Although only 34 kilometers (21 miles) wide at its narrowest point, it has been instrumental in protecting Britain from wartime invasion and in reinforcing, in a very symbolic way, the idea that Britain can somehow live a separate

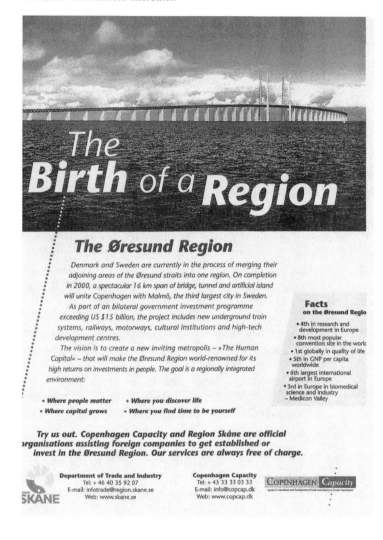

The Øresund Region

Denmark and Sweden are currently in the process of merging their adjoining areas of the Øresund straits into one region. On completion in 2000, a spectacular 16 km span of bridge, tunnel and artificial island will unite Copenhagen with Malmö, the third largest city in Sweden.

As part of an bilateral government investment programme exceeding US $15 billion, the project includes new underground train systems, railways, motorways, cultural institutions and high-tech development centres.

The vision is to create a new inviting metropolis – »The Human Capital« – that will make the Øresund Region world-renowned for its high returns on investments in people. The goal is a regionally integrated environment:

• *Where people matter*     • *Where you discover life*
• *Where capital grows*     • *Where you find time to be yourself*

**Facts**
**on the Øresund Regio**

• 4th in research and development in Europe
• 8th most popular convention site in the world
• 1st globally in quality of life
• 5th in GNP per capita worldwide
• 6th largest international airport in Europe
• 3rd in Europe in biomedical science and industry – Medicon Valley

**Try us out. Copenhagen Capacity and Region Skåne are official organisations assisting foreign companies to get established or invest in the Øresund Region. Our services are always free of charge.**

**Department of Trade and Industry**
Tel: + 46 40 35 92 07
E-mail: infotrade@region.skane.se
Web: www.skane.se
SKÅNE

**Copenhagen Capacity**
Tel: + 45 33 33 03 33
E-mail: info@copcap.dk
Web: www.copcap.dk

COPENHAGEN *Capacity*

FIGURE 4.5. "The Birth of a Region." A late-1990s advertisement extols the rise of a new Øresund region built on the linking of resources, people, and talent on either side of the historic strait between the Baltic and the North Seas.

and independent life from that of "the Continent." The existence of the Channel certainly has helped perpetuate insular prejudices against the continent, voiced in such quotable English sentiments as "the wogs [worthy oriental gentlemen] begin at Calais." But in fact the Channel has been equally important as a bearer of influences. Always alive with traffic and now crossable in record time via the new tunnel, or "Chunnel," which introduced high-speed cross-channel rail service in 1994, the channel hardly represents much of a physical barrier. Indeed, it has always been the crossing of the channel—whether by swimmers, ferries, airships and airplanes, or subterranean tunnel—that has most caught the public

imagination. All of the countries bordering on the North Sea enjoy numerous ferry links and business connections, which have the effect of bringing them closer together. Partly because of historic associations, partly because of proximity, Britain's natural "economic beachhead" on the continent is the Netherlands. Studies have shown that Dutch cities are, in fact, the most common place for British companies to set up European offices.

In a very real sense, then, it is important to recognize that the long and intense relationship with the seas—whether Mediterranean, Atlantic, or northern—has generated a particular kind of cultural solidarity among Europeans. The sea is the place where Europeans of diverse origins and backgrounds have always met. Traditionally they encountered one another in its harbors, today they are probably more likely to do so on its beaches or in its holiday resort towns, but the sea is a place of meeting and has come to be viewed as belonging to everyone. Europeans have evolved a common language or vocabulary associated with the sea and seafaring. There is a fraternity of seamen. There is a Law of the Sea that was essentially developed by Europeans to govern the behavior of all who use it. There is a common coastal landscape of harbor towns, seafront quarters, fortresses and arsenals, breakwaters, marinas, lighthouses, beacons, watchtowers, maritime museums, holiday resorts, and beaches. And finally, there is a shared imagination. All European cultures seem to share a common set of images, fears, and beliefs that stem from centuries of adventurous contact with the sea and still fire the imagination of those who look out upon its waters.

## Wild Beauty and Refuge: Europeans and the Mountains

A second landscape type that seems to have a special place in the European imagination is that of the mountains. Like the sea, the mountains are a place where people like to go, although for quite different reasons. The attraction of the mountains is less economic; it has more to do with breath-taking beauty and wilderness, or perhaps with romantic notions of freedom and refuge.

The mountains are because of their very nature sparsely populated places. Settlement is usually confined to the valleys and lower slopes. The people who live there have been traditionally thought of as rather remote and rustic, although increasingly this is hardly the case. For many Europeans, the peaks and flanks of the great massifs and ranges are viewed as relatively pristine natural wonderlands; the meadows and open heath above the tree line, used only for grazing by the local population, also have a romantic charm. In the Alps, and in parts of the Caledonian system, there is the added attraction of permanent snow and the occasional glacier. In short, the mountains are a recreational attraction, and Europeans have taken to them since the 18th century with great holiday enthusiasm, whether to hike, climb, ski, or just "take the air."

But there is also an aura of freedom and refuge that is associated with mountain environments. For their own populations, and for others, the mountains have traditionally been thought of as a place where difficulties of access could weaken the forces of oppression to the degree that they could be more successfully resisted. This idea has certainly been at the core of the national myth that binds together the cantons of Switzerland. Mountain refuges have been instrumental in the survival of Basque culture in northern Spain and have aided in the survival of the Rhaetian languages deep in the eastern Swiss and Italian Alps. Stone castles perched on craggy ridges above the Aude Valley in the south of France are silent testimony to the usefulness of the mountain environment to the Cathars, who fought a protracted battle in the 13th century to preserve their outlawed neo-Manichean religion against the crusading forces of the Catholic Church and the King of France. The idea that the mountains are a place of refuge where beleaguered peoples, cultures, and ideas can find the strength to survive is a common theme in European history. German propaganda used this very theme in the final months of World War II when it promoted the idea of a "mountain redoubt" to which a heavily embattled Nazi regime would retreat and survive to rise again.

Similar themes apply to the upland landscapes of Caledonian and Hercynian Europe. Although not as spectacularly vertical as true mountain chains, upland areas are also generally sparsely populated and lightly used. Moorlands and heath can be excitingly vacant and remote—witness the eerie and lonely settings of English mystery and horror novels set in such locales. And they too have often played a role as cultural refuges. The relative inaccessibility of the Caledonian highlands of the British Isles and of the Armorican Massif in Brittany have certainly played a role in pre-

**FIGURE 4.6. Mountain refuge.** A Cathar castle perches high above the strategic valley leading up from the Languedoc coast of the Mediterranean to Carcassonne and beyond to the Plains of Aquitaine.

serving the last vestiges of Celtic culture in Europe. The Massif Central in France was from early times a haven for embattled groups. It was the place where pre-Roman cultures managed to survive for a longer time than anywhere else. Its importance as a refuge area is underlined by the fact that the Roman annexation of the south of France (Narbonensis) in 121 B.C. was undertaken partly in response to the need to protect Roman trade in the Rhône Valley from the attacks of organized pirate bands based in the nearby massif.

Upland landscapes can also be romantically beautiful. The Hercynian formations of central Germany are storybook landscapes, with their elongated street villages set in deep valleys below wooded slopes and ridgelines. Equally captivating are the hedge-rowed landscapes of the Armorican Massif in Brittany, the deep V-shaped valleys and upland heaths of the Central Massif in the south of France, or the long lakes and glens of Caledonian Scotland. The grandeur of the peaks and ridges, waterfalls, and tranquil lakes of the English Lake District, which so enthralled the great romantic "Lake Poets"—Wordsworth, Coleridge, and Southey—hold a special place in the English imagination. Germans feel similar sentiments for the romantic Hercynian landscapes of the Rhineland or the

Harz, as do the Czechs for the forested ridges of the Bohemian Massif.

These landscapes are also home to a traditional way of life that has responded for ages to the patchy and limited quality of upland soils by favoring the extensive use of land for grazing animals. Thus, the uplands are often seen as the landscape of the shepherd or herdsman, which implies a certain openness and semiwildness, a setting in which human beings are constantly on the move, relocating their flocks or herds with the seasons in order to make the best use of available resources. These are the settings in which we might imagine ourselves stopped in our car on a winding road, unable to move as a mass of bleating sheep dolefully pick their way across our path on their way to an adjoining or distant pasture.

## The Soil of Our Fathers: Europeans and the Land

Our final theme highlights the relationship between Europeans and the continent's lowland landscapes of fields and pasture. We have already seen that Europe's greatest population densities favor the coastal lowlands and interior plains. While much of that density today is associated with urban living, earlier population densities resulted from the considerable agricultural carrying capacity of these lands. Local agricultural surpluses were, after all, an important precondition for the rise of urban market towns in medieval times, and many of those market towns became the foundations for modern cities.

It was not so far in the past, however, when good arable land was one of society's greatest reservoirs of wealth, and the relationship between agriculturists and the land was the primary one in many parts of Europe. This relationship runs deep. Europeans have long been among the great agricultural colonists of the world, systematically clearing woodlands, draining wetlands, and reclaiming land from the sea. Much emphasis is still placed by governments on preserving the viability of agriculture, protecting agricultural lands from urban encroachment, and protecting the livelihoods of those who till the land from the vagaries of the modern marketplace. Regardless of how much agriculture has modernized over the past century, we often think of traditional agricultural systems in Europe as examples of sensible accommodations between people and the environment.

The traditional Mediterranean system, for example, consisted of three elements—the cultivation of small grains, horticulture, and the grazing of livestock. This ancient "triad" was in many ways a natural adaptation to the region's unique environmental conditions.

FIGURE 4.8. Olive orchard. These olive orchards, surrounding the stronghold of Baños de la Encina built by the Caliph Al Hakam II in 967, illustrate the Mediterranean practice of combining grain farming with horticulture. The ground between the olive trees has been prepared for the planting of winter grains.

FIGURE 4.7. Traditional Mediterranean farming. In this scene, near Formia on the west coast of Italy, workers are pulverizing the topsoil of this field. This is a time-honored practice dating all the way back to the ancients, undertaken to preserve as much moisture as possible beneath the surface of the field before planting winter grains.

The first element, the cultivation of small grains, took place in the winter so as to take advantage of the cool and relatively wet winter months for germination and to have a harvestable crop before the onset of the region's desiccating hot and dry summers. Mediterranean agriculturists employed a two-field rotational system, in which grains were planted in a single field only every other year. The intervening year of fallow allowed the soil to recover sufficient nutrients to support the next year's grain crop.

The second element of the system consisted of orchards and vineyards. In these were cultivated both a variety of native drought-resistant horticultural plants, including the olive, the fig, the almond, and of course the grape as well as some later introduced exotic crops such as citrus fruits that required irrigation. These first two elements of the Mediterranean system were often closely linked. Both were commonly found within the lands of the large Mediterranean agricultural village. The grain fields often occupied low-lying and alluvial lands, while the orchards and vineyards covered the lower portions of the steeply sloped hillsides so common throughout the region. In some cases the two land uses were intermixed.

The third element, the grazing of small livestock, chiefly goats and sheep and to a lesser extent swine, on rugged upland and mountain pastures was often pursued quite independently of the other two. This was because the animals had to be herded back and forth, in a system known as transhumance, between summer and winter pasturages that were often quite remote from the home village. As a matter of adaptation to environmental conditions, the livelihoods of herders were separated from those of farmers and horticulturists.

The traditional farming system of the North European Plain also featured a carefully balanced relationship between fields, livestock, and the maintenance of soil fertility. Unlike the Mediterranean system, this system intimately mixed grain farming and animal husbandry. In many areas, it came to employ a three-field rotational system, in which two fields were planted each year in grain crops. One field was usually devoted to a bread grain, such as wheat or rye; the other to a grain used primarily, but not exclusively, for animal feed, such as oats or barley. The third field was left fallow. The livestock were fully integrated into the system. On the one hand, they provided draft power for plowing and the manure for maintaining the fertility of the fields. On the other, the feed crops harvested from the fields maintained them. From the livestock also came the meat and dairy products necessary to supplement the peasant's bread.

Yet another traditional system evolved on the less fertile uplands and in the peripheral northern and upland forestlands of Hercynian and Caledonian Europe. The poor soils of these regions necessitated a much greater emphasis on livestock. The extensive herding of livestock was therefore the dominant activity, supplemented by small-scale efforts at grain farming wherever local conditions permitted.

The classic field system for such regions is known as "infield–outfield." The infield was the small area near the village or farmstead where grain could be grown. The outfield consisted of the surrounding forests or wastes where the livestock were allowed to graze.

FIGURE 4.9. Ridge and furrow. At this living historical farm museum in Denmark, open fields are worked just as they were in the Middle Ages. The "up-and-down" topography of the field is a cumulative result of plowing long narrow strips with a wheeled plow whose moldboard threw the earth to one side as it moved along. The strips were plowed from the edges to the center, creating the alternating pattern of raised ridges at the center of strips and low furrows at their margins.

The outfields were often so extensive that livestock were moved about over long distances and tended by household members who were exclusively assigned to the task. The outfield was also used for cropping, but only small parts were used in any given year. These areas were then allowed to lie fallow, sometimes for a decade or more, before they were planted again. This practice of "shifting cultivation" is also sometimes called "slash-and-burn" or "swidden" agriculture. The infield, on the other hand, could often be planted every year, because an abundance of manure from the large numbers of livestock made it possible to maintain a constant and adequate level of soil fertility.

The old peasant cultures, built upon seasonal rhythms of working the land within these systems, are mostly gone today. Modern agriculture has, of course, changed the way in which the land is used and worked. Mechanization has reduced the necessary work force to just a fraction of what it once was. In many regions the scattered holdings of a single farmer have been consolidated far beyond the enclosures of a century or two ago to produce highly efficient agri-businesses or, in the case of large parts of eastern Europe, what were until just recently substantial collective enterprises.

For many Europeans the move from countryside to city was made not all that long ago, in some cases just a matter of decades or years. Roots in the countryside are not yet forgotten, nor are they ignored. Many urban-dwellers consider a trip to the countryside an appropriate or desirable weekend outing. Summer residences in rural areas are quite popular in many parts of Europe. Young people still go to the country to work in the summer, and upscale urbanites who can afford the commute gladly buy up old farmhouses as permanent exurban residences. There is much that is nostalgic and appealing about the fields and villages, the folk architecture of farmsteads, the hedgerows, stone walls, and pole fences, the windmills, country inns and pubs, tree-lined alleés, and great houses that dot the agricultural landscapes of lowland Europe. They are the visible reminders of soci-ety's ancient and deep-seated roots in the land.

## ENVIRONMENTAL CHANGE OVER THE AGES

Environmental change occurs as a result of both natural processes and human action. A great many changes result from natural causes. The natural world is constantly evolving, although we may often see it as static. We know, for example, that there have been considerable climatic changes over the ages. These variations have deeply affected European environments, as well as the people who made their living from them. The long period of climatic deterioration during the late 1500s, known as the "Little Ice Age," is a good example. This was an extended period of cold and stormy weather that resulted in significant vegetational change. It caused glaciers to move down mountain valleys to threaten villages and necessitated the retreat of agricultural frontiers in many of Europe's more northern and marginal upland regions. It was also responsible for a protracted period of stormy weather in the North Atlantic that probably sharply curtailed contact with Viking colonies in Greenland and Iceland. The loss of contact and deteriorating environmental conditions were important factors underlying a precipitous decline in the population of Iceland and the demise of the Viking settlements on Greenland.

From earliest times, however, human activity has also been an agent of substantial environmental change. Armed with an ever changing and more powerful arsenal of technological tools, human beings have possessed a unique capacity among biological creatures to challenge the physical limitations imposed on them by the natural world. We recognize, of course, that the interaction between humans and nature is a two-way street. Humans have not always been able to overcome the forces of nature. Often, too, their efforts have achieved results that are something other than what was intended. Nonetheless, the human impact over time on the European environment has been immense. Few, if any, land-

FIGURE 4.10. Natural disaster. The Greek island of Santorini consists of the rim of a gigantic crater formed when its volcano erupted around 1500 B.C. The debris that landed on the island of Crete, 75 miles to the south, and the massive tidal wave that followed largely destroyed the Minoan civilization in the Aegean. This event may be the origin of the story of the lost continent of Atlantis.

scapes exist today in Europe that we can truly say have not been seriously modified by human action.

## Deforestation

Certainly one of the most widespread and long-standing of human environmental impacts has been deforestation. The removal of forest cover by human agency began in earnest during Neolithic times, as systematic burning and clearing of forest vegetation accompanied the diffusion of farmers and herders over large parts of Europe. Indeed, recent paleoecological research has shown that the effects of burning during prehistoric times was probably much more dramatic than previously believed. The practice was responsible for bringing extensive human-induced environmental change to Europe for the first time and was clearly the first step in a long and inexorable process of deforestation for agricultural and other purposes that has lasted for thousands of years.

Perhaps the most striking example of this process is the near total destruction of the primeval Mediterranean woodlands. The forests of the region came under concerted attack as early as preclassical times. Using both fire and ax to clear fields and pasturelands, the removal of woodland cover was relentlessly pursued by the ancients for many centuries. Attica was reportedly stripped of all forest cover by the fifth century B.C., although there is certainly reason to believe that forest lands in other parts of the Greek homelands were as yet subjected to far less pressure. In addition to the clearing that was undertaken for agricultural purposes, Mediterranean forests were further decimated in both ancient and medieval times by a voracious demand for timber, which was used for fuel, for the construction of ships and buildings, and to produce charcoal for the smelting of metals. The timber requirements of the Venetian fleet alone are said to have been largely responsible for the disappearance by late medieval times of the extensive forests that once covered the Dalmatian coast of the Adriatic Sea.

The end result of all these activities was to produce a Mediterranean landscape of steep, barren slopes that were subsequently devastated by the erosional effects of winter rains. The wholesale stripping away of forest soils and the depredations wrought on young tree saplings by the grazing habits of ubiquitous herds of Mediterranean goats and sheep were enough to prevent any regeneration of the woodlands. With the exception of a few of the more remote areas of Iberia and the Balkans, the deforestation and accompanying erosion of soil material over the entire region was so

**FIGURE 4.11. Erosion.** Heavy erosion mars the landscape west of Corinth in Greece. Stripped of vegetation cover and left vulnerable to the effects of heavy winter rains, the gullied and eroded slopes seen here are forever lost to cultivation.

severe and widespread as to change forever the appearance and productivity of the land.

While large areas today have been reforested or are covered with some form of secondary vegetation, it is estimated that nearly a third of the Mediterranean region's soils continue to suffer severe losses from erosion. The predominant form of secondary vegetation that covers the lands around much of the Mediterranean basin consists, as we have seen, of drought- and fire-resistant low-lying evergreen shrubs. These plant communities are the present-day outcome of a centuries-old degeneration of the Mediterranean forest cover. An additional problem is that they, too, may now be subject to degradation as a result of continued human interference in the form of cutting and overgrazing. There is growing evidence that desertification is on the advance in certain areas throughout the region.

The clearing of the vast primeval forestlands that once covered most of temperate Europe was no less systematic. The main difference is that the conversion of many of these lands to productive cropland and pastureland has had a less detrimental outcome in terms of the carrying capacity of the land for humans than has been the case in Mediterranean Europe. In fact, it could be argued that centuries of mixed livestock and grain farming has generally left soils with

greater nutrient levels than those that are normally found in soils that have retained their forest cover.

As in Mediterranean lands, the agricultural clearing of forestlands in northern Europe was augmented by the exploitation of timber resources for fuel, building materials, the construction of wooden sailing ships, and the charcoal industry. The demand for tall and sturdy timbers for the building of ships was especially strong in northwestern European countries from the 1500s through the 1700s. In fact, the English, French, and Dutch quickly exhausted their native supplies and were soon forced to turn to sources in the Baltic, or to their overseas colonies, to meet their needs. Indeed, British capital helped to finance the so-called industrial breakthrough wrought by the forest industry in late 19th-century Scandinavia. An insatiable British demand for timber led first to the large-scale logging of the coastal forests of Norway, then to the systematic harvest of the northern forestlands of Sweden and Finland.

The charcoal industry was also a particularly powerful force in the removal of forest cover. Woodlands in many parts of western and central Europe were already under attack by medieval times. In their rush to supply local metal smelting industries, charcoal makers literally stripped parts of Belgium and northeastern France of trees. The practice was also widespread in Scandinavia. Indeed, by the 1700s and 1800s, local sources of wood for charcoaling had become so scarce in the iron and copper smelting districts of Sweden that many enterprises were forced to go extraordinary distances to secure adequate sources of charcoal timber.

The forest resources of temperate Europe probably reached their lowest point sometime during the 1700s. By that time, most of the natural forest, with the exception of some parts of northern Scandinavia and the northern interior of Russia, had disappeared. Since then there has been a gradual recovery. Over the course of the 18th and 19th centuries, country after country took up the cause of afforestation. The leaders were Germany and

FIGURE 4.12. Beech forest. Some sense of what the primeval woodlands of the North European Plain might have looked like can be gained here at the Royal Beech Forest at Fredensborg in Denmark. Royal hunting parks such as this were instrumental in preserving some forest tracts.

France, both of which reacted with special alarm to the deleterious effects of deforestation on agriculture and industry as well as national honor. The alarm led to the study of scientific forestry and the establishment of reserves and reforestation projects.

Along the Bay of Biscay coast of southwestern France, the reforestation of Les Landes, an ecologically troubled region in which advancing coastal dunes threatened to bury a once productive landscape, became a model of the benefits of afforestation efforts. The planting of huge plantations of pine trees dur-

ing the Napoleonic era not only stabilized the encroaching dunes but also had the added benefit of creating a source of scarce timber and resin for the French Navy. Afforestation has continued to the present and has resulted in a great many reforested areas both north and south of the Alps, many of them planted to a single species of tree. A particularly noticeable increase in the overall area covered by forests has occurred since World War II, partly due to an accelerated abandonment of marginal agricultural lands that has accompanied late-20th century efforts to rationalize and modernize agricultural production.

## Cultivation of Grasslands

Also forever altered by human actions are the natural grasslands of the long peninsula of steppe that once extended from Asia across southern Russia, Ukraine, and into the Maritsa, Wallachian, and Hungarian basins of southeastern Europe. Originally the domain of fierce nomadic peoples, who periodically swept out of Asia, these rich dark-earthed lands were eventually brought under European control and put to the plow. Eventually these regions became Europe's great eastern wheat belt. Much as is the case for the American Great Plains, little of the original prairie or tall grass plant communities that once covered

FIGURE 4.13. Afforestation. Scattered conifer plantations dot the crests and slopes of the Caledonian uplands that mark the borderland between England and Scotland. These trees were planted during the middle decades of the last century.

these regions has survived. In the case of the westernmost extensions of steppe into the intermontane basins of southeastern Europe, there is evidence that human influence goes back even further in time. These areas apparently were once forested. The grassland regimes we think of as their natural vegetative cover may have actually resulted from the removal of forest cover by humans in early times.

## Reclamation of Marsh and Fen

Marshlands are another natural landscape that has been systematically reduced. The ancients and the Romans undertook efforts to drain marshlands. But it was the Dutch, as we have already noted, who launched the most extensive effort at reclamation. They began perfecting elaborate techniques for reclaiming low-lying coastal lands as early as the 13th century and, by the end of the 16th century had begun to export their expertise to other countries. Over the next couple centuries, Dutch engineers assisted in literally dozens of projects across Europe aimed at reclaiming land from coastal marshes and river estuaries. Many of these projects were situated on nearby North Sea coastal sites in northern Germany and western Denmark, but Dutch engineers were just as likely to be found at work in places as far away as Sweden, Russia, England, Italy, and the south of France. One of the most extensive reclamations of the period took place in southeastern England, where hundreds of square kilometers of marshland were converted to agricultural land in the historic draining of the Fens.

The reclamation of marshlands continues to the present. Efforts to drain the vast Pripet Marshes of eastern Europe were initiated under state sponsorship in the 1870s and continue today. In more recent times a number of ambitious projects have been completed in the Mediterranean South. One of the most remarkable, as we have seen, is the draining of the Pontine Marshes on the west coast of Italy during the 1930s. Other modern projects include the ongoing Spanish efforts to drain the extensive marshes (*Las Marismas*) that follow the lower course of the Guadalquivir River.

## Disappearance of Heath and Moor

The heath lands of northwestern Europe are yet another form of vegetational cover that has historic associations with human agency. Heathlands are common throughout those parts of Europe that border the Atlantic and northwestern seas. In these areas the growth of the characteristic low-lying shrub vegetation that we refer to as heath is facilitated by the combination of Atlantic maritime climatic conditions and acidic soils. While some mountain and coastal heaths can be quite natural, the extensive areas of lowland and highland heaths of northwestern Europe are believed to occupy areas that were once covered by forests. There is some conflicting evidence about the degree to which these areas derive from natural processes as opposed to human action, but there is clear suggestion that human activity, particularly the practice of intentional burning, is at least partly responsible for their formation and continuance.

It is also interesting to note that the total area covered by Europe's heathlands has sharply declined over the past century and a half. The decline is due to the human agricultural colonization of heathlands and their conversion to grassland or forest through the cessation of burning practices. Some of the most marked declines have occurred in Sweden and Denmark; in the latter case, largely

FIGURE 4.14. Reclaimed heathland. The Lüneberger Heath is a vast sandy tract in the midst of the North German Plain. Originally covered with heath vegetation and grazed by flocks of hardy sheep brought here from Corsica, large areas have been forested and set aside as game preserves.

through organized effort during the late 19th and early 20th centuries to convert the heathlands of western Jutland to agricultural use. Similar losses have taken place in southern England.

## Introduction of Exotics

As natural forests, marsh, steppe, heath, and moor have gradually disappeared, humans have replaced them with new or modified forms of vegetative cover. Over the millennia agriculturists have brought to Europe a great variety of domesticated plants. The earliest examples, introduced from the Nile Valley and southwestern Asia, included wheat, the grapevine, and a wide range of horticultural plants.

Neolithic farmers brought the practice of growing wheat to Europe. It became the preferred bread grain of the classical world and remains today the most common cereal grain grown in southern and western Europe. The domesticated wheat strains that were introduced in very early times from southwestern Asia were all of the kind known as winter wheat—sown in the fall, cultivated in the spring, and harvested in the summer. They were perfectly adapted to the Mediterranean climate because they germinated and grew up during the wet winter weather and matured before the desiccating heat of summer. They

also did well north of the Pyrenees and Alps in the milder climates of western Europe but were never well established farther east or in northern Europe, where failure to ripen was often the consequence of late springs or prolonged dampness.

The ancient Greeks made wide use of the grape and were responsible, along with the Phoenicians, for its spread throughout the Mediterranean region. The Romans encouraged its production and took it with them as they extended the frontiers of the Empire northward to the Rhine and Danube, establishing the vine wherever local soil and climatic conditions permitted. Grapes were growing on the warm slopes of the Rhine Valley by the second century A.D. The Greeks and Romans developed the art of grape growing and wine making. They developed methods of grafting and budding to produce new varieties, techniques of cultivating and trellising, and the practice of protective terracing that ensures that the grapes ripen even in areas too far north to produce a really good harvest. Viticulture remains today as one of the continent's most extensive and valuable agricultural activities.

The introduction of intensive gardening of horticultural plants into the Mediterranean by Arabs and Turks also did much to transform the landscapes of the Mediterranean South, particularly in lowland and coastal ar-

**FIGURE 4.15. Viticulture on the Rhine.** Long rows of trellised vines climb the sunny-facing slopes along this stretch of the Rhine Valley in Germany. Other land uses visible here include the wooded heights above and the transportation corridor along the river's edge.

eas. The coastal plain of Valencia (*Huerta de Valencia*) in the southeast of Spain is, for example, nearly completely dominated today by intensively cultivated citrus groves. The early varieties of the orange, which were introduced by the Arabs, were small and bitter and were not well accepted. Better and sweeter varieties, however, were brought by the Portuguese—witness the word for orange in a number of languages (Arabic *bourtouqal*, Greek *portoka'li*, Turkish *portakal*, and Romanian *portocala*)—and became a sought-after delicacy by the late Middle Ages. Both the Arab and Portuguese varieties of the orange originated in Southeast Asia, which is why they require irrigation. Even the German/Scandinavian words *Apfelsine*, *apelsin*, and *appelsin* (Chinese apple) suggests its eastern origins.

Later introductions of exotics included maize, potatoes, and tomatoes, all of which came as a result of European contacts with the New World. Although brought back from America by the Spanish, maize was not readily accepted at first. The Spanish and Portuguese took the plant instead to Africa and India. Its successful introduction in Europe came later and via the Turks, who brought the plant to the Balkans and Italy, where it became known as Turkish grain. Maize subsequently became quite important in the Mediterranean, where it thrived in the warm, dry summer climate and responded better to irrigation than wheat or barley. In the 16th century, the potato was introduced to Spain as a garden plant. It appeared later in the Spanish Netherlands and eventually reached the British Isles, where it was first accepted as a large-scale field crop. Since potatoes are rich in carbohydrates and easily grown, even in cool climates, their cultivation spread rapidly throughout temperate Europe, not only as a food crop but also as a source of animal fodder and alcohol. By the 18th century the Irish population had become so completely dependent on the potato that it was terribly decimated by famine, disease, and emigration when the crop failed in 1845–1846 due to blight. Tomatoes have

had less impact. Initially used for ornamental purposes and generally regarded as poisonous, the tomato has only become a valuable food during the past century, although it was mentioned as a salad ingredient as early as the 16th century.

Native plants too have been domesticated and have spread far beyond their original ranges. Examples are barley, rye, and the sugar beet. Barley, which was known to the ancient Greeks and Romans, has a particularly short growing period and is easily adapted to a wide range of growing conditions, including high altitude. It enjoyed widespread cultivation as the chief bread grain in Europe until as late as the 16th century. Rye seems to have been domesticated later than the other grains. Because it grows well on poor soils and in climates too cool to produce a good crop of wheat, it became a staple grain crop throughout central and eastern Europe and Scandinavia. Sugar beets were once a relatively unimportant source of animal feed, but in 1747 a German apothecary, Andreas Marggraf, discovered a method of obtaining sugar crystals from the beet. Roughly half a century later, during the Napoleonic Wars, the sugar beet burst onto the scene as a major European field crop as a practical means of coping with the fact that Europe had been cut off from its customary source of West Indies cane sugar. By late in the 19th century, the beet had come to replace cane throughout the continent as the leading source of sugar.

Finally, changing field patterns and the abandonment of marginal lands have also had their environmental effects, particularly on the vegetation habitats of wild species. The enclosure of medieval open fields and commons that took place in various parts of Europe from the 1200s through the 1800s often resulted in the widespread planting of boundary hedges and trees. This was the process responsible for producing the characteristic patchwork landscape of fields and dense hedgerows that we associate especially with rural landscapes in parts of the British Isles, France, and Scandinavia. Although we may

FIGURE 4.16. Enclosure. The fields and pastures of this English–Welsh borderland landscape are enclosed with hedgerows. Settlement is dispersed—the old villages were broken up long ago—but confined to the lower slopes. Open heath lands lie beyond the boundaries of the upper fields.

not think about it, the introduction of boundary hedges and trees literally transformed the local ecology of the areas in which they were employed. They increased vegetative diversity and provided cover for birds and small animals. It seems ironic that the consolidation of fields that is taking place in today's Europe to accommodate trends toward larger agricultural holdings and greater mechanization has resulted in the wholesale destruction of hedgerows, and the habitat for abundant wildlife that they provide.

## Industrialization

The industrialization of Europe during the 19th and early 20th centuries was yet another source of significant environmental change. One of the key developments of the age was the industrial exploitation of the continent's major coalfields. The rapid and unrestrained development of these regions left in its immediate wake a whole series of grimly degraded landscapes covered with dirty industrial towns, slag heaps, poisoned rivers, and foul

FIGURE 4.17. Coalfield. The marble figure of a mourning woman overlooks the chalky edge of Vimy Ridge, where the Canadian Expeditionary Force fought a bitter and bloody battle in April 1917 to wrest the ridge from its German defenders. In the distance can be seen the pointed coal tailings that dot the coal-rich Artois Plain of northern France.

air, the most infamous example being the "Black Country" around Birmingham in the English Midlands, although the list can easily be extended to include the slag-heaped landscape of the Borinage (Sambre-Meuse Basin) in Belgium, the densely packed steel and chemical industries centered around the firm of Krupp in the Ruhr Basin, and the late 19th-century coal and steel industries of Upper Silesia and the Donets Basin.

Industrialization ushered in the building of extensive canal systems, the dredging and canalization of rivers, the development of a railroad net, the erection of cast iron and steel bridges and viaducts, and the blasting of tunnels to facilitate movement through mountain passes—all of which worked to alter the landscape and break the isolation, both economically and environmentally, of Europe's myriad natural regions. By 1888, it was possible to travel by rail from Paris to Constantinople on the Orient Express. Ease of transport stimulated the growth of industry beyond the coalfields and larger cities. New industrial zones emerged along railways and canals, and industrial landscapes penetrated into once bucolic agricultural areas.

This was also an age in which many cities expanded rapidly. Ports were expanded to carry increased trade, and large shipping canals such as the Manchester Ship Canal in Britain or the North Sea Canal in the Netherlands opened interior towns and cities to the movement of seaborne shipments of raw materials and goods. Early on the growth of cities largely took place within their already established boundaries. Open spaces were built over and the urban fabric became noticeably denser, packed in some areas with teeming industrial slums. By the latter half of the 19th century, however, this early centripetal phase was replaced by a tendency toward explosive outward expansion. Large cities began to sprawl, gobbling up enormous amounts of countryside in the process. As we shall see in Chapter 9, concern over the loss of agricultural land to low-density suburban sprawl was great enough by the middle decades of the 20th century to motivate, in some countries, the imposition of restrictions on urban expansion.

## CONTEMPORARY ENVIRONMENTAL PROBLEMS

Although environmental change has always accompanied human endeavor and has at times had long-term detrimental effects on the very people who effected the changes, Europeans today are faced with a wide range of new environmental problems. As everywhere on the planet, human indifference, along with our increased technological ability to alter and pollute the land, water, and skies on which we depend, seems to be responsible for far greater levels of environmental change than ever experienced before. Nearly everywhere in Europe the pace of environmental change has become uncomfortably fast.

### Eastern Europe

The most serious challenges seem to be concentrated in those parts of eastern and east-central Europe where, during the half-century that followed World War II, socialist regimes relentlessly pursued industrial development while doing next to nothing to protect the environment. The result has been a badly polluted environment, with landscapes literally resembling wastelands in some areas. Each new revelation to come out of these countries in recent years has seemed more shocking than the last. Ecosystems are deeply threatened everywhere and species extinctions are on the rise. Indeed, some east European countries have actually experienced a decline in human life expectancy, due to increased respiratory disease and other environmentally induced ailments.

A particularly telling example of the critical state of affairs in the East is the severe environmental contamination and public health hazards that were the legacy of massive Soviet era uranium mining and processing in the former East German borderland region south and west of the city of Chemnitz. A huge complex of mines and processing factories, employing as many as 150,000 people, was created in this densely populated region during the 1950s to supply the Soviet Union with weapons-grade uranium. The toxic legacy of this giant undertaking was a landscape of abandoned uranium mines, dilapidated yellow-cake factories, mountains of radioactive ash, and toxic waste dumps that have seriously contaminated soils and groundwater supplies with a deadly brew of arsenic, lead, iron, cadmium, sulfuric acid, low-level radioactive materials, and other poisons. All together an estimated 500 million tons of toxic wastes were spread over roughly 1,200 square kilometers. A number of lakes that were used as chemical dumps are so laced with harmful elements that they have been fenced off. Extraordinarily high levels of radon, a breakdown product of uranium, have affected thousands of dwellings situated on top of old underground mines. After the reunification of Germany in 1990, officials from the West were appalled at the scale of the disaster. An enormous effort had to be undertaken to cover the waste sites with millions of tons of fresh soil. Today the region looks green again, although the cleanup is far from complete. The estimated costs of the research and cleanup efforts necessary to restore the environment of this stricken region to even a reasonable level of environmental health have been staggering.

Unfortunately, this is not an isolated case. It is just one of a litany of environmental problems that many east-central and eastern European countries face. Recent appraisals now

suggest that Cesium 137 contamination from the 1986 nuclear disaster at Chernobyl covers much more of Ukraine, western Russia, and Belarus than was previously believed to be the case. Estimates suggest that as much as one-fifth of all farmland in Belarus may be unusable because of the disaster. Extensive strip mining for lignite coal has appallingly scarred the landscape of large parts of Poland, Bohemia, and the former East Germany. Strip mining for oil shale has done much the same in eastern Estonia. Romania is one of the world's "hot spots" for levels of cadmium and lead fallout. The country's Copsa Mica industrial region has been described as "an environmental disaster" that threatens the lives of its 200,000 inhabitants. Heavy industrial emissions and chemical dumping in the so-called dirty triangle that straddles the border regions between Poland, Slovakia, and the former East Germany have produced an array of pollution problems that rival those found anywhere in the world. Rates of respiratory disease, reproductive problems, and cancer among inhabitants of this region are far in excess of world norms.

Much of the damage strikes at the essential capacity to provide basic foodstuffs and clean drinking water. According to some reports, pollutants have rendered a quarter of Poland's soil unsuitable for growing food that can be safely eaten by people or livestock. Much of

FIGURE 4.18. Strip mining. These enormous slag heaps mark the site of the extensive oil shale mining that took place in eastern Estonia in the decades following World War II. In addition to the slag heaps, unsightly storage areas, decaying production facilities, and idle transport lines sprawl across the open countryside in this typically extensive Soviet era industrial development.

Poland's water is unfit even for industrial use. A 1989 study was able to classify a mere 4% of Polish rivers as possessing waters fit for human consumption. Biologically three-quarters were dead. Three-quarters of Bulgaria's agricultural lands have been classified as severely eroded, polluted, or destroyed. Only half of Russia's population has access to drinking water that meets recognized international safety standards. The waters backed up behind a flood control dam at the mouth of the Neva River at St. Petersburg are so contaminated by municipal and industrial wastes that the unhealthy character of the city's water supply has become internationally notorious. Some 80% of Romania's rivers are too contaminated to supply drinking water.

With western aid, the cleanup in the East has begun, but the task is Herculean. Most of the former socialist countries have by now developed plans to improve environmental conditions, although environmental quality legislation still lags behind western standards. The goal of joining the EU has been a strong stimulus in recent years to do much more, but the costs are enormous. Most eastern European countries simply lack the financial resources to tackle the problems, regardless of how ambitious their environmental cleanup and conservation programs may appear. It has been recently estimated that the cost of environmental cleanup to meet EU standards in Poland alone will be $300 billion.

Given the difficult environmental legacy of the socialist past, it is rather ironic that one of east-central Europe's most flourishing natural environments is the 1,400-kilometer-long stretch of territory that marks the no-man's land that once separated East and West Germany. For more than 40 years after World War II, the border zone was rendered inaccessible by thousands of kilometers of fencing. The strip of unoccupied land became a natural refuge for wildlife of all kinds. Known today as the "Green Band," and largely owned and watched over by a German conservationist group (Union for Environmental and Natural Protection in Germany), the former zone lives on as a protected environment for hundreds of species of birds and plants, many of which are officially endangered, as well as a reminder of the long postwar division of Germany and Europe between East and West.

## The Mediterranean

Some of the most striking environmental problems to be found outside of eastern Europe are in the Mediterranean Basin, where rates of population growth and economic development have accelerated very rapidly in recent years. There has been a general movement of population to coastal areas throughout the region. This general trend has been exacerbated by the phenomenal rise in recent decades of Mediterranean mass tourism, which adds as many as 140 million people to coastal populations every summer. Industrial and urban development, in particular, have steadily expanded all around the Mediterranean's shores since the end of World War II with scant attention, until relatively recently, to the dangers of dumping untreated sewage and industrial waste into the sea. It is estimated that as much as 70–85% of the sewage generated by the region's cities and towns is discharged into the sea untreated. This amounts to a staggering 600,000 tons a year by current estimates. Enormous amounts of nitrate and phosphorus fertilizers—perhaps four to eight times natural levels—also find their way into the sea, a by-product of efforts to modernize and intensify agriculture

**FIGURE 4.19. Dumping of wastes.** This truck is dumping garbage along a remote stretch of highway on the eastern side of the Peloponnese. From the looks of the refuse heaped below the highway's edge, dumping here is a common practice.

throughout the region. Added to this have been the effects of accidental oil spills and the now prohibited, but poorly monitored, practice of flushing the holds of oil tankers into the sea. Annual levels of oil pollution in the Mediterranean are substantial enough to account for one-fifth of the global total, making it one of the world's most oil-polluted seas.

High levels of pollution of all kinds, along with overfishing, have put tremendous strains on the Mediterranean marine environment. Because the sea lacks significant tides and has only one severely constrained outlet at Gibraltar, it lacks the ability to mix its waters efficiently or to exchange them very rapidly with the open sea. In fact, the waters of the Mediterranean change completely only once every 80 years. As a consequence, massive growths of algae blooms and periodic invasions of seaborne slicks of chemical pollutants have persistently plagued Mediterranean coastlines, as well as those of the neighboring Black Sea. The effects have been so bad that it has become fairly common for beaches in Italy and southern France to be closed on health grounds for periods of time in the summer.

Sources of pollution, or so-called black spots, abound in almost every country bordering the Mediterranean. One of the major sources of human waste and pollution in the eastern basin has been the dense urban agglomeration around Cairo, where the Nile is literally used as a huge open sewer. On Italy's west coast, illegal discharges of industrial waste and urban toxic waste from the industrialized area around Naples have helped to earn the entire Campagna region a reputation as the "rubbish tip of Italy." Industrial pollution problem areas also include Marseille and the Rhône delta, Gela on Sicily (center of the island's petrochemical industry), and Salonica and the Gulf of Thermaikos in Greece. The Adriatic has suffered enormously due to effluents that flow from the Po River, which drains the industrial heartland of northern Italy and flows through the area in which the region's highest density of intensive livestock breeding and highest levels of agricultural chemical use are found. Because of these effluents the Po delta and the coastal lagoons at the head of the Adriatic are in the slow process of dying in a morass of green algal scum, foul-smelling seaweed, and general ecological disequilibrium. The disappearance of oxygen in the water during the summer has almost completely eliminated fish and shellfish from the waters of the shallow Gulf of Trieste.

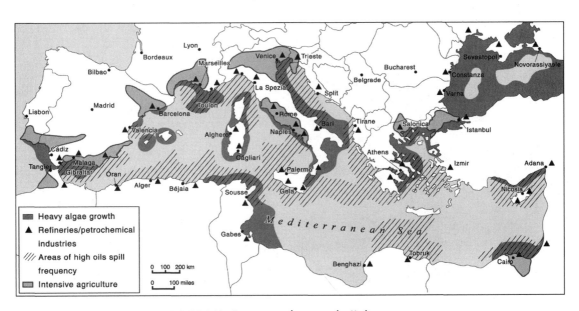

FIGURE 4.20. Environmental stress in the Mediterranean.

The city of Venice is in many ways an interesting example of many of these problems. Venice is situated in a lagoon at the head of the Adriatic. The city was developed on this site from the seventh century to provide its citizens with a safe haven from their enemies. Today, however, the city suffers from a number of severe environmental problems related to its unique location. A major threat is flooding. The city has been subjected to severe flooding with increasing frequency over the past 50 years. This is due to the fact that the three entrances to Venice's lagoon have been deepened for commercial purposes to the point where they can no longer protect the city from high tides and storm surges. The problem is exacerbated by subsidence caused by the pumping of water from aquifers beneath the city and by rising sea levels. St. Mark's Square, the focal attraction for the more than 2.8 million tourists who visit the city each year, is now flooded as often as 40–60 times a year, about 10 times as frequently as in the historic past.

Technical solutions are in the offing, such as the construction of immense mobile gates that would close off the lagoon's three entrances against tides and storm surges, but such solutions are controversial for a host of environmental and fiscal reasons, and no decision has been made to implement them. In addition to

**FIGURE 4.21. Flood.** Frequent flooding in Venice has become a serious environmental problem as rising waters take their toll on the foundations of buildings and monuments. Water damage is quite visible on the faces of these buildings.

forcing residents and tourists to traverse the city on raised wooden walkways in times of flooding, the higher water levels have begun to eat away at the soft brickwork of which most of the city's historic buildings are constructed, threatening the fabric of the historic city with rot and decay. To make matters worse, the city's nearly complete lack of a modern sewage collection and treatment system, along with the runoff from agricultural land, has turned the lagoon into a polluted lake. The lagoon fills each summer with decaying algae and has been increasingly unable to support aquatic life.

The degradation of the Adriatic environment also stems from postwar efforts in socialist Albania to rapidly industrialize a backward peasant economy with appalling disregard for environmental protection. The effort has resulted in the serious pollution of that country's more important riverine and estuarine areas. Waste from fertilizer, paper, and chemical plants, from urban settlements with no sewerage facilities, and from careless mining activity have rendered the coastal stretches of many rivers in central Albania organically dead. Serbia too has contributed to the release of untreated sewage into Adriatic coastal waters, especially along stretches of the coast subject to heavy tourist visitation, such as around Kotor.

While the strain has been severe, there has been significant international cooperation to arrest the deterioration of the Mediterranean marine environment. Much of the credit belongs to the Mediterranean Action Plan of the United Nations Environmental Program. The leaders of this effort have been successful since 1976 in persuading all of the Mediterranean countries including holdout Albania, which resisted signing on until 1990, to participate in a variety of programs to protect the Mediterranean from further pollution and to ensure the conservation of marine life. Under these programs, steps have been taken to prohibit polluting practices and begin to finance cleanup and protection efforts, such as the construction of urban sewage treatment plants. Primarily because of these actions, many of the catastrophic predictions for the environmental survival of the Mediterranean made back in the 1970s have fortunately not come to pass. Among the few remaining "pearls" of clear water in the Mediterranean, according to a recent World Wide Fund for Nature report, are the waters off the Spanish islands of Medas and Tabarca, the deep waters off Ustica near Sicily, and some coastal areas of the Ionian islands of western Greece and the southern coast of Turkey.

Changes in terrestrial environments around the rim of the Mediterranean are also marked. Ribbon developments of holiday complexes along the coast, especially in Spain, France, Italy, and Greece, have irrevocably altered vast stretches of what were once relatively unspoiled coastal environments. Spain's famous Costa del Sol has been caustically referred to as the "Costa Concreta" for the manner in which it has been completely built over with tourist accommodations. Intense coastal development of this kind has obliterated much of the Mediterranean coastal habitat from Portugal to Turkey for a variety of fauna. Particularly threatened are the species-rich wetland areas of southwestern Spain. According to one recent estimate, as much as 80% of the Mediterranean coastline is now "developed," most of it under only the laxest of building regulations.

The fast pace of development has also placed a heavy strain on renewable fresh water supplies, as aquifers have been drawn down in order to supply the needs of irrigated agriculture and proliferating urban areas, and as rivers have become more polluted. The Guadalquivir River of southwestern Spain now has the highest levels of nutrient pollution in all of Europe. Ground water withdrawals and existing and proposed water transfers from rivers and reservoirs in central Spain to irrigation districts in coastal areas have led to serious interregional conflicts, much exacerbated by a series of droughts in the 1980s and the 1990s and the contentious nature of Spanish regional politics. A combination of water shortages, sparse vegetative cover, soil degradation, and human activity has ultimately raised the specter of desertification for the semiarid regions of the Mediterranean countries. The southern and eastern parts of the Iberian Peninsula, Mediterranean France, the Italian Mezzogiorno, and almost the whole of Greece including the islands have been identified by authorities in recent years as seriously affected by widespread desertification.

## The Northern Seas

In northern Europe, similar stresses have affected the quality of marine environments. Dense population concentrations and high

FIGURE 4.22. Aegean coastal development. With roads already laid out, a new coastal development rises along the Peloponnese shore of the Aegean. In time, developments such as this threaten to eliminate much of what previously lay untouched.

levels of development flank the Baltic and North Seas, and, although waste discharge practices are more controlled in many of the surrounding countries than is the case for the Mediterranean, both seas absorb enormous quantities of pollutants. The fact that they are shallow and contain relatively modest volumes of water means that the pollution load in the northern seas is actually one of the heaviest in the world. Indeed, the North Sea has been found to contain measurable levels of every known source of contamination. The problem is made worse in the Baltic because the sea is virtually landlocked, and there is little chance of pollutants being carried off to other waters. The problem also seems to affect every part of these seas. Counterclockwise circulation patterns in both the North Sea and the Baltic tend to carry pollutants from the mouths of the large rivers of the North European Plain, where the majority of them first enter the marine environment, to less densely settled northern coastlines, where riverine discharges are more moderate.

A major problem in the Baltic has been the marked increase in nutrient levels since the 1970s. Today the Baltic receives an annual input of roughly 50,000 tons of phosphorus and over a million tons of nitrogen. The bulk comes from east-central Europe and is of agricultural origin, the largest source by far being the Vistula River, which accounts for two-thirds of the nitrogen that ends up in the Baltic each year. The rise in nutrient levels throughout the Baltic has led to advanced stages of a process known as eutrophication, through which the waters are choked by runaway production of algae and other vegetation. Rising nutrient concentrations and plankton production in surface waters have worked to greatly increase oxygen consumption in deeper parts of the Baltic. This condition exacerbates the oxygen deficiencies occurring quite naturally in the depths of the Baltic since the narrow Danish Straits provide only limited inputs of oxygen-bearing saline water from the open sea by way of the Kattegat. A sufficient supply of oxygen at these depths is extremely important to the survival of Baltic fish, such as the cod, which

reproduces in deep-water areas. Inadequate supplies of oxygen cause the eggs to die. Today, nearly 35% of the seabed of the Baltic is virtually lifeless, a condition that has generated considerable international concern. The Kattegat, which receives large quantities of nutrients from the Baltic and the German Bight, has also shown marked signs of advanced eutrophication.

One of the traditional bounties of the northern seas has been the annual harvest of fish. While fish stocks are affected by many factors, both natural and human, and have varied considerably over recorded history, many have been severely depleted in recent decades due to overexploitation. Norwegian and Icelandic herring have been particularly hard-hit. They were all but eradicated by overfishing in the 1960s and have only slowly shown signs of recovering. North Sea herring, at least, seem to have been saved from depletion by a ban imposed on fishing between 1977 and 1982, but new scientific reports published in the spring of 1996 suggest that the North Sea herring is again threatened by extinction due to excessive fishing. The European Commission has responded with plans to halve the fishing quota for herring in the North Sea and to introduce reductions in the quotas for the Skaggerak and Kattegat as well.

Overfishing in arctic waters off the coast of Norway, and especially in the Barents Sea, has been devastating. Stocks of cod in these waters have declined to only about one-fifth of what they were before World War II. The fishing of cod in these waters may now well have to be banned in order to allow the surviving adult cod adequate time to reproduce. Stocks of capelin, a fish upon which cod and many arctic fauna feed, were severely depleted in the mid-1980s when fishing fleets turned to them as a substitute for the disappearing cod. This caused a serious state of ecological imbalance in arctic waters, resulting in the tragic loss of tens of thousands of seals and whole colonies of birds in the Barents Sea region due to starvation. Only a complete suspension of capelin fishing at the end of the 1980s was able to restore the situation.

Less pressure has been exerted by the fishing industry on fish stocks in the Baltic. Indeed, the Baltic herring population has remained more or less stable. Here it has been the environmental disturbances mentioned above that have caused the most damage, particularly for the cod. While greater international cooperation and enforcement of negotiated fishing quotas seem to have largely stabilized the situation in the 1990s, the fact remains that fish populations in all the northern seas are far smaller than they have been at any time in recorded history. Experience has shown that recovery is seldom complete.

## Mountain and Upland Landscapes

Europe's mountain and highland landscapes have become increasingly threatened by a rising tide of mass tourism and economic development. The relative inaccessibility of many of these areas has been broken in recent decades by the construction of modern roads and highways. The opening of new communication links has been followed, in turn, by waves of tourist-related developments, such as luxury hotels and resorts, ski areas, amusement parks, and shopping centers, as well as the introduction of new industries and communities. The unfortunate consequence is that many formerly pristine mountain and upland areas have become sprawling scenes of congestion and noise during the high tourist seasons, with many harmful side effects in the form of pollution and environmental degradation.

Relatively unspoiled areas and endangered plants and animals are being protected. Although late in coming by American standards, a growing number of national parks have been established by European states to preserve these landscapes. The Parc National des Pyrénées Occidentales is a good example. This 100-kilometer-long reserve, established in 1968 along the Franco–Spanish border, was designed to protect at least part of the Pyrenees from the onslaught of tourism-related development. The park takes in some of the region's most spectacular cirques and valleys and provides sanctuary for many endangered

flora and fauna, including the Pyrenean brown bear, which now numbers no more than a dozen or so animals. Brown bears are also an endangered species in the Balkans. In Greece they are protected by a mountain reserve at Nymphaion, which contains a number of former "dancing bears" confiscated from their owners under a Greek law that outlaws the practice.

Switzerland has established a number of nature parks to protect threatened alpine plants and wildlife. Nature reserves and scenic areas in Scotland cover roughly 13 percent of the land area and are the last refuge for several threatened species native to the highlands of the British Isles. Numerous areas have been recently set aside as reserves in the Carpathians, often as cooperative efforts between countries such as Poland, Slovakia, and Romania. One example is Poland's Magurski Park, located on the mountainous Polish–Slovak border, which was founded in 1995 to protect extensive stretches of Carpathian beech forest and the wild lynx, wolf, bear, and boar populations that roam them. In northern Finland, as well as other Scandinavian countries, preserves and parklands have long been established to protect the traditional reindeer herding lands of the Sami (Lapps).

Also on the rise are efforts to subsidize and protect traditional cultural highland or mountain landscapes, such as the aesthetically pleasing mixture of forest and pasture often found in alpine areas. Austria, in particular, has received international attention for its recent experimentation with an idea that has come to be known as "ecotourism" or "green tourism." The object is to promote a form of tourism that strikes a careful balance between tourism-related development, so essential to the economic vitality of otherwise declining rural areas, and the need to protect both natural landscapes and the cultural landscapes that have resulted from centuries of traditional human land uses. The alpine landscape that attracts so many tourists to Austria is just such an environment—an aesthetically pleasing mixture of mountain forest, pasture, and village, which is every bit as much a cultural landscape as it is a natural one. The Austrians, who regard their alpine environments as a national treasure, have long promoted their perpetuation through agricultural subsidies to mountain farmers. The new ecotourism policies are an extension of these efforts. They encourage individual alpine villages and regions to take steps that ensure a gentle form of alpine tourism, mainly through the strict delimitation of spaces specifically designed to meet the recreational needs of visitors while setting apart and protecting the most fragile elements of the alpine environment.

## Atmospheric Pollution

Atmospheric pollution is a form of environmental stress that has become prevalent throughout Europe. While smoke and soot from manufacturing processes and from coal or wood burning for heat and cooking produced more than their share of foul-smelling and noxious air in towns and cities of a century ago, the problem has been magnified and redefined today as pollutants have become more complex and their source areas more widespread.

The major source area for airborne pollutants is the industrial heartland of northwestern Europe. Despite considerable efforts in recent decades to curb effluents, the high concentration of factories, power plants, refineries, and automobile traffic in this region still contributes much to air quality problems over Europe. Concentrations of heavy and highly polluting industry in many of the former socialist countries of east-central and eastern Europe are also major contributors. The problem is often exacerbated in many of the former socialist countries of east-central Europe where poor-quality high-sulfur lignite coals remain a primary source of energy for industrial plants and for the heating of buildings. Effluents are on the rise throughout the Mediterranean South, which has enjoyed high rates of economic development and growth in recent decades.

Concentrations of carbon dioxide and sulfur dioxide in the atmosphere are derived largely from the combustion of fossil fuels

FIGURE 4.23. Brown coal air pollution. The early autumn morning air over the city of Rostock in eastern Germany fills with smoke emitted by the burning of brown coal in homes and industries. This photo was taken during the early 1990s soon after German reunification and before Western pollution control technologies were introduced to reduce pollution over the cities of the former East Germany.

and are close reflections of modern industrial and transport activity. Both have increased rapidly over Europe since the end of the last century. Within the countries of the EU emissions of carbon dioxide have actually fallen slightly since 1990, but progress has been uneven. Some of the largest source countries in northwestern Europe, such as Germany, the United Kingdom, and France, have been able to reduce their emissions. Their success, however, has been largely nullified by substantial increases in other countries, particularly in the rapidly developing Mediterranean South. According to EU statistics the largest increases in carbon dioxide emissions over the period 1990–1995 occurred in Portugal (22.5%) and Spain (16.8%). Greece and Italy also posted substantial increases during the same period. The largest contribution to these increases came from electricity generation in thermal powered plants and road transport emissions. The problem of sulfur dioxide emissions, which is particularly strong in high-sulfur lignite burning areas of east-central Europe, continues largely unabated.

Prevailing westerly winds and the counterclockwise rotation of the cyclonic weather systems that move across northern Europe make atmospheric pollution a truly international problem. One consequence is that the environmental effects of air pollution often result from air contaminants that first enter the atmosphere over industrial areas in western and central Europe and are then transported east and north, and at times back west again, before returning to earth. Thus, for example, only 9% of the nitrogen oxide deposition that occurred in Denmark in 1994 could be directly attributed to Danish sources. For the same reasons, the high sulfur-content coals burned in the former socialist countries of east-central Europe have a particularly del-

eterious effect in downwind Belarus. Prevailing westerly winds similarly ensure that the noxious effects of burning oil shale in eastern Estonia are most noticeable across the Russian border in the St. Petersburg area. Cyclonic circulation patterns also have an effect as they spin air currents in a counterclockwise direction. Such patterns dictated that the first noted effect outside the Soviet Union of the disastrous nuclear accident at Chernobyl in April 1986 was the arrival of radioactive clouds over northern Sweden. Eventually it

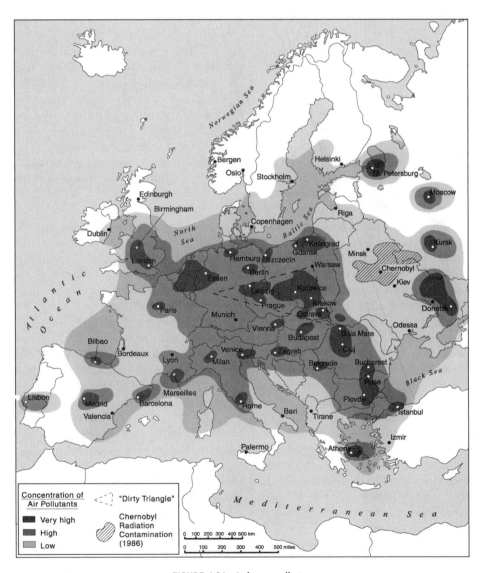

FIGURE 4.24. Airborne pollution.

was Poland that received the highest levels of contamination from the spiraling airborne cloud created by the Chernobyl accident.

One of the most notable large-scale effects of air pollution occurring in the 1990s was the high level of forest loss experienced all over Europe, but especially in east-central and eastern Europe, due to the dry deposition of sulfur dioxide and the wet deposition of both nitrogen oxide and sulfur dioxide in the form of acid rain. These pollutants tended to accelerate the acidification of soils, especially where soils and rock materials lacked the natural capacity to counteract the process, such as on the Fennoscandian Shield, in large areas of the Caledonian system, and on some Hercynian and Alpine formations. The problem of "forest death" first surfaced in the late 1960s in Scandinavia and Germany, but has come to affect forest cover over nearly the entire continent. According to estimates, slight to severe damage has been inflicted on trees across all of Europe. The hardest hit country was Poland, where an estimated 94.8% of all trees were affected. Other east-central and eastern European nations where the intensity of defoliation topped the 75% level include the Czech Republic (91.3%), Slovakia, Belarus, Lithuania, Latvia, and Ukraine. Most European countries experienced damage affecting at least 40–50% of the forest cover. Led by the Scandinavian countries, there has been considerable agreement among European countries in recent years to take steps to reduce significantly the amount of emissions responsible for acid rain.

At the more local scale, pollution in the urban environment is an ever-present fact of daily life for many Europeans despite efforts made by authorities to control or reduce it. As we noted above, programs to reduce concentrations of sulfur dioxide and nitrogen dioxide produced from the burning of fossil fuels have made strides since the 1960s, especially in the Scandinavian countries and in parts of western and west-central Europe. Nonetheless, local temperature inversions in winter can still bring these pollutants to serious levels over many cities.

But even where progress has been made in reducing the effects of these common pollutants on urban environments over the past couple of decades, gains have often been offset by heightened levels of lead, hydrocarbons, carbon monoxide, and nitrogen oxides released by an ever increasing number of motor vehicles. The growing adoption of lead-free fuels and catalytic converters in recent years is helping, but conditions in many traffic-congested European cities remain poor. Even cities like Madrid, which is situated high on the plateau of the Spanish Meseta, are more or less constantly blanketed today by a heavy brown haze. One of the most notorious cases is that of Athens, whose residents and visitors routinely endure the suffocating effects of *nefos*, the smog cloud that fills the city streets and darkens the sky. Authorities in Athens have been forced to restrict the flow of vehicles into the city during peak periods of air contamination. Oslo, which is particularly subject to temperature inversion, has recently attempted to reduce vehicular traffic in the city by installing a system of electronic tollgates on major roads leading into the city.

While the most serious effect of poor urban air quality is its considerable cost in human health, there has also been the problem of corrosion and crumbling that urban air pollutants visit on exposed surfaces of metal and stone. Façades of historic buildings and monuments that have stood for centuries have been literally eaten away in the span of a decade or two under the assault of modern urban pollutants. The most celebrated example of this is the shocking damage done to the Parthenon by the pollutants that blanket Athens.

The instances of contemporary environmental crisis are, of course, countless. There are in Europe few geographical areas or aspects of life that are not afflicted in some way. The diverse range of natural and humanized environments that so many Europeans take for granted, and often regard as a piece of their cultural identity, are changing today at a pace that is more rapid than ever experienced in the past.

## Environmental Awareness

Awareness of this fact is widespread and generally higher in Europe than in many other parts of the world. Evidence for this lies in the high visibility of environmental concern in public opinion polls and European politics, the degree of commitment to enlightened environmental policy exhibited by the European Union, national governments, and local governments, as well as the actions of a wide variety of popularly supported conservation organizations. Although the founding treaties of the European Community make no mention of environmental policy, an indication of a growing acceptance of a supranational approach to environmental problems is the fact that the 1992 Maastricht agreement committed all EU member countries to the pursuit of environmental policy initiatives that are endorsed by a simple majority vote. Loosely organized efforts at cross-national cooperation between environmental organizations sparked by such issues as the siting of nuclear plants or nuclear reprocessing plants near national borders or proposals for hydropower installations affecting whole river basins have become fairly common in recent years. They reflect a growing appreciation of the regional implications of many environmental issues.

On a more formal level, there has been a marked trend toward the internationalization of environmental decision making that parallels the recent general trend in Europe toward the internationalization of economic and political decisions. Important umbrella organizations headquartered in Brussels include the EEB (European Environmental Bureau), which represents more than 120 environmental groups from across the European Union countries; an organization known as CEAT (*Coordination Européenne des Amis de la Terre*), which generally represents the more conflict-oriented grassroots groups and pays greater attention to eastern European concerns; and such powerful international organizations as Greenpeace and the Worldwide Fund for Nature. An increasing recognition that environmental issues need urgent attention may be found throughout environmentally stressed east-central and eastern Europe. "Green" organizations have emerged as part of the political scene in many of the former socialist countries.

The international influence of Green politics is also visible in the deliberations of the European Parliament in Strasbourg. Since 1999 members of Parliament with ties to the Greens and various regionalist groups have formed a political group known as the Greens/European Free Alliance. This group, which in 2003 claimed 45 members from 12 countries, is the fourth-largest political action group in the European legislature (with about 7% of the 626-member body). Members of the group also hold key governmental posts in a

FIGURE 4.25. **Environmental awareness and politics in Germany.** A youthful "Green" demonstration gears up during the summer of 2001—somewhat incongruously beneath a L'Oréal cosmetic advertisement—in Bonn's central market square.

number of European states. In addition to supporting traditional environmentalist policies aimed at such things as sustainable development and the abandonment of nuclear energy, the group also advocates human rights, world peace, and the decentralization and democratization of decision making within the EU. In addition to representing various national Green parties, the group also fronts for the Green organizations of a number of "stateless nations," such as Andalucía, Catalonia, Flanders, Wallonia, and the Basque Country.

As in everything else, awareness and commitment are unevenly distributed. The highest levels of both are found in the Scandinavian countries and in Germany, Switzerland, and the Netherlands, followed by France, Italy, Austria, Spain, Belgium, Luxembourg, Ireland, the United Kingdom, and Portugal; significantly lower levels prevail in the Balkans and across much of east-central and eastern Europe. This ordering is reflective of the general environmental condition and of the degree of environmental protection that already prevails in each country. When it comes to the promulgation of international environmental policies, those that have achieved the greatest success seem to be most interested in lobbying for strong initiatives that will protect standards already in place at home. The greatest fear for these countries, now that the initiation of new environmental policies is becoming increasingly centralized within the bureaucratic apparatus of the European Union, is that weak regulatory decisions made in Brussels could undermine their own environmental standards. Those at the other end of the spectrum are often satisfied with relatively modest international standards, which are usually an improvement over what exists at home, and fearful of the potential economic costs of more aggressive environmental policies.

On the other hand, there are rapidly growing levels of concern in those countries that have traditionally been more complacent. A recent EU-sponsored survey measuring levels of concern shows that the most "very worried" answers came not from the high environmental standards countries such as

Sweden and Switzerland but from southern countries such as Greece, Italy, and Portugal (eastern countries were not surveyed). In other words, we are beginning to see a reversal in roles. Indeed, a 2003 referendum in highly environmentally conscious Switzerland surprised many observers when it turned back Green proposals to institute "car-free" Sundays four times a year, shut down the country's remaining nuclear plants (producing 37% of the country's electricity), and renew an existing moratorium on building new nuclear plants. The results of the referendum are hardly a significant erosion of otherwise staunch Swiss support for Green-minded policies, but they do suggest a growing reluctance to go beyond what has already been achieved.

Surveys show that the issues that concern Europeans most are the potentially catastrophic and dramatic, such as the dangers posed by nuclear power accidents, radioactive wastes, oil spills, and other industrial disasters. This is in large part the legacy of attention-grabbing events, like the 1986 nuclear disaster at Chernobyl or the 2002 sinking of the oil tanker *Prestige*, which broke in half in a storm off the Galician coast of Spain with more than 20 million gallons of crude aboard (threatening an environmental disaster twice

**FIGURE 4.26. Recycling.** Rows of various colored recycling bins like these are a ubiquitous street-side sight all across Europe and evidence of the degree to which the more mundane forms of environmentalism have become commonplace.

the size of the 1989 *Exxon Valdez* disaster off the coast of Alaska). Less concern is registered for environmental threats that have a long history of media exposure, such as air pollution and acid rain, or a more nebulous immediate threat, such as ozone depletion and the demise of tropical rain forests. As one might well expect, these issues are most hotly contested by the younger and generally most idealistic elements of the population, although environmentalism has been long enough on the European scene that it generally enjoys widespread support across all groups.

## FURTHER READING

Bode, W. K. H. (1994). *European gastronomy: The story of man's food and eating customs*. London: Hodder & Stoughton.

Bennett, C. F., Jr. (1975). Human influences on the ecosystems of Europe and the Mediterranean. In C. F. Bennett, Jr. (Ed.), *Man and the earth's ecosystems: An introduction to the geography of human modification of the earth* (pp. 121–144). New York: Wiley.

Carter, F. W., & Turnock, D. (Eds.). (1996). *Environmental problems in Eastern Europe*. London: Routledge.

Darby, H. C. (1956). The clearing of the woodland in Europe. In W. L. Thomas, Jr. (Ed.), *Man's role in changing the face of the earth* (pp. 183–216). Chicago: University of Chicago Press.

Evans, E. (1956). The ecology of peasant life in western Europe. In W. L. Thomas, Jr. (Ed.), *Man's role in changing the face of the earth* (pp. 217–239). Chicago: University of Chicago Press.

Grenon, M., & Batisse, M. (Eds.). (1989). *Futures for the Mediterranean basin: The Blue Plan*. Oxford, UK: Oxford University Press.

King, R., Proudfoot, L., & Smith, B. (Eds.). (1997). *The Mediterranean: Environment and society*. London: Arnold.

Lambert, A. M. (1985). *The making of the Dutch landscape: An historical geography of the Netherlands (2nd ed.)*. London: Seminar Press.

Marples, D. R. (1997). Legacy of Chernobyl in 1997: impact on Ukraine and Belarus. *Post-Soviet Geography and Economics, 38*, 163–170.

Mollat du Jourdin, M. (1993). *Europe and the sea*. Oxford, UK: Blackwell.

Olwig, K. (1984). *Nature's ideological landscape: A literary and geographic perspective on its development and preservation on Denmark's Jutland heath*. London: Allen & Unwin.

Plut, D. (2000). Environmental challenges of Europe: The state of environment and environmental trends in the EU (EU15) and the Accession Countries (AC10). *GeoJournal, 52*, 149–155.

Pyne, S. J. (1997). *Vestal fire: An environmental history, told through fire, of Europe and Europe's encounter with the world*. Seattle: University of Washington Press.

Saiko, T. A. (1998). Environmental challenges in the new democracies. In D. Pinder (Ed.), *The new Europe: Economy, society and environment* (pp. 381–476). Chichester, UK: Wiley.

Thirgood, J. V. (1981). *Man and the Mediterranean forest*. London: Academic.

Thorpe, I. J. (1996). *The origins of agriculture in Europe*. London: Routledge.

Tickle, A., & Welsh, I. (Eds.). (1998). *Environment and society in Eastern Europe*. London: Addison Wesley Longman.

Vogeler, I. (1996). State hegemony in transforming the rural landscapes of eastern Germany. *Annals of the Association of American Geographers, 86*, 432–458.

Warner, J. (1999). Poland: The environment in transition. *Geographical Journal, 165*, 209–221.

Zilhão, J. (1993). The spread of agro-pastoral economies across Mediterranean Europe. *Journal of Mediterranean Archaeology, 6*, 5–63.

Zohary, D. (1993). *Domestication of plants in the Old World: The origin and spread of cultivated plants in West Asia, Europe and the Nile Valley*. Oxford, UK: Clarendon.

# PART II

## Culture and Identity

# CHAPTER 5

# Language

The focus of the three chapters in this section is culture and identity. Who we are and where we belong are central questions that affect the lives of all people. These are issues that have always been important in Europe, given its tremendous cultural diversity and the fractious and often bloody history of past centuries. They are also of particular interest today, as more and more European states become or aspire to be members of the European Union. Thus, Europeans today must reconcile the meaning of embracing a newly imagined and shared European identity while continuing to grapple, as they always have, with the need to order their sense of place or rootedness at other scales.

In this chapter we begin our discussion of culture and identity by exploring the topic of language, before turning in subsequent chapters to religion and polity. We see language as an especially appropriate place to begin. Language, after all, underlies all communication. It is the principal conveyor of ideas and thoughts, our primary means of expressing what is familiar and intimate. As such it is a fundamental element of a person's identity and a badge of membership in a community. Language also has deep roots, going back to earliest times. In this sense, language can be thought of as more central to culture than perhaps any other trait. Language reflects the values and attitudes that lie at the core of hu-

man culture. Through the study of language and its development we can see evidence of the many links and borrowings among cultures and can gain a basic appreciation of many of the differences and the commonalities that Europeans share.

## THE STUDY OF EUROPEAN LANGUAGES

If we compare the vocabularies and grammatical structures of the 40-odd standard languages currently used by Europeans it becomes immediately clear that some are very much more similar to one another than they are to the rest. It does not take a trained linguist to recognize that Castilian (Spanish) is like Portuguese in many respects, as Danish is like Swedish, but that Spanish and Danish bear few resemblances to each other.

Why, we might wonder, would words having the same meaning in two different languages also have a similar form? There are three ways in which this could come about. One is simply by accident, but given the enormous number of combinations of possible consonant and vowel sounds available in any language this is highly unlikely. A second is that words have been borrowed from one language into another. As we shall see, this is a common occurrence, but loanwords are normally restricted to particular parts of a language's lexicon. Words are usually borrowed along with the objects or ideas they describe. This frequently, but not always, means that the elements involved were not present in the culture of the recipient language group. Thus, the very basic sectors of vocabulary, those relating to body parts and human relationships, for example, are seldom much affected by word borrowing. When there is considerable agreement in the fundamental vocabulary of two languages, the third possibility alone can be considered, namely, that the languages are related genetically, that is, they have descended from the same ancestral speech forms.

The idea that, as among human beings, there are genealogical relationships among languages was developed by linguists during the 19th century. When it became apparent that languages constantly undergo change, an analogy was quickly made with human evolution, the principles of which were outlined by Darwin in the middle of that century. Languages change largely because the societies that use them change, in their technology, in their mode of organization, and in their value systems. As two peoples speaking similar languages lose touch with each other, usually because of migration, their cultures diverge because their experiences are different, and, as a result, their speech forms drift apart. Thus, the distance between two related languages is in part a function of the amount of time they have been separated.

In the 1860s a German linguist, August Schleicher, expressed this by depicting related languages on a genealogical chart. All were seen as descending from a common parent (proto) language and being related to one another much as family members are (the tree-stem theory of language development). Today we recognize that this picture is simplistic. No "proto-languages" existed in the past, but rather groups of similar speech forms. While linguistic change is in part the result of simple separation in time and space, it is also due to innovations that have spread across space, affecting some members of the family more or less than others (the wave the-

ory of language development). Nonetheless, the impact of the 19th-century linguists has been so great that we still use their terminology (language families and subfamilies).

## THE INDO-EUROPEAN LANGUAGE FAMILY

By far the largest number of Europeans speak languages that belong to the *Indo-European* family. The other families represented in the region are the *Uralic* and the *Altaic*. One language isolate, Basque, whose genealogy is very much in dispute, completes the picture. What follows is first a presentation of the theories about the origins of these language groups and then a discussion of the emergence of the standards used in Europe today. An understanding of the relationships among languages is important both because people who speak closely related languages might be expected to see the world in a similar way and because, other things being equal, they are more likely to learn each other's languages and communicate with each other.

The Indo-European language family has received more intensive study than any other in the world. This is partly because it was the first family to be systematically researched by linguists (who spoke mainly Indo-European languages themselves) and the one in which the principles of historical linguistics were worked out. Interest in the history of these languages has also been heightened by the fact that they are spoken as mother tongues by nearly half the world's population and because they are closely associated with the European cultures that so greatly influenced the world after the Great Discoveries.

### The Origins of Indo-European Speech

Of particular concern to language historians has been the identification of the Indo-European homeland, the core region from which the languages spread. A related question is the timing of that diffusion. When did speakers of Indo-European tongues first settle in Europe? Based on the similarities among

**TABLE 5.1. The Languages of Europe, and Number of Speakers, by Region**

Northern Europe   28.1

| | | |
|---|---|---|
| *Indigenous languages* | 25.4 (90.4%) | |
| Indo-European | 19.4 | |
| Germanic | 18.0 | |
| North Germanic | 18.0 | |
| Swedish | | 8.3 |
| Danish | | 5.1 |
| Norwegian | | 4.3 |
| Icelandic | | 0.26 |
| Færoese | | 0.04 |
| Baltic | | 1.4 |
| Latvian | | 1.4 |
| Uralic | 6.0 | |
| Fenno-Ugric | 6.0 | |
| Fennic | 6.0 | |
| Finnish | | 5.0 |
| Estonian | | 0.95 |
| Saami | | 0.03 |

*Immigrant languages*   2.7 (9.6%)
(Russian, South Slavic, Arabic, Castilian, Iranian, Polish, Turkish)

Britain and Ireland   62.6

| | | |
|---|---|---|
| *Indigenous languages* | 61.6 (98.4%) | |
| Indo-European | 61.6 | |
| Germanic | 60.9 | |
| West Germanic | 60.9 | |
| English | | 60.9 |
| Celtic | 0.7 | |
| Brythonic | 0.7 | |
| Welsh | | 0.56 |
| Gaelic | | 0.14 |
| Irish Gaelic | | 0.06 |
| Scots-Gaelic | | 0.08 |

*Immigrant languages*   1.0 (1.6%)
(largely Indic languages)

Western Europe   84.8

| | | |
|---|---|---|
| *Indigenous languages* | 9.3 (93.5%) | |
| Indo-European | 79.2 | |
| Romanic | 56.0 | |
| French | | 54.0 |
| Occitan | | 1.6 |
| Corsican | | 0.17 |
| Catalan | | 0.21 |
| Germanic | 22.6 | |
| West Germanic | 22.6 | |
| Dutch | | 20.4 |
| German | | 0.2 |
| Alsatian | | 1.4 |
| Frisian | | 0.6 |
| Celtic | 0.6 | |
| Brythonic | 0.6 | |
| Breton | | 0.6 |
| Basque | 0.1 | |

*Immigrant languages*   5.5 (6.5%)
(Arabic, Portuguese, Italian, Turkish, Spanish)

West Central Europe   97.2

| | | |
|---|---|---|
| *Indigenous languages* | 91.1 (93.7%) | |
| Indo-European | 91.06 | |
| Germanic | 89.3 | |
| West Germanic | 89.3 | |
| German | | 89.3 |
| Romanic | 1.76 | |
| French | | 1.4 |
| Italian | | 0.32 |
| Rhaetian (Romansch) | | 0.04 |
| Slavic | 0.2 | |
| West Slavic | | 0.14 |
| Sorbian | | 0.14 |
| South Slavic | | 0.06 |
| Slovene | | 0.03 |
| Croatian | | 0.03 |
| Uralic | 0.04 | |
| Ugric | 0.03 | |
| Hungarian | | 0.04 |

*Immigrant languages*   6.1 (6.3%)
(Turkish, South Slavic, Italian, Kurdish, Greek, Polish, Spanish, Portuguese)

East Central Europe   79.0

| | | |
|---|---|---|
| *Indigenous languages* | 75.0 (100.0%) | |
| Indo-European | 64.2 | |
| Slavic | 60.2 | |
| West Slavic | 53.2 | |
| Polish | | 38.2 |
| Kashubian | | 0.2 |
| Czech | | 9.8 |
| Slovak | | 5.0 |
| South Slavic | 6.6 | |
| Slovenian | | 1.8 |
| Serbo-Croatian | | 4.8 |
| East Slavic | 0.4 | |
| Ukrainian | | 0.25 |
| Belorussian | | 0.15 |
| Baltic | 3.0 | |
| Lithuanian | | 3.0 |
| Germanic | 0.8 | |
| West Germanic | | 0.8 |
| German | | 0.8 |
| Indic | 0.2 | |
| Romany | | 0.2 |
| Uralic | 10.8 | |
| Fenno-Ugric | 10.8 | |
| Ugric | 10.8 | |
| Hungarian | | 10.8 |

*Immigrant languages*   0.0 (0.0%)

*(continued)*

137

TABLE 5.1. *(continued)*

| | | |
|---|---|---|
| Western Mediterranean | 107.1 | |
| *Indigenous languages* | 106.3 (99.3%) | |
| Indo-European | 105.7 | |
| Romanic | 105.0 | |
| Castilian | | 29.3 |
| Portuguese | | 9.9 |
| Catalan | | 6.7 |
| Galician | | 2.5 |
| Sardinian | | 1.5 |
| Italian | | 54.1 |
| Rhaetian (Friulian) | | 0.7 |
| French | | 0.3 |
| Germanic | 0.3 | |
| West Germanic | 0.3 | |
| German | | 0.3 |
| Slavic | 0.12 | |
| South Slavic | 0.12 | |
| Slovene | | 0.12 |
| Illyrian | 0.12 | |
| Albanian | | 0.12 |
| Hellenic | 0.04 | |
| Greek | | 0.04 |
| Indic | 0.11 | |
| Romany | | 0.11 |
| Basque | 0.62 | |
| *Immigrant languages* | 0.9 (0.7%) | |

| | | |
|---|---|---|
| Balkans | 65.0 | |
| *Indigenous languages* | 63.6 (97.4%) | |
| Indo-European | 60.46 | |
| Slavic | 20.7 | |
| South Slavic | 20.2 | |
| Serbo-Croatian | | 11.5 |
| Macedonian | | 1.7 |
| Bulgarian | | 7.0 |
| East Slavic | 0.5 | |
| Ukrainian | | 0.5 |
| Romanic | 23.4 | |
| Romanian | | 23.3 |
| Arumanian (Vlach) | | 0.1 |
| Germanic | 0.1 | |
| West Germanic | 0.1 | |
| German | | 0.1 |
| Hellenic | 10.1 | |
| Greek | | 10.1 |
| Illyrian | 5.4 | |
| Albanian | | 5.4 |
| Indic | 0.76 | |
| Romany | | 0.76 |
| Uralic | 2.0 | |
| Fenno-Ugric | 2.0 | |
| Ugric | 2.0 | |
| Hungarian | | 2.0 |
| Altaic | 1.14 | |
| Turkish | | 1.0 |
| Gagauz | | 0.14 |
| *Immigrant languages*<br>(largely Russian) | 1.4 (2.2%) | |

| | | |
|---|---|---|
| Eastern Europe | 208.3 | |
| *Indigenous languages* | 206.1 (98.9%) | |
| Indo-European | 192.0 | |
| Slavic | 190.3 | |
| East Slavic | 190.05 | |
| Russian | | 147.15 |
| Ukrainian | | 35.52 |
| Belorussian | | 7.38 |
| West Slavic | 0.09 | |
| Polish | | 0.09 |
| South Slavic | 0.16 | |
| Bulgarian | | 0.16 |
| Romanic | 0.45 | |
| Romanian | | 0.45 |
| Germanic | 0.35 | |
| West Germanic | 0.35 | |
| German | | 0.35 |
| Iranian | 0.37 | |
| Ossetian | | 0.37 |
| Indic | 0.13 | |
| Romany | | 0.13 |
| Armenian | 0.35 | |
| Uralic | 3.1 | |
| Fenno-Ugric | 3.06 | |
| Fennic | 2.9 | |
| Mordvin | | 0.74 |
| Mari | | 0.52 |
| Udmurt | | 0.50 |
| Komi | | 0.34 |
| Karelian | | 0.80 |
| Ugric | 0.16 | |
| Hungarian | | 0.16 |
| Samoyedic | 0.04 | |
| Altaic | 8.2 | |
| Turkic | 7.7 | |
| Tatar | | 4.7 |
| Chuvash | | 1.4 |
| Bashkir | | 1.0 |
| Yakut | | 0.4 |
| Tuva | | 0.2 |
| Mongol | 0.5 | |
| Buryat | | 0.35 |
| Kalmyk | | 0.15 |
| Caucasian | 2.8 | |
| Abkhazo-Adyghian | 0.5 | |
| Nakh (Chechen-Ingush) | 1.1 | |
| Dagestani | 1.2 | |
| *Immigrant languages*<br>(languages of the former Soviet Union) | 2.2 (1.1%) | |

*Note.* Data from Encyclopaedia Britannica Staff (1999).

modern members of the family, linguists are agreed that a set of common "proto-Indo-European" dialects could not date back over the many thousands of years that the archeological record tells us modern human beings (*Homo sapiens sapiens*) have lived in Europe. Rather, Indo-European speech at some point replaced the languages of earlier inhabitants of the region.

Two principal models have been advanced to explain how one language can replace another. In one, known as the *wave of advance* model, a larger and technologically superior population gradually absorbs another by very slowly encroaching on and occupying their territory, replacing the former languages with their own. No massive migrations are involved, only local ones at the frontier of the two cultures. The other paradigm, called the *elite dominance* model, also postulates a society with a superior technology but one with, in addition, a more sophisticated social, political, and military structure, which allows a relatively small group to dominate and impose their language on a larger one.

For some decades now the latter model has been in the ascendancy where the question of the origin and spread of Indo-European languages is concerned. Attention has focused on the steppe country to the north of the Black Sea where a pastoral nomadic culture has been identified by its particular type of burial mound (the kurgan) in the fourth millennium B.C. This culture can be shown to have expanded its territory over the next 1,500 years or so, something that has been linked to the domestication of the horse and the invention of wheeled chariots. There is some disagreement in the dating of all these events, but these *Kurgan* people have been claimed by many archaeologists to be an Indo-European elite who swept into Europe and wiped out almost all traces of pre-existing languages.

More recently doubts have been raised about this scenario. Some have protested that the social organization of these people at the time in question was not sufficiently advanced to allow them to accomplish these feats. It has also been pointed out that the density of population in Europe at the time was too high to permit such a wholesale linguistic replacement. A new theory stresses the *wave of advance* model and identifies the first Indo-Europeans with the Neolithic farmers who brought agriculture to Europe from Anatolia beginning about 7000 B.C. This theory has the advantage of not requiring long-distance migrations and the subjugation of large agricultural populations by small military elites. Rather, the pre-Indo-European populations are seen to be Mesolithic hunters and gatherers whose numbers were very much smaller and whose social organization was far simpler than those of the invading farmers. Here and there special circumstances may have promoted their survival into recorded history (i.e., the Etruscans in Italy and the Basques in the western Pyrenees), but the overwhelming numbers and technological superiority of the agriculturalists won the day for the Indo-Europeans.

This argument is predicated on the assumption that agriculture was introduced into Europe by people migrating from the Middle East and carrying their language with them, a point about which there is some disagreement. While a migration of farmers (demic diffusion) is supported by many, others insist

FIGURE 5.1. The origins of Indo-European speech. The Lions' Gate is one of three important entrances through the southern walls of the Hittite capital of Hattusas in central Anatolia, one of the most elaborately fortified cities in the ancient world. The now extinct Hittite language is known from texts that date back to the 17th century B.C. This is the earliest writing that has been found in any Indo-European language.

that it was the *idea* of plant and animal domestication, with its associated technology, that was diffused (cultural diffusion) and that there was little movement of people connected with it.

Although archeological evidence cannot help us much with this question, the science of genetics can. We have more information about the genetic profiles of modern European populations than we have of any other populations in the world. When analyzed these data show a remarkable pattern. There is a steady change in the genetic makeup of Europeans as one moves from the Balkans northwestward across the region to the North Sea. Exactly such a pattern would be expected if a Middle Eastern (Anatolian) farming population crossed into Europe, with successive generations migrating step by step ever farther from the homeland and absorbing ever increasing numbers of indigenous Mesolithics. Beyond this evidence, everything we know about hunting and gathering societies in more recent times suggests that such people strenuously resist the adoption of an agricultural economy, which requires a very different fund of knowledge and set of skills. Only prolonged contact with farming populations, involving intermarriage and cultural exchange, could bring about the wholesale abandonment of a foraging economy for an agrarian one.

The association of Indo-European peoples with the establishment of agriculture also makes the development of the distinctive subfamilies of the language group more understandable. The language of the Neolithic farmers must have undergone much change during the long, slow process of colonization. Regional differences would have arisen in part simply because of spatial separation and the diffusion of linguistic innovations from different centers, but also because of the incorporation of elements of the various Mesolithic languages encountered (substrata). Our task now is to examine the emergence of the six subfamilies whose homes are in Europe and the development within them of the standard languages spoken by modern Europeans.

## The Hellenic Subfamily

The first languages of Europe to achieve a written form belonged to the Hellenic subfamily. We can follow the history of the Greek language from as early as the 14th century B.C. In that century the Greeks developed a syllabary, a writing system in which symbols represent syllables rather than individual phonemes, as they do in an alphabet. This system, known to us as Linear B, was used largely in inscriptions during the height of the Mycenaean civilization that flourished from the 14th to the 12th centuries B.C. When this civilization was destroyed a Dark Age descended on the Greek peoples, and writing appears to have dropped out of use until the eighth century B.C. The new writing system was an alphabetic one, developed by the Greeks on the model of an alphabet used among Semitic peoples in the Middle East. One of the major innovations was the introduction of symbols for vowel sounds, which the Semitic alphabets lacked. This Greek invention has subsequently provided the model for virtually all alphabetic writing systems, including the Latin one.

The massive Greek literature, which comes down to us from the Archaic and classical periods (eighth to fourth centuries B.C.), is written in a variety of dialect forms, nearly all of them mutually intelligible. Inevitably, however, the prestige of Athenian literature and the political supremacy achieved by Athens meant that the language of this city and the region of Attica in which it was located rose to dominance. This was the Greek that was then imposed on much of the eastern Mediterranean by the conquests of Alexander the Great. From the fourth century B.C. to the sixth century A.D. this language, known as the *Koine* or Hellenistic Greek, reigned supreme in the cities of the east. Even after the region fell under the authority of the Roman Empire, Greek persisted as the everyday speech of urbanites, the language in which virtually all business and administration was conducted. Although remaining firmly rooted in the Attic dialect, the *Koine* absorbed many foreign elements, especially vocabulary from Latin.

After the fall of Rome and the Empire in the west, the center of Christian civilization shifted to Constantinople, the city that the emperor Constantine had founded on the site of the Greek colony of Byzantium. This city, which gradually reassumed its former name, remained the champion of eastern Christian civilization until its fall to the Turks in 1453. The *Koine* continued to be the official language and usual speech of the Empire, but a gulf began to develop between its written form and the way in which it was commonly spoken. The normal change that was taking place in the spoken language was decried by purists, called Atticists, as linguistic decadence. Under their influence the formal written language, Byzantine Greek, became characterized by a rather strict adherence to the Archaic forms of classical Greek. In this way a tradition of *diglossia* (from the Greek, meaning "two tongues") developed that, as we will see, resurfaced in the last century and has plagued the Greeks until quite recently.

With the fall of the city of Byzantium, the last of the Greek peoples passed under Turkish rule, and none would know independence again until 1830, when the first Kingdom of Greece emerged in the Peloponnese and the lands to the north of the Gulf of Corinth. The new state required a standard language in which to conduct its affairs, but little Greek had been written in the four centuries since the disappearance of the Empire. While the spoken language remained alive and well, inevitably considerable divergence in speech patterns had occurred, and the newly independent Greek state was presented with an array of dialects but no national language. It was at this point that the notion of *diglossia* was revived. While a standard spoken form (Demotic Greek) arose, based largely on the dialects of the Peloponnese, the national literary language, the *Katharevusa*, or "purified language," was modeled on classical Greek. The latter became the medium of law and administration, of education and publication, indeed of all official, public, and prestigious domains of social life. Even newspapers were published in a simplified version of the Katharevusa.

The result was, of course, that every Greek, in order to be literate, had to learn two languages. This was hardship enough, but another difficulty arose as Demotic Greek came to be identified with liberal, left-wing causes, while the Katharevusa was seen as symbolic of conservative, right-wing thinking. Following the fall of the military dictatorship, which had carried the nurturing of the Katharevusa to absurd levels, the decision was finally made to abandon the system of two languages. In 1976 a law was passed which proclaimed Demotic Greek, now known as Modern Greek, to be the single official language of the country. The change was not brought about without pain, however. Besides the difficulties of teaching and using the spoken standard as a written language, fears were widely voiced that the language was being vulgarized and impoverished. Today most of these obstacles have been overcome, but, as is the case with most small languages, there is apprehension about the future of the Greek vocabulary in light of the pervasive influence of the major international languages, especially English, but also French and German.

## The Romanic Subfamily

The second European language of which we have written evidence is Latin. The Latin language is a member of the Italic subfamily of Indo-European and was originally spoken by small groups of people living in the lower Tiber Valley near the present city of Rome. As these people grew more powerful they came to dominate the other peoples of the Italian peninsula, and their language supplanted the others of its group. With the expansion of Roman power beyond Italy, Latin was introduced as a second language in lands where quite different tongues were spoken. In most parts of the western Empire it ultimately came to replace these languages; in the east, however, it could not compete with the firmly established Greek language.

The Romanic languages of today, then, may be regarded as modern forms of Latin. The differences among them are the result of (1) the different speech forms upon which Latin

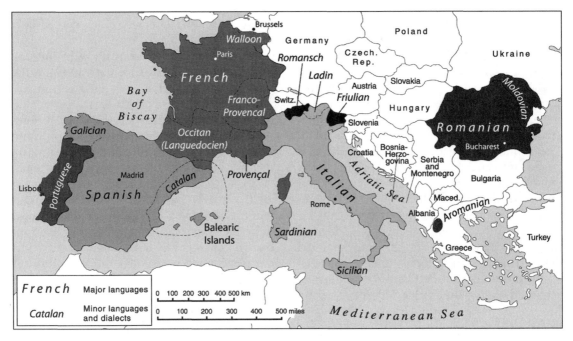

FIGURE 5.2. Romanic Europe.

was imposed (the *substrata*), (2) the different varieties of spoken Latin that were introduced (e.g., educated versus more popular speech patterns) and (3) the different languages that were superimposed on the Latin-speaking peoples by the (largely Germanic) invaders who brought about the fall of the Empire in the west (the *superstrata*). The diffusion of Latin speech is, then, an excellent example of the elite dominance model of language replacement.

Because we have Latin texts from the sixth century B.C., we know more about the history of the Romanic languages than we do about that of most of the other subfamilies. It must be emphasized, however, that these languages have descended from colloquial Latin, not from the classical written or oratorical forms of the language. Indeed it was probably not until the eighth or ninth century A.D. that people began to notice that the language they were speaking was different from that of the Classical texts. By the 12th century deliberate efforts were being made to write down the vernaculars, and from this time we must date the beginnings of standardization.

It is not easy to classify the Romanic languages, and linguists are divided on the question of what the relationships among them are. It is usual to make a first distinction between a western and an eastern group, the boundary passing across the Italian peninsula just to the north of Florence. The differences between these two groups of speech forms are usually explained by the persistence of Latin schools in the west, giving the language there a more correct character that contrasts with the rather popular speech of the east.

As for the modern standards, it is generally agreed that Italian stands closest to the original Latin and is the most central, that is, most easily intelligible to other Romanic speakers. It arose in the 13th and 14th centuries as the literary language of the city of Florence, the center of the Italian Renaissance. Its use by writers such as Dante and Boccaccio gave it great prestige. Subsequently this language has been greatly modified, borrowing heavily from classical Latin and, more recently, adopting features of the dialect of Rome, which became the national capital in 1870 following Italian unification.

Standing farthest from Latin and least intelligible to other speakers of Romanic languages is French, in great part because of the radically altered sound system. The standard is based on the speech of Paris, one of the so-called Francien dialects spoken in the Île de France. It is not entirely clear why linguistic change was so rapid and far-reaching in northern France, but clearly the Germanic language of the Franks, who organized the early state, played some role. Francien was not a prestigious literary language in the Middle Ages, taking a backseat to both the Norman French that was carried to the British Isles and to Picard. It was the Edict of Villers-Cotterêts in 1569 that firmly established Parisian Francien as the sole official language of the country.

During the 17th and 18th centuries the French grammar and vocabulary were strictly codified, producing a highly precise tool for communication but allowing for little individual deviation from the rules. The French revolutionaries who gained power at the close of the 18th century regarded as subversive the continued existence of dialects, patois, and regional languages. To rid France of multilingualism, the central authorities attempted to make the use of anything but the official form of French unacceptable, even shameful. Compulsory schooling was introduced in part to "Frenchify" the nation's children. Even the Catholic Church abandoned sermons and religious instruction in regional languages. By the late 19th century most French citizens could use the standard language. Some dialects were still preserved for use in the home, but this practice was strongly discouraged by the authorities.

Only since the 1990s has there been a movement to preserve or recover regional languages in France. A governmental decision in 1995, responding to a growing demand for teaching in regional languages, has made it possible for local authorities to organize instruction in the form of bilingual regional language courses. Seven regional languages are now taught in France—Basque, Breton, Catalan, Corsican, Creole, Gallo, and Occitan. Enrollments, however, are low.

The Ibero-Romanic languages, Spanish, Portuguese, and Catalan, owe their origins to the Reconquista, the reconquest of the Iberian Peninsula from the Muslims by the Christian kingdoms of the north. This "crusade" dominated the region's history during the Middle Ages, lasting from the 8th century to the end of the 15th. After the Moorish invasion in 711, Muslim authority was established everywhere in the peninsula except the far north. Arabic became the official language in this area and was adopted by many Latin speakers, some of whom also converted to Islam (*muwallads*). By the 14th century six varieties of colloquial Latin could be identified on the peninsula. Across the north from west to east the distinctive dialects were Galician, Asturo-Leonese, Castilian, Aragonese, and Catalan. In the Muslim lands a curious form of Latin was spoken by people who, although they had remained Christian, had nonetheless adopted the dress and customs of their Arab neighbors. They were called Mozarabs, from the Arabic word for "arabized," and we know the dialect they spoke as Mozarabic.

The reconquest of the western part of the peninsula was launched from both León and Galicia, but ultimately the latter took the upper hand, spreading Galician Latin to the south. In the east it was the Aragonese and the Catalans, politically unified in the 12th century, who led the crusade. In the center the initial base was León, but the Castilians soon took control, and it was their tongue, the most deviant of all the Ibero-Romanic speech forms, that was carried into central and southern Spain. As the Mozarabic population was absorbed into the expanding Christian kingdoms, a very large number of words that they had borrowed from Arabic passed into the languages of the north. These were primarily the names of things about which they had learned while living under Arab rule. They were terms dealing with administration and the organization of society, with commerce, agriculture, and industry, and with science and warfare. At the same time most of the map of Spain was renamed in Arabic (e.g., the river Guadalquivir—from the Arabic *wadi al kabir* [river the great one]).

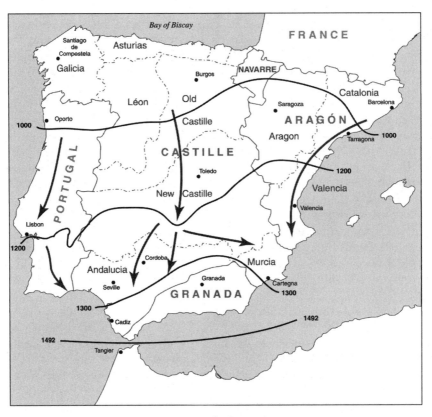

FIGURE 5.3. The *Reconquista*.

Castilian was standardized during the 16th and 17th centuries in Toledo. It became the official language of Castilian Spain, was exported in its Andalusian form to the New World and, after 1759, supplanted Catalan as the official language in the Aragonese part of the country. The rise of Portuguese out of the Galician dialect was the result of the reconquest of Lisbon in 1147 and the consequent establishment of an independent kingdom of Portugal. The language developed its own identity and standard form during the golden years of Portuguese expansion overseas, growing away from its parent Galician tongue (*Galego*), which sank to the status of a backwater dialect. Since the 18th century there has been a revival of interest in Galego, which, in spite of the invasion of Castilian forms, is still best viewed as a dialect of Portuguese. With the union of Aragon and Catalonia in 1137, Catalan became the official language of the new kingdom, though it lost

that position in the mid-18th century and suffered great discrimination from the end of the Spanish Civil War to the mid-1970s, a 40-year period during which the central government under Franco did everything it could to repress the regions, including the banning from public use of vernacular regional languages. Recognized by the new Spanish Constitution of 1978 as a language with the same status as Spanish, it is now the official language of the Autonomous Region of Catalonia and of the principality of Andorra.

Five minor Romanic languages are also spoken in western Europe. By far the largest is Occitan, still used by about 15 million people in the southern part of France. In the 12th century this language was the vehicle of a rich poetic literature and a flourishing culture, which was quite distinct from that of northern France. It was crushed, however, by the Papacy and the French Crown, who launched a crusade (1208–1229) against the Cathar heresy, which had gained wide popularity in the region. Nonetheless the standard language had sufficient prestige to survive into the 16th century. Thereafter it deteriorated into a group of local dialects and gradually retreated before standard French, especially after the Revolution. A literary revival in the mid-19th century led to the establishment of a modern standard based on the dialect of the Arles–Avignon region. Medieval Occitan was very close to Catalan, and until the crusade against the Cathars the two speech areas had close political and economic ties. Over the years, however, Occitan has grown nearer to French while Catalan has approached Castilian, and the classification of the two languages is now very much in question.

The language still spoken by most of the population living on the island of Sardinia is completely unintelligible to most Italians and is generally regarded as a separate language. As a written language for official matters, Catalan replaced Sardinian when the island came under Aragonese rule in 1322. Later Castilian and, more recently, Italian became the official languages. Today there is virtually no literature published in Sardinian, not even a newspaper, and the only "standard" is a normalized dialect form used in folk poetry.

The other three minor Romanic languages in the west are often grouped together under the rubric "Rhaetian." Two, Ladin and Friulian, are spoken in northeastern Italy, while the third, Romansch, is used in the eastern-most Swiss canton of Graubunden (Grissons). The former two have been heavily influenced by local Italian speech, and some scholars prefer to consider them members of the Venetian dialect group. Friulian is spoken by more than 700,000 people and has a vigorous local literature. Ladin has only about 20,000 speakers and is used as a language of instruction in the first two years of some elementary schools in various dialect forms. Since 1938 Romansch, though the mother tongue of fewer than 50,000 people, has been recognized as the fourth national language of Switzerland. It is used only in the cantonal government, but it supports five newspapers. There is no Romansch standard, but a lively local literature

is produced in several of the dialects. Unlike Ladin and Friulian, Romansch resembles French more than Italian.

Romanian is the only Romanic standard to be spoken in eastern Europe. Although the precise origins of the Romanians' linguistic ancestors are debated, they were clearly a non-Hellenized Balkan population (Illyrian, Thracian, or Dacian) who came under strong Roman influence when large numbers of imperial troops were stationed among them in an effort to more adequately fortify the north-eastern frontier. The language differs significantly from those of the Romanic west in that it retains many odd features of Latin grammar (though Portuguese does this as well) and in that its superstratum is not Germanic but rather Slavic. Indeed, Slavic loanwords abound in the vocabulary, as do, to a lesser degree, those from Hungarian and Turkish. The standard was developed in the 17th century and includes features from a number of dialects, though the Bucharest idiom now predominates. In the 19th century many foreign loanwords were replaced by borrowings from French in an effort to more thoroughly Romanize the language. Romanian is the official language today in both Romania and the newly independent state of Moldova. Historically the language has been written in the Cyrillic alphabet, as it still is in Moldova, but after the principalities of Wallachia and Moldavia were united in 1859 the Latin script was adopted for the new kingdom of Romania.

Two minor Romanic languages are also spoken in the Balkans. The Aromanian dialects, found in Greece, Albania, Yugoslavia, and Bulgaria, are related to Romanian but cannot be understood by speakers of that language. Literary texts have been published in dialect form since the 19th century. Many of the Jews expelled from Spain in 1492 found their way into the lands of the eastern Mediterranean. These "Sephardim" preserved the medieval Spanish they had spoken in their homeland, and many Balkan Jews use it today as a language of the home and of religion. The standard literary version is known as Ladino, but most speakers use forms that are considerably different and are better called Judeo-Spanish or Sephardi.

## The Celtic Subfamily

The ancient Greeks and their students, the Romans, were good geographers. They were keen observers of the world around them, and they have left many accounts of the peoples who inhabited the region they called Europe. Among these were tribes that, in Athenian times, lived in central Europe and spoke languages belonging to the Celtic subfamily of Indo-European. We can't be sure that all the peoples the Greeks called *Keltoi* and the Romans called *Galatae* spoke tongues ancestral to what we now understand as Celtic languages. The science of linguistics was not highly developed then. Probably most were, however, as the river names of their homeland (Rhine, Main, Tauber, etc.) reveal today. The material cultures of the Celts are well known to us today in the Bronze Age Urnfield and Iron Age Hallstatt and La Tène complexes.

The Celts were to fall on hard times, however. Many scholars feel that an abrupt change in climatic conditions bringing colder winters and cooler, wetter summers during the last half of the first millennium B.C. caused a massive outmigration of Germanic peoples from Scandinavia to the North European plain, displacing much of the Celtic population. Place names show that they migrated into eastern Europe (Galicia in Poland), to Anatolia (Galatia), and to Iberia (Galicia in Spain). By far the largest number, however, settled in France (Gaul) and in Britain and Ireland. In Gaul it was their fate to be conquered and Latinized by the Romans. In Britain some were Romanized, but most were driven into the western and northern highlands and some across the Channel to Brittany by the invading Germanic Anglo-Saxons. In Ireland the Celts remained undisturbed by foreign populations until the late Middle Ages.

Linguists distinguish between Continental Celtic, the languages of those peoples known to the classical writers as *Keltoi* (Greek) and *Galatae* (Roman), and Insular Celtic, which

was spoken in Britain and Ireland. The former was submerged by other languages, mainly Latin, but it may be traced in a few inscriptions, and vestiges of its vocabulary remain in some modern Romanic languages, especially French. Insular Celtic has given rise to the four Celtic languages that survive today, Irish and Scottish Gaelic, which belong to the Goidelic, or Gaelic branch, and Breton and Welsh, which constitute the Brythonic, or British, branch. All are spoken by small numbers of people today, and their survival over the long term is in question. In Britain and Ireland the Celtic tongues fell victim to the expansion of political domination from London, which promoted the use of the English language. Breton has suffered the same kind of competition from French, with the political ascendancy of the Paris region.

Of the four, Irish Gaelic (Erse) has the longest written tradition. It begins in the fourth century A.D. with the inscriptions on stone monuments carved in the ogham alphabetic script. There is no agreement about the origin of this writing system. Some scholars see a connection with the runic alphabet of the Germanic peoples; others would have it derived from the Latin alphabet. The latter appears with the conversion of the Irish to Christianity in the fifth century, and from this time the rich Irish oral tradition was put into writing. Viking activity in Ireland led to the adoption of some Scandinavian words, but the largest contribution of loanwords to the Irish vocabulary came from the Anglo-Normans. By the end of the Middle Ages a highly standardized literary norm was well established.

With the consolidation of English power in Ireland in the early 17th century, Irish became the language of an oppressed people. It was not taught in schools, nor was there an Irish-speaking upper class to support a literature. Children from Irish-speaking homes were even made to wear "tally sticks" around their necks in school, on which they received notches for every time they spoke Irish. The number of notches determined the severity of their punishment at the end of the day. After the famine of the mid-19th century, which hit the Irish-speaking west especially hard, the

FIGURE 5.4. Celtic and Germanic Europe.

portion of Ireland's population using Irish as a mother tongue declined to less than a quarter and became most prominently lodged in the remote western fringes of the island (the *Gaeltacht*).

Until just recently, the number of native speakers has continued to drop despite attempts at revival, the introduction of a new written standard since 1945, and the establishment of Irish as the country's first official language and as a compulsory language in all schools. The recent turnaround is due to the fact that the language has become fashionable. A new interest in Irish culture and language, helped along in part by the popularity of Irish rock groups and musicians who have begun to sing the language, has made spoken Irish trendy today among young people.

Irish settlers carried the Gaelic language to Scotland in the early sixth century. Although the Irish literary norm was used in Scotland,

the spoken language began to diverge significantly from Irish usage, both because it absorbed features of the British Celtic languages that had been spoken there previously and because, like colonial languages everywhere, it preserved some archaic forms that were lost in the home country. By the 15th century the two languages were no longer mutually comprehensible, and it is at this time that a separate Scottish written standard began to emerge.

The language was always at a disadvantage, however, because Scottish national culture developed in the Lowlands where a dialect of English called Lallans was spoken. This language became the vehicle of Scottish culture, not Gaelic, which was largely relegated to a peripheral position in the Highlands. On the other hand, Scottish Gaels became more literate than their Irish cousins because, as Protestants, they read the Bible in their native language and used the vernacular in religious services. Still, unlike Irish, Scots Gaelic has no official position in its country, and the recent literary revival finds its adherents not among the native speakers of the Highlands and Islands, but among their cousins who have moved to Edinburgh and Glasgow.

In contrast to Gaelic, British Celtic was heavily Romanized, and Latin continued to enjoy high prestige even after the withdrawal of the Roman legions in 410 A.D. It was Irish monks who, in the ninth century, introduced the custom of writing down the vernacular. A written standard began to develop in the 14th century and was fixed by the translation of the Bible into Welsh in 1588. The political union with England in 1536, however, proved a disaster for the language in that it was deprived of its official status in the country. By the 18th century, although the vast majority of the Welsh people spoke their native tongue, almost none was literate in it. The language was saved by the Methodist revival, embraced widely in Wales, which encouraged the laity to read the Bible and other religious literature in Welsh, and established schools that greatly raised the level of literacy in the language. The literary norm, however, differed greatly from the spoken forms in daily use and was rarely heard outside the church, chapel, or lecture hall. In recent years, though, there has been a great improvement in the official status of Welsh. It is used as a language of instruction, may be heard on radio and television, and appears in magazines and newspapers. Of all the Celtic standards it has the most secure future.

Just as the Gaelic form of Celtic was carried to Scotland from Ireland, so the British form was borne to Brittany (little Britain) from Cornwall. Thus, Breton has close affinities with Welsh and with the now extinct Cornish language. One popular theory has been that the language was carried across the English Channel by large numbers of emigrants from Cornwall in the fifth and sixth centuries A.D. who displaced the native Gauls and their Continental Celtic speech. This mass migration is seen as resulting from pressure exerted by the Anglo-Saxon invaders of Britain. An-other theory, more recently advanced, holds that the local (Gallic) idiom may merely have undergone a fundamental change as the result of strong cultural influences emanating from Britain, with relatively few migrants being involved.

Breton is the last among the extant Celtic languages to be standardized. Not until 1920 was this task undertaken, and it resulted in the adoption of two norms, each based on one of the two major dialectal groupings. This long delay is largely the result of French linguistic policy, which has aggressively discouraged the daily use of any language other than standard French. Today, a small group of educated people, known as the Diwan ("the sprouting of the seed" in Breton) Association, promotes the preservation of the language through the establishment of bilingual courses in local schools. Interest, however, remains slight. The majority of Bretons are literate only in French.

## The Germanic Subfamily

We noted earlier that the Celts appear to have been displaced from their homeland in west-central Europe about the middle of the first millennium B.C. by Germanic tribes coming from the north. The Germanic subfamily of Indo-European languages probably originated in the southern part of Scandinavia and the lands along the south coasts of the North and Baltic Seas.

Using both linguistic and archeological evidence, five fairly distinct dialect groups may be discerned by the third century B.C. The north Germanic peoples occupied the southern part of the Scandinavian peninsula. They subsequently spread westward across the Danish islands and Jutland, and their linguistic descendants today are the Scandinavians and the Icelanders. The North Sea Germans also moved to the west, many settling in Britain, where they displaced a Romano-Celtic population. These peoples spoke tongues ancestral to modern English and Frisian. Two other groups, one living between the Rhine and Weser Rivers and the second located in the valley of the Elbe, spread southward, occupying a large territory from the North European Plain into the Alps and even beyond. Their heritage is the large family of Netherlandic-German speech forms heard today from the Netherlands to Austria and still in some areas farther east. The east Germanic peoples crossed the Baltic from their early homeland in southern Scandinavia, settled briefly in the lower Vistula valley, then moved to the shores of the Black Sea and gradually infiltrated the crumbling Roman Empire. Here they adopted Latin speech, their Germanic tongues preserved only as superstrata in some of the Romanic languages.

Until the end of the Viking Age (ca. 1050) the dialects of North Germanic were relatively similar, and people from widely separated areas in Scandinavia probably had little difficulty understanding one another. By the end of this period, however, it is possible to discern the beginnings of a distinction between West Norse speech patterns, used in Norway west of the mountain divide, in the Færoes and in Iceland, and East Norse forms used in eastern Norway, Sweden, and Denmark. This split deepened in the Late Middle Ages, when one can differentiate between a deeply conservative Insular Norse spoken in the Atlantic and a much more innovative Continental Norse (or Scandinavian) used on the mainland. The final contrast developed within Scandinavian speech during the High Middle Ages as basic changes in the Danish sound system caused the spoken Danish language to move away from that of Norway and Sweden.

The four modern Scandinavian standards—Danish, Swedish, and two Norwegian forms—are largely the result of political events in the region. Scandinavians can read each other's languages without much difficulty; and, except between Danes and the others, conversation presents few problems given good will on both sides. If Scandinavian political history had been more like that of Germany, where multitudes of independent states were unified only in the 19th century, there might be a single Scandinavian standard today. The rise of separate Danish and Swedish languages is a consequence of the establishment of two independent states in the early 16th century just before the victory of the Reformation, which demanded access by all to the religious literature in the vernacular.

In Norway the situation was more complicated. Under Danish rule since the 14th century, Norway was declared an integral part of Denmark in 1536, and Danish became the language of church and state. In Oslo (renamed Christiania), the administrative center, a kind of Danish came to be used as the spoken language, but it was pronounced using native Norwegian sounds and included a number of words and constructions that were native. By the early 19th century, when Norway won its independence from Denmark and passed into a crown union with Sweden, the spoken standard was a kind of hybrid "Dano-Norwegian." As a written language this standard came to be known as *riksmål* or *bokmål*, the national or literary language. This was unacceptable to many nationalists who were pressing hard for an independent Norwegian identity and proclaimed that the national language should be untainted by Danicisms. Accordingly, an effort was made to collect words and grammatical forms from the rural dialects of western Norway, which, it was thought, preserved elements of the medieval Norwegian language that had been obliterated by centuries of Danish rule. The result was a constructed language that was first called *landmål*, the language of the country, but later came to be known as "New Norwegian" (*nynorsk*). For some time these two Norwegian standards did battle, *bokmål* with its supporters in Oslo and the east country, *nynorsk* strong in Bergen and the west country. Efforts to bring the two together have as yet yielded no definite results, but *bokmål*, the dominant language and the one taught as a foreign language abroad, has become less Danish in the process.

Like Norway, both Iceland and the Færoes came under Danish control in the 14th century. As in Norway Danish was also introduced as the language of secular and ecclesiastical administration. However, in Iceland, although Danish became a required subject in the schools, it never replaced the native idiom as the standard written or spoken language. Of all the medieval vernacular literatures of Europe, the Icelandic is by far the richest. Unlike medieval Norwegian, it was far too well established, and too different, to be ousted by a Scandinavian tongue. Modern Icelandic preserves Old Norse grammar almost intact, and an Icelandic schoolchild today can read the old sagas with minimal help. In equipping the language for modern use Icelandic linguists have eschewed international terms such as "telephone," substituting native constructions instead, for example, *talsími* (talking wire).

No literary tradition developed in the Færoe Islands during the Middle Ages, and Danish made stronger inroads into society there. When a standard was developed in the middle of the 19th century many Danish loanwords were retained. Nonetheless, the choice of an orthography close to that of Icelandic emphasizes its close relationship to that language, and Færoese is equally difficult for a Scandinavian to learn. Since the establishment of home rule for the Færoes in 1948 the language is the principal one used for instruction in the schools.

The Germanic speakers who first settled in the valleys of the Rhine, Weser, and Elbe and then moved south gave rise to the myriad speech forms sometimes called Continental West Germanic. Significant differentiation within this speech area began in the sixth century when a series of sound shifts occurred in the south and then spread north, some reaching farther than others. The result was the establishment of four main dialect regions: a southern one in which a much altered Upper German prevailed, a northern one where a little-changed Low German speech was heard and, in between, a West Middle German region in the middle Rhine–Main valleys and an East Middle German region in Upper Saxony where some sound shifts had occurred but not others.

The growth of trade in the Middle Ages under the hegemony of the Hanseatic League promoted an early standard based on the Low German of the south Baltic coast where Lübeck was the leading city and other towns such as Rostock and Stralsund were prominent members. This language never reached maturity, however, because by the 17th century the Hansa had been outcompeted in the Baltic by the English and Dutch and was in rapid decline. Instead it was Noord Holland, with its mercantile center of Amsterdam, which rose to prominence, spawning a Low German standard, which has come down to us as Netherlandic (*Algemeen Beschaafd Nederlands*). This serves today as the official language of the Netherlands and of the Flemish (Netherlandic-speaking) parts of Belgium.

Standard written German (Hochdeutsch) is based on the language that Martin Luther used in his translation of the Bible (1522–1534). Luther was a theologian at the University of Wittenberg and a favorite of the Duke of Saxony. The language he employed in his translation was that current at the Duke's court, a form of East Middle German. Because of the great popularity of Luther's Bible in the Protestant German lands, printers preferred to use this idiom in other works as well in order to reach the widest possible audience, and over the years it has developed into a quite uniform standard used across all of German-speaking Europe. In contrast to France, local dialects are alive and well in the German-speaking lands, and even the spoken standard (*Hochsprache*) may be heard with quite variable accents, although the Low German sounds of the Hanoverian dialect are preferred. In many urban areas a more colloquial German (*Umgangssprache*) is used.

Three distinctive dialects have attained the position of spoken standards in communities outside of Germany. Luxembourgish (Lëtzebuergisch) and Alsatian, the latter spoken in France, are both West Middle German dialects. Swiss German (Svitzertütsch), an upper German variety, is the majority language in Switzerland.

The language of the Ashkenazi Jews, Yiddish, developed out of a variant of West Middle German during the Middle Ages when many Jews lived in the valleys of the Rhine and Main and were active in commerce, banking, and money lending. Its vocabulary has, however, been strongly influenced by the Jewish ritual language, Hebrew, and by Slavic languages after the massive migrations of Jews from Germany into eastern Europe brought about by the persecutions that followed the Black Death. This history has yielded the basic dialectal division between Western Yiddish, spoken largely within the German language area, and Eastern Yiddish, which developed in the Slavic-speaking region. The early literary tradition had a strong Germanic bias, but the modern standard has a distinctly Eastern Yiddish base.

The Germanic dialects carried to Britain in the fifth and sixth centuries A.D. were mainly of the North Sea variety, though other elements were certainly present. The various linguistic communities settled in different parts of the island, and by the eighth century four distinct dialect areas may be identified: Northumbria in the north, Mercia in the center and east, Kent in the southeast, and Wessex (kingdom of the West Saxons) in the southwest. Although Northumbria took the early lead in literary activity, this advantage was lost with the Viking attacks and subsequent Norse settlement in the north and east. Cultural leadership passed to Wessex, and it was in Winchester, the center of King Alfred's realm in the late ninth century, that the great works of the Old English period were written. This Old English "standard" was thoroughly West Germanic in grammar and vocabulary and is more easily read today by German than by English students.

Norse settlement in the eastern portions of Britain did much to change the English language. How many Scandinavians actually colonized the Danelaw, as their territory north of the Thames came to be called, is a matter of dispute, but because the Norse and English dialects were still rather close, words could easily pass from one to the other without the presence of very large numbers of immigrants. The borrowings from North Germanic during this period are therefore impressive. Nouns as common as *egg*, *husband*, *knife*, *law*, *root*, *sky*, and *window*, verbs such as *call*, *die*, *drown*, *rid*, *thrive*, and *want* and even the personal pronouns *they*, *their*, and *them* are all Scandinavian contributions to the English language. In many cases the original West

Germanic word was lost, but in others it was retained in a somewhat different meaning. Thus the word for "to die" (modern German *sterben*) was preserved but came to mean to die in a particular way, that is, "to starve."

Hard on the Scandinavian invasions came that of the Normans, themselves originally Norsemen but by 1066 thoroughly Latinized. Norman settlement did not involve large numbers of colonists but rather was largely restricted to the nobility, to whom the new Norman monarch granted most of the estates in the land. Norman French thus became the language of the elite, while English remained the speech of the common people. For several centuries England was a bilingual country, and many people of all classes learned to use both languages. Inevitably the two forms of speech began to influence each other, and by the 14th century English contained a very large number of French words, especially in the areas of government, law, military life, fashions, food, and hunting—in short, the realm of the elite. Some scholars have suggested that up to 75% of the original Germanic vocabulary may have been lost. Where it was retained, however, the addition of French and Scandinavian words has given English a richness of vocabulary that few other languages can match. Thus, an English speaker can "wish" for something (West Germanic), "want" it (North Germanic), or "desire" it (French).

Gradually the ties between the Norman nobility and their compatriots across the channel weakened, and the long series of wars between 1337 and 1453 caused much enmity between the English and French courts. In 1362 the Statute of Pleading was passed, directing that all court proceedings thereafter be conducted only in English. A standard written form of English now began to evolve out of the dialects in the East Midlands. The prestige of these speech forms rested on the fact that London had been established as the clear capital of the kingdom and Oxford and Cambridge were leading centers of scholarship. In the 1390s Chaucer used this new Middle English to write Canterbury Tales, as did Wycliffe in his late 14th-century translation of the Bible. This is the language, vastly different from the Old English of Wessex, that has evolved into the modern English standard.

Spoken English varies enormously across Britain and Ireland. Since the late 19th century, speaking properly has meant using the Received Pronunciation (RP). Fostered by the public (read "private") schools, it was the traditional voice of the British Broadcasting Corporation and is based on the educated speech of the southeastern part of England. Still, estimates today place the number of RP users at just 3% of the population. Regional and class accents are alive and well, and the English still judge others very largely on the way they speak. As Henry Higgins put it in George Bernard Shaw's *Pygmalion*, "The moment an Englishman opens his mouth, another Englishman despises him."

Besides accents, however, true dialects have survived. One that has also attained a written form is Lowland Scottish (Lallans), the speech of most Scots and the vehicle of Scottish culture. It not only has sounds that are strikingly different from those of the RP, but it also preserves many more loanwords from Scandinavian as well as quite a number from Scottish Gaelic. The dialects of Northern Ireland are transitional between Lallans and Southern Irish. The latter has also achieved the status of a literary language and bears the strong imprint of Irish Gaelic in some of its grammatical structures. English was, of course, also imposed on the British Celts. Spoken Welsh English is also highly distinctive, but its impact on the written language has been less than in the case of Lallans or Southern Irish.

The closest relative of English, Frisian, has, of course, been far less successful than its big brother. Once spoken all along the southern littoral of the North Sea, it is now confined to the Dutch province of Friesland (West Friesian) and a few isolated districts in Germany (North and East Friesian). A literary language from the 11th to the 16th centuries, Friesian then ceased to be written until the 19th-century Romantic Movement caused a revival of interest in the regional culture.

By then the acceptance of Netherlandic and Hochdeutsch as the standards of the Friesian communities was too far advanced to be reversed, however, and although a standard form of West Frisian exists today it is little used.

## The Balto-Slavonic Subfamily

The Baltic and Slavic languages share many features, including quite archaic ones, suggesting that their speakers have been in close contact over a very long period of time. In the second millennium B.C. the Balts inhabited a relatively large territory north of the Pripet River, while the Slavs lived in a rather more compact area to the south. As they moved north to the coast of the Baltic Sea and east to the upper Dnepr, the Baltic peoples spread themselves thinly on the ground, favoring the early development of very different dialects. The Slavs, on the other hand, remained linguistically quite unified for a long time after the Balts began to disperse.

Slavic pressure from the south and east and the advance of German settlement from the west resulted in many Balts losing their language and culture. The westernmost of the thinly spread Balts, who spoke a language known as Old Prussian, were overwhelmed in the late Middle Ages by eastward-moving Germans. By the early 18th century only the Lithuanians and the Latvians remained. In neither case had a standard language arisen, although there had been literary forms since the 16th century. The medieval Grand Duchy of Lithuania had employed Polish, Latin, and Belorussian as official languages, while the Latvians had been under the rule of German landlords since the 13th century. Modern official standards for both languages were only developed after World War I in conjunction with the postwar establishment of the independent states of Lithuania and Latvia. Lithuanian preserves many archaic features, giving it special importance in the study of comparative Indo-European linguistics.

Of all the European tongues, the Slavic have been the last to undergo divergence. Unlike the Balts, the Slavic peoples remained

FIGURE 5.5.  Balto-Slavonic Europe.

in place for a considerable time, and did not begin to divide until roughly 200 A.D. This means that some form of Proto-Slavic speech was common to all groups at a relatively late date. Individual languages probably did not emerge until as late as the 10th century. Although the standards are distinctive, they are almost all linked by transitional dialects that grade imperceptibly into each other, as in the Romanic and Netherlandic-German worlds.

Divergence occurred as Slavic peoples began to wander outward from their original homeland south of the Pripet Marshes. Three major groups emerged from these wander-

**FIGURE 5.6. The politics of language.** For Baltic Europe, independence from Soviet rule has meant that Russian has ceased to be an official language. All citizens, including ethnic Russians still living in Latvia, must now conduct their business in Latvian. On this road sign outside the city of Riga in Latvia, the Russian place names have been painted over, leaving only the Latvian place names to guide travelers to their destinations.

ings: an eastern group, which spread out over the eastern portions of the North European Plain and eventually gave rise to the Russian, Belorussian, and Ukrainian languages; a southern group that wandered across the Carpathians and Danube into the Balkans, recognizable today as speakers of Slovenian, Serbo-Croatian, Macedonian, and Bulgarian; and a western group that initially stayed home but then moved west into areas vacated by Germans and Balts. The western group eventually spread as far west as the Elbe, but was later driven back again during the late Middle Ages by the eastward expansion of Germans. From this group derive the modern West Slavic languages of Polish, Czech, and Slovak.

The greatest linguistic differences are between the South Slavic languages, on the one hand, and the West and East Slavic ones, on the other. Here a wedge was driven through Slavic territory by the advance of the Germans into Bavaria and Austria, by the sudden appearance of the Uralic-speaking Hungarians (Magyars) in the middle Danube plain in the 10th century, and by the expansion of the

Romanians to the east. Even so, there are palpable similarities between Slovenian dialects and those spoken in the Czech Republic and Slovakia.

The location of the Slavic peoples on the boundary between the Byzantine and Roman Christian worlds has had a profound impact of the development of their written languages. In an effort to counteract the influence of the Western Christian Church, the Orthodox brothers Cyril and Methodius were invited as missionaries into the state of Great Moravia (modern Czech Republic) in the ninth century. They developed a form of written Slavic that came to be called Church Slavonic and was written in an alphabet that, in a variety of forms, is known today as Cyrillic. Church Slavonic was adapted to local speech patterns, which were still very close, and was used throughout the Slavic world. After the Schism between Eastern and Western Christianity and the beginning of the Crusades in the 11th century, Church Slavonic fell out of use in almost all Slavic lands that had come under the sway of the Catholic Church, and was replaced in the liturgy by Latin. This marks the beginning of a vernacular literature in Czech, Polish, Slovene, and Croatian, which, with strong western influences, have developed into modern standards written in the Latin alphabet. In the Orthodox lands the continued use of Church Slavonic as the liturgical language hampered the formulation of a vernacular standard, as did the long period of Turkish rule in the Balkans. A standard form of Russian, Ukrainian, Bulgarian, and Serbian arose in the 19th century, followed by Belorussian and Macedonian standards, all inscribed in the Cyrillic alphabet, in the 20th.

Serbo-Croatian is in a unique situation. The spoken language in Serbia and Croatia exhibits only slight differences, but the written standard uses different alphabets. The Serbs, who are Eastern Orthodox in religion, use the Cyrillic alphabet, while the Croats, who are Roman Catholic, have adopted the Roman alphabet. The role that politics plays in the definition of language can be seen in the demands made by many Croatians that their language, despite only slight lexical and syntactic differences from Serbian, be considered a separate language.

## The Illyrian or Thracian Subfamily

The Albanian language is the sole survivor of an Indo-European subfamily known as Illyrian or Thracian, once spoken in the Balkans to the north of the Hellenic lands. Albania became an independent state for the first time in 1912 as a result of Great Power efforts to keep Serbian territory from reaching the sea. The language was divided into two dialect groups: Gheg, spoken in the north and in the Yugoslav Kosovo region by a Muslim majority and a Catholic minority, and Tosk, used in the south by Muslims and a minority of Orthodox Christians. Two literary standards were recognized. In 1925 a Gheg became president and subsequently declared himself king as Zog I in 1928. He married a Catholic Hungarian princess and entered into a close association with Catholic Italy, which ended in 1939 with occupation by that country. After the war Albania was split into two factions, largely along

linguistic lines. The nationalist Ghegs laid claim to Kosovo while the communist Tosks, who were supported by their Yugoslav brethren, rejected this claim. After the communist victory, the government was headed by an "Orthodox" Tosk who was in league with Yugoslavia to deliver Albania as another federal state in that country. When Moscow denounced Yugoslavia in 1948, however, the Tosk leadership stood with its Russian allies and consolidated its hold on the country. This began a long isolation of the Kosovars from the land of their forefathers.

Linguistic unification became a priority of the Tosk government, and its Institute of Linguistics sought to create a United Literary Albanian (ULA). In spite of the fact that two-thirds of all Albanians speak Gheg, the new standard was thoroughly Tosk in grammar and phonology. Because Gheg is much richer in vocabulary and phraseology, 49% of the lexicon was Gheg, but no credit for this was given in the dictionary. ULA is an excellent example of how language may be used as an instrument of power and a criterion of social prestige. Because of the fundamental differences in the sound systems of Gheg and Tosk, Ghegs have a very difficult time speaking Tosk correctly. Not only does this place them at a disadvantage in the job market, but also not being able to speak the language of the ruling party could make them appear politically reactionary.

# NON-INDO-EUROPEAN LANGUAGES
## The Uralic Language Family

The Uralic languages belong to two distinct sub-families, the Samoyedic and the Fenno-Ugric, each thought to have descended from a group of common speech forms, called Proto-Uralic. Using paleobiogeographic methods, that is, the examination of words for different plants and animals in the vocabularies of the various languages, Finnish and Hungarian scholars have tried to identify the original home of the Uralic peoples. Although there is no complete agreement, most of this evidence points to an area in the northern Urals and along the lower and middle courses of the Ob in western Siberia. About 3000 B.C. the ancestors of the Fenno-Ugric speakers started their migration to the west of the Urals, where their language began to develop along different lines from that of the Samoyeds. Continued westward and southward movement has led to further differentiation and given rise to distinctive Fennic and Ugric tongues. The degree of similarity between two of the most distantly related members of the group, Hungarian (Ugric) and Finnish (Fennic), is comparable to that between English and Russian. Within the Fennic branch, on the other hand, some modern standards, such as Finnish and Estonian, both Balto-Fennic, differ little more than do divergent dialects of the same language. The Sami (Lapps) are seen as a non-Fenno-Ugric people who adopted the language of neighboring Fennic peoples, abandoning their own.

## The Altaic Language Family

The Altaic languages include those of the Turkic, Mongolian, and Tungus subfamilies. Historically they have been spoken over a large territory extending from the Balkans, through the steppes of central Asia and southern Siberia to northwestern China. In the European context it is the Turkic languages, especially the southwestern group, which includes Turkish, and Azeri; the northwestern group, including Tatar and Bashkir; and Chuvash that are important. Turkish is spoken as an indigenous language in Turkey and Bulgaria, Azeri is the official language of Azerbaijan, while Tatar, Bashkir, and Chuvash are languages with more than a million speakers each in Russia. The Tatars are the largest linguistic minority in the Russian Federation, and Tatar nationalism poses a significant threat to the state. In addition, Turkish is a major immigrant language in western Europe, with 2 million speakers, over two-thirds of them in Germany.

## The Afro-Asiatic Language Family

The Afro-Asiatic language family includes five branches that have historically been spoken across North Africa from Mauritania to Somalia and beyond into southwest Asia. They include Semitic, Chadic, Cushitic, Berber, and the now extinct Egyptian-Coptic. By far the largest number of people speak Semitic languages, especially Arabic. Although written Arabic has a standard form, the spoken varieties are widely divergent. Four spoken norms are recognized: Moroccan Arabic as spoken throughout most of the Maghreb; Syrian Arabic, the standard in most of the Middle East; Arabian Arabic, spoken in the Arabian peninsula; and Egyptian Arabic. The latter is most widely understood and is frequently used as a *lingua franca* among Arabic speakers from different parts of the realm. Arabic, especially the Moroccan form, is an important immigrant language in a number of European countries, particularly France, where there are more than a million and a half speakers. Maltese, an official language of Malta (with English), is an Arabic dialect but one so long isolated from other dialects and so heavily influenced by Italian that the resultant loss of mutual intelligibility with other Arabic speakers might justify classifying it as a separate Semitic language. Hebrew, the closest relative of Arabic, remains the sacred language of Jewish communities, though in everyday life they use Yiddish, Ladino, or the local vernacular.

## Basque

Basque (Euskara) represents the only speech form to survive the Romanization of southwestern Europe. Today it remains an isolated language with no known linguistic relatives, although some common features do point to a relationship between Basque and a group of languages indigenous to the Caucasus region. A theory gaining increasing recognition is that the language is a remnant of speech forms common to Mesolithic (hunting and gathering) peoples living in parts of Europe before the advent of Neolithic (agricultural) populations. After the Roman conquest, Basque, as the language of a largely rural population, was at a severe disadvantage vis-à-vis the Latin spoken in the cities, and since the 10th century it has steadily lost ground to Castilian Spanish. In the process, however, it greatly influenced that language, making it quite different from the other versions of Iberian Latin. There is still no universally recognized Basque standard, although one literary model seems to be gaining increasing acceptance.

## THE DIVERSITY OF EUROPE'S LANGUAGES

As we have seen, the peoples of Europe speak in many tongues. In few other regions of the world is there so much linguistic diversity over such short distances. The variety of languages is all the more remarkable when one considers that virtually all the speech forms have well-established written traditions and distinguished bodies of literature. The polyglot nature of the European linguistic heritage is a source of both pride and concern. Many view the large number of cultivated languages that have been spawned in the region as evidence of a high cultural achievement, something that sets Europe apart from the rest of the world and which, like any other precious asset, must be preserved at all cost. Others see it as a barrier to the kind of economic, political, and social unity that many Europeans have been working toward since the 1950s. Indeed, it can easily be argued that language often plays a decisive role, along with other political, economic, or social factors, in kindling the kind of collective identity that leads to demands for autonomy and sepa-

ratism. Whichever view one takes, linguistic pluralism is a fact of modern European life and therefore deserves our careful attention.

It will be useful here to compare the number of languages spoken in Europe with that used in other culture realms. There are 32 different languages that are recognized as either official or national and are used to conduct the affairs of government in one or more independent or autonomous states. All but one (Catalan in Andorra) are spoken as a mother tongue by the majority of the population in at least one of those states. Many of these languages are also spoken by minorities in other countries, and there are a number of other languages that are used in Europe only by minority groups. Within this latter category one should distinguish, as will be done later, between those indigenous to the region and those that have been brought by immigrants from other parts of the world.

We can compare the linguistic diversity in the major culture realms of the world by looking at the percentage of the population in each speaking the 10 most widely used languages. By far the greatest variation is found in sub-Saharan Africa, but it should be pointed out that the vast majority of these languages are used almost exclusively for oral communication and have little written tradition. For this reason and because of the great linguistic diversity, most states in the region use the European colonial language (dominantly English or French) for official purposes. The seemingly large number of official

TABLE 5.2. Linguistic Diversity in the World's Major Culture Regions[a]

| Culture region | Largest language | 2nd–5th languages | 6th–10th languages | The rest | Official languages |
|---|---|---|---|---|---|
| Europe | 15.96% | 38.45% | 21.94% | 23.64% | 32 |
| Latin America | 55.26% | 37.25% | 2.20% | 5.29% | 9 |
| Anglo-America | 83.89% | 11.36% | 1.35% | 3.39% | 2 |
| Main Islamic Realm | 53.26% | 32.83% | 7.82% | 6.09% | 8 |
| Sub-Saharan Africa | 4.37% | 13.86% | 13.41% | 68.37% | 22 |
| South Asia | 29.13% | 33.30% | 19.60% | 17.97% | 11 |
| Southeast Asia | 16.15% | 34.32% | 19.65% | 29.89% | 10 |
| East Asia | 55.72% | 24.63% | 14.10% | 5.55% | 5 |

*Note.* Data from Encyclopaedia Britannica Staff (1999).
[a] Percentage of total population speaking the 10 largest languages as a mother tongue.

languages (22) is due to the fact that, since the advent of a post-apartheid government in South Africa, the number of such languages in that state has risen from two to nine, the largest number for any single country in the world. The only other culture region to exhibit a pattern of linguistic diversity similar to that of Europe is Southeast Asia, where, nonetheless, the number of official languages is significantly lower.

Another way of looking at linguistic diversity is to assess the degree to which majority and minority languages are mixed together in different countries. If we disregard the microstates there are 64 instances in Europe where a minority language group comprises at least 1% of any single country's population. In 36 of these cases the minority forms a majority in at least one other European country; in 16 cases the minority is indigenous to Europe, but nowhere comprises a majority; in the other 12 cases the minority is an immigrant population (Romany, Arabic, or Turkish).

The large number of significant minority groups using a language spoken by majorities elsewhere is unique to Europe. The sole example in the United States is the Spanish-speaking community, while Canada and Australia can offer just three instances each. In many Third World countries there is no majority language, but where one does exist almost nowhere does it serve an important minority in another country. The significance of this phenomenon is that the minority in question has a base where its language is flourishing and dominant and from which it can draw nourishment in time of need. On the other hand, of course, the minority group can also become the object of (sometimes unwelcome) irredentist claims by the majority state.

## LANGUAGE POLICY IN THE EUROPEAN UNION

One may ask whether, in light of the supranational state now developing in Europe, this linguistic diversity should be preserved?

What should be the linguistic policy of the European Union? Should it have a linguistic policy at all? The EU and its institutions have long been based on the principle of the equality of member states and their languages. Prior to the most recent accession of new member states, there were 11 official languages in the EU, embracing at least one language that is official in each of the then 15 member states (neither Irish Gaelic [Erse], the first official language of Ireland, nor Lëtzebuergisch, the national language of Luxembourg, were included). Accordingly, the languages of the 10 new members will now have equal rights. The positive side of this policy has been that it gives equality to virtually all the languages spoken in the EU, but the downside is that it imposes an enormous financial burden for translation. Every document must be rendered in each of the official languages. This is a burden that amounts to millions of pages each year and currently consumes 0.8% of the EU's budget. More than this, the policy does not officially encourage any kind of linguistic uniformity within the EU that would foster greater interpersonal communication and a sense of all-Union identification.

To address these problems, two other strategies have been proposed. One is to adopt one or more (probably not more than three) languages of "wider communication" to be used as the sole official languages in the EU and to be learned in every member state as *foreign languages*. The majority languages within each state would continue to be used as languages of instruction. The second and more radical proposal is to use the languages of "wider communication" as the medium of instruction in all schools, thus making them *second languages*. Both suggestions raise problems. In each scenario, certain selected languages would be given a privileged position over all others. In addition, in the second alternative all other languages could in time cease to be used in the public sphere and thus be reduced to the status of "languages of intimacy," that is, employed only in the home and among close friends.

## Choosing the Languages of Wider Communication

In deciding which languages are to become privileged, the question of importance inevitably arises. Clearly the two or three official languages of the EU should be important ones. What, then, determines the importance of a language? This is not a linguistic issue. From the point of view of structure and vocabulary, all languages are of equal interest and value; all tell us something about the general phenomenon of human communication. The relative importance of languages is a social construct. Languages are made more or less important by the extent to which they are used and understood and by the purposes for which they are employed.

Certainly one measure of importance is the number of people who use a language as a mother tongue. Most people would agree that English and Spanish are more important than Dutch and Romanian. However, the largest single linguistic community in the world is the one that speaks Mandarin Chinese. Does this mean that Mandarin is more important than English or Spanish? Clearly more is involved here than just the number of native speakers. Another issue is how widely, that is, in how many different countries, is the language spoken. Worldwide, English is the majority mother tongue in 6 countries, Spanish in 18, and Mandarin in just 1. Also important is the number of countries in which a language is recognized as the official or national tongue and used as the primary language of instruction. English is official in 58 countries, French in 35, and Spanish in 21, while Mandarin Chinese has that position in only 3. The prominent position of English, French, and Spanish reflects, of course, the role that these peoples played in European colonialism. Lacking a dominant indigenous language, many former colonies have chosen to use the former colonial language in an official capacity, even though only the elite in the society speaks it.

The strongest indicator of the status of a language, however, is not its use as a mother tongue, second language, or official language. It is simply the number of people who take the trouble to study it as a foreign language. The languages most often studied as foreign languages generally have one or more of the following characteristics: they are useful in business and travel; they are the vehicles of popular culture (especially important among young people); they are widely used in scientific and technical publications and other scholarship; they enjoy prestige in journalism; and they have rich and well-respected literary traditions. Languages may be seen as commodities. Their acquisition incurs costs, so the benefit of the acquisition must outweigh the costs. Also to be reckoned with is a snowball effect. The more people who learn a language, the more useful it becomes and the more people want to learn it. Especially significant is "estimation," that is, the attitudes that groups regarded as important in the society have toward a particular language.

Data on foreign language acquisition in individual countries are not easy to obtain, but Table 5.3 gives some impression of the relative importance of the major foreign languages learned in the older western countries of the European Union. Several points are worth emphasizing. The study of foreign languages has increased dramatically over the past three or four decades. While 54% of those over 55 reported never having studied a foreign language, only 11% of those 15–24 did so. English is the dominant language studied by all cohorts, followed consistently by French, German, and Spanish. While the order among the four has remained the same, the gap between each has widened. English has gained in popularity against the other three, French against German and Spanish, and German against Spanish. Indeed, if we look at individual countries, Spanish is important only in France, while French is more widely studied than German everywhere except the Netherlands, Denmark, and Greece. German is also stronger than French in the rest of Scandinavia and Finland, in central Europe, and in the Balkans. Russian, once widely studied in the former Soviet bloc, has retreated rapidly before English and German, recently losing ground even in pro-Russian Bulgaria.

TABLE 5.3. The Study of Foreign Languages in Selected EU Countries

| | English | French | German | Spanish | Italian | None |
|---|---|---|---|---|---|---|
| Foreign languages learned by persons 15–24 years of age (%) | | | | | | |
| Belgium | 69 | | 24 | 10 | 0 | 13 |
| Denmark | 97 | 40 | 92 | 12 | 0 | 0 |
| France | 89 | | 35 | 34 | 9 | 5 |
| Germany | 82 | 32 | | 5 | 0 | 10 |
| Greece | 73 | 9 | 16 | 0 | 4 | 21 |
| Ireland | | 70 | 26 | 5 | 0 | 13 |
| Italy | 75 | 47 | 9 | 3 | | 7 |
| Luxembourg | 83 | 97 | 97 | 8 | 0 | 4 |
| Netherlands | 97 | 68 | 92 | 10 | 0 | 1 |
| Portugal | 63 | 64 | 4 | 12 | 0 | 24 |
| Spain | 60 | 21 | 2 | | 0 | 20 |
| United Kingdom | | 77 | 39 | 9 | 3 | 16 |
| Foreign languages learned by persons 25–39 years of age (%) | | | | | | |
| Belgium | 69 | | 38 | 9 | 0 | 14 |
| Denmark | 96 | 35 | 90 | 5 | 0 | 2 |
| France | 76 | | 27 | 25 | 6 | 17 |
| Germany | 72 | 27 | | 4 | 0 | 16 |
| Greece | 50 | 7 | 11 | 0 | 6 | 40 |
| Ireland | | 48 | 8 | 5 | 0 | 26 |
| Italy | 58 | 44 | 8 | 6 | | 19 |
| Luxembourg | 73 | 96 | 93 | 8 | 0 | 3 |
| Netherlands | 95 | 64 | 85 | 11 | 0 | 2 |
| Portugal | 35 | 42 | 2 | 12 | 0 | 52 |
| Spain | 35 | 27 | 4 | | 0 | 36 |
| United Kingdom | | 61 | 23 | 9 | 7 | 30 |
| Foreign languages learned by persons 40–54 years of age (%) | | | | | | |
| Belgium | 50 | | 34 | 3 | 0 | 23 |
| Denmark | 85 | 26 | 77 | 4 | 0 | 8 |
| France | 48 | | 17 | 18 | 5 | 39 |
| Germany | 53 | 20 | | 1 | 0 | 25 |
| Greece | 26 | 9 | 8 | 0 | 3 | 62 |
| Ireland | | 31 | 5 | 4 | 0 | 35 |
| Italy | 28 | 41 | 6 | 2 | | 46 |
| Luxembourg | 57 | 96 | 92 | 7 | 0 | 7 |
| Netherlands | 85 | 56 | 79 | 6 | 0 | 10 |
| Portugal | 17 | 19 | 3 | 8 | 0 | 74 |
| Spain | 11 | 17 | 4 | | 0 | 56 |
| United Kingdom | | 45 | 17 | 10 | 7 | 43 |
| Foreign languages learned by persons 55 years of age and older (%) | | | | | | |
| Belgium | 24 | | 18 | 4 | 0 | 41 |
| Denmark | 54 | 18 | 48 | 4 | 0 | 29 |
| France | 31 | | 13 | 11 | 5 | 49 |
| Germany | 34 | 16 | | 1 | 0 | 41 |
| Greece | 15 | 5 | 2 | 0 | 2 | 74 |
| Ireland | | 15 | 2 | 1 | 0 | 51 |
| Italy | 15 | 24 | 5 | 5 | | 65 |
| Luxembourg | 41 | 92 | 94 | 4 | 0 | 3 |
| Netherlands | 64 | 46 | 70 | 6 | 0 | 20 |
| Portugal | 6 | 10 | 3 | 3 | 0 | 85 |
| Spain | 3 | 6 | 1 | | 0 | 69 |
| United Kingdom | | 31 | 11 | 6 | 5 | 57 |

*Note.* Data from European Commission (1995).

## The Rise of English to World Prominence

English has developed into the world language par excellence. As a native language, with over 400 million speakers it is the second most widely spoken language in the world, after Mandarin Chinese, which has twice that number. It is an official or national language in 58 countries and is spoken by more than 800 million people as a second or foreign language. Some 70% of all mail is written in English, and 80% of all information stored in data banks is recorded in English.

How has this hybrid tongue, formed and developed on what was for a long time an obscure, sparsely populated island off the west coast of the Eurasian continent, attained this unique position? If we look for an economic explanation, no doubt the leadership of England during the Industrial Revolution and the influential role that the United States subsequently played in the development of technology helped English to become the language of science and industry. The overwhelming importance of these fields in the modernization of society meant that English became dominant in other areas as well. French, the great international language of the preindustrial era, held its advantage for a while in diplomacy and the arts but in the end surrendered pride of place even here. The penetration of English into every important aspect of modern life was also facilitated by its spread to the far corners of the earth. By the beginning of the 20th century, Britain, with her sea power and economic might, had amassed the greatest empire in the world, and English became the commercial and administrative language of that far-flung domain.

Some linguists maintain that, quite apart from the advantages with which historical circumstances have presented it, English has inherent characteristics that make it more suitable as a *lingua franca* than other languages. Some of these are related to the grammar or syntax. In spite of the fact that all Indo-European languages were originally highly inflective, that is, they had many verb endings indicating tense and noun endings showing case, most of these have been lost in English.

In the absence of inflections, a fairly rigid word order is now used to convey meaning. Because this word order is more natural and logical than that permitted in many other languages, the argument goes, it is relatively easy for a foreigner to gain a *reasonable* level of competency in English. On the other hand, *near native* competency in speech is quite difficult to achieve because the sound system is so different from that of most languages. The lexical characteristics of English are also favorable. We pointed out earlier that, because of its hybrid nature, English has a much larger and more varied vocabulary than most languages. This elasticity makes it easy to create new terms when they are needed and to accommodate new words, especially foreign loanwords.

Within Europe today there is little doubt that English is fast becoming the international language of choice. It is, without a doubt, the usual language of contact between two individuals who do not speak each other's language. There is much pressure to use English in education and research, in business, and increasingly in the job market. Indeed, according to a recent EU survey the idea that all Europeans should learn English was widely accepted (69% of respondents). Already well over half the EU either claims the ability to converse in English or claims English as their native language.

While language purists across the continent may fret, the march of English seems inexorable. Despite a 1994 law aimed at banning foreign expressions from the French language, the French are increasingly resigned to the corruption of their language with English words and phrases. In Germany, the seemingly ubiquitous mixture of German and English, known as *Denglish*, is made all the more noticeable by the German habit of running words together, as in "Businesssportcenter." The penetration of English is most advanced in countries like the Netherlands, where more than 80% claim to speak it, or in Scandinavia, where some jokingly say it is spoken better than in Britain. European languages tend to be increasingly riddled with "Americanisms"—such as "take away" food or "weekend getaway"—many of which are launched through advertisements, movies, and pop music. Sadly, its growing prevalence seems to have had a dampening effect on the desire of native English speakers to learn other languages. An estimated two-thirds of all Britons speak no other language than English.

## Learning the Languages of Wider Communication

It seems clear that, if the European Union moves to reduce the number of official languages to two or three, the first will be English, the second French, and the third German. The question then remains whether these "languages of wider communication" should be taught as mandatory *foreign languages* (treated as any other course) in all EU schools, leaving the local languages as the media for education, or whether they should replace the local languages in this latter function, that is, become *second languages*. The arguments for and against each strategy cluster largely around curricular and cultural issues.

If all students in EU countries are to gain competency in two or three languages, none of which may be their mother tongue, many school hours that might be used more profitably will be tied up in language training. The time spent on this at present varies considerably both from one country to another and among age groups. A second foreign language is usually introduced at age 13, but a few countries do not require two. On average, students between the ages of 13 and 18 spend 9–10 hours a week studying two languages in Germany, Belgium, and Luxembourg but devote just 3 hours to one language in Ireland and Greece. To achieve competency in two official EU languages that are not one's own would certainly require 10–12 hours a week. In addition, instruction would probably have to begin at the primary level, where there is at the moment little foreign language instruction. Clearly students' education in some other areas would have to suffer.

The European Union does presently offer a program to enhance the opportunities for students and teachers to study other languages in the countries where they are spoken. This program, entitled LINGUA, is aimed especially at the least widely used and least taught languages of the EU. Its aim is diversification, stressing the idea that Union solidarity is dependent on the recognition by those who speak the most widely used languages that a competence in other Union languages is essential. Although LINGUA has received wide support, it is telling that former Prime Minister Margaret Thatcher opposed British funding because it would be used to support marginal languages. Very evidently one of the problems of selecting "elite" languages to be used in wider communication is linguistic arrogance.

Under the second proposal students would be immersed immediately in one or more of these elite languages, using them as languages of instruction. The initial difficulties of this strategy are considerable, of course, because all teachers would have to be fluent in at least one second language, but eventually the system would feed itself, and there would be little or no foreign language instruction in schools, though this runs counter to the aims of the LINGUA program. Rather than having to take time from other subjects, more time would be available for them. In addition, having no need for foreign language teachers, more teachers could be trained to teach other subjects. From a curricular point of view, using languages of wider communication as the media of instruction would seem to make a great deal of sense.

The danger of the second strategy is that it might, in the long run, lead to the impoverishment of Europe's theater of cultures. A dominant feature of 19th-century nationalism, especially as it developed in Germany, was the notion that language is the single most important marker of culture. Even today, many linguists believe that the mother tongue is a fundamental part of people's identity and of enormous important in placing them within their culture.

One question is whether the major languages chosen for use in the schools and other public venues will eventually cause the demise of the local languages and, if so, whether the cultures they represent will die with them. Certainly historical experience is not encouraging. The Latin language and culture overwhelmed almost all competitors in the Roman Empire, and the minorities in the modern European nation states have not fared all that well. This underlines the importance of multilingualism, a fact recognized by the EU when it declared 2001 the "European Year of Languages." The aim was to celebrate publicly the EU's immense linguistic diversity and promote the learning of language skills as a means of better understanding others and appreciating their culture. Significantly, the focus was not just on national languages but on regional and minority languages, as well, which underlines the EU's public commitment to maintaining linguistic diversity in Europe

At the present time it appears that, although many European nations are willing to give up their economic and political independence to a central authority, they are not willing to abandon their distinctive languages and cultures. In other words, a rather strongly entrenched linguistic nationalism persists, especially with respect to the threatened hegemony of English. The Dutch are among the Europeans who are most comfortable with foreign languages, but when the Ministry of Education suggested that all university instruction be carried on in English there was heavy opposition. Thus, states continue to legislate to stem the tide of English, and a more or less constant barrage of proposals surface that seek to preserve multilingualism in Europe through such mechanisms as placing restrictions on the use of English, requiring that publications and product labels be multilingual and that access to education and employment be based, at least in part, on demonstrated multilingual skills.

On the other hand, loss of the mother tongue may not be so great a danger to cultural identity as some people fear. Only one-quarter of those who feel themselves to be ethnically Basque speak the language. Most have Spanish or French as their mother tongue, yet this does not seem to diminish popular support for a Basque identity, or even separatism. As the European Union expands, it would seem economically unfeasible to continue to increase the number of official languages. It seems most likely, however, that the languages of wider communication chosen for use in the EU will be learned by its citizens as foreign, rather than as second, languages.

## FURTHER READING

Aitchison, J. W., & Carter, H. (1999). Cultural empowerment and language shift in Wales. *Tijdschrift voor Economische en Sociale Geografie, 90,* 168–183.

Barbour, S., & Carmichael, C. (Eds.). (2000). *Language and nationalism in Europe.* Oxford, UK: Oxford University Press.

Comrie, B. (Ed.). (1990). *The major languages of eastern Europe.* London: Routledge.

Council of Europe. (2000). *Linguistic diversity for democratic citizenship in Europe: Towards a framework for language education policies, Proceedings, Innsbruck, 10–12 May, 1999.* Strasbourg, France: Council of Europe Publishing.

Encyclopaedia Britannica Staff, Britannica Editors. (1999). *Britannica book of the year 1999.* Chicago: Encyclopaedia Britannica.

European Commission. (1995). *Key data on education in the European Union.* Luxembourg: Author.

Greenberg, J. H. (2000). *Indo-European and its closest relatives: The Eurasiatic language family.* Stanford, CA: Stanford University Press.

Hindley, R. (1990). *The death of the Irish language: A qualified obituary.* London: Routledge.

Krantz, G. S. (1988). *Geographical development of European languages.* New York: Peter Lang.

Mackay, W. (1991). Language diversity, language policy and the sovereign state. *History of European Ideas, 13,* 51–6l.

MacAulay, D. (Ed.). (1992). *The Celtic languages.* Cambridge, UK: Cambridge University Press.

McCrum, R., Cran, W., & McNeil, W. (1986). *The story of English.* New York: Viking.

Mallory, J. P. (1989). *In search of the Indo-Europeans: Language, archaeology and myth.* London: Thames & Hudson.

Mamadouh, V. (1999). Beyond nationalism: Three

visions of the European Union and their implications for the linguistic regime of its institutions. *GeoJournal, 48*, 133–144.

Perez, S. (1998). Languages and regions in Europe and elsewhere: A revival of regional issues? *Prospects, 28*, 629–642.

Phillipson, R. (2002). *English-only Europe?: Language policy challenges.* New York: Routledge.

Posner R. (1991). Society, civilization, mentality: Prolegomena to a language policy for Europe. In F. Coulmas (Ed.), *A language policy for the European Community* (pp. 121–137). Berlin: Moulton.

Renfrew, C. (1987). *Archaeology and language: The puzzle of Indo-European origins.* New York: Cambridge University Press.

Rickard, P. (1989). *A history of the French language* (2nd ed.). London: Unwin Hyman.

Stephens, M. (1978). *Linguistic minorities in western Europe.* Llandysul, Wales: Gomer Press.

Van der Auwera, J., & van der Meer, J. (1995). *The Germanic languages.* London: Routledge.

Vestergaard, T. (Ed.). (1999). *Language, culture and identity.* Aalborg, Denmark: Aalborg University Press.

Withers, C. W. J. (1988). *Gaelic in Scotland, 1698–1981: The geographical history of a language.* London: Routledge.

# CHAPTER 6

# Religion

Religion may be defined as humankind's relationship to what it regards as holy or sacred. Holy powers are seen as external to human society, and belief in them stems from a human desire to relate to, even be dependent upon, forces outside the physical world. To be religious, then, is to feel connected in some way to the holy. One way of maintaining this connection is through worship, for example, prayer, sacrifice, contemplation, or magic. Another is through proper conduct. There may be rituals to perform, words to recite, holy days to keep, places to frequent or to avoid, leaders to follow, and a literature to be read and pondered. Religions thus develop a body of beliefs or doctrines about the nature of the supernatural world and how humans should relate to it. They also elaborate moral codes of conduct and normally construct some kind of an organization to oversee the practice of the religion and assist believers in that practice. Religion everywhere is closely bound up with family structure. It has a major impact on how sexual behavior and reproduction are regulated and how the socialization of children is carried out. Religion thus impinges strongly on both the values of a culture and on its institutions.

Because religion is so intimately associated with the well-being of the believers, groups that have very different religions often view one another with deep suspicion and lack of understanding. Religion, like language, is a fundamental element of a person's identity and membership in a larger collective community. Unlike language, however, religion is seen to be tied to the community's very survival. For this reason, religious rivalry can awaken much deeper antagonism than rivalry among linguistic groups.

Beyond its sacred content, religion shapes many other elements in society. The moral code is especially important in determining how people will behave in certain situations. Religion has a strong impact on art and literature, even that which is not explicitly religious. It has a strong influence on architecture and thus helps to shape the built environment, both ecclesiastical and secular. But most importantly it provides a worldview, an overarching way of looking at human life and at the environment in which humans live. This is why the religious traditions of a community remain important even when most of its members are no longer believers. It has been said that there is a great difference between being religious and having a religion. In today's Europe, only a minority of the population is religious, but virtually everyone has a religion.

## RELIGION THROUGH THE AGES

### The Three Great Western Religions

The three great religions of the West, Judaism, Christianity, and Islam, all evolved in the arid environment of the Middle East. The earliest of the three, Judaism, has its origins around 1500 B.C. in northern Mesopotamia. Before the rise of Judaism, the religions of the Middle East were tribal. They were animistic, endowing animals, plants, and even rocks with spirits, and they were particular to related groups of people, or tribes. Judaism was organized around the concept of monotheism, belief in a single god, and developed a complex philosophy. It remained, however, attached to a single ethnic group, and is often called an ethnic religion, similar in this respect to Hinduism and Chinese religion. Unlike the latter, however, its monotheism implied that it aspired to become the religion of all humankind. It did not become a universalizing religion, however, largely because of the doctrine that proclaimed the Jews to be the chosen people of God. Only at the coming of the Messiah would all people see the light and follow the God of Israel.

Christianity grew out of Judaism. Christ, a Jew, proclaimed himself to be the Messiah, but the Jews refused to accept him. Failing in this, the Apostles, especially Paul, interpreted this new "Jewish" religion to the non-Jews, those whom the Jews called Gentiles. These were mainly Greeks, and they played the major role in making Christianity a religion of Europeans. Its monotheism and lack of attachment to any particular ethnic group left Christianity free to be a universalizing religion. Such religions are also proselytizing, that is, one of their major goals is to convert others to their religion. Judaism, on the other hand, while welcoming converts, has never actively sought them.

Islam is the creation of the Prophet Muhammad. Born in Mecca on the Arabian Peninsula in 570 A.D., he married and fathered six children. A merchant by trade, he began to experience revelations in his late thirties and retired alone to the desert to meditate be-

**FIGURE 6.1. The spread of Christianity.** During a visit from St. Paul in the first century A.D. the inhabitants of Cappadocia in central Anatolia were so thoroughly converted that Cappadocia became the great stronghold of Christian monasticism. The monasteries and churches, dug deeply into the easily worked volcanic tufa cliffs, continued to fulfill their functions until the exchange of populations between Greece and Turkey in 1923. Here we have the Girls' Monastery, which accommodated some 300 nuns and is called by the Turks the "Virgins' Castle."

tween 610 and 613. When he returned to Mecca, it was to preach a religion, which, in stark contrast to the tribal religions of the Arabs, was monotheistic. His thinking was almost certainly influenced by Christian ideas, and perhaps by Judaism. Mecca possessed a large black stone, the Kabba, which was an object of pilgrimage for Arabs all over the peninsula. The wealthy merchants of Mecca, worried about the loss of their business were the old religion to be rejected, drove Muhammad and his followers from the city. Their flight, called the hegira, to the city of Medina in the north, marks the first year of the Islamic calendar. Eventually Muhammad won over the Meccans and built an Islamic state in central Arabia. After his death in 632, the Muslim religion, both universalizing and proselytizing, was spread to the west and to the east with lightning speed by the armies of the Arab faithful.

## The Roman Empire

The official state religion of Rome was a form of Emperor worship that also involved a polytheistic pantheon of gods. The religion and the state were solidly fused, and Judaism was just about the only other religion tolerated in the Empire. The favor with which the Romans regarded the Jews is illustrated by the obliging way in which they crucified Christ. Subsequently the privileged population of the Empire saw Christianity as a particular danger because it had a special appeal to the poor and the outcast. No doubt the universalizing nature of Christianity was also viewed as a threat to the state religion. Whatever the reason, the persecution of Christians was a major Roman sport until the conversion of the Emperor Constantine in 313. With this event, Christianity was declared legal in the Empire. In 337 Rome became the second state to make it the official religion; this had happened 34 years earlier in Armenia.

During the first century A.D. the position of the Jews worsened under Roman authority, and, as a result of a rebellion, the Temple in Jerusalem was destroyed in 70 A.D. This led to a major outmigration of Jews from Israel to other parts of the Empire, the beginning of a dispersal of the Jews that came to be known as the Jewish Diaspora. The greatest concentrations in the early days were in Mesopotamia, Syria, Egypt, and western Anatolia, but increasingly the Jews migrated westward, settling in the Iberian Peninsula and Gaul. As we will see later, this movement set the stage for the large European Jewish populations that suffered such tragic fates, first in the Middle Ages and later in the modern era.

## Divisions within Christendom

A scant century after attaining a dominant role in the Roman Empire, Christianity was rent by dissension. The source of the controversy was the extent to which Christ's nature was human or divine. The Monophysites, represented today by the Armenian Apostolic Church, the Syrian Jacobites, Egyptian Coptics, and Ethiopian Orthodox Church, maintained that his human and divine natures were completely fused. This view was opposed at the Council of Chalcedon in 451 by the majority of the Christian world, which took the position that the two natures were separate but commingled (the Orthodox view). Different still were the opinions of the Nestorians, who believed that the two natures were completely separate, and the Arians, who thought that Christ was a completely different being from God. Arianism was popular among many Germanic tribes that invaded the Empire, but it subsequently died out. Nestorianism survived only in South Asia, and the Monophysite view in the Middle East, where it is today referred to as Eastern Rite Christianity. Christianity in most of the ancient world, including Europe, however, remained Orthodox.

The early Church was organized administratively on the pattern of the Roman Empire. The seats of authority were cities, with higher levels of command located in larger centers and subordinate ones in successively less important towns. In this way the structure of the Church came to assume a hierarchical form. At the top of the hierarchy were five patriarchs, all theoretically with equal rank. These prelates had their seats at Rome, Alexandria, Jerusalem, Antioch, and Constantine's newly founded capital, Constantinople. However, since Rome had the relics of St. Peter, the principal apostle, it claimed the position of the first patriarch. When, in 451, the Council of Chalcedon assigned this position to the patriarch of Constantinople, the first of many rifts between the eastern and western Christian worlds occurred. It must be remembered, however, that these two worlds were already culturally rather different, the east being Greek and the west, Latin.

In the seventh century the position of the patriarchs at Alexandria, Jerusalem, and Antioch was seriously undermined by the fall of those cities to the armies of Islam, leaving

Rome and Constantinople as the two foci of the Orthodox Christian world. The latter was also the seat of the Roman Emperor, since the Empire in the west had fallen to the German barbarians, and only in the east did the Empire still survive. In a move to regain primacy in the Christian world, the Pope at Rome crowned Charlemagne Roman Emperor in 800. This infuriated the Emperor in the east and initiated a schism in which the patriarch in Constantinople excommunicated the Pope and the Pope excommunicated him. Although these edicts were subsequently revoked, further confrontations resulted in a series of similar events. The excommunications of 1054, however, were not to be revoked until 1965, and the year 1054 has traditionally been taken to mark the final break between the Eastern and Western Churches.

Many differences arose between what became known as the Roman Catholic and Eastern Orthodox Churches. One was that the Pope and Council of Cardinals in the West frequently reinterpreted the religious literature. In the East, on the other hand, there was little deviation from original doctrine, which is why the Eastern Church is known as Orthodox (Greek *orthos*, straight, + *doxa*, opinion). Another difference was in the realm of monasticism, where Eastern Christianity held onto the view that monks should isolate themselves from the world. Living in monasteries supported by wealthy patrons, they devoted themselves to contemplation, developing the liturgy and painting sacred images (icons). In Western Christendom, monks and nuns (the regular clergy) were organized into orders, which followed their own sets of rules and regulations and specialized in particular kinds of activity. They sometimes mingled closely with the general population, as in the case of the mendicant (beggar) orders.

In Church polity, too, Roman Catholicism and Eastern Orthodoxy developed very differently. The fall of the Empire in the West meant that leadership of the Church was separated from secular authority. The Pope was the sole head of the Church as an institution and he decided all religious matters, together with his clerical advisors. Because the Empire persisted in the East, however, a system of governance known as Caesaropapism devel-

**FIGURE 6.2. Monasticism.** Perched high on the walls of a cliff overlooking the zigzagging climb away from the Aegean coast of the eastern Peloponnese are the whitewashed walls of the Elonis monastery. Like many monastic sites, Elonis is remote, the lives of those who live there purposely separated from the secular events of the outside world.

oped. The term suggests a close association between Emperor and patriarch, and, in fact, the former was frequently able to exercise control over the institutional affairs of the Church. In matters of theology the patriarch normally prevailed, but even here the secular administration often interfered. As Orthodoxy spread in Europe, the alliance between Church and State persisted. In the West, on the other hand, the notion of the universal (catholic) Church, free of any connection to states, prevailed.

The gulf that developed between the theologies of the Eastern and Western Churches led the former to view the teachings of the latter as heretical. This belief was extended to virtually all intellectual development within Western Christendom, and prevented most Western ideas from penetrating the East. Beyond this, however, the memories of the fourth Crusade created a real revulsion among Orthodox Christians toward the Roman Catholic Church. Diverted from their goal of gaining control of the Holy Land for Christendom, the Catholic armies of the Fourth Crusade sacked Constantinople in 1204, took control of most of the Byzantine (Eastern) Empire for almost 60 years, and forcibly imposed their religion on the Greek population. After this event the line of demarcation between Catholicism and Orthodoxy became without a doubt the sharpest cultural boundary in Europe.

## The Spread of Christianity beyond the Empire

By 410, when the Visigoths sacked Rome and the Western Empire began to crumble, Christianity was established, however unevenly, throughout the Roman Empire. Perhaps the first attempt to bring the religion to the barbarians beyond the Roman world was Patrick's mission to the Irish. Patrick had been born in Wales, but as a boy he was taken prisoner by Irish raiders and grew to manhood in Ireland. Escaping from his Irish captors, he made his way to Brittany, where he entered a monastery and received religious training. Sometime around 432 he returned to Ireland

on a mission to bring Christianity to the land of his captivity. His message was well received and led eventually to the founding of the Celtic Monastic Church. The name suggests the fundamental difference in organization between this church and the Roman one. The Celts were not an urban people. The earliest towns in Ireland were founded in the ninth century by Viking invaders. The Church leaders, therefore, were the heads of the rural monasteries, not bishops seated in cathedral towns.

The Celtic Church carried on an active missionary activity in Scotland and among the Anglo-Saxons of northern England. This was of some concern to Rome, and in 597 Augustine was sent as a missionary to southern England. Establishing his base at Canterbury in Kent, he brought the Anglo-Saxons of the south within the fold of Christendom. Eventually an agreement was reached between the two churches, and they were merged to form the British Church in 644. From Britain a vigorous missionary activity was launched on the continent among the Franks and the Germans. Boniface of Wessex (d. 754), often called the Apostle of Germany, unified the missionary movement by bringing it under the control of Rome. In the 10th and 11th centuries German missionaries brought Christianity to the Scandinavians, West Slavs, and Hungarians and penetrated the territory of the South Slavs. In the 1380s, the Grand Duke of Lithuania accepted the religion for his people, completing the eastward march of Catholicism across northern Europe.

The successes of the missionary activity emanating from Byzantium were much more limited. In the 870s the leaders of both the Bulgarians and the Serbs were converted. Bulgarian influence among the Romanians eventually brought them within the fold, but the great coup was the conversion in 988 of the Prince of Kiev, the leading East Slavic state. Still, in 1400, fewer than 15% of Europe's population were Eastern Orthodox Christians. This percentage would increase significantly in later centuries, however, because of the higher fertility in the Orthodox world.

## The Muslim Incursions

On three separate occasions in history the forces of Islam assaulted the territory we have defined as Europe. Each time they were driven out, but only after centuries of domination, and the legacy they have left is unmistakable. The first was the Moorish invasion of Iberia in 711. It was accomplished by an army led by Arabs but consisting mainly of Berbers from the Maghreb. The Moors quickly defeated the divided Visigoths and overran the peninsula, threatening even the heart of France before being turned back across the Pyrenees in 732. Christian authority survived in the far north, and the medieval history of Spain and Portugal was totally dominated by the *Reconquista*, the centuries-long reconquest of the peninsula for Christendom. This was finally achieved in 1492 with the victorious entry of the Catholic Monarchs, Ferdinand and Isabella, into the last Moorish stronghold of Granada.

As noted in the preceding chapter, one legacy of the Muslim period in the history of the Iberian Peninsula is the large number of Arabic loanwords, especially in Castilian, and the multitude of Arabic place names. Another is the Islamic architecture, constructed mainly in the Moorish period but also after the Christian reconquest by Muslim architects, a style known as Mudéjar. In recent years there has been a movement in Spain en-

couraging people to return to their Muslim roots. Many Spaniards, especially in Andalusia and Valencia, are descended from Moors who converted to Christianity (Moriscos). The Spanish government now reports 450,000 Muslims living in Spain. Some have only just recently arrived as migrant workers from the Maghreb, a few are rich Arabs with fancy homes on the Costa del Sol, but many are Spaniards who have recently converted to Islam.

The second onslaught began with the destruction of Kiev by the Golden Horde in 1240. This khanate formed the western part of a great Mongol Empire that had been founded by Genghis Khan in the early 13th century. Not Muslim in the beginning, the Horde was gradually Turkified and Islamicized, especially during the early 14th century. Its capital was established on the Volga, near the modern city of Volgograd, and at its height it exacted tribute from virtually every Russian state but Novgorod. The empire collapsed at the end of the 14th century, and the principality of Muscovy emerged as the leader of the Russian people. Two important ideas emerged from the century and a half of the "Mongol captivity." One is that it had isolated Russian culture from the rest of Europe and infused it with a penchant for Oriental despotism. This is the foundation for the 19th-century argument that Russia belonged

FIGURE 6.3. Moorish architecture. As seen on this doorway to The Grand Mosque (Mezquita) in Córdoba, Moorish builders made inventive uses of brick and glazed tiles. Another common decorative feature was the horseshoe-shaped arch, which was likely inherited from the Visigoths who occupied the Iberian Peninsula prior to the Moorish conquest. Interiors were much more lavishly decorated than exteriors.

to Asia, not to Europe. The other is that Russia, in particular Muscovy, was the stalwart defender of the faith against the infidel. After the fall of Christian Constantinople to the Turks in 1453, Moscow capitalized on this reputation, assuming for itself the title of the "Third Rome."

The third Islamic invasion came from the southeast in the middle of the 14th century. Under the leadership of a man called Osman, who founded the Ottoman dynasty around 1300, the Muslim Turks overran Anatolia by 1400 and as early as 1349 had established a foothold in Europe, from which they advanced into the Balkans. In 1389, on the "field of blackbirds" near Pristina in modern Kosovo, they won a stunning victory over a Christian army led by the flower of Serbian nobility. The heroic exploits of various Serb chieftains in this battle have inspired a famous ballad poetry and a great cycle of legends, which helps to explain the importance with which Serbs regard the region known as Kosovo. The anniversary of this act of gallantry, even though in a losing cause, is still celebrated each year in Serbia on the feast of St. Vitus (Vidovdan, June 28).

In a second great battle, which took place in Kosovo in 1448, the Ottoman Turks further consolidated their hold on the Balkans. The Byzantine Empire, which carried forward the tradition of Roman rule in the east and was the center of Eastern Orthodoxy, was by this time literally engulfed by the rising tide of Ottoman expansion. In 1453, under Mehmet the Conqueror, the Ottomans closed in on the ancient imperial city of Constantinople itself and, much to the shock of the Christian world, succeeded in capturing it. The relentless westward advance of the fearsome Ottoman armies up the valley of the Danube continued into the 16th century and resulted in the fall of Belgrade in 1521, and of Buda in 1526. By 1529 they had reached the gates of Vienna, and although they failed to take the city, the Turks created a virtual no-man's land in Hungary, successfully guarding this frontier until the end of the 17th century.

The legacy of Ottoman rule in the Balkans is the presence of significant Muslim minorities in several parts of the region. The Turks themselves did not move in large numbers into the conquered territories. The descendents of the few who did are most numerous

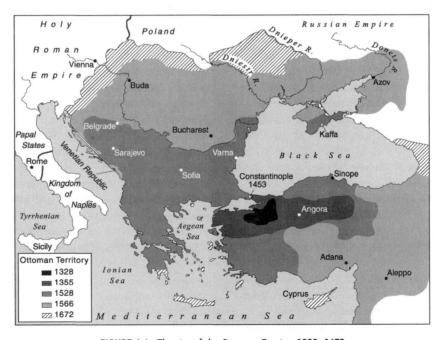

FIGURE 6.4. The rise of the Ottoman Empire, 1328–1672.

today in Bulgaria, where they are settled in the south and comprise about 9% of the population. More important were the conversions of indigenous peoples to Islam. Conversion meant that landholdings could be retained and also gave exemption from the special taxes placed on Christians living within the Ottoman Empire, such as the seizure of sons to serve in the Janissaries, an elite corps in the standing army of the empire. Some groups showed a particular penchant for adopting the Muslim faith. Before the Ottoman invasion, the Albanian Ghegs had been largely Catholic while the Tosk were, in the main, Orthodox. The majority of both groups converted to Islam. In Bosnia, many South Slavs, especially the landowners, had rejected both Catholicism and Orthodoxy and created their own Bosnian (Bogomil) Church. Like the Cathars in France, the Bogomils subscribed to a neo-Manichean heresy and were shunned by other Christians. Thus, it was not difficult for them to embrace Islam. This is the origin of the Bosnian Muslim community that became the object of Serb aggression during the mid-1990s.

## Jewish Settlement in the Middle Ages

By the 13th century, the Jewish Diaspora in Europe was concentrated in Iberia, especially Spain, and in the valleys of the Rhine and its tributaries. The Jews in Muslim Spain (Sephardim) were treated well by their Muslim hosts and rose to be prominent figures in trade, politics, and intellectual life. Indeed, the Jewish contribution to Spanish universities, which were among the best in Europe, was out of all proportion to their percentage of the population. Later, under Christian rule, their position worsened dramatically. Militant campaigns resulted in the forcible conversion of many Jews, but other Catholics remained suspicious of the new Christians' sincerity. Most were thought to profess Christianity only outwardly, while practicing the rites of Judaism in secret (cryptic Jews). The Spanish Inquisition, authorized by the Pope in 1478, was directed principally against these "conversos." Unconverted Jews were expelled

from Spain in 1492 and from Portugal in 1497, but the Inquisition continued to persecute the conversos, sometimes called Marranos (pork eaters) because they were said to use this act to prove their rejection of the Jewish faith. The fanatical hatred directed at converted Jews stemmed from the incredible success they had achieved in virtually every aspect of Spanish life. Ironically, even the Spanish monarch, Philip II, an avowed enemy of conversos, had some Jewish ancestry and was quite correctly described by Pope Paul IV as a Marrano.

Expulsions of Jews began much earlier in northwestern Europe. They were banished from England in 1290, and a major eviction from France occurred in 1306. For the German Jews (Ashkenazim) real trouble began with the First Crusade in 1096. Passing through the German lands on their way to the Holy Land, crusading armies attempted forced conversions, slaughtering all those who would not submit. The persecutions continued and reached a peak during the Black Death, when the Jews were made the scapegoats for the catastrophe and accused of poisoning the wells.

Some of the hatred directed against the Jews was certainly religiously inspired. Were they not the murderers of Christ? Yet, the principal motive was probably economic. In the 12th century the Church launched a campaign against usury, then defined as the practice of lending money at interest. Unfortunately, money lending was essential to the economy, and one could not make a living at it without taking interest. Thus it developed that the Jews came to fill this need. While many derived their livelihoods through money lending, many others were merchants involved in both local and long-distance trade. Whatever business they engaged in, the Jews seemed to be successful, and the wealth they amassed was envied and coveted by their Christian neighbors.

The upshot of the persecutions that became so commonplace in western Europe was a major migration of Jews to the east. For the Ashkenazim the principal destinations were the Kingdom of Poland and the Grand Duchy of Lithuania, which were united in 1569. The Polish kings in the 14th and 15th centuries were known to be especially tolerant for their time, and by 1450 Poland had long been known in Germany as the safest place for Jews. The vast territory embraced by the Polish-Lithuanian state in the 17th century meant that Ashkenazi settlement also spread into what is now Belarus and Ukraine. Russia, by contrast, had a strict no-admission policy, which ended only with the final partition of Poland in the late 18th century. Now faced with large numbers of Jews within the empire, Russia dealt with the problem by restricting all Jews to their current areas of residence, with the exception of certain areas near the Black Sea where Jewish colonists were allowed to settle. The main area of Jewish settlement within Russia came to be known as the Jewish Pale. At the end of the 19th century, it included all of Russian Poland, most of Ukraine, Lithuania, Belorussia, Bessarabia, and the Crimean Peninsula, and contained nearly 5 million Jews.

After their expulsion from Iberia, the Sephardic Jews moved eastward across North Africa and through the Mediterranean, many settling in the expanding Ottoman Empire. As in Poland, they were welcomed by the rulers and founded large communities in western Anatolia and the southern Balkans. In the Balkans they established themselves in every major city, but especially in Salonica, which they literally turned into a Spanish city. By 1660, Salonica was said to be home to as many as 40,000 Jews. As the activities of the Inquisition intensified in Iberia, many *Marranos* sought refuge in the Netherlands, where their Jewish background would be more difficult to uncover. They became especially numerous in Amsterdam, the rising center of Dutch world commerce once it had shaken off Spanish rule.

## The Protestant Reformation

In the early 16th century the position of Western Christendom seemed secure. The Muslims had been driven from Spain, and, although they now reigned supreme in the Balkans,

these were lands occupied largely by Eastern Orthodox peoples. Indeed, the Orthodox Church had been greatly weakened by the Ottoman advance, and its only secular champion was the distant Principality of Moscow. The Jews, too, were largely gone from western Europe. At this moment of seeming triumph, the Universal Church itself foundered.

It was not as if there hadn't been signs of the rupture to come. In the 1370s, John Wycliffe in England had challenged many practices of the Church and attacked the legitimacy of the office of the Papacy itself. His followers, the Lollards, though driven underground, appear to have played a substantial role in the success of the 16th-century English Reformation. In Bohemia, Jan Hus became the popular leader of a reform movement in the early 15th century. Much influenced by the writings of Wycliffe, he became involved in a power struggle between the Bohemian king and the German Archbishop of Prague. Incurring the wrath of the Archbishop, Hus was put on trial in Constance as a Wycliffe heretic and was burned at the stake in July 1415. After his death the Hussite movement spread widely and became a focus for anti-Austrian sentiment among the Czechs. It was crushed, however, in the Counter-Reformation and survived only in the exiled Moravian Church.

The Reformation of the 16th century involved two principal movements, Lutheranism and Calvinism, which was also known as the Reformed movement. In 1517 Martin Luther fastened his 95 theses, meant to open discussion about the weaknesses he saw within the Church, on the door of All Saints' Church in Wittenberg. As a German patriot, he was troubled by the wealth that poured into the coffers of Rome through the purchase of indulgences, which were supposed to reduce the time spent by sinners in purgatory. Central to his doctrine was the idea that salvation could not be bought but was attainable through faith alone. He also viewed the Scriptures as the supreme authority and insisted that lay people be able to consult them directly rather than through the mediation of a priest. This conviction lay behind his transla-

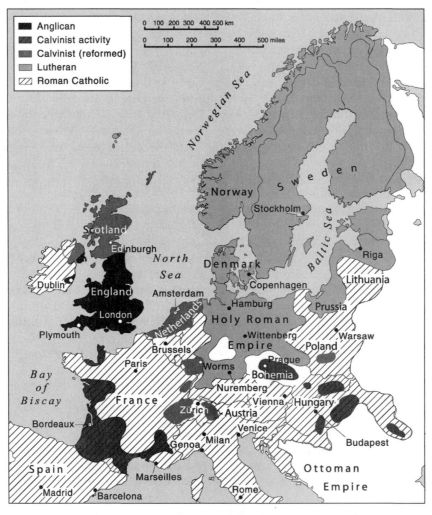

FIGURE 6.5. The Reformation.

tion of the Bible into German, an act that was to have an enormous impact on the rise of standard German, as we have seen. Lutheranism never gained much popularity outside the Germanic world, but it was accepted by the princes of many German states, by the King of Sweden for the Swedes and Finns, by the King of Denmark for the Danes, Norwegians, Icelanders, and Færoese, and by the Grand Master of the Teutonic Order for the peoples of the East Baltic.

The Reformed movement has its origin in Huldrych Zwingli, who first preached in Zürich in 1518. His sermons, denouncing many of the same excesses that Luther railed against, helped to initiate the Swiss Reformation in 1522. The movement quickly spread to neighboring urban cantons, especially Bern and Basel, but was stoutly resisted in the rural forest cantons. This began a long association between Reformed Christianity and urban, bourgeois populations. In the early 1530s, John Calvin, a French humanist who had fled from Paris to Basel because of his liberal ideas, was converted to Swiss Protestantism. In 1536 he was invited by the burghers of Geneva to help in the establishment of the new religion there. He created a Church in Geneva that was to provide a model for Reformed Churches everywhere. Key features of this branch of Protestantism were the doctrine of predestination and the idea of government by an assembly of representatives chosen by the congregation rather than by bishops (Presbyterianism). Aside from the urban cantons of Switzerland, Reformed Christianity was adopted in many territories in the Rhineland, in the Netherlands, and in Scotland. Reformed ideas were also widely accepted in France (the Huguenots) and in east-central Europe, but there they survived the Counter-Reformation only in eastern Hungary and among the Germans and Hungarians of the Transylvanian Basin.

While the Lutheran and Reformed movements lay at the heart of the Protestant Reformation, there were other groups as well. The Universal Church was not just split—it was shattered. The Anabaptists represented the radical left wing of the Reformation. Originating in Zürich among disillusioned followers of Zwingli, their aim was to restore the early Church of true believers. They held that true baptism was possible only when a person could publicly admit sin and seek salvation through faith, and thus rejected the baptism of infants. They also believed in the strict separation of church and state, and, for true believers, complete abstention from public life, especially service in the military. Their radical beliefs brought them into constant conflict with the secular authorities, and they were expelled from one city after another. Nonetheless, Anabaptist thinking also took root in Moravia and in the Netherlands and northern Germany. The former movement gave rise to the Hutterites and the latter to the Mennonites. The Amish descend from the followers of Jakob Ammann, whose teachings were at variance with those of mainstream Mennonites and who formed a breakaway sect in the 1690s. Because of their prowess in agriculture, Catherine the Great of Russia invited many Anabaptist groups to settle on the farming frontier in Ukraine, where they were given permission to use their own language and were exempted from military service. In the late 19th century many of these people left for the Great Plains of North America when they began to lose their privileges.

The Reformation in England followed a rather different course than in the rest of Europe. In 1534, Henry VIII essentially nationalized the Church by separating it from Rome and declaring himself head, but he gave it little theological direction. Henry had slight interest in religious doctrine; the reasons for his actions were purely personal and political. More attention was given to theological matters by his children who followed him on the throne. A brief effort, under Edward VI, at bringing the Church of England into line with Protestant thinking was reversed when the Catholic Mary Tudor ascended the throne in 1553. The major work of reforming doctrine would be left to Henry's daughter, Elizabeth. Her "Elizabethan Settlement" was based primarily on the teachings of the Lollards and the Lutherans, with some admixture of Calvinism. The tenets of faith as expressed in the Thirty-nine Articles of 1571, however, often contained ambiguities and made minimal demands on believers. Elizabeth's chief objective was to make the Church as inclusive as possible. What she wanted was universal acceptance of the Church and of the monarch's role as its supreme governor. She was totally unconcerned with the details of her subjects' beliefs. It was thus that, in doctrine, the Church of England became a branch of Protestantism, while in government, liturgy, and customs remained much closer to medieval Catholicism than the other Reformation Churches.

The ramifications of the Reformation, even outside the realm of religion, were wide-reaching. When the Universal Church in the West was shattered, national churches were established. The Church of Sweden and the Church of Denmark were Lutheran, the Dutch Reformed Church and the Church of Scotland were Calvinist, to name but a few. Latin gave way to the vernacular language in the service and the religious literature. These were important first steps in the development of nationalism, the idea that the nation-state is the only legitimate sovereign political entity. The new religions, especially Lutheranism, exalted the state of marriage. Not only were clerics permitted to marry and form families, but also the home was made perhaps the most important center of religion, providing a substitute for the monastery. In medieval Catholicism, religion had belonged unequivocally to the public realm. With the Reformation it began to be removed to the private sphere. In the 18th century, the Enlightenment would make religion a matter of personal choice, further privatizing it.

Around the turn of the 20th century, the German sociologist and political economist Alfred Weber developed the notion that there was a link between the Reformation and the rise of capitalism. He did not credit the new faith so much with furthering the capitalist *system* as with encouraging the development of the *spirit* of capitalism. The capitalist economy differed from the medieval one in that the individual entrepreneur replaced the corporate guild as the principal actor. Weber argued that the capitalist entrepreneur came to value work for its own sake, not merely as a means to meet the needs of daily life. In making the connection to the Protestant ethic, he cited Luther's idea that the work of God was best accomplished in the common occupations, not in monasteries. He further noted Luther's rejection of charity as a way to achieve salvation. This he saw as promoting an ethic of self-reliance, further strengthening the respect for work. In Calvin's preaching he emphasized the idea of predestination. Even before birth, he said, God had decided whether or not a person would be saved. Many of his followers reasoned that success in this world was a sign of being one of the elect, and this success was a result of work. Since Calvinism insisted that its followers lead a simple and frugal life, the wealth gained from hard work could not be lavished on luxury but only reinvested in economic activity. This is a principal tenet of capitalism. Many have raised objections to Weber's argument, but it remains a thesis open to discussion.

## English Nonconformism

The Nonconformist, or Dissenter, movement in England was a continuation of the Protestant Reformation. It originated in the late 16th century among a group of people who felt the Elizabethan Settlement had not advanced the Protestant cause far enough. These "Puritans" sought to rid the Church of England of the Roman Catholic "popery" that they felt it had retained. Many had fled from England to Geneva during Mary Tudor's reign and had absorbed a healthy dose of Calvinism. The Puritans won a brief victory in the mid-17th century when Parliament overthrew Charles I and the army established a government under Oliver Cromwell. One of their chief aims was to replace the Church's episcopal form of government with one more representative of the people. The restoration of the monarchy in 1660 smashed these hopes, but with the passage of the Act of Toleration in 1689 the Dissenters did win a substantial victory.

Several Protestant denominations descend from the Puritan movement. The Congregationalists distinguished themselves by establishing governance by the congregation of worshippers, independent of any higher authority. The Baptists also held to this form of governance but differed by maintaining that only believers (hence not infants) should be baptized. British Unitarianism was a product of the increasingly scientific view of the universe that marked the 18th-century Enlightenment and encouraged an increased emphasis on reason and morals among the liberal Calvinist clergy. Finally, the Society of Friends (Quakers) represents the extreme left wing of the Puritan movement. Eschewing ordained clergy and buildings specifically dedicated for religious functions, the early Quakers believed that God would come to any gathering of worshippers and spontaneously speak through one of the congregation. While all these outgrowths of Puritanism developed in England, they spread also to other parts of Europe and especially to North America.

The last important Nonconformist movement to arise in England is Methodism. Around 1740, John Wesley, an Anglican clergyman, began preaching to people living on the fringes of society, to those who felt overlooked by the Church of England. He was joined by others within the Church and formed a society that was dubbed "Methodist" by others because of its emphasis on methodical study and devotion. Methodism had special appeal to people in the rapidly expanding industrial areas of Britain, where it gave hope to the poor and taught them frugality so that they might improve their lot. Although it was never Wesley's intention to separate from the Church of England, a formal break did occur in 1795, 4 years after his death. Together with the Baptist movement, Methodism also made an impact on a number of continental societies, as well as becoming a major force in American life.

**FIGURE 6.6. Eglwys yng Nghwm Pennant.** "Cwm Pennant" is the name of a remote valley in North Wales and the title of one of the most famous poems in Welsh. This stone chapel, surrounded by its congregational graveyard, is typical of rural Welsh chapels built in the early to mid-19th century, when Nonconformist religion flourished in Wales. (Photo: A. K. Knowles)

## The Holocaust

During the 19th and early 20th centuries there was little change in the religious map of Europe. The most sudden and sweeping alteration in the religious composition of the European population took place during the 1930s and 1940s as a result of the Nazi effort to erase the Jewish population from the map of Europe. All through the 1920s there had been a rising wave of "racial" prejudice in Germany. It was both pro-Aryan and anti-Semitic. With the coming of the great economic crisis in 1929, the boycotting and vandalizing of Jewish businesses began. With the ascendancy of the Nazi Party in 1933 came dismissal of Jews from government and university posts. The Nuremberg Laws, published in 1935, stripped Jews of their citizenship and forbade them to marry other Germans.

The number of beatings and murders of Jews by Nazi youth gangs increased during the 1930s. The violence reached a crescendo on the night of November 9, 1938 (*Kristallnacht*, the night of broken glass), when nearly every synagogue in Germany and thousands of Jewish businesses and shops were destroyed. Next began the wholesale imprisonment of Jews in concentration camps and the confiscation of their wealth. Those not imprisoned were ordered to live in ghettos and barred from all public parks and buildings, including schools. By 1941, all use of the telephone and public transport systems was forbidden, and Jews over the age of 6 were required to wear the yellow star-of-David badge.

Anti-Jewish measures spread with the annexation of Austria in 1938, of Czechoslovakia in 1939, and the enactment of laws on the German model in Italy, Hungary, and Romania. With the early successes of the Nazi military machine nearly all of the Jews of Europe were brought under direct or indirect German control. The emphasis at first was on expulsion, but there was nowhere for them to go. In January 1942 the decision was taken to implement the "final solution." The official stated policy was to "resettle" (read "exterminate") the Jews in the East. Poland was chosen to be the center for the annihilation of all European Jewry. The six largest Nazi extermination camps (Auschwitz, Belzec, Chelmno, Majdanek, Sobibor, and Treblinka) were all located here. Jews from outside Poland were either sent to ghettos in eastern cities and then to the camps or they were shipped directly to the gas chambers, usually at Auschwitz. Not surprisingly, of the estimated 5.9 million who perished during the Holocaust, 55% were Polish.

In some countries, mainly in western and northern Europe, the Christian population tried to help the Jews. Virtually all Danish Jews escaped the death camps because they were smuggled across the Øresund to neutral Sweden by Danish fishermen. Some French Jews found refuge (ironically) in Spain and Portugal and also in Switzerland. The Finnish government, although allied with Germany against the Soviet Union, refused to turn its tiny Jewish population over to the Nazis. Perhaps most remarkable was the firm resistance put up by the Bulgarian people and their gov-

ernment, which saved the lives of all 50,000 of that country's Jews. But there was no hope for the Jews of most of eastern Europe. Anti-Semitism had been rife there from the 18th century onward. The population often cooperated with the Nazis in rounding up and destroying local Jewish populations.

The impact of the Holocaust on the Jewish population of Europe was devastating. The principal losses were in the occupied territories, especially Poland and the western Soviet Union, because this is where the bulk of Europe's Jewry was concentrated before the war. Whereas almost 60% of all the Jews in the world lived in Europe before the war, just one-third did so in 1946. That percentage has continued to decline because of emigration, largely from the territories of the former Soviet Union, to Israel and the United States. Today only about 2 million Jews remain in Europe, about half in Russia and Ukraine and half in France and England. More Jews now live in France than in any other European country, in part because of a large immigration of Sephardim from North Africa.

TABLE 6.1. Jewish Population Losses during the Holocaust

|  | 1939 population (in thousands) | 1946 population (in thousands) | Losses (in thousands) |
|---|---|---|---|
| Western Europe | | | |
| Belgium | 80 | 45 | 35 |
| France | 300 | 200 | 100 |
| Netherlands | 130 | 30 | 100 |
| West-central Europe | | | |
| Austria | 90 | 10 | 80 |
| Germany | 300 | 30 | 270 |
| East-central Europe | | | |
| Czechoslovakia | 275 | 35 | 240 |
| Hungary | 450 | 150 | 300 |
| Poland | 3,300 | 70 | 3,230 |
| Eastern Europe | | | |
| Russia | 3,000 | 2,000 | 1,000 |
| Balkans | | | |
| Greece | 75 | 10 | 65 |
| Romania | 800 | 425 | 375 |
| Yugoslavia | 75 | 15 | 60 |
| Western Mediterranean | | | |
| Italy | 60 | 30 | 30 |
| Europe | 8,425 | 2,775 | 5,650 |

*Note.* Data from Ben-Sasson (1976).

FIGURE 6.7. Neue Synagogue, Berlin. Once a symbol of the prosperity and prestige achieved by Berlin's large Jewish community, the Neue Synagogue was built in 1866, using a mock Moorish style popular at the time. The building served as the city's central synagogue until the time of the Holocaust. All but destroyed during the war, the structure was restored in 1995 and now serves as a Jewish museum and culture center.

## RELIGION IN EUROPE TODAY

### Affiliation, Practice, and Belief

It is useful to distinguish among three ways in which a person may be associated with a religion. The most distant form is *affiliation*, that is, some kind of formal, documented connection between an individual and an instituted religious body. Affiliation, however, tells us nothing about *practice*. In Europe, particularly, there is a large discrepancy between belonging and worshipping. There is also much variation in the frequency of worship. Finally, neither affiliation nor practice says much about *belief*. The relationships among these three elements of religious association are complex. One may belong without practicing or believing, believe without belonging or practicing, and even practice without believing—at least, in *all* the tenets of the faith. The term *nonreligious* usually means, therefore, nonaffiliated, though in some cases it can mean association with an atheist group. These data thus give only a general impression of how the major branches of religion are distributed in Europe.

Perhaps the most striking feature of modern data on religious affiliation in Europe is the large percentage of the population that is unaffiliated or atheistic. The figure for all of Europe is much inflated by the very high percentage for the former Soviet Union, where all religion was proscribed under the communists. Nonetheless, in every region it is higher

TABLE 6.2. Religious Composition of Europe's Major Regions

|  | Orthodox | Eastern Rite Catholic | Roman Catholic | Protestant | Jewish | Muslim | Other (mainly nonbelievers) | Total |
|---|---|---|---|---|---|---|---|---|
| Western Europe | 0.4% | 0.0% | 69.5% | 5.6% | 0.8% | 4.9% | 18.8% | 100.0% |
| Britain and Ireland | 0.9% | 0.0% | 8.6% | 45.6% | 0.4% | 1.3% | 43.1% | 100.0% |
| West-central Europe | 1.5% | 0.0% | 38.3% | 39.6% | 0.0% | 1.9% | 18.7% | 100.0% |
| East-central Europe | 1.8% | 0.3% | 76.4% | 4.6% | 0.3% | 0.1% | 16.5% | 100.0% |
| Nordic and Baltic Europe | 3.2% | 0.0% | 1.8% | 76.4% | 0.0% | 0.7% | 17.9% | 100.0% |
| Western Mediterranean | 0.0% | 0.0% | 76.5% | 0.9% | 0.0% | 1.2% | 21.4% | 100.0% |
| Eastern Europe | 23.7% | 2.7% | 1.5% | 1.9% | 0.7% | 8.5% | 60.9% | 100.0% |
| Balkans | 65.4% | 0.0% | 5.2% | 0.9% | 0.2% | 11.5% | 16.8% | 100.0% |
| Europe | 12.6% | 0.7% | 35.9% | 15.0% | 0.4% | 4.4% | 31.1% | 100.0% |

*Note*. Data from Encyclopaedia Britannica Staff (1999).

than the 9% reported for the United States. Outside of the former communist bloc, the percentage of nonreligious people is highest in the Netherlands and the United Kingdom, specifically England. Generally, nonaffiliation is lower in Catholic than in Protestant countries, but the specific historic context of each country must also be kept in mind. Thus, in Poland, where Catholicism is an integral part of Polish nationalism, it is under 10%. The same is true of Romania, where Orthodoxy has always defined for most Romanians what they are, setting them apart from the minority Hungarians and Germans. On the other hand, in Spain the Catholic Church was closely associated with the fascist regime, a fact that soured many Spaniards on organized religion. The high figure in the Netherlands may be associated with the strong humanist tradition there and the fact that the Dutch Reformed Church was not established. Nonaffiliation is much lower in Scandinavia, where strong state Churches have existed since the Reformation.

Table 6.3 shows data on affiliation, practice, and belief for some western European countries. The figures for church attendance and beliefs are from a survey taken in 1981. Some of these data are also available from a similar survey done in 1999. The differences between the two surveys are not large, but in general the later survey shows lower percentages of people professing most of the beliefs. Of the nine countries shown, five are dominantly Catholic, two are largely Protestant, and two are mixed. Comparing practice with affiliation, it is clear that, overall, church attendance is highest in the Catholic countries and lowest in the Protestant. The major exception is France, where, in spite of the fact that 76% of the population professes to be Catholic, 57% say they never go to church. Indeed, a comparison between nonaffiliation and nonattendance reveals that nominal affiliation is most widespread in France, Belgium, Denmark, and Britain.

A belief in God is probably the most fundamental tenet in Christianity. In most of the countries a portion of those who appear to believe do not practice. This is highest in Britain and France. Ideas about the nature of God vary greatly, however. For some, God is a be-

**TABLE 6.3. Affiliation, Practice, and Belief in Some Western European Countries**

|  | Denmark | Britain | Ireland | France | Belgium | Netherlands | Germany[a] | Spain | Italy |
|---|---|---|---|---|---|---|---|---|---|
| **Affiliation** | | | | | | | | | |
| Catholic | 0.6% | 9.0% | 91.5% | 76.5% | 88.0% | 32.0% | 33.9% | 66.7% | 81.7% |
| Protestant | 86.4% | 53.0% | 8.5% | 1.8% | 0.5% | 23.0% | 42.8% | 0.2% | 0.2% |
| None | 11.7% | 30.2% | 0.1% | 14.0% | 8.6% | 38.0% | 21.1% | 32.1% | 17.1% |
| **Church attendance** | | | | | | | | | |
| At least once weekly | 3% | 14% | 82% | 12% | 30% | 27% | 21% | 41% | 36% |
| Never | 43% | 46% | 4% | 57% | 34% | 41% | 20% | 25% | 21% |
| **Belief in . . .** | | | | | | | | | |
| God | 58% | 76% | 95% | 62% | 77% | 65% | 72% | 87% | 84% |
| A personal God | 24% | 31% | 73% | 26% | 39% | 34% | 28% | 55% | 26% |
| Sin | 29% | 69% | 85% | 42% | 44% | 49% | 59% | 58% | 63% |
| A soul | 33% | 59% | 82% | 46% | 52% | 59% | 61% | 64% | 63% |
| Life after death | 26% | 45% | 76% | 35% | 37% | 42% | 39% | 55% | 47% |
| Heaven | 17% | 57% | 83% | 27% | 33% | 39% | 31% | 50% | 41% |
| Hell | 8% | 27% | 54% | 15% | 18% | 15% | 14% | 34% | 31% |
| The devil | 12% | 30% | 57% | 17% | 20% | 21% | 18% | 33% | 30% |

*Note.* Data on affiliation from Encyclopaedia Britannica Staff (1999). Data on church attendance and beliefs from Harding, Phillips, & Fogarty (1986).
[a] Data on church attendance and beliefs are for West Germany.

ing that humans can relate to on a personal level and who takes an interest in their daily affairs. For others, the deity is more diffuse, a life force or spirit. The expression of belief in a personal God correlates much more strongly with other traditional Christian beliefs. Six of these are presented in the table, the last three representing a very literal interpretation of Christian theology.

A measure of the religiosity of these nine countries' populations can be obtained by combining the figures on frequent church attendance, belief in a personal God, and beliefs in heaven, hell, and the devil. By this definition the Irish are clearly the most religious, followed at some distance by the Spanish. Yet more secular are the Italians, Belgians, Dutch, Germans, and British. The French and the Danes appear to have the loosest tie to their Christian past. We may recall that the French were the leaders of the first Fertility Transition and the Danes were the leaders of the Second. The examples included here contain no Orthodox populations. In a survey taken in the three Baltic States of Estonia, Latvia, and Lithuania, 64% of Russians (40% of them Orthodox) declared they believed in God, but only 4% of these claimed that they went to church at least once a week. The devil was a reality for 35%, and 36% thought there was a life after death. This profile is closest to that of the French.

The fall of communism and the breakup of the Soviet Union have drastically altered the climate for religion in the eastern part of Europe. Many traditional religions, once vilified by the authorities, have been revitalized and are being enlisted in the service of nationalist causes. The importance of religion to Polish and Romanian nationality has already been mentioned, but Ukraine also offers an excellent example of this phenomenon. By the Union of Brest-Litovsk in 1596 a number of Orthodox bishoprics in the Ukraine entered into communion with Rome while retaining the Orthodox liturgy and other customs of the Byzantine Church. This body became known as the Ukrainian or Eastern Rite Catholic (sometimes called Uniate) Church. Because it had separated from Orthodoxy, and hence

Moscow, it early became a focus of Ukrainian nationalism. It flourished during the periods of Catholic Polish and Austrian rule but was suppressed under the Orthodox Czarist and atheist Soviet regimes. In 1989 it reemerged and reclaimed its role as the champion of Ukrainian independence. In response, a portion of the Orthodox Church broke from Moscow to form the Ukrainian Orthodox Church—Kiev Patriarchate. This Church also supported independence and found favor among Ukrainian political leaders. Moscow answered by giving autonomy to the Ukrainian Orthodox Church—Moscow Patriarchate. What this demonstrates is that the reawakening of interest in religion in the former communist bloc must be seen in part as a manifestation of national revival, as well as a long-term manifestation of a deep religiosity that in many ways distinguishes eastern Europe from the West.

At the same time as the traditional religions try to reclaim their positions, missionaries for nontraditional religions, especially from the United States, are taking advantage of what they see as a religious vacuum to spread their own faiths. In Russia, Protestantism, while still claiming less than 1% of the total population, is making remarkable inroads. This is especially true in the peripheral areas—northwestern Russia, Siberia, and the Far East. Alarmed by their success, the Russian Orthodox Church has put pressure on the government to marginalize them. In 1997 a law was passed that required new religious groups to function for 15 years before they could register permanently as national religious organizations. Elsewhere in the former communist bloc the ground is less fertile for this kind of foreign intervention. Religious persecution under the communists had a shorter history here than in the Soviet Union, and for a number of reasons persecution stemming from local conditions was less severe.

What can be said about the Christian religion in modern Europe today is that belief in the central tenets of the faith is not widespread. What lingers is a general belief in a God, but more as a spiritual force than as a personal presence in one's daily life. For many, however, religion is still closely associated with traditional culture. The major Church holidays, such as Christmas and Easter, have become secularized but still can elicit widespread attendance at church. Holy rites are still sought by many to mark the major occasions in the life cycle: birth (baptism), marriage (though this is declining), and death (funerals). The adherence to a particular form of Christianity is also for some a badge of national identity that sets them apart from their neighbors of different faiths.

It is difficult to generalize about Muslims in Europe today, divided as they are between the immigrant communities of the West and the indigenous ones of the East. Islamic identity is certainly strong among the Tatars and other Russian groups, as well as in the Balkans. It has also become important in western European countries, where in major cities such as Frankfurt, Berlin, and Paris the muezzin can be heard calling the faithful to daily prayer. There are now roughly 12.5 million Muslims living in the European Union, the majority of them from countries such as Morocco, Algeria, Pakistan, Indonesia, Turkey, Iran, and Iraq, and the product of the waves of labor immigration that swept into many west European countries during the postwar decades.

Almost everywhere, however, the Christian majority sees Muslims as a threat. The recent Serbian aggression against Bosnians and Kosovars amply demonstrates this fact. The prejudice has deep roots, going all the way back to the bitter struggles waged by Christian Europe against the "infidels" during the Middle Ages. The most recent spate of "ethnic cleansing" between Christian and Muslim populations in Bosnia follows on previous episodes of genocide and removal that took place immediately after World War I, and especially during World War II when Serb nationalists killed nearly 100,000 Bosnian Muslims in their villages (the Muslims were also responsible for atrocities against the Serbs).

Today's "war on terror," in which all Muslims are viewed with suspicion and rising alarm, has exacerbated religious, social, and economic prejudices already held among western European populations toward their immigrant neighbors of Islamic faith. Although the vast majority of western Europe's Muslim population are neither extremists nor have any ties to terrorist activity, they are all too often automatically condemned. Most European countries have in recent years officially espoused the goal of multiculturalism as a means of assimilating their sizable Muslim immigrant populations, but in fact little is

**FIGURE 6.8. Mosque in Hamburg.** A large mosque, replete with minaret and full-scale mural of a traditional mosque in Turkey, stands among a variety of commercial and residential buildings near the center of Hamburg. The building marks the presence of the city's large Turkish immigrant community. (Photo: J. Hagen)

done to integrate them, and most stick to their national groups, socializing and praying with one another. They are highly visible, not only in dress, speech, and skin color but also in the presence of their Muslim schools and mosques. Only in Spain and Italy does the general public seem to have a relatively relaxed attitude toward the Muslim population today, due in part to historic ties in parts of these countries with North Africa and a Muslim heritage.

## Religion and the European Union

As we have seen, of the three principal religious groups in Europe, Catholics are the most numerous. This is particularly true of the European Union. At its founding the EU (then the EEC, or European Economic Community) was a strongly Catholic bloc. With the admission of the United Kingdom and Denmark the balance shifted significantly toward the Protestants, although a Catholic majority was maintained. The entry of Greece brought the first significant Orthodox community, slightly reducing the relative importance of the others, but the admission of Spain and Portugal 4 years later once again increased the Catholic majority. Today, while Catholics remain most numerous, they are no longer in the majority. This first became true following the entry of Finland and Sweden in 1995, although now the admission of staunchly Catholic Poland and other Catholic parts of east-central Europe has returned the balance. The lack of a Catholic majority is also due to significant numbers of Spaniards and Italians now identifying themselves as nonreligious.

TABLE 6.4. Changes in the Relative Size of Major Religious Groups as the EU Has Expanded

|  | Catholic | Protestant | Orthodox |
|---|---|---|---|
| The 6 | 66% | 17% | 0% |
| The 9 | 54% | 30% | 0% |
| The 10 | 52% | 29% | 4% |
| The 12 | 59% | 25% | 3% |
| The 15 | 49% | 24% | 3% |
| The 25 | 53% | 19% | 3% |

*Note.* Data from Encyclopedia Britannica Staff (1999).

From the beginning, the Protestant Churches have had an uneasy relationship with the European Union. One of their problems is that since their inception they have identified strongly with national or regional entities. Indeed, as we have suggested, the Protestant Reformation was one of the forces behind the rise of nationalism. As the EU challenges the very existence of the nation-state, the Churches of the Protestant world have to wonder what their role in the new social order will be. This is especially so since the Pope sees the EU as an opportunity to return Europe to its former position as the bulwark of Christendom. The vision is one of a unified political, economic, and religious system, the latter under the leadership of the universal Catholic Church.

The position of Protestant Church leaders on European unification is that religious freedom is of the utmost importance. They want no part of a Christian state but rather take the position that the development of a secular society in Europe is a *fait accompli*. Indeed, they celebrate the role that Protestantism has played in the philosophical movements that have emancipated European society from the dominance of religious values. In their view autonomous thinking lies at the foundation of Europe's democratic institutions. A monolithic Christianity must not be allowed to reconquer Europe.

Tactically one of the main problems the Protestants have had is that they lack a single voice. No Protestant leader has the status of the Pope, whose position as head of a Church with over a billion communicants worldwide gives him the prestige of a major chief of state. The Vatican maintains diplomatic ties with Brussels. Its spokesmen command the attention of the media. It is not surprising that some Protestants complain that the Catholic Church monopolizes Christianity. A burning question is whether the Protestant community should become more institutionalized so it can more effectively compete, or whether it should remain true to its ideal of pluralism and accept the consequences. In spite of their handicaps, Protestant leaders have managed to maintain a lively dialogue with the EU

Commission and have made clear their views on many issues. The entry now of more Orthodox countries may also help the Protestant position. Their Churches, too, have a national base, and the two groups now work together within both the World Council of Churches and the Conference of European Churches.

## RELIGION AND PLACE

From earliest times specific places have been afforded special status for religious purposes. We know that many prehistoric sites and monuments mark the locations of sacred places. The circular complex of stones and ditches known as Stonehenge, which was built and rebuilt over two millennia beginning somewhere around 3000 B.C. in the midst of England's Salisbury Plain, was probably designed to function both as a temple and an astrological calendar. Much later, the Greeks and Romans built temples on sites they dedicated to the deities. The place of Rome's founding, atop the Capitoline Hill, was of profound religious importance and was graced by a series of temples intended as sanctuaries of the gods.

At times, the sacred sites of one religion could be co-opted by another. Some Roman temples survived as Christian churches. During the medieval expansion of Christianity into the lands beyond the former Empire, it was not uncommon for the sites of pagan practice and ritual to be simply incorporated into the Christian landscape. In northern Europe there are numerous examples of places where Christian churches were founded, for the sake of convenience or continuity, on or near sacred groves or hilltops traditionally deemed holy by the local population. In a similar fashion, a portion of the center of the Great Mosque (*La Mesquita* in Spanish) of Córdoba became a cathedral church following the Christian reconquest of the town, while the great Christian church of Hagia Sophia in Byzantine Constantinople was converted to a mosque after the Turkish conquest of the city in 1453.

The Christian veneration of holy places dates back to the fourth century A.D., when places in the Holy Land associated with the life of Jesus were first identified and enshrined with structures, such as the Church of the Holy Sepulchre in Jerusalem. Indeed, the Crusades were launched in medieval times, in part, to protect Christian access to these holy places. Also important in the Christian world was the cult of martyrs and saints, which held that the spirits of martyrs remained present at the place of their martyrdom or in the remains of their bodies, a belief that led to the establishment of holy places outside of Palestine. Thus, Constantine erected St. Peter's Basilica in Rome in the early fourth century over the site of a Roman cemetery (excavated in 1939) where St. Peter was believed to have been buried after his martyrdom in 64 A.D.

After the fourth century the cult of martyrs and saints spread from Rome to other places

**FIGURE 6.9. Christian conversion of pagan sites.** Sweden's most famous pagan site, located at Old Uppsala, features three immense royal burial mounds and a flat-topped assembly mound. Behind the mounds stands a Christian church, which once formed part of a much larger Christian church built in the 1130s on the site of a wooden pagan temple. This is also said to be the site of an elaborate pagan rite that took place every eighth year at the time of the midwinter full moon. On these occasions, human and animal sacrifices were hung from a holy tree for 9 days.

**FIGURE 6.10. Pilgrimage.** Pilgrims arriving in Santiago de Compostela to visit the shrine of St. James are met by the spectacular baroque façade of the town's gray-granite cathedral, designed in the mid-18th century by a local architect. The famous front features two massive bell towers and a statue of St. James himself, looking out over the cathedral square from high above the entrance.

in Christendom. In 813, for example, Christians in far-off Galicia miraculously discovered the remains of the apostle St. James, who had been martyred in Jerusalem in 44 A.D. His bones, which had somehow been transported to this remote location in the far northwestern corner of the Iberian Peninsula (according to Spanish tradition aboard a miraculous ship without sails), became a symbol and rallying point for Christian Spain in its long struggle against the Moors. The city of Santiago de Compostela, which grew up around the great cathedral church that was erected on the holy resting place of St. James, became the third most important place of pilgrimage in the Christian world after Jerusalem and Rome. Christians who managed to make their way to the site of James's grave at Compostela were

promised absolution. For those who were not able to make the trip, forgiveness for their sins was possible by sending someone else in their place. During the 11th and 12th centuries, when the cult of St. James was at its height, a system of pilgrimage routes that led from all over western Christendom to Santiago de Compostela brought as many as half a million pilgrims to the sacred site each year.

In time a cult of relics developed in which the Church, in both the East and the West, encouraged and facilitated the distribution of the remains of martyrs and other holy objects to as many places as possible. Thus, every major church came to possess some important relic of alleged miraculous power. The cathedral church (Dom) of Trier, for example, became a place of special attraction because its relic was the "seamless robe" worn by Christ before he was crucified. Bruges's Basilica of the Holy Blood boasted one of the holiest relics in all of Europe, a phial that purportedly contained a few drops of blood washed from the body of Christ, which, from the time of the phial's arrival in Bruges shortly after the Second Crusade until the year 1325, would miraculously liquefy every Friday evening. Each year on Ascension Day, the phial is still carried around the town in solemn procession, just as it was in the Middle Ages.

The most ubiquitous relics were the fragments of the "True Cross"—purportedly recovered in Jerusalem by St. Helena, the mother of Constantine, in 327 A.D. These fragments eventually found their way into the possession of countless cathedrals and abbeys across Christendom. So numerous were these relics of the cross that they became the focus of a general attack on the veneration of relics among 16th-century Protestant reformers, in support of which John Calvin is said to have caustically observed that nothing less than a very large ship would have been sufficient to carry all the extant fragments of the cross to Europe.

Today we might regard the sites of Holocaust atrocities and extermination camps as special places of religious pilgrimage and memory for Jews. Auschwitz, the most notorious of the Nazi death camps in Poland, where more than a million people died, mostly Jews, has been preserved since 1947 as a museum and place of memory. The museum, which became a UNESCO World Heritage site in 1979, receives nearly half a million visitors a year.

Perhaps one of the most moving, but least known, of the Nazi extermination sites is located at Salaspils, not far from the city of Riga in Latvia. Visitors to Salaspils encounter a 40-hectare open field in the forest, in which stand half a dozen monumental statues of hopelessly forlorn, yet defiant, human forms. Inscribed on the concrete building that guards the entrance to the grounds are the ominously evocative words "The earth moans beyond this gate." As one steps beyond, one notes that from somewhere beneath the earth comes an eerie and steady thumping noise meant to represent a human heart. Under this otherwise innocuous-looking piece of ground lie the remains of 53,000 men, women, and children killed by the Nazis.

Burial grounds of all kinds are among the most interesting of sacred places. Human societies have always developed elaborately ritualistic ways for disposing of and memorializing the dead. The practice of burial in the ground goes all the way back to earliest times, as evidenced by the many surviving fields of Paleolithic, Neolithic, and early Bronze Age

earthen burial mounds or barrows scattered across Europe, as well as by discoveries of deliberate prehistoric burials in caves. The pagan Norse sometimes honored fallen chiefs and heroes by setting them adrift in blazing ships, but also buried the dead along with their belongings, including ships, in great burial mounds. The ancient Hebrews placed their dead in niches cut into the walls of caves, a practice that became widespread among Jews, and later Christians, throughout the Roman Empire. The labyrinths of subterranean catacombs outside the city of Rome, which also became places of Christian worship, are perhaps the best example of the practice.

The Romans, who generally cremated the dead until about 100 A.D., placed the remains in niches set in the walls of an above-ground tomb, most commonly a rectangular and barrel-vaulted structure known as a *columbarium*. The remains of the poor were often placed in tall earthen pots, or *amphora*, the necks of which projected out of the ground for the purpose of pouring liquid offerings down to the dead. Christians, who placed such great emphasis on the idea of resurrection, eventually began to bury the dead in crypts beneath the pavements of churches and in churchyard cemeteries, often erecting elaborate markers or mausoleums to mark the resting places of the wealthy and important.

Interment grounds were intended from earliest times to be exclusive spaces. The Romans reserved the rights-of-way along the roads leading into the city for the tombs of the those with status or money, for it was important to such people to be publicly remembered after death and therefore to build their family tombs in places where they could be seen and visited by passersby. In contrast, the disposal of the remains of criminals, slaves, and the poor were relegated to special areas that were more remotely located. Christian cemeteries could also be quite morally exclusive, The interment of murderers and witches, and those who committed suicide—not to mention infidels and Jews, or even Christians from other towns and denominations—was often prohibited. Exclusion could

**FIGURE 6.11. Memory.** The stoic poses of the stone figures at Salaspils offer a poignant reminder of the horror of what happened in this open meadow outside of the city of Riga during the Nazi mass exterminations of World War II.

**FIGURE 6.12. Necropolis.** The necropolis, or "city of the dead," was customarily located outside the city in the ancient Mediterranean world, often along a road leading into the city. One of the most visited examples is found at Myra in southwestern Turkey, where the necropolis, which dates from the fourth century B.C., is cut into the stone face of the western side of the acropolis. Many tombs are elaborately cut to resemble the shapes of houses or temples. (Photo: J. L. Kramer)

even extend to nonfamily members, in the sense that individual burial plots and mausoleums were typically set aside, even by the Greeks and Romans, as the private spaces of families who wished to see the spirits of their loved ones remain together beyond death.

In the urban context, the issues of sanitation and overcrowding have always loomed large. The ancient Greeks and Romans, who recognized the inherent sanitation dangers posed by the disposal of the dead in concentrated places, permitted burials to take place only outside the city walls. In Rome, the law of the Twelve Tables barred burial or cremation within the confines of the city. Christians, however, began to bury their dead, as we have seen, in and around the churches where they worshipped. Their insistence on doing so soon placed them at odds with the town authorities, but the fact that church properties had become exempt by the Middle Ages from most secular laws meant that the practice was

allowed to continue. As a result, overcrowded churchyards, which were literally filled with coffins, often stacked on top of one another to levels barely beneath the surface of the ground, became a breeding ground for disease and a public sanitation threat. The need for space was so pressing that barely decomposed corpses were often disinterred in the dead of night and thrown into nearby pits to make way for fresh burials. As concerns over public health (which were often tied to a greater understanding of the connection between public health and environmental causes) began to mount in the 19th century, the practice of burial on the grounds of churches in towns and cities was gradually discontinued in many parts of Europe.

A related 19th-century development, which also relieved some of the pressures of overcrowding and sanitation, was a revival of the practice of cremation. Cremation was common among the ancients, as well as among many pagan groups in northern Europe. The common belief was that the consumption of the body by fire was a beneficial practice because it purified the body, which was commonly thought to otherwise be capable of defiling anyone who came into direct contact with it. The fire was also thought to light the way of the deceased to another world. After around 100 A.D., however, the practice died out among the Romans, in part because of the influence of Christianity, which associated the practice with pagan beliefs and held that cremation might prevent the resurrection of the body. With the exception of the period around the Black Death, when mass cremations of bodies became necessary, the practice of inhumation became nearly universal in Europe and persisted until late in the 19th century. The revival of cremation began in Britain, only after the publication of an influential book on the subject by Queen Victoria's personal surgeon, Sir Henry Thompson. Legalization in many countries, and the acquiescence of both the Protestant and Catholic Churches (but not Orthodox Jews) soon followed and paved the way for a general return to the practice in many parts of Europe.

**FIGURE 6.13. Christian burial grounds.** Rows of weathered gravestones grace the grounds of England's Malmesbury Abbey, dissolved by Henry VIII in 1539. The remains of the abbey church date from the 12th century, although a monastery stood on this site from as early as 676 A.D. Local legend tells of the ghost of a monk who wanders among the gravestones at night, looking for something.

## RELIGION AND THE BUILT ENVIRONMENT

Religion is deeply intertwined with European history and has left a dramatic impression nearly everywhere on the European cultural landscape. In the classical and especially the medieval periods more time, resources, and energy were put into the construction of places of worship than any other building endeavors. Even in the early modern period religious edifices were still among the most conspicuous elements in the landscape. Only in modern times have secular buildings become the prime concern of architects. The often monumental projects of Europe's great religious institutions provide a rich catalog of the changing styles of European architecture. We now turn our attention to the religious architectural history that can be read in the modern European landscape.

### Classical Beginnings (500 B.C.–400 A.D.)

The buildings left to us from the classical Greek period are almost entirely religious in nature. They are the temples built as the homes of deities important to the local population. Most are concentrated in southern Greece, the Aegean islands, and the western parts of Anatolia, but some may be found in the colonies established on Sicily and in the south of the Italian peninsula. In Greece itself the majority are constructed of white marble, though other stone was used. That is especially true in the western colonies, where marble was not available. The structures are typically rectangular in form with an inner room reserved for the statue of the deity and outer porches lined with rows of columns, often topped by elaborately carved capitols.

The acme of classical Greek architecture is to be seen on the Athenian Acropolis. An acropolis (Greek for "upper city") was a prominent feature of most Greek cities. Built atop a prominent hill, it contained the chief religious and administrative buildings and formed a kind of defensible citadel to which citizens from the lower town could retreat in times of danger. It was not impregnable, however, and the Athenian Acropolis was left in ruins by the Persians in 480 B.C. It was rebuilt under Pericles between 447 and 406 B.C., and the remains of the buildings one sees today date from this period.

By far the greatest achievement of the Periclean Age is the construction of the Parthenon, the temple of Athena, which contained a 12-meter-high gold and ivory statue of the goddess. Outside the temple stood a colossal bronze statue of Athena that could be seen from the sea 45 kilometers away. Both of these statues were taken to Constantinople by the Byzantines and were among the treasures lost during the sack of that city by the Crusaders in 1204. For such a large structure, the

Parthenon gives a remarkable feeling of weightlessness. This is achieved through the inward bowing of the columns such that, if they were extended upward, they would meet at an elevation of roughly 3 kilometers above the building. The Parthenon was converted first into a Byzantine church, then into a mosque, and finally into a powder magazine, which was hit by Venetian fire in 1687. Modern air pollution has taken a further toll, and the building is now being restored.

The built religious environment of the Romans covers a much larger territory, extending from the eastern Mediterranean, where Ephesus in modern Turkey, for example, was renowned for its Temple of Artemis or Diana, to the western Iberian Peninsula. Even north of the Alps, in France, Britain, and Germany, the ruins of Roman civilization can be seen in many places. The Romans advanced the technology of construction well beyond what the Greeks had achieved. The principal innovation was the use of the rounded arch. This allowed the building of higher and roomier structures, since the arches distributed the weight laterally and thus could support much heavier loads. Arch construction was greatly facilitated by the Roman improvement of an old building material, concrete. Most Roman monumental buildings, such as the Colosseum, were erected using concrete, which was then faced with a rock such as travertine (limestone) to make them more attractive. Marble was used

**FIGURE 6.14. The Parthenon.** This temple to the goddess Athena was built as a massive public works project during the fifth century B.C. Some of Athens's citizens even thought, at the time of its construction, that the structure was far too extravagant for the city. Conservators have worked hard, in recent years, to repair some of the damage caused by the 1687 explosion that shattered the temple, as well as to restore some of the features damaged by latter-day airborne pollutants.

mainly for decoration, applied in slabs to brick or concrete walls.

Early Roman temples were built on Greek models, rectangular with colonnaded porches, but later the Romans began to experiment with the new technologies of construction. A remarkable example of this experimentation is the Pantheon in Rome. Originally erected in 27 B.C. in the traditional temple style, it was completely rebuilt by the Emperor Hadrian between 118 and 128 A.D. The result is a circular building of concrete faced with brick and crowned by an immense concrete dome.

**FIGURE 6.15. The Pantheon.** Visible in this photo is the classical columned porch of the Pantheon, which fronts the cylindrical outer walls and domed interior of the structure. The building is remarkable for the precision of its design. The dimensions of the cylindrical casing and the dome are exactly equal. Atop the dome is a 9-meter-wide hole through which shafts of light descend to the floor below.

At 43 meters in diameter and 22 meters in height, it was the largest dome built anywhere in the world until modern times. This pagan temple has survived because it was rededicated in 609 as a Christian Church, which it remains today.

After Constantine's Edict of Toleration (313) gave legitimacy to Christianity within the Empire, the new religion began to construct churches that were adaptations of a secular building type, the basilica, that was used by the Romans as a hall of assembly, commerce, reception, or law-making. The general form of the building was rectangular, with a long, high hall (nave) flanked by lower aisles and ending in a rounded apse. Constantine commissioned three large churches with this form in Rome, the largest of which was the original St. Peter's (replaced in the 16th century by the present church). In the plans for these he added a transept that crossed the nave just before the apse, giving the buildings the form of a cross. This remained the model for churches in the Western Christian world throughout the Middle Ages.

## The Byzantine and Orthodox Traditions of the East (330–1712)

When Constantine began to build his new capital on the Bosporus, the "Second Rome," he assembled a mass of builders and artisans for the purpose. The majority came from Rome, so that the early official art was virtually all Roman art, and the classical basilica was adopted as the usual style of Christian Church. Change was in the air, however, since the new city arose in the Greek-speaking world, a fertile center of artistic ideas that had developed quite independently of Rome. The religious structures of Constantine's new capital were of two main types: longitudinal basilicas and centralized churches. The former, usually with three aisles, were intended for congregational worship; the latter, which were circular, square, or even octagonal in shape, were for burial or commemorative use. It was through a subtle combination of the two types that the characteristic Byzantine church emerged.

The Byzantine style made great strides in the sixth century, during the reign of the Emperor Justinian, one of the greatest builders of all time. He was responsible for the erection of four major churches in Constantinople, the most famous of which is the great cathedral of Hagia Sophia, where the ideas of the longitudinal basilica and the centralized building were combined in a wholly original manner. The distinctive feature of all of these buildings was the form of the roof, the dome. By the ninth century, Byzantine churches generally conformed to a single pattern, usually termed the "cross in square." Like St. Mark's Basilica in Venice, these churches typically had five domes, one at the center of the cross

**FIGURE 6.16. Hagia Sophia.** Built for the emperor Justinian as an imperial temple, Hagia Sophia (the Cathedral of Holy Wisdom) was intended to proclaim forever the glory of God and empire. The best mathematician of the time was employed to design what became the world's largest domed space; and it remained so for a thousand years until surpassed in the 16th century by the dome of St. Peter's in Rome. The church was converted to a mosque and surrounded by minarets after the Turkish conquest of Constantinople in 1453. In 1935 the new secular-minded Turkish Republic turned the building into a museum.

and one at each of the outer points. The building material varied with the locality, although brick was preferred to stone. The exterior decoration became increasingly elaborate, using intricate patterns in brickwork or colorful glazed pottery tiles.

The Principality of Kiev was converted to Christianity in 988, and Byzantine art in Russia was first established there. From Kiev the Byzantine style of architecture soon spread through the principalities of Novgorod and Vladimir-Suzdal. Everything connected with the design and decoration of the new churches followed the Byzantine pattern. The standard plan of the Greek church—the cross inscribed in a rectangle surmounted by a central dome—became the accepted type for Orthodox churches. Novgorod later became the center of a quite original style. It was here that the fundamental features of later Russian architecture were developed. The severe climate and heavy snowfalls of the north necessitated various modifications of the Byzantine architectural forms. Windows were narrowed; roofs became steeper and flat domes took on the bulbous form that, in different varieties, became the most notable feature of Russian church architecture.

After Constantinople fell to the Turks in 1453, hegemony in the world of Orthodox Christianity shifted to Muscovite Russia, and the city of Moscow became the "third Rome." Eager to rival the other centers of culture, the princes of Moscow launched a building program designed to give the city a new look in keeping with its new international importance. The city's citadel, the Kremlin, and two of its important churches were entirely rebuilt by Italian architects between 1475 and 1510. The Italians were required to incorporate the basic features of Byzantine planning and design into the new cathedrals, but also managed to introduce Italian motifs into the exterior decoration of the buildings.

The most thoroughly Russian of all the churches built in Moscow during this period was the Cathedral of St. Basil the Blessed (Pokrovsky Cathedral) in Red Square (1554–1560). Built by Czar Ivan IV (the Terrible) in gratitude for his victories over the khanates of Kazan and Astrakhan on the Volga, the church's structure exhibits no apparent architectural order. The lavish use of color and design in the decoration of the exterior is also at variance with Byzantine models. St. Basil's is essentially a copy of the wooden churches of

**FIGURE 6.17. Cathedral of St. Basil the Blessed.** Set in the midst of the windswept expanses of Moscow's Red Square, St. Basil's broods silently over a passing young couple. Although the church was actually designed by two local architects, legend has it that an Italian architect was employed to do the job, and that the Czar, Ivan the Terrible, had the poor fellow's eyes put out so that he could never duplicate or improve on the design.

northern Russia done in brick. As such it evokes the spirit of medieval Russia in a way no other church in Moscow can match.

## Muslim Religious Architecture in Iberia and the Balkans

Islamic architecture graces the European landscape in two widely separated areas. One is Iberia, where it is the remnant of a Moorish civilization that lasted from the 8th to the end of the 15th century. The other is the Balkans, which formed a part of the Ottoman Empire from the late 15th to the early 20th century. In the former the Muslim religion has largely disappeared, and the building styles come down to us as relics of the past or as features incorporated into later Christian buildings. In the latter the religion lives on, however, and many of the Islamic structures function as places of worship today.

The most important religious structure to survive from the Moorish period in Spain is the Great Mosque of Córdoba (La Mezquita). This is one of two classic early mosques to be built in the western Islamic world, the other being the Great Mosque of al-Quayrawan in Tunisia. By the 10th century Córdoba had become the largest and most prosperous city in Europe, outshining Byzantium and rivaling Baghdad, the new capital of the eastern caliphate. The completed mosque was described as having "as many bays as there are days in the year," and its 1,293 marble columns, 280 chandeliers, and 1,445 hanging lamps were much extolled. The interior walls were decorated with rich marbles, porphyries, and alabaster, and the domed Mihrab, which indicated the direction of Mecca and amplified the words of the imam, or prayer leader, was thought to be among the most perfect in the Islamic world. This monumental edifice is, however, marred by a Christian cathedral choir that was unfortunately built in its very center during the Renaissance. Fortunately, the cathedral occupies just 48 of the 365 bays of the mosque.

With the fall of the Umayyad dynasty in Córdoba, power in Muslim Spain fell into the hands of Berber families from Morocco.

**FIGURE 6.18. The Giralda.** This Moorish minaret turned Christian Gothic cathedral tower is the city of Seville's best-known cultural landmark. According to legend the tower was saved from destruction by the conquering Christian leader Alfonso, who let it be known before the city was taken that he would put to the sword anyone who attempted to destroy it. The beauty of the tower derives from its intricately patterned brick trelliswork and delicate windows and balconies.

The architecture of these puritanical dynasties, the Almoravid (1056–1147) and the Almohad (1130–1269), was massive and austere. The greatest monument from this period is the Giralda in Seville, the minaret of the Muslim mosque, which was embellished and served as the bell tower of the great Gothic cathedral that replaced the mosque after the Reconquest. Built at the end of the 12th century, this crowning achievement of Almohad architecture became the model for the minarets in Rabat and Marrakesh.

After the fall of Granada to the Catholic monarchs in 1492 and the subsequent expulsion of the Muslims, things made in Muslim style continued to be produced by *Moriscos*, Moors who had ostensibly converted to Christianity. This art is referred to as Mudéjar and is well represented in, for example, the Alcazba in Seville. Although generally confined to secular buildings the Mudéjar style was also applied to Jewish synagogues (later converted into Christian churches), two very fine extant examples being Santa Maria La Blanca and El Tránsito in Toledo. The Mudéjar spirit, in fact, permeated most of Spanish architectural ornament and decorative arts for centuries, and its influence can even be found in Spanish America.

The grand tradition of Ottoman architecture, established in the 16th century, differed markedly from that of the earlier Moors. It was derived from both the Byzantine Christian tradition, outlined above, and native Middle Eastern forms used by the Islamic Seljuk Turks, who preceded the Ottomans. The Byzantine tradition, particularly as embodied in Hagia Sophia, was perhaps the major source of inspiration. Byzantine influence appears in such features as the use of stone and brick together and in the details of dome construction. Also influential were the contacts that the early Ottomans had with Italy. A distinctive feature of Ottoman architecture is, then, that it drew from both Islamic and Christian sources. Ottoman architecture reached its pinnacle with the building of the great mosques that still define the Istanbul skyline. Their imposing central domes, surrounded by a cascade of smaller half-domes, totally dominate these structures, while the tall, slender minarets from which the imams call the faithful to prayer (now via loudspeakers) stand as guardians around them.

## Early Medieval Church Architecture in the West: The Romanesque and Gothic

The classical age of the Romanesque in Western church architecture is usually dated 1050–1140, although the term *Romanesque* was not coined until 1818. It describes a type of architecture that descends from, but is different than, Roman architecture, much as Romanic languages are the distinctive offspring of Latin. Like the churches of the early Christian era, Romanesque churches derive basically from the Roman basilica. The basic form consisted of a central nave with side aisles, ending in a rounded apse in the east and having a single or twin towers at the west end. The transept at right angles to the nave, originated by Constantine, was also preserved, the crossing being surmounted by a central tower. Like the Romans, the builders of the 11th and 12th centuries continued to employ rounded arches between columns to support the roof. This allowed the columns to be spaced more widely but still meant that the bulk of the weight of the roof was borne by thick walls and massive columns. The result was a rather heavy, bulky building with few windows, allowing relatively little light inside. The Romanesque period coincided with the great era of monasticism in western Christendom. The style, therefore, is often closely as-

FIGURE 6.19. Blue Mosque. Built in the early 17th century by Mehmed Aga, the royal architect of the Ottoman Court, Istanbul's Blue Mosque exhibits a perfectly symmetrical profile, with its large central dome flanked on all sides by matched half-domes, cupolas, and minarets. Known as the Blue Mosque because of its blue tile decor, the structure was partly built using marble from the ruins of the nearby Roman Hippodrome.

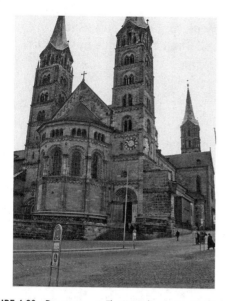

**FIGURE 6.20. Romanesque.** The Kaiserdom in Bamberg is one of Germany's "imperial" cathedrals. Consecrated in 1012, the cathedral burned and was rebuilt twice during its first two centuries, becoming in the process a transitional structure between the Romanesque and the newer Gothic style. The heavy protruding choir here at the east end of the building with its rounded arches and windows is typical of the Romanesque.

sociated with the Benedictine, Cluniac, and Cistercian orders.

The demise of the Romanesque is first apparent in new structural developments that began about 1090. These were a response to the desire on the part of builders to achieve several objectives that could not be reached using Roman or Byzantine technology. Primary among these objectives was to create taller structures that admitted more light. Three innovations made by progressive Romanesque engineers enabled this to be done: ribbed vaulting, pointed arches, and the flying buttress. The first two enabled weight to be concentrated to massive columns inside the structure while the third carried it to pillars outside the walls of the church. All of this meant that walls could be taller and thinner and have much greater window space. The result was buildings that appear to soar toward the heavens rather than being bound to the earth, and buildings with huge stained glass windows that throw light into the farthest corners.

The Gothic style was born in the western part of Europe, in the Île de France around Paris, and is conventionally dated from about 1140 to 1400. The earliest building in which these techniques were used was the abbey church of Saint-Denis (1135–1144) in Paris. Something similar was attempted soon after at Notre Dame in Paris (1163) and also at Laon to the northeast (1165). One of the most influential of the early Gothic buildings was Chartres (1194). Outside of northern France, the early stages of development in the Gothic period show, as did the Romanesque before them, strong regional influences. These depended on the availability of building materials, for example, stone versus brick, but also cultural ties and the routes along which ideas were channeled. Swedish Gothic was heavily influenced by French, for example, while in Norway English models dominated. Italy developed its own style, influenced to some degree by antiquity but also by Byzantine Constantinople. Here, where cheap building stone was not available, churches were built of brick and faced with decorative marble.

The new technology tempted builders to experiment with ever larger buildings, but eventually it was seen that there were limits. Beauvais cathedral in France had a disastrous history, which included the collapse of its vaults, and it was never completed. By the High and Late Gothic periods the emphasis was on decoration. Windows were enlarged, the tracery made more complex, and the stained glass colored less heavily, letting in more light. This is known in France as the Rayonnant style and in England as the Decorated and Perpendicular. English Perpendicular gave rise to a phase of Gothic unique to England in which the most characteristic feature is the fan vault. Italy produced its own unique version of Rayonnant styling, perhaps best seen in the front of Sienna Cathedral or in the cathedral bell tower in Florence.

One might argue that the Gothic took imagination to an extreme. For many the flamboyance of form and decoration had become too much. New Renaissance forms derived from classical antiquity now provided an alternative form of art, one with more order and so-

**FIGURE 6.21. Gothic.** The Cathédrale Notre-Dame at Chartres is one of the most magnificent examples of Gothic architecture in Europe. Built over a relatively short period from 1194 to 1260, the building has a unity of architectural style achieved by few other churches. The church provided, in many ways, a stylistic template for other Gothic cathedrals built across northern France during the first half of the 13th century, such as Reims, Amiens, and Beauvais. (Photo: J. Ostergren)

lemnity and one founded solidly on a highly revered tradition. The result was the wholesale abandonment of Gothic art on the grounds that it was barbaric. Indeed, it is the Renaissance artists, themselves, who coined the name "Gothic" to express their loathing for an art form, which they believed, like the Goths, had destroyed the noble classical heritage.

## Early Modern Church Architecture in the West: The Renaissance and Baroque

The Renaissance (1400–1600) began in Italy, close to the remains of the classical past from which it took its inspiration. Rome had, of course the largest stock of classical ruins, but the Renaissance was born not there, but in Florence. While Rome at this time was a relatively small and poor city, under the control of the Papacy, Florence was economically prosperous and politically stable.

The Renaissance reintroduced the dome, which, as we have seen, became the hallmark of Byzantine and Russian architecture but which was notably absent from Western Christendom during the Middle Ages. It is Brunelleschi's great dome over the *duomo*, or cathedral, of Florence that marks the beginning of this development. Another innovation of the Italian Renaissance was the adoption of the centralized plan. Many Renaissance archi-

tects came to believe that the circle was the most perfect geometric form and, therefore, the most appropriate to use in structures dedicated to a perfect God. In addition, Renaissance architects were determined that their buildings be more orderly and rational than those of the uncivilized Gothic designers.

From Florence the early Renaissance style spread gradually over Italy, becoming prevalent in the second half of the 15th century. Many of the churches and palaces of Venice are built in this manner. In the early 16th century political and cultural leadership shifted from Florence to Rome, largely because a succession of powerful popes wanted to develop the papacy as a secular power and wished to embellish the city with ambitious new building projects. By the end of the 16th century the new style pervaded almost all of Europe.

A variation of Renaissance architecture found in Spain is known as Plateresque. It takes its name from the word *platero*, meaning silversmith, because of its rich ornamentation, resembling silversmith's work. There has always been a long tradition in Spain of elaborate decoration, often explained in part as an influence from Moorish art. The Renaissance Plateresque style is purely one of decoration; there is no change in structure from the earlier Moorish and Gothic periods. The richness of classical ornamentation imported from It-

FIGURE 6.22. **Renaissance.** Florence began building its massive cathedral in 1294. Envisioned was a great vaulted basilica with an enormous dome as the church's crown. The problem was that no one knew how to build a dome that large and high until a local goldsmith and sculptor turned architect, Filippo Brunelleschi, arrogantly insisted that only he could construct such a dome and that he could do it without scaffolding! Brunelleschi, who had studied the work of Roman architects, was given the commission and succeeded in making good on his claim. The distinctively ribbed dome was completed in 1436 and topped with its lantern in 1468.

aly blended effectively with the elements of the Moorish and flamboyant Late Gothic styles to form the new Plateresque style. The greatest center of the Plateresque, as demonstrated on cathedral and university façades, was Salamanca.

The last great historical period of Western church architecture, lasting roughly from the early 17th to the mid-18th century, was the Baroque. Baroque was at first a term of abuse, probably derived from the Italian word *barocco*, which was used by philosophers during the Middle Ages to describe an obstacle in schematic logic. Baroque church architecture was inspired in part by the fervor of the Counter-Reformation. Indeed, Baroque is often seen as the flamboyant architectural expression of the "Roman Church Triumphant." It had its greatest impact in a belt of territory extending from Italy, through the German Catholic lands of Switzerland, Germany, Austria, and into Bohemia and Poland. It was here that the Protestant threat to the Church was both most strongly felt and most vigorously opposed. It is also associated with Catholic Spain and her overseas possessions. Outlying examples may be found in France and the Protestant lands, as well as in Russia.

The Baroque style differed from that of the Renaissance in that it was essentially concerned with emotion and the senses rather than with reason and the mind. The center of

the early Baroque was Rome, and the three great masters there were Gian Lorenzo Bernini, Francesco Borromini, and Pietro da Cortona. In this early Roman phase, Baroque builders returned to the medieval longitudinal axis plan where the nave promoted a

FIGURE 6.23. **Baroque.** The countryside of Catholic Germany is rich with examples of Baroque church architecture. The Cistercian Abbey at Waldsassen, in the Upper Palatinate, has a reputation as one of the masterpieces of German High Baroque. Built in the late 14th century by George Dientzenhofer, one of the masters of Baroque building, the abbey houses a spectacular library encased in galleries of fancifully carved wooden shelving beneath a vaulted frescoed ceiling.

sense of movement toward the altar. They also gave greater prominence to the façade of the church. Later, leadership in the genre passed to the lands north of the Alps, and by the end of the 17th century the imperial cities of the Catholic Hapsburgs, Vienna and Prague, had emerged as the capitals of High Baroque. In the countryside, it was the great abbeys of the German lands that most fervently embraced the new style.

## Modern Church Architecture in the West: Neoclassical and Revival Styles

The majority of historic Christian church buildings erected since the end of the 18th century are either neoclassical in style or belong to one of the revival styles popular in the 19th century. Neoclassicism, which swept through Europe between 1750 and 1830, was a reaction against what were seen as the excesses of Baroque architecture. It corresponded with a new interest in antiquity, one that, unlike that of the Renaissance, was scientific and focused especially on the archeological investigation of the classical sites of past civilizations. Neoclassical structures, unlike the more imaginative Renaissance and Baroque structures, were intended to be true to documented examples of the past, focusing on the grandeur and simplicity of Greek or Roman forms.

Although neoclassical buildings continued to be erected until the 1930s, the 19th century was dominated by a Romantic inclination to draw inspiration from a variety of historical styles (Historicism), and sometimes to combine them even in the same buildings (Eclecticism). Particularly noteworthy was a nostalgic fascination with the medieval past, which produced a spate of neo-Gothic style church building first in England and then spreading across much of western and central Europe. Much church building in the latter part of the 20th century conforms to the new international architectural style, which utilizes modern materials and emphasizes function over form. Relatively few new church edifices have been constructed, however, and the impact of modernism on the built religious environment has been both scattered and slight.

**FIGURE 6.24. Neoclassicism.** The neoclassical Basilica of Esztergom is the largest church in Hungary. Although the present building is from the 19th century, the city, at the western entrance to the Danube Bend, has been the seat of Roman Catholicism in Hungary for more than a thousand years. The crypt is the burial site of Cardinal Mindszenty, who is revered by Hungarians for his unyielding opposition to both fascism and communism.

## FURTHER READING

Badone, E. (Ed.). (1990). *Religious orthodoxy and popular faith in European society*. Princeton, NJ: Princeton University Press.

Ben-Sasson, H. H. (Ed.). (1976). *A history of the Jewish people*. Cambridge, MA: Harvard University Press.

Dogan, M. (1998). The decline of traditional values in Western Europe: Religion, nationalism, authority. *International Journal of Comparative Sociology*, 39, 77–90.

Encyclopaedis Britannica Staff, Britannica Editors. (1999). *Britannica book of the year*. Chicago: Encyclopaedia Britannica.

Frend, W. (1988). Christianity in the first five centuries. In S. Sutherland, L. Houlden, P. Clarke, & F. Hardy (Eds.), *The world's religions* (pp. 142–166). Boston: G. K. Hall, pp. 142-166.

Fulton, J., & Gee, P. (1994). *Religion in contemporary Europe*. Lewiston, ME: Mellen.

Geanakoplos, D. J. (1966). *Byzantine East and Latin West: Two Worlds of Christendom in Middle Ages and Renaissance*. New York: Harper Torchbooks.

Gilles, S. (1988). Christianity in Europe: Reformation to today. In S. Sutherland, L. Houlden, P. Clarke, & F. Hardy (Eds.), *The world's religions* (pp. 216–242). Boston: G. K. Hall.

Graham, B. J., & Murray, M. (1997). The spiritual

and the profane: The pilgrimage to Santiago de Compestela. *Ecumene, 4,* 389–409.

Greeley, A. M. (2003). *Religion in Europe at the end of the second millennium: A sociological profile.* New Brunswick, NJ: Transaction.

Halman, L., & Riis, O. (Eds.). (2003). *Religion in secularizing society: The Europeans' religion at the end of the 20th century.* Leiden, The Netherlands: Brill.

Harding, S., Phillips, D. R., & Fogarty M. P. (1986). *Contrast in values in western Europe.* London: Macmillan.

Kostof, S. (1995). *A history of architecture: Settings and rituals.* (2nd ed.). Oxford, UK: Oxford University Press.

McLeod, H. (1997). *Religion and the people of Western Europe, 1789–1989.* Oxford, UK: Oxford University Press.

Meldgaard, H., & Aagaard, J. (1997). *New religious movements in Europe.* Aarhus, Denmark: Aarhus University Press.

Nolan, M. L., & Nolan, S. (1989). *Christian pilgrimage in modern western Europe.* Chapel Hill: University of North Carolina Press.

Peach C., & Glebe G. (1995). Muslim minorities in Western Europe. *Ethnic and Racial Studies, 18,* 26–45.

Smart, N. (1989). *The world's religions: Old traditions and modern transformations.* Cambridge, UK: Cambridge University Press.

Sopher, D. E. (1967). *Geography of religions.* Englewood Cliffs, NJ: Prentice Hall.

Sutherland, S., Houlden, L., Clarke, P., & Hardy, F. (Eds.). (1988). *The world's religions.* Boston: G. K. Hall.

Wilson, N. J. (Ed.). (2001). *The European Renaissance and Reformation, 1350–1600.* Detroit: Gale Group.

# CHAPTER 7

# The Political Landscape

For more than four decades following World War II the most salient and immutable feature of the political map of Europe was its division into an East and a West. This was the legacy of Yalta, the historic meeting in 1945 between Churchill, Roosevelt, and Stalin that determined the geopolitical configuration of postwar Europe. In the aftermath of the defeat of Nazism, a bipartite Europe replaced a prewar Europe that had consisted of not two but a number of politically and culturally definable regions, including a "Central Europe" that for all practical purposes ceased to exist after 1945. The two halves of postwar Europe became estranged from each other through sharply contrasting political and economic systems. Whatever else of political importance may have happened during these postwar decades—and there was much that did—Europe's two-way division was an ever-present reality. The political landscape, in a sense, was frozen in place by the chilling winds of the Cold War.

All that changed rather suddenly in the 1990s. The political landscape of Europe was suddenly transformed, taking on new shapes and possibilities on a scale not seen since 1918–1921. The most spectacular change was the breakup of the Soviet Union and the elimination of Soviet hegemony over eastern Europe, which in turn unleashed a wave of democratization and nation building all across the eastern half of the continent. The process dramatically increased the number of sovereign nations on the map from 32 to 43; extended the aggregate length of political frontiers, many of them contested, by thousands of kilometers; and raised the possibility of new regional associations in the Baltic, central Europe, eastern Europe, and the Balkans. Second, Germany was reunited, creating a powerful and potentially domineering state of some 80 million people in the heart of Europe. Third, the idea of a union of European states, long anticipated, and embodied today in a European Union of as many as 25 states, emerged as an attractive, although not always fully embraced, means of achieving a peaceful and prosperous European future. And finally, threatening to alter the fabric even further has been the recent wave of regional and ethnic demands for political and territorial recognition—ranging from the open warfare and "ethnic cleansing" that have plagued the Balkans and other parts of the East to the demands for greater political and cultural autonomy pursued by regions within some of the states in the West.

Depending on one's point of view, these changes are either exhilarating or fraught with political danger. There has been no shortage of optimism for the future of an integrated Europe, and the rush of political events after 1989 generated widespread hope

FIGURE 7.1. Cold War Europe.

for the success of the new democracies in the East. On the other hand, enthusiasm for the deepening of EU ties has been far from universal. Britain and other member states remain cautious about, and in some cases openly opposed to, many of the new integrative initiatives. In addition, unsettling political events in the East and elsewhere have begun to temper the euphoria with which the momentous political developments of the past decade were first welcomed.

The political culture of contemporary Europe, then, is one that is buffeted by a variety of forces and circumstances, placing it in a state of considerable flux. Our purpose in this chapter is to attempt some understanding of the forces that shape the modern European political landscape. These are forces that sometimes act in concert, sometimes as counterweights to one another. We focus on three: nationalism, supranationalism, and regionalism. We begin, because of its immense impact on the political structure of Europe and on the lives and identity of contemporary Europeans, with nationalism. We then turn to supranationalism and its potential to bring the

**FIGURE 7.2. Berlin Wall.** Only small graffiti-covered sections remain of the wall that once cordoned off West Berlin from the surrounding territory of socialist East Germany. Long the symbol of Cold War tensions, the wall is fast becoming a distant memory following the reunification of Germany more than a decade ago.

nations of the continent into a larger and lasting harmony. We end with regionalism, the relatively recent but powerful trend to refocus political action and identity at the regional or local level.

## NATIONALISM

### The Rise of Nationalism

Nationalism is undoubtedly one of the most powerful political forces to affect modern Europe and, indeed, the world as a whole. It may be defined as a collective state of mind or consciousness in which groups of individuals become cognizant of a common culture and history, and thus identify themselves as a distinctive people, or nation. It further requires that this nation place its primary sense of loyalty and duty with its own independent state, the nation-state, which is seen as the only legitimate territorial and political expression of national identity. Indeed, nationalism is a force that is usually not deemed satisfied until all members of the perceived nation are embraced within the territory of the state. Moreover, the perfect nation-state is not attained until all persons not belonging to the nation are excluded from the state. These principles of nationalism are the primary forces, along

with the legal systems and formal institutions of society, that support the system of national states that has prevailed in Europe over the past century.

Nations are something that must be invented. While there is some sense that national identity can be primordial, we know that it is normally a phenomenon that develops from the activities of elites who, often for purposes of their own, wish to generate around them a popular sense of nationhood and belonging. The process of nation building thus involves the identification or invention of an ethnic past, of national myths and heroes, of common history, cultural institutions, heartland, and territory. The success of a nationalist movement depends on a general acceptance and embracing of this complex of ideas by the general populace.

Although we often may not think of it as such, nationalism is a relatively recent phenomenon. While its antecedents may be traced deep into the past, nationalism did not become a widespread and powerful force in Europe until the beginning of the 19th century. Before that time most political allegiance was personal. People felt a sense of loyalty to a sovereign prince or an important local ruler who, in turn, may have owed fealty to others. Or they may have identified with a much more vague and universal entity, such as the Christian Church. Throughout much of history Europe's major political units consisted of dynastic states and empires, whose legitimacy and power was built around the rights and prerogatives of the royal household and court, and whose alliances and foreign adventures were often dictated by marriages and intrigues between the various houses of the continent's ennobled elite. Few, if any, were ethnically homogeneous.

Sixteenth-century England is often cited as the first place in Europe to experience a form of nationalism, but its emergence as a real force in European society is one of the great transformations that accompanied the French Revolution and the Napoleonic Wars. Many of the philosophical underpinnings of nationalism are associated with the ideas of the French Revolution, in which the state and the

FIGURE 7.3. Europe after the Treaty of Vienna (1814).

nation were seen as one and the same, and deserving of a government that reflects the popular will. Nationalism, therefore, was a revolutionary dogma whose first success was its central role in transforming the great absolute monarchies of western Europe into nation-states. In addition to the transformation of dynastic states to nation-states in western Europe, the 19th-century Romantic interest in national culture and heritage, the drives for national unification in Germany and Italy, and the various struggles for national recognition in the multinational Austro-Hungarian, Russian, and Ottoman Empires are all generally seen as expressions of the rising spirit of nationalism.

But it is not always clear how widely this spirit was felt by the masses as opposed to national elites. Indeed, one of the striking conclusions of Eugen Weber's book, *Peasants into Frenchmen*, is that most of the people who lived in the small towns and countryside of France did not see themselves before 1870 as members of a French nation, and that a good many still failed to do so even as late as World War I. This finding is made all the more interesting in light of the fact that France is commonly thought of as one of the more unified and long established nation-states in Europe. It is important to recognize that nationalism is a process that can take many forms, that there can be a significant lag between its initial embracement by a few and its acceptance by the masses, and that it is not a foregone conclusion that all Europeans, even today, have developed a deep sense of national identity.

The point that nationalism can take many forms becomes relevant when we consider the fact that the movement emerged first in the West and later diffused to central and eastern Europe. As nationalism spread eastward, it encountered very different social and political situations, which caused the ideas surrounding it to be interpreted differently. The main transmitters of western ideas to the East were German Romantic thinkers such as

Johan Gottfried von Herder, whose concepts of nationalism contained the essentials of and actually differed relatively little from the western meaning of the term. German thinkers such as Herder, though, wrote in a context where no nation-state as yet existed and therefore paid much lip service to the idea of nationality in the form of a culturally and linguistically defined people, or *Volk*. Herder maintained that people had to find themselves by rediscovering their language and history, but he intended that this process should result in a world of free nationalities cooperating peacefully with one another as equals. Central and eastern European elites tended to reinterpret this cultural nationalism in starkly political terms, where *Volk* stood for a group with a distinctive history, culture, rights, and a mission; and where the individual, who had no rights of his or her own, was ruled from birth by the will of the *Volk*, which in turn was dedicated to the realization of the political nation.

As a consequence, a distinction can be made between what nationalism came to mean in the West and in the East. In western European countries such as England, France, and the Netherlands, the rise of nationalism was primarily a democratizing phenomenon, whereby sovereignty was transferred from a ruler to a relatively homogeneous citizen population already residing within a long-recognized political unit. Nationalists were able to capitalize on this already given political, cultural, and territorial reality and were thus able to direct their attention toward the consummation of a national democratic society in the present without having to focus too much on the past. In the East nationalism arose much later in an environment where social and political development were far less sophisticated and where existing political units and culturally homogeneous populations only rarely coincided. In this setting nationalists became much more preoccupied with ethnic descent and dreams of liberation from the rule of others. In addition, eastern nationalism became much more intimately tied to religion. Nationalism in the East, therefore, has a tendency to be more exclusionist and messianic in its drive to realize the nationalistic rights of a chosen people. While the two forms are hardly mutually exclusive, it is useful to use the words *civic* and *ethnic* to differentiate between nationalism in western and eastern Europe.

Most would agree that nationalism has been the dominant political force of the 20th century and that it, unfortunately, has not always been the kind of liberal and progressive force envisioned by its early champions. As strong national states emerged across Europe toward the end of the 19th century, nationalism became an increasingly conservative and reactionary force that was used to thwart political reform and socialist movements both at home and abroad, as well as to fuel national rivalries and conflicts. This was certainly true of the German Empire after 1871, which became a highly authoritarian and militaristic state, and it festered throughout a central and eastern Europe still encumbered by aged and increasingly anachronistic dynastic empires, ruled by the Romanovs, Hapsburgs, and Ottomans. Nationalism's darker side infected the West as well. By the late 19th century, nationalistic pride and a general denigration or indifference to all things foreign had become perhaps no less a British or French way of thinking about themselves and their neighbors. The outbreak of World War I, and the cataclysmic bloodbath that followed, was certainly abetted by such strong nationalistic passions and rivalries.

Moreover, the peace settlement that followed in 1919 unleashed two new nationalistic developments that helped to set the stage for renewed conflict in 1939. One was the postwar political reorganization of central and eastern Europe according to liberal principles of national self-determination. This idea, which was vigorously promoted by the American President Woodrow Wilson at the Paris Peace Conference, led to the creation of a large number of new "nation-states"— Czechoslovakia, Poland, Lithuania, Latvia, Estonia, Austria, Hungary, and Yugoslavia—in place of the defeated multinational empires of central and eastern Europe. However high-minded the intentions, there was a certain

FIGURE 7.4. Europe between the World Wars.

naiveté involved in the application of this concept to a region with as complex a cultural history and as confused an ethnic geography as this part of Europe. Although envisioned as national states, most of the new states were nearly as multinational as the empires they replaced. Nor were the masters of these new states any more tolerant of national minorities than their imperial predecessors. In most cases, the promise of a stable and democratic national society went unfulfilled. The new states eventually began to slip into a condition in which they became inclined toward authoritarian regimes, the suppression of minorities, and conflict with their neighbors. Weak and

unstable, they became pawns in the coming European conflict. Hitler thus found it remarkably easy to exploit the resentments and territorial claims that Hungarians harbored toward Romanians, Romanians toward Russians, Croats toward Serbs, and so on.

The other development that took place between the wars was the rise in Italy, Spain, and Germany of a particularly intense and xenophobic form of nationalism, which we know as fascism. Totalitarian fascist regimes in these countries appealed to extreme nationalist sentiments by glorifying the state and extolling the superiority and virtue of one nation over others. This was particularly true in Germany, where the doctrine of the superiority of the "Aryan" race over the Jews and the Slavic peoples of the East became a cornerstone of national identity. Although ideologically different, communism in the Soviet Union under Stalin also took on many of the same nationalistic and authoritarian features. We might conclude that it was in the political environment of interwar Europe that nationalism reached its zenith as a powerful, though often misdirected, force.

## Nationalism in Europe Today

Many believe that there has been an erosion of national feeling in Europe since World War II. Some would claim that Europe today has entered a "postnational" era. This is perhaps most true in the West, where a number of recent surveys suggest that there is evidence of mitigated "national pride" across all nations; that ever lower proportions of national populations feel "very proud" of their country, have confidence in the army, or show much enthusiasm for other common indicators of nationalistic feelings. Surveys also show that individualism is on the rise, an indication that people increasingly see themselves as part of a complex society in which people have multiple roles and allegiances and move freely between them as the situation warrants. As we shall see, a growing reliance on a supranationally organized Europe, as well as a "Europe of regions," are part of this process by which the role of national identity in the West appears to have been downgraded. At the same time, it is important not to take the idea too far. Nationalism is far from being extinguished as an element of European identity in a relatively small continental space that is politically partitioned into more than 40 nation-states.

Germany has long been held up as the premiere example of nationalism's retreat in western Europe. For decades a profound sense of guilt over Nazi crimes during World War II has dominated the way in which Germans have regarded themselves and their country. Postwar German governments characteristically bent over backwards to portray themselves as committed first and foremost to the ideals of European integration and cooperation. A commitment to these ideals was long a cornerstone of postwar German foreign policy in Europe. Overt expressions of national pride were avoided at all costs. Critical references to things Jewish, or about the Jewish state in Israel, were especially taboo. On the other hand, more recent developments in Germany are demonstration of the fact that national pride is not necessarily a thing of the past. Since German reunification in 1990, it has become more acceptable in Germany to break the old taboos. For a new generation of Germans the horrors of World War II seem distant. There no longer appears to be any reason to feel personal guilt for Nazi crimes of the past, no reason not to rekindle a sense of German national identity and pride. Germans now seem to be cautiously willing to stand up for what are seen as German rights and views.

It is much more difficult to judge the condition of nationalism in the East, given the recent emergence of these countries from the long repression of their national independence during the postwar years, and the accordant need to proclaim a renewal of national spirit and purpose. Ironically, the communist years may have worked to keep nationalism alive in east-central and eastern Europe since various efforts at integration in a Soviet-dominated eastern bloc were both ineffective and strongly resisted. The collapse of communism and Soviet influence in the 1990s seems to have opened up space for a "national renaissance" in which nation-state and nation could once again be reaffirmed. Some view what happened as a sort of "catching up," the completion of a process that was cut short roughly half a century ago. At least in the short term, there has been a rush of popular support for the new national democracies established in the wake of communist rule. For the long term, however, the status of nationalism seems clouded. Across most of the new postcommunist democracies there is a near universal desire to become a part of a new and integrated Europe, and a certain willingness—perhaps even stronger than in the West—for people to think of themselves first as European.

**FIGURE 7.5. Historic connections.** The Alexander Nevski Church in Sofia, built at the end of the 19th century as a memorial to the 200,000 Russian soldiers who died in the Russo-Turkish War of 1877–1878, which resulted in Bulgarian independence. A Russian saint, Alexander defeated the Swedes on the banks of the Neva in 1240, thus winning his sobriquet. Admiration for the Russians, as distinct from the Soviets, is evident elsewhere in the Bulgarian capital.

The most visible and disturbing form of nationalism in the East, however, is a radical ethno-nationalism. This is a divisive force that threatens the integrity of states and is, at least in some sense, a kind of throwback to the difficulties of the interwar period that were generated by the more exclusionary and messianic character of eastern nationalism, outlined above. This is the nationalism that fuels the killing and "ethnic cleansing" that have convulsed some of the territories belonging to Yugoslavia and the former Soviet Union. In this sense, nationalism in the East today can be seen as an ambivalent force, caught between the desire to resume the process of nation building interrupted by World War II and the long socialist years, on the one hand, and the reawakening of old conflicts among ethnic and cultural groups, on the other.

A type of ethno-nationalism also exists in the West, primarily in the form of radical populist political movements whose demagogic leaders denounce the increasing cultural heterogeneity of many western societies. The examples of this new xenophobia are legion. Jörg Haider of the Freedom Party (FPÖ) in Austria built his political reputation by warning against the threat of "Umvolkung" (ethnic

transformation) that may result from a continued influx of people from eastern Europe and the Balkans. Neo-Nazis in Germany shout *Ausländer raus!* (foreigners out!) and commit acts of violence against Turks and other immigrant groups. Jean-Marie Le Pen warns his French supporters of the perils of the "Arab invasion" from the Maghreb, while Belgium's far-right Vlaams Blok profitably pursues the inflammatory politics of an anti-immigrant stance.

This is a "scavenger" type of nationalism, wherein an alien threat to a preexisting sense of nationhood is identified and publicized for the purpose of generating hate and prejudice. While ostensibly limited in its appeal to the traditional political right, or "center-right" as it is often known in Europe, this ethno-nationalism persists and, at times, garners real popular support at the polls. In France, Le Pen's National Front has been around now for nearly two decades. It won 15% of the vote in the first round of the 1995 presidential elections and has captured as much as 30–35% of the vote in some local elections. More recently Le Pen made an unexpectedly strong showing in the first round of the 2002 presidential elections, coming in second with 17% of the vote and a majority vote in 35 of the country's 100 *départements*. Le Pen's challenge was later beaten back decisively in a run-off election with incumbent President Jacques Chirac, but not before serious questions were raised about the mood of the French electorate. These concern both the degree to which crime is related in the public mind to race and immigration, and the growing discomfort of the populace with a perceived loss of French national identity and prestige, for which it blames a failed governmental policy of multiracialism.

The recent electoral appeal of western right-wing political parties, espousing a chauvinistic brand of nationalism and racism, is hardly limited to France. Xenophobic right-wing parties have recently come to power as coalition partners in several countries. Jörg Haider's Freedom Party came in second with 27% of the popular vote in Austria's 1999 national elections, gaining a place in the national government. In May 2002, just nine days after the assassination of Pim Fortuyn, its outspoken right-wing, anti-immigration leader, the Lijst Pim Fortuyn found itself the second-largest party in the Dutch Parliament and a coalition player in the new government. Quite remarkably, the party didn't even exist just 3 months before the election. In 2001 Italy's National Alliance Party, which descends from Mussolini's fascists, joined the country's ruling coalition. The maverick right has also done well in recent years in such seemingly unlikely settings as Norway (Progress Party), Denmark (Danish People's Party), and Switzerland (Swiss People's Party). The political success of these parties is marked in regions and cities where immigrant populations are particularly large, such as Antwerp, where the nationalistic and anti-immigrant Flemish party Vlaams Blok has captured as much as one-third of the vote in city elections.

Such recent electoral successes, however, are not necessarily portents of a surge of the extreme right in European politics reminiscent of the interwar period. The record of success is, in fact, highly uneven. Most rightist parties have surged to prominence rather suddenly and then fallen back to obscurity almost as quickly as they have risen. Nor has there been anything resembling a continent-wide sweep of electoral success. The successes of the xenophobic right wing have for the most part occurred only here and there, and in some parts of Europe hardly at all. Germany, for example, has not experienced any kind of national demonstration, despite occasional flareups in industrial cities. Britain has seen relatively little at the national scale, and the problem seems to scarcely exist in countries such as Spain, Portugal, and Greece. What extreme-right politicians have sometimes been able to capitalize on is not so much the racist and rabidly nationalistic sentiments of the electorate but rather a general sense that mainstream parties, whether center, left, or right, have become too arrogantly bureaucratic, complacent, and seemingly out of touch with the needs and concerns of ordinary citizens. Voters are genuinely concerned about such issues as chronic unemployment,

crime, and illegal migrants. They express their concerns by occasionally voting the leaders of left- and center-leaning parties out of office. Such instances derive as much from the failure of the incumbent political elite as from the allure of the extremist populists.

## SUPRANATIONALISM

The nation-state remains the essential building block of the international political order and will undoubtedly remain so for the foreseeable future. At the same time, though, it faces a certain diminishment of its importance in our global postindustrial society. There is evidence that the power and authority of the state are gradually eroding, both upward to new supranational institutions and downward to the level of the region and locality. As some would say, there is an ongoing "hollowing out" of the state that is taking place in this age of heightened interest in the global and the local. Again, all of this is not to say that the nation-state is in any danger of disappearing, or that national populations may come to see themselves no longer in nationalistic terms. But as an object of popular allegiance and devotion, and as the holder of all sovereign powers, the nation-state is increasingly being forced to share its former preeminence with other contenders.

Among these contenders is the idea of a "united Europe" governed by supranational laws and institutions. This is an old idea that has been partially realized at various times and in different forms over the ages. One might, for example, view the Roman Empire or Charlemagne's Empire as early supranational organizations of European peoples. The universal power once held by the medieval Christian Church over sovereigns across Europe is another example. Even Hitler's New Order sought to unite Europe, however unwillingly. There is evidence that, for a brief moment, many Europeans might even have been willing to embrace a German-led authoritarian "New Order" in place of what was widely perceived as the failure of the liberal democratic order created after 1918. It was the Nazi insistence that it be a "German" New Order of brutality and slavery that quickly quashed any such support. The converse of this, the idea of a fully integrated and democratic Europe, therefore, has made its most solid advances only in the years since the continent experienced the ultimate catastrophic consequence of nationalistic ambition: World War II. Today's European Union is the most successful example of the many steps taken toward the supranational ideal over those decades, and the best hope for the realization of the postwar dream of European cooperation and integration.

## Postwar Recovery and Economic Cooperation

The postwar dream of a united Europe was articulated as early as 1943 by French economist Jean Monnet, who called on European nations to form a federation, or a "European entity," that would ensure prosperity and vital social progress. In 1946 Winston Churchill seconded the notion in an influential speech delivered in Zürich in which he called for a new spirit of cooperation in Europe. The first concrete attempts at cooperation, however, emerged from efforts to recover from the economic chaos that threatened Europe at war's end in 1945.

American Marshall Plan aid, which was administered under the auspices of the Organization for European Economic Co-operation (OEEC), provided an important impetus toward integration in that it required, as a first step, that a level of economic and political cooperation be established among recipient nations. The offer of American aid, however, was rejected by the Soviet Union and, with little choice in the matter, by its satellite states in east-central Europe. Indeed, the Czechs and Poles, who had originally accepted Marshall Plan aid, soon found themselves forced to reverse their decisions. As a consequence most of the Marshall Plan aid, and the cooperative planning that accompanied it, went to western Europe, where it set the stage for the wide range of integrative initiatives that followed.

The negative Soviet reaction to the American aid initiative eventually led to an independent nexus of supranational cooperation among the nations of east-central and eastern Europe, although from the very beginning these cooperative efforts were more imposed than voluntary. The umbrella organization for international cooperation in the East was the Council for Mutual Economic Assistance (CMEA), which was organized in 1949. Through a series of 5-year plans, running from 1956 to 1985, CMEA undertook measures to promote the industrial development and coordination of the socialist economies of eastern Europe and later of two non-European states—Cuba and Mongolia—as well. In practice, however, most cooperation and trade among member states was strictly bilateral. CMEA never evolved into the kind of integrative supranational organization that emerged in the West, in part because member states remained cautious to the end of the intentions of the Soviet Union and of one another. Political events after 1989 quickly made CMEA irrelevant. It was formally dismantled and replaced with a looser consultative body in 1991. Also dismantled in 1991 was the Warsaw Pact, the defensive alliance founded in 1955 by the Soviet Union and its east-central European satellites.

In the West, a plethora of supranational organizations emerged during the first decades after the war: OEEC (1948), the North Atlantic Treaty Organization (1948), the Council of Europe (1949), the Nordic Council (1952), the Western European Union (1954), the European Economic Community (1958), or "Common Market," and the European Free Trade Association (1960). Each was established for particular purposes; memberships were overlapping. The North Atlantic Treaty Organization (NATO) and the Western European Union were founded as defensive military alliances. The Council of Europe and the Nordic Council were founded as deliberative bodies dedicated to promoting international understanding and cooperation. The European Economic Community and the European Free Trade Association were primarily organized in the interests of economic cooperation. However, only one organization, the European Economic Community, developed a vision broad enough to achieve real integration across a wide range of policy issues.

## The European Economic Community

The European Economic Community (EEC), which was the forerunner of today's European Union, was established by six western European states—the Netherlands, Belgium, Luxembourg, France, West Germany, and Italy—in a 1957 agreement known as the Treaty of Rome. The EEC was built on the foundation of two earlier economic agreements. The first was the Benelux Union of 1947, which bound the Netherlands, Belgium, and Luxembourg together in a customs union. The second was the European Coal and Steel Community (ECSC), which was set up by France, West Germany, Italy, and the three Benelux countries in 1951 to pool their coal and steel resources. The brainchild of Monnet, this effort by six countries to integrate one of the most basic industrial sectors of their economies under a supranational authority was very successful and provided a strong impetus toward the further efforts at economic integration embodied in the Treaty of Rome agreement. The ECSC was also important in establishing an atmosphere of reconciliation and shared interests between the former antagonists France and Germany, which would evolve into one of the key relationships in the development of the European Community.

Building on these earlier agreements, the Treaty of Rome established a supranational organization committed to four goals: the elimination of internal barriers to trade, a common external tariff, the free movement of capital, services, goods, and people among the member states, and common integrative policies in key areas such as agriculture, energy, fisheries, monetary policy, and regional policy. While primarily economic in its specific goals, there was also a recognition, embodied in the nature of its stated goals as well as the structure of its deliberative and administrative institutions, of long-term movement toward shared governance and the subordination of national sovereignties over a wide range of issues. Together with the ECSC, which remained in existence, and the European Atomic Energy Community (Euratom), which was also a product of the Treaty of Rome, the EEC was poised by the end of the 1950s to begin the process of bringing Europe together.

Meanwhile, seven nations outside the EEC—the United Kingdom, Norway, Sweden, Denmark, Portugal, Switzerland, and Austria—formed the European Free Trade Association (EFTA) in 1959. During the 1960s they were known as the "outer seven," as opposed to the "inner six" of the EEC. EFTA was not intended as a customs union. The focus was instead on the promotion of free trade among its members and improved trade relations throughout western Europe. It also eschewed any language that committed its members to policies that would entail any loss of sovereignty, a feature that further differentiated it from the EEC and made it especially appealing to countries with strong traditions of political independence and neutrality, such as Sweden and Switzerland. EFTA was originally organized by the United Kingdom, which eventually came to see the organization as a means of gaining leverage in its own coming negotiations for EEC membership.

During the 1960s the EEC achieved startling economic success as the economies of the six "Common Market" countries surged ahead and enjoyed a sustained period of remarkable growth and prosperity that lasted until around 1973. The thriving EEC underwent reorganization in 1967. The "three communities"—the EEC, ECSC, and Euratom, were merged into a single structure, which became known as the European Community (EC). The name change was indicative of a gathering shift in emphasis away from a predominantly economic focus. By this time, the stated long-term goals had clearly become a single market economy, a single currency, and a federalist political union.

## The EC "Widenings" of the 1970s and 1980s

Success was attractive and pressures to enlarge the Community began to mount. As early as 1961, four EFTA members—the United Kingdom, Ireland, Denmark, and Norway—began negotiations for membership in the EC. These negotiations lasted for over a decade, primarily because French President Charles De Gaulle opposed the idea of Britain's accession. The first enlargement of the EC was finally agreed to in 1971. Two years later, the United Kingdom, Ireland, and Denmark became members, expanding the Community from six to nine members. After a referendum, in which concerns over concessions that would have to be made to the Community's Common Fisheries Policy loomed large, Norway chose to decline its membership invitation. In the aftermath of the enlargement, relationships between the EC and what remained of the EFTA were restructured so as to strengthen ties and bring western Europe closer to the goal of a single economic space. By the mid-1970s, the European

FIGURE 7.6.  EEC/EU enlargements, 1973–2004.

Community had already become the economic core and was in position to become the political core of western Europe.

The first enlargement was followed by a second and third. The "EC-Nine" became the "EC-Ten" with the accession of Greece in 1981, and then the "EC-Twelve" when Spain and Portugal were admitted in 1986. These expansions were moves that advanced the geographic frontiers of the Community into the western and eastern basins of the Mediterranean. They brought the EC to the natural southern limits of the continent and into direct contact with Europe's southeast and Maghreb peripheries.

Economically and politically, they also broadened the Community to include areas that were distinctively different from the core. The accession of Ireland in 1973 was the first instance in which a state with an economy situated at a considerably lower level of development was included. The three Mediterranean additions were, however, even more underdeveloped and potentially burdensome, given the priority the Community placed on bringing its constituent regional economies toward some level of convergence. Moreover, the political history of all three countries, each of which had only recently emerged as a democratic state after a prolonged period of dictatorship, was a major issue. On the other hand, the new accessions represented significant gains in resources and population. They nearly doubled the geographic area of the EC and increased its population by 22%. Their relatively lower levels of development also offered certain economic complementarities that would benefit the Community in the long run.

## The EC "Deepenings" of the 1970s and 1980s

Alongside the geographical "widenings" that took place through the first, second, and third enlargements was a growing movement toward a "deepening" of economic, institutional, and political integration. Indeed, it is useful to think of the developmental history of today's European Union as consisting of a se-

ries of "widenings" and "deepenings." The latter process began at the end of the 1970s when preliminary steps were taken toward a European Monetary System with fixed exchange rates and when direct elections to the European Parliament in Strasbourg were initiated. This was followed during the mid-1980s by a series of discussions leading toward an initiative that would bring the Community to a greatly expanded level of integration. That was achieved in the "The Single European Act," which was drawn up by the European Council and approved in 1987. It called for implementation of a series of measures that would result in the development of a Single European Market by the end of 1992.

These measures sought to remove remaining physical, technical, and fiscal barriers to the movement of capital, people, and goods; to extend EC policy to include such areas as environment and research and technology; and to advance common economic and monetary policy. Equally important were decisions to streamline the Community's decision-making processes by replacing unanimity with majority voting in the Council of Ministers and by increasing the power and role of the European Parliament. The act also provided for the formulation and implementation of a European foreign policy. Although there were certain misgivings along the way, the implementation of these measures in 1992 was widely expected to usher in an expansive "New Europe without frontiers." To a considerable degree these expectations have been met.

## Birth of the European Union

An additional major step toward integration was taken in 1992, when the Treaty of European Union (also known as the Maastricht Treaty) was signed at an intergovernmental conference held in the Dutch provincial city of Maastricht. The treaty, which was ratified in 1993, provides for the continued "deepening" of cooperation among member nations in a great variety of areas and organizes all cooperation into three forms, officially referred to as the "pillars" of the union. These are the

European Community (EC), the Common Foreign and Security Policy (CFSP), and the Cooperation in the Fields of Justice and Home Affairs (JHA). The European Union is the umbrella organization that stands over these three constituent "pillar" organizations.

Now as the European Union, the community was "widened" again in 1995 by the admission of three new members—Austria, Sweden, and Finland—who joined following referenda approving the move in each of these countries. Norway was also invited to join but once again voted the measure down in a national referendum. This fourth enlargement brought the number of member states to 15, increased the area of the community by roughly a third, expanded its population by 11% to some 370 million citizens, and shifted its geographic center of gravity eastward. The absorption of former East Germany into the German Federal Republic in 1990 also contributed to the eastward shift.

Among the important integrative goals of the 1990s was the removal of all obstacles to the free movement of people of all nationalities across the internal borders of the Union. This process began in the mid-1980s when Belgium, France, Germany, Luxembourg, and the Netherlands signed the Schengen Agreement, committing themselves to the gradual removal of checks at shared borders. In 1995 the Schengen Agreement came into full force, establishing the Schengen Area within the EU, consisting at that time of the original five signatories of the agreement plus Spain and Portugal. Under the Amsterdam Treaty, which came into force in 1999, the Schengen provisions governing the free movement of people and common police and border controls were extended across the entire community, although special provisions were applied to Denmark, Great Britain, and Ireland.

## A Single Currency

The most significant integrative development of the 1990s, however, was the move toward a single European currency. This began with the 1992 Maastricht Treaty, which set a specific timetable for achieving monetary union.

A second step was the establishment in 1994 of a European Monetary Institute (EMI), charged with strengthening the coordination of the monetary policies of the member states and preparing the way for the eventual establishment of a European Central Bank. In early 1995 the European Commission adopted a plan for the implementation of a single currency, and later that year the European Council dubbed it the "euro" and specified a launch date of January 1, 1999. On that date 11 states—Austria, Belgium, Finland, France, Germany, Ireland, Italy, Luxembourg, the Netherlands, Portugal, and Spain—irrevocably fixed their exchange rates, and the euro became a part of the financial landscape of Europe. A 12th country, Greece, was added in January 2001.

Three EU member countries remained outside the so-called euro zone. In a September 2000 national referendum, Denmark rejected participation, in part because voters feared adoption of the euro would signal an unacceptable further erosion of Danish political sovereignty (a threat stressed by the country's anti-immigrant and nationalist Danish People's Party). Sweden too chose to follow a go-slow approach, hoping to join only after bringing its economy into closer alignment with the other states and after the then strong weight of Swedish public opinion against the euro abated. The United Kingdom also delayed, declaring that five specific criteria must be met before a national referendum on the issue could be held. Among British concerns were the impact on investment and unemployment at home, the effect on the European primacy of London's financial service markets, and whether entry into the euro zone would actually do anything to promote growth and prosperity in the United Kingdom.

For its initial two years, the euro was strictly a currency of business and investment, bought and sold on financial markets. Nonetheless, the adoption of the euro by so many states meant that, for all practical purposes, the EU became a single integrated capital market. The introduction of the euro had a substantial impact on European busi-

**FIGURE 7.7. Introduction of the euro.** The introduction of euro currency has been a remarkable success, but initially the idea drew skepticism from many. The message written on this Paris expressway bridge in the summer of 2001 expressed something less than a supportive attitude.

ness culture, unleashing a wave of American style hostile takeovers and the advent of serious cross-boundary investment strategies. It took Europe a long way toward eliminating the vexing problems of price transparency and foreign exchange costs and risks. Also important was the creation of the European Central Bank in Frankfurt, which placed EU monetary policy, for the first time, in the hands of an independent institution capable of wielding power second only to that of the U.S. Federal Reserve. It soon became clear that the EU countries that remained outside the euro zone could not escape its influence. They were in effect virtual members of the euro zone, if not formal members. London's enthusiastic welcome of euro trading and an unprecedented decision by the London Stock Exchange to forge an alliance with the Frankfurt Exchange and smaller European exchanges was evidence of this.

The introduction of euro banknotes and coins on January 1, 2002, marked the most dramatic step to date in the move toward a single European currency. On that date national currencies disappeared in 12 European countries as they adopted the euro as official tender. In what had been billed as the "biggest money swap" in history, Europeans began to spend bills and coins whose face designs pay homage to the theme of European supranational unity. Banknotes carry motifs

that are symbolic of Europe's architectural heritage. On one side are images of windows and gateways as symbols of the spirit of openness and cooperation within the EU. On the reverse side are stylized images of bridges from different ages (none of them represents a specific existing monument) meant to be a metaphor of communication. Coins carry a map of Europe and the 12-star symbol of the union on one side, but in a bow toward national pride each member state is allowed to place motifs of their own choosing on the other side.

To European integrationists, acceptance of the euro has been seen as a powerful force for closer political union. By agreeing to abandon

**FIGURE 7.8. Euro banknote.** The backside of the 5-euro note features a stylized image of an aqueduct. The intent is to recognize Europe's unique architectural heritage, although not too specifically. The structure on the note is reminiscent of a number of well-known Roman aqueducts but is an exact match for none of them.

national currencies and the independent right to set national fiscal policies, member nations have surrendered a significant piece of their political sovereignty. That Germany, for example, could abandon the deutsche mark, the symbol of its postwar stability and prosperity, is a remarkable sacrifice to make for greater European integration. Also remarkable is the relative ease with which the transition has taken place. Some commentators have been fond to point out that no other currency has been so widely circulated in Europe since the Roman Empire.

Indeed, as Europeans move about and spend the new currency, one of the interesting things will be to see how the coins, which are minted and introduced by each country within its own borders, spread across Europe. Researchers are already tracking this process, which promises to be a unique window on the extent of European integration. How long will it take before a state of equilibrium is reached, in which coins (which are predominantly carried and spent by individuals) will be found everywhere in Europe in rough proportion to the number minted by individual countries? Based on earlier returns, some experts predict that the process will be complete in as little as 5–7 years.

The euro, however, still faces potential political problems. Although official obstacles and potential political costs discourage them from doing so, some of the east-central European states now joining the EU are considering making the euro their official currencies, even though applicant countries are required to wait 2 years after joining the EU before adopting the euro. Perhaps the biggest political problem facing the euro zone, though, is an internal one. Underlying the EU's single monetary policy is a "stability and growth pact" that requires member countries to keep their budgets in balance or face very stiff penalties. Ironically, Germany and France, two of the strongest proponents of the policy, have been among the first to experience difficulty meeting this requirement, forcing the EU into the embarrassing position of having to water down the pact in order to allow them to escape its provisions.

## The 2004 Enlargement

Since the accession of Austria, Finland, and Sweden in 1995, the EU has taken steps toward further enlargement. Formal bilateral negotiations began in 1998 on the accession of a "first wave" of six applicant countries: Cyprus, the Czech Republic, Estonia, Hungary, Poland, and Slovenia. These countries were considered to be most able to meet the strict political and economic criteria for membership set down by the European Council. A year later negotiations were opened with a "second wave" of six applicant countries (Bulgaria, Latvia, Lithuania, Malta, Romania, and Slovakia). Turkey was recognized as a 13th candidate, although negotiations have yet to get under way officially. All of these countries were given associate member status, which means that they were guaranteed eventual full membership. Despite the apparent implausibility just a few years earlier of such a thing happening, the EU made the historic move at its Copenhagen summit at the end of 2002 to admit as many as 10 of the applicant countries in May 2004.

The 2004 enlargement is an historic undertaking that adds, in its initial phase, more than 100 million new EU citizens. It is also a difficult undertaking that will undoubtedly dominate EU politics and policy for a long time to come. The enlargements extend the boundaries of the EU ever farther from the original core in western Europe, taking them for the first time into east-central Europe as well as extending them along the southern Baltic rim of northern Europe. With the addition of Cyprus, and assuming that Turkey will eventually be admitted, the EU is also being thrust deep into Europe's Southeastern Periphery. This has been paralleled by a contemporaneous eastward extension of membership in NATO. In fact, NATO moved to embrace potential new east-central European members even far more quickly than the EU, admitting Poland, the Czech Republic, and Hungary as early as 1999.

What also makes this unique is the fact that the new member states are significantly different from the West in political culture and economy. These are, for the most part, fragile new democracies whose populations are still relatively unaccustomed to western ways of governance and civil responsibility. The economic differences, in particular, are on a scale far beyond that experienced in any of the previous enlargements. While this enlargement raises the population of the EU by more than 25%, its total gross domestic product is increased by only about 5%. With the exception of a couple of capital cities, nearly every region within the new member countries in east-central Europe will qualify for development funds. The accession of these countries brings per capita wealth across the EU down sharply. Given the potential costs and difficulties of the entire undertaking, it is hardly surprising that a large part of the debate over enlargement policy has concerned itself with setting minimum conditions that will make the new member countries more like the old member countries (they are required, for example, to assimilate 80,000 pages of EU law into their legal systems), and with the thorny problem of devising terms of accession that bestow the benefits of membership on new members without undermining the stability of the existing EU and its institutions. Long and difficult negotiations were necessary to clear a host of issues, and a myriad of special concessions had to be granted for each of the applicants—the Latvians, for example, needed dispensation to take undersized herring in the Baltic—before the final decision to admit all 10 countries could be announced.

One of the most difficult hurdles has been agricultural policy. Most of the new member countries are two or three times as dependent on agriculture as present EU countries. This means a restructuring of the EU's cumbrously byzantine Common Agricultural Policy (CAP), which delivers an enormously complex system of subsidies and protections to the community's farmers that currently consumes nearly half of the EU's annual budget. To date the EU has been loath to extend the same agricultural benefits to newly acceding countries in east-central Europe, preferring instead to limit the newcomers to just 25% of the level of subsidy currently given to west-

ern farmers (rising to 100% only after 10 years). The EU also plans to impose restrictions and quotas on agricultural production in the East in order to protect western farmers from competing with eastern surpluses. These proposals are seen in the new member nations as highly discriminatory and have unleashed a storm of protest, particularly in Poland, where as much as one-fifth of the population earns its livelihood directly from agriculture. Indeed, it is much feared in Poland that expensive EU restrictions on the processing of meat will likely drive thousands of small-scale producers out of business.

With billions at stake, vested interests in the West, on the other hand, are likely to resist any future proposed softening of the EU's agricultural policies toward the newly acceded members. Even in its present form, the agricultural aid package will, according to estimates, pour a staggering 25 billion euros into east-central Europe in the first 2 years after accession, with almost half of it going to Poland. Current members fret that over the long term the buildup of direct payments to eastern farmers will simply become too expensive to bear and that the entrenched interests of new member states in perpetuating the subsidies will wreck any chance of ever bringing about a much needed reform of the CAP.

FIGURE 7.9. Farming in east-central Europe. What will become of east-central Europe's antiquated but potentially cheap and productive farming economy is one of the key questions surrounding the latest enlargement of the EU. These Polish farm workers ride a horse-drawn cart as they go about their work.

Enlargement also promises to place a severe strain on "structural" development funds. In its ongoing effort to equalize development and living standards across the community, the EU spends billions each year in development funds. Taken together, development funds and agricultural subsidies account for roughly 80% of the EU budget. Development funds have traditionally gone primarily to the poorer countries and regions within the EU, especially to Spain, Greece, and Portugal as well as to southern Italy and parts of Ireland. Under those rules, nearly every new member country could immediately qualify for generous expenditures of structural funds, which means that either more funds would have to be raised or that current recipients would have to do with less. Countries such as Spain are adamantly opposed to sharing. As with the case of farm subsidies, the EU has tried to solve the dilemma by holding back on benefits to the newcomers. By invoking a new rule restricting aid to no more than 4% of a country's GDP, the relatively small economies of the new member countries are limited in how much aid they can absorb. These countries have been quick to charge that the potential financial burden to the EU is being grossly exaggerated, pointing out that in relative terms the EU will spend in the first 3 years only one-fifteenth as much in aid on 10 new member countries as the United States spent on Marshall Plan aid during an equivalent period.

Controls over borders constitute another broad area of concern. The accession of so many new member states in east-central Europe advances the external frontiers of the EU far to the east, bringing them into direct contact with Russia (in the past this only occurred on the Finnish frontier), and with other ex-Soviet states, such as Belarus and Ukraine. Kaliningrad, the detached western enclave of Russia on the Baltic, which was once Königsberg in East Prussia, has suddenly become an island surrounded by EU territory. The prospect of border troubles makes many current EU members uncomfortable. How can this long and potentially leaky eastern frontier be made secure against illegal cross-border movements of goods and people? The resources of the poorer new member countries in east-central Europe are clearly insufficient to control their eastern frontiers effectively.

Moreover, a sealed border with fences and electronic surveillance, even if it could be built, sends the wrong exclusionary message to an eastern Europe whose friendship and cooperation the EU now works hard to cultivate. Inevitably it could result in a new economic and political division of Europe rather than the open and whole Europe held by many to be so important to future peace and prosperity. The fear of exclusion has already prompted an angry official protest from the Russian Parliament: "The attempt by the European Union to divide inhabitants of the European continent into first and second category citizens goes against the EU's declared policy—that of the construction of a unified, free, democratic Europe, without frontiers and without discrimination." In parts of east-central and eastern Europe the new frontier zone has already come to be known as the "Belgian Curtain," a present-day takeoff on the old "Iron Curtain" of Cold War days, but this time signifying the eastern limits of power exercised by the European Commission in Brussels.

A good part of the concern over borders has to do with migration. It is generally assumed within the older EU community that enlargement will be accompanied by huge population pressures from the East. This will come in part from the newly admitted east-central European countries, from which researchers estimate hundreds of thousands will take advantage of the right that EU residents have to move freely within the Union. That prospect is especially troublesome, for example, in the already economically struggling borderlands of eastern Germany, where workers fear an invasion of cheap labor that might cost them their jobs (wages in Poland are only a fraction of what they are in Germany). The EU has insisted on imposing a 7-year transition period during which such migrations from new member countries would be controlled. But perhaps even more frightening is the possibil-

**FIGURE 7.10. Migrants.** The older members of the EU fear a new wave of immigrants from those parts of Europe that remain outside the community. This photo captures the long line of people that forms each day outside the Austrian Embassy in Belgrade to apply for visas. Recent reports from nearby Bulgaria suggest that the flow of the young and the talented to the West, whether legally or illegally, is a major national concern.

ity of large numbers of people in the former Soviet republics, who seek a better life, crossing weakly controlled borders to enter the EU. Even before enlargement, with relatively tight borders, an estimated half a million illegal migrants from the East were smuggled or managed to sneak into the EU each year. Not surprisingly, given the current anti-immigrant politics in many EU countries, the issues of border controls and illegal labor movements have and will continue to loom large in the discussions over enlargement.

A final stumbling block is a political one. Now that enlargement is a reality, the EU must resolve how power and influence will be wielded in a newly expanded Union, with both large and small states. This was, in fact, the focus of a summit of EU leaders that took place in Nice in 2000, and remains a central issue as the EU now debates the draft of a constitution. One critical issue is whether each member state will, as in the past, have its own commissioner in the all-important European Commission. The larger countries fear that in an enlarged commission would be unwieldy, and too much power would go to the small states. The EU's new draft constitution proposes a commission of just 15 voting

members, with the member countries holding these positions in turns, according to a strict rotation. Related to this is the issue of how to define a voting majority in the Council of Ministers. The Nice Treaty of 2000 introduced a complex system of determining a majority, in which three big countries plus one small one would be able to muster enough votes to block a decision. The draft constitution proposes that a majority be constituted by a simple majority of the states equaling at least 60% of the population of the EU.

The EU has long committed itself officially to a policy of enlargement and with the current enlargement has delivered on its commitment. Within the old EU-15 it has generally not been politically acceptable to come out openly against the goal of enlargement. Nonetheless, doubts have definitely been present. Just beneath the surface, the French in particular have always held deep reservations—partly for political reasons, fearing that enlargement enhances the importance of Germany at French expense, and partly for economic reasons, fearing a diminishment of EU farm aid. This failure to generate real enthusiasm in the West, among governments and citizens alike, has made people in the new member countries anxious and sometimes angry. A certain level of "EU skepticism" prevails today in many of these countries. The referenda held during 2003 in each of the applicant countries to formalize their acceptance of admission into the EU all delivered a positive "yes" vote, often by greater margins than pollsters predicted. In Slovenia, almost 90% of those who turned out cast a yes vote. And even, Malta, where the outcome was considered most in doubt, delivered a majority of 53.7%. Yet, turnout was often not what it was expected to be, and according to pollsters yes votes were often cast in a spirit of reluctance to oppose, but masked deep-seated reservations. Ironically, enthusiasm is highest in countries that are furthest from achieving accession, such as Bulgaria and Romania.

The desirability of the new member states, as seen from within the old EU, has been quite uneven. Some definitely have had their champions. Northern European countries,

**FIGURE 7.11. New minorities.** These Russian women are protesting the loss of rights suffered by Russian nationals in Latvia following that country's assertion of its independence from the collapsing Soviet Union. Independence for the Baltic States cost many longtime Russian residents the jobs and special status they enjoyed during the Soviet years.

such as Sweden, Denmark, and Finland, for example, pushed strongly from the beginning for the rapid accession of the three Baltic States, which are seen by these countries as an integral part of a developing Nordic–Baltic community. Estonia and Latvia were the best qualified of the three to join the EU, with Lithuania running far behind, but for political reasons it was difficult to separate them and all were allowed to join the EU together (rather ironically, Lithuania now has the fastest-growing economy in Europe). Admission for the Baltic States brings unique problems in that they alone among the new members were once part of the former Soviet Union rather than satellite states, and are the only new members to contain large minority populations of ethnic Russians. Germany too has played a strong role in supporting the admission of certain countries, favoring for economic and political reasons the inclusion of Poland, the Czech Republic, and Slovenia.

There has been a general reluctance, on the other hand, for anyone to accept the idea of Turkish membership. Although Turkey submitted its application for membership back in 1987, it was not formally offered candidacy until 1999. The EU has since declined to set a start date for membership talks. The EU cites Turkey's poor human rights record with

respect to its Kurdish minority (14 million strong in a country of nearly 70 million) as the major stumbling block, along with the as yet not entirely resolved deadlock between Turkey and Greece over the future of the Turkish-speaking minority on Cyprus. Although never openly stated, EU countries react instinctively to the fact that Turkey is a Muslim country. Moreover, there is the fact that the bulk of Turkish territory lies in Asia, which raises the issue of where Europe should properly end geographically. If Turkey is to be admitted, then why not Iraq, Tunisia, Algeria, or Morocco? There is also the fact that within the space of only a decade or two Turkey's fast-growing population could make it the EU's most populous member, deserving of considerable political sway in EU decision making. As the EU equivocates, Turkey becomes increasingly restless and fed-up. Turkey's frustration is further heightened as it watches 10 other candidate countries assimilated into the EU as a single group. Ominously, some voices within Turkey even call for a turn away from the West in favor of forging connections with eastern neighbors such as Russia and Iran, instead.

Nor do many seem eager to consider the Balkan countries, although Bulgaria and Romania have associate status, which guarantees them eventual membership. Both have yet to

**FIGURE 7.12. Turkish pride.** This young man has wrapped himself in one of the flags he is selling on the streets of Istanbul on the occasion of the country's national day. Many Turkish citizens feel a sense of resentment over the EU's long delay in agreeing to open negotiations for Turkey's accession to EU membership.

complete negotiations and hope to join, rather optimistically, by 2007. Bulgaria, especially, has worked hard to present itself as both European and "civilized" by cleaning up its human rights record vis-à-vis its Turkish minorities and ending its hostility toward neighboring Macedonia. The countries of the "western Balkans"—a term that is applied to Albania and the five former republics of Yugoslavia that remain outside the EU now that Slovenia has been admitted—are eager to join as soon as they possibly can. Albania and Macedonia have recently become quite vocal in demanding that they receive accelerated consideration for EU associate membership on the grounds that such action is necessary to ensure the stability of the Balkan region in the wake of the Kosovo crisis. The EU makes

**FIGURE 7.13. In line for accession.** Romania hopes to be among the next to join the EU. The memorial in the foreground of this photo of Nicolae Belascu Boulevard in Bucharest is dedicated to the victims of the December 1989 revolt against the Ceausescu government. Crowds of people gathered in this street, many of them university students, were slaughtered by security forces following the spread of an uprising in western Transylvania to Bucharest and the flight of the Ceausescus by helicopter from the roof of the Communist Party headquarters.

no promises and refers to the "Regatta Principle," which suggests that they will be allowed in one by one as they qualify, rather than in a group as in the current enlargement. Croatia is probably the strongest candidate.

No one, within or outside the EU, expresses any serious hope that Russia or any of the other remaining eastern European states, such as Belarus, Ukraine, and Moldova, might be considered anytime soon, although as a matter of policy the EU invests in the project of upgrading their economic infrastructure and encouraging democratic government through its Technical Assistance for the CIS (Commonwealth of Independent States), or TACIS Program, so that they may one day qualify.

## The Future of the European Project

Everyone would agree that the "European Project" has come a long way since the end of World War II. Each new level of supranational agreement and legislation has nourished a rising public awareness and commitment. In most member countries European political, economic, and social issues now receive regular and serious public discourse alongside national issues; and, although most citizens may not be fully aware of the fact, more than half of the laws and regulations by which they live emanate from Brussels. Nonetheless, the process is far from complete. Whether the move toward a truly integrated Europe can be realized remains to be seen. "Euroscepticism" has become a common political term, and it epitomizes the concerns that remain, especially among some member states, about the incremental loss of national sovereignty that accompanies each new step toward integration. In addition, there is always the question of whether the process, given our uncertain world, can be maintained in the face of unknown crises and conflicts that may yet lie in its path.

There is also the question of whether a true supranational identity, that can overcome long-standing national identities, can ever be truly forged. Europeans, without a doubt, share a certain common historical and cultural heritage, but there are no ritual celebratory European events that have the same kind of emotive meaning as, for example, a Bastille Day—although a Europe Day (May 9) has been established, a flag has been unfurled, and an anthem set to Beethoven's "Ode to Joy" has been written. A recent survey revealed that a majority of EU citizens believed that their country's membership is a good thing, but approval levels were characterized as "precarious" in more than a few states. In none of the three states granted EU membership in 1995—Sweden, Finland, and Austria—do a majority of people still think that membership is a "good thing." Sweden, in fact, has been lukewarm about its membership ever since voting to join in 1994, and frequently demonstrates by its actions the uneasiness of its relationship with Brussels. The Danes are known for their penchant for bucking European trends, and the British have always been of two minds about their relationship with the continent. Quite significantly, approval of EU membership has recently fallen to less than the EU average in France and Germany, both of which have traditionally been firm supporters of the European project.

An ongoing debate remains between integrationist and decentralist views about the long-term shape of the Union, and this debate is likely to sharpen in the years ahead as the current attempt to reform the constitutional architecture of the Union is discussed and voted on. Integrationists are keen to extend majority voting rules to a range of policy areas in such key areas as taxation, social security, and subsidies to poor nations (about 20% of EU decisions) that are currently still subject to national vetoes. Opponents, who have a more federalist vision of the future, hope to halt the advance of centralization and preserve national and regional rights. One outcome, for which there is already some precedence (e.g., border controls, currency, etc.), may be that smaller groups of countries will push ahead with greater integration in certain contested areas, while others refrain, producing in the end a Union of overlapping internal communities.

## REGIONALISM

A resurgence of regionalism in Europe is a much noted phenomenon. The circumstances behind this trend are varied. It is part of what has been called the "hollowing out" of nation-state authority and a reaction to the growing impact of supranational organizational activities and processes. It is also a product of the wave of technological revolutions and economic restructuring associated with the 1980s and 1990s, which have caused cities and regions across Europe to see themselves, rather than the state, as principal competitors for investment and development funds. Many have accordingly felt the need to promote or even sell themselves as distinctively important actors on the European scene, self-confidently in charge of their own destiny. In many areas, the renaissance in regional awareness also has to do with a heightened cultural identity, based on a resurgence of ethnic community or on perceptions of long-standing cultural or economic differences from other parts of the national realm, or both. In any case, it is a matter of fact that many European states in the West, and now in the East as well, are under strong devolutionary pressures.

Regional assertions of political and cultural identity are nothing new. We often take the nation-state for granted, forgetting that Europe is a much compartmentalized place in which provincial and regional cultures, developed over many centuries, have been around for a far longer time. The regions have always been contenders for political power. In the past, some nation-states have tried to overcome this fact by centralizing authority. Napoleon, for example, acted to neutralize the power of the old feudal provinces of France by introducing an administrative system of 96 small and roughly equally sized *départements*, so artificial that they were mostly named after rivers, or in some cases mountain ranges. Each was functionally subordinated to the central government and ruled by a prefect who was appointed in Paris. Similar efforts at centralization were pursued in Italy, after the country was unified in 1861, and in Spain and Germany under strongly nationalistic regimes during the 1930s. In other countries the region fared better, successfully preserving traditions of provincial or regional autonomy alongside national authority. Official policy in the Soviet Union during the 1920s and 1930s, which attempted to equalize the political and economic status of Russian and non-Russian populations through the creation of a federated state of republics and autonomous regions, may have actually worked to foster territorial ethnic and national identities instead of the intended Soviet brotherhood of peoples. Switzerland is the extreme example of a state in which local authority has remained strong, protected by a constitution that guards the cantons and communes against any transgressions against their authority by the national government.

## Regional Political Authority

Political authority is today divided between European nations and regions in a number of ways. The range of different types run the gamut from highly centralized or unitary political systems to highly decentralized or federalist systems. At one end of the continuum are the so-called unitary states, in which legal political authority is vested exclusively with the national government. In western Europe these include all five of the Scandinavian countries, the Netherlands, Ireland, and Greece. The former communist states of east-central Europe may also be placed in this category, partly because of the centralized administrative traditions of their distant imperial past and partly because of their recent history, in which communist regimes strived to eliminate or reduce the powers of regional units in order to protect the state and the party from any challenge to its authority. Administrative reforms now under way in some of these states, however, may eventually lessen their unitary qualities.

A weaker version of the unitary state is found in France and the United Kingdom, where a limited amount of political authority is traditionally found at the regional level, but without constitutional recognition. The role of the central government has been in decline in both states for much of the late 20th century and continues today. France has taken steps to reduce the centralized power of the state by devolving more authority to lower-level units of government, primarily the *départements* but also including the regions, which were first established in 1960 for regional planning purposes. The United Kingdom has just recently recognized some of the demands for greater self-governance put forward by its principal regional components. The people of Scotland now elect a parliament, while Wales and Northern Ireland have their own assemblies to govern their affairs. In the case of Northern Ireland, it was the so-called Good Friday agreement of 1998 that ended many long years of strife and paved the way for a devolutionary transfer of powers to a Northern Ireland Assembly in 1999 (renewed political unrest, however, has forced a temporary suspension of the Assembly). In the wake of these changes, the English regions may also receive greater local powers, and there has even been discussion in some quarters of the need to establish an English parliament since the English may now ironically become the only citizens of the United Kingdom without their own parliament or national assembly.

At the other end of the continuum are the "federal states," in which a clear constitutional division of powers exists between federal and regional authorities. Germany, Belgium, Switzerland, and Austria all belong to this category, although it should be recognized that Belgium has only recently adopted federalism. Austria, however, also possesses some of the features of a unitary state, and Switzerland is confederal in that the central government is actually limited by the powers of the individual cantons and communes. Germany is the one truly federal state, in which constitutional provision is made for a set of exclusive federal powers, a separate set of exclusive constituent state (*Länder*) powers, and conditions under which the federal power may influence constituent state actions or under which the constituent state may legislate if the federal power does not. The federal system in Germany, with its considerable emphasis on checks and balances, is much in-

**TABLE 7.1. Nation-States and Governments**

| Official name | Type of government | Most recent constitution/ independence |
|---|---|---|
| Republic of Albania | Parliamentary democracy | 1998 |
| Principality of Andorra | Parliamentary democracy (with two princes as heads of state) | 1993 |
| Republic of Austria | Parliamentary democracy | 1920 |
| Republic of Belarus | Republic | 1994 |
| Kingdom of Belgium | Parliamentary democracy (under a constitutional monarch) | 1830 |
| Bosnia and Herzogovina | Parliamentary democracy | 1995 |
| Republic of Bulgaria | Parliamentary democracy | 1991 |
| Republic of Croatia | Parliamentary democracy | 1991 |
| Republic of Cyprus | Republic | 1960 |
| Czech Republic | Parliamentary republic | 1993 |
| Kingdom of Denmark | Constitutional monarchy | 1953 |
| Republic of Estonia | Parliamentary democracy | 1992 |
| Republic of Finland | Parliamentary democracy | 1919 |
| French Republic | Republic | 1958 |
| Federal Republic of Germany | Federal republic | 1949 |
| Hellenic Republic (Greece) | Parliamentary republic | 1975 |
| Republic of Hungary | Republic | 1949 |
| Republic of Iceland | Semipresidential, parliamentary | 1918 |
| Ireland | Parliamentary republic | 1937 |
| Republic of Italy | Republic | 1948 |
| Republic of Latvia | Parliamentary democracy | 1991 |
| Principality of Liechtenstein | Hereditary constitutional monarchy | 1921 |
| Republic of Lithuania | Parliamentary democracy | 1992 |
| Grand Duchy of Luxembourg | Constitutional monarchy | 1868 |
| Malta | Republic | 1964 |
| Republic of Moldova | Republic | 1994 |
| Monaco | Constitutional monarchy | 1962 |
| Kingdom of the Netherlands | Parliamentary democracy (under a constitutional monarch) | 1848 |
| Kingdom of Norway | Hereditary constitutional monarchy | 1905 |
| Republic of Poland | Republic | 1997 |
| Portuguese Republic | Republic | 1976 |
| Romania | Republic | 1991 |
| Russian Federation | Federation | 1993 |
| Republic of San Marino | Republic | 1600 |
| Slovak Republic | Parliamentary republic | 1993 |
| Republic of Slovenia | Parliamentary democracy | 1991 |
| Kingdom of Spain | Constitutional monarchy | 1978 |
| Kingdom of Sweden | Constitutional monarchy | 1975 |
| Swiss Confederation | Federal state | 1848 |
| Republic of Turkey | Republic | 1982 |
| Ukraine | Presidential–parliamentary | 1991 |
| United Kingdom of Great Britain and Ireland | Constitutional monarchy | unwritten |
| Vatican City | Monarchial–sacerdotal state | 1929/1985 |
| State Union of Serbia and Montenegro | Federation | 2003 |

*Note.* Data from U.S. Department of State (2003).

fluenced by that of the United States. An important consideration in its design was to provide safeguards against the extreme centralization of power that occurred in Germany during the Nazi era.

Situated nearby on our continuum are the "quasi-federal states" of Spain, Portugal, and Italy, where clear divisions of power have been made between the center and the regions but without the formal structures of the federal state. Spain is the strongest example, where provisions enacted in the 1978 constitution to reduce the strongly centralized state of General Franco allow the country's 17 regions to enjoy varying degrees of constitutionally guaranteed autonomy. The arrangements for self-governance that have been negotiated for each of the regions vary quite considerably, and for three—the Basque Country, Catalonia, and Navarre—include wide powers. Ultimately, however, these powers are held at the pleasure of the central authority in Madrid due to a clause in the post-Franco constitution that says that a region may forfeit all or part of its rights of self-governance if it fails to meet its constitutional obligations or if it poses by its actions a threat to the interests of the rest of Spain. The regional assembly of Spain's Basque Country, from which the terrorist separatist movement *Euskadi Ta Askatasuna* (Basque Homeland and Freedom), or ETA, has been operating for more than three decades, was recently threatened

**FIGURE 7.14. Regional autonomy.** The regions of Spain have already won varying degrees of guaranteed autonomy from Madrid. The graffiti on this wall in Galicia calls for more—total independence.

with such loss of powers for its refusal to participate in the national government in Madrid's banning of Batsuna, the political wing of ETA. Conversely, Catalonia, which holds more powers than any of the regions, pushes continually and often successfully for even more autonomy from Madrid. Portugal's 1976 constitution declares it to be a unitary state, but provisions for new regional government arrangements are being implemented. In Italy government reforms have recently given greater autonomy to the provinces.

Russia too is a special case. In the aftermath of the collapse of the Soviet Union, Russia has officially declared itself a federation. The Federal Treaty of 1992 formalized a federal system that was largely incorporated into the new Russian constitution of 1993. The treaty and the constitution provide the two most important territorial elements of the Russian Federation, the republics and the regions (*oblasts*), with equal federal status. While the central government can claim defense and foreign relations as its exclusive domain, the republics and regions are supposed to enjoy far-reaching self-governance rights in domestic affairs. In fact, however, the division of responsibilities between the republics and the center remains ill defined in many areas. This is especially true of issues surrounding the ownership of land and natural resources and control over taxation mechanisms. The regions, despite their legally equal status, are in an even more disadvantageous position vis-à-vis the center than the republics. In a very real sense, Russian federalism has failed in that the relationships among republics, regions, and the center are defined as much by the practical political and economic leverage that individual republics and regions are able to wield as they are by formal constitutional arrangements. There are thus de facto differences among the federal units. Much of this is a reflection of the practice of negotiating separate bilateral treaties between the republics and Moscow, many of which have produced dramatically different results. The regions have also sought to jockey, with even more uneven results, for a greater degree of self-rule.

One of the difficulties with the new regionalism is that, as we have seen, regions have real political status in only a handful of European countries. From an administrative point of view, there is no European standard on what constitutes a region. They may be, as is the case with France's regional units, the artificial product of a penchant for regional planning that has long been common to many European countries. They may, at the other extreme, be cultural regions or historic provinces that possess significant ethnic, linguistic, or religious identities and are quite willing to demand a degree of political autonomy, or even a separate political future, for themselves.

Examples of the latter are many, including Catalonia or the Basque region in Spain, Flanders and Wallonia in Belgium, Scotland in the United Kingdom, Friuli-Venezia Giulia and the South Tyrol in Italy, and Corsica in France (which, in fact, just recently won unprecedented guarantees from the French government that it will enjoy greater autonomy in the future). They might also be the constituent member states of a federalist structure, such as the *Länder* in Germany. But even the German *Länder* are, in fact, mostly artificial administrative creations, replete with their own regions for planning and administration. Or they can be relatively low-level administrative units. Poland, for example, has recently restored and given new powers to the district (*powiat*), a governmental unit that was abolished in 1973 and lies between the commune and the county. Administrative reforms in France, despite the new powers afforded to the regions, have devolved the most important responsibilities to the local administrative level of the *département*. Considerable authority also remains with the district (*Kreis*) in Germany.

Thus, there is much debate over the form that the region should take in its new role as a governmental authority responsible for making policy decisions in cooperation not only with national governments but in concert with the policies of supranational institutions as well. It is often suggested that the regions likely to emerge from this new regionalism as really significant are the city-regions. This is a reflection of the increasingly urban-oriented spatial structure of European economy and society. As national governments gradually surrender their powers and responsibilities, cities and their regions are logically the most appropriate subnational units to make decisions and provide services that are responsive

**FIGURE 7.15. Mini-state.** Often forgotten in any discussion of European polity are the continent's mini-states, which are also relevant to any discussion of regionalism because they all have a strong historical regional identity. Europe's mini-states include Andorra, Liechtenstein, Monaco, San Marino, and the Vatican City. Most of Monaco's 1.9 square kilometers of territory are visible in this photo, which looks west across the Mediterranean front of the famous principality.

to the needs of their populations, and to enter into cooperative arrangements with other city-regions on matters of common interest. The rise of the city-region has been aided by a wave of local government reforms that took place in both western and eastern Europe since the 1960s. In many cases, these reforms created metropolitan or city–hinterland administrative units, which are being raised today to the level of administrative regions or provinces. This was the case, for example, in 1990 when Italy took steps to introduce metropolitan units into its reorganization of provincial-level government functions.

## A "Europe of the Regions"

In recent years it has become quite fashionable to advance the idea that the region may be the most relevant political unit of the future. The various debates over Europe's future often address the notion of a "Europe of the Regions" in which regions of varying size and origin, some of them even crossing national boundaries, are seen as potentially the most dynamic political and economic units of a new Europe. The rise of the region, and the concomitant erosion of the nation-state, is often viewed as a simple merging of long-standing popular regional identities and aspirations with the new political realities of our time. In the idealistic words of Denis de Rougemont (as quoted in Bassand, 1993, p. 11), an early proponent of the idea of a new Europe built on regions, "the regions will very quickly form, organize and assert themselves. And since they will be young and flexible, full of vitality and open to the world, they will enter into exchange relationships as frequently and extensively as possible. They will group together according to their affinities and complementarities, and according to the new realities, which have formed them. . . . It is on these regions that we shall build Europe."

The EU has given legitimacy to this idea by emphasizing the importance of regional diversity and interregional cooperation in its blueprint for the building of a more perfect union. Following a long decade of European regional activism in the 1980s, exemplified by the creation of an Assembly of European Regions in 1985 and by the establishment of lobbying missions in Brussels by individual substate regions, the EU began to design official regional policies and initiatives in the early 1990s. In 1991, for example, a consultative "Committee of the Regions," consisting of representatives of European regional and local authorities, was created along with a Council of European Municipalities and Regions. There is also an Assembly of European Regions. Official EU support for the devolution of decision making to the regional level was articulated in the 1992 Maastricht Treaty, under the so-called concept of subsidiarity. The idea has been widely accepted. As integration proceeds, many EU countries have attempted to decentralize and deconcentrate the activities of the state in the interest of providing a more regional and democratic response to the needs of people.

Also important is a new kind of emergent region that crosses international boundaries and which, in many cases, may not have previously existed at all or may not have been recognized in any formal sense. The most common examples have arisen out of efforts by regional governments to promote cooperation between specific adjacent border regions. Well-known examples include the *Regio Basiliensis*, which combines adjacent border regions in France, Germany, and Switzerland, or EUREGIO, which consists of the Dutch–German borderlands between the Rhine, Ems, and Ijssel Rivers. One survey, published in the mid-1990s, identifies no fewer than 116 European examples of this form of cross-border regional cooperation.

Cross-border region building has been encouraged in a number of ways. One motivating force, as described above, is the desire on the part of local or regional forces to establish for themselves an advantageous position relative to the global economy. A second impetus comes from the European Union, which has supported cross-border regionalism as a means of deepening the integration of member states. The EU encourages such activity through the provision of specially earmarked funds. A third motivation derives from the numerous unique opportunities for east–west cross-border cooperation (also encouraged by the EU) that sprang up in the wake of the collapse of socialist governments in east-central Europe. The latter has made border cooperation between regions situated along Europe's former east–west divide a particularly common phenomenon. A good example is Euroregion Pomerania, established in 1995 to bring together the border regions of historic Pomerania, which includes a number of towns and districts in the eastern most parts of the German *Länder* of Mecklenburg-Vorpommern and Brandenburg and much of Szczecin voivodship in northwestern Poland. Since 1998, some 33 communes from across the Baltic Sea in the old Swedish province of Skåne have also been linked to this cross-border cooperative initiative.

At yet another level, Europeans have become aware of what might be called "macro-" or "superregions." Macro regions occur at a much larger scale and typically cross a far larger number of boundaries. They are in many ways a looser construction, built without some of the formal institutional structures and agreements that often characterize either subnational regions or the cross-border initiatives that link specific border areas together. At this macro scale of regional development,

the general awareness that "regions do matter" was officially sanctioned and heightened by the publication in 1991 of *Europe 2000: Outlook for the Development of the Community's Territory*, which identified eight large regional groupings (superregions) in the space of the Community that could be justified on the basis of geographical proximity and developing mutual relationships. For European decision makers these regions have become potentially useful as vehicles for strategic planning, rendering the continent more easily understood by contrasting transnational zones of growth and dynamism, such as the so-called Blue Banana (a European core region stretching from London to Milan), and zones that are relatively peripheral or are otherwise lagging in development. The so-called Atlantic Arc, stretching the length of Europe's western coast from Lisbon to North Cape and consisting of lands that have traditionally looked away from Europe toward the Atlantic as well as containing areas that are today some of the EU's most economically depressed, is a case in point.

The idea of macro regions has also caught the public imagination. Indeed, in 1994 American journalist Darrel Delamaide produced a popularized exposition of macroregionalism in Europe, titled *The New Superregions of Europe*, that outlined eight European regions, replete with evocative labels, such as "Latin Crescent," "Baltic League," "Mitteleuropa," and "Alpine Arc." The idea was to present the spatial organization of Europe in entirely new terms by delimiting macro-scale regional units that both ran across contemporary state boundaries and captured Europe's most recent macro-scale spatial patterns of business and economic development. For the most part, however, such regions exist only in the imagination or as analytical tools.

## Baltic Europe: A Region in the Making

At the same time, some macro regions have begun to take on a measure of true regional identity. An excellent case in point is Baltic Europe. Although this is only one example,

**FIGURE 7.16. Euroregion.** The EU has gone out of its way to lend support to the formation of cross-border regions. This is the official logo, replete with a EU flag for a sail, of Euroregion Pomerania—a cross-border regional association of neighboring areas of Poland, Germany, and Sweden.

FIGURE 7.17. Macro regions (after Delamaide).

we will examine it in some detail to illustrate the kind of macro-level regional development that the current political, social, and economic climate in Europe is fostering.

While there seems to have been little sense of a Baltic identity over the decades extending back to World War II, there has recently been a flurry of activity that has led many to conclude that a new Baltic regional identity has emerged. The novelty of the current situation is heightened by its sharp contrast with that of the postwar decades, when the long political and economic rivalry between East and West effectively turned the Baltic into a zone of ideological conflict. The Baltic Sea, during that period, was in many ways more of a barrier than a bridge between its opposite

shores. Only since 1989–1990, with the end of the Cold War and the dissolution of the Soviet Union, has it been possible to think about the prospect of bringing the lands and peoples around the sea together into some kind of new regional construct.

The problem has been how to build a new Baltic regional identity. Given its sharply divided recent history, some proponents of the idea of a new Baltic regional identity have been fond of looking to the more distant past for precedent; and there is some basis for doing so, for historically there have been brief examples of lively connectivity, and at times even unity of a kind, across the waters of the Baltic. The Vikings were long ago active in establishing a series of trading posts around its shores as they drove eastward to access markets along the rivers of Russia. In the 12th and 13th centuries crusading knights from the Christian West imposed both their overlordship and faith on those who lived around the eastern margins of the sea. Later, the Hanseatic League, a powerful association of German trading cities, succeeded in turning Baltic commercial trade into a monopoly that lasted from the 13th to the 15th century. Still later, the Swedes succeeded in asserting their hegemony over the entire region for a period of time during the 17th century. But the current coming together of Baltic interests seems to bear little resemblance to any of these instances from the past. The phenomenon is essentially a response, both politically and economically, to the perception of new structural situations and opportunities in a changing Europe that, in turn, has found resonance, for one reason or another, among a broad range of interests across the Baltic area.

The region-building process in the Baltic has been going on now for a little over a decade and is the product of an interesting collection of actors. Its earliest instigators were business-oriented leaders, particularly from northern Germany, who in the late 1980s were concerned about the southward shift in Germany's economic center of gravity taking place at the time. They began to promote the idea of a "Mare Balticum" as a counterweight.

**The Hanse-Office**

Joint office of the States of
Hamburg and Schleswig-Holstein

**FIGURE 7.18. Mare Balticum.** Part of the impetus for the creation of a new Baltic identity came from northern Germany. This is the logo of the Hanse-Office, set up by the north German states of Hamburg and Schleswig-Holstein to help coordinate Baltic regional initiatives and facilitate lobbying for support from the EU in Brussels.

Another early actor was an intellectual community of Nordic-Baltic peace researchers, environmentalists, planners, and international specialists who wished to promote a new Baltic identity as a means of ensuring the survival of a certain quality of "Nordicness" in a developing "Europe of the Regions." Yet another impetus emerged out of a general concern over security issues. The Baltic had long been a source of Cold War tensions, and the many uncertainties unleashed by the dissolution of the Soviet Union made the idea of macroscale regional cooperation an attractive means of ensuring peace, security, and stability throughout the Baltic. Concern about the increasing pollution of the Baltic was also a factor in bringing people from across the region together.

A final element of early region-building activity came through the establishment of formal international institutions and networking organizations of various kinds. One of the first was the Union of the Baltic Cities, set up with 32 charter members at a conference in Gdansk in 1991. A Baltic Sea Ports Organization was created later that year, and shortly thereafter representatives from the governments of the Baltic States, the Nordic countries, Poland, Germany, and the European Union met in Copenhagen to establish a framework for a Council of the Baltic States (CBSS) dedicated to serving "as an overall forum focusing on needs for intensified cooperation and coordination among the Baltic Sea States." Numerous additional initiatives, many of them quite spontaneous and representing a rather wide and diverse range of actors, soon appeared. These include the Baltic University Programme, a network of universities from across the region; ARS BALTICA, a forum devoted to organizing and coordinating cultural events across the region for the purpose of fostering a common sense of cultural identity; and the Baltic Center for Writers and Translators, founded in the Swedish city of Visby in 1993. All have contributed undeniably to the emergence by the mid-1990s of a Baltic Sea region endowed with certain strong features of community and identity.

What is interesting about the macro region-

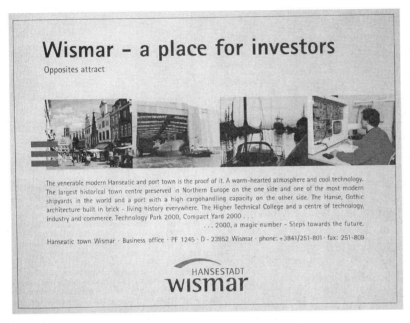

**FIGURE 7.19. Cities and regions.** One beneficiary of Europe's new regionalism has been cities. Many find it economically advantageous to build their image around regional identities as they compete for investment. In this advertisement, the north German city of Wismar reminds readers of its historical tradition as a Baltic Hanseatic town while at the same time depicting itself as a modern and forward-looking place. The punch line: "opposites attract."

building process in the Baltic, as well as in other parts of Europe, is the extreme importance of both myth making and networking. The various actors clearly understood from the beginning that it was essential to engage in active myth making—that is, to take steps to generate the image or impression that a Baltic Sea region exists, that something is happening that makes it natural and desirable for businesses, chambers of commerce, activitists, students, and tourists to both see and act on the potential connections and sense of identity the region has to offer. This was a process not unlike that which we have generally come to accept as basic to nation building. It was undertaken by an elite, consisting of intellectuals, politicians, business leaders, and journalists. It meant inventing or rediscovering historical precedents, however superficial they might be. It also meant creating icons and images, such as the notion of a new Hanseatic region. Equally important was the establishment of multiple networks at the grassroots level. While intergovernmental cooperation was deemed useful, much more emphasis was placed on a type of popular and democratic involvement that one might think of as "subsidiarity-in-action."

While there is a definite political element to the much heralded late 20th-century emergence of Europe's regions, it appears also, as the Baltic example demonstrates, to be just as much a phenomenon of civic and economic boosterism. As such, it is something that we will return to in later chapters on urban and economic life. In many ways, Europe's new subnational, cross-border, and macro regions appear to be proclaimed and extolled primar-

**FIGURE 7.20. Networking.** Ultimately, Europe's macro regions depend heavily on networking on the grassroots level. Indeed, formal associations at the national level are often shunned in an effort to maintain spontaneity and independence. In this spirit, The Baltic Institute, a Swedish foundation for Baltic cooperation, maintains an Internet website solely for the purpose of providing an open forum and information center to promote decentralized cooperation in the Baltic region.

ily by local economic and political elites, who are engaged in projecting an attractive climate for capital investment and in networking with people of similar circumstance elsewhere in Europe. One commentator has christened them "bourgeois regions." Indeed, the most common way that one becomes aware of them is through glossy investment advertisements, tourism promotions, and Internet webpage sites.

The degree to which regions such as the Baltic may, for ordinary citizens, be real objects of political or cultural identity capable of competing effectively with state or other territorial units is unclear. They do, however, speak to the growing diversity of territorial and political frameworks within which Europeans live and work, and they have raised a lively academic discussion as to what they may mean. Some have argued that they are yet another contribution to a developing "deterritorialized consciousness," in which the loyalties to the rigid spatial structures of the past are dissolving and being replaced by allegiances that are much more fluid and overlapping. Others have raised the romantic notion of a "new medievalism"—a return to the old city-states and trading alliances of the High Middle Ages. Still others choose to dismiss them as nothing new and of little political consequence.

## FURTHER READING

Bassand, M. (1993). *Culture and regions of Europe*. Strasbourgh, France: Council of Europe.

Blouet, B. W. (1996). The political geography of Europe: 1900–2000 A.D. *Journal of Geography*, 95, 5–14.

Delamaide, D. (1994). *The new superregions of Europe*. New York: Dutton.

Dogan, M. (1998). The decline of traditional values in Western Europe: religion, nationalism, authority. *International Journal of Comparative Sociology*, 39, 77–90.

Gellner, E. (1983). *Nations and nationalism*. Oxford, UK: Blackwell.

Giordano, B. (2000). Italian regionalism or 'Padanian' nationalism—the political project of the Lega Nord in Italian politics. *Political Geography*, 19, 445–471.

Greeneld, L. (1992). *Nationalism: Five roads to modernity*. Cambridge, MA: Harvard University Press.

Habermas, J. (1996). The European nation-state: Its achievements and its limits. In G. Balakrishnan & B. Anderson (Eds.), *Mapping the nation* (pp. 281–294). London: Verso.

Harvie, C. (1994). *The rise of regional Europe*. London: Routledge.

Heffernan, M. (1997). *Twentieth century Europe: A political geography*. New York: Wiley.

Herb, G. (1997). *Under the map of Germany: Nationalism and propaganda, 1918–1945*. London: Routledge.

Hooson, D. (Ed.). (1994). *Geography and national identity*. Oxford, UK: Blackwell.

Hough, J. F. (1998). The political geography of European Russia: Republics and oblasts. *Post-Soviet Geography and Economics*, 39, 63–95.

Jervell, S., Kukk, M., & Joenniemi, P. (Eds.). (1992). *The Baltic Sea area—a region in the making*. Oslo: Europa Programmet and the Baltic Institute.

Jönsson, C., Tägil, S., & Törnqvist, G. (2000). *Organizing European space*. London: Sage.

Kaiser, R. (1994). *The geography of nationalism in Russia and the USSR*. Princeton, NJ: Princeton University Press.

Newhouse, J. (1997). Europe's rising regionalism." *Foreign Affairs*, 76, 67–84.

O"Loughllin, J., & van der Wusten, H. (Eds.). (1993). *The new political geography of eastern Europe*. London: Belhaven.

Paasi, A. (1996). *Territories, boundaries, and consciousness: The changing geographies of the Finnish–Russian border*. Chichester, UK: Wiley.

Sellar, C., & Pickles, J. (2002). Where will Europe end? Ukraine and the limits of European integration. *Eurasian Geography and Economics*, 43, 123–142.

Smith, A. D. (1995). *Nations and nationalism in a global era*. Oxford, UK: Basil Blackwell.

Unwin, T. (1999). Contested reconstruction of national identities in Eastern Europe. *Norsk Geografisk Tidsskrift*, 53, 113–120.

U.S. Department of State. (2003). Fact sheet: Independent states in the world [On-line]. Available www.state.gov/s/inr/rls/4250.htm

Weber, E. (1976). *Peasants into Frenchmen: The modernization of rural France, 1870–1914*. Stanford, CA: Stanford University Press.

# PART III

## Towns and Cities

# CHAPTER 8

# Cities and Urban Life to World War I

Our purpose in Part III, and Part IV to follow, is to explore the questions of where and how Europeans live. This is a complex issue, but in many ways the simplest answer is that Europeans today live predominantly in towns and cities and pursue the lives of urbanites. With nearly three-quarters (72%) of the continent's population living in places that are commonly regarded as "urban" (i.e., 2,000 or more inhabitants), it is not much of an exaggeration to say that the city is home for most Europeans. To say so is not to deny the existence of the millions of Europeans who live in rural communities, nor to ignore the vast areas of open countryside to be found even in the continent's most densely populated areas. It is, however, a simple acknowledgment of the fact that Europe is one of the world's most highly urbanized regions. Moreover, one might easily argue that a large majority of the rural population is under the influence of an urban way of life that today reaches out almost effortlessly to engulf nearly everyone. Modern transportation and communication technologies have so increased the accessibility of the city to those who live in surrounding areas and vice versa that the countryside has become in many ways an extension of the urban realm, making the differences between urban and rural life less perceptible than they once were.

Metropolitan Paris, for example, now en-compasses for all practical purposes the entire Paris Basin. Even though most of the basin would technically still be considered rural, it is also a vast zone of "exurban" development in which the exact outer boundaries of the city are becoming increasingly difficult to delimit. Indeed, one of the latest housing trends affecting the outer portions of the basin involves the conversion of thousands of second homes, previously established by Parisians for weekend use, into first homes for affluent urbanites willing to commute long distances to the center or able to conduct their business transactions from afar. Similar pressures prevail in the southeast of England, where serious housing shortfalls in London and its surrounding counties have recently raised pressures on local councils to relax planning controls and expand housing development programs in rural areas.

All over Europe one can readily observe the outward-radiating impact of a highly mobile, leisure-oriented urban lifestyle. As the trend continues, more and more of the countryside seems dedicated to serving either the residential or leisure needs of the urban dweller. Consider, for example, the picturesque town of Bad Münstereifel, which is located in a relatively secluded part of Germany's Eifel region but within easy driving distance of major Rhine cities such as Cologne, Bonn, and Koblenz. The town, which

**FIGURE 8.1. Exurban retreat.** Only a handful of people stroll down the main street of Bad Münstereifel on a quiet weekday afternoon. This popular retreat for urban dwellers from nearby cities in the Rhineland is usually crowded with visitors on weekends and holidays. Although tucked fairly deeply into the rural expanses of Germany's Eifel region, the town is very much within reach and a part of today's urban society.

caters to the urban daytripper's desire to eat, shop, and be seen in a pleasing locale outside of the city, is virtually deserted on weekdays but completely overrun by a crush of recreating urban dwellers on weekends and holidays. It is almost as though the town leads two completely separate lives, depending on the time of the week. Although it may seem counterintuitive at first to most visitors, it is no accident that the town's car parks and meters levy a charge only on weekends.

One might also argue that the city—and its way of life—is one of the very foundations of European society, that in a very real sense Europe is defined by its cities. This is because the city embodies so many of the ideas, innovations, and lines of development that we associate with European history and identity. It is, after all, from the legal foundations of medieval towns and cities that we derive such fundamental notions of governance as the right of local independence against princely or state powers. The city has been and continues to be the place where trade, industry, finance, learning, justice, government, high culture, and the arts achieve their greatest expression. Aspects of its built landscape are often purposely fashioned to symbolize human achievement in all of these areas. Towns and cities are also the organizational foci of European space. They each occupy a specific niche

in a hierarchical urban network, whose elaborate web of functional interconnections is the primary means by which the continent's myriad local societies and economies are melded together into some kind of larger framework.

It is difficult, therefore, to speak of where and how Europeans live without entering into a discussion of urbanism, and that is the subject of the two chapters in this section. In this chapter we look to the past to understand how urban places and urban life have evolved; that is, we try to identify the critical transformations in the organization and use of urban space that have brought us to the present condition. Although an almost infinite amount of space could be devoted to the long evolution of European urbanism, our purposes here are to describe the major transformations that have taken place over the centuries leading up to the Great War of 1914–1918. We take a more contemporary perspective in the chapter that follows.

## CLASSICAL FOUNDATIONS

### The Greek City-State

The ancient Greeks, who around the eighth century B.C. began to organize themselves politically and territorially into hundreds of city-states, or *poleis*, first introduced urbanism to

Europe. Most of these city-states, which reached the height of their development by the beginning of the fifth century B.C., were relatively small places. Usually located on small plains tucked between the mountains and the sea, their economies were predominantly agricultural. A few grew to be exceptionally large places. Athens may have had as many as 200,000 or more people, but most were of a far more modest size; many were really no more than very large villages. Whatever their size, the Greek *polis* was a novel departure in city development in that it intimately bound a local tributary area to an urbanized central place and claimed for itself a sovereign political status based not on the power of a deified ruler, but on the democratic participation of its citizens.

In time these places developed an urban form that was widely replicated. Most Greek cities were built on defensible sites and walled. Many were dominated by a fortified height of land, or *acropolis*, beneath which the city developed. Near the center was the *agora*, an open space that served as a combination market, public forum, and casual meeting place for a people accustomed to carrying out their daily business and social activities outdoors. The *agora* was often grandly edged

with *stoae*, long open-fronted buildings framed by colonnades and used for conducting business of various kinds. Stretching beyond these monumental spaces, and in sharp contrast to them, were the cramped and tangled residential quarters of the common citizenry.

In response to mounting population pressure at home, many of these city-states sent out colonists who carried their urban culture and institutions far beyond the Greek homelands. This organized exportation of the Greek city-state to other lands occurred between roughly 734 and 585 B.C. It spawned clusters of colonial daughter settlements along the shores of the Black Sea, as well as along the Mediterranean coasts of southern Italy and southern France, and on the islands of Sicily and Corsica.

At the same time, similar settlements were being established in the western Mediterranean by other peoples. The Phoenicians, a seafaring and commercially oriented people from the Levant, established daughter colonies in North Africa, southern Spain, and on the islands of Sardinia, Sicily, and Malta. The most important of these Phoenician colonies was Carthage, situated on the coast of Africa opposite the Straits of Sicily. Totally devoted

FIGURE 8.2. Acropolis. On the Isle of Rhodes, the ancient acropolis looms over the modern town of Lindos. Occupied since perhaps as early as the ninth century B.C., the acropolis is typical of the fortified heights that served as sanctuaries in many Greek cities.

to commercial endeavor, the city grew wealthy from the exploitation of silver and copper mines in the south of Spain and from the control of commerce in the western Mediterranean basin. The Etruscans, a people of obscure origin who occupied northern and central Italy, also evolved a distinctive urbanized culture, which reached its height about 500 B.C. The loose federation of city-states formed by the Etruscans even included, for a time, the homelands of a group of Italic peoples known as the Romans.

## Roman Urbanism

The Romans eventually came to inherit the urban traditions of the classical world. This inheritance was in large part a function of Rome's location on the western side of the Italian peninsula, roughly midway between the civilized cultures of the Etruscans to the north and the colonial Greek city-states to the south. Although originally nothing more than a collection of Iron Age village settlements scattered across the hilltops flanking the east bank of the Tiber River, Rome emerged, while it was still under the control of the Etruscans, as a city-state of some importance. From the Etruscans, who eventually were forced to withdraw, the Romans acquired advanced engineering and building skills. Religion, art, and an urbane culture were borrowed from the Greeks.

Over the next several centuries Rome became embroiled in a long series of hegemonic wars. Italy and Sicily were subdued first, an accomplishment made easier by the fact that the power of the Etruscans had been destroyed by the invasions of Celtic tribes from the north and that the Greek city-states were too divided among themselves to put up much of a concerted defense. Upon the defeat and destruction of its great commercial and military rival Carthage in 146 B.C., Rome emerged as the master of the entire western Mediterranean basin. After that each new conquest led inexorably to another. Rome went on to exert its authority by the first century A.D. over the eastern Mediterranean basin, as well as much of western and southern Europe.

In the process, Rome was transformed from a city-state to a great empire, a fact that had profound implications for the direction that European urbanism was to take by the latter part of the classical period. Despite its early success, the city-state was simply too small and weak to maintain its independence in a world increasingly dominated by large territorial powers. The decline began in Greece in the fifth century B.C., as the old Hellenic city-states fell under the control, one by one, of a powerful and expansive Macedonian state. The rise of Roman hegemony over much of Europe by the first century A.D. was the culmination of that process.

All this meant that urbanism under the Romans would fulfill a somewhat different political and functional role. Cities and their *territoria* became the building blocks of empire. They functioned as centers of imperial administration and consumption. They were also the conveyors of Roman culture and values, which included urbane and civilized living, to the heterogeneous peoples who made up the Empire. Under the Romans the main purpose of the city was no longer to anchor small and proudly independent societies, but to link diverse and subservient populations administratively to the center of power.

Thus, the Romans were responsible for bringing urbanism in Europe to new heights. The Roman system of towns and cities extended to every corner of the Empire. Provinces were divided for administrative purposes into *civitates*, or city-regions, each centered on an urbanized central place, or *civitas*. The existing cities of conquered regions throughout Mediterranean Europe were incorporated into the Empire's extensive urban system, while in western Europe urbanism was introduced into areas where it had been previously absent. The Romans accomplished this with minimal disruption to the existing spatial organization of conquered regions by simply converting the primitive central places of the native population, such as hill forts and tribal meeting places, into Roman towns and cities. The process by which the Romans established towns and cities throughout the West is generally seen as one of the major achievements of the period. It is be-

**FIGURE 8.3. The Roman past.** The Porta Nigra (Black Gate) is by far the most imposing Roman building of northern Europe. The structure, which dates from the end of the second century, was the imperial gate to the city of Trier. The massive sandstone exterior has been weathered black by the passage of time (hence the name bestowed in medieval times).

cause of this achievement that so many European cities today are able to take such pride in directing visitors to the excavations and artifacts of their Roman past.

At the very top of the Roman urban system was the city of Rome. Although estimates are crude at best, the population of this great city is believed to have been somewhere around a million, which made it by far the largest city in the Empire and the greatest concentration of people known to Europe until this time. The city was the cosmopolitan center of the Empire, filled with peoples of diverse origins. It seemed to produce little but require much. Likened by some scholars to a giant "parasite," the city depended on the provinces to satisfy its insatiable appetite for food, slaves, luxuries, and tribute.

Elsewhere, the cities and towns that formed the skeletal framework of the Empire varied greatly in number, size, and function. The greatest concentrations were found in the more densely populated parts of Mediterranean Europe—in Italy, Greece, France, and the coastal areas of the Iberian Peninsula. In the Balkans, Britain, the German lands, and in the interior of Iberia, where populations were thin, towns were scattered and few, although their densities increased along the Rhine and Danube frontiers of the Empire, where settlements supported the Legions defending the frontier.

Certain common features distinguished Roman cities. Like the Greeks, the Romans put considerable emphasis on the construction of finely built public buildings and monuments. Most cities of any importance possessed a focal or central space—the forum. In addition, there would be a basilica, which served the functions of courthouse and market, temples, public baths, a theater, perhaps an amphitheatre or stadium. Roman cities differed from those of the Greeks, however, in the great size and splendor of their public buildings. As time went on, the Romans also distinguished themselves from the Greeks by the fact that public buildings and spaces were increasingly constructed to glorify and legitimize not just the state but also the Roman emperors themselves. The authority and honor of each new emperor was highly dependent on his ability to make his power seen not only in deeds but also in monuments and public works. This was particularly evident in Rome itself, where successive emperors went to great lengths to outdo their predecessors, forever adding new fora, triumphant arches, and victory columns to the center of the imperial capital—even stooping at times to the practice of stripping the monuments of their predecessors of the building materials, sculptures, and medallions needed to complete their own projects. Finding open space in the center of the city for the construction of new buildings and monuments soon became a major problem.

The Romans, who placed such high value on order and authority, made extensive use of geometric forms in the layout and construction of public spaces and buildings. The Imperial Fora, which came to cover the center of the city, were laid out as rectangular spaces, with precise dimensions (the Roman architect Vitruvius stipulated an ideal length-to-width ratio of 3:2) and clear axes of movement and perspective. The colonnaded public buildings and temples that flanked them were meant to be viewed from particular directions, and were carefully aligned with adjoining spaces and structures for visual effect. The achievement of a very linear sense of space and visual order was extremely important. The effect was meant to be reassuring, to give credence to the notion that the authority and power of the Empire was timeless and unchanging.

The Romans also tried to impose some degree of regularity on the overall layout of urban places. In many parts of Mediterranean Europe, especially in the East, where city foundations long predated Roman rule, there were often difficulties in achieving this. Indeed, no regular plan was ever possible for Rome itself, which evolved early and literally overflowed with unplanned and dangerously crowded development. But in the West, where towns were more likely to have been founded later, or were developed exclusively by the Romans themselves, they were often arranged according to a gridiron plan that featured two intersecting main streets, the *cardo maximus* and the *decumanus maximus*. Public buildings were located near the intersection of these main streets. A similar geometric order was often imposed on the surrounding countryside in the form of carefully surveyed roads and long rectangular fields. The abandonment of many Roman sites during the Dark Ages and their subsequent redevelopment during medieval times and succeeding centuries has meant that the old Roman grid

**FIGURE 8.4. Foro Romano.** Built on a marshy valley between the hills of Rome, the Roman Forum was the heart of public life in the ancient city. Down the center of the immense complex ran the Sacra Via, flanked on either side by temples, basilicas, and monuments to the glory of Rome. The ruins were used in the Middle Ages as a quarry for building material and as a pasture. Archeological excavation began in the late 19th century and has continued ever since.

is not readily apparent in most modern city centers. Its pattern is often only subtly present, at best. But in some cities, such as Córdoba, Nîmes, Cologne, Verona, and Ljubljana, it is still quite recognizable despite the distortions of time.

Roman towns contained a variety of residential building types, ranging from spacious villas to carefully laid-out rows of arcaded buildings that combined living quarters and workshops, to masses of extraordinarily large and often rather shoddily constructed apartment blocks, or *insulae*. Well known are the cramped quarters and appallingly unsanitary conditions of the great numbers of the latter erected in the city of Rome by profiteering contractors and landlords. According to one record from the fourth century A.D., there were as many as 46,602 of these, containing an average of 200 people each. By contrast, the villas of the elite were spacious affairs, facing inward on an entrance hall or *atrium*, elegantly appointed with tile mosaics and marble wall facings, and sometimes even equipped with water closets and central heating. Living conditions in towns far from the center of Roman power were usually less crowded and more livable for the common citizenry, but probably appeared hopelessly "provincial" in the eyes of the elite residents of the capital.

Like the ancient Greeks, the Romans spent much of their time outdoors and away from home. The morning hours for male citizens were filled with business activities, which might mean craft production or the sale or purchase of goods, or possibly stationing oneself near the villa of a wealthy citizen to receive a favor or perform a service or errand. Much of Roman society was built around networks of client–patron relationships, which had to be attended to on a regular basis. Afternoons might be devoted to social activities and entertainments. One could visit the baths, which were the social centers of the city, or take pleasure in the spectator thrills and excitements of the circus or amphitheater. Evenings meant a return home to host guests for dinner, attendance at a dinner to which an

invitation had been secured during the day, or simply eating out at a bar or inn on the street. Women spent more time at home, but might also go out on their own, and in Roman society enjoyed the right to join their husband and his associates at the table. This was in sharp contrast to Greek society, where women led far more restricted lives.

The games and entertainments, and the massive facilities in which they took place, were part of the effort to maintain public order and to provide public works. Roman urban society was underlain with a great mass of people belonging to the plebeian class, for whom there was little work to fill their days. To maintain order, the authorities fell into the practice of providing free bread (the dole) and a constantly expanding number of entertainments for the masses. By the end of the third century A.D., as many as 200 days of the year were devoted to staging games and entertainments at public expense. The Roman Colosseum was built by the Emperor Vespasian and dedicated by his son Titus in 80 A.D. Ori-

**FIGURE 8.5. The Games.** The Colosseum in Rome (Flavian Amphitheatre) stood nearly 50 meters tall. The outside of the building consisted of three arcaded façades and an "attic" story, from which the *velarium*—a great canopy that shaded the spectators—was hung. A special unit of the Roman navy, whose job it was to unfurl and secure the canvas, was permanently stationed here.

ginally known as the Flavian Amphitheater (Flavius was the family name of Vespasian and Titus), the massive concrete and stone structure hosted the city's gladiatorial contests as well as other bloodthirsty spectacles and held an estimated 55,000 spectators. The Circus Maximus, a heavily monumentalized elongated racetrack on which teams of charioteers competed in wild and thrilling races, could handle crowds as large as 385,000. Similar structures were built in other Roman cities, although on a much smaller scale. The amphitheaters at Nîmes, Arles, and Verona, for example, all of which have survived, seated roughly 20,000 spectators each.

The Romans invested heavily in massive engineering works intended to supply the city with water and discharge its waste. The city of Rome consumed a prodigious amount of water, which was brought to the city from tens of kilometers away via large aqueducts, and then directed through open channels and lead pipes to street fountains, the public baths, and private houses, with any surplus used for cleaning streets. A system of underground sewers carried wastewater away. Sections of some of the great aqueducts that supplied Rome and other Roman cities have survived to the present as reminders of the immense wealth and engineering expertise expended by the Romans to provide the infrastructure necessary to support large urban places. Indeed, the Romans did much to introduce a tradition of urban public works to Europe that would be picked up and carried on in later eras.

Relatively little, on the other hand, was invested during the height of the Empire on urban fortifications. Few towns were walled until relatively late in the Roman period. This was largely due to the fact that the Empire was long able to ensure relative peace and safety—the so-called *Pax Romana*—behind its territorial frontiers. Thus, the main focus of defensive construction took place on the military frontiers, where elaborate systems of forts, ditches, and walls were developed. It was not until the latter part of the third century A.D. that Rome, under the threat of barbarian invasions, undertook the construction of the city's massive 19-kilometer-long Aurelian Wall, which survives to the present day. In response to similar pressures, Roman towns in the third century erected walls and transformed themselves into fortified administrative centers, a process that began to distinguish them from their surrounding *territorium* and helped to bring about a separation of city and countryside that would characterize the Middle Ages.

**FIGURE 8.6. Public works.** Built in the first century A.D., the aqueduct at Segovia brought water from the River Frio to the Roman settlement and military camp at Segovia. Nearly 30 meters tall at its highest point, the double-tiered arched construction carried water until late in the 19th century.

## MEDIEVAL TOWNS AND CITIES

### Decline during the Dark Ages

A sharp break exists between the classical urbanism of the Romans and Greeks and the new urbanism that overtook Europe during medieval times. A major reason is the precipitous decline of Roman cities and towns that occurred during the so-called Dark Ages, which lasted from roughly the fourth to the ninth century A.D. The decline was the result of the dire circumstances and calamities of the times, not the least of which was the disintegration of the western Empire before the advance of invading Germanic tribes. These invaders, who came not so much to destroy the Empire as to share in its wealth and power, brought with them a much lower material culture, which included little in the way of experience with urban living. This, coupled with a general decline in climatic conditions, diminished agricultural productivity and opportunities for trade, and substantial losses in population due to famine and disease, eventually led to the wholesale deterioration of urban living as the Romans had known it.

Cities in the Mediterranean South suffered the least. Most continued to be occupied and to carry on urban functions, even though their populations may have declined. Elsewhere in Europe the effects of invasion and other depredations were often devastating. Some towns and cities simply ceased to exist altogether. Others became mere shadows of their former selves, with small populations sheltered behind defensive walls built hastily during the latter part of the Roman period to protect residents from the increased onslaughts of marauders. These walls, which as time went on were built and rebuilt to protect ever smaller areas, often encompassed in the end only a fraction of the area previously occupied by the Roman city. The walled area of Nîmes, for example, contracted during this period from 550 acres to just 20 acres.

As cities declined, life all over Europe was reduced to a much more rudimentary level in which people lived more or less self-sufficiently on the land, with few social, economic, and political relationships that extended beyond locality, kin, and tribe. During the rebirth of urbanism that followed the Dark Ages, the city arose not so much from, but alongside, what had become a predominantly rural society, built around an inelastic and self-sufficing system of land tenure and feudal obligation. In this sense, the medieval city was a very different place than the Roman *civitas* or the Greek *polis* before it, both of which were intended to bind together the city and its rural environs.

### The Rise of Medieval Towns and Cities

A renewal and spread of urbanism began to take hold in Europe during the ninth century and continued for about 400 years. It came to a rather abrupt end around the middle of the 14th century, as the population declined and conditions deteriorated with the spread of plague. During this prolonged period of growth, existing cities expanded greatly in size and function. Large numbers of new towns were also founded, principally in those parts of Europe that lay beyond the old frontiers of the Roman Empire. In all, the number of places in Europe that might be thought of as urban by today's standards—that is, those with roughly 2,000 or more inhabitants—may have reached as many as 900 by the end of the 13th century. If we take into account the fact that most places of a few hundred or more were probably urbanized places by the standards of the Middle Ages, the number of urban places may have actually numbered well into the thousands.

Medieval towns were founded and grew for a variety of reasons. Defense was a key factor from the beginning, and became even more so during the Viking raids and invasions of the 9th and 10th centuries. In these times of danger, the safest place that could be found in many parts of Europe was behind the crumbling walls of an old Roman settlement or beneath a fortified strong point established by a local prince or bishop. This place of refuge became a focal point around which an embryonic urban settlement might develop. Improvements in existing town defenses or the extension of the walls of a castle or monastery to include the small built-up area that began to develop in its shadow were common and necessary first steps toward the physical development of a town.

A second factor was the rise of a local market. This occurred largely because of a series of economic developments. As the Dark Ages waned, Europe experienced a general extension of arable land and an improvement in husbandry, which led to food surpluses and renewed population growth. Feudal lords were quick to recognize the potential profits to be gained by sponsoring a central place somewhere on their holdings where agricultural produce and locally produced crafts and wares could be bought and sold. The benefits to the feudal lords came in the form of tolls and taxes that could be levied on the sales activities. This, in turn, led to the possibility that the commercial activities of the towns would expand to attract merchants engaged in long-distance trade. Thus sprang up urbanized communities of merchants and craftsmen, whose right to carry on their business freely and whose obligations to pay for the privilege were carefully stipulated in charters granted by kings and local lords. Over time, the legal guarantees of the town charter gave the "commune" a degree of autonomy that clearly differentiated it from that of the predominantly feudal and manorial countryside.

A third factor was the close connection that existed between the Christian Church, the one universal institution in medieval life, and urban places. As in Roman times, the town remained the principal seat of ecclesiastical authority and administration, and therefore the site of numerous Christian institutions and edifices—cathedrals, parish churches, monasteries, almshouses, and hospitals—both within and just outside its walls. The power of the Roman Catholic Church, which commanded vast wealth in medieval times, rested in the city. Indeed, the protection afforded to towns by bishops often rivaled that of counts and princes. And, in this sense, the business of the city was as much the glorification of God as it was the production of goods and trade. The spires of its cathedrals and other churches, visible from far beyond its walls, were symbolic expressions of its individual identity, recognized by residents and nonresidents alike.

## Size

Most medieval towns and cities grew largely by immigration, drawing their population from elements in the surrounding countryside somehow able to leave the land. A few places became quite large. The vast majority, however, remained relatively small. By the beginning of the 14th century the very largest were those whose populations topped 50,000 and in a few cases exceeded 100,000. These were found mostly in Mediterranean Europe, where rural population densities were high and the urban legacy from the past was strongest. Included among these Mediterranean mega-cities were Córdoba, Granada, Seville, Milan, Venice, Genoa, Florence, Naples, Palermo, and Constantinople. North of the Alps there were only three extraordinarily large places: Paris, Ghent, and Cologne. Cities with populations between 25,000 and 50,000 would also have been considered large for the times. They were fairly numerous—there were more than 50 of them—but also heavily concentrated in Mediterranean Europe and in France. Much more evenly distributed, however, were the many modest-sized cities of 10,000 to 25,000 inhabitants. The same was true of the smaller cities of a few thousand souls and the great mass of small places whose population numbered in the hundreds.

## Types of Places and Networks

It is useful to think of medieval Europe as having three broad zones of urban development. The first comprised those parts of Mediterranean Europe where urban life had been least affected by the decline of Roman power. Cities throughout this zone were often smaller than they had been in Roman times, but few had disappeared altogether and there had been relatively little need to found completely new towns. Continuity with the Roman past was greatest here, and overall levels of urbanization remained relatively high. This was especially true in the south of Spain, where under Moorish rule large urban places like Granada, Córdoba, and Seville grew and prospered. These cities not only retained their Christian populations but also grew through the addition of densely settled Arab quarters. Meanwhile, at the other end of the Mediterranean, the spectacular city of Constantinople continued to hold its place as one of Europe's greatest wonders. For much of the medieval period, Constantinople could lay claim to being the richest and most sophisticated city in the world—heir to the Roman tradition, major market for luxury goods and raw materials, site of hundreds of fabled Christian churches and chapels, and gilded seat of power for the Emperor of Byzantium.

A second zone consisted of the remainder of what had once been Roman Europe, the former provinces and frontier zones of northwestern Europe. It was here that cities suffered the worst destruction and depopulation during the Dark Ages. The urban renewal of the Middle Ages took place selectively within this zone, with some places prospering more than others, depending on their location relative to the developing routeways of commerce and whether they were fortunate enough to acquire important ecclesiastical or administrative functions. This zone also experienced the occasional founding of entirely new towns. But most important to the development of a distinctive urban network in this zone was the medieval expansion of long-distance commerce between northern and southern Europe. This particularly enhanced the fortunes of towns and cities situated along a broad commercial axis that stretched from northern Italy to the Low Countries.

Located at either end of this axis, and dominating the conduct of the lucrative north–south trade, were two highly urbanized regions. In the north was a network of towns in northeastern France and Flanders, which prospered from the manufacture and sale of woolen cloths. The most powerful of these was the city of Bruges, which benefited not only from the productivity of its own cloth manufacturers but also from its roles as the chief import center for English wool and the main distribution point for cloth made in other major Flemish cloth-making towns such as Ghent, Ypres, and Douai. Home to the offices of merchants from all over Europe, and especially from Italy, Bruges was the most important medieval trading center of northern Europe, although its importance began to wane in the 14th century as other regions began to establish their own cloth industries.

Dominating the other end of the axis were a number of north Italian trading cities, which competed with one another for control of the trade in highly valued spices, oriental silks, perfumes, ivory, and other luxuries that could be obtained from Byzantium, the Islamic Near East, and even India and China. They did so by securing commercial privileges in Constantinople and other eastern Mediterranean and Black Sea ports. Indeed, many of these eastern ports had special quarters set aside for the numerous Italian merchants and traders who settled there. At one point in time, Constantinople is said to have had as many as 60,000 Italians living within the city. Most important among the competing towns were Venice, Genoa, and Pisa, although the power of Pisa declined rapidly near the end of the 13th century due to a series of defeats by its rival, Genoa. Venice and Genoa continued to vie with each other for the eastern trade until the late 14th century, when Venice was eventually able to establish its supremacy.

The great family-based trading companies from the various Italian towns found themselves in excellent geographic position to profit as middlemen from the movement of goods between east and west as well as north and south. The Italians succeeded in monopolizing, for example, the trade in alum, a powdered substance obtained in Asia Minor that was highly prized in the Flemish textile towns in the north for its ability to fix dyes in fabrics. The Italian merchant houses also prospered because of the sophistication and effectiveness of their methods. They pioneered the most advanced business methods of the time, maintaining permanent offices in all of the

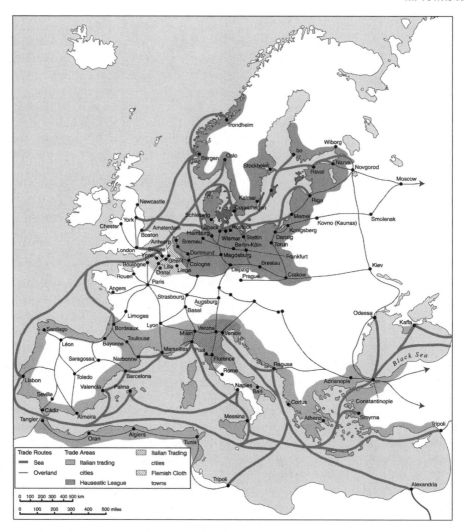

FIGURE 8.7. Trading cities and trade routes at the end of the Middle Ages.

towns in which they did business and even developing an elaborate system of drawing up bills of exchange designed to solve the financial problems of conducting long-distance trade in a world of myriad and difficult-to-convert currencies.

The remainder of Europe fell into a third zone, a vast area in which no earlier tradition of urban life had ever been established. Across this region stretched a broad scattering of mostly modest to small-sized places. The most highly urbanized area occurred along the axis of the *Hellweg*, a broad avenue of relatively easy transportation stretching across

the great *loess* plains of central Germany from Dortmund to Goslar. Elsewhere the more important places were more widely spaced and built around royal or ecclesiastical nuclei, or located to take advantage of the trade opportunities offered by sites that placed them astride major gaps or corridor routeways, at major river crossings, and at selected points along the coasts of the Baltic and North Seas. Great numbers of smaller places were more evenly scattered. These grew up for the most part from pre-existing agricultural villages, or they were deliberately planned in conjunction with the *Drang nach Osten*, the great

**FIGURE 8.8. Venice.** As early as the 10th century, Venice had established trading routes through concessions granted by Byzantium that placed the city in an advantageous position to dominate the trade between Europe and the Levant. Within two centuries the city had achieved fabulous wealth and prominence, which were reflected in the fabric of the city. Seen here is one of two great symbols of the city's might, the Basilica of St. Mark (the other is the Ducal Palace). Fronted by a magnificent piazza completed in the 15th century, the stunning façade of the 11th-century basilica leads to the shrine of St. Mark, whose body was stolen from Alexandria in 828 and brought here.

eastward agricultural colonization of Slav lands relentlessly pursued by the Germans throughout the course of the 13th and 14th centuries. Beyond the zone of German settlement or colonization—in the interior reaches of Scandinavia, across the great interior plains of eastern Europe, within the arc of the Car-

pathians, and south of the Danube into the Balkans—the density of urbanized places dropped off sharply.

Beginning in the late 12th century, the German merchants of a number of towns across northern Germany began to band together for the purpose of organizing and controlling trade throughout the Baltic and North Sea regions. Based on the Law of Lübeck, the merchant associations of these towns agreed on common policies to protect shipments and sought to create favored privileges and monopolies over the northern European trade in commodities such as grain, timber, herring, furs, honey, copper, and iron, all of which could be obtained in the east from Russia, Poland, and the Baltic region, and exchanged for cloth, spices, salt, wine, and other goods from the west. This confederation of north German trading cities became known as the Hanseatic League. At the height of its power during the 14th century, the Hansa consisted of approximately 100 towns. German merchant interests of the Hansa helped develop trading towns throughout Scandinavia and the Baltic, such as Bergen, Visby, Stockholm, Danzig (Gdansk), Riga, and Reval (Tallinn). The League met regularly to coordinate policy and settle disputes. It also maintained foreign trading offices, or *konotore*, in such places as Bruges, London, and Novgorod.

**FIGURE 8.9. Hansa.** One of the most important of the German Hansa towns that dominated the trade of the Baltic was Lübeck. Seen here is the city's Holtentor (Holstein Gate), whose two towers, built in 1477 and joined by a gabled façade, became the city's emblem. In the background are the restored towers of the 13th-century Marienkirche, the city's largest and most important church, which was damaged badly during the 1942 bombing of the city.

## Medieval Townscapes

Medieval towns took a variety of forms. Many were built on Roman foundations, as we have seen, and were constrained in their development by that fact. Others developed in a chaotically organic fashion around defensive strong points or ecclesiastical sites, or from large agricultural villages. Still others, often distinguished by their carefully planned rectilinear layout, were "planted" in open country for colonial or strategic purposes. Perhaps the classic example of the latter is the walled town of Aigues-Mortes in the south of France, which was laid out in the 13th century by Louis IX as a fortified staging point for the Seventh and Eighth Crusades. The layout of medieval towns could also be quite complex, as in cases where towns grew from multiple nuclei, or in cases where planned towns were grafted onto existing settlements. The classic example here is Hildesheim, which by the early 14th century had developed from the coalescence of a number of discrete settlements focused respectively on castle, cathedral, monastery, and a 13th-century planned town.

The confining element for all towns was the defensive wall. In these unsettled times, no town did without one. If the town grew too large for its walls, they were often torn down and rebuilt to envelope a suburb or to enclose more open space. Some towns went to the trouble of moving their walls several times. Cologne, for example, rebuilt its walls four times. The town wall, with its towers and gates, provided protection from attack, but it also separated the town politically, economically, and socially from the surrounding countryside, which lived under an entirely different set of rules. The wall, then, had psychological importance as a symbol of the town's individual identity and independence, much as did a citadel or cathedral tower. Its gates were the key places where the worlds of townspeople and outsiders of all kinds met and where interactions between them were controlled by customs and tolls. Certain noxious activities, such as tanning industries and livestock markets, were relegated to places

**FIGURE 8.10. Medieval curtain wall.** The city of Ávila in Spain is surrounded by one of the best-preserved medieval curtain walls in all of Europe. Spanning for a total distance of 2 kilometers and punctuated by 88 cylindrical towers, the walls were built by Alfonso VI after he conquered the town from the Moors in 1090. Alfonso forced his Moorish prisoners to labor on the construction of the walls until the project was completed, a task that took them 9 long years.

beyond the walls, and unwanted elements of the population such as lepers were often forced to live there. Abbeys and hospitals, many of which were not founded until the citizens of towns had developed the necessary wealth to endow them, also sometimes occupied space outside the city walls.

The focal point of the town was the central marketplace (other squares might also exist for lesser or more specialized markets). This was the site of the weekly market, as well as the annual or semiannual fair that was organized around the exchange of goods brought from or destined for more distant places. Most were originally open-air markets, but many were eventually embellished with a market hall where goods could be stored before sale and in which business could be conducted in inclement weather. In towns where a particular craft or industry prevailed, a large hall devoted to that product or activity sometimes dominated the marketplace. The grandest of the Flemish cloth halls, built in Ypres between 1200 and 1304 to hold the annual cloth fair, was an astounding 433 feet long. The structure survived until World War I, when it was destroyed in an artillery bombardment. Merchant's buildings and the headquarters of individual guilds might also typically front on the market square. The

FIGURE 8.11. **Market square.** One of Europe's finest market squares is Brussels's Grand Place. In the 13th century this was the commercial center of the medieval town. Covered markets for the sale of goods of all kinds covered the square, while the halls of the influential guilds lined the perimeter, along with the city's ornate Gothic town hall. This view features one side of the square, with its ornately decorated baroque guild halls, erected by the guilds after the original medieval structures were destroyed during a French bombardment of the city in 1695.

guilds were exclusive associations of merchants or craftsmen that attempted to control the conditions of trade and production for the benefit of their members through various regulations and restrictions. They played a powerful role in the trade and administration of the town, usually locating their headquarters as close to the marketplace as possible.

Although most towns were initially dominated by a feudal ruler, who might maintain a castle or palace within the walls, the usual pattern was for them gradually to acquire sufficient independence so that the administration of the town shifted to some form of city government, usually run by magistrates overseen by a council. Considerable wealth was typically lavished on the construction of a building worthy of housing the town's administrative and legal organs. The town hall normally fronted on the market square and sometimes provided space on the ground floor for market activities. In many Italian towns, where internal feuding often made public administration contentious, administrative and judicial functions were often separated and housed in different buildings. Italian town halls were frequently built at least partially with defensive needs in mind, and typically sported tall watchtowers. They also differed from their northern counterparts in that the authorities both lived and worked within their

walls. They were known accordingly as Palazzi Pubblici rather than as town halls.

As the most important institution in the medieval world, the Church also took an active hand in overseeing many of the essential facets of town life. The town's great church—or cathedral if the town was the seat of a bishop—was built to reflect the importance and power of the town's religious establishment. It was invariably one of the largest and most impressive structures, its size and deco-

FIGURE 8.12. **Rathaus.** Lübeck's mid-13th-century town hall is a solid example of the characteristic medieval brickwork of northern Germany. The high wing on the right dates from around 1440. The high façade features spire-tipped turrets and huge holes to lessen wind resistance. Coats of arms are embedded in the brickwork.

**FIGURE 8.13. Palazzo Pubblico.** During the 12th and 13th centuries, Sienna was one of the major cities of Europe. Almost the size of Paris, it controlled most of southern Tuscany and its rich wool industry, dominated the trade routes between France and Rome, and maintained Italy's richest Medici banks. The prosperity came to an abrupt halt with the Black Death, which reached the city in 1348 and in just five short months reduced the population from 100,000 to 30,000. The city's main square, the Campo, was laid out and paved with elaborate brickwork on the city's old marketplace in 1347 (the year before the plague). At the foot of the down-sloping square stands the Palazzo Pubblico, with its 102-meter bell tower, the Torre del Mangia.

ration an expression of the wealth and prosperity of the town. The church square, set before the portals of its towering west front, served both as an important meeting place and as a place of ritual and ceremony. It was the starting and ending point for the religious processions that periodically wound through most towns, and the place for staging various religious celebrations and plays.

In fact, the presence of the Church throughout the city was extensive and multifaceted. Towns were organized ecclesiastically into subordinate parishes, each of which was focused on its own church, which was often founded or endowed by a local benefactor who lived and worked nearby. A host of other religious houses were also scattered throughout the city, including hospitals and almshouses, university chapters, friaries, and ab-

beys, whose authority and revenues came from disparate sources. The Church, which tended over time to accumulate the rights to a considerable amount of property through the pious bequests of residents of means who wished to ensure their place in the afterlife, was typically the town's largest property owner. It also frequently managed to acquire a great many special privileges, such as the right to hold a market or fair, or even the right to regulate and profit from the practice of prostitution. Alongside the burghers, the men of the Church wielded considerable authority and claimed an important place in the power structures of the town.

But the medieval town was also a very decentralized place. It was subdivided into quarters and districts, each with its own individuality and measure of autonomy. This was a reflection of the highly spatialized organization of economic activity, in which certain crafts and vocations, such as cloth making, tanning, goldsmithing or woodworking, as well as distinctive groups, such as the city's Jewry or its foreign merchants, were concentrated in their own quarters. Jurisdictions over specific places and activities within the town were typically complex, falling quite variably under the authority of king, bishop, count, guild, city council, or whoever else might have secured the necessary rights and privileges.

This economic and social partitioning of the medieval town was further underlined by the fact that its streets and alleys were, for the most part, never intended as thoroughfares. Narrow and winding, and seldom paved, they were poorly adapted for wheeled traffic. They were used primarily as places of intense commerce and production rather than as facilitators of movement between different parts of the city. There was, accordingly, great commercial importance in possessing frontage on the street. In cities north of the Alps, this was reflected in the placement, building style, and layout of individual houses. Houses were built up tightly against one another, and typically four to six stories high. Their tall and narrow gabled fronts faced the street, while they backed on the green space of checkered gardens that filled the interior of blocks. The lower floor opened to the street and served as a shop or workplace. The middle stories were reserved for the master and his immediate family, while an extended household of apprentices, journeymen, and other family members, or storage space, occupied the upper stories. Houses in many northern European cities were constructed of timber, with wattle and plaster between the studding, which made them highly susceptible to fire, the bane—along with the plague—of most medieval towns.

Housing in Mediterranean cities displayed a greater continuity with the Roman past, featuring squarish house lots and buildings that were more squat and prone to be constructed of stone or masonry due to the shortage of wood for building purposes in that part of Europe. Houses were less open to the street, focusing instead on an inner courtyard. Rooftops were flat or slightly pitched, in contrast to the steep gables necessary in the north to cast off rain and accumulations of snow. Also common to the Mediterranean town, especially in Italy, was the presence of tower constructions that soared high above the rooftops of the rambling and multiunit housing compounds of the town's most important, and often feuding, families. The constant feuding was emblematic of the fact that the nobility were more likely to settle in Italian towns, where they took readily to commerce and finance, and competed incessantly with one another for control of town affairs. The skylines of some Italian cities literally bristled with these family towers (Florence is said to have had as many as 400), rising to heights of up to 100 meters and contending with churches and civic buildings for pride of place. In some cases, formal agreements had to be drawn up to limit the escalating heights of private towers.

While densities along streets may have been very high, it is also important to note that medieval towns usually contained plenty of open space and on the whole were not exceptionally crowded. Enclosing walls were moved outward with some frequency, and it often took decades for the built-up area to fill

**FIGURE 8.14. Private towers.** The cathedral square of medieval San Gimignano is paved with stones set in a herringbone pattern and flanked by medieval houses and towers. Across the square on the right is the 13th-century Palazzo del Podesta, with its tower. Nearby, at the mouth of one of the town's important thoroughfares, the Via San Matteo, may be seen three towers belonging to two of the town's most important families—the Chigi Tower and the twin Salvucci towers.

the walled space. Indeed, some towns were so overly optimistic in laying out their defensive perimeter that they never filled the enclosed area. Open space meant that agriculture could be a part of the town's economy. Garden plots and animals were commonly found within the walls, and the citizens of most towns also controlled nearby fields outside the walls. Indeed, an often overlooked feature of the medieval townscape is the large number of barns and granaries built to store food reserves for times of trouble.

As in Roman days, the provision of water was a matter of major concern. Water came from springs and streams, often located some distance away. The flow from these sources had to be canalized, brought through fortifications and into the town, and then distributed to public wells or to specialized industrial users such as tanners, dyers, and brewers. Wells and channels were always subject to contamination from the seepage of urban refuse, which accumulated in streets and back lots due to poor or sporadic efforts to collect and remove it. Moreover, whenever growth reached the point where the town began to bump up against the limits of the walls, interior space began to disappear, resulting in congestion and increased exposure to infection and disease. These problems contributed to the period of urban stagnation that we associate with the 14th and 15th centuries. The concentration of people in cities made them especially vulnerable to disease, not least to the rapid and devastating spread of plague during both the period of the Black Death and its subsequent reoccurrences.

## THE EARLY MODERN CITY

Unlike the Middle Ages, the period from the mid-15th to the close of the 18th century is not known for the founding of great numbers of new towns. Nor did it see a general rise in the overall level of urbanization. The proportion of the European population that lived in urban places at the end of the period is thought to have been somewhere between 15–20%, roughly the same as at the beginning. Growth did occur, but it was highly selective. Only certain types of cities were affected. The majority remained much as they were at the end of medieval times, many of them still enclosed within their 14th-century walls. It was, nonetheless, an important age for the development of European urbanism. What made this period of "early modern" urban development important were the significant changes that occurred in the role that some cities played in European society and the revolutionary ways in which many thinkers of the time dreamed of reshaping the layout and organization of cities.

### Urban Growth

The cities that experienced real growth at this time were of three types: capitals, port cities, and a small number of new places established to perform specialized functions. Underlying the rapid growth of capital cities was the rise of the centralized dynastic state, which by the 16th century was gradually brushing the old

feudal order aside. This was the Age of Absolutism, and along with it came a growing centralization of government and its attendant bureaucracy in the great capital cities. The aristocracy, who dared not be too far from access to central power, also became increasingly concentrated there, along with all their retinues and consumptive tastes.

Thus capital cities, especially in the West where the centralization of administrative functions was most advanced, experienced phenomenal growth and rose to commanding positions in the urban hierarchy. The city of Paris, for example, doubled in size between the end of the 15th century and the start of the 19th, to reach a population of just over 550,000 inhabitants. Over the same period London grew from just 50,000 inhabitants to nearly 950,000, making it the largest city in Europe. Other great capital cities that reached a population of 150,000 or more during the period included Constantinople, Naples, Moscow, Vienna, Amsterdam, Dublin, Lisbon, Berlin, Madrid, and Rome. As a matter of fact, by the close of the 18th century every European city that had achieved a population of 150,000 or more was a capital.

The second type of city to experience rapid growth at this time was the port city. This was, in part, a reflection of the fundamental shift in European trade patterns that followed the discovery and colonial exploitation of overseas lands. While a good share of Europe's trade had always been carried by sea, and many Mediterranean, North Sea, and Baltic ports had been important places in medieval times, the focus now shifted to the Atlantic trade. This shift favored those port cities that were in a position to take part in the great oceanic trade with Asia and the New World. Overseas colonial trade contributed to the exceptional growth of cities like London and Amsterdam, which were both port cities and capitals, but it also produced a whole new class of important coastal cities on the western margins of Europe.

Into a third category of "high-growth" urban places fall two types of planned towns. These places were newly founded during this period for reasons of military defense or for the aristocratic pursuit of pleasure and status. The first of these types includes garrison towns and naval bases, which in the 16th and 17th centuries were planted in strategic locations by government authority for the purpose of securing national frontiers or projecting military might. Classic examples of garrison towns are Palm Nova in northern Italy, Naarden in the Netherlands, and Neuf Breisach on the Rhine frontier between Germany and France. Towns like Rochefort and Brest are examples of towns built as naval bases. These towns were carefully planned according to the leading ideas of the time to include wide streets and avenues laid out geometrically. Elaborate and deep girdles of defenses, consisting of star-shaped bastions, redoubts, and glacis, also encircled them. Built strictly for strategic defense, these towns were never intended to expand beyond their planned size, and rarely did so.

A second type of planned town was built to accommodate the tastes and special needs of the upper classes. One version was the "residence city," an elegantly planned urban setting for princely palaces, which often featured an elaborate system of radial streets focused on the royal residence. Examples of such places include the towns of Richelieu and

**FIGURE 8.15. Garrison town.** Strategically located on the Spanish–Portuguese border astride the main highway from Lisbon to Madrid, the town of Elvas has an event-filled military history going all the way back to the Romans. In the 17th century, the Portuguese turned the town into a key garrison city, surrounding it with a massive system of fortifications. Based on the principles of the French military architect Vauban, the defenses were laid out to protect the defenders from every conceivable angle of attack.

Versailles in France, The Hague in the Netherlands, or Mannheim, Karlsruhe, and Potsdam in Germany. Such places could be founded in entirely new locations, or they could be grafted onto existing cities. Although built nearly everywhere in Europe, many of the best examples of residence cities were found among the many small principalities of Germany and in other regions that were as yet not a part of the system of larger states.

## Revolutions in Layout and Design

All urban development during this period was heavily influenced by new concepts of urban layout and design. During the 15th and 16th centuries Renaissance thinkers began to develop concepts of urban planning based on the rational principles of geometric order. Their plans placed great emphasis on single-focus radial layouts, on the provision of vistas, and on a highly proportional and formalistic repetition of forms. Renaissance builders were also influenced, as we have seen in our earlier discussion of church architecture, by the rediscovery of the monumental structures of classical antiquity, especially those of Rome, and took pains to reintroduce classically inspired domes, arches, and decorative forms into their structures. Also important to these developments were the biases of the military engineer, who wished to open the city to the rapid movement of troops. By the middle of the 17th century, new organizational principles gave a different twist to Renaissance urban design. These Baroque-era conceptions of urban space, which we may collectively refer to as the "Grand Manner," were an attempt to shape the entire city so as to reflect its position in the hierarchical social and political order of the time. In short, the Grand Manner ideal called for "gilded" urban landscapes that simultaneously embraced ostentatious display and demonstrated the stability and legitimacy of princely power and authority.

While it was physically impossible to completely transform European cities to reflect these ideals, an attempt was made to do so whenever possible. This was easily accomplished in the case of the new garrison towns and residence cities, where now pre-existing urban fabric could get in the way. Radical new layouts were also enthusiastically pursued in existing cities when great fires or other natural disasters presented the planners with unique opportunities to build on a clean slate. The grand rebuilding of central Lisbon on a grid plan after the disastrous earthquake that struck the city in 1755 is a prime example. On the other hand, circumstances could just as easily work against the realization of the new plans—witness the frustration of the elaborate plans drawn up for the rebuilding of London after the great fire of 1666. The jealously guarded property rights and the tenaciously conservative building habits of the London populace simply proved too difficult to overcome, and only a small portion of the postfire plans were ever implemented.

Where catastrophic disaster or a need for an entirely new town were lacking, planners did succeed in implementing their designs on a more modest scale in select parts of the city. One of the most common efforts was to develop a grand avenue or boulevard, which was often boldly pushed through sections of the city with little regard to what was there before. The purpose was usually to give the city a grand ceremonial passageway, or to provide an axis for a new quarter of prestigious residential development. One of the earliest examples of the new avenues is the Strada Nuova in Genoa, which is famous for the splendor of its Renaissance residences. The best-known is Paris's Champs Élysées, which was built during the reigns of Louis XIV and Louis XV to provide a processional route extending westward from the palace and gardens of the Louvre. Just about every major European capital had one.

Associated with the development of avenues was the opening of spacious squares or circles, from which the avenues might radiate. Examples are the Place Vendôme in Paris, Piazza del Popolo in Rome, or St. James' Square in London. Perhaps the grandest example is the Place de la Concorde in Paris, which served as the focal point connecting the gardens of the Louvre, the street that led to the Church of the Madeline, and the grand axis of the Champs Élysées. Although few in number and affecting only small portions of the city, the new avenues and squares were a symbolic modification of the fabric of the city. They were purposely laid out as demonstrations of Renaissance order and regularity in the midst of medieval confusion, and were later embellished as Baroque tributes to high fashion, splendor, and magnificence. The buildings that faced them were harmonized with the street and with one another to reflect uniform principles of proportion and alignment. Their construction and design emphasized the horizontal through the repetitive placement of cornices, lintels, windows, and doors. The striking horizontality of their collective façades and unbroken rooflines, which carried the eye to the distant vanishing point, gave a grand sense of movement to the whole ensemble. All movement and all perspectives seemed ultimately to lead to symbols of power: the grand monuments, palaces, and courts of the regime. Filled with wheeled carriages, whisking the upper classes back and forth on their daily business, these great ave-

**FIGURE 8.16. Disaster leads to order.** On the morning of All Saints Day, 1755, the city of Lisbon was struck by a terrible earthquake. The entire center of the city was destroyed by the combined effects of the shock and a tidal wave, and an estimated 30,000 people lost their lives. In a monumental undertaking, the city center was rebuilt according to a grand design employing a grid of 48 streets leading inland from a grand Commercial Square on the waterfront. The streets were fronted with uniformly designed buildings of four stories, topped by an attic level with tiers of dormers.

**FIGURE 8.17. Renaissance arcades and gables.** Long harmonious lines of Renaissance mansions lend grace to Arras's historic Grand Place, which is completely surrounded by these stylishly arcaded and gabled buildings. This northern French industrial town suffered greatly during World War I, but has managed to reconstruct and restore much of the historic elegance of the city center.

nues contrasted sharply in function, as well as appearance, with the localized activity and plodding pace of the medieval street.

## Class Differences

Baroque planning played unabashedly to the needs and values of the upper classes. Along with the grand avenues, the planners introduced spacious parks and gardens, fountains and monuments, magnificent theatres, and prestigious new residential quarters. All were reflections of the elite's fondness for ostentatious display and the leisurely pursuit of pleasure. The era marked the beginning of a growing segregation of the classes. Many aspects of medieval popular culture—such as the town-wide celebrations of patron saints or the ceremonial traditions of the craft guilds—which had long served as unifying bonds between the layers of society, now became less acceptable to the upper classes, who turned to indoor balls and specialized leisure pursuits, and who even tried to suppress the popular celebrations that they now viewed as rowdy, vulgar, and superstitious.

Urban society was becoming more formally stratified, and this was reflected in residential patterns. Whereas in the medieval city the living spaces of rich and poor were often thoroughly intermixed, a function of the common practice of living and working as master and apprentice in the same structure, the baroque city was a place where work and living quarters were becoming more physically separated, especially for those on the extreme opposite ends of the social order. The elegance of the quarters of the upper classes contrasted sharply with the squalid housing of the lowest classes, who were attracted to the city in immense numbers and crowded into cramped quarters. A particularly striking example of this growing physical separation was the appearance of the "residential square," an open space surrounded solely by residential buildings occupied by people of high social class or rank. Over time these developments took on a variety of forms, including ellipses, crescents, and circles. Perhaps best known for its fine residential squares is London's West End, but they were built in many cities all across the continent.

Cities were also becoming more crowded, with dire consequences for the poor. Like the new garrison towns, many older European towns and cities were now ringed by the elaborate geometrical defense works of the age. They were no longer able to expand outward to accommodate new demands for space, as they had in the past, by simply moving the walls. The new defenses were too large and expensive to tear down and rebuild. Moreover, they were developed in great depth and required large open "fields of fire" beyond

FIGURE 8.18. Residential square. Completed in 1612, Place des Vosges was one of Paris's first elegant residential squares. The square's 36 houses were designed to exhibit a symmetrical appearance. The façade features a continuous arcade, topped by two stories with alternate brick and stone facings and steeply pitched and dormered slate roofs. Two larger structures face each other across the square—the King's Pavilion and the Queen's Pavilion.

them. This meant that suburban development beyond the defenses was not feasible. Cities were forced to build more densely. Open spaces for gardens and fields were gradually built over and, when open space was gone, existing structures were built higher. As Renaissance and Baroque cities became more crowded than their medieval predecessors, they also neglected to compensate for this with improvements in the provision of water or the elimination of sewage and wastes. In the end, they became unhealthier places as well.

## THE INDUSTRIAL CITY

Many of the great social and economic changes that we associate with the 19th and early 20th centuries were born of the revolutionary developments in the technology and organization of production that accompanied the Industrial Revolution. Among these developments were the replacement of hand labor with machines, the movement of production activities from small workshops to factories, the use of new and more powerful sources of power, and the invention of a vast array of new products. The influence of industrialization on the spatial patterns of Euro-

pean urbanism was profound and may be thought of as having two important phases: an early period in which a new type of industrial town evolved from the reorganization and intensification of a "proto-industrial" economy that had long existed in some rural or semi-rural areas; and a later period in which improved transportation and new technologies led to a locational shift of industrial growth toward existing cities.

### Phases of Industrial Development

The industrialization of Europe began in the countryside. While medieval towns and cities, as we have seen, were highly successful in establishing themselves as principal places of production, as well as trade, they were never exclusively so. The manufacture of cloths, metal products, glass and pottery, and many other wares continued to take place also in rural areas. By the 18th century, some of these activities that took place outside of the towns had become quite highly organized, and a fairly large number of rural or semirural proto-industrial regions had emerged. The economies of these regions were mostly based on metallurgy or the production of textiles, and were generally located in areas peripheral to major centers of population in order to take advantage of rural underemployment and to escape the guild restrictions of the big towns. Production was based on extremely small units. Iron-producing areas, for example, depended on the output of many small furnaces scattered across the countryside. In cloth-making areas, women working in their homes converted raw materials, supplied to them by a local entrepreneur, to finished or semifinished products—a form of industrial organization referred to as the "domestic" or "putting-out system."

What changed, especially in the key textile and metal industries, was that entrepreneurs began to invest more capital and inject technological innovations into these systems. Gradually production began to be pulled together into larger units as the introduction of machinery and the need for power to run it made the concentration of activities in a sin-

FIGURE 8.19. Early industrialization. This woolen mill was built on the banks of the River Avon near the edge of the small town of Malmesbury, England. The town had been active in the woolen industry from the 16th century and benefited for a time from the introduction of machine production at the end of the 18th century. Later technical developments, however, found better employment elsewhere, and the town's importance waned.

gle place necessary. Industry began to concentrate first along rivers and streams to take advantage of waterpower. Later, with the introduction of coal-fired steam power to run machines and a whole series of innovations in coal-based metallurgy, there was a shift to the coalfields, which in many cases coincided locationally with areas of proto-industrial development. Over time the sleepy hamlets, villages, and small towns where these new factories, mines, and foundries were located evolved into industrial towns. Some grew up literally overnight from almost nothing. For the first time since the Middle Ages, Europe experienced the founding of a great many new urban places.

Over time, clusters of these new industrial towns and cities began to emerge. In England, where the process began, the textile industries of Lancashire and Yorkshire and the metallurgical industries of the West Midlands each produced their own regional agglomerations of industrial towns and cities. In France the foci were the textile industries of Nord

and the metals, lace, and silk industries around Lyon and St. Etienne; in Germany it was the textile and the iron and steel industries of the Rhineland, Saxony, and Upper Silesia; and in Sweden the iron industries of the Bergslagen. Not all of the urban places in these industrial agglomerations were new. Many existing places also grew, usually small towns and regional centers that were engulfed as industrial development overtook them. Many even became synonymous with their region's newfound industrial reputation, as in the cases of Nottingham hosiery, Sheffield cutlery, Lyon silk, or Essen steel.

Relatively unaffected by this early phase of industrial urban development, however, was the great majority of European market towns, and small or medium-sized cities. These places continued to perform the traditional functions demanded of their place in the established hierarchy of central places, and remained apart from the emerging industrial order until later developments began to shift the focus of industrialization away from the coalfields and the old proto-industrial regions.

This shift signaled the beginning of a second, and more broadly based, phase of indus-

FIGURE 8.20. Resource location. Early industry gravitated toward sources of power, raw materials, and labor. The lower Swansea Valley in Wales began to industrialize late in the 18th century when local seams of coal suitable for smelting became accessible. Copper ore was brought to the coalfields by boat from the nearby Cornwall peninsula, and a large copper smelting industry developed. By the 1860s the production of copper reached its peak in the Swansea Valley, which supported a number of large works like the one pictured here.

trial urbanization. It occurred as a result of a series of changes that began to extricate industry from its early locational bonds. Most important was a new freedom of movement offered by an expanding railroad system. Long-established cities, with their large reservoirs of human capital, business services, and consuming markets suddenly became attractive locations for industries now able to move bulky raw materials to labor, rather than the other way around. Also important was a broadening of the industrial base, beyond textiles and metallurgy, to a wide range of activities such as chemicals, light engineering, the manufacturing of clothing and footwear, food processing, and the mass production of an expanding range of consumer products. The rise of the electrical industry, in particular, led to the founding of countless new firms in and around large cities. Berlin, for example, which grew at a breathtaking pace around the end of the 19th century, owed much of its industrial development to the growth of electrical giants such as Siemens and AEG. Thus, by 1900 the impact of industrialization on European urbanization included not only the rise of a few great industrial regions but new growth for countless older towns and cities, as well.

## Growth and Distribution

All told, the developments of the 19th century led to a tremendous increase in the urban population of Europe, as well as in the proportion of the European population living in urban places. The total population of Europe more than doubled between 1800 and 1910. During the same period, however, the number of people living in urban places grew from roughly 25 million to somewhere in excess of 160 million, a more than six-fold increase! The proportion of the population living in urban places tripled, from around 12% to an unprecedented 36%. Remarkable as this growth in urbanization was, it is nonetheless important to keep it in perspective. The fact remains that the European population at the beginning of the 20th century, taken as a whole, was still more rural than it was urban.

As might be expected, given its pioneering role in the whole process of industrialization, Great Britain claimed the highest levels of urbanization. As much as three-quarters of the British population already lived in urban places by 1910. The populations of the Netherlands, Italy, and Belgium were all well over half urbanized by this time, while levels in Germany, France, and Switzerland exceeded the European average and were rising rapidly. At the other end of the scale, relatively low, but accelerating, levels of urbanization were still the rule around the peripheries of Europe—in Portugal, the Balkans, across northern Scandinavia, and the interior spaces of east-central and eastern Europe.

Whatever regional differences in levels of urbanization may have existed, European cities had become, nearly everywhere, much larger places. Whereas a population of around 55,000 was all that was required in 1800 to make the list of the 50 largest cities in Europe, by mid-century the threshold had been raised to more than 90,000. By the end of the century it was 300,000. The city of London, which topped the European urban hierarchy throughout the period, had become an urban giant by 1900, with a teeming population of nearly 6.5 million people! Eight other cities had surpassed the million mark. Most were the capitals of the Great Powers of the time, but also included among the continent's new "millionaire cities" were a few of the leading early centers of industrial agglomeration in Britain—Manchester, Birmingham, and Glasgow. All told, there were more than 150 places in Europe that could claim a population of 100,000 or more by 1900. Only 21 could have made the same claim just a century earlier.

The Industrial Age was also marked by considerable volatility in the hierarchy of urban places. At the very top a degree of stability was maintained in that most of the great capitals managed to more or less hold their own. But at lower levels, many lesser capitals and port cities, especially in Mediterranean Europe and in France, lost ground. Nineteenth-century industrial growth affected the towns and cities of Iberia, Italy, and western France only weakly. Thus, a number of cities that had long held a position of rank—such as Lisbon, Cádiz, Seville, Granada, Palermo, Venice, Bordeaux, and Nantes—disappeared from the highest orders of the urban system after 1800. Prominent among the newcomers and rapidly rising stars, especially after 1850, were the middle-sized industrial cities of Britain, such as Leeds, Bradford, Sheffield, Nottingham, Bristol, and Belfast, and the emerging centers of the string of new industrial regions that stretched eastward across Germany and into Poland—places like Cologne, Dresden, Leipzig, Breslau (Wroclaw), Gleiwitz (Gliwice), and Lódz.

Indeed, a list of the top 50 urban places in 1900 would include, for the first time, not only individual cities but large agglomerations of industrial settlements, such as the intensely developed coalfield conurbations of the German Ruhr, or the Rhondda Valley in South Wales. Among the top 50 urban places in 1900, at least half could be said to have earned their place primarily on the basis of rapid industrial development during the course of the preceding century. The rest might be described as more multifunctional, but nonetheless still owed a substantial portion of their growth to their ability to attract industry.

## Changes in the Urban Landscape

With rapid growth and increased size came a very different urban fabric. No longer confined by fortifications, and encouraged by an improved transportation infrastructure, cities began to spread outward. Open space with good access to transport was required to build factories, mills, and housing for workers, and such space was most readily available on the urban periphery. Thus, cities became girdled with sprawling new districts of interspersed factories and housing. The shape of the city, which heretofore had been compactly drawn in around the old medieval–Renaissance–Baroque core, began to take on rather irregular configurations. The introduction of railroads revolutionized transportation and rail lines, which emanated outward in various directions from cavernous iron-and-glass cano-

pied stations erected around the edges of the old-city cores, quickly connected cities to one another. As the city expanded, there was a tendency for tentacular fingers of urban development to follow these transportation lines, leaving interstitial areas of open countryside between these fingers.

The problem of providing housing for burgeoning populations of workers and their families spawned expedient solutions that were emblematic of the age. In the absence of any apparatus for planning and control, developers were free to pursue their own ends, which usually meant the minimization of wasted space and the maximization of profit. The housing they put up was generally monotonous, crowded, shabbily constructed, and only inadequately equipped with basic amenities. In Britain, as well as in the Low Countries, street after street of narrow-fronted row housing, set back-to-back with housing on the next street, was built to house working populations. When the streets were filled, efficiency-minded developers often cut cul-de-sac passages into the interiors of the larger blocks to build even more dwellings in backlot spaces. New construction was never sufficient to meet the need. The demand for space in some cities was so great that people were forced to live in dank cellars.

FIGURE 8.21. Row housing. This residential street in an English town is typical of 19th-century industrial era row housing. Built closely together, with common walls, each house fronts close to the street and is backed by a small extension to house a kitchen. Bylaws enacted late in the century ensured that such dwellings benefited from more space and light.

Elsewhere on the continent, the preferred solution was the construction of enormous, multistoried tenement buildings that virtually covered entire city blocks. In Berlin, which experienced spectacular growth during this period, a lack of building regulations led to the invention of the *Mietskaserne*, or "rental barrack," a massive tenement that became the city's most characteristic building form. Other cities developed their own distinctive versions of the tenement. Individual apartments within these huge structures were small and dark, often without exterior windows. Residential densities were remarkably high, exacerbated by the fact that many apartment tenants rented part of their meager space to lodgers. By 1900 Berlin possessed the highest population density, at 1,000 per hectare, of any city in Europe. There were five people, on average, for every room in the city. The provision of open space, water supply, and sanitary facilities for the entire resident population of these colossal structures was usually relegated to just a few small interior courtyards. Open spaces in the interiors of some tenement blocks were even occupied by light industry.

Our worst images of living conditions in the industrial slums of 19th-century cities derive from the writings of contemporary observers such as Charles Dickens and Friedrich Engels. In some ways, these images are perhaps too simplistically drawn. They reflect the then prevailing middle-class view of such areas as dens of squalor, disease, and immoral or sociopathic behavior, and the failure of middle-class reformers to appreciate the fact that their immigrant inhabitants may have seen them quite differently—as socially familiar and manageable havens from which they might cope with the vagaries of the urban industrial world they had so recently entered. The industrial quarters of European cities were, nonetheless, relatively unhealthy places, as the documented high incidence of infant mortality and periodic spread of communicable diseases such as cholera, tuberculosis, and influenza clearly reveal. During the middle decades of the century, some industrial cities in Britain recorded shockingly high infant mortality rates. The problem, which was poorly understood by public health officials at the time, was as much environmental as it was social. It persisted until the very end of the 19th century when the efforts of reformers to make improvements in urban sanitation and housing, along with improvements in the diet of the working population, began to bring some relief.

The appearance of cities was also altered during this period by a number of dramatic changes that took place in and around their historic centers. One development was the gradual transformation of the old medieval/renaissance center to a modern administrative and commercial district, filled with offices, banks, retail stores, hotels, and entertainment services. A symbol of the concentration of these new activities was the rise of the department store. One of the best examples was London's Harrods, which from relatively modest beginnings became one of the marvels of its age, boasting London's first escalator, installed in 1888, an amazing range of goods for sale from around the world, and the appropriately imperial slogan "Harrods serves the world." Not to be outdone, Berlin's sumptuous Wertheims, which dazzled shoppers with

**FIGURE 8.22. Tenements.** These 19th-century tenement buildings in Berlin's Prenzlauer Berg district survived the bombings of World War II and are today being refurbished by largely new residents who have moved here from the western parts of the city to buy up property. The building on the right still bears the scars wrought by war and neglect during the socialist years, while the building on the left sports a freshly stuccoed façade and new windows and roof.

its walls of glass and mirrors, grand staircases, chandeliers, and fountains, all blazingly illuminated by 100,000 lights, claimed to be the "greatest store in the world." A construction boom in grand hotels, all claiming the best address in the city, was also symptomatic of the grand transformation that was taking place as cities all across the continent vied with one another for greatness. One consequence of these functional changes was that the central city gradually came to employ a growing middle class, white-collar work force.

Some cities developed entire new districts near the old core where the new political, cultural, and economic foci of the city could be concentrated. Vienna, for example, built its "Ringstrasse" complex of public and cultural buildings in the 1850s on open land released for development following the dismantling of the city's ring of inner defenses. Madrid and Barcelona pursued the concept of *ensanche*, in which the walls around their respective

medieval city cores were replaced with new urban areas linked together by a peripheral boulevard and connected to the center by a series of arterial roads. Development plans put forward for the city of Rome in the 1870s and 1880s called for a new administrative district on open ground to the east of the existing city. They also envisaged the opening up of the city center with new axial crossroads and the construction of a series of monumental structures meant to foster feelings of national pride. Kaiser Wilhelm II of Germany, ever determined to outdo his rivals in Paris, Vienna, and London, unleashed a vast rebuilding of Berlin's medieval/renaissance center to create a new imperial capital dominated by monumental statuary and numerous pieces of overbearing neo-Gothic and neoclassical architecture.

The classic example, however, is the Second Empire transformation of Paris into a city of great boulevards, open spaces, monuments and parks. This vast remake of the city took place under the direction of Baron Georges-Eugène Haussman, who served as Prefect of the Seine between 1853 and 1870. Haussman's Paris is in many ways a realization of the ideals of the Grand Manner, although ironically more than a century too late and for the benefit of the new rich—the bourgeoisie—rather than for the aristocracy. In place of the city's deeply congested and foul-smelling medieval quarters, he created an open and stylish urban landscape. This took place often at the expense of the poor, who were ruthlessly expelled from the great masses of ramshackle housing demolished to make way for grand boulevards and squares, lined with majestic Second Empire-style houses, topped with mansard roofs and faced with rows of wrought iron balconies. Haussman was an engineer by training. In addition to laying out boulevards and squares, he saw that the city underwent a thorough cleansing and an upgrading of its infrastructure. The slums on the Île de la Cité facing the Cathedral of Notre Dame were cleared and the Cathedral restored. The city received new sewers, and a series of modern bridges to span the Seine. So successful was Haussman in all

**FIGURE 8.23. Galleria.** New retail establishments set in rather grand surroundings were an important addition to the changing centers of 19th-century European cities. Milan's Galleria Vittorio Emanuele II was one of these opulent settings. Built in the 1860s, the cruciform-shaped iron-and-glass-canopied gallery was one of the most fashionable places to shop and be seen in the city. Tragically, the architect, Giuseppe Mengoni, fell to his death while inspecting the roof just days before the gallery opened.

of this that today we regard the open, "city of light" urban environment of Paris as one that has deep historic roots, rather than the product of a 19th-century reformulation of the city's fabric.

Another feature of the age was the variety of historical styles that were used to build the host of new government ministries, financial institutions, hotels, academies, museums, opera houses, and arcaded department stores that sprang up in cities across Europe. The urban architecture of the period was dominated by the revival of classical, Gothic, Romanesque, and even Byzantine building styles. The eclectic use of these styles, sometimes in combination, was romantically intended to connect a new era of modern government, technological advance, and economic progress with its perceived classical or national foundations. The Gothic Revival style was thus favored in England for the construction of public buildings, as for example in the new Houses of Parliament built in London between 1837 and 1867, because of its strong associations with the glories of the country's past. Although there was some experimentation with modern iron and glass building materials, especially in the vast interior spaces of train stations and department stores, a pervasive historical ornamentation remained the fashion of the times. More often than not, modern structural frames of iron or steel were clad in brick and fanciful historic ornamentation. A prime example is London's Tower Bridge, completed in 1894 in a neo-Gothic style designed to reveal not a trace of the bridge's internal steel frame structure or modern hydraulic machinery.

Only at the very end of the century was there a reaction against the historical emphases of 19th-century building styles. The Art Noveau movement, also known as *Jugendstil* in Germany and *modernisme* in Spain, flourished briefly from the end of the 19th century to the outbreak of World War I. It produced an array of unusual and highly varied structures all across Europe. The decorative exuberance that characterized much of this architecture is manifested in the works of its most singular practitioner, the Catalan Antonio Gaudí, who produced an array of startlingly new buildings in his home city of Barcelona. His Casa Milá apartment house and Exploratory Church of the Holy Family (Sagrada Familia) are illustrative of the organicism that was so much a part of the Art Noveau design.

The rapid growth of European cities required that massive investments be made to

**FIGURE 8.24. Opera.** Haussman's ambitious renewal projects for Paris were intended to open up the city and highlight its monumental buildings and squares. The Avenue de l'Opéra was designed to showcase the Opéra Garnier, which opened in 1875. The Avenue was deliberately left bereft of trees, which might mask the vista of the huge edifice of the Opéra. The uniform façades of the Second Empire-style buildings facing the avenue further enhance the view.

**FIGURE 8.25.** *Modernisme.* Toward the end of the 19th century a new style of art and architecture, *modernisme*, a variant of Art Noveau, was born in Barcelona. It became a means of self-expression for Catalonian nationalism. The architect Antoni Gaudí (1852–1926) was among its greatest exponents. Gaudí's buildings employed fluid and uneven organic forms and inspiration from Islamic and Gothic architecture as well as from the natural world. Pictured here is Casa Mila "La Pedrera" (the stone quarry), built between 1906 and 1910, with its remarkable wave-like façade and roofscape of chimneys and vents resembling abstract and terrifying sculptures. There are no straight walls anywhere in the building.

improve the systems of urban transportation and infrastructure. Most new industrial towns lacked such things entirely, and existing cities were only poorly equipped to handle the rapid growth that they experienced during this period. The construction of new bridges, for example, was a commonplace and necessary activity, as was the encasing of flood-prone rivers within massive stone embankments, atop which were placed stylish promenades with wrought iron benches, railings, and lampposts. Most cities sited along the banks of major rivers—even great ones like London—made do with only one or two bridges prior to the 19th century, but could boast of many before the century was out. Another of the prominent additions to the city-scape was the circle of railroad stations built

at the places where the great rail corridors leading into and out of the city terminated. The latter part of the century also saw the introduction of electric tramways and underground metro systems. The widespread occurrence of pollution and epidemics eventually prodded public officials to redesign and expand underground water and drainage systems. An elaborate subterranean system of gas and water mains, drainage pipes, and sewers began to develop beneath central city streets. The city began to glow by night as gas, and later electrical, street lighting systems were added.

## Social Class and Leisure

These improvements, however, largely benefited city center and middle-class residential areas. Many services were only slowly extended beyond the line of the old city walls to the new belts of industrial suburbs that lay beyond, and even then the dwellings there were often not hooked up because landlords refused to pay the cost. Nor were there sufficient means to bring services to the inner slums. As late as 1919, a survey of workers' dwellings in Vienna revealed that 77% lacked gas and electricity and that 95% had no running water. Paris's so-called Red Belt of shanty housing located on the glacis beyond the old city walls (filled in part with the flotsam of Haussmanization) was virtually without any municipal services until after it was cleared and redeveloped in the 1930s.

Indeed, a distinctive feature of the social geography of the 19th-century industrial city was the marked residential segregation of the social classes. By this time the process of class separation that had begun in the previous era reached its inevitable conclusion. Elite and middle-class populations ensconced themselves in well-appointed suburban developments, or in areas of fashionable redevelopment on the fringes of city centers, such as along Vienna's Ringstrasse, while the working class and the poor were left to occupy either the more congested quarters of the inner city or the new industrial suburbs. The physical separation between the living quarters of the classes was further reinforced by obvious differences in dress, manners, language, and leisure activities. Whereas the social world of the elite and middle classes revolved around boardroom, club, concert, and theater, that of the working classes focused on the camaraderie of the neighborhood street and pub.

For most middle-class residents, the poorer areas of the city were distant and dangerously mysterious. Few ever ventured there. Berlin, which rapidly became one of Europe's industrial powerhouses during the latter decades of the 19th century, attracted poor immigrants from the countryside and beyond as though it were an immense magnet. Between 1871 and 1914 the population of the city nearly quadrupled from roughly 1 million residents to over 4 million! So rapidly did the immigrant populations arrive in Berlin that huge tent cities sprang up on the city's edge to receive them and authorities scrambled to devise schemes to house them. The majority came from the German lands to the east, although substantial numbers came from other countries, particularly Russia. Desperate to find work in the city's burgeoning industries, they crowded into and were swallowed up by the vast and teeming industrial slums that mushroomed

beyond the elevated ring railroad that encircled the city center.

On the other hand, a rich variety of new amusements and attractions intended for mass consumption brought classes together at least for brief periods, especially during the latter part of the period. A proliferation of music halls and cheap theaters offering variety entertainment, and later moving picture shows, along with public concerts, became the most popular recreational outlets of the times. Sidewalk cafés multiplied as important locales where people congregated out of doors during their leisure hours. Equally important were various forms of outdoor recreation and sports, excursion trains to seaside amusements, and visits to public parks and monuments. Promenading in the parks, which were now open to the public rather than set aside as royal preserves as they had been in earlier times, or along the river embankments was a common activity popular with all classes. Rising incomes and mass-produced goods with recreational utility, such as the bicycle, helped to create a new popular urban culture of broad appeal. The early motion picture images of happily recreating crowds, that seem to be so common an artifact of the times, suggest to us an "innocent age" in which the classes mingled, if only on Sunday, to take in the many pleasures of a new cultural capitalism.

Indeed, a profound sense of progress marked the end of the age. The staging of great international expositions and fairs in the major capitals was an outward demonstration of a growing pride of accomplishment. These extravagant affairs, which featured the technological and scientific wonders of the times—as exemplified in the Crystal Palace, an immense iron-and-glass hall built in London's Hyde Park to house a grand display of "the Works of Industry of all Nations" and serve as the centerpiece of the Great Exhibition of London held in 1851—were attended by enormous crowds drawn from all walks of life. More than 6 million people came to see the Crystal Palace, which was regarded as a wonder of its time. Nearly half a century later, the 300-meter-tall Eiffel Tower, the breathtak-

**FIGURE 8.26. Regency London.** Increasing segregation of the classes created demand for new residential areas for the urban elite. During the 1820s and 1830s, John Nash, planner and architect for England's Prince Regent, who later became George IV, created palatial residential developments of white stuccoed and columned townhouses set on terraces, squares, and crescents around London's Regent Park. Seen here is the gentle curve of one of Nash's creations—Park Crescent.

**FIGURE 8.27. Eiffel Tower.** More than a century after its controversial birth as a world exhibition attraction, the Eiffel Tower still dominates the Paris skyline. Although the tower was a technological wonder, at the time of its construction critics portrayed it as monstrous, useless, and a barbaric affront to French culture and sensibility. It was to be torn down after the exhibition, but the structure survived, in part because it found new importance as a radio, and later television, transmission tower.

ingly modern open-lattice wrought iron structure built (not without controversy) as the focal point of the Paris Exposition of 1889, became an overnight sensation. To the millions who attended these and other great urban exhibitions, and indeed to Europeans of all walks of life, the world did appear to be poised on the edge of a new and more prosperous age, and faith in the future seemed strong, even as the gathering clouds of a cataclysmic war threatened.

## FURTHER READING

Benevolo, L. (1993). *The European city*. Oxford, UK: Blackwell.

Briggs, A. (1979). *Iron bridges to crystal palace: Impact and images of the industrial revolution*. London: Thames & Hudson.

Connolly, P., & Dodge, H. (1998). *The ancient city: Life in classical Athens and Rome*. Oxford, UK: Oxford University Press.

Dennis, R. (1986). *English industrial cities of the nineteenth century: A social geography*. Cambridge: Cambridge University Press.

Ennen, E. (1979). *The medieval town*. (N. Fryde, Trans.). Amsterdam: North-Holland.

Friedrichs, C. R. (1995). *The early modern city, 1450–1750*. London: Longman.

Gilbert, D., & Driver, F. (2000). Capital and empire: geographies of London. *GeoJournal, 51,* 23–32.

Girouard, M. (1985). *Cities and people: A social and architectural history*. New Haven: Yale University Press.

Hall, P. (1998). *Cities in civilization: Culture, innovation, and urban order*. London: Weidenfeld & Nicolson.

Hohenberg, P. M., & Lees, L. H. (1995). *The making of urban Europe, 1000–1994*. Cambridge, MA: Harvard University Press.

Kostof, S. (1991). *The city shaped: Urban patterns and meanings through history*. Boston: Little, Brown.

Kostof, S. (1992). *The city assembled: the elements of urban form through history*. Boston: Little, Brown.

Mumford, L. (1961). *The city in history: its origins, its transformations, and its prospects*. New York: Harcourt, Brace, Jovanovich.

Pirenne, H. (1925). *Medieval cities: Their origins and the revival of trade*. Princeton, NJ: Princeton University Press.

Pounds, N. J. G. (1969). The urbanization of the classical world. *Annals of the Association of American Geographers, 59,* 135–157.

Sennett, R. (1994). *Flesh and stone: The body and the city in western civilization*. New York: Norton.

Smith, C. T. (1978). *An historical geography of western Europe before 1800* (2nd ed.). London: Longman.

Vance, J. E., Jr. (1977). *This scene of man: The role and structure of the city in western civilization*. New York: Harper's College Press.

Verhulst, A. (1998). Towns and trade, 400–1500. In R. A. Butlin & R. A. Dodshon (Eds.). *An historical geography of Europe* (pp. 100–113). Oxford, UK: Clarendon.

Wycherley, R. E. (1976). *How the Greeks built cities: The relationship of architecture and town planning to everyday life in ancient Greece* (2nd ed.). New York: Norton.

# CHAPTER 9

# Modern and Postmodern Urbanism

When Europe marched exultantly off to war in 1914, everyone on both sides expected the entire affair to be over quickly and gloriously. This was, after all, the beginning of the modern age. Efficiently mobilized and elaborately equipped, the imposingly machine-like modern armies of the day appeared unstoppable to the cheering crowds that lined the streets of towns and cities to see them off. Victory would surely be decisive and swift. It was not to be. In fact, the fighting dragged on for more than four exhausting years. More than 10 million soldiers were killed, a lost generation, and a political and social order with which Europe had grown comfortable was thoroughly discredited and, in some countries, ignominiously upended.

The war was a watershed, its true fateful portent epitomized in the famous remark on the eve of the outbreak of hostilities by British Foreign Secretary Sir Edward Grey: "The lamps are going out all over Europe: we shall not see them lit again in our lifetime." While there may have been a sense among Europeans some 14 years earlier, as they celebrated the birth of the 20th century, that they enjoyed the enviable good fortune of riding the cusp of an enlightened and modern industrial age, the war brought into question much that people previously held

to as a matter of faith. True modernity, in the sense of a highly complex and specialized society that embraces the rights and prerogatives of the individual, and enjoys an unprecedented material abundance generated by rapid and seemingly endless advances in science and technology, did come to Europe over the remaining course of the century. The age of its coming, however, has been a tumultuous and, at times, a barbarously murderous one. No other century can be said to have witnessed such momentous changes in the political, social, and economic fabric of European life as the past one.

The continent's towns and cities have been no less affected by the events of the modern age than anything else; they are in fact the places most strongly identified with the new cultures of modernity. In this chapter we trace the evolution of modern urban development in Europe from the end of World War I to the present. The first half of the chapter focuses on the many changes that took place before and after World War II, including the somewhat divergent course of development imposed on eastern European cities by the dictates of socialist planning. The latter half of the chapter turns to the contemporary scene and attempts to delimit some of the seminal features of what may be regarded as an entirely new age of "postmodern" urbanism.

## THE MODERN CITY

The modern era of urban development in Europe may be thought of as extending from the end of World War I into the 1980s. Like the industrial age before it, this was a time of rapid urban expansion and development. Over this period the number of people living in urban places swelled from roughly 160 million to more than 400 million, while the proportion of people living in urban places rose to nearly 70% of the total population. As a consequence of this immense growth, society as a whole may be viewed during this period as having become predominantly urban for the first time in European history.

Across the entire continent, cities of all sizes and ranks grew significantly larger, both in population and area. By the mid-1970s, it took a population of roughly a million to make the list of Europe's 50 largest urban areas, more than three times as many as in 1900. Even by as early as the 1930s, the upper ranks of the urban hierarchy had become the exclusive domain of a growing class of "millionaire cities" that wielded tremendous political, cultural, and economic influence as the continent's metropoli, *grand villes*, and *grosstädte*. The growth that took place at all levels over the period came to be distinguished by processes of decentralization and sprawling suburbanization, and in many areas by the coalescence of nearby towns and cities into giant urban conurbations.

The process, however, was not a continuous one. The pace of development in the modern era was slowed significantly by the depression of the 1930s and interrupted by the widespread destruction and dislocations of World War II. Because of this fact, the era is most usefully thought of as having two distinct parts: an interwar period, lasting from the end of World War I in 1918 to just before the start of World War II in 1939; and a postwar period, lasting from the late 1940s to the mid-1980s.

## Interwar Urbanism

Horrific as it was, the Great War of 1914–1918 had little material effect on cities. Most of the fighting took place in the open countryside. Only the relatively few cities and towns unfortunate enough to be directly caught in the battle zones, chiefly in the northeast of France and in southwestern Belgium, and here and there in east-central Europe, suffered serious bombardment and destruction. Veterans of the war largely returned home at its conclusion to familiar haunts and pursuits, although they also found the populations of the cities to which they returned to be swollen with new migrants who had been drawn there to meet the labor demands of war production. For many, the difficulties of the war and the peace that followed generated a restless sense of disillusionment with the old order. Particularly in defeated Germany, armed struggle over the political future took place in the streets between rival ideologies. But even in more peaceful corners of Europe, a certain willingness after the war to embrace new ideas and radical political solutions was commonplace.

One of the hallmarks of urban development during the years after World War I was an explosion of suburban growth. This was spurred by a number of factors. These included a growing middle class of white-collar workers who were attracted to, and possessed the necessary credit to finance ownership of, new housing on the urban fringe far from the crowded inner-city quarters; a general depression in the costs of materials and labor, which made such new housing affordable; and continued improvements in transport technology—suburban trams, electric trains, and later motor buses and cars—which made commuting into the city from ever more distant locations possible.

An important influence on these new suburban developments was the ideal of the "garden city," first developed and publicized before the war by the English visionary Ebenezer Howard as an appealing alternative to the problems presented by the rapid, uncontrolled growth of industrial cities during the 19th century. Many of the stylish new suburban developments that soon began to pop up around the fringes of cities after the war consisted accordingly of great numbers of semidetached or freestanding houses. Most were built in vernacular or modern architectural styles, situated on gently curving streets, and surrounded by modest-sized garden spaces.

This was especially the case in England, where a tradition of living in one- or two-story houses was already in place; the trend was less pronounced on the continent, where a tradition of high-density tenement housing was the rule. There, the new suburbs still tended to feature a high proportion of apartment blocks, but with much more green space than was common in the past. Most continental cities eventually also came to possess examples of "villa suburbs" built on the garden city model, especially after Howard's 1902 book, *Garden Cities of Tomorrow*, was translated into French in 1917. One of the most interesting examples is found in Germany's *Ruhrgebiet*, where progressive industrialist owners of mines and factories chose to meet the region's extraordinary demand for housing in the 1920s through the construction of large suburban developments of semidetached single-family houses with gardens.

As the Ruhr example suggests, not all interwar suburban development was for the middle class. So great was the working class de-

mand for inexpensive new urban housing that Paris, during this period, became literally surrounded by vast areas that were subdivided by speculative developers into small, cheap building plots. These plots were sold to relatively poor people, who then put up their own dwellings using whatever materials they could lay their hands on. In other places, development was more controlled. Municipal authorities in Britain subsidized sizable tracts of low-cost "homes fit for heroes" in order to provide housing alternatives for people living in crowded working-class neighborhoods. Similar motives lay behind publicly constructed low-income housing estates on the outskirts of Berlin, where authorities succeeded in laying out a ring of model "garden city"-style developments astride sizable tracts of land annexed by the city in 1920. Paris too managed to develop several socialist-inspired municipal housing developments beyond the fringes of the city.

Whatever their form, the new low-density suburbs were highly consumptive of land. They sprawled outward from suburban rail, tram, and bus stations to gobble up great chunks of open countryside. One consequence of this suburban sprawl was that the built-up area of cities, which during the preceding century had begun to take on highly irregular, almost tentacular, shapes as development moved out along main transport lines, began to become more rounded once again as

FIGURE 9.1. Interwar garden city suburb. These semidetached houses face a gently curved suburban street outside London. Built with traditional styling during the post-World War I housing boom, the dwellings were intended to meet middle-class dreams of quiet suburban living quarters within easy commuting distance (via rail or bus) of jobs and shopping in the city center. Each house has its own garden space, both in front and back.

the interstitial areas between radiating transport corridors filled with new suburban housing. One by one, nearby villages and towns were engulfed by and incorporated into laterally encroaching cities. A great deal of prime agricultural land was also lost in the process, so much so that voices of concern began to be raised in some quarters. In areas where cities were already closely spaced, continued unrestrained suburban expansion brought on the specter of massive coalescences of towns and cities into great urban agglomerations. "Conurbation" was the new term for this phenomenon, coined in 1915 by the British sociologist Sir Patrick Geddes. The term has an almost ominous ring to it, reflective of the cautionary view of what was happening held by such visionaries as Geddes, who foresaw the need for comprehensive urban and regional planning.

In fact, the interwar years are known for producing a host of revolutionary ideas about how to plan and reorganize the urban environment. The ideal of the garden city, which emerged in England around the turn of the century and spread to the continent by the 1920s and 1930s, has already been mentioned. In Britain, the coalescence of towns and cities, especially around London as well as in the industrial districts of the Midlands and Scotland, led to the suggestion that urban sprawl might best be contained by the practice of encircling cities with "green belts" in which urban development would be prohibited. Europe's first green belt was established around the built-up area of London in 1938, and persists despite all challenges to the present day.

Many architects and planners advanced ideas on how to redesign the urban environment to make it more humane, functional, and efficient. Perhaps the most influential was the French-Swiss architect Le Corbusier, who proposed as early as 1922 to relieve the ill effects of congestion in the city by concentrating people and activities in a sort of vertical "garden city" of tall modern-design buildings spaced widely and evenly on a geometric layout, thereby freeing up large amounts of ground space between the structures for transportation systems and, even more im-

portantly, for open green space devoted to parkland and leisure activities. Most of the thinkers of the time focused on what might be viewed as rather technocratic, or functionalist, solutions for the problems of overcrowding and urban sprawl. Few of their grand proposals to redevelop existing urban environments were ever carried out. More often than not, it was physically impractical to implement them at the time. But the ideas behind them would survive to influence post-World War II urban and regional planning.

A fresh sense of modernity, with all its attendant virtues of energy, efficiency, and progress, came to pervade the life of the city by the 1920s. This was epitomized in the built landscape by a radically new kind of architecture, which reflected the view that the 20th century had given birth to a "modern man" who should live in a nonhistorical and highly functional space, constructed of modern materials such as concrete, steel, and glass. The center of this modern (international) school of design was in Germany, where one of its leading practitioners, Walter Gropius, headed the Bauhaus—the famous institute of modern

FIGURE 9.2. Interwar model housing. Flamensiedlung is the name of this model housing development built at the end of the 1920s on the outer edge of the Prenzlauer Berg district in Berlin. The intention was to create a new modern style of mass housing that broke away from the old tenement house concept. While the project consisted of rows of long box-like buildings such as this one, the rectangular monotony of the apartment blocks was offset with corner windows and balconies. Open garden areas also separated buildings from one another.

arts, whose architectural staff and students pioneered a wide range of revolutionary solutions to the construction of public buildings, factories, and individual houses, as well as the furnishings that should go into them. Convinced that modern technology had the power to create an entirely new and better world, Gropius and his associates put their ideas on display between 1927 and 1931 in model developments built at Dammerstock near Karlsruhe and at Siemenstadt, Prenzlauer Berg, and Reinickendorf in Berlin.

As the centers of modernity, cities—and especially large cities—came to be viewed as the crucially important places of the times. Paris reveled in its reputation as the cosmopolitan cultural center of not only the French nation, but also the world. London was a world metropolis of astounding variety and complexity. Berlin earned a special notoriety as a *Weltstadt* that projected itself both as a model of modern disciplined productivity and enlightened governance and as a fascinatingly *avant garde* society of restless souls indulgently caught up in the devil-may-care pursuit of pleasure and extravagance. Indeed, the most strikingly vivid image of this electrifying, and sometimes darker, side of modern urbanism to come out of the 1920s and 1930s is that of the wildly intoxicating and decadent Berlin night life of cabarets, cafés, showgirl revues, prostitution, and fighting between rival fascist and socialist street gangs. Potsdamer Platz, the fashionable crossroads located at the pulsating center of Berlin life, earned a fabled reputation during this period as the place that never slept.

Not everyone, however, was swept up in the whirlwind of gaiety and risqué adventure. The majority of urbanites experienced a much more mundane, but purposeful, version of modern city life, hurrying to and fro in their unchanging daily routines of work and domesticity. This seemingly cold and mechanistic daily existence of contemporary urban industrial workers partly inspired the 1926 science fiction film *Metropolis*. Lavishly produced in Berlin's Ufa Studios by Austrian-born director Fritz Lang, the silent film employs fantastic imagery to portray a futuristic urban world populated by impoverished masses of workers who live underground and toil endlessly at running the machines that support the life above of a carefree and privileged elite. In 1933, after the Nazis rose to power in Germany and banned many of his films, Lang fled to Hollywood.

Fascism and communism, the two great contending political movements of the period, each had their own designs for the organization of urban life and infrastructure. The Italian fascist regime, under Mussolini, attempted to turn cities into political statements. Fascist town planners purposely revived features of Roman architecture and urban layout and applied them to their projects as a means of underlining the historic connections between the glories of the Roman imperial past and the modern fascist imperial future. Thus, a number of new towns, built as public works projects on the newly drained Pontine Marshes and in Sardinia, were laid out like ancient Roman towns on a gridiron plan, complete with central forum at the crossing point of the major north–south (*cardo maximus*) and east–west (*decumanus maximus*) arterial roads. Italian fascist architects tended to favor the modern (international) style, but to emphasize nationalist claims of continuity with the imperial grandeur of Rome they also took to adorning buildings and monuments with classical style statuary, arches, and columns, and to making heavy use of ancient building materials, such as marble and travertine.

The Italian dictator Mussolini was in many ways obsessed with the reshaping and refurbishing of the Italian capital. He took an extraordinarily strong interest in the excavation, preservation, and display of the ruined monuments of Rome's imperial past, sponsoring archeological work to expose extensive new areas of the half-buried Imperial Fora. He also authorized extensive demolition and construction work in different parts of the city for the purpose of opening "breathing" space around important monuments. One of these projects near the center of the city was to enlarge the Piazza Venezia and the adjoining approaches to the Vittoriano, the colossal neoclassical white marble monument to King Victor Emanuel II and Italian nationhood, which had been built between 1885 and 1911 in the center of Rome on the slope of the Capitoline Hill. Another project sought to develop a grand piazza fronted by modern government buildings around the ruins of the mausoleum built by the Emperor Augustus in the first century A.D. In an effort to improve circulation within the city, extensive demolitions were undertaken to make way for new thoroughfares, such as the Via dell'Impero, which connected the Colosseum with the city center at the Piazza Venezia via a grand 130-meter-wide avenue that rather ironically paved over large sections of recently excavated classical ruins with modern roadway; or the Via del Mare, which was driven through the heart of the city center to improve access to the new *autostrada* leading to the sea at Ostia.

While never fully implemented, the fascist renewal plans for the city simultaneously served two purposes. The enormous investment in public works projects reaped political dividends by alleviating unemployment. At the same time, the rehabilitation and veneration of the city's imperial past helped to glorify the regime and cement in the minds of Italians the much-prized ideological con-

nection the fascists attempted to make with the past. On the downside, the sweeping "Hausmannization"-style projects managed to destroy the homes of substantial numbers of the city's citizens. The Via dell'Impero project, for example, resulted in the demolition of more than 5,000 dwellings.

Ultimately Mussolini's architects abandoned the effort to redevelop the city center in favor of pursuing new projects on the city's edge that would project a truly modern fascist utopian landscape. One example is the Foro Mussolini (known today as the Foro Italico), built in 1932 on the northern edge of the city as a huge sports complex, consisting of multiple stadia embellished with grandiose nude statues of athletes in martial poses, intended to showcase the fascist cult of physical virility and athletic achievement. Most impressive, however, was an extensive new planned development located to the south of the city. Known as EUR (Espozione Universale di Roma), the project was originally intended as an international exhibition of Italian cultural and scientific achievement. It was scheduled to open in 1942 on the occasion of the 20th anniversary of Mussolini's triumphant march on Rome, but the war intervened and the event was never held. Laid out in the classic Roman orthogonal plan with two main axes

**FIGURE 9.3. Fascist thoroughfare.** The Roman Colosseum stands at the end of the broad thoroughfare the Via dell'Impero, built by Mussolini through the heart of the area once occupied by the ancient Roman fora. The intent was to both improve circulation in the city center and to provide a ceremonial axis for fascist parades that symbolically connected the classical past to the new city center at the Piazza Venezia. The new avenue also swept away the homes of thousands and ironically paved over acres of classical ruins at the same time that the Italian dictator was sponsoring archeological work to uncover them.

**FIGURE 9.4. Espozione Universale di Roma.** The best-known and most impressive structure of the fascist-era EUR development south of Rome is the Palazzo della Civiltà del Lavaro. Also known as the "Square Colosseum," the building, with its 216 rounded arches, is somewhat reminiscent of a Roman amphitheater. Built between 1938 and 1943, the monumental structure anchors one end of an avenue that crosses the central axis of the development's gridiron plan.

crossing at right angles, and employing vast quantities of concrete, marble, and travertine, this formal city of modern buildings set in imperial grandeur gradually came to be seen as a new fascist core of Rome, separate from but connected symbolically to the traditional center by a highway known as the Via Imperiale. Conceived as a monumental center, the development still stands today as a stylish administrative and residential suburb of the city.

In Germany, the Nazis professed a deep disdain for the softness and self-indulgent decadence of urban life, preferring instead to extol the traditional values and virtues of life in the countryside. Nevertheless, Hitler, who had an amateurish passion for architecture and building, and believed that the principal problem faced by the nation's heavily industrialized cities was a lack of any suitable focus for community life, was eager to refashion German cities as monuments to the ideals of National Socialism. Thus, the Nazis attempted to mix politics and planning, believing that if the physical center of public life in German cities could be properly organized, the power of community would be enhanced and all urban problems would somehow work themselves out. Hitler, accordingly, ordered giant building plans drawn up for some

30 German cities. The most ambitious were those for Berlin (the capital), Nuremberg (the site of the Nazi party congresses), Munich (the capital and birthplace of the Party), and Linz (the Austrian city of Hitler's youth and his personal favorite among the cities of the new, enlarged Reich).

The building projects, the majority of which were never completed, were essentially intended to be unabashed displays of power. They featured enormously intimidating public buildings and monuments, set to vast and linear configurations of public space in a manner reminiscent of the Roman Imperial Fora. Hitler also wished that they be built of durable materials (chiefly granite and concrete) to stand the test of time. His favorite architect, Albert Speer, even championed the fanciful idea that modern materials should be eschewed in the construction of the Third Reich's monumental buildings because they would fail someday to produce impressive ruins of the kind left by the Romans. His theory was accepted in Nazi architectural circles as the "law of ruin value" (*Ruinengesetz*). Although architecture under the Nazis exhibited many aesthetic contradictions—borrowing traditional ideas from the past as well as modern functionalist principles from Bauhaus designs—the preferred style was a stripped-down form of neoclassicism, with an emphasis on bigness and the projection of authority.

Thus, one of the first projects to be undertaken was the 1931–1932 redevelopment of Munich's neoclassical Königsplatz, originally built by Bavaria's King Ludwig I, into a Nazi forum. The reworking of this historic landmark featured the paving over of the immense square to serve as a rally and parade ground, grandly framed on two sides by 19th-century neoclassical public buildings, and on a third side by a Propelaeum modeled after the one on the Acropolis in Athens. The remaining side of the square opened to an avenue, the approach to which was set between two rectangular Doric-columned "Honor Temples" that were erected in 1935 to hold the remains of the 16 Nazis who died in the 1923 Beer Hall Putsch. Flanking the two temples was a pair of identical party buildings designed

**FIGURE 9.5. Königsplatz.** Today sunbathers occasionally stretch out on the broad grassy expanse of Munich's Königsplatz. During the National Socialist era the square was paved over and used for mass rallies and parades. Seen here on the far side of the square is the Grecian-styled Propelaeum, modeled after the one leading to the Acropolis in Athens.

under Hitler's supervision by the Bavarian architect Paul Ludwig Troost (one of them the so-called Brown House, named after the Brown shirts of the SA).

The most ambitious building plans, however, were reserved for Berlin. The historic center of the capital was slated for extensive demolition and redevelopment. The master plan for the new National Socialist capital, which was developed from some of Hitler's ideas by Albert Speer, envisioned such grandiose changes to the existing fabric of the city center that the demolitions necessary to clear the way for construction would have eliminated over 50,000 dwellings. Scheduled for completion in 1950, the redesigned and newly refurbished capital was to be renamed Germania. A fair portion of the demolition work was actually completed (in part with the aid of Allied bombing raids), and a few buildings were constructed, but most of the work on the project was cut short by the war. Our most vivid sense of what the new capital might have looked like comes from surviving plans and from photos taken of a modeled mock-up of the rebuilt city center.

The plan for the city was organized around three principal elements: a grand axial boulevard, a Great Hall, and a Triumphal Arch. The first, an extraordinarily broad 120-meter-wide north–south boulevard, lined on either side

with impressive public and private buildings intended to demonstrate architecturally the power and prestige of the German nation, was to extend ponderously across the city for a distance of 5 kilometers (twice as long as the Champs Élysées in Paris). Along the way, the boulevard was to cross a widened version of the city's existing "Unter den Linden–Charlottenburger Chausee" east–west axis. Planned for its northern end was an immense square dedicated to Adolf Hitler, flanked by palaces and ministries and dominated by the Great Hall—a stupendous domed structure modeled after the Pantheon in Rome that would hold up to 150,000 standing people. Ever mindful of the need to outdo the competition, the diameter of the dome, at 250 meters, was so great that just the oculus at the top would have been large enough to engulf the domes of both the Pantheon in Rome and St. Paul's in London. Near its southern end a

**FIGURE 9.6. Footing.** Almost nothing remains of Hitler's grandiose designs for a postwar Berlin. One of the few pieces is the giant concrete cylinder, which was poured as test footing for a planned triumphal arch, so enormous that it would dwarf Paris's Arche de Triomphe and have sufficient surface space to carry the names of millions of German soldiers who gave their lives in sacrifice. Today it sits quietly on a vacant lot on the south side of Berlin.

Triumphal Arch was to tower above the grand boulevard, reaching a height of 120 meters (exactly two-and-a-half times that of the Arc de Triomphe) and memorializing on its surfaces all 1.8 million names of Germany's martyred dead in World War I. Visitors to the city, who might arrive at the South Station located at the extreme southern end of the grand axis, would step out onto a grand square in front of the station from which they might gaze up the avenue at the white dome of the Great Hall, framed in the distance beneath the curve of the Triumphal Arch. A giant cylindrical-shaped concrete "test-footing" for the arch still stands today, looming silently and long forgotten over a vacant lot on the south side of the city.

In the Soviet Union an intense debate took place during the 1920s about the role and form that cities should take in the modern socialist state. At one extreme was a group of "deurbanists," who expressed a deep distrust of the city, seeing it as an unredeemable den of iniquity, corruption, and class distinction. They called for the complete abolition of cities on the grounds that they were capitalist in origin, form, and function—or, at the very least, a turn toward Ebenezer Howard style ideas of garden city development. Others regarded the city as a potent instrument for advancing Marxist–Leninist ideological doctrines and accordingly focused their attention on experimenting with blueprints for fashioning communal forms of urban living that would hasten the breakup of the family and other bourgeois institutions. Perhaps the most influential of the new ideas about the shape of future Soviet cities was N. A. Milyutin's concept of a "linear city," in which urban space would be organized into long belts, broken by green belt dividers between neighboring zones of residence, industry, and transport. Milyutin's concepts were used during the latter half of the 1920s in the planning of Stalingrad (Volgograd) and the new steel town of Magnitogorsk.

Nonetheless, due to the many disruptions and generally unstable conditions of the post-revolutionary period, little was actually accomplished during the decade following the 1917 revolution, other than the subdivision and redistribution to workers of urban property previously owned by the bourgeoisie and aristocracy, the desultory clearing of some urban slum areas, and what is today regarded as a rather tragic destruction of a great many historic buildings and churches. It wasn't until 1931 that the debate about what to do with Soviet cities was officially resolved. The leadership issued a decree declaring all cities to be already socialist, thereby ending any further theorizing about the need to deurbanize or come up with utopian forms of development. The new and overriding national priority would henceforth be industrialization, and over the course of the series of 5-year plans lasting from 1928 to the outbreak of war with Germany in 1941, the command economy would be the greatest force shaping Soviet cities.

The official obsession during the 1930s with heavy industrialization meant major growth for Russian cities. Floods of labor moved from the countryside to existing cities, and scores of new industrial towns were founded near sources of raw material and power. Moscow, which already had a substantial industrial base, literally doubled in size, reaching a population of more than 4 million by the end of the decade. Overall, the urban proportion of the country's population grew from less than one-fifth in 1926 to more than one-third by 1939. So important was the emphasis on industrial development, however, that only scant resources, if any at all, were available to provide the infrastructure needed to support the growing urban populace. Despite the rapid growth of urban populations, very little housing was constructed during the 1930s, resulting in an appalling overcrowding that quite ironically exceeded at times the worst conditions prevailing in Russian cities before the Revolution.

While the extraordinary circumstances of the time may have brushed the planning ideals of the 1920s aside, many of these ideas lingered on through the 1930s and would later play a role in Soviet urban planning after World War II. Some of them were embodied in the 1935 Plan for the Reconstruction of

Moscow. Although the plan was never really carried out, it called for such measures as a limitation on the growth of the city, the construction of high-quality housing for workers, an improved transport infrastructure, a spatially equitable distribution of services, and most importantly a series of grandiose central-area building projects intended to reflect the grandeur of socialist achievement. A few of these projects were undertaken, such as the widening of some arterial streets to accommodate multiple lanes of traffic in either direction (e.g., Gorki Street, now Tverskaya Street), the opening of large spaces capable of holding mass rallies and demonstrations (e.g., the Square of the 50th Anniversary of October, today's Manezhnaya Square), and the construction of the first stages of the city's Metro, which became world-renowned for the lavish adornment of the interior spaces of its stations.

Most remarkable of the projected but never completed central-area projects, however, was the Palace of the Soviets, an enormously overdone Gothic-style skyscraper topped by a gigantic statue of Lenin—the whole ensemble reaching some 413 meters in height (1/25th the radius of the city, and one-third again as tall as the Eiffel Tower). This immense structure, which was to be erected on the site of the 19th-century Cathedral of Christ the Savior, built to commemorate the defeat of Napoleon and demolished by Stalin in 1931, never got beyond the drawing boards. In fact, the site was for a long time jokingly known as "Europe's largest hole in the ground." Eventually, a giant open-air swimming pool was developed there in 1958. Since 1997, a reconstruction of the original Cathedral, undertaken as part of the effort to commemorate the 850th anniversary of the founding of the city, has occupied the site. But the original plan to build as large a structure as the Palace of Soviets, along with a host of other monumental central city improvements, all designed to signal in architecture and space the inevitable victory and glory of Marxist–Leninist ideology, is an indication that the Soviet state under Stalin was no less interested than the fascist regimes of Italy and Germany in seek-

**FIGURE 9.7. Cathedral of Christ the Savior.** Visible from all over Moscow today is the golden dome of the newly rebuilt Cathedral of Christ the Savior. The original church was commissioned by Czar Alexander I in 1812 to commemorate the Russian defeat of Napoleon and was constructed between 1839 and 1881. It was subsequently demolished in 1933 to make way for a planned but never built skyscraper, the Palace of the Soviets. The present re-creation of the church, the largest in Russia, is seen as symbolic of the country's recent spiritual and nationalistic revival. (photo: V. Bogorov)

ing to legitimate its existence through a grand redevelopment of the center of its capital.

## World War II and Its Effects

These interwar developments came to an abrupt end in 1939 as World War II intervened to cast its somber pallor or, worse yet, its awful shadow of destruction across Europe's towns and cities. The calamitous effects of aerial and artillery bombardment, bitter house-to-house fighting, and demolitions set in the wake of retreating armies would soon be commonplace in the devastated city centers, gutted tenements and houses, and disrupted infrastructures of thousands of towns and cities stretching from Brest to Stalingrad and from Tromsø to Palermo. The war years also brought a cessation of urban growth, as the resources and the productive energies of the combatants were turned to other purposes. Even nations that escaped direct involvement in the war, such as neutral Sweden, experienced a dearth of construction and urban development during these years.

The effects of the war set the agenda for much of what happened to European cities during the first decades of the postwar period. The first priority in those countries that bore the brunt of the fighting was the restoration of services, the clearance of rubble, and the reconstruction of homes and buildings. Roughly half of the built-up area of the larger German cities had been laid waste by the end of the war. The centers of cities like Berlin, Cologne, Hamburg, Dresden, and Budapest, which were subjected to massive bombings and heavy fighting during the latter part of the war, were nearly totally destroyed. The city of Stalingrad, scene of one of the most climactic battles of the war, was a sea of devastation and ruin. In the waning months of 1944, the Germans systematically reduced nearly the whole of Warsaw to rubble by demolition prior to abandoning the city to the advancing Russians. Countless millions faced the severe winters of 1945 and 1946 with only makeshift shelter. Rebuilding was a matter of necessity as well as pride. Indeed, one of the common images we have of life in Germany's battered cities immediately after the war is one of gangs of women engaged in clearing rubble from the streets and stacking undamaged bricks for use in rebuilding.

## Postwar Development

All across Europe one of the highest postwar priorities in urban areas was the provision of new housing. Wartime losses, the cessation of home construction during the war, renewed rural to urban migration, and the onset of high rates of family formation and an attendant postwar baby boom combined to produce huge housing shortages. The most pressing need was in badly battered German cities, such as Berlin, Hamburg, Hannover, and Essen, where up to 60% of residential dwellings had been destroyed or damaged. But the

problem extended, in one form or another, to nearly all countries. In 1950, the shortfall of housing in the Netherlands came to more than 300,000 units. Long waiting lists for housing were the rule even in the city of Stockholm, which as the capital of a neutral country experienced no wartime damage at all, but still had difficulty in providing an adequate supply of housing for its citizens nearly 30 years after the war in spite of a government-sponsored "one million homes program."

In the Soviet Union and other east European nations, housing shortages were especially severe, but they did not receive the same kind of immediate attention after the war that they received in the West. This relative inattention to housing problems resulted from government policies that placed the highest priorities on economic reconstruction and development rather than on the provision of housing. The situation was also exacerbated by Stalin's obsession with expensive "showpiece" urban construction projects, such as the seven excessively flamboyant "Stalinesque style" skyscrapers planned for various locations around central Moscow during the early 1950s. By the time of Stalin's death in 1953, the housing situation had become critical. Existing housing stocks had been subdivided into ever-smaller dwellings, and even these were often inhabited by multiple or extended family units. Densities of up to one family per room were not uncommon in many postwar Soviet cities. Concerted action was finally taken under Stalin's successor, Khrushchev, who launched a crash housing construction program dedicated to end the housing crisis in just 20 years. The effort eventually succeeded in placing a majority of Soviet citizens in "improved housing," but only after more than two decades of frenzied activity.

The postwar housing shortage led nearly everywhere in Europe to an emphasis on large, municipally planned, and often prefabricated apartment-block housing estates, the cheapest and most efficient means of housing large numbers of people quickly. Stopgap developments of this kind quickly came to surround most cities. Many, like the hastily con-

FIGURE 9.8. Flak tower. Across Europe, much of the effort after World War II to provide large amounts of housing quickly and cheaply went into building large multiunit apartment buildings. Here, on the south side of Berlin, a modern apartment building was constructed, rather nonchalantly, right over a wartime concrete flak tower that was used to shelter people from air raids and provide a platform for antiaircraft guns. The massive concrete structure was part of the Sportspalast complex from which Hitler made many of the speeches seen in newsreels.

structed *grands ensembles* that mushroomed up around the edges of Paris, were roundly criticized for their monotonous architecture and lack of adequate transportation and services, but they continued to be built well into the 1970s. In many ways, Soviet planners succeeded in surpassing all others in this "cookie cutter" process of stamping out housing estates. The Soviets developed a more or less standardized approach, in which clusters of apartment blocks were grouped together to form housing estates of 8–12,000 people, known as *mikrorayons*. Each of these developments was intended to be connected to the city center by public transportation, supplied with standard amounts of green space and community services, and to contain a representative cross-section of the population in terms of occupation, ethnicity, and so on. Purposely designed to generate a sense of community, they in fact turned out to be coldly sterile environments that generally failed to meet the expectations of such attempts at social engineering.

An important effect of the destruction and dislocations of the war was to provide an opportunity for a general wave of state-led, comprehensive urban planning efforts. Many of the criticisms of big cities and the ideas about how they might be redesigned that floated about during the prewar years were revived, as planners worked to replace old, poorly designed cities with modern ones. A highly technocratic form of planning for the future of urban areas quickly became a respectable and indispensable part of the administrative machinery of government. In England, planners were influenced by the Barlow Report, a prewar study that focused on the need for decongestion and decentralization of urban areas. Plans drawn up for the Greater London

FIGURE 9.9. Prefabs. A virtual wall of Soviet-style prefab apartment blocks stretches across the horizon in this photo taken on the outskirts of the city of Kaunas in Lithuania. Developments such as this housed millions of urbanites and helped to relieve the severe housing shortages that plagued cities in the Soviet Union. They were often built with shoddy materials and deteriorated quickly.

Area during the latter part of the war by Sir Patrick Abercrombie accordingly called for the control of population and building densities in the damaged city core. Also called for was the dispersal of "overspill" populations to planned New Towns, located out beyond the green belt imposed in 1938 to control the sprawl of the city. Similar ideas were pursued in other countries. By the 1960s, most large European cities had instituted some kind of centrally planned program designed to divert new growth to planned satellite settlements on the urban fringe and had undertaken various efforts to redevelop city cores.

The dawn of the automobile age also influenced the evolving postwar structure of European cities. Particularly in the West, transportation planners were forced to place increased emphasis on improving automotive access to the various parts of cities and providing space for people to park their vehicles in and around congested city centers. London began planning for an elaborate system of radial and ring roads. Paris began construction of its Boulevard Périphiqué and outer motorways. Such policies of motor vehicle accommodation diffused rapidly across the continent. The webs of new transportation arteries that resulted from these efforts served to divide and delimit, as well as connect. City after city became differentiated through its various ringways and expressways into new constituent parts—inner and outer zones, residential neighborhoods, industrial parks, and commercial strips. The automobile also facilitated, again particularly in the West, a massive redistribution of population to new suburban residential areas far beyond the center of the city. Planners increasingly developed plans that tied urban development to expansions of the transportation network. Thus, the 1965 *Schéma Directeur* plan for the Paris region envisioned a multicentered city region linked together by a system of motorways and an improved rapid transit system.

While postwar planning brought much change in the form of reorganized town centers, new transportation infrastructure, and modern housing developments, most cities also directed considerable resources into the

FIGURE 9.10. **Restoration.** The buildings seen here across Warsaw's old town square were completely wrecked during the war. In a remarkable restoration effort, they were meticulously rebuilt from old photographs, plans, and memory to replicate the scene as it appeared before the war.

reconstruction of their war-damaged architectural heritage and in so doing managed to preserve, amid the new and the modern, certain familiar characteristics of national and regional urban environments. Warsaw, for example, expended tremendous effort and resources on the meticulous re-creation, from old photos, plans, and memory, of the city center as it appeared before the war. In countless towns, burned-out cathedrals, town halls, opera houses, and palaces re-emerged from the ashes, along with carefully refurbished old town quarters and streetscapes, to reclaim their traditional place of pride in the urban fabric and to offer residents and tourists alike a welcome relief from the monotonous sameness of the modern urban landscape.

Meanwhile, the populations of cities continued to grow. In some parts of Europe, large cities were becoming more than agglomerations or conurbations. Some had evolved into massive urban regions, consisting of dozens of individual but highly integrated towns and cities. Thus, by the end of the 1970s the London region had come to encompass the entire southeastern part of England and contain more than 12 million people. Across the English Channel lay a horseshoe-shaped belt of cities in the Netherlands, containing roughly 5 million people and known as Randstad Holland. A vast urban region of nearly 10 million people surrounded Paris, and another 10 million or so lived in a sprawling cluster of cities extending along the Ruhr and lower Rhine Valleys of Germany. Together, these large urban regions, along with smaller and more peripherally located conurbations in the English Midlands, northeastern Belgium, southwestern Germany, and northern Italy came to be recognized as the modern urbanized core of western Europe.

Postwar growth in socialist east-central and eastern Europe, on the other hand, did not share the same widespread characteristics of urban sprawl and coalescence. Much of the new growth remained concentrated in the larger cities, particularly the capitals. An unswerving postwar emphasis in Europe's socialist states on high-density housing development, together with a generally greater distance in the east between major towns and cities, worked to inhibit the occurrence of a western-style melding together of towns and cities into extensive urban corridors and regions.

The remarkable growth of western cities and their regions, which was based on the rapid economic and demographic growth enjoyed by the western democracies during the immediate postwar decades, eventually began to slow in the 1970s. Economic recession, significant declines in birth rates, as well as changes in lifestyle and attitudes, all worked to alter the circumstances of postwar urban development. As a consequence, many of the comprehensive plans developed at the end of the 1960s and the beginning of the 1970s, which were still primarily attuned to accommodating scenarios of unending growth on the urban periphery and to pursuing a modernizing redevelopment of urban cores, suddenly had to be revised or even shelved altogether.

Planning became more conservation-minded as the public began to question the radical changes embodied in the modernist agenda. Motorway construction and large-scale urban renewal projects began to give way to smaller, more ecologically friendly and historically sensitive improvements of the urban fabric. Aging housing stock, for example, began to be rehabilitated rather than demolished and replaced with brand-new construction. A policy of accommodation to motor vehicles began to be replaced by policies that placed restraints on vehicular access to central areas, many of which in turn began to be redesigned, at least in part, for primarily pedestrian use. But most importantly, western European planners and city government officials were forced to switch their attention to the problems of urban contraction. By the late 1970s, deindustrialization and depopulation had replaced decongestion and decentralization as the most pressing urban issues of the day.

The key developments that came to define the transition in western Europe during the 1980s from the modern era to our present postmodern era were the flight of capital, jobs, and people from the city. By the start of the decade, analysts had begun to talk about "counter urbanization," a process in which people, jobs, and businesses abandoned the city, not for the suburbs, but for smaller settlements and rural areas well beyond the urban fringe, as well as for environmentally attractive locations far outside the urbanized core of Europe. Throughout the early 1980s, censuses across western Europe, with the exception of some Mediterranean areas, began to record substantial downturns in the populations of major cities and towns. Faced with such losses, the most important issue for city governments became finding ways to ensure that cities would somehow be in a position to play a leadership role in a globalized and technologically advanced postmodern world. This, in turn, led to the self-conscious rehabilitation of city centers, waves of investment in technopoles and office parks, and touting of gentrified and amenity-rich urban environments that seem to characterize European cities today.

## POSTMODERN URBANISM

It has become fashionable to describe today's urban systems, cityscapes, and urban life as "postmodern" or "postindustrial." The terms suggest that somehow we seem to have left the modern or industrial age behind and embarked on something entirely new. The changes that we associate with these labels are most evident in the cities of the West, but also appear to be rapidly spreading to those parts of Europe recently freed of the restraints of socialist economies and political systems.

What are these changes? They involve things that may not be so apparent to the casual everyday observer. But imagine the reactions of someone who may have just recently returned after an absence of a couple of decades. This individual would be struck immediately by the manner in which the city has been transformed. The familiar skyline and the fabric of the old city core would have a very different appearance to our time traveler. It might even be scarcely recognizable. It would seem disrupted by clusters of new office and luxury apartment towers, and modified in texture and style by new uses of spaces and by the introduction of aesthetically oriented postmodern architectural forms. There would be abundant signs of new investment and rehabilitation; in many places there would be evidence of a new and rather self-conscious attention to historical preservation. The city center would somehow appear more vigorous and clean, clearly an object of renewed civic action and pride, although the incongruent presence of homeless people and

**FIGURE 9.11. Homeless.** A homeless man sleeps on a bench at the Forum des Halles in Paris. Judging from the carton near him, he has just recently dined at the nearby Kentucky Fried Chicken outlet.

beggars on the streets might also detract from that impression.

Our returned resident would undoubtedly sense that the city contains new social divisions of space. Some of the older parts of the city, mostly within close proximity of the center, would have a startlingly new look. The ravages of time and the wear and tear of repeated occupancy and neglect would appear to have been washed away. The original look of individual structures, as well as entire streetscapes, would seem to have been lovingly restored or "upgraded." The people who live on these streets would strike our visitor as relatively young and active, fashionably dressed. They would appear to be living mostly as singles or in pairs. The whole area would seem to have been taken over by a "gentrifying" new urban elite of young professionals with plenty of money to spend at scores of nearby upscale shops and restaurants. By contrast, some of the housing tracts farther out along the city's fringe, many of them thrown up hastily after World War II to relieve the housing shortage, would appear to be headed in exactly the opposite direction—taken over and "downgraded" by elements of a new urban poor, displaced from the city center, often of recent immigrant origins, and therefore racially or ethnically distinct from the majority of the population.

Also striking would be evidence, throughout the city, of completely new modes of urban culture and consumption: trendy waterfront developments of shops, restaurants, and condominiums in place of old industrial warehousing and dockyards; hypermarkets, discount outlets, fast-food restaurants, and cut-rate chain motels clustered along suburban commercial avenues; mall-like regional shopping centers; and a sprinkling of garishly promoted theme parks and water parks located just beyond the urban fringe. Urban life would appear to have become keyed to a much higher and more visible level of consumerism and to a far more standardized, or internationalized, array of consumption opportunities than was ever the case in the past. The consumer electronics revolution would be everywhere apparent: visible in the form of

**FIGURE 9.12. Blockbuster.** Just like anywhere else in the world, the video rental shop has become one of the most common retail outlets on urban streets. This Blockbuster store is on Rome's Via XX Septembre, the route by which Garibaldi's troops entered the city on September 20, 1870, ending more than 12 centuries of papal rule and paving the way for a new united Italy.

street corner automated bank machines, electronics store window displays, video rental shops, and by the ubiquitous presence of cellular telephones pressed to the ears of passersby and motorists.

## Reurbanization: The Restructuring of Urban Places

All of these changes are symptomatic of a vast restructuring process that has profoundly affected urban places and systems throughout the world. At root is a force that is commonly known as "globalization." The term refers, in the most general sense, to the great acceleration in world trade that, since the 1970s, has come to link inextricably activities and events occurring in regions and places around the world. More specifically the concept incorporates a number of trends. These include the liberalization of global financial, commodity, and labor markets through the decline of the regulatory powers of the nation-state, the emergence of great supranational or continental trading blocs, the growth in the number and influence of transnational corporations, and the rise of informational technologies capable of providing the necessary infrastructure for a truly global economy. In essence, it means that the new global economy is built around the coordination of production inputs that are drawn from an international web of suppliers. The key to navigating the system is to concentrate the strategic and high-value managerial inputs of informational and technological expertise at some central point. The location of traditional factors of production, such as capital, labor, industrial plant, and raw materials, is less important, because they may be summoned as needed from wherever they may be currently available at an advantageous cost.

## Deindustrialization

In western Europe, the urban impacts of these developments have been many. One of the most important is the transformation that cities experienced in their employment structure during the 1980s and 1990s. The ready availability of low-cost production units abroad caused many European cities to endure repeated waves of "deindustrialization." This has been especially true in places unfortunate enough to be saddled with great concentrations of older and less competitive manufacturing establishments. There has also been a decentralizing flight of manufacturing employment within Europe to smaller towns and rural locations. Deindustrialization cost Paris and its suburbs, for example, roughly 800,000 industrial production jobs during the 1980s, a decline of 45.7%. The inevitable outcome has been that ever-smaller proportions of the urban labor force are employed in traditional manufacturing jobs.

At the same time, employment in retail, insurance, banking and corporate service occupations has surged, and in select cities great emphasis has been placed on securing the "command and control" kind of managerial employment associated with large transnational firms. The city has become less and less a place of material production and more a place of managerial and tertiary activities. Taking Paris again as an example, it is instructive to note that a quarter of the current workforce of the city and its environs consists of directors, managers, and self-employed persons. Another quarter hold intermediate managerial positions, while only the remaining half are employees or manual workers.

## Residential Polarization

One effect of these shifts in employment structure has been an increased social and economic polarization of the residential city, a condition sometimes referred to as the "dual city," or perhaps more accurately as the "fragmented" or "heterogeneous" city. With the wholesale decline in traditional manufacturing jobs, today's urban employment market has come to offer two principal types of opportunity: a limited pool of high-income professional and managerial positions and a mass of low-income, temporary, and part-time forms of employment. The situation has tended to squeeze the middle classes and create an urban housing environment in which there is heightened competition between groups of vastly unequal economic power for housing with convenient access to places where jobs are concentrated.

Since a substantial portion of the new service and informational industry jobs have become concentrated in city centers, many managerial and professional workers have invaded and gentrified older neighborhoods near those centers in order to be simultaneously in close proximity to their jobs and to sources of upscale shopping, dining, and entertainment. Low-income households have

been displaced by this process to inner-city locales where the housing stock offers less potential for upgrading or to housing areas that are simply more distant from the center. Meanwhile a growing "underclass" of individuals whose skills and educational background are of limited value in the new urban economy have become more or less permanent wards of the state or allowed to fall into difficult straits. Statistics show that the proportion of people on permanent social assistance in cities across western Europe has risen precipitously through the 1980s and the 1990s, a trend that contrasts sharply with the 1960s and 1970s, when the demand for social assistance remained stable or even declined.

The concentration of large numbers of newly arrived immigrants in many west European cities has also contributed to the growing sense of social differentiation. As we have noted in earlier chapters, nearly all western countries have accepted large numbers of immigrants over the past few decades. These immigrants have come from former colonial areas in Africa, Asia, and the Caribbean, as well as from poorer areas of eastern and southern Europe. Many came as "guest workers" during the 1970s to help meet labor shortages in rapidly expanding European economies. A sizable number have come

FIGURE 9.13. Multicultural. This photo of a tenement-lined street in Berlin just happens to capture three people crossing the street—a black, an Asian, and a Caucasian. The presence of sizable immigrant populations is quite noticeable in many European cities.

more recently as illegal immigrants, refugees, and asylum seekers. Most have made their homes in cities, where they have formed their own communities despite government efforts to integrate them into the society and culture of their new homelands. As a consequence, spatially distinct immigrant neighborhoods have become a commonplace part of the urban scene across much of western Europe. Relatively high birthrates among these groups have often made them the most rapidly growing segment of the urban population, even after additional influxes have been cut off by the imposition of government controls on immigration. Thus, in many urban areas the immigrant element can make up a startlingly high and growing proportion of central city residents.

The picture that emerges is one of a deeply divided urban society of haves and have-nots, separated by different economies and increasingly forced to occupy two urban environments that are spatially discrete but never very distant from each other. Nonetheless, one must be careful here. A number of studies have shown this view to be too neat and a bit overdrawn. The average city, in fact, contains not just two, but a wide variety of residential areas, each with its own distinctive social and housing characteristics. Moreover, levels of residential segregation vary considerably among cities, depending on a variety of factors, such as local employment conditions, market availability and condition of housing stock, and the degree of intervention exercised by local and central government authorities through their planning and social housing policies. It is clear, however, that due to societal changes urban poverty has in general become more spatially concentrated in well-defined inner-city pockets and in residential areas that were developed on the municipal periphery during the decades following World War II.

## Office Space

To meet the infrastructural requirements of doing business in the new global economy, city governments have undertaken rather am-

bitious renewals of city centers. They have also invested heavily in the development of suburban office and technological research parks. Such activities are motivated by the need to compete with other cities for a share of what is essentially a footloose industry. Modern telecommunications have given the new informational sector tremendous locational leeway. While access to the infrastructure and services of a large or medium sized city will always be essential, few of the traditional locational concerns such as proximity to raw materials, transport, or markets matter much any more. Corporate managers may base their locational decisions instead on such matters as the attractability of a place to their workforce. Cities have accordingly become very eager to polish their images as forward-looking, amenity-rich environments where educated and highly skilled people might prefer to live and work.

One means of accomplishing this has been to place a high priority on "new-age" office space. Most cities have experienced a substantial building boom of modern office structures designed to facilitate the use of computer-age information technologies. These constructions have often taken the form of highly concentrated developments intended to link business functions with access to recreation, shopping, entertainment, hotels, and high-rent housing. Perhaps the best-known example is the city of Paris's massive office–hotel–convention–shopping–entertainment development at La Défense. This shining complex of office towers anchors the far west end of Paris's "Historic Axis," which now stretches some 8 kilometers from the Louvre up the Champs Élysées to the Arc de Triomphe and then outward along L'Avenue Charles De Gaulle to La Défense. An immense modern arch (Arche de la Défense) ties the new business center in visually with the rest of the historic axis. Meanwhile, other office complexes have sprung up in peripheral locations around Paris, especially in a large crescent-shaped area of new development along the curve of the Seine River in the west, to the east of the city center along the riverfront in Bercy, and in New Town suburban lo-

**FIGURE 9.14. New-age office space.** Rising like a phoenix at the end of Paris's historic transportation axis is the city's business office center at La Défense. Begun in the 1960s, the complex is noted for its architectural achievement, its dazzling array of public sculptures, terraces, and fountains, and its strong representation of companies in communications, transportation, finance, and technology. The open rectangular structure at the end of the avenue is the 110-meter-tall Grande Arche, which is large enough to enclose completely the Cathedral of Notre Dame.

cations like Marne La Vallée. Much of the construction boom in and around the city has occurred since 1985, when the government decided to remove restrictions on office development.

Across the English Channel, a growing demand in the mid-1980s for new office space also forced the Corporation of London to abandon a long-standing policy intended to preserve the city's architectural heritage. The old policy placed restrictions, among other things, on the height and density of buildings. The City's sudden decision to depart from this stance stemmed in part from fears that the development of new office complexes around London and especially at downriver locations, such as Canary Wharf on the Isle of Dogs, might draw office tenants away from the traditional city-core location. Whereas only the dome of St. Paul's Cathedral and the spires of Christopher Wren's churches once stood above the London skyline, today it is pierced by the growing number of tall office structures that loom over the City proper, or cluster a bit farther out around central London's major railroad stations as well as along the south bank of the Thames River. Indeed, the London building boom has been so extensive that the demand for office space has been greatly exceeded. Many of the developments are currently plagued by high vacancy rates.

The office boom has hardly been limited to

a few major western capitals like Paris and London. It extends across all of Europe from Lisbon to Moscow and reaches well down the urban hierarchy. Most western cities have at least one high-profile center city or suburban project and are steadily adding other new office and residential towers to their skylines. Amsterdam, for example, has its high-rise waterfront office area on the edge of the

**FIGURE 9.15. Docklands.** Canary Wharf Tower (245 meters) soars over London's burgeoning new office complex, an ambitious government/free-market development scheme that has created a major business center on the Isle of Dogs, where dilapidated warehouses and abandoned docks once stood. The development has been controversial since its inception in the 1980s because of issues regarding its mix of public and private financing, its effect on land values, and especially its effect on the predevelopment population, many of whom were forced to leave. In the foreground are the tracks of the Docklands Light Railway (DLR), opened in 1987 to connect the complex to London's center.

FIGURE 9.16. London's skyline. This view from the waters of the River Thames captures the striking new business tower skyline that has mushroomed over "The City" in recent years. Whereas once the Tower of London, visible in the right-center of the photo, might have been the major feature in this scene, today it seems dwarfed by the steel and glass behind it. The tall tower in the center of the photo is the Nat West Tower (183 meters), built in 1980.

city center. Frankfurt, the "office city" of Germany, has its Mainhattan project and its Burostadt Niederrad office park; Hamburg, its City Nord project. The list could go on and on. Not wanting to be left out, eastern cities, as we shall see later in this chapter, are scrambling to catch up.

## Center Renewal

A general refurbishing of city centers and a boosting of civic pride have accompanied much of this office building activity. Over the past couple of decades cities have introduced fashionable pedestrian shopping streets, taken steps to clean up and restore historical monuments, improve and extend parklands, and commission new image-producing monuments. The most elaborate example of the practice of adding new monuments to enhance the cultural prestige of the city (as well as the political prestige of the ruling party) is the series of grandiose projects commissioned for Paris in the late 1980s by François Mitterrand, the so-called *grands travaux* (grand works) of the President (the Opéra Bastille, Musée d'Orsay, the Grand Louvre, the Institut du Monde Arabe, the new Ministère des Finances at Bercy, and the Arche de la Défense). The provision of high-quality cultural and leisure amen-

ities, including the hosting of internationally recognized festivals, trade fairs, and hallmark sporting events, is much emphasized, as is investment in high-quality transportation and communications facilities, such as modern state-of-the-art airports and high-speed trains. An intense promotion of tourism typically rounds out the effort to project the right image.

Waterfront developments are another very common feature of this revitalization process. For historical reasons, most European cities are located on the banks of major rivers or es-

FIGURE 9.17. Infrastructure. One important step that cities are taking to improve their image in today's competitive investment climate is to upgrade infrastructure. Cities are investing in state-of-the-art public transportation, airports, and communications links. In this photo a gleaming new tram pulls into a passenger stop in the French provincial capital of Nancy.

FIGURE 9.18. Waterfront development. A residential boom has taken place along the length of the Thames between The City and the Canary Wharf Development to meet the demands of office workers. Old and in most cases derelict warehouses, such as the Gun Wharves building seen here, have been converted by developers into trendy condominiums and loft apartments. New buildings, such as the one on the left, have also been built, usually with stylistic attention to the area's historic waterfront heritage.

tuaries. The decline of many old waterfront industries and the migration of dockland facilities to new sites more accessible to modern container ships and road or rail services, has left many cities with extensive areas of abandoned warehouses and lofts. These areas have become prime targets for municipal and private development schemes, usually distinguished by a mix of postmodern architectural nostalgia for a district's industrial past with the provision of an amenity-rich milieu for an urban elite. Examples include Manchester's Salford Quays development, Oslo's Aker Brygge development, Barcelona's Olympic village and Barceloneta district, and of course the much publicized and controversial Canary Wharf development in London's old Docklands area.

## Research Parks

Finally, one of the most revolutionary developments has been the rush to establish research and technology parks, or "technopoles," on the edge of European cities. This is again a function of the growing competition between cities to capture a piece of the new global science and technology economy. The idea is to lure companies not only with the infrastructural and amenity advantages of the host city but also by providing a building site where firms may benefit from interaction with other firms and with educational institutions engaged in scientific and technological innovation and high-risk ventures.

The phenomenon is widespread, but especially associated with cities whose universities are able to provide strong technical support and with cities that can offer the kind of cultural and environmental advantages (e.g., climate and scenery) that are especially appealing to the highly educated professionals employed by these firms. Cities in the Mediterranean South have been particularly successful in serving up the right mix of enticements. The best-known of these Mediterranean science and technology parks is Sophia Antipolis, a sprawling 6,000-acre complex outside of the cities of Antibes and Cannes on the French Côte d'Azur. Other notable Mediterranean technopole developments are found outside Valencia, Barcelona, Toulouse, Montpellier, Grenoble, Turin, Milan, and Genoa; but nearly all European cities have endeavored, with varying degrees of success, to create some kind of local version of "Silicon Valley."

FIGURE 9.19. Technopole. With its university and forward-looking image, the city of Montpellier self-consciously styles itself "the Mediterranean Technopole," confidently predicting its role over the coming decade as the "emergent" market between Marseilles and Barcelona. The city is already home to a number of new companies that have built their headquarters in the city's new office and research parks. It is also one of the leading members of Genepole, a network of French centers of biotechnology.

## Changes in the Urban System

At the broadest scale, the result of all these developments has been to make fluid the hierarchical system of relationships that orders European cities. Cities are in competition with one another to promote and market themselves in this postindustrial economic environment; and there have already been winners and losers. Geographers and other social scientists have attempted to gauge these trends, although most of their studies have so far applied only to western Europe, where good comparable data are most readily available. They attempt to accomplish this principally by assessing the attractiveness of cities as places to live and do business according to a range of economic, demographic, and sociocultural variables. The results are used to construct hierarchical rankings of cities.

A number of generalizations may be drawn from these studies. First, whereas in the past the relative success of cities clearly had a lot to do with the internal urban structure and economic strength of the country within which they were located, there now seems to be a growing tendency for cities to break free of their national identities and their traditional relative position in national hierarchies. This is due to the fact that national frontiers have come to mean less in a supranationally organized Europe. Cities are essentially competing for position in a transnational mobile market of capital, labor, and services. Thus, national capitals no longer necessarily have as advantageous a position over other cities as they once had, although there is certainly no indication that they are in any danger of losing their absolute advantage. Nor do such stereotypical images as the depressed state of industrial cities of the English Midlands, the provinciality of cities in the south of France, or the backwardness of Spanish or south Italian cities necessarily hold true any more.

Germany is a particularly interesting case and a model for what may well be happening to urban systems across all of Europe. The highly federalist structure of the postwar German state has always allowed individual cities the freedom, more than has been the case in other countries, to stake out their own identity and place in the national urban system. As a result the West German urban system that emerged over the decades following World War II was conspicuous for its lack of a city that could claim any kind of national primacy. Recent developments following reunification, such as the transfer of the German capital from Bonn to Berlin, the ongoing incorporation of East German cities into the larger urban system, and continued competition among West German cities for capital investments, seem to have led to even greater levels of differentiation and fluidity at all levels of the national urban hierarchy. Now that Europe as a whole has begun to take on a federalized structure similar to Germany's, there is likely to be an even far greater latitude for individual cities to be successful irrespective of their place in the national hierarchy.

The striking upward mobility of such places as Manchester, Glasgow, Toulouse, Grenoble, Barcelona, or Bari demonstrates the new volatility within national urban systems. Cities in a variety of locations and situations are finding new potential for growth. Many medium- and small-sized cities that have long lain in the shadow of great centers like London, Paris, or Frankfurt are benefiting from decentralizing tendencies that are driving some firms out in search of quieter, less congested, surroundings. Some cities with old declining industrial bases, like Glasgow or Duisburg, have demonstrated a capacity to reshape their image and begin to overcome the deleterious effects of deindustrialization. Meanwhile cities such as Bristol, Toulouse, Stuttgart, Düsseldorf, Bologna, Luxembourg, Copenhagen, Stockholm, and Dublin, whose main function has traditionally been to provide administrative, educational, and financial services to a region or in some cases a small nation-state, are now finding themselves particularly well equipped to attract much-sought-after information-technology firms.

A second observation is that the postwar conventional wisdom—that location within the urban-industrial core of Europe offers a built-in advantage—seems to have lost some of its truth. Whereas for decades it was commonplace to speak of the rapid growth of cities within the "golden triangle" bounded by London, Frankfurt, and Paris, or along the arc of the so-called Blue Banana stretching from the English Midlands to northern Italy, today we hear a lot about growth on the peripheries. A number of telecommunications companies, for example, have chosen to locate in Irish cities, responding to what they perceive as a favorable Irish business climate, convenient access to the European market, and good cross-Atlantic connections.

There is, of course, little reason to doubt that the traditional urban core of western Europe will continue to dominate urban development, but geographic centrality seems to matter less today, given the current decentralizing trends in the location of production and services. Related to this is a lessening of the former distinction in western Europe between a more developed North and a less developed South. While most economic indicators generally still favor northern cities, the cities of the South have tended, throughout the 1980s and 1990s, to outperform those of the North across a broad range of economic indicators. They are clearly catching up, and it has therefore become fashionable to view the urban development occurring along what has become known as the "Mediterranean Crescent" or "Second Banana" as among the most vibrant in today's Europe.

Finally, we can point, as we did in an earlier chapter, to a growing sense of cooperation and identity between cities and their regions. As cities strike out on their own in this newly internationalized environment, the relationship between them and their immediate regions or hinterlands has taken on new importance. Such connections were important historically when cities and their regions were often autonomous economic units, but became less so in modern times as cities took their respective places in the more elaborately integrated economic apparatus of the nation-state. Today old relationships between centers and tributary areas are being rekindled and new relations are being forged as cities look to themselves and their regions as the basic building blocks of a new Europe.

A renaissance of provincial and medium-sized cities is therefore taking place, built on a potent brew of new economic investment and resuscitated pride in local cultural heritage. Hamburg, for example, makes much of its medieval Hanseatic traditions, while Munich and Barcelona combine their newfound international economic muscle with a spirited affirmation of their respective Bavarian and Catalan heritages. As we have seen in an earlier chapter, it has also become common for these new city regions to "network" and form alliances with one another for the purpose of undertaking cooperative projects in education and the arts, or in providing new infrastructure or in jointly offering incentives for investment capital. As if an indication of the times, these alliances quite typically extend across national boundaries.

## Urban Transformations in Postsocialist Europe

Most of what has been said so far applies especially to the West. Cities and urban systems in the East may be said to be rapidly headed in much the same direction, but they have started from a very different baseline. This is not to say that urban development in eastern and east-central Europe has not proceeded historically along lines similar to those in the West, but it is true that the onset of the whole process of modern urbanization occurred much later. Urbanization in the eastern half of Europe generally lagged behind that of the West by at least a step or two throughout most of the 20th century. That fact was further exacerbated in the second half of the century by more than 40 years of socialist rule, which imposed its own peculiar ideological stamp on the more recent evolution of eastern and east-central European cities.

Among the most critical developments of the socialist period was the decision to abolish the urban land market and introduce centralized decision making and fixed property values in its place. The effect was to make location within the city largely irrelevant from an economic point of view. Except to repair war damage, there was really no incentive to in-

**FIGURE 9.20. Time warp.** The physical appearance of streetscapes in many east-central and eastern European cities changed little over the socialist years. The façades of the buildings on this street in the city of Wismar, as seen in the early 1990s not long after German reunification, are gray and dingy. Individual apartments within the buildings were kept up, of course, but there was little incentive to paint and maintain exterior walls and entrances or interior entrée ways or staircases. Rather ironically, places like this became the best places to see—at least for a brief time—what city streets might have looked like before World War II.

vest in the city center, and, in fact, relatively little in the way of new development actually occurred there. Thus, many city centers in the socialist bloc countries became locked in a kind of time warp. By the late 1980s, the physical appearance of city centers in socialist Europe had not changed all that much from prewar times. Historic buildings and the existing housing stock were simply left in place, although the latter was routinely subdivided due to massive postwar housing shortages and often allowed to fall into a rather dilapidated state. The modern office buildings, banks, hotels, boutiques, and department stores so commonplace in western cities after the war were largely absent. Central city development projects more often took the form of massive public monuments to socialism or, as in the case of Ceausescu's Bucharest, to the personality cult of a national leader. Transportation system improvements and a few "showcase" inner-city housing developments were completed, especially in areas totally destroyed during the war, but for the most part planners directed the lion's share of development funds toward the building of grandiose industrial complexes and housing estates on

the city's edge, an emphasis that was more in line with the high priority placed by socialist regimes on rapid industrialization.

Sprawling suburbanization and increased residential polarization, two trends that have often characterized postwar housing development in western cities, were never very important. Most eastern cities remained relatively compact. Residential densities were generally higher, both at the center and on the periphery, than was the case for western cities. As we have seen, housing policy after the war focused on two priorities: nationalizing and partitioning existing housing stock within what socialist planners referred to as the "capitalist city," and the construction of large, densely settled, and architecturally undifferentiated housing estates on the urban fringe. The construction of villas or semidetached housing was extremely rare. Residential segregation based on socioeconomic status, while certainly present, was never as extreme as in the West. One of the priorities was to see that

**FIGURE 9.21. Ceausescu's Bucharest.** Monumental public projects were not uncommon during the socialist years. This was especially true in Bucharest where Romanian communist dictator Nicolae Ceausescu bulldozed large sections of the historic old city, including many churches, to create a grand axis flanked by government buildings and leading up to the steps of the pompously oversized Palace of Culture pictured here. Construction of the massive Stalinist structure employed 60,000 workers for 5 years. At 330,000 square meters in area, it is the second-largest building in the world after the Pentagon. Likened for its sumptuous extravagance to an 18th-century Versailles, Bucharest today is left with this highly visible and monstrously ugly reminder of the past.

egalitarian principles were applied in the provision of housing, which was accomplished through planning decisions rather than by market competition. Middle-class suburbs or inner-city neighborhoods of poor or low-income workers were not supposed to exist, although in reality "black market" dealings sometimes did lead to significant differences in who might occupy housing in certain areas. A lessening of the influence of socialist ideology in some countries in the latter part of the 1980s has also led to increased socioeconomic residential segregation.

At the level of urban systems, the experience of the socialist countries also diverged significantly from that of their western counterparts. With the exception of a few very large places, most notably Moscow, there has been far less differentiation within the urban system. Socialist policies favored capital cities as centers of decision making and invested heavily in their economic growth, but the agglomerating effects of the relatively few really large centers on their orbits of medium- and smaller-sized cities has been far less than in the West. The East, as we pointed out earlier, lacks the great conurbations and growth belts that we associate with western urbanism. Cities are much more widely spaced, and the socialist ideal of fostering an even distribution of settlement and economic development across regions has tended to enhance the importance and distinctiveness of medium-sized cities, once the central primacy of the capital is acknowledged. One might say that the system is best developed at the lower and middle levels of the urban hierarchy, but, with the exception of a few primate cities, only weakly so at the upper levels.

As the postsocialist cities of eastern and east-central Europe now compress both time and space in an effort to catch up to their western counterparts, the changes that take place will undoubtedly be much more profoundly noticeable than those observed over the past couple of decades in the West. Among these changes are the privatization of property and reintroduction of a free land market, and a revitalization and restructuring of old historical city centers with emphasis on

luxury-item shops, office space, banks, and hotels in combination with international investment and tourism. We are also seeing an expansion of city center functions into nearby residential zones and a selective gentrification of those zones. This, in turn, is creating a new social division of space, associated with the commodification and rise in the cost of housing and featuring greater levels of socioeconomic homogeneity. A new suburbanism beyond the city periphery, based on private construction of villas and other forms of low-density housing, is also under way. Within the urban system, medium- and small-small sized cities are becoming more differentiated as individual places struggle with varying success to upgrade their endogenous economic base and attract investment funds, while capital cities experience a period of especially rapid growth.

Indeed, the current pace of development in many of the larger central and eastern European cities is astounding. The construction of western-style office towers, trade centers, shopping malls both above and below ground, and showy new condominium complexes appears to be occurring everywhere. In this sense, the former capitals of the socialist states are clearly the biggest beneficiaries of the opening to the West. Indeed, it has often been said that the three largest "construction sites" in today's Europe are the cities of Moscow, Warsaw, and Berlin.

Led by its popular and powerfully autocratic mayor, Yuri Luzhkov, Moscow, the former capital of world communism, has strived to define an entirely new image for itself. Since becoming mayor in 1992, Luzhkov has worked tirelessly to engineer an ambitious program of high-profile construction projects, both in the city's center and as part of a $5-billion "New Ring" development scheme for the city's periphery. The Moscow City Council, which along with the mayor controls the city's urban development process, has been active in encouraging a host of speculative investments. These include showy symbolic gestures, such as the 1997 rebuilding of the massive Cathedral of Christ the Saviour as part of the city's 850th anniversary celebra-

**FIGURE 9.22. New villa construction.** New wealth generated in Russia's free-ranging market economy is safely invested here in property as well as lifestyle. The construction of new villas, such as these, is a common site around the outskirts of the Russian capital.

tions, or the raising of an immense statue of Peter the Great on the banks of the Moscow River. Also included are massive commercial ventures, such as the construction near the Kremlin at Manezh Square of a modern four-level underground shopping center, which boasts more than 80,000 square meters of retail and office space.

Moscow's private redevelopment efforts have featured such varied projects as the rehabilitation of the city's turn-of-the-century Art Nouveau-style Metropol Hotel and the construction of dozens of new office and luxury apartment towers. Many of the new structures are stylishly postmodern in architectural design. In an effort to break away from the coldly modernist architecture that characterized Moscow's more recent socialist past, they typically incorporate decorative elements that reflect the historic building styles of the city. A prime example is the new 43-story Edelweiss residential tower complex, whose outline so much resembles the familiar profiles of the city's seven Gothic-like Stalinesque skyscrapers that it has been dubbed the "eighth sister." Since the mid-1990s, Moscow has added more than 30 new high-rise towers to its skyline. Another 40 or so are currently under construction in a city whose skyline continues to sport a veritable forest of building cranes, and at least 10 more are on the

drawing boards or in the proposal stage. Aglow at night with garishly illuminated corporate logos and advertisements, Moscow's center has begun to morph itself into a mainstream emporium of the global economy, and the tendency to reach for the colossal remains strong. Among the proposed new structures is the 640-meter "Tower of Russia," the plans for which are currently commissioned with the American architectural firm that designed the Sears Tower and the John Hancock Center in Chicago. If built, the tower would become the world's tallest structure.

In addition to the raising of new structures, a sizable portion of the center of Moscow's rather dilapidated stock of apartment buildings has undergone refurbishment as part of the rush to provide upscale residential space near to the hub of the city's new commercial economy. A seemingly insatiable demand for office space and high-end housing has driven rents in the city center, despite the wave of new construction, to levels comparable to, if not even higher than, those found in many western European capitals. Depending on the amenities and the view, affluent Muscovites may currently spend up to $3,000 per square meter for luxury apartment space at or near the city center. The city center is gradually becoming more exclusive. The steep rise in property values and rents has begun to drive people on lower or fixed incomes from their homes, replacing the formerly mixed population of the city center with so-called New Russians, the rising class of *nouveau riche* who have profited handsomely from Russia's transition to a market economy.

Warsaw, too, has experienced considerable change since 1989. The relatively quick restoration of private land ownership rights and revitalization of the market economy in Poland has sparked a building boom in the Polish capital. Since the mid-1990s over $5 billion has been spent, largely by foreign investors, on a series of downtown building projects. More than two dozen new high-rise commercial and residential towers now dot a city skyline that prior to 1989 had just five tall buildings, the most notable of which was the 231-meter Palace of Culture and Science. This huge Moscow-style wedding cake skyscraper erected during the 1950s as a gift from Stalin to the Polish people is now regarded by many as Warsaw's anachronistic monument to the country's socialist years. The pace of new construction in the city continues unabated. Another 30 new towers are currently proposed, planned, or under construction, including a proposed European Trade Center building, which at nearly 300 meters would take its place among Europe's tallest structures. Like Moscow, the city is awash with new commercial activity. In the center of the city a sprawling underground shopping mall has been opened next to the central station, while out on the periphery Warsaw has become home to a half-dozen suburban western-style shopping complexes—each surrounded by ample parking, anchored by large "hypermarkets" such as the French-owned Carrefour and Géant stores, and featuring familiar western chain outlets like Dunkin' Donuts and The Athlete's Foot.

After a decades-long postwar existence as a city divided between East and West and as a relative economic backwater compared to major West German rivals like Frankfurt, Hamburg and Munich, Berlin is aggressively reinventing itself as the "New Metropolis Between East and West." Once again in the spotlight as the new German capital, the city

**FIGURE 9.23. Wedding Cake.** Originally called Stalin's Palace, and often nicknamed "the Wedding Cake" or "the Vertical Barracks," Warsaw's huge concrete neo-Gothic Palace of Culture was a gift from Josef Stalin to the people of Warsaw in the early 1950s. The building, which stands in the commercial center of the city, is surrounded by a very large green park area, which says something about the lack of value placed on central location in socialist Europe, since any similar area in a western city would have been heavily built over because of its high land value.

is moving rapidly ahead. A top priority is the task of overcoming a critical shortage of modern office space. Much of the city's new construction activity has been concentrated in and along the former no-man's land buffer zone that followed the line of the wall through the city's center. Major development within the zone is focused in three areas. First, around the newly refurbished Reichstag building, where a new quarter has been laid out to house the ministries and government offices transplanted from the former capital in Bonn. Second, in the historic downtown shopping and office district located just to the east of the former wall around Friedrichstrasse. And third, around Potsdamer Platz, which once held the reputation of being the liveliest crossroads hub of prewar Europe but was leveled by bombing during the war, and because of its location just to the west of the wall was left to sit vacant during the postwar decades.

**FIGURE 9.24. Western retail outlets.** Shoppers in this suburban Warsaw shopping mall must pass a Dunkin' Donuts outlet on their way to shop at the modern hypermarket owned by the French retail grocery chain Géant, which anchors the mall. Western companies like Géant have invested heavily in east-central Europe during the 1990s.

Billed as Europe's single "biggest construction site" and viewed by crowds of curious onlookers from the roof of a temporary promotional structure known as the Infobox, a revitalized quarter of new office buildings, hotels, restaurants, theaters, and retail shopping rose quickly from the wasteland around Potsdamer Platz during the 1990s (although the early stages of construction proceeded very cautiously due to the presence of occasional unexploded shells left over from the fighting for Berlin in 1945). Two major multinational companies, Daimler-Chrysler and Sony, have played central roles in the development of the site, each developing a complex of buildings on land they acquired adjacent to the square shortly after the fall of the Berlin Wall. The more eye-catching of the two is the Sony Center, an ensemble of eight buildings that occupies a wedge of land touching and extending to the northwest of Potsdamer Platz. The focal point of the Sony Center complex is an ellipse-shaped forum topped by a 100-meter-diameter tented roof of laminated glass and Teflon-coated fabric, which floods the interior with shifting tones of light and shadow. Its exclamation point is the 103-meter blue-tinged steel and glass tower, one side flat and the other gently curved, which faces the Platz at the apex of the Sony complex.

While criticized by some Berliners for its lack of sensitivity to any historic sense of the city's landscape or community ideals, the development is hugely successful and perhaps emblematic of the increasingly dominant role exerted by large multinational firms in shaping the public landscapes of cities. While the designers of the new Potsdamer Platz developments in Berlin have made a conscious effort to create public space—there are museums, restaurants, boutiques, multiplex cinemas, even an IMAX theater, and thousands of visitors stream through the Daimler-Chrysler and Sony Center foras and atriums daily—the public space is primarily a carnival-like landscape of consumption, while the tower spaces above are reserved exclusively for the serious day-to-day work of the corporate world and for luxury apartments.

As development proceeds along such lines, it seems reasonable to assume that we can expect a growing reintegration of former socialist cities into the larger European urban system. The new "peripheries," such as the so-called Mediterranean Crescent, that have arisen around the traditional west European core will eventually have their counterpart in some kind of new urban constellation in the East. Most likely to emerge as anchors will be the capitals and more progressive provincial cities in the parts of east-central Europe most closely linked with the West. Among the capitals, Berlin certainly, but also such places as Warsaw, Prague, Vienna, and Budapest are

**FIGURE 9.25. Potsdamer Platz.** Visitors to Berlin's Sony Center gawk at the gleaming glass walls and the eye-catching tented fabric and glass roof as they pass before the IMAX theater. Along with the nearby Chrysler Atrium and other restaurants and attractions, the Sony Center has restored Potsdamer Platz to its former importance as one of Berlin's busiest locations. Except for the small remnant preserved in the pavement outside, it is difficult to tell that this spot stood just to one side of the infamous Berlin Wall.

likely to be major players. Together these cities dominated the urban system of east-central Europe at the beginning of the 20th century and continued to do so up until World War II, after which they fell into decline as their natural economic and cultural links to one another and the rest of the continent were severed by the political bifurcation of postwar Europe. All have now shown signs of vigorous recovery and growing integration within the new transnational urban economy. Their rapid development has even led to nostalgic conjecture in some quarters, however unrealistic it may actually be, about a return to a pre-1914 urban ordering of central Europe.

Europeans today live in a thoroughly urbanized society. In the two chapters of Part III, we have traced how they have come to this point. We have seen how the spatial forms and built environments of towns and cities have evolved over the ages from the early classical foundations of European urbanization to its present "postmodern" form. All of this helps us to appreciate, as we walk the streets and squares of European cities, how historically "layered" our surroundings may be. More often than not, the cityscape we see is an intricate mixture of surviving elements from past and current developmental periods. We have also seen how the functions

and relative importance of towns and cities have changed with the ages—how they have at various times been either integrated with or separated from the surrounding countryside, how at various times towns and cities in different parts of Europe have been more or less advantageously situated with respect to the currents of trade or technological advancement, or how they may have risen or fallen with the ebb and flow of political power. In other words, we have tried to appreciate the fact that the functional and spatial characteristics of the urban system are dynamic. Today's urban hierarchy is certainly different from, for example, that of the industrial era, the Middle Ages, or classical times, and continues to evolve. The same might be said of the internal social organization of towns and cities.

All of this suggests that there is nearly always something unique about any European town or city. No two have exactly the same cityscape, history, or even prospects for the future. Yet, their inhabitants share a distinctly European heritage of urban development and life, and, as we have noted, the circumstances of that existence seem to be becoming more homogenized in an increasingly globalized world. What are some of the principal characteristics of the everyday lives that Europeans live? We have now seen that the majority live in urban places, and have suggested that even those who live beyond the confines of towns and cities are influenced in countless ways by the dictates and fashions of the continent's larger and dominant urban society. We now turn in the last section of this book to examining how Europeans spend their time—whether at work, in school, in retirement, or simply at leisure.

## FURTHER READING

Argenbright, R. (1999). Remaking Moscow: New places, new selves. *Geographical Review, 89,* 1–22.

Ashworth, G. J. (1998). The conserved European city as cultural symbol: The meaning of the text. In B. Graham (Ed.), *Modern Europe: Place, culture and identity* (pp. 186–209). London: Arnold.

Bekemans, L., & Mira, E. (Eds.). (2000). *Civitas Europa: Cities, urban systems and cultural regions between diversity and convergence.* Brussels: Presses Univesitaires Européenes.

Castells, M. (1993). European cities, the informational society, and the global economy. *Tijdschrift voor Economische en Sociale Geografie, 84,* 247–257.

Danta, D. (1993). Ceausescu's Budapest. *Geographical Review, 83,* 170–182.

Dawson, A. H. (1999). From glittering icon to . . . *Geographical Journal, 165,* 154–160.

Dieleman, F. M., & Faludi, A. (1998). Randstad, Rhine-Ruhr and Flemish Diamond as one polynucleated macro region? *Tijdschrift voor Economische en Sociale Geografie, 89,* 320–327.

Forest, B., & Johnson, J. (2002). Unraveling the threads of history: Soviet-era monuments and post-Soviet national identity in Moscow. *Annals of the Association of American Geographers, 92,* 524–547.

Glebe, G., & O'Loughlin, J. (Eds.). (1987). *Foreign minorities in continental European cities.* Stuttgart, Germany: Franz Steiner.

Grava, S. (1993). The urban heritage of the Soviet Regime: The case of Riga, Latvia. *Journal of the American Planning Association, 59,* 9–30.

Ladd, B. (1997). *The ghosts of Berlin: Confronting German history in the urban landscape.* Chicago: University of Chicago Press.

Meller, H. (2001). *European cities, 1890s–1930s: History, culture and the built environment.* Chichester, UK: Wiley.

Notaro, A. (2000). Exhibiting the new Mussolini city: Memories of empire in the World Exhibition of Rome (EUR). *GeoJournal, 51,* 15–22.

Ragulska, J. (1987). Urban development under socialism: The Polish experience. *Urban Geography, 8,* 321–339.

Siderov, D. (2000). The resurrection of the Cathedral of Christ the Savior in Moscow. *Annals of the Association of American Geographers, 90,* 548–572.

Sutcliffe, A. (Ed.). (1984). *Metropolis, 1890–1940.* Chicago: University of Chicago Press.

van der Wusten, H. (2000). Dictators and their capital cities: Moscow and Berlin in the 1930s. *Geojournal, 52,* 339–344.

White, P. D. (1998). Berlin: Social convergences and contrasts in the reunited city. *Geography, 83,* 214–226.

# PART IV

## Work and Leisure

# CHAPTER 10

# Making a Living

Most Europeans today make their living in a manner that is very different from the way they might have just a century ago. Europe's new industrial age was then in full swing. Millions of workers lived in industrial towns and cities and labored daily in mines, foundries, shipyards, mills, and factories. In Europe's most heavily industrialized zone, running from Britain across northeastern France and the Low Countries and into Germany, but also in scattered locations across the length and breadth of the continent, the industrial worker had become the backbone of the economy. Alongside this working class, an even newer group of urban workers was emerging. These workers were also wage earners, but they served an expanding office and retail services sector as clerks, secretaries, bank tellers, and retail sales assistants. At the same time very large sections of the continent were still essentially rural, inhabited by people who made their living from the land or sea. Indeed, despite the rapid late 19th- and early 20th-century growth of industry and cities, agricultural work still supported the largest number of Europeans, although the balance was slowly tilting toward urban and industrial life.

These classical features of industrial society have been transformed over the past century as Europe's economies have evolved and matured. Among the many changes is a vast reduction in the proportion of the population earning a living from agricultural work. This has happened at the same time that food production has been maintained or even increased. Manufacturing employment has also fallen in most countries, in addition to being transformed by the introduction of automated technologies, by the decline of traditional heavy industries, and by the rise of newer electronic and high-tech consumer-oriented industries. At the same time, employment has expanded tremendously in the service sector, which now accounts for the majority of jobs in nearly every European country. The typical European worker today is a white-collar employee who holds a service job in government, or in the health, finance, retailing, leisure, or entertainment sectors. This is as true in the former socialist economies of east-central and eastern Europe as it is in the traditionally capitalist western economies. Processes of globalization and integration have made the economies of individual countries, and by extension the jobs that Europeans hold, whether agricultural, manufacturing or service, more similar and more interdependent than ever before. And, in one of the great transformations of the age, these economies are more likely to contain large numbers of women, both married and single, working outside the home.

The emergence of a modern service economy and a concomitant rise in the qualifications necessary for employment have been paralleled by a rapid expansion of education systems. Europe's population today is notably more highly educated than it was a century ago, with most young people now completing at least some form of secondary education. A growing percentage now goes on to higher education or specialized vocational training. Thus, one of the great changes has been the considerable extension of the length of time spent preparing for a life of work. Young people on average have come to enter the labor force today at a far later stage of life than did either their parents or grandparents. They have also found a working life that is more flexible and varied but in some ways less certain in its conditions of employment.

A third major change has been the remarkable growth in individual wealth and living standards that has occurred since World War II. In the aftermath of the war much of Europe lay in economic as well as physical ruin. Wartime destruction, deprivation, and dislocation had severely disrupted or impoverished the economies of entire nations and countless individual citizens. Only slowly did Europe begin to restore some semblance of normalcy during the years immediately following the war. In the 1950s and 1960s, however, the pace of recovery quickened and, particularly in the West, Europeans enjoyed the beginnings of an extended period of economic growth and prosperity that has continued, with only minor slowdowns and setbacks, to the present.

This remarkable development has meant that throughout the latter half of the 20th century real incomes rose substantially, allowing most western Europeans the luxury of a disposable income to spend on a range of goods and services, such as cars, appliances, electronics, and vacations, that went far beyond what would normally be regarded as the mere basics of life. Although measurably different in many ways, a similar improvement in living standards also occurred in the socialist East. Even though levels of income and wealth accumulation have lagged significantly behind those of the West, and certain luxury goods may have often been out of the reach of ordinary people, eastern Europeans by and large have also enjoyed a level of prosperity and economic security that, by the late 1970s and the 1980s, was vastly superior to that which they had known previously.

In addition to generally rising levels of prosperity, Europeans have also benefited from a remarkable willingness on the part of the state to guarantee people's long-term welfare. The so-called postwar economic miracle provided the wherewithal by which most western European countries were able to institute comprehensive and generous provisions for the welfare and social protection of their citizens. The idea that the state should provide economic and social security for the disabled, the elderly, and the disadvantaged, as well as for families with children, became an ideological underpinning of the late 20th-century welfare state in western Europe. However, the question of whether and for how long society can bear the costs of the seemingly open-ended provisions that have become the norm in most countries has been a matter of political debate in the West since the late 1980s. The issue of sustainable levels of social welfare provision is no less critical in the former socialist states of the East. There during the postwar decades the state intervened even more comprehensively in the business of providing economic and social security for its citizens, going far beyond the usual provision of pensions, health care, and welfare, to the subsidization of housing and food costs, day care for children, and even family vacations.

Our purpose in this chapter is to explore each of these four developments—the transformation of labor markets, the expanding length and breadth of education and training, the real growth of personal income and wealth, and the struggle to provide adequate but affordable levels of welfare and social security—that so profoundly shape the way in which Europeans economically ground their daily lives as they enter the 21st century. As we do so, we will be especially interested in contrasting and comparing the changes occurring in both the old democracies of the West and the new democracies of the East.

## LABOR MARKETS

### Agriculture, Forestry, and Fishing

Only a relatively small part of Europe's population today is dependent on the land or the sea for its livelihood. Employment in agriculture, forestry, or fishing is proportionately least important in the heavily urbanized and service-oriented economies of western and northern Europe. Throughout this area, less than 5% of the economically active population is employed in these primary sectors of the economy. Britain has the smallest proportion in all of Europe, at less than 2%. Even in France, where agriculture has traditionally enjoyed a favored place in the national economy, the proportion of the labor force actually employed in this sector today barely exceeds 4% of the labor force.

The relative importance of the primary sector grows, however, as one moves out from the urbanized core of western Europe toward the peripheries. To the west, agriculture and fishing play a notably larger role in the more traditional employment structures of the regions along Europe's Atlantic fringe. The same holds for the poorer parts of the Mediterranean South. Agriculture is also a relatively more important way of making a living in the highlands and basins of central Europe,

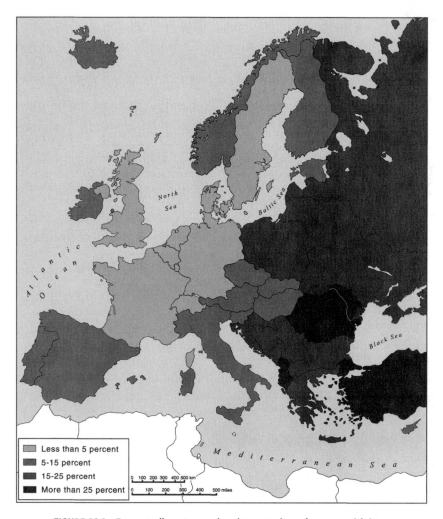

Less than 5 percent
5-15 percent
15-25 percent
More than 25 percent

0  100 200 300 400 500 km
0  100  200  300  400  500 miles

FIGURE 10.1. Economically active employed in agriculture, forestry, and fishing.

and its significance becomes even more pronounced on the broad expanses of the eastern European plain that extend through Poland and on into the Baltic States, Belarus, Ukraine, and Russia. The same is generally true of the Balkans. Indeed, agricultural employment is at its highest in the least economically developed Balkan countries of Albania, Moldova, and Romania, reaching levels of nearly 40% or more.

The modernization and mechanization of agriculture have a relatively long history in the West. Significant progress was already under way in some regions during the 18th and 19th centuries as farmers began to adopt innovations, such as new crops and fertilizers, and to organize into cooperatives. But the pace of change has been most rapid over the latter half of the 20th century. During the 1960s and 1970s, the rate of change was particularly high as agriculture was simultaneously intensified and specialized. During this period farming also became more intimately linked in many areas to agribusiness and food retailers. These changes were accompanied by a steady decline in the number of small farmers and a concentration of land into larger and larger operations. This was especially true in some of the richest regions, such as East Anglia in England, the Paris Basin in France, the southern Netherlands, the

**FIGURE 10.2. Agribusiness.** Agriculture in western Europe is highly capitalized, mechanized, and productive. Surplus production is a perennial problem. Here a tractor works the soil to prepare the ground for a crop of winter wheat on the High Meseta in Spain.

north German plain, and Italy's Po Basin and Emilia Romagna regions.

Many of these changes led to extensive gains in productivity. This has meant that policymakers throughout the 1980s and 1990s have chiefly sought, although often with little success, to reduce agricultural output. Overproduction remains a persistently difficult issue in Europe. The complicated and controversial agricultural subsidy system of the EU, known as CAP (Common Agricultural Policy), essentially encourages farmers to overproduce and absorbs roughly half of the annual budget of the EU. This continues despite a number of recent efforts to bring about reform.

At the same time, there has been a long-term trend toward fewer and fewer agricultural jobs. According to EU statistics, agricultural labor in the 15 (pre-enlargement) member states has fallen from the equivalent of nearly 13 million full-time workers at the end of the 1970s to fewer than 7 million today. While three-quarters of all agricultural labor in these EU countries is family-based, there has also been a growing shift toward non-family labor as women and youthful family members continue to drift out of agriculture to find employment in other sectors. The trend is especially marked in Spain, where the employment of seasonal workers, imported from the Maghreb countries of North Africa and elsewhere, has become increasingly common in the orchard, vineyard, and olive grove harvests.

Both the role of agriculture in national economies and the level of employment in agriculture have remained much higher in the East, despite various efforts to restructure production during the decade of the 1990s. Collectivization, which was introduced during the socialist years in many countries, resulted in fewer and larger units but not necessarily in wholesale reductions in the size of the agricultural labor force. Wherever it was introduced, agriculture became more industrialized but remained generally inefficient in its use of human resources. Where collectivization was not extensively applied, as in Poland and the former Yugoslavia, agriculture

**FIGURE 10.3. Collective farm.** With multiple silos and extensive outbuildings, a collective farm sits in the midst of hundreds of hectares of grain fields. When this photo was taken in the early 1990s, there was little evidence that this operation in Lithuania had yet been privatized.

basically remained as traditional and labor-intensive as it had been in the past.

Since 1989 there has been a drive in many east-central and eastern European countries for privatization. Events have shown, however, that many collective farm members actually prefer the familiar and relative security of co-operative farming to the higher level of risk entailed in private farming. As a consequence, some privatization initiatives have been rejected or delayed. While there has been a general increase in the number of small family farms in some of the formerly socialist countries, production has fallen nearly everywhere, and at present the success of an expected transition to a western-style agricultural economy appears mixed, at best. In the countries that have been most successful in making the transition to a market economy, such as Estonia, Hungary, Slovenia, the Czech Republic, and Slovakia, the share of agricultural employment has been slowly declining toward levels comparable to those in the West. It remains high, on the other hand, in Poland and has actually grown in Romania, where other employment opportunities have been particularly scarce.

## Manufacturing

The present map of manufacturing employment in Europe looks notably different from that which existed in the not-so-distant past.

The hub of European factory employment today lies well to the east of the area that we might think of as the traditional industrial heartland. The highest levels of employment in this sector are centered instead on the countries of east-central Europe. Relatively high levels also extend westward from this core region to include much of Germany, eastward to include Ukraine and Belarus, and southward to take in some but not all of the countries of the Balkans.

It is important to remember that this high employment zone does not necessarily contain the most productive or efficient examples of European manufacturing. It is simply the area where employment in this sector is relatively most important. This is to a very large extent the legacy of the intensive drive for industrial development that preoccupied nearly all of the socialist countries in the decades following World War II. This zone of proportionately high industrial employment persists today despite the substantial losses in manufacturing jobs that have occurred in the 1990s as exposure to a competitive open market has forced industry in these countries to close obsolescent plants and eliminate widespread employment redundancies. Russia might also be included, but with just under 25% of its economically active population now employed in manufacturing, it falls more properly among a group of countries such as Finland, Denmark, the United Kingdom, Italy, and Portugal, in which manufacturing employment remains relatively high but more modestly so. The lowest levels of manufacturing employment, with the exception of the southern Balkans, are generally found in the once industrialized but now more service-oriented economies of western and northern Europe.

The decline of manufacturing employment is, however, a European-wide phenomenon related to a process, known as deindustrialization, in which certain traditional industries begin to lose, for a variety of reasons, their ability to produce competitively. These industries find themselves unable to innovate or reorganize and typically enter a cumulative process of decline that may eventually

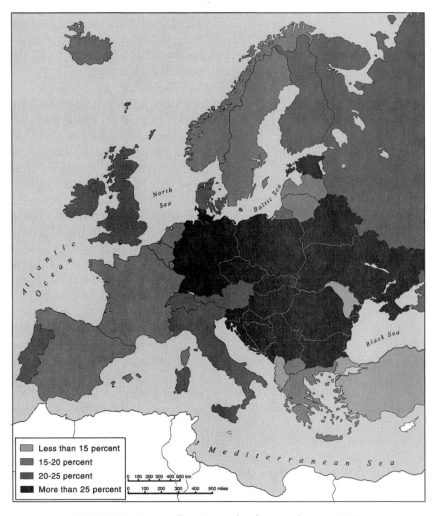

FIGURE 10.4. Economically active employed in manufacturing, 2000.

threaten to depress the entire economy of the city or region in which they are situated. Deindustrialization is often blamed on the rise of transnational companies, which are known to have no qualms about closing inefficient plants and shifting production overseas to reduce costs, although there is evidence that this is far too simplistic an explanation. Since the 1970s deindustrialization has resulted in substantial job losses across Europe and has contributed to persistently high levels of unemployment in many of the continent's older industrial cities and regions. The impact has been concentrated especially in the traditional manufacturing sectors of steel, metal

fabrication, chemicals, and energy, but also in textiles, clothing, and footwear.

A progressive and long-term spread of deindustrialization from the oldest industrial areas to the newest is reflected in the dates at which industrial employment has peaked in each European country. The earliest countries to peak did so as early as the 1960s. These include Britain, Belgium, Germany, the Netherlands, Switzerland, and Sweden. From these long industrialized and relatively rich countries, the downturn in manufacturing employment spread outward to include the entire West by the end of the 1980s. The only exceptions to the rule were Portugal and Greece, where the peak was not reached until the early 1990s. Since then the retreat has begun and continues also in the former socialist states of east-central and eastern Europe, whose relatively inefficient state-run enterprises find themselves in no position to compete in the open market. Industrial employment is estimated to have fallen by roughly one-third in east-central Europe since the early 1990s. In Romania there has been a decline of nearly 50%.

This is not to say that manufacturing is in any danger of disappearing as a major sector of European employment and economy. The continent still ranks high among the world's most productive industrial regions. Europe produces a full range of industrial products and is known for quality goods, particularly in telecommunications, textiles and clothing, food products, chemicals, and pharmaceuticals. What is happening, though, is a massive restructuring of how Europe produces goods and materials.

Among a number of restructuring trends is privatization. In the decades following World War II many countries nationalized key industries, both to protect them from foreign competition and to combat domestic unemployment. These publicly subsidized industries soon became bloated and inefficient.

They proved uncompetitive outside of their very limited and protected domestic markets. Beginning in the 1980s, many western European countries began to privatize, selling off large portions of their public holdings to buyers in the private sector. They were led by Britain, which began by breaking up its telecommunications monopolies as well as such state-managed giants as British Rail, British Airways, and British Steel. Even France, which has one of the strongest traditions of state ownership among western countries and which initially resisted the trend, joined in eventually.

In the former socialist countries, where the vast majority of production units have been state-owned, there has been an even greater eagerness to divest. In former East Germany, the Treuhand organization, which became the postunification holding company responsible for selling off state-owned companies, began operations with more than 11,000 companies to put on the block. Poland began its privatization drive with more than 8,000 state firms to sell. Romania had 40,000. The process has been long and difficult. Among the many barriers has been a lack of potential buyers as well as uncertain systems of corporate law and taxation. Despite bargain basement prices, most countries were successful in sell-

FIGURE 10.5. Privatization. The privatization of state enterprises in former East Germany was handled after reunification by the Treuhand organization, which worked out of this building in Berlin. The building has an interesting history. It was originally built during the Nazi era as Herman Göring's Air Ministry. After the war, which it survived, it became the House of Ministries for the East German regime. Most recently it has been given over to the Finance Ministry of the German Federal Republic.

ing off only a portion of their state-owned firms, and failure rates among newly privatized manufacturing enterprises have been high.

A second trend is an accelerating wave of transnational takeovers and mergers. At first the only large transnational companies to operate in Europe came from abroad. American and Japanese firms like Ford, IBM, and Sony demonstrated that they could produce more flexibly and capture larger markets by operating on a truly pan-European scale. Most European companies, which were nationally based, lacked the ability to organize in this fashion and were soon disadvantaged. Since the 1980s, however, there has been a rising tide of European cross-boundary acquisitions and alliances. This has come with the encouragement of the EU, which as part of the drive toward the Single Market has eased controls on international mergers and takeovers and promoted the adoption of European rather than national product standards. As a result of this trend, the likelihood that a European worker may work for a large international firm that is actively organizing production and distribution on a pan-European basis is far higher today than it was just 10 or 15 years ago.

A third trend is the move toward the higher technology and microelectronics manufacturing sectors. Recent data suggest that as many as 12 million EU citizens (roughly 8% of the labor force) now hold high-tech manufacturing jobs and that these jobs are heavily concentrated in a handful of regions, such as Scotland's "Silicon Valley" between Glasgow and Edinburgh, the Netherlands' Noord-Brabant region, the south of France, the area around Stuttgart in Germany, and along the M4 motorway corridor to the west of London. Many cities or city-regions have invested heavily, as was pointed out in an earlier chapter, in setting up new research parks for the purpose of attracting high-tech firms, the majority of which are relatively small in size and prefer an environment in which they can interact with others. Towns or cities that host the corporate headquarters of major global high-tech firms have also benefited, such as

Espoo, Finland, the home of mobile phone giant Nokia, or Walldorf, Germany, the headquarters town of SAP, one of the world's largest business software firms.

This highly visible trend has given rise to the notion that the industrial landscape of Europe is being regenerated as a series of micro-regions containing specialized networks of high-technology firms. There are other manufacturing sectors that also appear to be undergoing a similar process of regional agglomeration and networking, such as designer clothing in northern Italy. But it is also important to remember that there is much in the manufacturing sector that is traditionally organized and located, and that the old remains every bit as important as the new.

## The Service Sector

It is an inescapable fact that Europe's economy has become increasingly service-oriented and that a large part of the employment losses that have occurred in other sectors have been absorbed by the service industries. Indeed, service is the only sector that has generated an increased number of jobs over the past two decades. It now accounts for more than half of all employment in nearly every European country. The only exceptions are Romania and Moldova, both of which still have very large agricultural sectors, and war-torn Bosnia and Macedonia.

The move toward a service economy is most advanced, as one might expect, in the economic heartland of northwestern Europe, where more than three-quarters of the working population hold service jobs of one kind or another. In two west European countries, the Netherlands and tiny Luxembourg, the proportion of service industry workers exceeds 80%! The dominance of service employment over all other forms then shades off as one travels away from the core regions of western and northern Europe. Ireland, Iceland, and Finland, along with all of west-central Europe and the western Mediterranean countries of Italy and Spain, form the immediate periphery. They are followed in turn by Portugal, Estonia, Latvia, and the

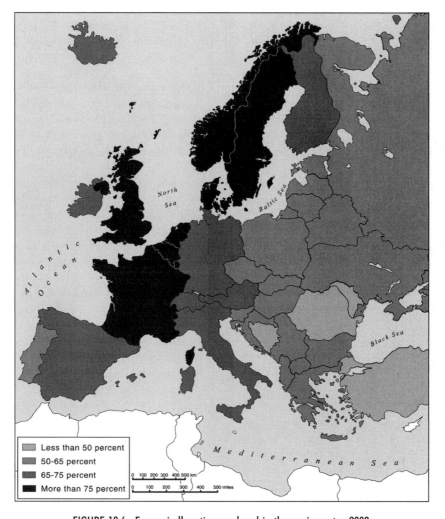

FIGURE 10.6. Economically active employed in the service sector, 2000.

countries of east-central Europe, eastern Europe, and the Balkans. The entire pattern is roughly concentric and classically reflective of what we generally understand to be the "core to periphery" sequence of European economic development.

The largest service industry sector in the West is the distributive services, consisting predominantly of retailers and their suppliers. The EU, which keeps detailed economic statistics, counts more than 5 million distributive enterprises within the 15 pre-enlargement member states, employing nearly 22 million people, or roughly one-fifth of all workers. Most European retailing enterprises are small to medium-sized establishments, al-

though the numbers of large chain stores, hypermarkets, and discount outlets have long been on the rise, especially in some western countries. The United Kingdom has been a leader in this trend, as have France, Spain, and Italy.

Other commonly recognized nongovernmental service categories include finance, communications, transportation, and the so-called hotel, restaurant, and cafe sector. Of these, the financial sector, which consists primarily of the banking and insurance industries, is proportionately the most important. Also, as one of the most exposed sectors to ongoing forces of globalization and deregulation, it is both growing and changing very rapidly.

Communications and transportation is the least important as an employer, despite its reputation as the focal point of the global information society. Employment in communications and transportation is also heavily concentrated in large firms—a legacy of a disappearing era of state-owned monopolies. The hotel, restaurant, and cafe sector is the most dispersed, with most establishments (94%) employing fewer than nine people.

The fastest-growing of the service sectors, however, is "producer services," which is made up of firms that provide other firms with specialized forms of assistance and support. These specialized business services include such things as computer and software support, financial and legal consulting, market research, and security protection. Over the past decade, the number of producer services enterprises has doubled in most countries. Growth has been especially dynamic in the continent's economic heartland. In a handful of western countries—the Netherlands, Germany, France, Luxembourg, and the United Kingdom—this sector now claims over a quarter of the total economy, and in the Netherlands over a quarter of all workers. Producer services tend to be concentrated, as one might expect, in the larger metropolitan areas and cities. Because it is such a primary component of today's restructured economies, the possession of a healthy producer

services establishment has become one of the most essential factors in the competition among cities to attract new investment and employment.

The rapid rise of a private service sector in the former socialist countries of east-central and eastern Europe since 1990 has been most remarkable, especially in light of the fact that it has been created almost from scratch. According to recent EU statistics on the eight new member countries in east-central Europe, nearly 2.5 million private service enterprises were created in these countries during just the first half-dozen years following the fall of the Berlin Wall, with Hungary (which began privatizing even before the 1989 and 1990 revolutions), Slovenia, Poland, the Baltic States, and the Czech Republic leading the way. In all countries, these new ventures have been largely the product of local entrepreneurship. Relatively few enterprises have benefited from outside capital. Most are small-scale, employing only a few people. Many are "micro-enterprises," operated in many cases by people who probably hold another job. In only rare cases have they resulted from the privatization of state-owned concerns.

At the same time, there is ample evidence that the going has been tough and that over the short term the number of such enterprises in the former socialist countries is likely to de-

**FIGURE 10.7. Franchise.** One overnight European business success story is Telepizza. This fast-food franchise began in Spain and rapidly spread over all of western Europe. The rapidly expanding company has opened branches in Poland and Romania as well as in such far-flung places as Chile and Mexico. It is also setting up in the Maghreb. Seen here in Paris is a typical franchise outlet, with its trademark motorbike delivery vehicles lined up outside.

**FIGURE 10.8. Entrepreneurship.** The 1990s saw an explosive increase in small service businesses in the new democracies of east-central and eastern Europe. One major growth area was the provision of security. This advertisement (in English for potential foreign business clients) offers around-the-clock protection to help deal with the dangers and pitfalls of the new capitalism.

cline. Many are already dormant and a majority face serious problems. In responding to survey questions, many entrepreneurs complain of high levels of competition due to the fact that too many enterprises have been set up and there is an insufficient number of customers with strong purchasing power or credit, as well as a lack of resources necessary to engage in the kinds of marketing activities necessary to make their small service businesses well known.

## Conditions of Employment

The length of time that Europeans spend at their jobs has declined steadily over the past half-century, a reflection both of the influence of organized labor and the transition to a service-oriented economy. In the 1950s a workweek that stretched to 45 hours or more was not unusual. Today, according to EU statistics, Europeans spend on average just under 40 hours per week (39.3 to be precise) at their jobs. Manufacturing workers put in slightly more time than service workers, while agricultural workers generally work longer hours, averaging a little over 43 hours per week.

There is considerable variation between countries. Workers put in the least amount of time in Belgium, Italy, and Denmark. Those in the Mediterranean countries of

Spain, Portugal, and Greece work longer hours—although the workday is customarily broken by a long mid-day break. In the United Kingdom, whose "long-hours" culture seems to stand apart from that of the rest of the continent, the average workweek remains unusually long at nearly 44 hours, although there has been a slight decrease in recent years. Moreover, nearly a quarter of British workers put in up to 48 hours per week, the maximum allowed under the EU "working-time directive" rules adopted in Britain in 1998. In contrast, the average proportion of workers putting in this much time across the EU is only around 9%. British workers are also more likely to work on Sunday. In France, on the other hand, the socialist government has recently moved to cut the workweek from 39 to 35 hours, albeit amid misgivings about the possible negative effect on the country's ability to compete in the marketplace.

To date, the French experiment, which has been phased in gradually (the average workweek now stands at 37.7 hours), has defied the dire predictions that the move would hurt productivity. In fact, French worker productivity has risen since the implementation of the shorter workweek, and unemployment has fallen sharply. In contrast British worker productivity remains lower than it is in most other western European countries. French hourly productivity has been shown to be one-third higher and German productivity one-quarter higher. Such differences, however, may be as much cultural as anything else. The French have perhaps enjoyed a longer trend toward flexible and temporary work practices, and French firms may be freer to find sensible ways of making good use of shorter working hours than their British counterparts.

Today's labor market has, in general, become far more flexible than it was just a decade ago. Europeans today are more likely than in the past to have part-time jobs, to be working under fixed-term contracts, and to be employed for greatly differing numbers of hours per week. In the EU in 1999, nearly one in five employees (18%) held part-time jobs, the vast majority of them (80%) women.

Another 13% were working under some kind of fixed-term contract. There is also a substantial, but often inestimable, share of employment that takes place in the so-called informal sector, where no reportable contracts exist (activities such as hairdressing, repairs of all kinds, and the making of goods at home). Particularly in Mediterranean countries, as well as across large parts of central and eastern Europe, such "flexible employment" in the "black economy" is widespread and often correlated with areas where "official unemployment" stands at relatively high levels. Its incidence is also on the rise in parts of northern and western Europe where it has previously been less important. What this means, when taken all together, is that traditional full-time work has come to be somewhat less important for a sizable segment of today's population.

Finally, as a consequence of the breaking down of national barriers to the movement of labor within the European Union, the potential labor market for an EU citizen has been opened up to include the entire EU space. This is reflected in a greater mobility of workers, particularly those in seasonal or in certain service industry jobs such as waiters, maids, and harvest or sanitation workers. It is also quite evident among business elites. Europe is rapidly developing a new cosmopolitan business class—much larger than in the past, fluent in several languages, essentially borderless, and aggressively nonnationalistic. This kind of mobility is, however, much less

evident among other professionals, such as doctors, lawyers and in some cases even academics, for whom legal barriers to permanent employment in other countries still remain. Nor does it seem to apply very much to industrial and skilled workers. The huge labor migrations that many economists once predicted would follow the creation of open labor markets simply have not occurred. Throughout the restructuring of the 1990s, there has in fact been a marked stability of working populations, at both the regional and national levels. Only quite small percentages of EU citizens have actually moved to other countries for reasons of employment, although for younger and highly educated workers the trend is definitely upward.

In a few industries a shortfall of qualified labor within the EU is causing EU countries to look outside the Union. High-tech and computer specialists have been shown to be especially prominent among these. Skilled labor shortages in this rapidly expanding sector of the economy have created extraordinary pressures. Germany has, for example, recently begun accepting thousands of resumes from computer specialists in non-EU countries who are now eligible for special 3-year renewable work permits specifically targeted at workers who possess appropriate technology skills. Austria is also considering a short-term relaxation in its immigration laws to meet an anticipated deficit of thousands of skilled information technology workers. In

**FIGURE 10.9. Informal economy.** These African men are selling purses and handbags on a Rome street corner. Activities such as this are part of the informal economy, and may also, in this case, be part of the illegal migration problem.

the United Kingdom, the current shortfall of information-technology specialists is estimated at more than 200,000 workers. As in Germany, the government has recently announced plans to ease work permit requirements for companies who wish to recruit information technology workers from outside the EU.

## Unemployment

Western Europeans have experienced two distinct labor markets since the end of World War II. The first, which lasted into the mid-1970s and was associated with the so-called postwar economic miracle, was a period of relatively low unemployment. Indeed, many western countries were forced, as we have seen, to import foreign guest workers during this period in order to meet labor demands. Over the past quarter century there has been, however, an extended period of relatively high unemployment resulting from a series of economic downturns, ongoing processes of deindustrialization, and relatively low levels of job creation. Indeed, the persistence of double-digit unemployment during this period has plagued most western European economies. Governments have come under much criticism for their inability to develop economic policies that generate jobs on the same prodigious scale as the U.S. economy seems to have done during the same period. Indeed the term *Eurosclerosis* has entered the lexicon to describe the relative inelasticity of late 20th-century, as well as current, western European labor markets and economies.

Although the numbers rise and fall from time to time, the overall geography of unemployment in western Europe seems to have changed little over the past decade or two. There is, however, considerable regional variation. At the broadest scale, a clear core and periphery pattern exists. A core of more prosperous areas, where unemployment levels are relatively low, covers much of the European heartland from southeastern England to northern Italy. Beyond that is a peripheral belt of high unemployment that includes the traditional western and southern peripheries

of Ireland, Spain, Portugal, southern Italy and Greece, but also Sweden, Finland, and the former East Germany. At a more intimate scale, considerable variation exists within these larger zones. Many regions within the heartland that suffer from the eclipse of traditional industries exhibit persistently high unemployment rates. This has been particularly true of the old steel and coal areas of northern France and southern Belgium, the Saarland and Ruhr, and parts of the English Midlands, as well as some of the old shipbuilding areas. Meanwhile, other regions surrounding large metropolitan centers such as London or Brussels, or centers of new high-tech industries and services clusters such as Baden-Württemberg, Bavaria, or Emilia Romagna, have prospered and largely escaped the burden of high unemployment.

The socialist countries of east-central and eastern Europe also enjoyed a protracted period of full employment after World War II. Unlike the West, universally high levels of employment continued here through the 1970s and 1980s as a matter of public policy, although they were accompanied by seriously

FIGURE 10.10. **Deindustrialization.** Traditional heavy industries were hit hard during the last decades of the 20th century. Seen here is the gate to the Gdansk Shipyard (Stocznia Gdanska), where the famous Polish workers' movement Solidarity staged an uprising in August 1980. Their protest caught the world's attention and played a major role in sparking a gathering tide of rebellion within east-central Europe that eventually brought socialist rule to an end. The Gdansk Shipyard, however, has been no more immune than other heavy industry to the pressures of today's economy, suffering bankruptcy in 1996.

declining levels of productivity that resulted in part from problems of labor redundancy and absenteeism. The market economy transitions of the 1990s, however, have led to widespread and unusually high levels of unemployment, reduced living standards, and increased job insecurity, often accompanied by a sharp rise in self-destructive behavior, especially among men. Such problems have been particularly evident in parts of Russia, Ukraine, and the Balkans, but also in other east-central and eastern European countries. Most of the formerly socialist countries posted a rise in unemployment percentage rates from zero or negligible to the middle- or even high-teens by the mid-1990s. These levels have eased off more recently, however. A recent EU-sponsored report assessing the labor market in the countries of east-central Europe found an average unemployment rate of around 13%—considerably higher than the average figure of a little over 9% for the countries of the EU, to be sure, but better than just a few years earlier. There is, however, little prospect of ever returning to pretransition employment levels, which has necessitated a considerable readjustment in the labor market expectations of a significant segment of the population. One consequence has been the rising specter of what some have referred to as a "postsocialist underclass."

Nonetheless, overall rates of participation in the labor market, despite the difficulties of the transition period, remain higher overall than those found in the West, part of which has to do with higher levels of female participation in the East. During the socialist years in eastern Europe, women were strongly encouraged to participate in the labor force. They were in a sense "emancipated" from domesticity, although not entirely so, since they were still expected to shoulder family responsibilities. Nonetheless, female participation was everywhere high, and women made real and substantial inroads into many of the professions, in addition to taking traditional jobs in the services and labor-intensive sectors of industry and agriculture.

Indeed, one of the many difficulties associated with the transition from a planned to a market economy in the former East Germany has been the severe dislocation of a labor market in which female participation had been much higher than in West Germany. At the time of reunification, women's share of the East German labor market was around 47%, as compared to something less than 40% in the Federal Republic, where female participation levels have traditionally been among the lowest in Europe. Such relatively high levels of participation had long been promoted in East Germany, as in other socialist states, for ideological reasons as well as to meet the needs of the economy. They had been made possible by social policy measures designed to lessen conflicts between workforce participation and family responsibility, such as provisions for on-site child care, work leaves, and financial grants. Although women had been accorded an official equality in the workplace with men under the old state regime, a gender bias seems to have remained beneath the surface. For under the pressures of restructuring, it has been women who have been most strongly affected by cutbacks in employment and in child care services used to employ women. Within a short time after reunification, unemployment among women in the former territory of the old German Democratic Republic rose from nearly zero to more than 20%. For many East German women, reunification brought not only unemployment but also an unanticipated sense of confusion over their role in economic life outside the home.

## Feminization

While women's participation in the labor force has long been high in the socialist East, the feminization of the labor force in the West has been a more recent and much more varied phenomenon. Important to the process have been the ongoing changes in the employment structure toward increased services, which has greatly expanded the kinds of part-time and flexible employment opportunities so often regarded in many western societies as especially attractive to females. The rise in women's work and careers must also be seen in the context of a revolution in attitudes. In most western countries there was once a very strong negative relationship between female participation in the labor force and the presence of children. Recent studies, however, show ever-increasing overall levels of women's employment and a marked decline in the traditional "braking effect" of child rearing. According to EU surveys, 42% of women reportedly stop work because of child-rearing responsibilities, but there is evidence that women are generally returning to work sooner after having children and are becoming more persistent in their engagement with work outside the household.

Studies have also shown that there seem to be three distinctive European types or pat-

terns of female participation. The first features a very high rate of participation, in which women are engaged in paid work for most of their working lives. In this type the work pattern for women is much the same as for men; and even though substantial numbers of female employees are part-time workers, the hours worked are relatively long, the jobs tend to have status, and they are often relatively well paid. This type seems to exist across much of east-central and eastern Europe, in Scandinavia, and until recently in eastern Germany. A second type, which is more typical of the core regions of northwestern Europe, exhibits more moderate rates of participation. Here the age-specific pattern of

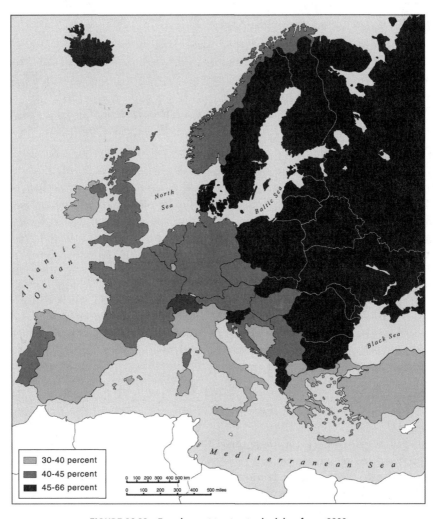

FIGURE 10.11.  Female participation in the labor force, 2000.

women's work is bimodal, with women starting out as full participants, then exiting the labor market during child-rearing years, but returning, usually to part-time work, when their children reach school age. In contrast to the first type, work tends to be for shorter hours and more often is concentrated in traditional female sectors, such as clerical or retailing work, with lower pay and fewer employment rights. The third type predominates in the Mediterranean South as well as along the western Atlantic fringe. It is characterized by relatively high initial participation rates but then a more or less permanent exit from the labor force in favor of homemaking and child rearing. According to a 1997 EU poll asking women to describe what they did for a living, 60% of women in Ireland identified themselves as "housewives," as did 49% in Spain, 42% in Greece, and 40% in Italy. This is in sharp contrast, for example, to Denmark, where only 4% responded in the same way.

Explanations for these patterns are many. Part of it is cultural or ideological. Catholic countries have usually placed greater emphasis on traditional patterns of patriarchy and household structure, while socialist countries have placed greater emphasis on social equality. These differences can also be explained as simple reflections of historical patterns of labor demand—northern and western European countries have experienced significant labor shortages, while Mediterranean countries and peripheral western regions have not. Deindustrialization and the expansion of a service sector rich in part-time job opportunities have also been strongest in the countries of northern and western Europe. And finally, employers in different parts of Europe have used part-time jobs to satisfy different needs. It is also important to remember that even within countries there are differences, for example, between rural and urban areas, and among regions.

Inequality in the value placed on the labors of women and men in the workplace is a persistent feature of our society, and it comes as no surprise that on average European women earn less than men. According to the latest EU data, it would appear that women, on av-

FIGURE 10.12. **Women's work.** In rural areas on Europe's periphery, where agricultural economies are most traditional, the woman's role has changed little from what it has always been—a grueling combination of domestic chores and field labor, burdened further by responsibility for child rearing. Seen here is a Turkish peasant woman on her way into the fields to harvest apricots. (Photo: J. L. Kramer)

erage, currently earn roughly one-fourth less than their male counterparts. Even when some of the structural differences between the employment circumstances of women and men are removed—for example, the fact that women generally work different kinds of jobs and are on average younger and less educated than men—and the focus is placed on pay differences among people who have the same qualifications and job characteristics, women still earn 15% less than men. The geography of pay differentials between the sexes corresponds closely to that of the above-mentioned three types of female participation—that is, the least inequality is found in eastern Europe, Scandinavia, and in the new *Länder* of Germany (former East Germany). Conversely, the highest levels of inequality are found in the Mediterranean countries and in Ireland, although levels of inequality are also relatively high in the United Kingdom, Austria, and the Netherlands.

## EDUCATION AND TRAINING

There is no doubt that in today's era of relatively high unemployment and rising demand for workers who possess advanced qualifications, greater and greater emphasis is being placed on education and training. As compared to just a few decades ago, young people in Europe are spending more time in school and taking longer to make the transition from school to career employment. Nor is the boundary between the two as clearly demarcated as it once was. Europe's young people find it far more difficult to enter the labor force today than their counterparts did in the 1950s and 1960s, and public authorities have responded by extending and placing a higher priority on educational systems.

### Trends

Today's conceptions of the beginning and end of youthful learning and preparation are widening. At one end of the educational system, it has become increasingly common for children of 4 years, and even 3 years, to be enrolled in preprimary education. EU data show that 50% of all 4-year-old children participated in some form of pre-primary education in 1997. In many western countries, such as Belgium, France, Italy, Spain, and the United Kingdom, the level of participation was over 90%. In the first three countries listed above, participation at the 90% or greater level even extended down to 3-year-olds. Although levels are overall somewhat lower, a similar extension of formal education for preprimary age groups seems to be under way in other parts of Europe as well. At the other end of the educational system, the numbers in which and the ages at which young people are engaged in various forms of higher education or vocational training have also risen sharply since the 1960s. It is no longer unusual for young people to continue their education beyond the age of 20. Indeed, the upper limit for education is now often regarded as 30.

Concomitant with the trend for later and longer education is the fact that young people are staying in the parental home far longer than in the past, often well into their 20s. Whereas an early departure from home for the purpose of becoming independent was relatively common among young people in the 1960s and 1970s, especially in northern Europe, the last couple of decades has seen a marked reversal of the trend. EU-wide, it is estimated that some 65% of young people, aged 20 to 24, now live with their parents, and surveys suggest that a majority see "living at home" as a good thing. This trend, as one might expect, parallels today's tendency for delayed formation of unions and families noted in Chapter 3.

The currently high emphasis placed on education and training received its initial impetus during Europe's long period of postwar economic growth between 1950 and 1973. Labor

FIGURE 10.13. Education. Uniformed schoolchildren head off to school in the early-morning hours on a Istanbul street. Europe's population is highly educated, with near universal literacy in all countries. Attaining the appropriate knowledge and skills to make a living in today's society requires an increasingly long period of education, extending well into their 20s for many people.

shortages in many countries during this period underlined the need for highly qualified workers. This was accompanied by a parental desire to see their children better qualified for the workforce and a general move toward the democratization or opening up of access to educational systems, many of which were traditionally elitist in nature. A slowdown in the economy and rising levels of unemployment in the late 1970s and during the 1980s then precipitated a long-term trend toward greatly expanded and accelerated participation in education, which continues right up to the present time. Ever greater demands for technical expertise and knowledge on the part of workers has also raised the level of education and training necessary to succeed in the marketplace.

The official policies of the EU, as well as of individual countries, have encouraged the trend. The EU made improving vocational qualifications one of the priorities of the 1992 Maastricht Treaty and has reiterated the importance of this goal at subsequent summits and meetings. National examples are many. Ireland, which established a free and open educational system in the 1960s, became a magnet for high-tech investment by instituting educational policies in the 1970s and 1980s that produced one of the world's best-educated workforces, particularly in the fields of science and technology. France has broadened and reformed its educational system a number of times since a period of intense student dissatisfaction in the 1960s. The notoriously difficult *baccalauréat* exam, which has performed the function of determining who is admitted to France's traditionally elitist university system since 1808, has been moderated and democratized over the past 30 years to the point that more than three-quarters of those who take it today are able to pass. It has also been extended beyond the three classical exams in the sciences, literature, and economics to include testing across a wide range of technical subjects. Reforms in Britain's educational system have done much to extend both its accessibility and content. In 1998, for example, the British government launched a high visibility 5-year program intended to raise standards and make British youth more competitive in the marketplace.

At the same time that the comprehensiveness and quality of European education is on the rise, there is a growing challenge to provide an adequate supply of primary and secondary teachers. According to EU data, an alarming proportion of trained teachers are nearing retirement age. In many states we are seeing reports suggesting that as many as one teacher in five will retire in the next 5–10 years. In such countries as Sweden, Germany, Austria, and Italy, the situation is particularly acute, prompting real concern over potential shortages. Sweden has already experienced teacher shortages, especially in the northern parts of the country and in the primary grades. Fed up with low salaries and recognition, there have even been reports that some Swedish educators have actually begun to offer their services to the highest bidder via Internet auction.

## National Distinctions

While overall these trends seem to extend across Europe, there are of course differences based on national or cultural traditions. No two countries seem to have quite the same approach to education, despite the widespread respect for learning that seems to prevail everywhere. Moreover, education is one arena in which the EU so far has only modest influence. Educational policies and standards are traditionally the domain of national or, in some cases, local governing bodies.

Despite, for example, the widespread trend for longer periods of schooling, the duration of educational training varies widely among countries. While within the EU as a whole half of all 20-year-olds are still in school today, in Britain, Denmark, and Austria half of all young people have left school by the age of 16 or 17. Meanwhile, in France and Belgium half are still in school until at least the age of 22. The variation reflects the complexity of career routes taken by young people in different national situations. In countries like France and Belgium, and to a somewhat lesser extent in the Mediterranean countries, the most common sequence is a lengthy period of formal training followed by direct integration into the labor market. Young people in these countries are less likely to receive vocational training as opposed to general education courses as part of their secondary-level schooling (Italy is the exception). The experience of young people in other countries is more mixed. In west-central European countries such as Denmark, Germany, Austria, and the Netherlands, there are high proportions of young people who are simultaneously engaged in training and active in the labor market. Students in these countries are also more likely to pursue vocational training courses as part of the secondary school curriculum and to take advantage of formal links between courses and on-the-job training provided by employers. In Britain, where participation in the world of work seems to come earliest, there is both a high incidence of early and direct entry into the labor market and of studying while working in order to get a better job.

In addition to rather striking differences in the importance and form of vocational training, national education systems differ in a variety of other ways. There are real but diminishing differences in the degree to which educational systems are geared toward universal training versus the education of an elite. Reforms in both the English and French systems have moved them significantly away from their elitist historical foundations, although vestiges of the past are still quite visible. The practice of segregated schooling, in which students pursuing different courses of study are tracked into different schools, has a long tradition in German-speaking countries. Common secondary schools were, in contrast, adopted early in the Scandinavian countries. Some countries have taken steps to temper the competitiveness of the educational experience. Denmark, for example, has eliminated any kind of tracking up to age 16 and refrains from marking student achievement until the last 3 years of lower secondary education. Italy abolished grades and exams in 1977, substituting a personal record that is maintained by teachers and shared with parents every 3–4 months.

There are also important differences in the degree to which education is administered locally versus centrally. In France, across much of the Mediterranean, and in eastern and east-central Europe, school systems are centrally administrated, whereas in Britain schools have a long tradition of local control, although a growing centralization of curricular authority and funding has certainly taken place since the 1980s. In Scandinavia, there is a tradition of local organization and responsibility at the primary level but less so at the secondary level. The Netherlands is unique in that there are parallel systems of Protestant, Catholic, and public schools, all of which are state-funded but not necessarily centrally controlled. Germany, with its strong federal structure, devolves responsibility for education onto the individual *Länder*.

Education also differs in intensity and emphasis. Mediterranean countries generally require more hours of school than do the countries in northern Europe. The annual number of classroom hours required of 16-year-olds who have opted for the "science" track is, for example, nearly one-third less in such countries as Sweden, Germany, and Britain than in Spain and Portugal. Until recently, school days in Germany were confined largely to the morning hours. Some countries devote much more time to the humanities than others. There are also wide discrepancies in linguistic training. Romance language countries are generally more inclined to favor instruction in the mother tongue over foreign languages, although Britain and Ireland are perhaps unique among European countries in that foreign language instruction is not a compulsory part of the primary school curriculum.

There has, however, been a more or less universal trend toward expanding the emphasis placed on foreign language training, principally by extending the period over which students are required to take a foreign language. France, for example, has experimented since 1989 with introducing students to foreign language study earlier than before, during the last 2 years of primary school. Spanish children now begin studying foreign languages 3 years earlier than their counterparts did a decade ago. This earlier and longer trend in language training follows a EU initiative, "Europe in the classroom," which advocates placing increasing emphasis in the curriculum on European unity and integration.

The recommendation adopted by the EU ministers of education and cultural affairs calls for the incorporation of a heightened awareness of "Europe" in common social studies classroom subjects such as geography, history, economics, and political science, as well as an earlier introduction of foreign languages into the curriculum.

## Higher Education

European systems of higher education have moved inexorably over the past 30 years toward an American-style mass-production process. As a result, enrollment in university and polytechnic institutions has risen sharply. Between 1980 and 1995 there was a 75% in-

crease in students in higher education within the then 15 countries of the EU. Some countries, notably Greece, Ireland, and Britain, posted increases well in excess of 100%. At the same time higher education became more open to women. In 1995 there were 103 women per 100 men in higher education across the EU, which means that the gender gap had all but disappeared among EU countries, with the exception of Germany, where the participation of women remained significantly lower.

One consequence of all this growth is that nearly all European systems of higher education have been faced with difficulties of adaptation and change. In France and Germany, both of which opened their universities to a

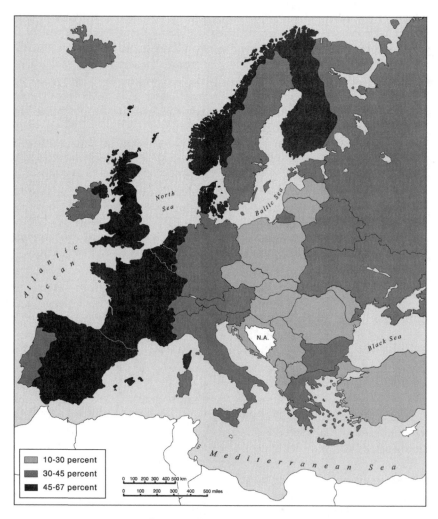

FIGURE 10.14. Education—third-level gross enrollment ratio, 1996.

broader segment of society in the wake of student unrest and public criticism in the 1960s,
resources have lagged far behind growing student numbers. The French system has been
described as literally straining at the seams, a
situation that has generated calls for a shift
back toward higher requirements for those
entering the university. German universities,
which lack formal structures that push students through to degrees in a timely manner,
are chronically overcrowded and slow to produce graduates. Indeed, less than a fifth of the
students who enter German universities ever
actually get a degree. German universities
have also suffered terribly from stagnant
funding. Dutch universities have recently responded to similar problems by tightening requirements and forcing universities to accelerate the processing of students. Over the last
decade or two, Britain's system of higher education has undergone some of the most radical changes. The system has been broadened
to include a whole new tier of colleges and
polytechnics, a process that doubled the number of institutions with "university status." Its
institutions have also been forced to compete
with one another, under a system of periodic
nationwide quality reviews of research and
teaching, to attract both more students and a
larger share of ever scarcer resources.

The problems of universities in the formerly socialist countries of eastern and east-
central Europe are particularly pressing.
Under socialist regimes, higher education was
well supported. It received a high priority and
could boast of modern facilities and adequate
funding, although researchers, teachers, and
students were often subject to unwanted political influence. Since the fall of communism,
however, university systems in these countries have been beset by drastic declines in
funding. Severe shortages of money have had
devastating effects on the morale of educators
and researchers and on efforts to reform the
systems and bring them more into line with
their western counterparts. One legacy of the
socialist past, for example, is the division of
faculty into separate institutions for teaching
and research, the latter of which were more
highly privileged with resources. Current
thinking favors both an updating of curricula

FIGURE 10.15. Gustavium. Europe has a long and distinguished
tradition of university education. This photo is of the Gustavium, for
long the main building of Uppsala University—the first to be founded
in Scandinavia (1477). The Gustavium was built in the 1620s by the
Swedish King Gustavus Adolphus, who was a major benefactor of the
university and for whom the building was named. The onion-shaped
dome was added later in order to build an amphitheatre for the university's Renaissance genius, Olof Rudbeck, who made pioneering discoveries about the human lymphatic system. The domed amphitheater
provided a space where dissections could be performed under adequate
lighting.

and the merging of research and teaching institutions to bring researchers and students
back into contact. Progress on such reforms,
however, is exasperatingly slow. Moreover,
the problems are exacerbated by a rapid expansion in student numbers. The number of
students matriculated at Warsaw University,
for example, nearly doubled during the 1990s.
At the same time, and rather ironically, there
has been a troubling shortage of students and
faculty in the sciences, as talent has drifted
away from the universities to better opportunities in an emerging market economy.

Perhaps the most recent development that
brings European higher education closer to
a more American-style system is a EU-
sponsored accord, now agreed to by 32 countries, to introduce a single system of awarding
degrees. Between now and 2010, the signatories have agreed to replace traditional degrees
and degree programs with a 3-year undergraduate degree and a 2-year master's degree.
The aim is to eliminate the confusion caused
by the current bewildering array of national
degree systems by establishing one univer-

sally accepted, or "portable," degree system. The change is expected to increase job mobility across Europe. It is also expected to produce a rush of new applicants to MBA programs, which currently lag behind their American counterparts in popularity and acceptability. As students are freed from the burden of previously lengthy university degree programs, it is anticipated that they may be more likely to choose to continue their education at international business schools.

Another area of impending change has to do with the funding of higher education. The belief that higher education is a public good and that the costs of access to it, for those who are qualified, should be borne by the state has always been held strongly in Europe, much in contrast to the United States, where students or their families are required to make substantial contributions to the cost of their education in the form of tuition and fees. However, the rapid democratization of European education in recent years and the concomitant failure of public funding to keep pace have begun to undermine this formerly unassailable ideal. Although not yet a universal trend, there are clear signs that costs in the future may be increasingly shifted from the state to students.

This has particularly been the case in Mediterranean and in some of the former socialist countries, where private contributions, either in the form of increased fees or through growing enrollments in for-profit institutions of higher learning, have been on the rise since the mid-1990s. Faced with limited opportunities to take up meaningful studies in cash-strapped state institutions, a growing number of eastern Europeans have shown themselves willing to pay for courses of study offered by newly founded institutions financed through private tuition payments. Especially in demand is high-quality training in business, law, computing, and foreign languages—all areas seen by residents of the former socialist East as essential to getting ahead in today's free-market economy. Some east-central European countries, such as Poland, Romania, and Hungary, as well as most of the former Soviet states have been quick to pass legislation opening the field to private colleges and universities. One of the leaders in this trend is Poland, which is now home to nearly 200 private institutions of higher education, many of them business schools, with a rather astounding combined enrollment of nearly 400,000 students, more than one-quarter of all higher education students in the country. Romania is said to have roughly 130,000 students enrolled in more than 50 private tuition-financed institutions, and Hungary claims nearly 30,000 attending 32 different private institutions. A few east-central European states, such as the Czech Republic, have proceeded a bit more cautiously, but now seem resigned to follow along much the same path.

Such an overt trend toward fee-based higher education has generally not been the case in western Europe, although in some countries precedents have already been set for a future move toward requiring the payment of fees. Within Germany the State of Baden Württemberg has experimented with a scheme that imposes fees on students whose university studies have extended beyond 6½ years. When other German länder began to consider doing the same or, worse yet, charging fees to all students, a storm of protest forced the German government to pass legislation banning fees for anyone earning their first degree. In Britain, where the idea of introducing tuition fees has long been a matter of public discussion, no action has yet been taken. Proponents see "top up" fees, as they are called in Britain, as an effective means of bringing funds into the nation's cash-starved higher education system and of relieving those who do not get a university education from the burden of paying for those who do. On the other hand, the imposition of fees is opposed by many in the middle and working classes, who view it as a loss of entitlement and as a potential barrier placed across the path to higher education for children of poor families.

One other interesting development in higher education that has received substantial support from the EU is the movement of students across national boundaries to study in other countries. Whereas the opportunity to study abroad was once restricted to the sons and daughters of Europe's elite, the EU is

FIGURE 10.16. **Bosporus University.** One interesting institution of higher education is Bosporus University in Istanbul. Originally founded in 1863 as Robert's College, the institution was the gift of New England philanthropist Christopher R. Robert and other Americans who wished to encourage the higher education of Turkish men. In 1971 the college became a state institution and was renamed Bosporus University. This photo of the quad looks as though it could have been taken at any small New England college.

now funding a program that enables students to attend courses lasting between 3 months and a year in any of 29 participating European countries, and to have that time credited to their degree course. Known as "Erasmus," the program has enjoyed remarkable success. Since its inception at the end of the 1980s, participation has grown by roughly 8–10% a year, so that by the 1998–1999 academic year 181,000 students had taken part. Among participant countries the United Kingdom is the most popular destination for foreign students, followed by Germany and France. Nonetheless, taken as a whole, mobility remains relatively low, affecting only a very small proportion of the entire EU university population.

## WEALTH

Economically, the decades since World War II have been remarkably good ones for Europe overall. To be sure, western Europeans have experienced periods of recession and stagnation, and eastern Europeans have of course endured the economic deprivations of communism's decline and, more recently, the turbulent transition toward a market economy. Few could say today, however, that they are not materially better off than generations that have gone before them, or that Europe does not generally enjoy what might be regarded by global standards as remarkably

high levels of prosperity and well-being. Indeed, Europe has long been, and continues to be, one of the great players in the global economy. As measured by gross national product (GNP), Europe claims 5 of the world's 10 largest economies. The economies of Germany, the United Kingdom, France, and Italy rank 3rd, 4th, 5th, and 6th, respectively, behind the "mega-economies" of the United States and Japan, while Spain's comes in at 10th, behind those of China, Brazil, and Canada. In particular, western Europe, in the form of the EU, constitutes a major trading bloc on the world stage; the combined economic weight of its 15 pre-enlargement member countries exceeds that of the United States. Europe as a whole is a relatively wealthy part of the world and continues to grow in prosperity relative to much of the world. For most of the latter half of the past century, Europe's annual growth in GNP has been at or above average world rates.

Although relatively prosperous overall, there are clear differences in the wealth of individual European countries, and especially between East and West. Per capita GNP is highest in Luxembourg, Switzerland, Norway, and Denmark, where it exceeds $30,000 a year by rather substantial margins. By comparison, the figure for the United States is around $29,000. The remainder of Scandinavia and the core of continental western Europe follows close behind, with annual per-capita GNP figures falling in the $25–30,000 range. More moderate levels are found in the peripheral EU countries of Ireland, the United Kingdom, Spain, Portugal, Italy, Greece, and Finland. Far more modest levels pertain across the entirety of the former socialist states of east-central and eastern Europe. Among these, the various recently admitted EU states can claim relatively higher levels of national wealth, although these levels are still only one-quarter to one-half of the norm in the West, with the exceptions of Slovenia and the Czech Republic. For a relatively large number of the remainder, per-capita GNP barely exceeds $1,000. In the case of poor Albania and Moldova, it is only $760 and $460, respectively.

The significance of differences in GNP per capita among countries is not always clear. The figures often mask differences in the relative domestic buying power of local currencies and the specific circumstances of local market conditions. One way of better approximating relative income is to adjust for these factors by converting GNP per capita to a measure known as Purchasing Power Parity (PPP). When this is done and applied to Europe, several things happen. First the wealthier western continental core of the EU expands outward to include the United Kingdom, Italy, and Finland. Only Ireland, Spain, Portugal and Greece now remain on

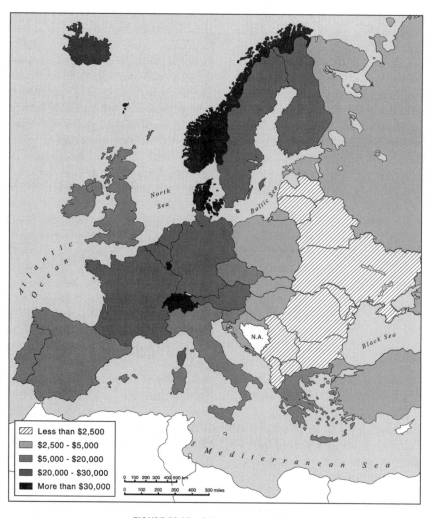

FIGURE 10.17. GNP per capita, 2000.

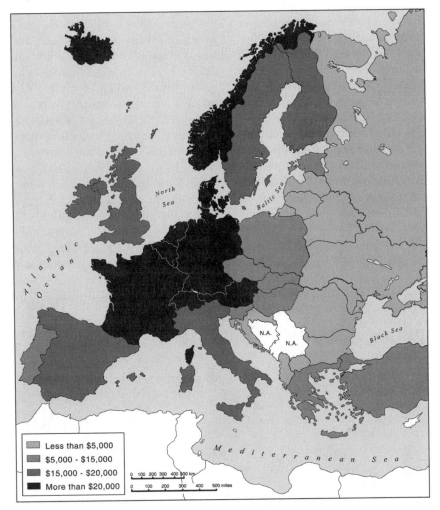

FIGURE 10.18. Purchasing power parity (PPP) per capita, 2000.

the more "moderately wealthy" periphery. Central and eastern Europe look much the same, although two of the new additions to the EU, Slovenia and the Czech Republic, are now elevated to join the other moderately wealthy states.

Another important distinction revealed when the PPP is used is that the absolute difference, if not the relative difference, between the West and the East is lessened, thereby softening the impression that the East is completely impoverished compared to the West. Differences within West and East also become less apparent. Individual purchasing power in the majority of the western countries is strongly clustered around the

$20,000 figure. The range among central and eastern European states is also smaller. Apart from relatively prosperous Slovenia and the Czech Republic, individual purchasing power in the remaining states cluster thickly around the $5,000 figure.

Income distribution is another useful measure of how countries may differ in terms of individual wealth accumulation. We generally think of the social democracies of western Europe as places where government taxation and wage policies have worked to lessen income extremes. We also think of the former socialist regimes of east-central and eastern Europe as having placed even greater emphasis on this goal during the postwar decades by overtly holding down the levels of compensation for many professionals and, of course, by barring the rise of any capitalist business class. This view is generally borne out by current data on income inequality. With the exception of Russia, where the rise of a new wealthy elite in the 1990s—the so-called New Russians—has been most marked, the majority of the former socialist states exhibit a very low ratio between the share of all household income held by the wealthiest 10% of all households and the share held by the poorest 20%. In the West, there is more variation. The Low Countries, Germany, Sweden, Spain, and Italy exhibit the lowest levels of income inequality, with relatively modest concentra-

tions of wealth at the top and relatively high levels of wealth at the bottom. Ireland, Britain, France, Austria, Denmark, Finland, and Iceland are somewhat more inclined to display upwardly skewed income distributions, while in Portugal and Norway a marked imbalance toward the top exists.

While income disparities in the West are greater than in the East, they are overall certainly less than in the United States. On the other hand, people do live in poverty, at least officially. According to EU data taken before the 2004 enlargement, roughly 18% of the population of the then member states fell below the official poverty line, which was defined as less than 60% of median national in-

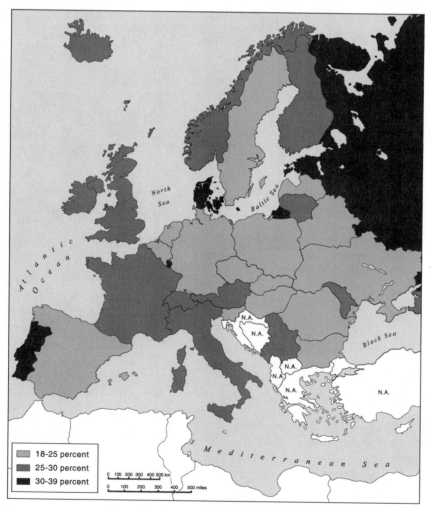

FIGURE 10.19. Income distribution: Proportion of household income received by the wealthiest 10% of all households, 2000.

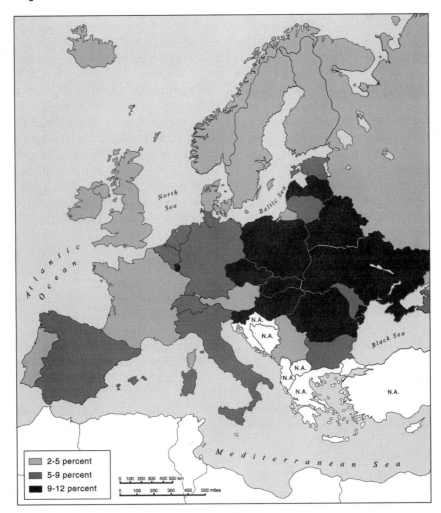

FIGURE 10.20. Income distribution: Proportion of household income received by the poorest 20% of all households, 2000.

come. The poverty rate was highest on the Mediterranean and Atlantic peripheries (Greece, Portugal, Ireland, and the United Kingdom), in isolated rural areas elsewhere, and in the immigrant quarters of many cities. It was lowest in the highly developed core areas of the northern and north-central states. Persistent unemployment and recent structural transformations in the economy have contributed in many parts of the West to a growing sense of barely making enough to make ends meet. The EU reports that nearly one-third of EU households claimed in 1999 that they couldn't afford a week's holiday away from home. This claim was especially common among Mediterranean households. More than half in Greece, Spain, and Portugal said this was true. But rather implausibly the perception also held in relatively prosperous Sweden, where 56 percent insisted on making the same claim.

The economic situation of households in the new democracies of east-central and eastern Europe is more difficult to assess. For all of these countries, the rather sudden transition from a planned economy to a market economy has been a dramatic experience that has raised a host of uncertainties. The national economies of most countries in this part of Europe had stalled during the 1980s, and their populations were already experiencing a slow and steady slippage in living standards. During the post-1989 transition, however, these economies were beset by a frightfully rapid and substantial decline. Output of services and goods dropped precipitously, unemployment and inflation rose, all at the same time that the social securities so long provided by the former socialist governments threatened to disappear.

Still, survey data suggest that poverty has not increased dramatically, particularly in the new democracies of east-central Europe. This is not to say that income levels have not fallen, but that the fall in income has been felt across most of the population and that the effects of the transition on individuals has been less dramatic than it has been on national economies as a whole. Data for east-central European countries do show a general increase in income inequality. These increases, however, are from fairly low levels to begin with and are still modest in comparison to those in the West. In many cases they are not at all dissimilar to increases in income inequality posted during the same period in such countries as Sweden, the United Kingdom, and the United States. Poverty levels have also increased, in some cases doubling, but again from relatively low levels to levels that are still modest by international standards. Moreover, at least in some of the east-central European states, like Poland and the Czech Republic, the situation of pensioners, who are normally thought to be most vulnerable, has actually improved because governments acted during the early years of the transition to protect pensions from the effects of inflation.

This, however, was certainly not the case, at least initially, in Russia and some other parts of the former Soviet Union, where many subsidies were eliminated or severely reduced. In fact, Russia stands out as one part of the East where some of the worst dislocations seem to have occurred. It is in Russia that the emergence of both a new and extravagantly wealthy capitalist class and an impoverished underclass has captured the most popular attention. But even for Russia, recent survey data show that most of the population has sufficient, if not abundant, income to make ends meet; that poverty is often transitional rather than persistent, with many families moving in and out of poverty over time; and that, where poverty is persistent, it most commonly affects children in families headed by single parents rather than pensioners, as is commonly assumed. Of all of former socialist Europe, Moldova holds the dubious honor of having suffered the most dramatic decline in personal income and growth in income inequality over the decade of the 1990s.

## WELFARE

Since the end of World War II Europeans, East and West, have come to expect levels of social protection that are both generous and comprehensive. By the standards of the United States, and most other parts of the world, Europeans have enjoyed a remarkably secure existence, knowing that they were protected by the "cradle to grave" welfare state from the privations that might result from a wide range of stressful conditions, such as unemployment, sickness, disability, as well as old age or survivorship. Many states have also provided, as a matter of course, liberal health benefits, free education, and a range of family-based benefits, such as child allowances, protected parental leave, and subsidized preschool and child care services.

Beginning in the 1990s, however, social security systems began to come under a great deal of pressure. In the West the pressures have been both economic and demographic. The rather long period of sustained and very high unemployment experienced by most countries over the last couple of decades has meant that a sizable proportion of the population has been dependent on state handouts, which in turn has severely strained the ability of governments to meet the costs of maintaining generous unemployment and social services programs. As we have seen in an earlier chapter, a steadily aging population has also meant that governments have been forced to pay out more in pensions and to meet ex-

**FIGURE 10.21. Pensioners.** Pensioners were one of the hardest-hit elements of the Russian population during the transition of the 1990s. Caught on fixed incomes in a time of rapid inflation and by a government that often fell behind on meeting its obligations to pay, many were forced to find seemingly desperate ways to make ends meet. In this scene, photographed in the mid-1990s, a long line of pensioners stands near the entrance to Moscow's Kazan station. Each person is holding bottled drinks and sandwiches, hoping to sell them to passing commuters.

tended demands on health services. Prognosticators now believe that the cost of pensions in France will top 16% of the country's gross domestic product (GDP) by midcentury—up from a current 12%, and more than four times the 4% of GDP spent on pensions in 1960. On top of all this, those countries that have worked to position themselves for membership in the "euro zone" have been forced to bear unusually severe budgetary pressures as they strive to meet the stringent fiscal requirements necessary for membership in the currency group, which has placed a severe squeeze on funds available for social security programs.

All of this has led to a spate of social spending cutbacks and political maneuvering over the future shape of social protection programs. Perhaps the greatest changes have come in Sweden—and these have possibly been the most shocking, because of the country's long reputation as Europe's leading welfare state. Indeed, Sweden stood out in 1990 as the only European country to commit more than half of all government spending to social security and welfare. By 1993, public spending in Sweden had grown to a high of 67.5% of GDP. The country, however, was hit in the early to mid-1990s by a major recession, which caused a severe budgetary crisis. Faced with rising unemployment and one of Europe's most rapidly aging populations, the

government was forced to undertake serious reforms of its generous pension system. Limitations on sick pay and reductions in child support benefits were also imposed, although the country's system of universal health care was largely maintained. Since 1997, the economic situation has improved and benefits have risen, but the Swedish welfare state today is less generous overall than it was just a decade ago.

Other western countries have faced similar problems and have attempted to curtail spending on social protection programs in various ways. Norway has devised more restrictive pension benefit regulations. Finland has reformed unemployment benefits. The Netherlands privatized its health benefits system. The Danes cut the duration of unemployment benefits and reformed the country's pension system. The Swiss both trimmed unemployment allowances and extended the waiting period for benefits. France embarked on major health care reform and looked for ways to cut social security costs. Germany, which was forced to deal with the economic burdens imposed by reunification in addition to other fiscal pressures, proposed changes in the retirement age and reductions in sick-leave pay. As part of its struggle to meet European Monetary Union requirements, Italy raised the minimum retirement age and overhauled its welfare system. Austria lowered welfare and unemployment benefits, and Britain moved to contain social spending and prevent social security fraud, most recently announcing a variety of welfare cuts as well as expressing an interest in raising the official retirement age. In short, nearly every western government faced a public spending dilemma during the 1990s and became engaged in loosening the social welfare safety net wherever it was politically feasible to do so. No country has yet seemed to hit on the perfect solution to the cost-control pressures of the times, and the experimentation will undoubtedly continue.

The shock to existing systems in the East came with the post-1989 transition away from communism. Initially, there was a sharp decline in health and social security benefits of all kinds due to the pressures exerted by the high levels of inflation and unemployment that accompanied the transition. In some countries there simply wasn't any money available to pay out, or runaway inflation cut so deeply into the value of benefits that they became virtually worthless to recipients. The new democracies of east-central and eastern Europe have, nonetheless, struggled to continue the payment of benefits. Indeed, most countries have attempted to raise payment levels and even introduce new protections, such as unemployment insurance. There has also been an effort to find ways to reform existing social security systems, such as experimenting with the establishment of privatized supplementary pension funds. By the mid- to late 1990s, the situation had largely stabilized, with most countries managing to maintain or improve slightly on pretransition social spending levels.

The mix of spending on social programs varies widely across Europe, depending on local circumstances. In the EU, where detailed statistics are kept, old age and survivorship benefits take the greatest share—an average of nearly half of all expenditures. As one might expect, the importance of these benefits for each country is related to the relative aging of its population. In western countries where the retirement age population exceeds 35% of total population (Austria, Bel-

gium, Denmark, France, Germany, Greece, Italy, Norway, and Sweden), expenditures on public pension programs currently exceed 10% of GDP. The only exception is the United Kingdom, where expenditures fall just short of that mark (9.5%). By comparison, expenditures in the United States stand at roughly 6.5% of GDP. Among the former socialist countries, where the proportion of retirement age people is generally lower, public pension expenditures as a percentage of GDP tend to run in the 6–8% range.

The burden of unemployment compensation has also grown substantially in recent years. In western Europe, persistent double-digit unemployment over the past couple of decades has made this form of social protection a major expense, while the former socialist countries, where unemployment officially did not exist prior to 1989, have been forced to launch unemployment insurance programs virtually from scratch. This was done out of necessity in the years immediately following 1989 as unemployment soared, and initially with unsustainable generosity. In 1990 Poland, for example, set unemployment compensation at 79% of average national earnings. Since the mid-1990s, program benefits in the former socialist states have been forced down to more affordably realistic levels. Eligibility rules have been tightened, and the duration of benefit periods has been shortened.

Most western countries—the exceptions being the United Kingdom and Ireland—continue to provide quite generous unemployment insurance coverage, usually with compensation levels in excess of 60% of average national earnings, and with layers of supplementary benefits, such as work training programs and unemployment assistance. The wisdom and sustainability of such policies, however, has become an important political issue. The extraordinarily generous benefits that exist in countries like Denmark, for example, have been criticized as an impediment to reducing levels of unemployment. The ready availability of relatively high unemployment benefits that extend over long periods of time can act as a fairly powerful disincentive to the search for employment. For this reason,

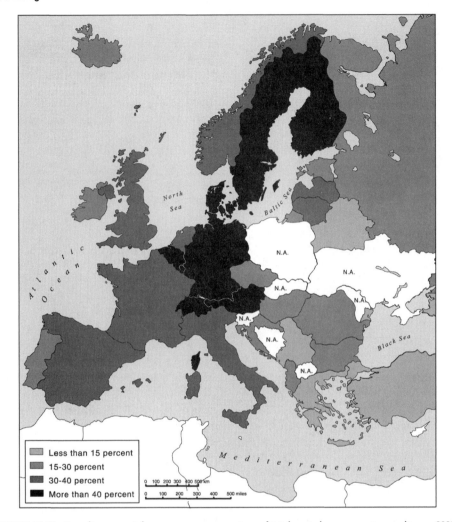

FIGURE 10.22. Spending on social programs as a percentage of total central government expenditures, 2000.

there has been a growing interest among policymakers in the curtailment of benefits as well as in experimentation with various "welfare to work" schemes.

Health care too is a major social cost that is largely borne in Europe through state-funded delivery systems. The most comprehensive systems are those that spend more than $2,000 per capita a year. These include, according to World Health Organization statistics, the Belgian, French, Danish, Dutch, German, Icelandic, Norwegian, and Swiss health care systems, all of which also invest better than 8% of national GDP in health care. Although the per-capita dollar invest-

ment is less, Austria, Croatia, Greece, and Slovenia also commit better than 8% of GDP. At the other end of the scale, Romania spends just $238 per person and only 3.8% of GDP, while Bulgarians on average receive $161 each for a total health expenditure of 3.9% of GDP. The United States, by comparison, spends $4,055 per person and 12.9% of GDP in a primarily private and for-profit health care system.

Like other social protection services, health care systems have come under stress in recent years. Fiscal restraints and reforms of various kinds have been imposed on the provision of health services in most western European

**FIGURE 10.23. Unemployment.** Relatively high levels of unemployment have become a more or less accepted norm across much of western Europe. Their arrival in the East, as a painful accompaniment to the transition to a market economy, has been more jarring, given the far less developed system of benefits and retraining opportunities in place in these countries. This man has spent the night on the streets of Budapest sleeping on a hard bench. (Photo: J. L. Kramer)

countries. People now complain in most countries of having to wait months, in some cases even years, for necessary operations. Cost-cutting moves have also resulted in reduced access to preventative care services and in substantial rollbacks in the state subsidies that reduce the out-of-pocket costs of medications. In countries where it is permitted, private health care insurance has become increasingly popular among those who can afford it. The trend has raised the specter that a multitiered system, in which the better care will go to the rich, will soon replace Europe's long tradition of universal health care provision. One country, the Netherlands, already requires people with higher incomes to take out private insurance. In the former socialist states, public health systems have suffered serious decline since the early 1990s due to dramatic budget cuts and the shifting of responsibilities from state to local authorities, in the worst cases leaving many poorer rural areas with virtually no access to effective modern health care.

Despite the changes and shocks of the 1990s, health and social protection throughout Europe remains strong by global standards. With relatively few exceptions, European governments routinely spend a quarter or more of their annual budget on social security and welfare programs of all kinds. The countries that proportionally commit the greatest overall investment to welfare and social protection programs are found in central and northern Europe. The Scandinavian states of Sweden, Finland, and Denmark spend proportionately more than anyone else, although considerably less than they did in 1990. They are followed closely by Germany, Austria, Switzerland, and Belgium. The rest of western Europe tends to spend less. Norway, the Netherlands, France, Italy, Spain, and the United Kingdom (just barely) form a secondary outer tier, while Iceland, Ireland, Portugal, and Greece, each of which have considerably lower levels of investment, sit on the periphery. Their relatively low level of investment is partly explained by demographic factors. Ireland, for example, is the youngest country in the EU, with roughly one-third of its population under 20 years of age and only a little more than one-tenth over 65. While Ireland's overall investment in social protection programs is among the EU's lowest, the country's spending on family and child benefits is higher than that of anyone else. The former socialist countries also sit on the periphery. In real terms, levels of investment there are perhaps lowest of all. While most currently spend at least 20% of GDP on social protection, that doesn't take into account the fact that GDP is often lower than it was during the socialist years.

In conclusion, then, we have seen quite ample evidence that Europeans enjoy a relatively high and secure standard of living. They find employment in a market-oriented and highly integrated service economy, belong to an increasingly highly educated and well-trained labor force, receive on the whole relatively generous compensation and benefits in return for their labor, and are comprehensively protected from personal misfortune and the vagaries of the marketplace by a far-ranging system of comprehensive health and social protection programs. All of these conditions have made Europe's population one of the most prosperous in the world. With this in mind, we now turn our attention in Chapter 11 to how Europeans make use of their considerable wealth as they consume and play.

## FURTHER READING

Amin, A., & Thrift, N. (Eds.). (1995). *Globalization, institutions, and regional development in Europe*. Oxford, UK: Oxford University Press.

Bailly, A. S. (1995). Producer services research in Europe. *Professional Geographer, 47*, 70–74.

Bloteevogel, H. H., & Fielding, A. J. (Eds.). (1997). *People, jobs and mobility in the New Europe*. Chichester, UK: Wiley.

Bradford, M. (1998). Education and welfare. In T. Unwin (Ed.), *A European geography* (pp. 261–273). Harlow, UK: Addison Wesley Longman.

Brock, C., & Tulasiewicz, W. (Eds.). (1996). *Education in a single Europe*. London: Routledge.

Carter, F. W., & Maik, W. (Eds.). (1999). *Shock-shift in an enlarged Europe: The geography of socioeconomic change in east-central Europe after 1989*. Aldershot, UK: Ashgate.

Fielding, T., & Blotevogel, H. (1994). *People, jobs, and mobility in the New Europe*. New York: Wiley.

Garcia-Ramon, M. D., & Monk, J. (Eds.). (1996). *Women of the European Union: the politics of work and daily life*. London: Routledge.

Loshkin, M., & Popkin, B. M. (1999). The emerging underclass in the Russian Federation: Income dynamics, 1992–1996. *Economic Development and Cultural Change, 47*, 803–829.

Pickles, J. (1995). Restructuring state enterprises: Industrial geography and eastern European transitions. *Geographische Zeitschrift, 83*, 114–131.

*Science*. (1996). Special issue: European universities in transition. *Science, 271*, 681–701.

Silbertson, A., & Raymond, C. P. (1996). *The changing industrial map of Europe*. New York: St. Martin's Press.

Smulders, G. W., Kompier, M. A. J., & Paoli, P. (1996). The work environment in the twelve EU-countries: Differences and similarities. *Human Relations, 49*, 1291–1313.

Stratigaki, M., & Vaiou, D. (1994). Women's work and informal activities in Southern Europe. *Environment and Planning A, 26*, 1221–1234.

Townsend, A. R. (1997). *Making a living in Europe: Human geographies of economic change*. London: Routledge.

Unwin, T. (1998). Agricultural change and rural stress in the new democracies. In D. Pinder (Ed.), *The new Europe: Economy, society and environment* (pp. 359–378). Chichester, UK: Wiley.

Williams, A. M. (1987). *The western European economy: A geography of post-war development*. London: Hutchinson.

# CHAPTER 11

# Consumption, Leisure, and Popular Culture

As Europeans became relatively more prosperous in the decades following World War II, they entered into a new age of heightened consumer tastes and consumption. This became especially true in the West, where access to fashionable and quality goods and enjoyments has long been a desirable and attainable goal for many. Indeed, for a lot of west Europeans the accumulation and display of material wealth has become an essential measure of social differentiation. Such things as the kind of automobile one drives and one's choice of residential property, vacation venue, or, most recently, cellular phone or digital television service are generally regarded as symbols of personal status and achievement. In the East, the desire to share more fully in this opulent consumer's world was partly behind the crisis of confidence in the socialist regimes that took place in the late 1980s. A long pent-up demand for conspicuous consumption remains an important, and as yet often unfulfilled, force in the various market economy transitions currently under way in the formerly socialist countries.

Our purpose in this chapter is to examine some of the major ways in which Europeans consume goods, spend their leisure time, and absorb popular culture. Where and how do

Europeans shop for necessities as well as luxury items, where do they choose to go on holiday, and how do they entertain themselves at home? As we explore these issues we will be especially interested in the trends currently under way in both the old democracies of the West and the new democracies of the East, and in the general question of whether we are witnessing a convergence or divergence of living standards, consumer tastes, and popular culture across European space.

## CONSUMPTION

Over the last quarter-century, Europeans have managed to translate their growing sense of prosperity and social security into a burgeoning "consumer culture." The importance of this culture of consumption has been greatest in the West, where it first arose and is so clearly dominant, but it is now well along in the process of diffusing, if somewhat unevenly, to all parts of the continent. What is happening is part of a worldwide trend, linked to the increasing globalization of information, services, and products. We now live in a global society in which precedence is given—above all else and despite humanistic, environmental, and religious strictures to the contrary—to the pursuit of the good life through consumption.

Europe's "boom" in consumer spending began rather dramatically in the mid-1980s, following a lengthy period of economic recession and uncertainty. This upsurge in consumer confidence coincided with the general optimism or "Europhoria" that surrounded new initiatives set in place with the 1985 Single European Act that swept away a whole range of barriers to cross-border business by 1992. It was fueled in part by low interest rates, and was both cause and effect of a revolution in credit and banking, which saw an explosion in the number of credit cards in circulation and the advent of the ubiquitous cash-dispensing machine. The process slowed briefly in the early 1990s, with the return of recession, but has continued more or less unabated since—consolidating its hold on the West and rising rapidly from a comparatively low base in the East.

Materialistic consumption is, of course, nothing new. It has long been an accepted fact of life for society's elite; and for at least the last couple of centuries it has been one of the defining ambitions of the rising urban middle class. What is different, though, about today's consumer culture is that it has become

**FIGURE 11.1. Smart car.** One of the hottest things to hit the consumer market in recent years is Daimler-Chrysler's "Smart City Coupe." Touted as the perfect solution to navigating and parking in Europe's congested cities, the smart car is only 2.5 meters long and 1.5 meters wide. The car is uniquely styled and fuel-efficient. Its manufacturer also likes to remind consumers that it is environmentally friendly and 100% recyclable at the end of its days.

a truly mass phenomenon and that there are such a variety of forms that it may take. Modern consumer culture is built on an ever widening array of goods marketed through aggressive media advertising that assaults the senses in all places and at all times of day. Under this constant media barrage, consumers are made ever conscious of rapidly changing styles and fashions and encouraged to buy impulsively. Modern consumer culture has introduced entirely new ways of retailing. Shopping has, in itself, become one of today's leisure activities, which increasingly takes place at new and specialized sites that are specifically designed to enhance the personal pleasure and allure of consumption. It also features the plethora of leisure and sport activities, health-related services and products, and electronic communication and amusement devices that have become so symptomatic of our age.

## Retailing

A large part of retailing in Europe has traditionally been dominated by small, independently operated shops and outlets, at which people shop locally to meet their everyday needs. England, after all, was once referred to as a nation of shopkeepers; and what could be more French than the local food shop, or *boulangerie*. The advent of large department stores and shopping arcades or "galleries" in the centers of 19th-century cities was certainly, as we have seen in an earlier chapter, revolutionary for its time and caused much excitement, but it did relatively little to change the way in which most people did their routine daily shopping. Today's marketplace is distinguished, in contrast, by a greater dynamism and growing diversity. There are a number of noteworthy trends, all of which are most evident in the West, although their effects are now being felt in the rapidly privatizing consumer markets in the East as well.

One major trend is consolidation. Retailing has become increasingly concentrated within larger and more highly capitalized firms, the majority of which are corporate rather than

**FIGURE 11.2. Food shop.** Europeans have traditionally shopped at small shops, such as the small food market seen here on a Berlin street. Local shops, though, face increasing competition from large chains and suburban hypermarkets.

family-run enterprises. The new large-scale form of marketing typically takes place in supermarket- or hypermarket-style large floorspace emporia, located at accessible points on the edges of built-up urban areas. The retailing strategy is to attract consumers either by providing exceptional choice on particular lines of merchandise or by offering the convenience of picking up a wide range of merchandise in a single trip. The trend began during the 1970s in the food retailing sector, as British and French retailers, such as Sainsburys and Carrefour, developed chains of hypermarkets. Early concentration in the food sector reflects the fact that this was the sector in which economies of scale and other cost benefits could most easily be achieved. Current estimates suggest that food supermarkets and hypermarkets account for over half of all packaged groceries sold in the EU, while in France, where the trend originated and has perhaps now reached the saturation level, more than four-fifths of all groceries are sold in this way. The consolidation process then spread during the 1980s from food retailing to such things as furniture, lawn and garden products, do-it-yourself home improvements, and consumer electronics. Indeed, by the early 1990s, large furniture outlet stores had become one of the more ubiquitous and commonly accepted sights on the fringes of urban areas. Today, supermarket, hypermar-

ket, or discount store settings have become commonplace for the sale of everything from clothing and toys to sporting goods and office supplies.

Consolidation has been accompanied by an accelerating trend toward the internationalization of retailing. As barriers to trade within the EU have tumbled, many firms have been prompted to look beyond their own domestic markets to increase their sales and profits. This is often an easier avenue to pursue than developing new product lines and finding new markets at home. Success in the European marketplace has also led some companies to look for new markets even beyond the continent. The Swedish home furnishings retailer IKEA, which operates outlets all across Europe as well as in many other parts of the world, is probably one of the very best examples of this. Another example is Carrefour, the French retailer whose hypermarkets can be found almost everywhere in France and Spain. Carrefour has recently expanded to other Mediterranean markets in Portugal, Italy, and Turkey, and has set up operations in parts of Latin America and Asia as well. Other major international retailers include such firms as Marks & Spencer, the British-owned clothing, footwear, and household goods giant; Virgin Megastore, Britain's upstart purveyor of everything from entertainment media to wedding gowns and cars; Tenglemann,

FIGURE 11.3. Hypermarket. Rows of automated checkout points await customers at this Carrefour supermarket in northern France. Banners hanging from the ceiling encourage consumers to use company credit and receive discount advantages. Inside is a vast array of packaged, frozen, and fresh food guaranteed to satisfy their every need.

the large German food retailer; and the Swedish clothier Hennes & Mauritz. In western Europe, a majority of the largest retailers have by now begun to run operations in at least several countries. Many have also managed to establish outlets in parts of east-central and eastern Europe.

Technology has also come to play a pivotal new role in retailing. Modern communcations and data-storage technologies have greatly improved retailers' ability to control the flow of merchandise to stores and to manage stock, handle credit, and expedite the checkout process. Today's average hypermarket is graced by a seemingly endless array of computerized checkout stations, where scanners check bar codes to ring up charges while simultaneously controlling stock and generating marketing data on consumer tastes and preferences. Of course, the automobile, above all else, has made it possible to bring the necessary masses of shoppers to the peripheral sites

FIGURE 11.4. Abundance of choice. A young Polish couple eye the enormous variety of goods and produce available inside a large Géant hypermarket outside of Warsaw. It wasn't that long ago that grocery shoppers chose from a relatively limited line of brand items, packaged only in relatively small units suited to daily shopping—quite different from the diverse offerings served up by retailers today. In eastern countries such as Poland, that day was even more recent.

where most of the new superstores are built. Also important is the now nearly universal ownership of freezers and refrigerators among households, at least in western Europe, that allows consumers to drive to a hypermarket and "stock up" on perishable items.

Technology is also opening a new retailing frontier in cyberspace, which is only just beginning to fulfill its promise. Although mail-order merchandising has been around a long time—particularly in Germany, Denmark, the United Kingdom, and to a somewhat lesser extent in France—advances in communications technology are providing a major boost to "home shopping," particularly in an age when increasing numbers of people are working at home or do not have the time or inclination to shop in the traditional way. *Virgin.com*, one of the more successful commercial Internet sites, is a leader in the art of providing "hot links" that connect millions of web-surfing consumers to the tantalizing array of business interests controlled by that British conglomerate.

The flip side to the growth of mega-retailers and chain stores is the decline of small and independent retail firms. Most western countries have experienced a loss in the number of shops over the past couple of decades that runs into the tens and even hundreds of thousands. Hardest-hit have been small food retailers, but also a great many shops and stores in other sectors. The extent of the decline varies enormously across Europe, depending on a number of factors, including distance from the epicenter of supermarket and hypermarket development in France and Britain, the resistance of local cultures to changes in shopping habits, and in some cases government regulatory policies. In France, for example, where the onward march of hypermarkets has been nearly irresistible, the government intervened in 1996 to protect small food retailers by passing legislation that prevented large retailers from using the term *boulangerie*, which has such a powerful association in the minds of the French with the act of shopping for food.

Behind most attempts by government to regulate the growth of hypermarkets has been the fear that the accompanying disappearance of small shops will hasten the decline of inner-city and neighborhood commercial areas, as well as concern about a current lack of environmental planning controls over the construction of hypermarkets and shopping centers outside built-up areas. In a number of countries, local planning agencies have been empowered to limit the development of large stores on the edges of cities. Norway has gone so far as to impose a complete moratorium on the building of shopping centers, pending results of a study by planning authorities. Among western countries the numbers of small retail outlets remain proportionately highest in Spain, Portugal, Italy, and Belgium—in the three Mediterranean countries largely for cultural reasons, in Belgium because of governmental intervention.

Nonetheless, it is important to point out that small to mid-size retailers still abound, are not in any danger of completely disappearing soon, and may still be seen lining the commercial storefront avenues, or "high streets," of Europe's towns and cities. Indeed, there has been growth in some sectors, such as the convenience store, which provides ready access over longer hours to quickly needed goods, particularly for motorists. In many of the nongrocery sectors, small specialty stores and shops still maintain a majority share of the market. Their overall distribution, however, shows a slight shift toward suburban shopping center and mall locations; and they are less likely nowadays to be independent due to trends toward the organization of small specialty retailing into chains and franchises, or cooperative buying groups.

Suburban shopping centers and malls are a rapidly expanding venue for retailing, and certainly part of the creation of a whole new landscape of consumption sites, which also includes theme parks and discount outlet and warehouse parks designed to cater to the motorized and affluent European consumer. The newest ones are carefully managed to present the consumer with an attractive mixture of shops, set in a planned environment of sights and sounds, along with plenty of parking. Within the cities, there has also been a parallel expansion of small and specialty retailing in association with newly gentrified and revitalized city centers, typically set on pedestrian streets, in underground malls or business tower complexes.

Recent years have seen rapid and revolutionary changes in retailing in the former socialist countries of east-central and eastern Europe. Under the old state-run retailing systems in these countries, little attention was paid to consumer demand. Products were distributed according to centralized bureaucratic decisions. Decisions about the location of shops and the display and sale of goods were made in a perfunctory manner, with little thought about enhancing the convenience or satisfaction of consumers. Since 1989, however, shopping has suddenly become big business. People are eager to join the consumers' world, and there has been a tremendous burst of private entrepreneurial initiative to meet the demand. Most east-central and eastern European countries have recorded soaring levels of retail sales, along with a spectacular rise in the number of retail establishments, some of which are the result of the privatization and restructuring of the old public-sector enterprises, while others are the product of a widespread enthusiasm for new capitalist ventures of all sizes and shapes. Credit cards have become far more common, and western-style cash machines are widely available, at least in the larger towns and cities.

Rather ironically, in comparison to the West, the East can be viewed, at least initially, as having taken quite the opposite direction in the evolution of its retailing structure. The early trend was to move from a system of centralized control of retail distribution to the proliferation of small-scale retailing, rather than the other way around, although the instrument of central control in the East had been the state rather than the giant corporation. According to one survey, the number of retail outlets in Poland soared remarkably immediately after the introduction of a free market, rising from just 165,000 in 1988 to 415,000 in 1994. More recently, however, there has been a steady growth in larger outlets and chain stores, similar to those of, and

often even owned or franchised by, large western retailing firms. Many have been established for ease of automobile access in outlying suburban locations. Indeed, in some urban areas the major obstacle to more development of this kind is the present inability of the road network to handle the traffic.

While the overall density of wholesale and retail outlets in the East remains well below that of the West, it is steadily rising; and in some east-central European countries, such as Poland, the Czech Republic, and Hungary, it has reached levels at least comparable to those in the West during the 1970s or 1980s. The process is, however, far from complete. It

**FIGURE 11.5. IKEA shopping bus.** Suburban shopping malls with lots of parking space have become commonplace, even in the former socialist states of east-central and eastern Europe. Retailers do everything they can to entice central city residents to these new emporia. Here an IKEA bus stands ready in front of Warsaw's Central Station to transport buyers out to the suburban location of its store on the outskirts of the city. The tall building in the background is the city's 1950s era Palace of Culture.

is so far largely restricted to the major urban centers, and in many areas has been severely hampered by the persistence of certain structural features of the old system, including poor wholesale distribution, weak management and marketing skills, and the entrenched presence of black-market retailing—particularly in the countries that were formally part of the Soviet Union. Nonetheless, there is every indication that the processes of privatization and investment will continue and that shopping in the East will increasingly resemble shopping in the West.

## Convergence or Divergence?

Given the retailing trends outlined above, it would appear that Europeans today are experiencing a process of homogenization in tastes and buying habits. The race to consolidation in retail marketing would certainly suggest that social and cultural differences in consumption patterns are being swept away and that Europe is converging inexorably on a single market dominated by powerful Eurobrands distributed through integrated international networks of wholesalers, advertisers and retailers. Yet, the case for convergence may not be quite that overwhelming, for there remain numerous examples of regional or national differences in consumer tastes for such things as food and drink, styles of clothing, home furnishings, autos and housing—even the packaging (i.e., size and shape) of individual products—that appear to defy the expected trend. In some cases, regional or national proclivities even seem to run in the opposite direction, toward more specialized products and services that satisfy local desires and needs, or a nostalgia for a simpler past. Politically, this tendency has been reflected at the highest level in the resistance that certain national governments, particularly in the Mediterranean, have offered to various harmonizing directives from Brussels that have demanded the replacement of national with EU-wide product standards. Many Europeans are naturally suspicious and a bit afraid of an all-encompassing homogenization of their lives.

## Food and Drink

One way in which we might examine the question of convergence versus divergence is to look at changing patterns of food and drink consumption. This seems an important area to explore because, after all, it was the food sector that first experienced the consolidating effects of hypermarkets and chain stores. As a consequence, it is a fact that processed and packaged foods of all kinds have been readily available to consumers for some time, both within and outside of urban areas; and that shoppers throughout most of Europe have become increasingly accustomed to choosing from a wide, but at the same time very standardized, range of food options.

There is, of course, a long history of changing dietary patterns to be kept in mind. Food availability in Europe was once heavily influenced by an inability to transport perishable items over long distances. What people ate and drank coincided roughly with what could be produced locally, depending on climate and soil. Diets were nearly everywhere rather monotonous and often low in caloric intake. They tended to be dominated by starchy staples, which were a relatively cheap and convenient source of calories for a population that was largely poor. The starchy staples usually came in the form of breads, porridges, and gruels made from locally available cereals. In certain parts of Europe, potatoes were also an important source of nourishment. Only small amounts of livestock products were consumed, and sugar, fruits, and vegetables were generally absent or of only minor importance.

All of this changed during the 19th and the first half of the 20th centuries. Change came as a result of increased and more varied agricultural productivity, a general long-term rise in real wages, a much-improved ability to preserve perishable foods and transport them over long distances, and a growing availability of food imports from other parts of the world. In short, food supplies became generally more abundant and affordable. During this period Europe passed through what might be called a nutritional transition, characterized by a rise in total calorie supply per capita, and a substantial decline in the proportion of the diet—although not necessarily the absolute amount of food—derived from starchy staples. Wheat became the dominant grain, replacing the wide variety of local grains from which flour was made. There was a growing consumption of animal products. There was also an increase in the consumption of fruits and vegetables, oils and fats, as well as sugar, which had been a great luxury for the majority of Europeans before prices began to fall in the late 19th century. In the end, the nutritional transition had a modernizing effect. It made regional diets more robust at the same time that it brought about a degree of convergence in European diets as a whole. The process was, however, very much extended over time and space. It began in northwestern Europe, where it was in some ways complete by the end of the 19th century. The nutritional transition came far more slowly and less completely to eastern and Mediterranean Europe, where it was still very much in progress as late as the 1960s, and in some respects still continues.

Despite the transition, important geographic distinctions in food and drink patterns still remained by the postwar decades of the 1950s and 1960s. In the case of alcoholic beverages, for example, consumption patterns in the 1960s were not dissimilar to those that had prevailed in the latter part of the preceding century. Europe was still divided into three broad zones: a northern zone extending from western Scandinavia to Russia, where spirits were the dominant drink; a middle zone running from the British Isles through the Low Countries and Germany to east-central Europe, where beers were preferred; and Mediterranean Europe, where the consumption of wines outdistanced everything else. While total consumption had declined somewhat since the 1890s, there was little change in the pattern of preference by the decades immediately following World War II— the only exception being Denmark, which had moved from the spirits to the beer zone sometime during the 1950s.

These distinctions had much to do with long-standing connections between environment and culture. The grape flourishes in the warm Mediterranean South, and wines have been important in Mediterranean Europe since Greek times. On the other hand, the best regions for producing the malting grains from which beer is produced are found north of the Alps, and the consumption of beer has long prevailed over much of Europe outside the Mediterranean. Spirits are distilled from a variety of grains and plants, including potatoes, found throughout northern Europe. They are a relative newcomer on the scene, replacing beer and emerging during the 18th

FIGURE 11.6. Place and taste. Strong associations exist between certain kinds of consumables and regional environments and cultures. This beer advertisement in a Berlin subway station tries to connect the taste and desirability of the Löwenbräu brand name with the invigorating mountain landscapes and carefree culture of Bavaria.

and 19th centuries as the leading drink in Scandinavia and Russia. Spirits were also briefly dominant in Britain, the Low Countries, and in Germany before being overtaken again by beer.

The use of cooking oils is another example of the long and pervasive influence of environment and culture on food preferences. The traditionally dominant source of natural cooking oil in Mediterranean Europe is the olive, while elsewhere in Europe it is butter and lard. The olive, which until this century was the only edible oil-bearing crop that could be grown in Europe, is produced for climatic reasons only in the Mediterranean South. Environmental conditions conducive to the production of swine and cattle and the absence of any kind of edible domestic oilseed led to a traditional reliance in the rest of Europe on butter and lard, and to a lesser extent on oils derived from fish. Oils were subsequently made from tropical oilseeds and margarine made from animal fats, and vegetable oils were introduced in the latter part of the 19th century and grew steadily in popularity as Europe's nutritional transition progressed. Nonetheless, as late as the 1960s in both northern and southern Europe, they were still less popular than traditional cooking oils.

The 1970s are viewed as the beginning of a whole new set of food consumption trends, the most notable of which is a growing con-vergence in tastes. These trends began in the West, particularly in the most developed areas of northern and western Europe, where incomes and prosperity rose to unprecedented heights during the postwar decades. Higher incomes meant that people were freer to buy what they desired rather than what their means forced them to consume, and the introduction of modern multinational marketing strategies and the internationalization of food distribution encouraged them to exercise their newfound freedom. In most western countries rising incomes led to significant increases in the consumption of meat during the 1970s and 1980s. At the same time, preferences for different kinds of meat gradually became more uniform. Pork, for example, has become the most important meat in every European country except Iceland, Albania, and Russia. In the great majority of countries, the order of preference is for pork, followed by beef, poultry, and mutton. By 1990 people in EU countries were deriving roughly one-third of their total calories from animal products, a level far in excess of any time earlier, although levels of consumption have more recently stabilized or begun to decline.

By the late 1990s many dietary clichés from the not-so-distant past had become passé. Scandinavian countries today consume more bread and cereals than Mediterranean countries. More fish products are eaten in Spain

FIGURE 11.7. **Olive production.** The olive grows everywhere throughout the Mediterranean. Here olive groves range endlessly over the mountainous Andalusian landscape of southern Spain. The fruit, which is harvested in winter, is either pickled in brine for eating or pressed to extract the oil used for preparing food. Spain is the world's largest producer of olives.

and Portugal than in Scandinavia. Coffee shops have begun to supplant tearooms in Britain. And the traditional three zones of alcoholic beverage consumption outlined earlier, while still recognizable, have become more muted. In most countries the leading drinks of the past have lost their supremacy. Beer, which is now marketed in easily transportable and refrigerative aluminum cans, is closing in on declining wine consumption in Mediterranean countries and, along with wine, which can now be shipped in tankers to far-away northern distributors, has overtaken spirits consumption in Scandinavian countries. Whereas differences in alcoholic consumption were once a largely north–south phenomenon, the major difference today is between a more homogenized pattern in the West and a preference for spirits in the East—the latter most recently underlined by a shift in the most favored beverage from wine to spirits in Romania and Bulgaria.

Evidence for convergence may be seen today in nearly every aspect of what Europeans eat and drink. This is definitely, however, a very complex trend, and there is some indication that it may be slowing. Even as overall dietary structures converge, regional differences may be found in how they are evolving. Mediterranean countries, for example, are in some ways still completing the nutritional transition that countries in northwestern Europe put behind them more than a half-century ago. The formerly socialist countries

of the East are just now grappling with the adjustment to western consumerism. Even as new products are accepted, local or regional cultures often choose to adapt the use of these products to their own particular circumstances and traditions. Some traditional forms of consumption also remain remarkably resistant to change. Ireland, for example, maintains a higher-than-average consumption of potatoes. The United Kingdom consumes more sugar and corn than anyone else, the Germans more beer, the French more wine, and Mediterranean countries in general consume more fruits and vegetables.

Moreover, despite the internationalization of food marketing, cultural differences still affect the basic way in which food shoppers approach the marketplace. A very good example of this is a recent survey of food shopping in western European countries. When asked what they thought was the most important factor in choosing a food store, consumers in France and Spain said price; for the Germans, Dutch, and British it was the range of food available; Italians placed the greatest emphasis on proximity or ease of access. These kinds of attitudes have served to encourage a more recent, and some would say postmodern, fragmenting trend in the retail food market, featuring regional brands and market distribution systems. Examples of such regional grocery chains include Eroski in the Basque country of northern Spain, Morrisons in northern England, and Cora in Alsace.

FIGURE 11.8. Fast food. A major force for dietary convergence is fast food. McDonald's and other fast food outlets have pretty well blanketed the European consumer landscape. Here, Muscovites grab a quick dinner at McDonald's as they head for home on a dark winter night.

## Social Change and Consumption

Analysts are very quick to point out that there is no such thing as a "Euro-consumer" yet. Culture is an important influence in maintaining differences, but much also depends on demographic and social change. Europe's aging population is, for example, an important factor in determining certain consumption patterns. It lies behind the increasingly extensive availability of health aids and cosmetic products that have to do with aging. Seniors are also more likely to demand familiar tried-and-true products and full-service attention to their needs when they go to market. The fact that older people are often more densely distributed in some areas than others can have a powerful effect on local marketing strategies and consumption patterns.

European families have also become smaller; in some residential areas there are relatively few children and many young people living alone. This is especially true in northern and western Europe. It is reflected in the kinds of products available for local consumption and by the willingness of consumers to shop around. Gentrified areas of urban professionals, for example, often demand quality lines of consumer products and generally prefer convenience over lower prices and

**FIGURE 11.9. Senior consumers.** These two German seniors are strolling past a storefront display of hygiene and health goods. Marketing in Europe is influenced, as anywhere else, by the tastes and needs of the local population. As Europe ages, more and more retailing will be aimed at meeting the special needs of this growing segment of the population.

greater variety. Time is a valuable commodity for these people, so they are often interested in one-stop, self-service shopping. They are also inclined to purchase food in simple single-serving packaging. The fact that more women work outside the home is another factor. Workingwomen spend far less time preparing meals and are therefore more interested in buying frozen, easily prepared processed foods. All of this has led to a growing provision of specialized products and marketing venues that stand alongside those of the mass-merchandising chains.

The substantial immigrant populations now quartered in many western cities add another divergent ingredient to the marketplace. Ethnically owned shops, food stores, and restaurants that cater to the immigrant's nostalgic ties to the tastes and smells of home are a commonplace sight. Ethnic food outlets, in particular, are often even able to "cross over" and find popularity with host populations. The ubiquitous Italian pizzeria is certainly one obvious example. Another is the countless fast-food street kiosks in German cities that sell the *Döner Kebap*, a wedge-shaped sandwich of spit-roasted meat and sauce on foccacia-like bread, introduced by Turkish immigrants but now popular with German consumers as well. In eastern Europe divergence often takes the form of a rising demand for locally produced products, particularly beverages and cigarettes, that were commonplace during the socialist period—a phenomenon that reflects both frustration with the higher costs of western goods and a nostalgia for old and familiar consumer habits and pleasures.

Finally, there is a far greater emphasis in today's society on individualistic lifestyles. Identity is important to people, and perceptions of personal identity and gratification—whether culturally, regionally, or individualistically based—are a strong determinant of a wide range of specialized consumption activities. People tend to display their individuality, or personal style, through what they consume, wear, or involve themselves in, and are increasingly more prone, as they do so, to reject traditional mass consumption goods and ser-

FIGURE 11.10. Crossover. Ethnic foods originally brought to Europe by immigrant workers in the 1960s and 1970s have become universally popular fare. Seen here is a Döner Kebap stand, a nearly ubiquitous sight in most large German cities. Introduced there by Turkish immigrant workers, the Döner Kebap is a big street-side seller, right alongside falafels, schnitzel, bratwurst, hamburgers, pommes frites, and Coca-Cola.

vices. Especially important here are the ways in which people use their leisure time for recreation and relaxation.

## LEISURE

Along with much higher levels of personal wealth and consumption, one of the most important changes in the lives of Europeans to take place during the latter part of the 20th century has been the expansion of leisure time. As late as the closing decades of the 19th century, the vast majority of Europeans spent most of their waking hours working or attending to the essentials of life. Most workers toiled for 10 hours a day, 6 days a week. The luxury of having significant amounts of free time to dispose of was strictly the province of the elite. And even as the enjoyment of leisure time gradually became more commonplace for the middle and working classes, it was usually restricted to relatively brief holiday periods, or to the free time that by tradition came to all on Sundays and public or religious holidays. It has only been since the

1960s that labor organizations and governments have steadily increased the amount of time that workers could rightfully claim as their own, and only since then that relatively abundant leisure time has become the norm for the majority of the population.

Europeans have come to have an exceptionally large amount of free time at their disposal, more so than their counterparts in America or Japan. Most European workers today are guaranteed 5–7 weeks of annual paid leave, including public holidays, and some receive even more. The Finns, for example, currently are entitled to 39 days of paid holidays a year. The French get 36, the Germans 33, and the Italians 30. The long-working British receive the least, with 28 days. Across the EU, the average leave and public holiday entitlement is 34 days. In contrast, the average American is entitled to just 16 days a year. A majority of the population has the necessary disposable income to do something special with it and actively seeks opportunities to do so. There is even a German Leisure Association dedicated to offering Germans information and advice on how best to take advantage of their free time.

## Tourism

Tourism has become one of the most popular ways for Europeans to spend their leisure time. Indeed, Europeans have literally come to expect to go on holiday, often one involving foreign travel, at least once a year; in many ways it has almost come to be viewed as a basic human right. This point was quite recently underscored in France, where the government has set up an official state-funded agency to help fill vacant beds in French tourist hotels with people who could not otherwise afford a holiday. The premise behind the scheme is that the right to leisure is something that all French citizens are entitled to regardless of social standing or economic situation—just as they are entitled to housing, education, and welfare. Germans also tend to view vacation travel as an entitlement.

Holidaymaking is something that often takes place at specific times of the year. In most European countries there is, for instance, a definite period, usually during one of the summer months, that is generally accepted as "the time" for lengthy summer holidays. In Sweden, for example, the summer holiday period begins in June around the time of the summer equinox. In France, it comes much later in the summer. During this time, many shops and businesses are closed and large portions of the population are away from their homes and jobs on holiday. The exodus can also be quite specific in terms of destination, as most national populations have long been in the habit of spending their holidays at the same venues or engaging in the same activities, although these predilections are, as we shall see, a matter of fashion and appear to be becoming much more diverse and individualistic. In this sense, tourism is what has been called a "positional good," meaning that it is something that people may use to define their social position and personal lifestyle. While tourism may be in part the pursuit of pleasure and relaxation, it may also be a matter of being seen in the right places and among the right people.

Given the great popularity of holiday-making and tourism among Europeans, and the considerable attraction that Europe holds as a holiday destination for people from other continents, Europe has the distinction of being the world's biggest tourism market. It has held this favored position for many decades, and although its relative importance has slipped somewhat over the past 20 years, Europe still claims 58% of world tourist arrivals and half of all global tourism receipts—which puts it well ahead of its nearest rival, North America. Tourism in Europe is a mega-industry, every bit as important as agriculture, construction, or automobile manufacturing. In 1998 tourism in the EU generated a whopping $1.15 trillion, or 14% of the combined gross domestic product of the EU's 15 member nations. According to World Travel and Tourism Council statistics, 19 million people in western Europe are employed by this sector of the economy, either directly or indirectly. An additional 16 million are thought to be dependent, in at least some way, on the

FIGURE 11.11. Tourism. One of Europe's most popular tourist attractions is the small German town of Rothenburg ob der Tauber, whose well-preserved medieval townscape has since the latter part of the 19th century been the epitome of what many believe to be quintessentially German. In this photo crowds of tourists wait, cameras in hand, for the moment when the clock on the Councilor's Tavern strikes the hour and mechanical figures emerge to reenact the Meistertrunk, the colorful legend of how the town was saved from destruction by its mayor, who managed to drink an entire tankard of beer (3.25 liters) in one go.

tourism industry in east-central and eastern Europe. Within the EU, the industry continues to grow at rates faster than the economy as a whole. According to EU data, more and more Europeans are visiting one another's countries every year. The growing demand is met continent-wide by an astounding 186,000 hotels and similar establishments with almost 9 million beds.

France is currently the most important tourist destination in the world, with as many as 70 million visitors a year. The United States is in second place, but is followed by a string of European destinations including Spain, Italy, the United Kingdom, Hungary, Poland, and Austria. Other major European destinations, by world standards (i.e., more than 10 million tourist arrivals from abroad annually), are the Czech Republic, Germany, Switzerland, and Greece. Greece, in fact, possesses the fastest-rising tourism market of the group.

Among Europeans, the Germans holiday and spend more money abroad per capita than any other national group, followed by the British and the French. The Germans actually spend more than three times as much on their foreign holidays as all Europeans together spend on trips to Germany. More than half of all Germans take at least one international trip a year, and many take more than one. The Dutch, Norwegians, Belgians, Icelanders, and Swedes also spend significantly more abroad than they take in. Overall, there is a definite net flow of tourist money from northern to southern Europe, although somewhat surprisingly the country with the largest net outflow of tourist money, next to Germany, is Russia. Russian tourists are currently spending more than two-and-a-half times as much abroad as the Russian tourist industry is able to take in at home. Russian cruise ships, loaded with high-spending tourists looking for bargains on all kinds of western goods, have become a common sight in Mediterranean ports, particularly in Istanbul, but even as far away from their Black Sea home ports as Spain and Portugal. With the exception of Russia, the remainder of the eastern half of Europe is a net recipient of international tourism expenditures.

The most favored international destination for travelers from within Europe is Spain, which is the preferred destination, in particular, for travelers from Germany and the United Kingdom. It is indeed no small wonder that, at the height of the holiday season, every other car on the streets of Spanish coastal towns seems to sport a German or

FIGURE 11.12. **Russian cruise ships.** Tied to the wharf is a line of Russian Black Sea cruise ships, which have brought holiday-seeking and bargain-hunting Russian shoppers to Istanbul. Long prohibited from visiting the West, today Russian and other eastern Europeans are a small but growing new source of international tourism revenues.

British license plate. Portugal and Greece also cater to a predominantly German and British clientele. Italy is another favored German tourist destination. Germans are by far the largest single tourist contingent in Italy, accounting for more than half of all nights spent in Italy each year by foreign tourists. Other countries tend to draw their largest influx of foreign visitors from neighboring states. Belgium's most numerous tourism customers, for example, come from across its common border with the Netherlands. Similarly, the Danes, the Dutch, and the Austrians receive more tourists from Germany than from any other place, while throngs of visitors from Britain spill over the Channel to become the largest foreign holidaymaking group in France. British tourists also exert an overwhelming presence in nearby Ireland. Curiously, the French fail to establish a strong presence anywhere, except in the United Kingdom where they are second in importance to the Germans.

## The Development of European Mass Tourism

Mass tourism is a phenomenon that first emerged in late 19th-century Europe, particularly in Britain. It was largely built around the development of places of outdoor pleasure and recreation that were open and accessible to the urban masses.

The first of these to appear were urban pleasure parks that provided a nearby recreational setting where people of all classes might promenade, picnic, and relax on Sundays and holidays. In London, such places had long been available to high society and the more fashionable elements of the middle class, who enjoyed privileged access to the royal parks and for whom a host of privately run pleasure and tea gardens, such as the famous Vauxhall Gardens, were maintained from the early 18th century. Working-class people and the poor, however, were excluded. Nineteenth-century social reformers and moralists, however, took the view that providing the working classes with access to open space and appropriate recreational and cultural opportunities could raise their general health and moral respectability. Access restrictions to the royal parks were lowered, and in 1841 public funds were used to develop Victoria Park, which, complete with fountains, follies, lake, flowerbeds, and cricket lawns, soon attracted 30,000 visitors a day, largely from working-class areas of the city's industrial East End. Even more successful in this respect was Battersea Park, opened in 1858 in the hopes of improving leisure activity in one of the city's more squalid working-class neighborhoods.

London's example was quickly copied elsewhere. Napoleon III, who was impressed by London's parks during a visit to the city, ordered that two royal preserves on the western and eastern approaches to Paris—the Bois de Boulogne and the Bois de Vincennes—be made into public pleasure parks, while in the midst of working-class Paris, Haussman set about creating the Buttes-Chaumont Park, transforming an unsightly low hill riddled with abandoned quarries and covered with the city's refuse into a romantically wooded landscape graced with waterfall, lake, winding trails, and lovely bridges. Copenhagen's Tivoli Gardens, founded in 1843 by Georg Carstensen and built on the site of a section of the city's fortifications, was modeled after urban pleasure parks he had seen in London and Paris. He envisioned Tivoli Gardens as a magic garden and playground, where Copen-

hageners and visitors alike could find amusements and nature in abundance, right in the midst of the city. The park's natural qualities are ensured by its original charter, which stipulates that at least 75% of its land be preserved as open space.

The great exhibitions that opened in major cities across Europe during the latter half of the 19th century—from the 1851 Great Exhibition of the Works of Industry of all Nations in London with its extraordinary 19-acre Crystal Palace exhibition building to the Paris International Exhibition of 1889 with its revolutionary and astounding 300-meter-tall Eiffel Tower—are also examples, as we noted in an earlier chapter, of elaborate, if temporary, urban amusements designed to attract, entertain, and educate great masses of visitors from all walks of life. So too were the great outdoor museums of rural buildings and lifestyles assembled by Romantics near the end of the century to foster appreciation of national culture. The first and most famous of these was Skansen, established in 1891 by Artur Hazelius on the grounds of what was formerly a royal deer park on the edge of the Swedish capital of Stockholm.

All of these developments were instrumental in establishing the practice of mass enjoyment of public places of entertainment and recreation. But, for mass tourism, by far the most important development was the emergence of large seaside resorts and amusement parks, made easily accessible from the large industrial cities by steamboat or train. In the case of London, steamboat excursions to downstream attractions on the Thames, like the Royal Terrace Pier and public gardens at Gravesend, or to seaside bathing resorts beyond the Thames Estuary on the coast of Kent, like Ramsgate and Margate, were popular among the middle classes from as early as the 1840s. In later decades, an ever larger number of seaside resorts that could be reached from London by rail began to spring up all along the Channel coast. Gradually these resorts also began to cater to holiday-makers from the working classes. By the 1880s and 1890s, holiday excursion packets consisting of as little as a day or as much as a

FIGURE 11.13. Buttes-Chaumont Park. Created virtually from scratch in the 19th century by Haussman from refuse dumps and abandoned quarries, Buttes-Chaumont Park is a green oasis in the midst of eastern Paris, frequented by joggers, strollers, and sunbathers.

week or two at resort towns along the coasts of Sussex, Kent, and Essex were within the means of and open to working-class East End Londoners. English industrial conurbations in the Midlands and elsewhere soon developed their own nearby seaside attractions. Similar developments took shape on the continent. In addition to public bathing, these seaside towns offered a wide range of lodgings, pubs, tearooms and restaurants, and a carnival atmosphere centered on the array of shops and kiosks, dance halls, and sundry amusements, all gaily illuminated at night by colored lights that lined the seaside promenade or clung to the decks of the great rambling timber piers that jutted far out into the harbor.

A few of these popular seaside resorts were especially well known. Blackpool, located on the Irish Sea coast within easy striking distance of the industrial towns of Lancashire, was Britain's largest and most popular resort town, boasting 7 miles of sandy beach and extensive amusements, including the 158-meter-tall Blackpool Tower, built in 1895 and modeled after the Eiffel Tower in Paris. On England's Channel coast, the best known was Brighton, where sea bathing first came into vogue among the upper classes during the latter part of the 18th century. The town received the powerful patronage of King George IV and was graced with Regency squares and distinguished landmarks, including the unusual and ornately styled Royal Pavilion. Brighton was connected to London by rail in 1841 and grew rapidly as open coaches of tourists descended on the town for the purpose of enjoying its 7 miles of pebbly beach, enclosed on each end by the imposing lengths of the Palace and West Piers.

Examples of well-known fashionable seaside resorts on the continent from the same period include Ostend, whose glamour was enhanced by the frequent patronage of the Belgian King, Leopold II; Trouville, which was a favorite summer playground in the 1860s for France's Napoleon III and his court; and Scheveningen, whose magnificently wide sandy beaches have made it the most popular of all Dutch coastal resorts since bathing was established there in 1818.

From its introduction in the late 19th century until after World War II, mass tourism remained essentially a domestic industry, spatially constricted to serving nearby industrial workforce markets. International tourism continued, as always, to be a specialized and relatively small-scale activity for the elite. Beginning in the 1960s, however, all of this suddenly began to change. Mass tourism went international and the favored destinations became the sun-drenched beaches of the Mediterranean and, a little later, the ski slopes of the Alps. The trend, which accelerated during the 1970s and peaked during the 1980s, was in part a product of the newfound profusion of time and money found at the middle and lower socioeconomic levels of European society. It was also made possible by the emergence of air travel as a form of mass transportation, and was built around a revolution in the provision of the tourist product.

The new international mass market featured a standardized good—sand and sun, or snow and ski slopes—that could be enjoyed in a specialized built environment at a competitively low price. Media advertising was used to promote the idea that the good was the equivalent of an exotic fantasy sensation of pleasure and fun that was completely beyond the familiar experience of normal everyday living. The good was most commonly purchased from an international tourist company in the form of a "package vacation" that included air transport, hotel, and a variety of ancillary privileges and services. The international tour companies, operating primarily out of northern European countries, profited from the fact that the large volume of their business made it possible to acquire and sell exclusive charter air flights and whole blocks of tourist hotel rooms at discount prices. So pervasive was the system that entire hotels, or even resort towns, were often dominated by package tourists from a single country.

The success of the new international package tours contributed enormously to the overbuilt beachfronts of countless Mediterranean seaside resort towns. The typical scene in these places is one of modern concrete and glass hotels standing shoulder to shoulder,

**FIGURE 11.14. Seaside promenade.** This photo looks south from Constitution Hill over the Welsh town of Aberystwyth on Cardigan Bay. Along the near sweep of the bay is the town's promenade, built in the Victorian era to accommodate and amuse tourists from English industrial towns on their summer holiday. The arm of land reaching out toward Ireland holds the crumbled ruins of one of Edward I's ring of castles around the Welsh coast. The round hill on the other side of the town is Pen Dinas, the site of one of Wales's many iron-age hill forts. (Photo: A. K. Knowles)

each looking down over a hotel-front outdoor café onto a demarcated stretch of sand on which the hotel provides the obligatory array of changing houses, beach furniture, and brightly colored beach umbrellas for its guests. International tourism has transformed the towns themselves into garish assemblages of souvenir shops, restaurants, and kiosks, ringed by row upon row of tourist apartments and condos. It has also turned their economies into low-wage seasonal labor markets.

The phenomenon first took root in the western Mediterranean along the mainland and island coasts of Spain (Costa del Sol, Costa Blanca, Costa Brava, Majorca, Minorca, and Ibiza), along almost the entire south coast of France, and on the Ligurian and Adriatic Rivieras in Italy. In the eastern Mediterranean it was somewhat later established on the Greek islands and subsequently spread to the Adriatic coasts of the former Yugoslavia, western Turkey, and Cyprus, in addition to appearing in its own specialized forms along the Black Sea coasts of Romania and the former Soviet Union. Similar developments are found on the Atlantic coasts of Portugal, especially the Algarve, on the Canary Islands, and on the Basque and Vendée coasts of the Bay of Biscay. All together, an estimated 140 million tourists are attracted each year to the European shores of the Mediterranean. With the growth of trans-Mediterranean tourism during the 1990s, additional millions of European tourists now populate the beach resorts of North Africa as well.

The advent of mass tourism in alpine regions has had similar effects. Switzerland, the most popular destination for winter sports-related holidays, now boasts more than 600 ski resorts scattered throughout the country's alpine region, many of which constitute major developments. Given the intense competition of mass tourism, most resorts in the High Alps have come to offer elaborate facilities and services, which has meant intense development in the form of modern buildings, shops, car

**FIGURE 11.15. Adriatic beachfront.** Chairs, umbrellas, and other beach paraphernalia are piled up in front of their respective hotels in this off-season photo of the beachfront at Riccione, one of a string of holiday towns strung out along the Adriatic coast of Italy. Known as the "Green Pearl" of the Adriatic, the town is thronged in the summer season with thousands of recreating visitors.

parks, and alternative entertainment, not to mention transportation links. Alpine centers such as St. Moritz and Zermatt have lost much of their traditional appearance and charm in an effort to cater to the mass market. As we pointed out in an earlier chapter, this has also come at a cost to mountain environments.

## The New Tourism

The last decade or so of the 20th century has seen yet another major shift in European mass tourism. While the traditional mass tourism to beach and mountain resorts continues, we have begun to see the emergence of a variety of new tourist markets that have very different characteristics. These new markets are highly specialized and relatively small-scale. They cater to an emerging consumer preference for something different and more varied than the standard mass-package tour. One important factor in this new development has been the growing influence of a new

middle class that consciously strives for individuality in its lifestyles and tastes. Such predilections have generated a more sophisticated outlook on leisure travel that demands opportunities for interaction with nature, rugged outdoors action, isolation and privacy, learning and self-knowledge, cultural and heritage appreciation, or novel experiences and thrills. Another influence has been the growing length of paid holiday time, which now allows people to consider taking two or even three vacations rather than just the traditional summer break. For example, vacation travel abroad around the Christmas and New Year's holiday season, which was almost non-existent a decade ago, has now become a very popular activity.

The demand is for more flexible travel arrangements, extending from "short breaks" to extended holidays, and that demand is currently being met by some revolutionary changes in European transport. Especially important here is the recent rise of the "no-frills" airlines, which have made it possible to travel cheaply to almost anywhere in Europe and to take advantage of popular "short break" opportunities. The proliferation of such airlines is a direct result of the EU's third liberalization package of 1992, which essentially allows any European carrier to demand landing spots at any destination. The development and competition is most advanced in the United Kingdom, where such upstart carriers as EasyJet and Ryanair have moved quickly to dominate the low-cost airline business by offering, in addition to no-frills service, such innovations as one-way fares and direct marketing. EasyJet flights, for example, may only be booked directly via the Internet. Irish-based Ryanair has been so successful that it is credited with making London–Dublin the second-busiest route in Europe after London–Paris. The British based no-frills airlines have invaded the continental market by setting up new hubs in busy airports such as Amsterdam and Geneva. They, along with continental budget carriers like Brussels-based Virgin Express are forcing the mainline flag carriers, like British Air, Lufthansa, SAS, and KLM, to introduce their own subsidiary entries into the no-frills market or to cut off-peak fares in order to compete. Advertisements placed conspicuously in Berlin subways by the Hamburg-based low-cost airline Hapag-Lloyd Express hype the fact that one can fly to Cologne for no more than the cost of a Berlin taxi ride (19.99 euros). The rise of these new air travel options,

along with an expanded system of high-speed inter-city rail service and the now nearly universal ownership of automobiles (and the ready availability of caravan trailers to tow behind them), has done much to free today's European travel consumers from the traditional package tour holiday arrangement.

The wide variety of tourism activities associated with the new tourism in Europe seem to fall into three broad categories: rural and ecotourism, urban and heritage tourism, and theme parks. The first of these reflects a growing perception, particularly on the part of the urban middle class, that the rural countryside can offer a serene and idyllic retreat from the stresses of everyday urban life and that its therapeutic effect can be far greater than a week on the beach teeming with other holidaymakers. After all, as we have pointed out earlier in this book, there is much that is nostalgic and appealing about the fields and villages, the folk architecture of farmsteads and villages, the hedgerows, stone walls and pole fences, the windmills, country inns and pubs, tree-lined alleés, and great houses that dot the agricultural landscapes of Europe. Moreover, in some areas the countryside can contain extensive open spaces, often seemingly wild and unspoiled, that are ideal for hiking, jogging, bicycling, picnicking, fly fishing, and other peaceful and healthful pursuits. The countryside also lies, in many cases, within easy reach of a population that largely has access to automotive transportation, and

FIGURE 11.16. No frills. A loosening of regulations governing the air travel industry has revolutionized Europe's internal tourism transportation market. Seen here, docked at Amsterdam's Schiphol Airport, is a "no-frills" Easy Jet airliner with its direct-booking telephone number emblazoned on its side.

FIGURE 11.17. Getaway? Even the big national carriers have gotten into the short "getaway" market. This advertisement for British Airways alerts passersby on a Paris street that quality round-trip service to London is available for a mere 69 euros.

whose free time can be easily organized into "short break" or weekend outings in the countryside.

It is estimated that within the EU roughly a quarter of all tourism is now directed toward the countryside, that a growing share of it is international, and that it has had a positive impact on rural economies. The provision of tourist accommodations on farms is commonplace and an important part of the tourist industry in such countries as Austria, Sweden, and Ireland. The term *ecotourism* has also emerged to connote the widespread involvement in rural tourism of governmental planning to protect the attractions of the local landscape. Austria even has an association of "Holiday Villages," which sets strict environmental standards and limitations on visitor crowding for its member villages. Such planning efforts place emphasis on avoiding rapid and haphazard development by concentrating on "high-end" specialty tourism rather than on the mass tourism market and by taking steps to ensure that tourist services and facilities reflect rather than contradict local traditions in architecture, landscape, and economy.

A second area of growth may be called urban and heritage tourism. We noted in earlier chapters that European cities have recently been forced to compete aggressively with one another for investment and that part of this effort has been to promote themselves as magnets for tourism and leisure activity. The great cities, particularly the capitals, have always been tourist destinations of considerable importance, but there is today a heightened emphasis, as in rural tourism, on the "getaway" or "short break" market. Indeed, the fastest-growing segment of the European tourism market is the two- or three-night "citybreak" package, which normally includes airline, hotel, and entertainment reservations. The no-frills airlines have aided in this by bringing international flights into secondary city airports rather than the major international hubs. Cities are promoting themselves as exciting places to visit, places where people can go for uniquely rewarding experiences in shopping, eating, entertainment, cultural appreciation, and sightseeing. Given its very high potential for conferring simultaneous financial benefit on business, retailing, entertainment and civic interests, tourism has thus become a major instrument of urban regeneration policies in countless cities. Major investments in new multipurpose city-center

FIGURE 11.18. Trek. Bicycling has become an avid leisure pastime for many Europeans. This well-equipped and stylishly outfitted French biker, balancing to snap a photo while pedaling uphill, is one of thousands who swarmed up and down the steep roads of the Vosges during a recent long weekend holiday.

attractions have become commonplace, including trendy waterfront redevelopments as in Barcelona, Oslo, and Glasgow, or showy shopping–business–hotel–entertainment complexes such as the new Potsdamer Platz redevelopment in Berlin. Also important is the staging of major cultural, sporting, and commercial events to bring in visitors and add to a city's prestige and visibility.

But perhaps one of the most vital elements is the promotion of "heritage" in the form of historic architecture and associations with historical events, personalities, and artifacts. We tend to take the conservation and promotion of urban heritage for granted, but it is interesting to note what a modern phenomenon it is. Beginning with a few late 19th-century pioneering examples and proponents, the movement became more widespread in the earlier half of the 20th century as a municipal responsibility to identify and preserve selected monuments, but only gained universal acceptance in the last couple of decades as an absolute priority of urban planning and development. Heritage tourism, as it is called, has become one of the most powerful tools in attracting visitors to cities, and has touched off a rush to conserve and refurbish historic monuments and buildings, even entire historic districts, that can be used to instill in a city's im-

age an appropriate aura of past glories and historic relevance. It has also played a role in the development of specialized rural tourism.

The third and final category involves the creation of spectacle and adventure in the form of American-style theme parks. The most significant development and trendsetter here was the opening of EuroDisney just outside of Paris in April 1992. Although the park struggled at first due to high prices and a regrettable insensitivity on the part of its American management team to local customs and tastes, the problems were quickly corrected and attendance took off, reaching more than 10 million visitors annually by the end of 1993. The American-style family theme park boom has now blanketed Europe, and holidaymaking Europeans are choosing to travel in record numbers to theme park destinations. Europe's 80 major theme parks were estimated to have attracted more than 100 million visitors in 2000. More and more parks continue to be developed amid a constant cycle of one-upmanship as promoters compete to entice easily jaded visitors with better quality attractions, bigger sensations, and more amazing thrills. For many parks the thrill element is especially important. The thrill sensation of the early 1990s was the 80-meter-tall "Pepsi Big Max One" roller coaster at Plea-

**FIGURE 11.19. Heritage.** It is sometimes hard to imagine that the preservation of historical buildings and landscapes that we take for granted today is only a relatively recent phenomenon. The city of Carcassonne in the south of France is an early example. The seemingly untouched walled medieval town was actually resurrected from a state of ruin during the 19th century when the wave of Romanticism sweeping Europe at the time made the Middle Ages seem fashionable. The restoration was planned by the architect Viollet-le-Duc and was only completed in 1910.

sure Beach Park in Blackpool, England. A short time later, it was the "Dragon Khan" roller coaster, erected at Universal Studio's Port Aventura theme park outside of Barcelona and capable of negotiating a series of eight inverted loop-the-loops at speeds of more than 90 kilometers per hour. Then it was the "Nemesis" at Alton Towers Park in Staffordshire, capable of delivering a maximum force of 4Gs. Each year the parks seem to get bigger and the thrills flashier, with no immediate end in sight.

Although the model for the theme park is American, combining a full range of overnight accommodation, meals, and services with amusement park attractions, European parks are often targeted to distinctively European tastes and interests. EuroDisney's biggest competitor near Paris, Parc Asterix, is built, for example, around the persona and antics of Asterix the Gaul, the popular French comic book character. Europa Park in southwestern Germany is organized around separate theme areas that reflect the cultures of various European countries and regions.

Heritage can also be important, as many parks have attempted to capitalize on a broadening public interest in and fascination with history, which includes not only witnessing but even participating in the past, at theme parks that feature "imagined" or "living history" demonstrations and activities. Flambards Village in Cornwall is an excellent example of this. The park features two very popular historical attractions. One is a recreation of a lamp-lit Victorian village in which visitors may wander among costumed players going about their daily business in more than 50 shops and homes; the second is a harrowing life-sized re-creation of the sounds and hazards of a typical London street at night during the World War II blitz. A major attraction in the French city of Caen these days is an elaborately designed museum exhibition on the 1944 D-day landings.

Technology is another draw—witness the success of Parc du Futuroscope near Poitiers, where roughly 3 million visitors a year wander about 53 acres of giant-image screens and interactive video entertainment in search of

**FIGURE 11.20. Memory and heritage.** The site of the June 1944 D-day landings in Normandy has become a major tourism site. The beaches and the towns behind them are filled with museums and shops commemorating the landings. It is also a site of memory for the thousands of aging veterans who return there each year in package tours or on their own. These two, one French and the other American, are conversing in front of the visitor center to the American cemetery at Omaha Beach, just before the Memorial Day ceremony put on there each year by the American authorities.

what the park touts as an experience in "distraction and learning." Warner Brothers' Movie World theme park in Germany is another example. In such pursuits, much is aimed at children. One of the leading family attractions in Europe is the Netherlands' Efteling Park, which draws roughly 3 million visitors a year to a world of fairy tale wonders intermixed with thrill rides. Young and old alike are similarly attracted in huge numbers to the Legoland parks, now operated by Lego, the Danish manufacturer of children's blocks, in Denmark and the United Kingdom, with a new park under construction in Germany.

Also big, but a little different from the typical theme park attraction, is the "exotic getaway." One of the most successful examples of this genre is the series of holiday villages now operated in a number of northwestern European countries by the Dutch firm Center Parcs. The idea is to offer urban families an opportunity to make a quick getaway to a natural setting without really having to travel very far. The parks feature comfortable well-appointed family accommodations in cottages along with a healthy supply of family-oriented activities and attractions. The villages attract millions of guests and are currently leading the European market for short holiday breaks.

When all is said and done, these newer forms of specialized tourism have not exactly replaced Europe's annual mass migration to the traditional seaside or mountain tourist resorts. These are still the dominant attractions. Recent developments, nonetheless, have begun to provoke change in the traditional mass tourism industry. One indication of this is the fact that Mediterranean countries have actively begun to take steps to diversify their tourism industries by placing more emphasis on the development of interior holiday destinations that offer more in the way of heritage and scenic tourism. Spain, for example, is now experiencing a very rapid expansion in cultural tourism, based on the country's colorful and multicultured historic heritage. There has also been a surge in specialized rural niche markets. At the same time, authorities are

making a concerted effort to give coastal tourism a new image, in large part by attempting to control the ugly and sprawling commercial growth that has tended to destroy the attractiveness of the country's popular seashore destinations.

There has also been a move, throughout Europe, to revitalize or refurbish some of the historic places of mass tourism, especially the older beaches and resorts that were established during the 19th and early 20th centuries. New investment has come in the 1990s, for example, to places like Blackpool or Brighton, which have experienced a long decline and are now hoping to reverse the trend. The renovation of Brighton's famous West Pier is a prime example. Long a forlorn symbol of neglect, the West Pier has recently received a structural facelift and is set to shine again with nightclubs, pubs, a health spa, and a casino. Proceeds from the lottery were used to shore up the foundations and restore the overall look of the Pier itself. Private money took care of the attractions and concessions, while Brighton Council completed a project to upgrade the rather seedy appearance of the area between the Palace Pier and the West Pier. The Brighton experience is one that is being repeated in old seaside resort towns all

**FIGURE 11.21. Exotic getaway.** One of the fashionable and highly successful CenterParcs, "Domaine des Bois Francs en Normandie" is located west of Paris, just outside the town of Vernuil-sur-Avre. Laid out on the grounds of a historic chateau, shown here, the resort offers guests such varied activities as horse riding, golfing, archery, fishing, boating, bowling, and exclusive dining, not to mention access to an exotic glass-domed, climatically controlled "aquatic tropical paradise." Guests can book by the week, for short weekend getaways of three nights, or for mid-week "holidays" of four nights.

around Britain. The lottery has channeled millions into restoring coastal piers, while government regeneration grants for seaside tourism are improving the physical appearance of beach towns by replacing decaying beachfront façades with new and smartly appointed promenades, fronted by attractive assortments of shops, eateries, and night clubs.

## East-Central and Eastern European Tourism

During the socialist era, the countries of east-central and eastern Europe developed their own special brand of mass tourism. It was essentially a form of collective consumption, in which groups of workers and their families set off on state-run package tours and holidays. The group-oriented structure of the experience was intended to spotlight and reward the virtues of worker solidarity and achievement. The principal destinations of this mass tourism were Black Sea beach resorts and health spa resorts, although also important was a type of heritage tourism that promoted a sense of pride in socialist sacrifice and accomplishment, especially during World War II. Nearly every city and region in the East came to possess some kind of attraction in the form of an elaborate monument or shrine to the struggles of the past. As we noted in Chapter 9, restorations that alleviated the extensive damage visited on many cities by the war, such as the reconstruction of Warsaw's completely destroyed Old Town, were also a part of the heritage scene.

During the Stalin era, most tourism activity took place within the boundaries of the respective eastern-bloc countries. Later the market became more international, and holiday travel to a wide variety of destinations within the Soviet-dominated Council for Mutual Economic Assistance (CMEA) bloc became possible. Tourism to western or other markets, however, was restricted to a very small and privileged segment of the party elite. The scale of tourism was very large. Paid holiday vacations were a nearly universal experience, and each country maintained a sprawling state tourism organization or bu-

FIGURE 11.22. The great patriotic war. An important holiday activity in the Soviet Union was the visitation of memorials and monuments commemorating the heroic Russian sacrifice during World War II. Seldom visited by anyone but Russian tourists, this memorial at Treptow in East Berlin commemorates the Soviet Union's 305,000 casualties during the 1945 Battle of Berlin, and is the resting place for 5,000 of them. The memorial grounds are dominated by a gigantic symbolic statue, atop a pedestal made of marble from Hitler's Chancellery, which in turn is set on top of a conical hill modeled after a *kurggan*, or traditional warrior's grave of the Don region. On either side of the mass graves are sculpted frescoes of stylized scenes from the Great Patriotic War.

reau to provide the necessary services and facilities and, as the need for foreign hard currencies became a major state concern in the late 1960s and 1970s, to facilitate and manage international tourism coming from outside the Soviet bloc. Yugoslavia, which during this period became increasingly politically estranged from the rest of the bloc, turned its Adriatic coast into a favored destination for western tourists seeking a Mediterranean-style sea resort holiday. To win foreign hard currencies, the Soviet Union even operated a western market-oriented trans-Atlantic steamship passenger service for a time between Leningrad and New York or Toronto, with intermediate stops in major west European ports.

The fall of communism has resulted in a major restructuring of tourism in the East. For one thing, it has opened western markets to travelers from the former socialist countries. Rather ironically, a rash of new travel agents and tour operators in east-central and eastern Europe that offer package holidays to western Mediterranean coastal resorts have contributed to the staying power of those resorts in a changing western tourist market. At the same time, the traditional mass tourism markets internal to the east-central and eastern European countries have stagnated. The flow of tourists to seaside resorts on the Adriatic has been affected by the uncertainties of ethnic conflict, and to Black Sea resorts due both to the loss of traditional markets in central Europe and to shaky economic and political conditions in all of the former socialist states that border on the Black Sea. All countries seem to have placed some priority on the rebuilding of their tourist industries, particularly with respect to attracting international tourism from the West, as part of the postcommunist restructuring process. Perhaps the greatest indicator of what has happened is the burgeoning number of Internet websites advertising tourism opportunities and services across all of east-central and eastern Europe.

The countries that have had the most demonstrable success in rebuilding their tourist industries are all in east-central Europe. Most have been able to build their success largely on trendy urban-based cultural and heritage tourism, and to a lesser extent on rural tourism. Poland has capitalized on its proximity to Germany, attracting large numbers of German tourists who come primarily by automobile to visit, among other things, the country's faithfully reconstructed historic city centers. Indeed, the main roads leading into Poland from the German frontier are lined with dozens of small enterprises that sell handicrafts, kitsch, and other goods to passing tourists. The country has also profited from a healthy flow of tourists from the United States, which has a large Polish American population. The old socialist era Polish state travel agency, Orbis, has undergone privatization and is expanding rapidly. There has been a rush to build new hotels and tourist accommodations across the country, many of them under the aegis of international chains, such as Best Western, Hilton, Sheraton, Global, and Accor. The roughly 1,000 hotels currently operating in Poland represent, according to recent estimates, a 70% increase over the number extant in 1994. Poland has quickly risen to be one of the most frequented of international tourist destinations in Europe. The country is ranked an impressive sixth in international arrivals among all European countries, although a rather large proportion of all visitors are of the short-term getaway or weekender variety.

The Czech Republic has also done well. Glittering Prague, midway between Berlin

**FIGURE 11.23. Black Sea resort.** The sandy beaches along the southern half of Romania's tideless Black Sea coast attract most of the country's summer vacationers and before the fall of communism were big draws for people in other Soviet-bloc countries. Mamaia, just north of the port city of Constanta, is the most popular destination for the sunbathing, beer-drinking crowd.

and Vienna, has proven to be a stellar attraction. The city has enjoyed an enviable reputation in recent years as one of "the" places to visit. Hungary, which had already experienced substantial western tourism before 1989, continues to attract foreign visitors to its capital, Budapest, with its elegant Danube river embankments and magnificent views from the Buda Hills, but also to a variety of other attractions. Hungary is currently second among all the east-central European countries in international arrivals. And finally, Slovenia, which shares common borders with Italy and Austria, has been able to establish a niche for itself as a specialized short-term tourist market. Tourists have been flocking to Slovenia in ever larger numbers to visit its small tidy cities, to enjoy the country's relatively pristine forested and mountainous landscape, and to participate in the increasingly popular outdoor activities on the wild rushing alpine waters of the Soča River, such as rafting, kayaking, and canyoning.

On a tawdrier note, a growing sex tourism industry has also emerged, especially in areas of east-central Europe most easily accessible to short-term western visitors. Many Czech and Polish towns near the German border have developed a conspicuously thriving trade in prostitution, capitalizing in part on the extensive recruitment of eastern European women who answer deceptive advertisements offering well-paid work and the possibility of relocation in western countries.

## Popular Culture and Entertainment

Europeans, of course, spend the greatest portion of their leisure time near home, where they engage in an enormous variety of cultural activities and entertainments. There are many traditional leisure pursuits that are more or less universal. Gardening, for example, is a common and time-honored leisure activity, especially among older citizens. Taking a simple walk also ranks high. Indeed, on evenings or weekend and holiday afternoons, the public parks and formal pedestrianized spaces of European cities and towns are typically thronged with people, young and old, who venture out to take the air, window shop, or relax alone or with others on a park bench or at an outdoor café. Much time is also devoted to self-improvement of the mind or body. Adult education classes, study groups and cultural clubs, associations, and activities of all kinds are popular; and museums, galleries and concerts, theater and ballet performances, and the cinema are all well attended. Europeans, as a whole, are avid leisure readers. Sports and physical fitness too are fervently pursued. Opinion polls show that walk-

FIGURE 11.24. Leisure time. A young Parisian couple chat on a park bench in front of the elaborate façade of the city's 19th-century Hôtel de Ville. Europeans, in general, seem more disposed than their American counterparts to relax and enjoy the time when they are not working.

ing or cycling for exercise rate among the most popular physical activities for Europeans in all countries and walks of life.

At the same time, Europeans are increasingly subjected, like everyone else in our world, to new and globalizing forms of popular culture, the majority of which are delivered through the media of modern telecommunications. Largely inescapable, such influences are seemingly everywhere, and their omnipresence raises questions in many quarters about the potential homogenizing impact they may have on national and local cultures and identities. The debate becomes especially pointed when globalization is seen as the equivalent of Americanization, a form of cultural imperialism in the eyes of many that threatens to inundate and take over virtually everything in an avalanche of American television shows, movies, music, and fashions.

Such fears about impending American cultural hegemony are usually overdrawn, since the invading American pop cultures are in themselves highly varied and are received, in turn, by diverse European national cultures, each of which instinctively tends to modify and interpret them to suit local tastes and needs. With the exception of Britain, Belgium, the Netherlands, and some of the Scandinavian countries, American films and television shows are almost invariably dubbed into local languages, and undoubtedly understood in local terms. American television imports, such as MTV, CNN, the QVC Shopping Channel, and a host of popular game shows, are typically Europeanized in terms of personalities, content, and format to the extent that they may, at times, appear scarcely recognizable to an American viewer. Nonetheless, the electronic revolution has become as much a fact of life in Europe as anywhere else in the world, and undoubtedly has introduced a new and surprisingly varied range of entertainments and activities to the leisure scene.

Television is easily the most powerful of the modern media conveyors of popular culture. Nearly every European household has a television set, which people typically watch for several hours per day. Indeed, statistics even suggest that the average European spends nearly as much time watching television as they do engaging in other activities such as work and school. Over the past seven decades television has developed from humble beginnings to become the most universally pervasive feature of the modern cultural landscape.

Television broadcasting made its first appearance in experimental form during the late 1930s. In 1937 the BBC began regular broadcasting, although only to an extremely limited number of receivers. At about the same time the French began construction on the world's

FIGURE 11.25. American cultural hegemony? A Hollywood film release is advertised on Berlin's Karl Marx Allee, the former showcase "socialist street" of East Berlin. In the background are the twin Stalinist towers that mark the beginning of the section of the avenue flanked by the ornate apartment buildings that were to be "palaces for the people."

most powerful television transmitter, which was placed atop the Eiffel Tower. The onset of World War II, however, put an end to further development until the end of the 1940s. After the war development followed a fairly common pattern. During the 1950s and early 1960s, all European countries developed national television broadcasting systems, which, unlike their American counterparts, were placed under public ownership and control. This meant that television programming was, in most cases, restricted to one or two channels. These public channels were generally on the air for a limited number of hours, during which they offered up a fairly mundane schedule of news reports, public service features, talk shows, and—depending on the size and sophistication of the domestic film and programming industries—a variable mixture of home-produced or imported entertainment programs and films. Commercial advertising was banned. Television receiver owners in nearly all countries were required to purchase a license to watch their sets, the proceeds from which were used to help pay for public broadcasting. In some cases, particularly in the eastern socialist countries, governments were successful in turning television into an effective propaganda tool.

By the 1980s, however the television landscape began to undergo significant change. As a consequence, what we have today is in many ways radically different from the traditional state-sponsored systems of the post-World War II decades. One precedent was set in Luxembourg, which uniquely chose from as far back as the early days of radio to turn broadcasting over to the private sector rather than establish a state-owned monopoly. Luxembourg's commercially formatted RTL (Radio and Television Luxembourg) television station, which was established in 1954, could be received (due to Luxembourg's small size and strategic location) in neighboring Belgium, France, and Germany. The station rapidly became a popular alternative to the more staid public programming then available in those countries. In 1955 a commercial channel funded by advertising appeared in the United Kingdom. A further impetus came in the 1960s, when "pirate" radio stations began beaming commercial broadcasts into the Netherlands from ships anchored in the North Sea. Although legal sanctions were undertaken to discourage such activities, the commercial mix of programming broadcast from these stations proved enormously popular with viewers. Open internal market rules introduced by the EU and the development of new transmission and receiving technologies eventually made it possible for independent broadcasters to set up shop virtually anywhere. Since the end of the 1980s television viewers in most countries have been rewarded with a veritable cornucopia of commercial viewing opportunities, accessible through the proliferation of free broadcast channels, satellite and cable systems, and now through the new digital technologies being introduced into some markets.

"Pay TV," in particular, has made significant inroads over the past decade or so. Roughly half of all European households now subscribe to some form of satellite or cable system, and literally dozens of operators have emerged to provide subscription services, a few of the largest being BSkyB (from Britain), Canal Plus (France), Kirch Pay TV (Germany), and Sogecable (Spain). On the other hand, Europeans seem less willing than Americans to pay for so-called premium services: only one-fifth of subscribers do so in Europe, as compared to four-fifths in America. The vast majority seems to be satisfied with purchasing just the basic packages. Part of the problem for subscription operators may be that so many public and commercial broadcast channels are already available in most markets that consumers see no great advantage in paying for premium programming. Indeed, many operators have lost money, and a serious shakeout seems to be currently under way in the industry. One answer is digital television, which cable and satellite operators, as well as the major telecom companies, are hoping will redefine the media through such features as interactive entertainment. Digital television has the added attraction for entrepreneurs of being especially well suited to the promotion and sale of products. Considerable invest-

**FIGURE 11.26. Programming choice.** This advertisement on the wall of a Paris subway station hawks the choice of 78 channels. Subscription to pay TV has become commonplace throughout Europe, with various system operators vying for the attention of consumers.

also a valued staple of the public broadcasting media.

At the same time, viewers have turned to other venues to satisfy an appetite for more sports, theatrical films, and a growing variety of "lowbrow" entertainment programs. Sports ranks especially high in audience share ratings. According to television rating statistics, as many as half of the most highly rated programs are football (soccer) matches. Indeed, television has been instrumental in enriching football clubs across Europe, helping to make celebrities of star players and managers and generally moving football to a position near the forefront of the European mass entertainment industry (some would say it has had a corrupting influence). The screening of domestic and international theatrical films, the latter dubbed in most countries into the local language, are a mainstay of evening, and especially late-evening, programming on commercial channels. Also common is an ever-present sprinkling of episodes from American television sitcoms and drama series, often scheduled in random chronological order; a more or less constant barrage of glittery and typically inane home-produced variety shows; and the inevitable game shows, usually cloned for each market from successful American or British models.

Most recently the popular entertainment television landscape seems to have been captured by reality shows and soap operas. The reality show sensation originated with an innovatively voyeuristic program called *Big Brother*, which was produced by Endemol Studios, a Dutch entertainment company that has been enormously successful in creating and exporting popular programs to other countries. The premise of *Big Brother* was to confine a group of people plucked from their everyday lives to a house and to film their every activity as members of the group vote one another out until only one remains. The show became an international hit that has been enormously successful in spawning licensed domestic versions in other countries, as well as stimulating the production of a host of imitation productions that continue to pull in big audiences.

ment is presently under way to install and upgrade systems to deliver digital multichannel television. The earliest ventures are developing fastest in Scandinavia and the United Kingdom, where the proportion of households already possessing digital television sets is highest.

What do Europeans watch on their television sets? In many respects, the high ground is still held by the more venerable of the "flagship" state-owned broadcasting channels, such as the BBC, which continue as they have always done to offer quality news, current affairs programs, and documentaries, along with the very best in drama and arts programming. Reputable news programming, in particular, is held in high esteem by an information-addicted public, which according to EU opinion polls tunes into news and current affairs programs more regularly than they do to any other kind of television fare. The BBC news, which is widely seen via cable or satellite in many countries, is generally regarded as the unvarnished truth. High-quality dramas, especially historical period dramas, turned out in those countries that have the necessary production resources to do so, are

The other recent ratings phenomenon is the "telenovela," a Latin American product that has become all the rage in some parts of western Europe (mostly in the Mediterranean countries) and across much of central and eastern Europe. Produced in Mexico and Brazil, the telenovelas are formulaic soap operas that exhibit a certain sensuously Latin appeal that seems to project well across cultures. People in eastern European countries are especially addicted. The standard telenovela plots, which feature "rags-to-riches" stories and titillating glimpses into the flamboyant but troubled lives of the "rich and famous," have been shown to strike a responsive chord among audiences in the formerly socialist countries. In Moscow, where half of all television channels regularly broadcast dubbed Mexican telenovelas, the city is sometimes said to come to a virtual standstill during the broadcasts of certain eagerly awaited episodes.

Such developments have, in turn, prompted some state-owned television systems to diversify. In the United Kingdom, for example, where there were once only two BBC channels—BBC1 and BBC2—there are now a BBC3 aimed at the 25- to 34-year-old market, two children's channels (Cbeebies and CBBC), and a new highbrow channel (BBC4). Critics bemoan what they see as a "dumbing down" of state broadcasting as it races to compete with commercial television for viewers and ratings—a recently cited example being the decision by ORF, Austria's national television channel, to jump into the realm of reality show programming with its own show, *Taxi Orange*, which follows a group of young people dragooned into encountering the challenges of the everyday world as taxi drivers. ORF defends its decision to enter the reality show market by pointing out that its show is different from others in that it promotes the idea of community rather than competitive chicanery. In *Taxi Orange* the young drivers have to be successful in coping with the job rather than successful in undermining one another in order to survive.

Has television worked to promote cultural convergence? In a large sense it has. Where there was once a nation-based system of television broadcasting that exhibited a considerable diversity from country to country in programming standards, content, and viewership patterns, there is today an increasing homogeneity in which more and more viewers have access to a broadly international, but largely undifferentiated, variety of programming choices to choose from. This ongoing internationalization of television both reflects and underpins the declining importance of state boundaries and the growing globalization of culture and consumerism that seem to be such hallmarks of our society.

Yet, as we have seen, there is much that remains distinctive about television culture in individual countries and regions. The scheduling of programs in many countries makes allowances for local habits and predilections, taking into account, for example, the differences in evening meal times between such places as Britain and Spain. The insistence on the part of viewers in most countries that foreign language programming be dubbed makes language and culture a key determinant in how television programming is consumed, and even in the amount of foreign produced programming that is made available to viewers. Location has also made a difference. The homogenization tendencies have perhaps been greatest where borders are nearby and permeable, such as in the Low Countries and adjacent areas of France and Germany. Conversely, the Irish for years have been sufficiently isolated by distance from everyone else to have little choice but to tune into domestic or U.K. channels. The introduction of cable and satellite subscriber systems has helped, but even there local differences in availability and programming exist. The "cabling" of some countries, such as Belgium, began as early as the 1970s, while others have only recently completed the process or are still without adequate service. In some of the former socialist countries, where the advent of commercial television is still in its infancy, and the difficulties of switching from programming designed to meet the goals of the state to programming geared to satisfy consumer tastes and the demands of advertisers are still being worked out, the television land-scape has become more westernized but remains highly idiosyncratic.

Europe's changing landscape of leisure consumption has also been deeply affected by the Internet. According to statistics gathered in the summer of 2002, the proportion of households in EU countries with direct access to the Internet had reached 40%, up from just 28% as recently as the fall of 2000. Internet penetration continues to advance rapidly, although rather striking differences remain between regions and countries. The most "wired" countries are found in Scandi-navia, where current penetration rates generally fall in the 60% range. The Netherlands also belongs to this high penetration group. Relatively high but somewhat more modest levels of access are obtained among other EU countries north of the Alps, with the exception of France and Belgium, where people seem to have been initially slower to embrace new computer technologies but have become enthusiastically passionate once the idea has caught on.

The Mediterranean countries have generally lagged behind their northern counterparts, partly because home computer

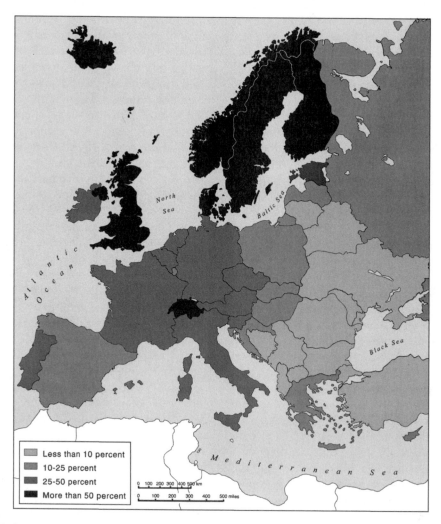

**FIGURE 11.27. Internet penetration.** Proportion of the population (adults and children) accessing the Internet at least once over a 2-month period, 2003.

ownership is limited and partly because the telecommunications infrastructure is less advanced. In Portugal, where Internet access rates have recently surged, the country is currently basking in the pride of having overtaken neighboring Spain, as well as having reached levels of penetration comparable to parts of northwestern Europe. The weakest of the EU countries is Greece, where the necessary infrastructure is perhaps most outdated and Internet access hovers at only around 10% of all households. In an effort to remedy the situation, the country plans to invest billions in EU development funds in coming years to improve its telecommunications infrastructure.

The leaders in east-central Europe are Estonia, Slovenia, the Czech Republic, and Poland, all of which boast Internet usage rates roughly comparable to those of moderately wired western countries such as Belgium, France, Italy, and Spain. Demand in Russia is very high, but Internet usage is severely hampered by the country's antiquated phone system, which is poorly equipped to handle digital communications. Nonetheless, usage is expanding rapidly. The proportion of Russian adults with access to the Internet is currently around 13%, roughly on a par with the level in Greece. Elsewhere in east-central and eastern Europe penetration levels fall off rapidly, reaching barely 1–2% of all households in such places as Serbia, Ukraine, Bosnia, Moldova, and Albania.

In addition to adopting e-culture at different speeds, Europeans differ in the kinds of online cultures that have developed. Surveys show that all across Europe the Internet is used most commonly for exchanging e-mails and searching for specific pieces of information. European users seem, on the whole, to be less prone than American users to engage in what might be called spontaneous surfing. One reason for this more focused use of the Internet may have to do with the relatively high access time charges incurred by users, many of whom still access the Internet from home via telephone modem rather than through lower-cost broadband hookups. Varying rates of home computer ownership

also affect online culture. Relatively low levels of home computer ownership in eastern and Mediterranean countries, and even in some western countries, have made the "Internet café" one of the newest and most popularly frequented places in central city and suburban neighborhoods, as well as in countless small towns and hamlets. On the other hand, in parts of Europe where home computer ownership is high, such trendy e-culture locales are scarcely to be found.

Europeans have been relatively circumspect about embracing e-commerce. The British are the most enthusiastic of Europe's on-line shoppers. Among U.K. Internet users, more than a third (37%) report regular on-line purchases of products, as compared to an EU average of only around a fifth. Much more modest but above-average use of the Internet as a shopping emporium is also found in Luxembourg, Germany, and the Netherlands. But elsewhere, and even in prosperous and fully wired Scandinavia, where credit card usage is also very common, the advantages of shopping on-line are widely spurned. The most

FIGURE 11.28. Internet café. A common sight over much of Europe is the Internet café, a convenient place for travelers or those who lack home computers to log on and check their e-mail or just surf the Net.

common explanation is that most Europeans are reluctant to give their credit card numbers to strangers, much less entrust them to cyberspace regardless of the security guarantees made by on-line merchants. Another factor is the relatively low use of credit card transactions that still prevails, even for in-person purchases, in many countries. Although this is changing, cash is still the most common way to make a purchase over large parts of Europe. Part of the explanation also lies with prevailing on-line marketing strategies, in which products are offered at essentially the same price for which they can be purchased at a store.

Nonetheless, there is little doubt that the electronic revolution has succeeded in adding a whole new layer to the ways in which Europeans spend their money and entertain themselves, and has contributed both to the growing homogeneity and continuing diversity of everyday living across the continent. Perhaps the most pervasive symbol of the new age is the cell phone, whose presence has become more or less ubiquitous in the hands of Europeans everywhere. The use of cell phones has become so widespread that the phenomenon has generated scathing editorials in nearly every country on the general lack of cell phone manners. They have revolutionized the way in which parents keep track of their offspring, as teenagers and even younger children are

**FIGURE 11.29. Cell phone.** The use of the cell phone has become so widespread that Europeans may be seen almost anywhere, cell clasped close to the head, listening or engaged in animated conversation. In this case, the conversation takes place in Rome on the steps of the fountain in the Piazza della Rotunda in front of the Pantheon.

entrusted with their own phones, almost as a right of passage. And, like every other new gadget that has come along in recent years to provide enjoyment and ease the burden of everyday coping, they have changed the landscape. Just try to walk down any city sidewalk, or ride any bus, tram, or subway, without noticing the ever-present and intense chattering going on over scores of small devices pressed tightly to the sides of their owners' heads.

## FURTHER READING

Apostolopoulos, Y., Loukissas, P., & Leontidou, L. (Eds.). (2001). *Mediterranean tourism: Facets of socioeconomic development and cultural change*. London: Routledge.

Beyerle, S. (2001, July/August). Mexico's entertaining export: Telenovelas titillate European audiences and viewers. *Europe*, pp. 20–21.

Carroll, M. (2001). American television in Europe: Problematizing the notion of pop cultural hegemony. *Bad Subjects: Political Education for Everyday Life, 57*, 11–14.

Dawson, J., & Burt, S. (1998). European retailing: Dynamics, restructuring and development issues. In D. Pinder (Ed.), *The new Europe: Economy, society and environment* (pp. 157–176). Chichester, UK: Wiley.

Delamont, S. (1995). *Appetites and identities: An introduction to the social anthropology of western Europe*. London: Routledge.

Graham, B., Ashworth, G. J., & Tunbridge, J. E. (2000). *A geography of heritage: Power, culture and economy*. London: Arnold.

Grigg, D. (1993). The European diet: Regional variations in food consumption in the 1980s. *Geoforum, 24*, 279–289.

Grigg, D. (1995). The nutritional transition in Western Europe. *Journal of Historical Geography, 21*, 247–261.

Grigg, D. (1998). Convergence in European diets: The case of alcoholic beverages. *Geojournal, 44*, 9–18.

Hall, D. R. (1998). Tourism and travel. In T. Unwin (Ed.), *A European geography* (pp. 311–329). Harlow, UK: Addison Wesley Longman.

Montanari, A., & Williams, A. M. (Eds.). (1995). *European tourism: Regions, spaces and restructuring*. Chichester, UK: Wiley.

Montanari, M. (1994). *The culture of food*. Oxford, UK: Blackwell.

Padidison, R., & Paddison, A. (1998). Consumption and retailing: Sameness and difference. In T. Unwin (Ed.), *A European geography* (pp. 220–237). Harlow, UK: Addison Wesley Longman.

Pells, R. (1997). *Not like us: How Europeans have loved, hated, and transformed American culture since World War II.* New York: Basic Books.

Perfiliev, Y. (2002). Development of the Internet in Russia: Preliminary observations on its spatial and institutional characteristics. *Eurasian Geography and Economics, 43,* 411–421.

Richards, G. (1996). Production and consumption of European cultural tourism. *Annals of Tourism, 23,* 261–283.

Shaw, G., & Williams, A. (Eds.). (1997). *The rise and fall of British coastal resorts: Cultural and economic perspectives.* London: Pinter.

Torrjman, A. (1995). European retailing: Convergences, differences and perspectives. In P. J. McGoldrick & G. J. Davies (Eds.), *International retailing: Trends and strategies* (pp. 17–50). London: Pitman.

Turnock, D. (1999). Sustainable rural tourism in the Romanian Carpathians. *The Geographical Journal, 165,* 192–199.

# CHAPTER 12

# Epilogue
## EUROPEAN FUTURES

We conclude our treatment of the European culture realm with a brief look into the future. Such an undertaking is always fraught with uncertainty. Only a few decades ago who would have predicted the momentous political realignments that took place in the 1990s? And no one would deny, especially after the events of September 11, 2001, that we live today in a highly volatile and remarkably interconnected world where occurrences in sundry places around the globe can suddenly alter all that feels familiar and predictable. Still, we think it might be useful here to speculate a bit about how Europe may look a decade or so from now.

Probably the greatest and most far-reaching change that will have taken place during this first decade of the 21st century is in the political realm, namely, the addition of 10 new members to the European Union. This fact alone must loom large in any discussion of what may happen in Europe over the coming years. After years of negotiation and waiting the EU15 became the EU25 in May of 2004. This was the outcome of a historic decision, made at the December 2002 Copenhagen Summit, to approve the applications of the AC10, as the accession countries came to be known. Joining the Union as new members

are the three Baltic States of Estonia, Latvia, and Lithuania, former states within the now defunct Soviet Union, five countries in east-central Europe that were satellites of the USSR—Poland, the Czech Republic, Slovakia, Hungary, and Slovenia—and the two island republics of Malta and Cyprus. The EU enlargement means that the Europe we have defined as a denoted culture region has moved one step closer to becoming an instituted region. It certainly means that, even more so than today, a sense of European identity will revolve around inclusion in, or close affiliation with, the EU Club. Dominated as it is by the countries of northwestern Europe, the Union will in turn stand for many of the cultural, philosophical, and institutional traits that we identified with Europeanness in Chapter 1.

And, within a decade or so, the EU25 will likely become larger still. Turkey has been promised a review, and if it meets EU demands on human rights it will be given an immediate date to start talks. We think it likely that Turkey will be admitted for a number of reasons. Foremost among them is that some political accommodation must be made between Greece and Turkey. This is necessary both to secure the EU's southeastern flank against the highly volatile Middle East and to facilitate the smooth accession of Cyprus with its divided Christian and Muslim communities. In addition, many within the EU would prefer that it not be seen as a purely Christian Club, but rather a Union that is free of religious bias. As a state that is overwhelmingly Muslim yet maintains a strictly secular government, Turkey would seem to be an ideal member through which to make this point. Even if Turkey gets the green light, it will take some time before its accession can be realized. The best that could be hoped for as things stand now is sometime early in the next decade.

Bulgaria and Romania are also likely candidates for admission within the foreseeable future. The year 2007 has been bandied about as a possible entry point for them, although few really believe that is possible, given the backward state of their economies. Russia, Belarus, Ukraine, Moldova, and the three states of Trans-Caucasia will likely remain beyond the pale for a very long time to come, as will the North African states of the Maghreb. But there are two Nordic countries that may yet want to join. Norway has twice rejected EU membership in national referendums, but there is now evidence that support within the country for joining the EU is growing. If Norway joins, that will exert pressure on Iceland, which would then become the only Nordic country left on the outside, even though 70% of its trade is already with the EU. Iceland has remained aloof primarily because it fears that EU common fishing policies would be detrimental to its fishing industry. At the same time, though, it would not like to see its chief fishing rival, Norway, gain a more favorable access to the EU market.

And what of the remainder of the Balkans? Of the five states that made up the former Yugoslav Federation, only Slovenia has succeeded in breaking away and earning admission to the E.U. Albania, too, remains on the outside. Accommodations of some kind will eventually have to be made with these countries, and there is some hope. The EU, prodded in part by the Greeks, who see themselves as the potential leader of a Balkan bloc

within the EU, has at least formally, if somewhat unenthusiastically, declared that the so-called western Balkans republics can all expect to join the EU—once they have met the stringent conditions imposed on all applicants, of course.

Political realities, however, may force the EU to make early concessions. The EU is already deeply involved in peacekeeping within the region and needs to ensure stability there. To meet this goal it will likely be forced to negotiate arrangements whereby the Balkan enclave (and possibly Kaliningrad too) will receive certain benefits of membership, even though they remain officially outside the EU for the immediate future. As we pointed out in Chapter 7, it is most likely that these countries will gain admittance one at a time (the so-called Regatta Principle) rather than as a group.

As if things weren't already difficult enough in this part of Europe, there is also the worrying prospect of further political fragmentation within the Balkans. Although the Republic of Yugoslavia has just recently been reconstituted as the State Union of Serbia and Montenegro, it is still not clear yet whether Montenegro will remain in the union. During the worst of the recent strife in the Balkans, Montenegro operated pretty much as an independent country, even though it was officially tied to Serbia. The present "state union" comes as a result of western pressure, in large part from the EU itself, to keep Montenegro and Serbia together. The fear is that Montenegrin independence would prompt renewed demands for independence from Kosovo, whose predominantly ethnic-Albanian population lives under a U.N. protectorate in the aftermath of the recent separatist fighting with Serbia that took place there. We think that it is probably in the best interests of everyone that accommodations be worked out that will encourage the reintegration of Montenegro with Serbia, and bring their union into the queue for EU membership. Failure to do so could result in two new independent political entities in an already highly fragmented and volatile Balkan region.

Another potent consequence of the present

EU expansion is that the newly enlarged EU is now much more differentiated internally than it has been in the past—a fact that is likely to make its politics more sectional. Relatively well-defined regional blocs are already visible, and they are likely to begin to want to play a much more significant role in EU decision making. These roughly approximate those presented in Chapter 1. What we referred to there as the Heartland remains in place, as does our three-region "Europe proper" core. These regional groupings will continue to see their role as central, much as they did before. The former western Mediterranean and a new and enlarged Nordic–Baltic bloc, however, can now be expected to take on a more assertive role in EU affairs, distinguished by the need to assert or protect the regional cultures and the special interests of these peripheral areas. The new members of east-central Europe and those parts of the Balkans that are able to attain membership status (along with Turkey) will stand apart because of the considerable economic and cultural differences that will continue to exit between them and the rest of the EU. With one or two possible exceptions, most of the new accession countries will in this sense remain second-class citizens for some time into the future.

In terms of further integration or deepening, we are likely to see more internal differentiation in the form of multitiered acceptance of EU initiatives. We have already seen precedents for this within the old EU-15, as, for example, in the adoption of the euro, or the Schengen agreement. For the 10 newest members, entering the euro zone was once thought to be almost an afterthought following the long tough road to accession, but now seems distant. The problem is that, according to new EU rules, newcomers must maintain the value of their currencies within a narrow band of 2.25% on either side of a central parity rate against the euro. This is far tougher than the 15% band previously announced by the EU. Moreover, once new member states adopt the euro, they will be obligated to keep their national budget deficits within 3% of GDP, a feat that even some of the older mem-

bers have had difficulty in accomplishing recently.

Given the runaway budget deficits currently prevalent in most of the new member states, which have been experiencing substantially slower growth and lower levels of foreign investment, entry into the euro zone is a dream that is likely to be delayed. This will be a major factor in perpetuating the multitiered nature of EU membership alluded to above. Remaining outside the euro zone means that these countries will be at a disadvantage in that their currencies will be more vulnerable and their costs of borrowing money higher. Moreover, they will forgo having any influence on major fiscal decisions made within the EU.

Regardless of what may happen with respect to the euro zone, or with other "multitiered" initiatives, the slow but inexorable deepening of EU integration is likely to continue. Ever since the decision in 1985 to establish a true "single market," the long legal and regulatory arm of Brussels has reached deeper and deeper into the affairs of the EU countries. Indeed, estimates suggest that as many as half of the new laws promulgated in member states today are simply national versions of legislation already drafted in Brussels. While the urge to Europeanize everything may be resisted by some—Denmark is a good example of a country that has resisted EU initiatives on such things as defense, citizenship, and social policies, not to mention adoption of the euro—most countries demurely accept each new expansion of power in Brussels. The long arm of Brussels even extends to nonmember states. Although still firmly an outsider, Norway is said to have already integrated thousands of EU directives into its own national law.

That being said, it is also important to realize that the EU remains far from being a "superstate," and many Europeans are uncomfortable with it becoming one. The urge to Europeanize is, in many ways, amply offset by the powers and prerogatives of the nation-states, which work very hard, both at home and in Brussels, to defend their individual interests and resist surrendering any more sovereignty than necessary to the larger "European Project." While EU legislation and directives may permeate the regulation of many aspects of the lives of Europeans, particularly in the economic sphere, the individual states still control most of the other essential areas of public decision making—for example, the right to determine public spending and policy on such things as pensions, welfare benefits, education, immigration, internal security, and defense. Moreover, the states control the all-important fiscal means of governing. Although the EU's regulatory powers may be many, in relative terms the EU budget is miniscule, amounting to only 1% of the collective GDP of the member states. In contrast, the federal budget of the United States is equivalent to almost one-quarter of the country's GDP.

As the EU looks to its future, a lively debate has developed over how the governance of the ever-widening Union should be structured. This debate was launched at the Intergovernmental Conference held in Nice in December 2000, which was designed to encourage an exchange of ideas not only among Europe's politicians but also among private institutions and organizations and individual members of the public. Contributions were invited from the applicant countries as well as from the present members of the Union. One hope was that the debate launched at Nice would bring the European Union closer to its citizens and counteract the widespread impression that there is a lack of true democratic participation in EU governance.

The debate that took place in Nice involved many issues, but it centered on what the relative importance of the Council of Ministers and the European Parliament should be. The majority opinion seemed to favor the Community Model, in which the Council and the Parliament wield equal power. This model recognizes the dual nature of the EU as both a union of member states, on the one hand, and a community of citizens on the other. Two other models were also put forward in various forms, however. The Intergovernmental Model sees the Council as the principal wielder of authority and thus underlines the Union as primarily an association of member states. This model has appeal to the larger member states. At the other extreme is the Federalist Model in which the European parliament would be greatly strengthened and made the primary source of power. This is the most democratic form of governance since the Parliament is a representative body elected directly by the citizens of the Union.

The kind of governance that the European Union will have in the future has since been taken up by a gathering of delegates—known as the Convention on Europe's Future—who met in the spring of 2003 to draft a constitutional treaty that would set the EU's course for the next 50 years. The resulting document is a complicated affair of more than 200 pages, much of which simply consolidates the past treaties among the EU countries into a single document. Part of it, though, enters new territory. Among other things, the treaty adopts a Charter of Fundamental Rights, expands the EU's legal and regulatory reach into criminal law, taxation, and social policy, reforms EU institutions, creates an EU foreign minister, and extends majority voting into perennially contentious areas, such as agricultural policy and the allocation of regional development funds. For the constitutional treaty to come into force, the member countries must each ratify it, a process that will likely extend for some time into the future. Indeed, the very fact that this is a constitutional "treaty" says volumes about the EU—a treaty being generally something that is agreed upon between states, as opposed to a constitution, which is adopted by a state.

What is interesting, though, about the draft of the constitutional treaty is that it does not appear to resolve the perpetual tug-of-war between advocates of the federalist and intergovernmental models of how the EU should be defined and run. On balance, it seems to lean to the federalist side. The very act of adopting a constitutional treaty and the creation of a foreign minister lends the EU a more formalized "state-like" identity (it will now have the legal right to sign treaties with other states). But, as so often is the case with the EU, things are not quite as they appear to be. The foreign minister will have no real power over national governments, which may veto any foreign policy initiative coming from Brussels and which will retain control over their armed forces. Nor does the treaty extend any new powers of taxation to Brussels. Thus, while the treaty expands the writ of Brussels into a number of new areas, it does little to take away any of the fundamental powers of the constituent member states. Indeed, to even take force it must be approved by everyone; it only takes a single rejection to derail the project. Even future constitutional amendments must be unanimously agreed to by all the member states.

One thing is certain, however. Regardless of its future exact shape or form, the European Union will be the third-largest political entity in the world after China and India, and by far the richest of these top three. And it will undoubtedly continue to be an important integrating force in the lives of its 450 million people with their different histories, languages, religions, and cultures. Whether it can successfully bring them together on all issues, or even achieve any kind of lasting relevance to their daily lives, remains to be seen. We would expect the member states to maintain their individual sovereignties and for national and regional cultures to persist, as they always have. British Prime Minister Tony Blair may have captured the future best when he called for the new Europe to become "a superpower, not a superstate."

It may be useful at this point to reassess some of things we have said about the Europeans in the light of a growing European Union. In Chapter 5 we made reference to the burden placed on the EU by the current policy of translating all documents into the official languages of the member states. The present enlargement adds nine new languages, four Slavic (Czech, Polish, Slovak, and Slovene), two Baltic (Latvian and Lithuanian), two belonging to different branches of the Uralic language family (Finnish and Hungarian), and one Arabic (Maltese). Depending on how Cyprus is handled, there may also be a Turkic (Turkish). This almost doubles the number of official languages spoken in the EU, with perhaps Bulgaria, Romania, Mace-donia, Albania, Norway, and Iceland yet to come sometime in the future.

Very clearly the present language policy, which we discussed in Chapter 5, will have to be reconsidered. It seems inevitable that a few languages of wider communication will have to be designated as the official languages of the EU. However, in a federation with 20 deeply entrenched national languages there can be no question of these official languages becoming second languages, that is, languages of instruction, across the region. Rather, we suspect that they will be studied as foreign languages by schoolchildren in all the member states.

Very likely these languages will be English, French, and German. As an established world language being made even more popular through the high-tech electronics revolution, English would seem to be the logical first foreign language studied. The later addition of both French and German would seem to take too much time from other important studies. More likely, one or the other will be learned. German has a history of use as a *lingua franca* in the Baltic and east-central European countries joining the EU, though its prestige was somewhat damaged by the events preceding and culminating in World War II. French is more popular in western Europe and the Mediterranean, so perhaps some kind of linguistic regionalization may be expected to develop.

The enlargement of 2004 also introduces more ethnic minorities into the EU, that is, cultures unlike those of the majority in the nation-states where they reside. Examples are Hungarians in Slovakia (and later on in Romania), Russians in Latvia and Estonia, and Romany (gypsies) in much of east-central Europe. The EU has human rights standards regarding how minority peoples are to be treated that are far more rigid than those formerly applied in some of the new member states or currently applied in many of the states that may be admitted in the future. Indeed, a major hindrance to the admission of Turkey at the moment is the government's treatment of its Kurdish minority. Only under the pressures of gaining admittance to the EU have the Turks begun to forge a new relationship with the country's Kurdish minority, which might someday even lead to some kind of Kurdish autonomy within the Turkish state. One may expect better social conditions for many minority peoples in the future, but how long their cultures can survive the convergence we alluded to earlier is another question. Certainly such examples from western Europe as Gaelic and Frisian are not encouraging.

In Chapter 6 we raised the issue of whether the Catholic Church because of its strong political institutions wields more influence in the EU than the Greek Orthodox or the Protestant Churches. The 10 new admissions add some Orthodox communities (Cyprus, Estonia, and Latvia) and some Protestants (Estonia and Latvia), but the overwhelming majority of new EU'ers are Roman Catholic. This is mainly the result of the accession of Poland, the most devout of the former Soviet satellites, with some 35 million Catholics. All of the east-central European states, together with Malta, are Catholic, but some, like the Czech Republic, were highly secularized during the communist period and now report large numbers of "atheists and nonreligious." Clearly the Vatican will continue to provide a major focus of loyalty for the peoples of the EU. The leadership of most of the Union countries, however, seems committed to a multicultural policy that rejects a strong religious involvement of any kind in secular government.

With the new admissions the population of the EU has been suddenly increased by 20% to 450 million. The prospects for significant growth of the new populations in the future are poor. Fertility levels in all but Cyprus and Malta are lower than the average for the old EU15, and 6 of the 10 are currently losing population because of an excess of deaths over births. Except in the two island republics, death rates are significantly higher than anywhere else in the EU. Life expectancy for males is 5–10 years lower, and in many cases is more than 10 years lower than for females in the same country. Still, the populations are aging more rapidly than those in the pre-en-largement EU simply because so few births are adding numbers to the younger age groups.

Overall, as we suggested in Chapter 3, Europe, for some decades to come, will have a population that is declining in size and steadily aging. Many demographers now predict a total population decline for the 25 EU countries of about 5% (roughly 25 million people) between now and 2050. In the coming years the aging of the population will become quite noticeable, if not a bit alarming. According to one recent study, the average age of the European population at mid-century will rise to a little over 52 years from just under 38 years today!

Thus, the problem of an inadequate working population to support the elderly will continue or even be exacerbated. While most countries will attempt to combat this problem by increasing taxes, reducing pension benefits, and delaying retirement, there are many experts who believe that such reform efforts will prove inadequate. The admission of Turkey and agreements with the Maghreb countries, with their far younger and more rapidly growing populations, could help to right the imbalance, but the attitudes of many Europeans toward the presence of Turks and Arabs in their midst would have to change appreciably for this to be a viable solution. A relaxing of immigration restrictions may help, but even here it has been calculated that the rate of immigration would have to be raised to more than 10 times its current level in order to offset the aging process already under way. The most effective answer would be a combination of renewed immigration and higher birthrates, but it remains very difficult at this point to predict exactly what may happen.

Economically speaking, the new accessions have brought into the EU new and rather large populations that make their living directly from the land. Viewed in another way, the EU has added a new and less developed rural economic periphery, much as it did in previous expansions but this time on a far grander scale. The agricultural productivity of these new rural populations will have to be accommodated within a EU that already produces sizable agricultural surpluses and struggles in vain to find a workable common agricultural policy. Agriculture can thus be expected to undergo further rationalization and modernization over the coming years in all of the newly acceded east-central European countries. This process will undoubtedly move large numbers of people off the land. Rates of urbanization can be expected to rise in the East, as they already have been doing for some time, bringing the relative importance of urban living ever closer to the levels known in the West.

Within urban systems we can expect continued competition for new-age investment between large and medium-sized cities across the breadth of Europe as they try to position themselves advantageously vis-à-vis the global economy. A reduction of the importance of international boundaries in the expanded areas of the EU should accelerate the integration of east-central European cities into the larger and more developed urban systems of the West and allow them to operate more freely in the new supranational context. Competing urbanized poles may be more common in the future. In addition to the traditional urban heartland of western Europe, there will likely be counterbalancing regional foci in such places as the so-called Latin Crescent of the western Mediterranean, a Hamburg–Ørestad axis at the juncture of the North and Baltic Seas, a Berlin–Warsaw–Prague triangle, or perhaps even a Vienna–Budapest Danubian corridor.

We can expect at least the larger urban places in east-central and eastern Europe to continue to transform their local economies and social and built environments to something closely approximating those in the West. During the past decade, we have already seen much evidence of western-style gentrification and commercial investment in the centers of eastern cities. These changes show no signs of slackening. Indeed, Moscow just recently announced the grand opening of its new "Mega-Mall," the largest such development yet seen in eastern Europe. Financed and developed by the Swedish home furnishing giant IKEA, the $250-million project features hypermarkets and hundreds of shops, two kilometers of

storefronts, a skating rink, and a multiplex cinema. Already a huge success, the complex attracts hordes of shoppers—an estimated 25–40 million a year—many coming from as far away as St. Petersburg. This development, and many more like it, exemplifies the new western-style urban commercialization now under way in cities across the former socialist countries.

Environmentally, we see some reason for optimism. As we sought to demonstrate in Chapter 4, human impacts on the natural environment are never-ending, and we will undoubtedly see new problems, accidents, and crises. At the same time, we have already witnessed some marked improvements over the past decade in the health of some European terrestrial and marine environments. Airborne pollutants, for example, have been reduced over western Europe thanks to international cooperation; and, as we have seen, the absolutely dire predictions made a couple of decades ago for the Mediterranean have largely been averted. There are even signs that the pace of environmental degradation has slackened in the former socialist countries, in part due to increased awareness and ongoing cleanup efforts, but perhaps due even more so to the widespread failure and closing of many outdated and polluting industrial facilities across the region. The EU's commitment to strong environmental policies (a fast-growing area of EU legislation) and the spreading reach of Brussels—with the latest enlargement to cover an ever larger portion of European environments—will certainly help future efforts at cleanup and conservation.

We end, finally, by returning to the issues of convergence and identity. We began this book in Strasbourg, calling attention to the way in which that city and its inhabitants seemed to fit so easily into many different Europes, and even into the world at large. We saw that Strasbourg could at once be small and provincial, French (or even a bit German), as well as urbanely European or global. The amazing interconnectedness of our world, advanced in so many ways by the high-tech electronics revolution of recent decades, makes it easier than ever to access or be a part of our converging world on a multitude of scales and dimensions, and Europeans are just as able to do so as anyone else in the world. Yet, place (the local as opposed to the global) remains both important and distinctive as "home." And it is ultimately in the context of specific places that Europeans live, work, recreate, and form their most intimate sense of identity; and it is through lenses derived from their experience with the distinctive cultures and environments that inhere in these places that they see and access the rest of the world.

# Index

# About the Authors

**Robert C. Ostergren, PhD,** is Professor of Geography at the University of Wisconsin–Madison. He has lived, studied, and traveled extensively in Europe, and is the author of many publications that pertain to European and North American cultural and historical geography, including the prize-winning book *A Community Transplanted: The Transatlantic Experience of a Swedish Immigrant Settlement in the Upper Middle West, 1835–1915*. In 1998 his university honored him with the Chancellor's Award for Distinguished Teaching.

**John G. Rice, PhD,** is Professor Emeritus of Geography at the University of Minnesota, Twin Cities. Educated in the United States and Sweden, Professor Rice has spent a long and distinguished career in the study of European population and culture and has traveled widely in the region over a period of almost 50 years. Of particular interest to him have been questions in the fields of ethnic studies and historical demography. His writings have focused on 19th-century Swedish population movements, especially those to North America.